MW01531485

Discovering AutoCAD

2000

MARK DIX
and
PAUL RILEY

CAD Support Associates

Prentice
Hall

PRENTICE HALL, Upper Saddle River, NJ 07458

Library of Congress Cataloging-in-Publication Data

Dix, Mark
    Discovering AutoCAD 2000 / Mark Dix and Paul Riley.
      p.   cm.
    Includes bibliographical reference (p.).
    ISBN 0–13–084264–8
    1. Computer graphics.   2. AutoCAD.   I. Riley, Paul.
  II. Title.
  T385.D588   1999
  604.2'0285'5369—dc21   99–39149
                                             CIP

for

Katelyn, Jesse,

Kathleen, and Michael

Editor-in-chief: *Marcia Horton*
Acquisitions editor: *Eric Svendsen*
Production editor: *Prepare*
Assistant managing editor: *Eileen Clark*
Executive managing editor: *Vince O'Brien*
Art director: *Jayne Conte*
Cover design: *Bruce Kenselaar*
Manufacturing buyer: *Beth Sturla*
Assistant vice-president of production and manufacturing: *David W. Riccardi*

Prentice Hall

© 2000, by Prentice-Hall, Inc.
Upper Saddle River, New Jersey 07458

All rights reserved. No part of this book may be
reproduced, in any form or by any means,
without permission in writing from the publisher.

The author and publisher of this book have used their best efforts in
preparing this book. These efforts include the development, research,
and testing of the theories to determine their effectiveness.

Printed in the United States of America

10 9 8 7 6 5 4 3 2 1

ISBN 0-13-084264-8

Prentice-Hall International (UK) Limited, *London*
Prentice-Hall of Australia Pty. Limited, *Sydney*
Prentice-Hall Canada, Inc., *Toronto*
Prentice-Hall Hispanoamericana, S.A., *Mexico*
Prentice-Hall of India Private Limited, *New Delhi*
Prentice-Hall of Japan, Inc., *Tokyo*
Prentice-Hall (Singapore) Pte. Ltd., *Singapore*
Editoria Prentice-Hall do Brasil, Ltda., *Rio de Janeiro*

AutoCAD, AutoLISP, and 3D Studio are registered trademarks of Autodesk, Inc. dBase III is a registered trademark of Ashton-Tate. DMP-61, DMP-29, and Houston
Instrument are trademarks of Amtek, Inc. IBM is a registered trademark of International Business Machines Corporation. LaserJet II is a trademark of Hewlett-Packard.
LOTUS 1-2-3 is a trademark of Lotus Development Corporation. MultiSync is a registered trademark of NEC Information Systems, Inc. MS-DOS and Windows are
trademarks of Microsoft Corporation. Summagraphics is a
registered trademark of Summagraphics Corporation.
Zenith is a trademark of Zenith Data Systems, Inc.

The AutoCAD Primary Screen Menu Hierarchy and Pull
Down Menus are reprinted with the permission of Autodesk, Inc. The AutoCAD Table Menu, Screen Menu,
and Pull-Down Menu are reprinted from the AutoCAD
Reference Manual with permission from Autodesk, Inc.

CONTENTS

PART III   **Isometric Drawing and Three-Dimensional Modeling**   **455**

Chapter 11   **Isometric Drawing**   **455**

Commands: ELLIPSE, ISOPLANE, SNAP (isometric), VIEW   455
Tasks:

Chapter 12   **Wireframe Models**   **484**

Commands: RULESURF, UCS, UCSICON, VPOINT   484
Tasks:

PREFACE

Get Active with *Discovering AutoCAD 2000*

Designed for introductory AutoCAD users, *Discovering AutoCAD 2000* offers a hands on, activity-based approach to the use of AutoCAD as a drafting tool—complete with techniques, tips, short cuts, and insights designed to increase efficiency. Topics and tasks are carefully grouped to lead students logically through the AutoCAD command set, with the level of difficulty increasing steadily as skills are acquired through experience and practice. Straightforward explanations focus on what is relevant to actual drawing procedures, and illustrations show exactly what to expect on the computer screen when steps are correctly completed. This edition features **new Web-based exercises and projects** included in each chapter. These optional exercises both assess a student's understanding of the material and increase their ability to manage documents across the Internet.

Features

This book uses a consistent format for each chapter that includes the following:

- Objectives, Key Terms, and Introduction
- Exercises that introduce new commands and techniques
- Exercise instructions clearly set off from the text discussion
- AutoCAD drawings and screen shots
- A Summary of key concepts and techniques
- 10 or more end of chapter Review Questions
- 4-6 Realistic Engineering "drawing problems"—fully dimensioned working drawings
- *New Optional Internet Projects at the end of each chapter*
- **Companion Web site—http://www.prenhall.com/dixriley/**

High-quality working drawings include a wide range of applications that focus on mechanical drawings but also include architectural, civil, and electrical drawings. This book contains an appendix with 10 drawing projects for additional review and practice, as well as 3D models of 24 objects drawn in 2D in earlier chapters.

Companion Web site—http://www.prenhall.com/dixriley/

This dedicated site is designed to support both professor and student users of this text. We hope it closely supports the book and serves as a useful tool that both complements and increases the value of the text. In particular, students will find **multiple choice assessment questions** for each chapter. These questions serve as check-ups to see whether students have mastered new AutoCAD commands. Students can answer these questions as either check-up exercises or quizzes. They receive the results of these quizzes instantly and can email these directly to their professor. Each chapter is also supported by an **extended AutoCAD project**. These extended projects complement the book and provide extra challenges for students. Finally, this Web site contains a Netsearch capability that helps lead students to different sites dealing with AutoCAD topics. Professors can take advantage of this site's **syllabus builder feature**. Following a step-by-step interface, this tool quickly helps create a graphic Web page containing class information and assignments. Professors control access to this site and maintain it with their own user ID and password. Syllabus Builder makes managing your class in either a local or distance learning situation a snap.

Our Approach

It has been a great pleasure to dig into this impressive new version of AutoCAD, to explore its many treasures, and to continue to face the challenges we have set for ourselves in each of our AutoCAD books. That is, to create an optimum learning sequence, to get students involved in drawing as quickly as possible, to keep the learning process active, and to give students a thorough and practical understanding of AutoCAD concepts and techniques. In teaching something as content rich as the AutoCAD 2000 software package, it is often necessary to keep in mind that less is more, and that "coverage" can be the enemy of understanding. The AutoCAD world is full of books, many of which do little more than duplicate the function of the *AutoCAD Command Reference*. We have all seen them at the bookstore, huge books that grow larger with every new release. However, the job of teaching is not to try to tell everything all at once, but to anticipate what the student will need at each new phase of the learning curve.

This book is designed as a teaching tool and a self-study guide and assumes that readers will have access to a CAD workstation. We also hope that many who use it will have access to the Internet and our exciting new companion Web site, *http://www.prenhall.com/dixriley/*, which adds a whole new dimension to the interactive possibilities of this teaching method. WWW activities, including explorations, drawing projects, and self-scoring tests, are optional components of every chapter.

The book itself is organized around drawing tasks that offer the reader a demonstration of the commands and techniques being taught at every point, with illustrations that show exactly what to expect on the computer screen when steps are correctly completed. While the focus is on the beginning AutoCAD user, we have found over the years that experienced CAD operators also look to our books for tips, suggestions, and clear explanations of AutoCAD commands and principles. It has not been unusual for seasoned pros working with our books to recognize connections and concepts they had not noticed or considered previously.

But this is a by-product. Our target audience is the beginning AutoCAD student with a serious professional interest. We strive to present a highly efficient learning sequence in an easy to follow format. Topics are carefully grouped so that readers progress logically through AutoCAD commands and features. Explanations are straightforward and focus on what is relevant to actual drawing procedures. Review questions, drawing problems, and WWW activities follow new material. And, most important, drawing exercises are included at the end of every chapter so that newly learned techniques are applied to practical drawing situations immediately. Retention and skill development are optimized as the level of difficulty increases steadily and facility is acquired through experience and practice. At the end of the book we have included additional drawing projects for those who want to go further.

All working drawings have been prepared using AutoCAD. Drawing exercises at the end of all chapters are reproduced in a large, clearly dimensioned format on each right-hand page with accompanying tips and suggestions on the left-hand page. Drawing suggestions offer time-saving tips and explanations on how to use new techniques in actual applications. The book is not a drafting manual, yet the drawings include a wide range of applications. While the focus is on mechanical drawings, there are also architectural drawings in most chapters and anyone completing all the drawings will be well equipped to move on to more advanced and specialized applications.

Instructor's CD

Qualified instructors using this text may order an instructor's solutions disk. To order this disk, either contact your local Prentice Hall sales rep, order online at *http://www.prenhall.com*, or call 1-800-922-0579. The ISBN for the instructor's CD-ROM is 0-13-086475-7.

Bundle This Book!

To make the cost of purchasing several books for one course more manageable for students, Prentice Hall offers discounts when you purchase this book with several other Prentice Hall textbooks. Discounts range from 10 to 20% off the price of the two books separately. At press time, you may bundle this text for discounts with any core Prentice Hall graphics text by Giesecke, Earle, Lockhart/Johnson, or Sorby. To request more specific pricing information, get ISBNs for ordering bundles, and learn more about Prentice Hall's offerings in graphics and CAD, either contact your Prentice Hall Sales rep, or go to *http://www.prenhall.com/cadgraphics/*. For the name and number of your sales rep, please contact Prentice Hall Faculty Services at 1-800-526-0485.

About the Authors

Mark Dix began working with AutoCAD in 1985 as a programmer for CAD Support Associates Inc. He helped design a system for creating estimates and bills of material directly from AutoCAD drawing databases for use in the automated conveyor industry. This system became the basis for systems still widely in use today. In 1986, he began collaborating with Paul Riley to create AutoCAD training materials, combining Riley's background in industrial design and training with Dix's background in writing, curriculum development, and programming. Dix and Riley have created tutorial teaching methods for every AutoCAD release since version 2.5. Dix has a Master of Arts in Teaching from Cornell University and a Masters in Education from the University of Massachusetts.

Paul Riley has been an Instructor and designer specializing in graphics and design of mutlimedia. He is a founding partner of CAD Support Associates, a contract service and professional training organization for computer aided design. His 15 years of business experience and 20 years of teaching experience are supported by degrees in education and computer science. Paul has taught AutoCAD at the University of Massachusetts, Lowell and Mt. Ida College in Newton, MA. He has developed a program, Computer Aided Design for Professionals, that is highly regarded and has been an ongoing success for the past 15 years.

Reviewers:

We would like to thank everyone who reviewed this book for the new edition and provided useful comments and suggestions:

Tom Bledsaw, *ITT Educational Services-Indianapolis*
Robert M. Koretsky, *University of Portland*
James G. Raschka, *Delaware County Community College*
Tom Bryson, *University of Missouri-Rolla*
James Devine, *University of South Florida*
Kathleen Kitto, *Western Washington University*
Larry G. Richards, *University of Virginia*
Timothy S. Sykes, *Houston Community College*

Acknowledgments:

We would like to thank the many people who have helped us in the preparation of this book. Most of all, thanks to Eric Svendsen, our editor at Prentice Hall, for his continued encouragement and support.

Thanks also to the people at Autodesk, Inc., for the use of software and support, and for the creation of this great software package. Thanks to Houston Instruments for the use of plotters and to Summagraphics for the use of digitizers.

We are grateful to Mike Pilarella for technical advice and support, and to John Williams at Mount Ida College for his interest in this project and his commitment to CAD education.

Thanks to Brian Cook, Jeremy O'Hara, and Matt Rose for classroom testing this manuscript.

Mark Dix and Paul Riley

PART I

BASIC TWO-DIMENSIONAL ENTITIES

1 — Lines

COMMANDS

ERASE	REDO
LINE	SAVE
NEW	SAVEAS
OPEN	UCSICON

OVERVIEW

Drawing in AutoCAD can be a fascinating and highly productive activity. AutoCAD 2000 is full of features that will enhance your CAD performance. Here and throughout this book, our goal will be to get you drawing as quickly and efficiently as possible. Discussion and explanation is limited to what will be most useful and relevant at the moment, but also give you an understanding of the program to make you a more powerful user.

This chapter introduces some of the basic tools you will use whenever you draw in AutoCAD. You will begin to find your way around AutoCAD 2000 menus and toolbars, and learn to control basic elements of the Drawing Window. You will produce drawings involving straight lines and learn to undo your last command with the U command. Your drawings will be saved, if you wish, using the SAVE or SAVEAS commands.

TASKS

1.1   Beginning a new drawing
1.2   Exploring the drawing window
1.3   Interacting with the drawing window
1.4   Exploring command entry methods
1.5   Drawing and undoing lines
1.6   Saving and opening drawings
1.7   Review Material
1.8   WWW Exercise #1 (Optional)
1.9   Drawing 1-1: Grate
1.10 Drawing 1-2: Design
1.11 Drawing 1-3: Shim
1.12 Drawing 1-4: Stamp

1.1 Beginning a New Drawing

When you load AutoCAD 2000 you will find yourself in the Drawing Window with the Start Up dialog box open. The Drawing Window is where you do most of your work with AutoCAD. You can begin a new drawing from scratch or open a previously saved drawing or template file. In this task you will begin a new drawing using the "Start from Scratch" option.

⊕ From the Windows 98 Start Up screen, choose Programs, then the AutoCAD 2000 folder, and then the AutoCAD 2000 program.

Or, if your system has an AutoCAD 2000 shortcut icon on the Windows 98 desktop, double click on the icon to start AutoCAD.

⊕ Wait…

When you see the AutoCAD 2000 screen with the Start Up dialog box in the foreground, as shown in Figure 1-1, you are ready to begin.

The Start Up dialog box gives you four options, indicated by the four icons at the top. You can open a previously saved file, start from scratch, use a template, or use a Wizard, which guides you through setup. For our purposes it will be best to start from scratch to ensure that your Drawing Window shows the same AutoCAD 2000 default settings as are used in this chapter. We will explore other possibilities later.

You should see your cursor arrow somewhere on the screen. If you do not see it, move your pointing device to the middle of your drawing area or digitizer. When you see the arrow, you are ready to proceed.

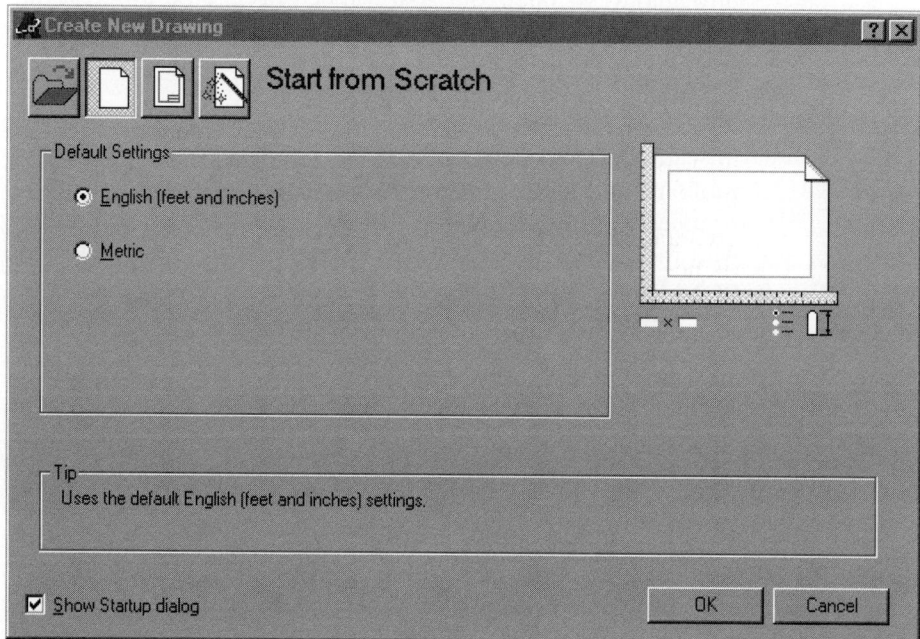

Figure 1-1

⊕ Move your pointing device until the arrow is inside the second icon.

> You should see the words "Start from Scratch" to the right of the icons in the startup dialog box.

⊕ Click on the second icon so that "Start from Scratch" shows in the dialog box.

⊕ Click on "English" in the Default Setting box.

⊕ Click on Okay to exit the dialog and start your new drawing.

> Pressing Enter will also work.

> The dialog box will disappear and your screen should resemble Figure 1-2. You are now ready to proceed to Task 1.2.

1.2   Exploring the Drawing Window

You are looking at the AutoCAD Drawing Window. There are many ways that you can alter it to suit a particular drawing application. To begin with, there are a number of features that can be turned on and off using your mouse or the F-keys on your keyboard.

The Screen

The AutoCAD 2000 Drawing Window has many features that are common to all Windows 98 programs. At the top of the screen you will see the title bar, with the AutoCAD 2000 icon on the left and the standard Windows 98 minimize, maximize, and close buttons on the right.

Below the title bar you will see AutoCAD 2000's pull-down menu bar, including the titles for the File, Edit, View, Insert, Format, Tools, Draw, Dimension, Modify, Window, Express, and Help pull-down menus. Pull-down menus work in AutoCAD just as in other Windows applications and are discussed later in this task.

The next line down is the standard toolbar. This toolbar is one of many toolbars that can be displayed on the AutoCAD 2000 screen. There are 24 toolbars available in the standard AutoCAD 2000 toolbar dialog box. Toolbars can be created and modified. They can be moved, resized, and reshaped. They are a convenience, but they can also make your drawing area overly cluttered. For our purposes you will not need more than a few of the available toolbars. The use of toolbars will also be discussed later in this chapter and in Chapter 3.

The next line is the Object Properties toolbar, which displays the current layer and linetype. It also includes tools for changing other object properties. Layers and linetypes are discussed in Chapter 4.

Below these toolbars you will see the drawing area with the Draw and Modify toolbars positioned vertically along the left side. You may see a bar at the top of the drawing area with the current drawing name, "Drawing1" on the left side. This indicates that you are in an AutoCAD 2000 drawing window. You can have more than one drawing open in a single AutoCAD 2000 session, but this will not be necessary at this point. If the drawing name bar is showing, you can eliminate it and expand your drawing window slightly by clicking on the maximize button at the top right of the drawing name bar.

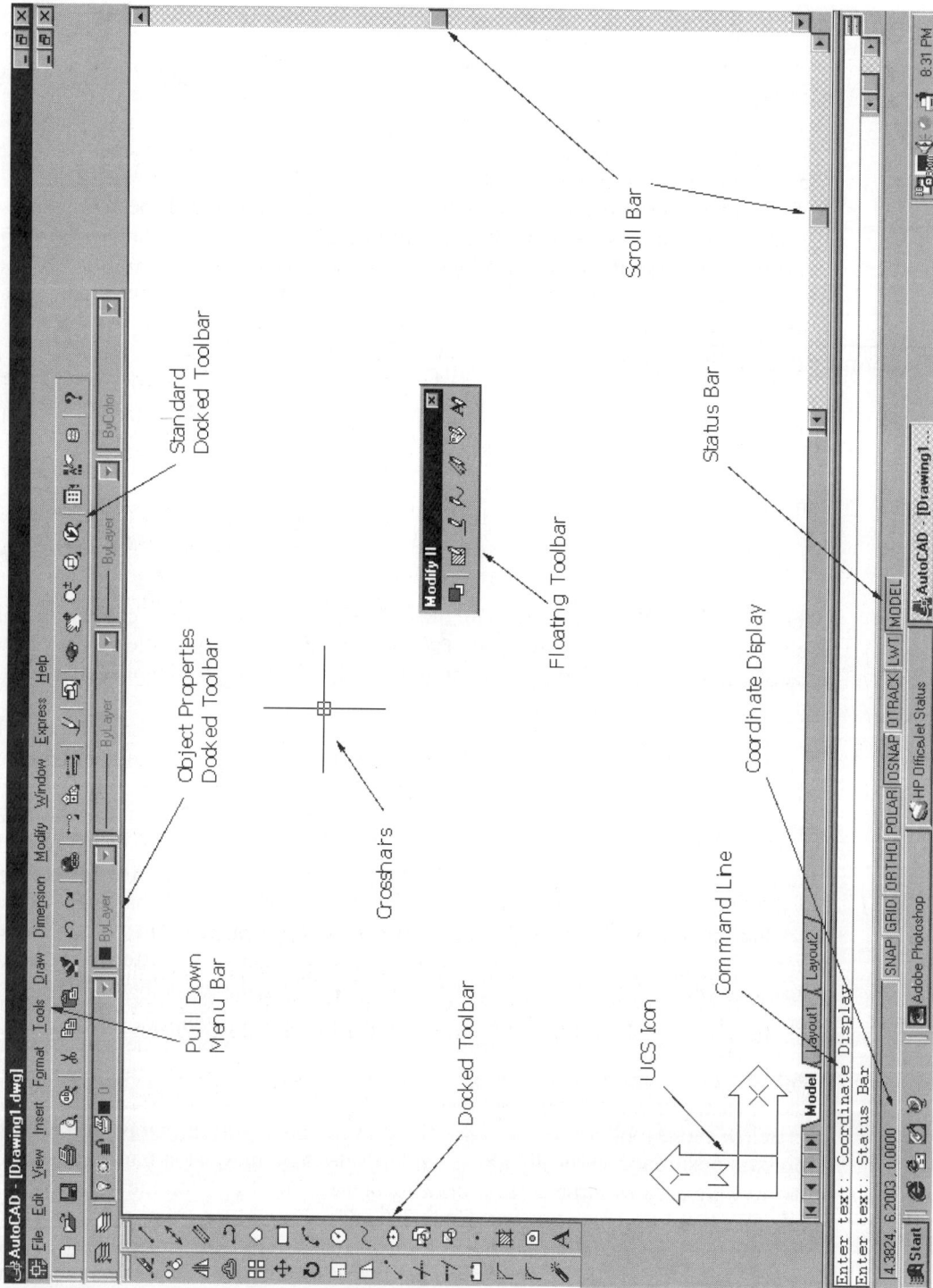

Figure 1-2

At the bottom of the drawing area you will see arrows and tabs with the words "Model", "Layout 1", and "Layout2". These tabs allow you to switch among the drawing and different layouts that you create for printing or plotting. You will have no immediate need for this feature. At the bottom and along the right side of the drawing area you will see scroll bars. These work like the scroll bars in any Windows application. Clicking on the arrows or clicking and dragging the square sliders will move your drawing to the left or right, up or down within the drawing area. We will demonstrate these in a moment.

Beneath the scroll bar you will see the command prompt area. Typed commands are one of the basic ways of working in AutoCAD.

At the bottom of the Drawing Window is the status bar, with the coordinate display on the left, currently showing three four-digit numbers, and eight mode indicators (Snap, Grid, Ortho, Polar, Osnap, Otrack, LWT, and Model) on the right. The coordinate display and mode indicators are discussed shortly.

Finally, the bottom of your screen will show the Windows 98 taskbar, with the Start button on the left and any open applications following. You should see the AutoCAD 2000 icon here, indicating that you have an AutoCAD window open.

Tip: You can gain more room for your drawing area by hiding the Windows 98 taskbar. This can be done by pointing to the top of the taskbar and dragging it down off the bottom of the screen. It will move down, leaving only the top edge showing. To get it back, point to this top edge again and drag it upward.

Switching Screens

⊕ Press F2.

This brings up the AutoCAD text window. AutoCAD uses this window to display text that will not fit in the command area. As soon as the text window opens, Windows adds a button with a text icon on the taskbar at the bottom of the screen. Now you can open and close the text window using the taskbar buttons or F2.

⊕ Press F2 again, or click on the AutoCAD icon button on the taskbar.

This brings you back to the Drawing Window. Once used, the AutoCAD Text Window operates like an open application. It remains "open" but may be visible or invisible until you close it using the close button in the upper right corner.

⊕ Press F2 or the AutoCAD text window button to view the text window again.

⊕ Click on the close button (X) in the upper right corner of the text window to close the text window.

Note: Sometimes AutoCAD switches to the text window automatically when there is not enough room in the command area for prompts or messages. If this happens, use F2 when you are ready to return to the drawing area.

1.3 Interacting with the Drawing Window

There are many ways to communicate with the Drawing Window. In this task we will explore the mouse, cross hairs, arrow, and other simple features. In the next task we will begin to enter drawing commands.

The Mouse

Most of your interaction with the Drawing Window will be communicated through your mouse. Given the toolbar and menu structure of AutoCAD 2000 and Windows 98, a two-button mouse is sufficient for most applications. In this book we will assume two buttons. If you have a digitizer or a more complex pointing device, the two button functions will be present along with other functions that we will not address.

On a common two-button mouse the left button is called the pickbutton and will be used for point selection, object selection, and menu or tool selection. All mouse instructions refer to this left button, unless specifically stated otherwise. The right button sometimes functions as an alternative to the enter key on the keyboard, but more often calls up short cut menus as in other Windows applications. The menu that is called depends on the context. Learning how and when to use these menus can increase your efficiency. We will point them out as we go along. In this task, most instructions are for the left button. If you hit the right button accidentally and open an unwanted short cut menu, close it by clicking with the left button at any point not on the short cut menu.

Cross Hairs and Pickbox

You should see a small cross with a box at its intersection somewhere in the display area of your screen. If you do not see it, move your pointing device until it appears. The two perpendicular lines are the cross hairs, or screen cursor, which tell you where your pointing device is located on your digitizer or mouse pad.

The small box at the intersection of the cross hairs is called the pickbox and is used to select objects for editing. You will learn more about the pickbox later.

⊕   Move the pointer and see how the cross hairs move in coordination with your hand movements.

⊕   Move the pointer so that the cross hairs move to the top of the screen.

     When you leave the drawing area, your cross hairs will be left behind and you will see an arrow pointing up and to the left. The arrow will be used as in other Windows 98 applications to select tools and to pull down menus from the menu bar.

     Note: Here and throughout this book we show the AutoCAD 2000 and Windows 98 versions of AutoCAD screens in our illustrations. If you are working with another version, your screen may show significant variations.

⊕   Move the cursor back into the drawing area and the selection arrow will disappear.

The Coordinate Display

The coordinate display at the bottom left of the status line keeps track of coordinates as you move the pointer. The coordinate display is controlled using the F6 key or by clicking on the display itself.

⊕ Move the cross hairs around slowly and keep your eye on the three numbers at the bottom of the screen.

They should be moving very rapidly through four-place decimal numbers. When you stop moving, the numbers will be showing coordinates for the location of the pointer. These coordinates are standard coordinate values in a three-dimensional coordinate system originating from (0,0,0) at the lower left corner. The first value is the x value, showing the horizontal position of the cross hairs, measuring left to right across the screen. The second value is y, or the vertical position of the cross hairs, measured from bottom to top on the screen. Points also have a z value, but it will always be 0 in two-dimensional drawing and can be ignored until you begin to draw in 3D (Chapter 12). In this book we will usually not include the z value if it is 0, as it will be until we get into 3D drawings.

⊕ Press F6 or click on the coordinate display.

The numbers will freeze and the coordinate display will turn gray.

⊕ Move the cross hairs slowly.

Now when you move the cross hairs you will see that the coordinate display does not change. You will also see that it is grayed out. The display is now in static mode, in which the numbers will only change when you select a new point by pressing the left button on your mouse. Try it.

⊕ Move the cross hairs to any point on the screen and press the left button on your mouse.

Notice that the first two numbers in the coordinate display change, but the display is still grayed out. Take a moment to ensure that you understand these values: the x value measuring horizontally, the y value measuring vertically, and the z value (0).

⊕ Move the cross hairs to another point on the screen.

You will see that AutoCAD opens a box on the screen, as shown in Figure 1-3. *You are not drawing anything with this box.* This is the object selection window, used to select objects for editing. It will have no effect now since there are no objects on your screen. You will give two points to define the window and then it will vanish because there is nothing there to select. Object selection is discussed in Chapter 2.

AutoCAD prompts for the other corner of the selection window. You will see this in the command area:

                    Other corner:

⊕ Pick a second point.

This will complete the object selection window. The window will vanish. Notice the change in the static coordinate display numbers.

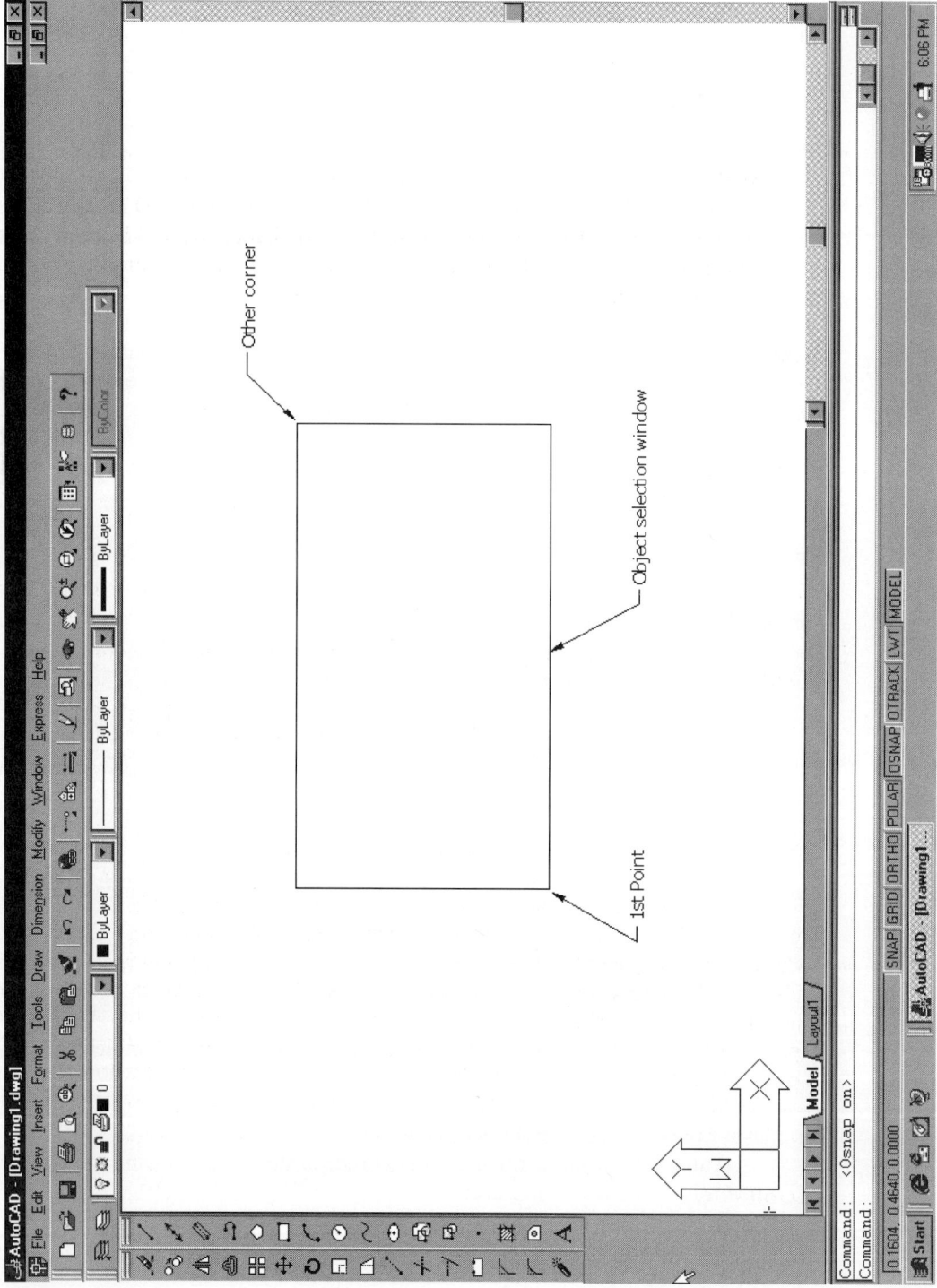

Figure 1-3

⊕　Press F6 to return the coordinate display to dynamic mode.

The coordinate display actually has two different dynamic modes, but this will not be apparent until you enter a drawing command such as LINE (Task 1.3), which asks for point selection.

Note: The units AutoCAD uses for coordinates, dimensions, and for measuring distances and angles can be changed at any time using the UNITS command (Chapter 2). For now we will accept the AutoCAD default values, including the four-place decimals. In the next chapter we will be changing to two-place decimals. The F-keys are switches only; they cannot be used to change settings.

The Grid

⊕　Press F7 or click on the word GRID on the status bar.

This will turn on the grid. When the grid is on, the GRID button will appear in the "down" position on the status bar, as illustrated in Figure 1-4. The grid will initially appear at the left side of the drawing area, as illustrated. In a moment we will center it.

The grid is simply a matrix of dots that helps you find your way around on the screen. It will not appear on your drawing when it is plotted, and it may be turned on and off at will. You may also change the spacing between dots using the GRID command, as we will be doing in Chapter 2.

The grid is presently set up to emulate the shape of an A-size (12 × 9 inch) piece of paper, with grid points at 0.50-inch increments. There are 20 grid points from bottom to top, numbered 0, 0.5, 1.0, 1.5, etc., up to 9.0. There are 26 points from left to right, numbered 0 to 12, including all .5 unit increments. The AutoCAD command that controls the outer size and shape of the grid is LIMITS, which will be discussed in Chapter 4. Until then we will continue to use the present format.

You should be aware from the beginning that there is no need to scale Auto-CAD drawings while you are working on them. That can be handled when you get ready to plot or print your drawing on paper. You will always draw at full-scale, where one unit of length on the screen equals one unit of length in real space. This full-scale drawing space is called "model space." Notice the word "MODEL" on the right end of the status bar, indicating that you are currently working in model space. The actual size of drawings printed out on paper may be handled in "paper space." When you are in paper space you will see the word "PAPER" on the status bar in place of the word "MODEL". For now, all your work will be done in model space, and you do not need to be concerned with paper space.

Scroll Bars

⊕　Click on the left arrow on the horizontal scroll bar at the bottom of the screen.

Your grid will move a little to the right.

⊕　Click the left arrow again.

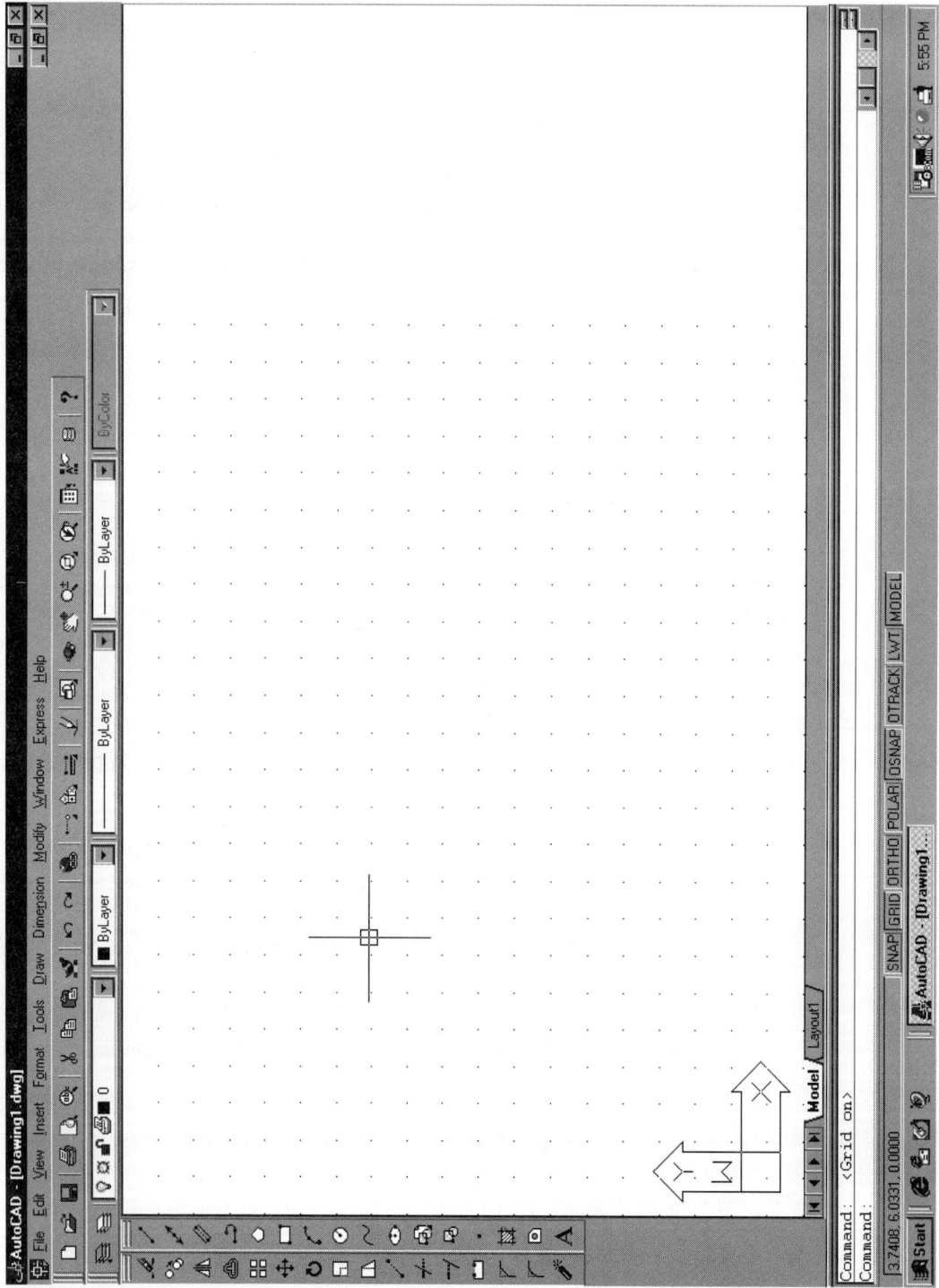

Figure 1-4

As you see, the movement is slight and the grid moves in the direction opposite to where the arrow is pointing. This may seem backward. Think about the scroll bars controlling the drawing window rather than the drawing itself. As you move the window to the left, the drawing within the window appears to move to the right.

⊕ Hold the mouse button down so that the grid moves continuously across the screen.

⊕ Work with the left and right buttons until the grid is centered within the drawing area, as shown in Figure 1-5.

Notice that moving the grid in this way does not change the coordinate value of dots on the grid. The position of grid points has changed relative to the screen but not relative to other points on the grid.

Snap

Snap is an important concept in AutoCAD 2000 and CAD in general. There are several AutoCAD features through which an approximate screen cursor location will lock onto a precise numerical point, a point on an object, or the extension of an object. All of these features enhance productivity in that the operator does not have to hunt or visually guess at precise point locations. In this chapter you will see examples of several of these related techniques, but we will leave in-depth discussion and demonstration for later chapters. The simplest form of snap is called incremental snap or grid snap, because it is conceptually related to the screen grid. Try this:

⊕ Press F9 or click on the word SNAP on the status bar.

The SNAP button should go into the down position, indicating that the snap mode is now on.

⊕ Move the cross hairs slowly around the drawing area.

Look closely and you will see that the cross hairs jump from point to point. If your grid is on, notice that it is impossible to make the cross hairs touch a point that is not on the grid. Try it.

⊕ If your coordinate display is in the static mode, press F6 to switch to dynamic mode.

⊕ Move the cursor and watch the coordinate display.

You will see that the coordinate display shows only values ending in .0000 or .5000.

⊕ Press F9 or click on SNAP again.

Snap should now be off and the SNAP button will be in the up or off position on the status bar again.

If you move the cursor in a circle now, you will see that the cross hairs move more smoothly, without jumping. You will also observe that the coordinate display moves rapidly through a full range of four-place decimal values again.

F9 turns snap on and off. With snap off you can, theoretically, touch every point on the screen. With snap on you can move only in predetermined increments. With

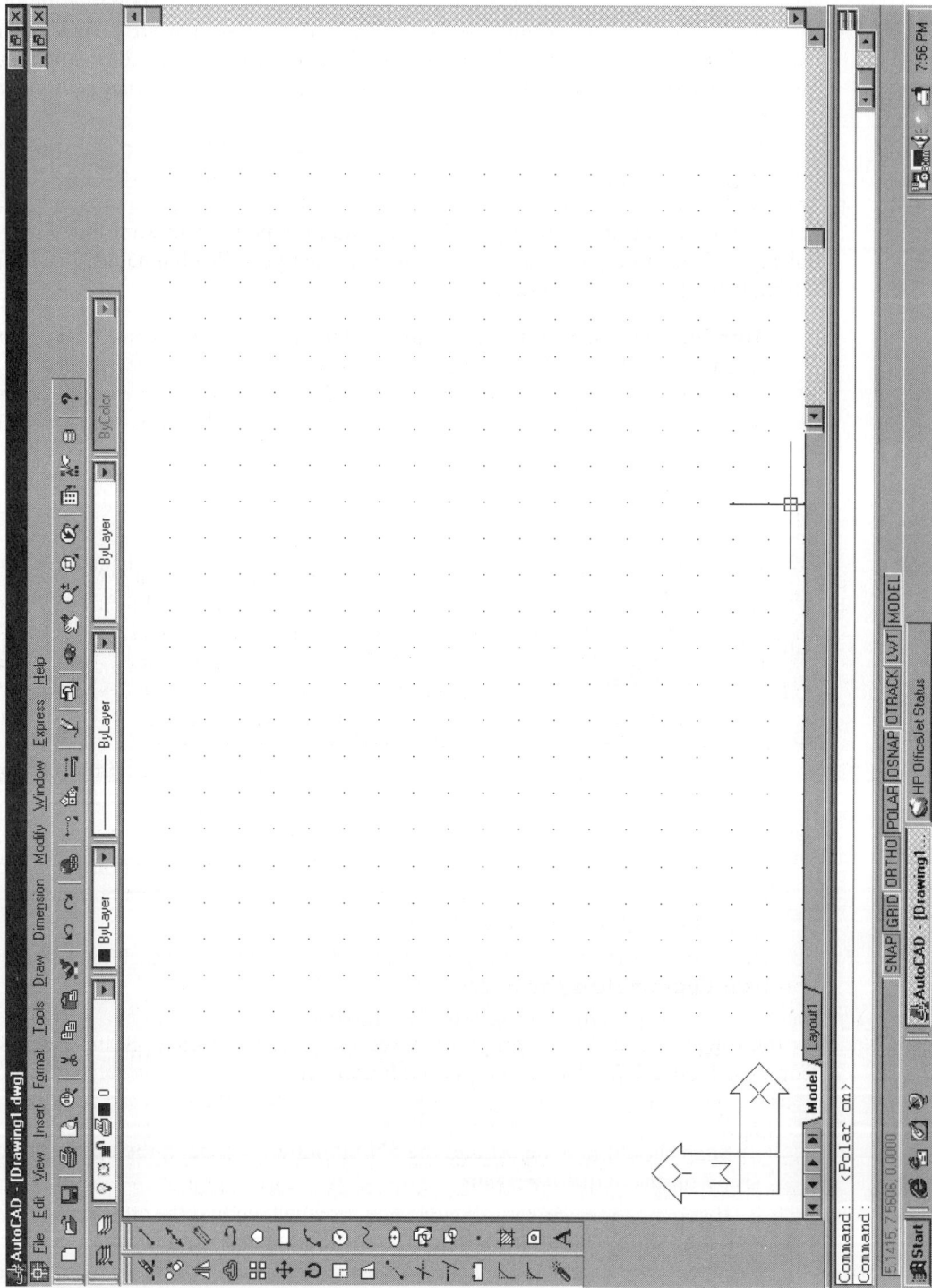

Figure 1-5

the Start from Scratch default settings snap is set to a value of 0.5000 so that you can move only in half-unit increments. In the next chapter you will learn how to change this setting using the SNAP command. For now we will leave the snap setting alone. A snap setting of 0.5000 will be adequate for the drawings at the end of this chapter.

Using an appropriate snap increment is a tremendous timesaver. It also allows for a degree of accuracy that is not possible otherwise. If all the dimensions in a drawing fall into 1-inch increments, for example, there is no reason to deal with points that are not on a 1-inch grid. You can find the points you want much more quickly and accurately if all those in between are temporarily eliminated. The snap setting will allow you to do that.

> **Tip:** Incremental snap is more than a convenience. In many cases it is a necessity. With snap off it is virtually impossible to locate any point precisely. If you try to locate the point (6.5000,6.5000,0.0000) with snap off, for example, you may get close, but the probability is very small that you will actually be able to select that exact point. Try it.

Other Buttons on the Status Bar

All of the status bar buttons are important and can be used to turn powerful features on and off. Some of the features are so powerful, however, that they will interfere with your learning and ability to control the cursor at this stage. For this reason we will encourage you to keep some features off until you need them. Generally you will want Snap, Grid, and Model to be on and all other buttons to be off. Ortho and Polar are discussed later in this chapter and you can use them at your discretion. Osnap, which stands for Object Snap is a very important feature that will force the selection of a geometrically definable point on an object, such as the end point or midpoint of a line. We will leave Osnap alone until Chapter 6 so that you have the freedom to select points without the interference of an Object Snap selection. Otrack stands for Object Snap Tracking. Otrack is an outgrowth of Object Snap and we will save it for Chapter 6 as well. LWT stands for Lineweight, which we will introduce in Chapter 3.

The User Coordinate System Icon

At the lower left of the screen you will see the User Coordinate System (UCS) icon (see Figure 1-2). These two perpendicular arrows clearly indicate the directions of the *x* and *y* axes, which are currently aligned with the sides of your screen. In Chapter 12, when you begin to do 3D drawings, you will be defining your own coordinate systems, which can be turned at any angle and originate at any point in space. At that time you will find that the icon is a very useful visual aid. However, it is hardly necessary in two-dimensional drawing and may be distracting. For this reason you may want to turn it off now and keep it turned off until you actually need it.

⊕   Type "ucsicon".

Notice that the typed letters are displayed on the command line to the right of the colon.

⊕ Press the enter key on your keyboard.

AutoCAD will show the following prompt on the command line:

```
Enter an option [ON/OFF/All/Noorigin/ORigin] <ON>:
```

As you explore AutoCAD commands you will become familiar with many prompts like this one. First comes the prompt, then a series of options inside brackets [ ] separated by slashes (/). The current setting is shown between the arrows < >. For now we only need to know about "On" and "Off".

⊕ Type "off" and press enter.

The UCS icon will disappear from your screen. Anytime you want to see it again, type "ucsicon" and then type "on". Alternatively, you can click on "View" on the menu bar, then highlight "Display" and "Ucsicon" and click "On". This will turn the icon on if it is off. If the ucsicon is on, the word on the menu will be "Off". In this case selecting Off will turn the icon off.

1.4 Exploring Command Entry Methods

In the last section you entered your first command, the UCSICON command, using the keyboard. You can also communicate drawing instructions to AutoCAD by selecting items from a toolbar, a pull-down menu, a short cut menu, or a tablet menu. Each method has its advantages and disadvantages depending on the situation and most tasks can be accomplished in several different ways. Often a combination of two or more methods is the most efficient way to carry out a complete command sequence. The instructions in this book are not always specific about which to use. All operators develop their own preferences.

An important concept in the creation of AutoCAD 2000 is what is termed "Heads-up Design". What this means is that optimal efficiency is achieved when the CAD operator can keep his or her attention focused on the screen, in particular, the drawing area and the objects being worked on. The less time and effort spent looking away from the screen the better. Staying heads-up certainly works as a general rule, and we will provide you with many techniques to support it as we go along.

Each of the basic command entry methods is described briefly. You do not have to try them all out at this time. Read them over to get a feel for the possibilities and then proceed to the LINE command.

The Keyboard and the Command Line

The keyboard is the most primitive and fundamental method of interacting with AutoCAD and is still of great importance despite the goal of staying heads-up. Toolbars and menus all function in part by automating basic command sequences as they would be typed on the keyboard. Being familiar with the keyboard procedures will increase your understanding of AutoCAD even if other methods are sometimes faster. The keyboard is the most basic, the most comprehensive, and changes the least from one release of AutoCAD to the next. It is literally at your fingertips and if you know the command you want, you will not have to go looking for it. For this reason, some excellent CAD operators rely too heavily on the keyboard. Do not limit yourself by typing everything. If you know the keyboard sequence, try out the other methods to see how they vary and how you can use them to save time and to stay screen-focused. Ultimately, you will want to type as little as possible and use the differences between the toolbar and menu systems to your advantage.

As you type commands and responses to prompts, the characters you are typing will appear on the command line after the colon. Remember that you must press enter to complete your commands and responses. The command line can be moved and reshaped, or you can switch to the text screen using F2 when you want to see more lines, including previously typed entries.

Many of the most often used commands, such as LINE, ERASE, and CIRCLE, have "aliases." These one- or two-letter abbreviations are very handy. A few of the most commonly used aliases are shown in Figure 1-6. There are also a large number of two- and three-letter aliases, some of which we will introduce as we go along.

Pull-Down Menus

Pull-down menus and toolbars have the great advantage that instead of typing a complete command, you can simply "point and shoot" to select an item, without looking away from the screen. The pull-down menus are always available and contain most commands that you will use regularly. Menu selections and toolbar selections often duplicate each other.

COMMAND ALIAS CHART	
LETTER + ENTER	= COMMAND
A ⏎	ARC
C ⏎	CIRCLE
E ⏎	ERASE
F ⏎	FILLET
L ⏎	LINE
M ⏎	MOVE
O ⏎	OFFSET
P ⏎	PAN
R ⏎	REDRAW
S ⏎	STRECH
Z ⏎	ZOOM

Figure 1-6

Pull-down menus work in AutoCAD as they do in any Windows application. To use a menu, move the cross hairs up into the menu bar so that the selection arrow appears. Then move the arrow to the menu heading you want. Select it with the pickbutton (the left button on your mouse). A menu will appear. Run down the list of items to the one you want. Press the pickbutton again to select the item (see Figure 1-7). Items followed by a triangle have "cascading" submenus. Submenus open automatically when an item is highlighted. Picking an item that is followed by an ellipsis (...) will call up a dialog box.

Dialog boxes are familiar features in all Windows and Macintosh programs. They require a combination of pointing and typing that is fairly intuitive. We will discuss many dialog boxes and dialog box features as we go along.

Toolbars

Toolbars are also a standard Windows feature. They are comprised of buttons with icons that give one-click access to commands. Twenty-four toolbars can be opened from the Toolbars dialog box accessible from the bottom of the View pull-down menu or from a short cut menu opened by right clicking on any open toolbar.

Once opened, toolbars can "float" anywhere on the screen, or can be "docked" along the edges of the drawing area. Toolbars can be a nuisance, since they cover portions of your drawing space, but they can be opened and closed quickly. Beyond the Standard, Object Properties, Draw, and Modify toolbars, which are open by default, you will probably only wish to open a toolbar if you are doing a whole set of procedures involving one toolbar. In dimensioning an object, for example, you may wish to have the Dimensioning toolbar open. Do not use too many toolbars at once, and remember that you can move toolbars or use the scroll bars to move your drawing right, left, up, and down behind the toolbars.

The icons used on toolbars are also a mixed blessing. One picture may be worth a thousand words, but with so many pictures, you may find that a few words can be very helpful as well. As in other Windows applications, you can get a label for an icon simply by allowing the selection arrow to rest on the button for a moment without selecting it. These labels are called "Tooltips". Try this:

⊕   Position the selection arrow on the top button of the Draw toolbar, as shown in Figure 1-8, but do not press the pickbutton.

You will see a yellow label that says "Line", as shown in Figure 1-8. This label identifies this button as the LINE command button.

When a tooltip is displayed, you will also see a phrase in the status bar in place of the coordinate display. This phrase will describe what the tool or menu item does and is called a "Helpstring." The LINE helpstring says "Creates straight line segments: line". The word following the colon identifies the command as you would type it in the command area.

Tablet Menus

If you are using a digitizer with a tablet (as opposed to a mouse) you may have a tablet menu available. Tablet menus were once very popular but are less common now since everything you need is accessible in menus and toolbars. With a good

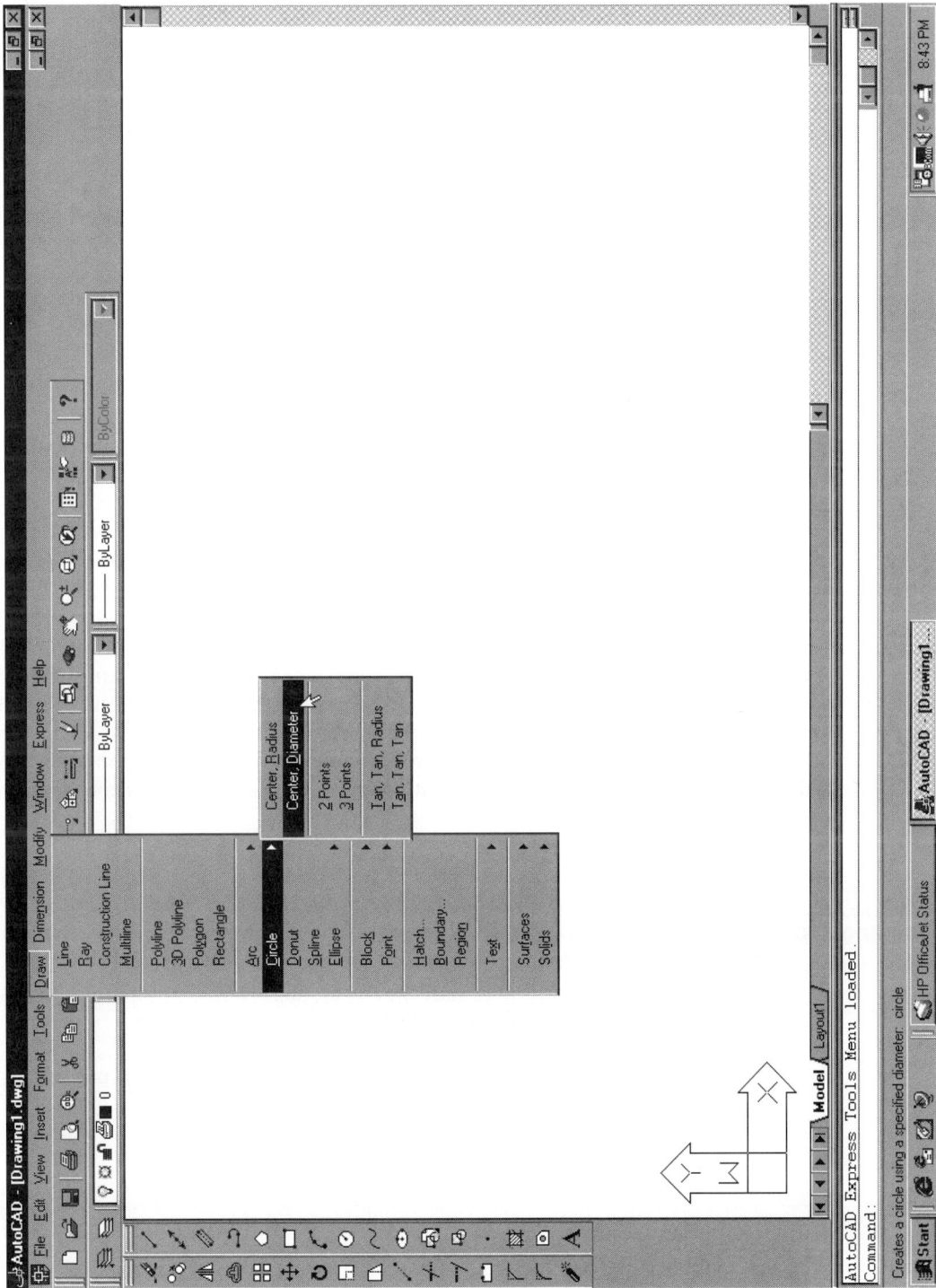

Figure 1-7

Figure 1-8

menu system there should be a large number of commands and subcommands available on the tablet, and you will not have to search through submenus or toolbars to find them. The major disadvantage of the tablet menu is that it is the antithesis of heads-up design; in order to use it you must take your eyes off the screen.

On a digitizing tablet move the pointing device over the item you want and press the pickbutton. Also be aware that tablet menus can turned on and off using the F4 key.

Now let's get started drawing.

1.5   Drawing and Undoing Lines

GENERAL PROCEDURE

1. Type "L", select Line from the Draw menu, or select the Line tool from the Draw toolbar.
2. Pick a start point.
3. Pick an end point.
4. Pick another end point to continue in the LINE command, or press enter or the enter button on your mouse to exit the command.

The procedure listed above is a general list of how to enter and use the LINE command. We offer these General Procedures throughout the book as a quick reference and overview. They do not in any way substitute for the more detailed and specific exercises that follow them.

| SNAP | GRID | ORTHO | POLAR | OSNAP | OTRACK | LWT | MODEL |

Figure 1-9

⊕ In preparation, make sure that your status line resembles ours, as shown in Figure 1-9.

In particular, note that SNAP, GRID, and MODEL are in the on position (down), while ORTHO, POLAR, OSNAP, OTRACK, and LWT are off (up). This will keep things simple and uncluttered for the present. ***This is very important***. While features like Osnap and Polar tracking are very powerful, they also can get in your way when used at the wrong time. You will have plenty of use for them later on.

Now it is time to enter the LINE command and start drawing.

⊕ Type "L" or select the Line icon from the Draw toolbar, or Line under Draw on the pull-down menu (remember to press enter if you are typing).

Look at the command area. You should see this, regardless of how you enter the command:

```
Specify first point:
```

This is how AutoCAD asks for a start point for your line.

Also, notice that the pickbox disappears from the cross hairs when you have entered a drawing command.

Most of the time when you are drawing you will want to point rather than type. To do this you need to pay attention to the grid and the coordinate display.

⊕ If snap is off switch it on (F9 or click on SNAP).
⊕ Move the cursor until the display reads "1.0000, 1.0000, 0.000".
⊕ Press the pickbutton.

AutoCAD registers your first point and asks for a second point. You should see this in the command area:

```
Specify next point or [Undo]:
```

This prompts you to pick a second point. The "Undo" option will be discussed shortly.

Rubber Band

There are several other new things to be aware of. One is the "rubber band," which extends from the start point to the cross hairs on the screen. If you move the cursor, you will see that this visual aid stretches, shrinks, or rotates like a tether, keeping you connected to the start point. In this case the rubber band represents the line you are about to draw.

Absolute (xyz) and Polar Coordinates

Another feature to watch is the coordinate display. If it is off (no change in coordinates when the cursor moves), press F6 to turn it on. Once it is on it will show either absolute coordinates or polar coordinates. Absolute coordinates are the familiar coordinate numbers (x,y,z) discussed previously. They are distances measured from the origin (0,0,0) of the coordinate system at the lower left corner of the grid. If your display shows three four-digit numbers, then these are the absolute coordinates.

If your display shows something like "4.2426<45,0.0000", it is set on polar coordinates.

⊕   Press F6 or click on the coordinate display and then move your cursor.

Which type of coordinates is displayed?

⊕   Press F6 and move your cursor again.

Observe the coordinate display. As you continue to press F6, you will see that there are three coordinate display modes: static (no change until you select a point), xyz (x, y, and z values separated by a comma), and polar (length<angle, z).

⊕   Press F6 once or twice more until you see polar coordinates.

Polar coordinates are in a length, angle, z format and are given relative to the last point you picked. They look something like this: 5.6569<45,0.0000. There are three values here: 5.6569, 45, and 0.0000. The first number (5.6569) is the distance from the starting point of the line to the cross hairs. The second (45) is an angle of rotation, measuring counterclockwise, with 0 degrees being straight out to the right. The third value (0.0000) is the z coordinate, which will remain zero in 2D drawing. In LINE, as well as many other draw commands, polar coordinates are very useful because the first number will give you the length of the segment you are currently drawing.

Now switch back to absolute coordinates and complete a line between (1.0000,1.0000,0.0000) and (8.0000,8.0000,0.0000), as follows.

⊕   Press F6 to read *xyz* coordinates.

⊕   Pick the point (8.0000,8.0000,0.0000).

Your screen should now resemble Figure 1-10. AutoCAD has drawn a line between (1,1) and (8,8) and is asking for another point.

                Specify next point or [Undo]:

This prompt allows you to stay in the LINE command to draw a whole series of connected lines if you wish. You can draw a single line from point to point, or a series of lines from point to point to point to point. In either case, you must tell AutoCAD when you are finished by pressing enter or the space bar.

Note: When you are drawing a continuous series of lines, the polar coordinates on the display are given relative to the most recent point, not the original starting point.

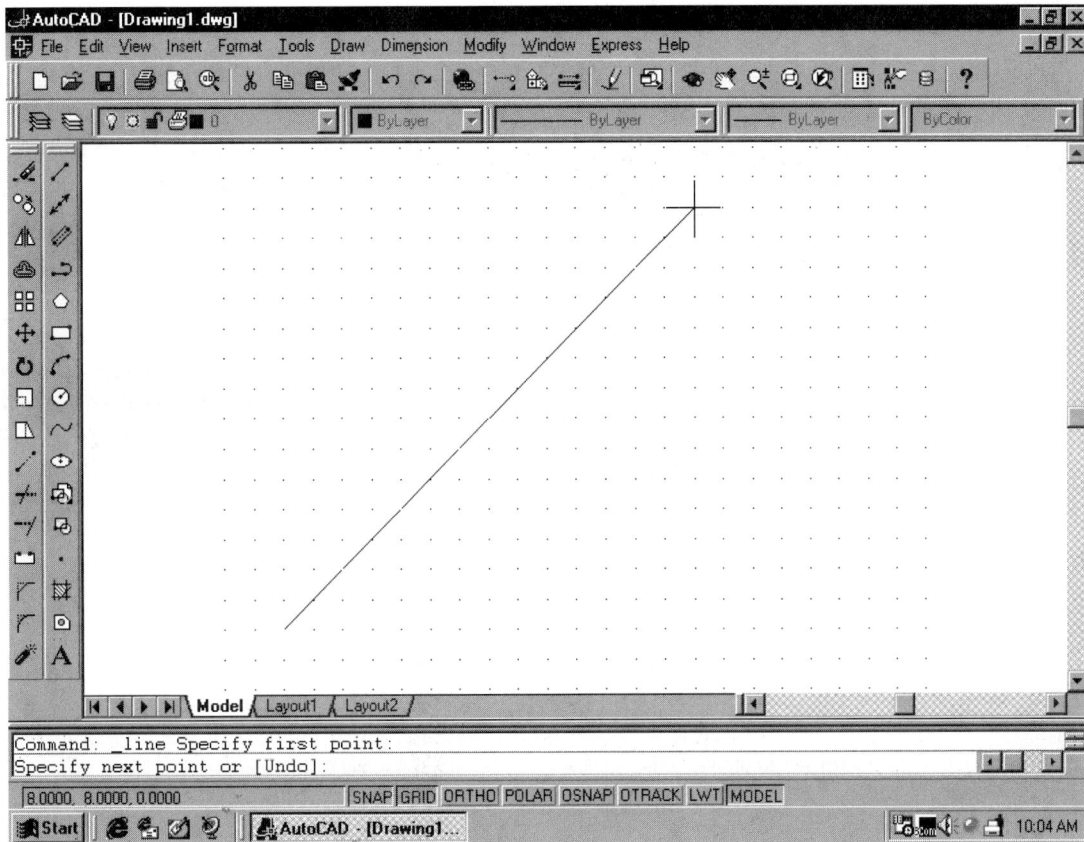

Figure 1-10

⊞ Press enter or the space bar to end the LINE command.

You should be back to the "Command:" prompt again, and the pickbox will have reappeared at the intersection of the cross hairs.

Space Bar, Enter Key, and Right Mouse Button

In most cases AutoCAD allows you to use the space bar as a substitute for the enter key. Although this is one of the oldest of AutoCAD features, it is a major contributor to the goal of heads-up drawing. It is a great convenience, since the space bar is easy to locate with one hand (your left hand if the mouse is on the right side) while the other hand is on the pointing device. For example, the LINE command can be entered without removing your right hand from your pointing device by typing the "L" on the keyboard with your left index finger and then hitting the space bar with your left thumb. The major exception to the use of the space bar as an enter key is when you are entering text in the TEXT or MTEXT commands (Chapter 7). Since a space may be part of a text string, the space bar must have its usual significance there.

Short Cut Menus

The right button on your mouse may also be used in place of the enter key sometimes, but in most cases there will be an intervening step involving a short cut menu
with choices. This, too, is a major heads-up feature, which we will explore as we
go along. For now, try this:

⊕ Press the right button on your mouse (this action will be called right-
click from now on).

This calls a short cut menu, as shown in Figure 1-11. The top line is a Repeat Line option that can be used to re-enter the LINE command. You will
have no use for the other options until later chapters.

Short cut menus are context sensitive; the menu that is called depends on
the situation. Often the last command entered can be repeated by selecting
the top option.

Tip: You can also repeat the last command by hitting the space bar or the
enter key at the command prompt. We recommend that you use this major
convenience often.

⊕ Move the cursor anywhere outside of the cursor menu and press the
pickbutton (the left mouse button).

The cursor menu will disappear but AutoCAD 2000 will take the picked
point as the first point in an object selection window.

⊕ Pick any second point to close the object selection window.

There are many context-sensitive short cut menus in AutoCAD 2000 and Windows
98. We will not attempt to present every one, but encourage you to explore. You
will find many possibilities simply by clicking the right mouse button while in a
command or dialog box.

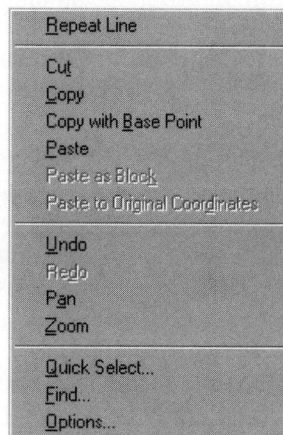

Repeat Line
Cut
Copy
Copy with Base Point
Paste
Paste as Block
Paste to Original Coordinates
Undo
Redo
Pan
Zoom
Quick Select...
Find...
Options...

Figure 1-11

Relative Coordinates and "@"

Besides typing or showing absolute *xyz* coordinates, AutoCAD allows you to en-ter points using coordinates relative to the last point selected. To do this, use the "@" symbol. For example, after picking the point (1,1) in the last exercise you could have specified the point (8,8) by typing "@7,7", since the second point is over 7 and up 7 from the first point. Or, using polar coordinates relative to (1,1), you could, in theory, type "@9.8995<45". All of these methods would give the same results.

Direct Distance Entry

Another convenient drawing method is called Direct Distance Entry. In this method, you pick the first point and then show the direction of the line segment you wish to draw, but instead of picking the other end point you type in a value for the length of the line. Try it:

⊕ Repeat the LINE command by pressing enter or the space bar.

AutoCAD prompts for a first point.

Tip: If you press enter or the space bar at the "Specify first point:" prompt, AutoCAD will select the last point entered, so that you can begin drawing from where you left off.

⊕ Press enter or the space bar to select the point (8,8,0), the end point of the previously drawn line.

AutoCAD prompts for a second point.

⊕ Pull the rubber band diagonally down to the right, as shown in Figure 1-12.

Moving along the diagonal set of grid points will put you at a −45 de-gree angle, as shown. The length of the rubber band does not matter, only the direction.

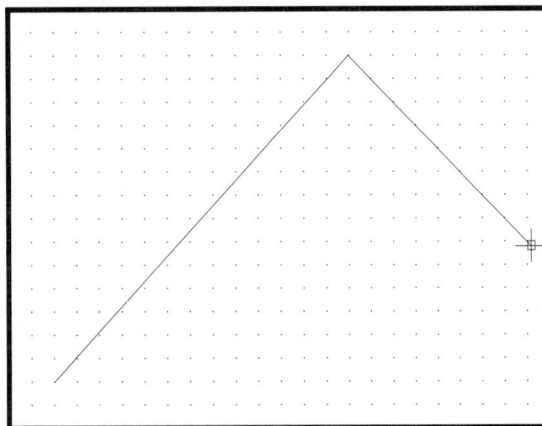

Figure 1-12

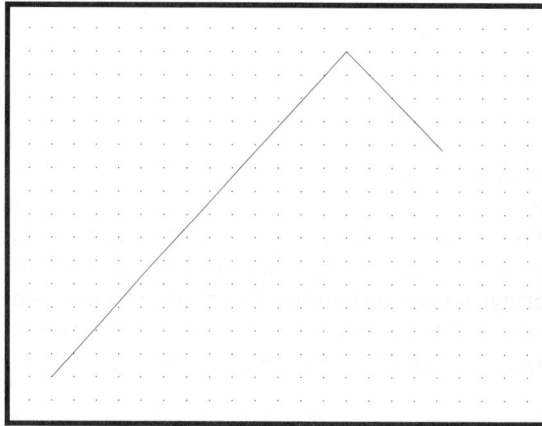

Figure 1-13

⊕ With the rubber band stretched out as shown, type "3".

⊕ Press enter or hit the space bar.

  AutoCAD will draw a 3.0000 line segment at the angle you have shown.

⊕ Press enter or the space bar to exit the LINE command.

  Your screen should resemble Figure 1-13.

Undoing Commands with U

⊕ To undo the line you just drew, type "U" <enter> or select the Undo tool from the Standard toolbar, as shown in Figure 1-14.

  U undoes the last command, so if you have done anything else since drawing the line, you will need to type "U" <enter> more than once. In this way you can walk backward through your drawing session, undoing your commands one by one. As mentioned previously, there is also an Undo option within the LINE command so that you can undo the last segment drawn without leaving the command.

⊕ Select the Redo tool, which is to the right of the Undo tool on the Standard toolbar.

  REDO only works immediately after U, and it only works once. That is, you can only REDO the last U and only if it was the last command executed.

  Note: The Undo tool executes a command called U. AutoCAD also has an UNDO command that can be entered at the command line by typing "undo".

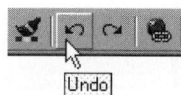

Figure 1-14

U is not an alias for UNDO, which is more elaborate. REDO can be used to reverse either U or UNDO. Also note that R is not an alias for REDO.

⊕ Use the Redo tool to ensure that there is at least one line in your drawing. Or, draw a new line.

Erasing Lines

The ERASE command will be explored in Chapter 2, but for now you may want to have access to this important command in its simplest form. Using ERASE brings up the techniques of object selection, which are common to all editing commands. The simplest form of object selection requires that you point to an object and then click the pick button. Try this:

⊕ Move the cross hairs so that they are over one of the lines on your screen, as shown in Figure 1-15.
⊕ Press the pickbutton.

You will see that the line becomes dotted, indicating that it has been selected. You will also see small blue boxes at the middle and at each end of the line. You can ignore these for now. They will be discussed in Chapter 2.

Now that the line is selected, you can enter the ERASE command to erase it.

⊕ Type "e" with the middle finger of your left hand and hit the space bar with your left thumb.

The line will disappear. Notice the left-hand alias and space bar technique again.

⊕ Before going on use U or ERASE to remove all lines from your drawing, leaving a blank drawing area.

Be aware that undoing ERASE will cause a line to reappear.

Ortho

Before completing this section on line drawing, we suggest that you try the ortho and polar tracking modes.

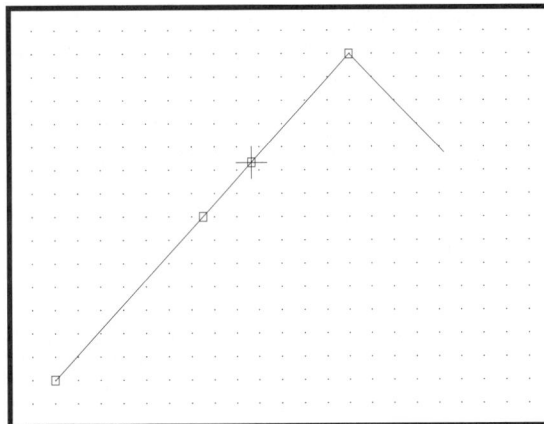

Figure 1-15

⌗ Type "L" <enter> or select the Line tool from the Draw toolbar.

⌗ Pick a starting point. Any point near the center of the screen will do.

⌗ Press F8 or click on the word ORTHO, so that the button goes down.

⌗ Move the cursor in slow circles.

Notice how the rubber band jumps between horizontal and vertical without sweeping through any of the angles between. Ortho forces the pointing device to pick up points only along the horizontal and vertical quadrant lines from a given starting point. With ortho on you can select points at 0, 90, 180, and 270 degrees of rotation from your starting point only (see Figure 1-16).

The advantages of ortho are similar to the advantages of snap mode, except that it limits angular rather than linear increments. It ensures that you will get precise and true right angles and perpendiculars easily when that is your intent. Ortho will become more important as drawings grow more complex. In this chapter it is hardly necessary, though it will be convenient in drawings 1 and 3.

Polar Tracking

Polar tracking is a new AutoCAD 2000 feature that may replace ORTHO for many purposes. Try it out:

⌗ Press F10 or select the POLAR button to turn on polar tracking.

Notice that POLAR and ORTHO are mutually exclusive. They cannot both be on at the same time. When you turn POLAR on, ORTHO shuts off automatically.

⌗ Move your cursor in a slow circle around the starting point of your line, just as you did with ORTHO on.

With POLAR tracking on, you will see that when the rubber band crosses a vertical or horizontal axis (i.e., when the rubber band is at 0, 90, 180, or 270 degrees),

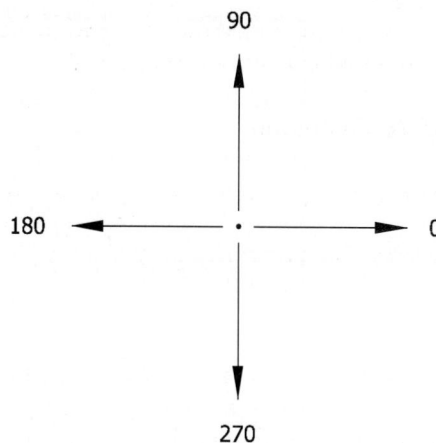

90

180 ← · → 0

270

Figure 1-16

Figure 1-17

a dotted line appears that extends to the edge of the drawing area. You will also see a tooltip label giving a value like "Polar 6.5000<0°" (see Figure 1-17). The value is a polar coordinate, without the *z* value. By default, polar tracking is set to respond on the orthogonal axes. In later chapters you will see that it can be set to track at any angle. For now you should leave it off and focus on basic line drawing and point selection.

⊕ Press F10 or click on the POLAR button to turn polar tracking off.

⊕ Move the cross hairs in a circle and observe that polar tracking is no longer in effect.

The Esc key

⊕ While still in the LINE command, press the "Esc" (escape) key.

This will abort the LINE command and bring back the "Command:" prompt. Esc is used to cancel a command that has been entered. Sometimes it will be necessary to press Esc twice to exit a command and return to the command prompt.

1.6 Saving and Opening Drawings

Saving drawings in AutoCAD 2000 is just like saving a file in other Windows 98 applications. Use SAVE to save an already named drawing. Use SAVEAS to name a drawing as you save it or save a named drawing under a new name. In all cases, a .dwg extension is added to file names to identify them as AutoCAD drawing files. This is automatic when you name a file.

The SAVE Command

To save a drawing without leaving the drawing window, select "Save" from the File pull-down menu, or select the Save tool from the Standard toolbar, as shown in Figure 1-18.

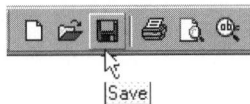

Figure 1-18

If the current drawing is already named, AutoCAD 2000 will save it without intervening dialog. If it is not named, it will open the SAVEAS dialog box and allow you to give it a name before it is saved. SAVEAS is described following.

The SAVEAS Command

To rename a drawing or to give a name to a previously unnamed drawing, type "Saveas", select "Saveas..." from the File pull-down menu, or, in an unnamed drawing, select the Save tool from the Standard Toolbar.

Any of these methods will call the Save Drawing As dialog box (see Figure 1-19). The cursor will be blinking in the area labeled "Files:", waiting for you to enter a file name. Include a drive designation, (i.e., "A:1-1") if you are saving your work on a floppy disk. AutoCAD will add the .dwg extension automatically. SAVEAS will also allow you to save different versions of the same drawing under different names while continuing to edit.

OPENing Saved Drawings

To open a previously saved drawing, type "open", select "Open" from the File pull-down menu, or select the Open tool from the Standard toolbar, as shown in Figure 1-20.

Once you have saved a drawing you will need to use the OPEN command to return to it later. Entering the OPEN command by any method will bring up the Select File dialog box shown in Figure 1-21. You can select a file directory in the box at the left and then a file from the box at the right. When you select a file, AutoCAD 2000 will show a preview image of the selected drawing in the Preview image box at the right. This way you can be sure that you are opening the drawing you want.

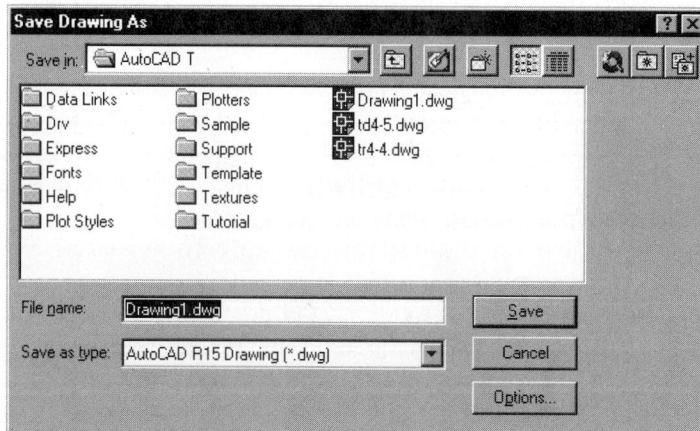

Figure 1-19

Figure 1-20

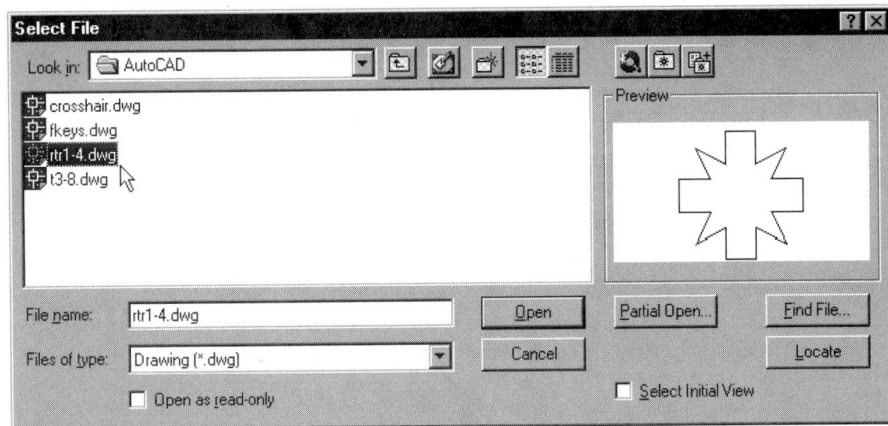

Figure 1-21

Exiting the Drawing Window

To leave AutoCAD, open the File pull-down menu and select "Exit", or click the Windows 98 close button (X) at the upper right of the screen. If you have not saved your current drawing, AutoCAD will ask you if you wish to save your changes before exiting.

1.7   Review Material

Questions

Before going to the drawings, review the following questions and problems. Then you should be ready for Drawing 1.

1. What function key opens and closes the text window?
2. What are the three different modes of the coordinate display and how does each mode appear? What are two ways to switch between modes?
3. What is Heads-up Design? Give three examples of heads-up design features from this chapter.
4. Explain and describe the differences among absolute, relative, and polar coordinates.
5. You have just entered the point (1,1,0) and you now wish to enter the point two units straight up from this point. How would you identify this point using absolute, relative, and polar coordinates?
6. What is the value and limitation of having SNAP on?
7. Name three different ways to enter the LINE command.
8. Name and describe three different methods of point selection in AutoCAD.
9. What does the U command do?
10. What is the main limitation of the REDO command?
11. What is the keyboard alias for the ERASE command?
12. What key do you use to cancel a command?
13. What command would you use to save a new version of a drawing under a new file name? How would you enter it?

Drawing Problem

1. Draw a line from (3,2) to (4,8) using the keyboard only.
2. Draw a line from (6,6) to (7,5) using the mouse only.
3. Draw a line from (6,6) to (6,8) using the direct distance method.
4. Undo (U) all lines on your screen.
5. Draw a square with corners at (2,2), (7,2), (7,7), and (2,7). Then erase it using the ERASE command.

> **Tip:** Closing a Set of Lines
> For drawing an enclosed figure like the one in step 5, the LINE command provides a convenient Close option. "Close" will connect the last in a continuous series of lines back to the starting point of the series. In drawing a square, for instance, you would simply type "C" <enter> in lieu of drawing the last of the four lines. For this to work, the whole square must be drawn without leaving the LINE command.

1.8   WWW Exercise #1 (Optional)

AutoCAD 2000 is a fully integrated Internet program. If you have Internet access you can go online from within the AutoCAD program or launch your browser from the Windows 98 taskbar. You must first be connected to your Internet provider. Beyond that you can move easily in and out of AutoCAD as you access all the resources available on the World Wide Web. Later in this book you will also learn how AutoCAD drawings can be published to the Web, transferred as email attachments, uploaded, downloaded, and included as part of Web sites and homepages. Further, you will learn how objects in a drawing can be designated as hyperlinks so that selecting them will take you directly from the drawing to an associated URL. If any of this language is not familiar to you, don't worry. You will learn everything you need to know for these exercises as you go along. To facilitate this, this book has its own (very cool) Companion Web site, which you are encouraged to access. At this site you will find self-scoring tests for each chapter of the book, special Web projects related to the material in the chapter, and links to other important and interesting CAD-related Web sites.

So, for your first AutoCAD 2000 Web trip we will teach you how to reach our Web site. Once there, take the test or go to the Web Project page for further instructions.

⊕ First, you must be sure that you are connected to an Internet service provider.

Do not exit AutoCAD, but use the minimize button, or the Windows 98 Show Desktop button, illustrated in Figure 1-22, to temporarily leave the drawing window. We cannot give you specific instructions for connecting to the Internet from your system. For these, consult your internet software documentation, instructor, or system manager.

```
┌──────────────────────────────────┐
│ 0.0086, 0.0086, 0.0000  Show Desktop │
│ ┌──────────────────────────────┐ │
│ │ 🚩 Start ║ 🌐 🔗 ◰🖱️        │ │
│ └──────────────────────────────┘ │
└──────────────────────────────────┘
```

Figure 1-22

⊕ Once you are connected to the Internet, click the AutoCAD icon on the Windows 98 taskbar to return to AutoCAD.

⊕ At the command prompt, type "browser".

This is the BROWSER command through which you can access Internet addresses. AutoCAD will prompt for an address:

```
Enter web location (URL) <C:\program files\AutoCAD...>:
```

The default location is shown within the brackets (< >) and is likely to be different from the one shown here. In Chapter 2 we will show you how to change this default.

⊕ Type "www.prenhall.com/dixriley".

If you are properly configured and connected, this will open our Companion Web site homepage shown in Figure 1-23.

⊕ Maximize the window, as shown, and enjoy your visit!

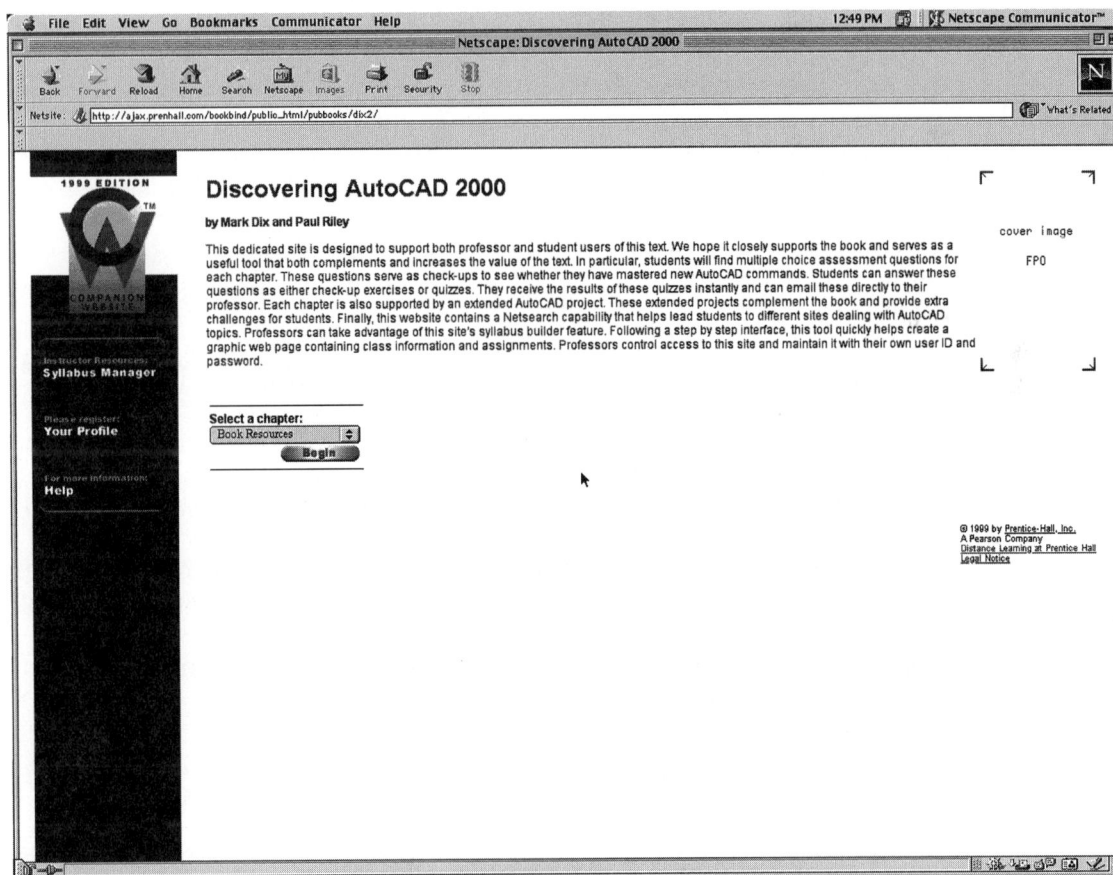

Figure 1-23

1.9   Drawing 1-1: Grate

Before beginning, look over the drawing page. Notice the status bar mode reminders and other drawing information below. *It is important to keep the modes as shown.*

The first two drawings in this chapter are given without dimensions. Instead, we have drawn them as you will see them on the screen, against the background of a half-unit grid. All of these drawings were done using the default half-unit snap, but all points will be found on one-unit increments.

DRAWING SUGGESTIONS

- If you are beginning a new drawing, type or select "New..." and then select Start from Scratch in the Startup dialog box. Notice that AutoCAD 2000 remembers your last selection and it becomes the default. Because of this you may be able simply to press enter or select OK to get started.
- Remember to watch the coordinate display when searching for a point.
- Be sure that GRID, SNAP, and the coordinate display are all turned on and that OSNAP, OTRACK, and LWT are turned off. ORTHO or POLAR may be on or off as you wish.
- Draw the outer rectangle first. It is six units wide and seven units high, and its lower left-hand corner is at the point (3.0000,1.0000). The three smaller rectangles inside are 4 × 1.
- The Close option can be used in all four of the rectangles.

IF YOU MAKE A MISTAKE—U

This is a reminder that you can stay in the LINE command as you undo the last line you drew, or the last two or three if you have drawn a series.

- Type "U" <enter>. The last line you drew will be gone or replaced by the rubber band, awaiting a new end point. If you want to go back more than one line, type "U" <enter> again, as many times as you need.
- If you have already left the LINE command, the U command will undo the last continuous series of lines. In Grate this could be the whole outside rectangle, for instance.
- Remember, if you have mistakenly undone something, you can get it back by using the Redo tool. You cannot perform other commands between U and REDO.

3,1

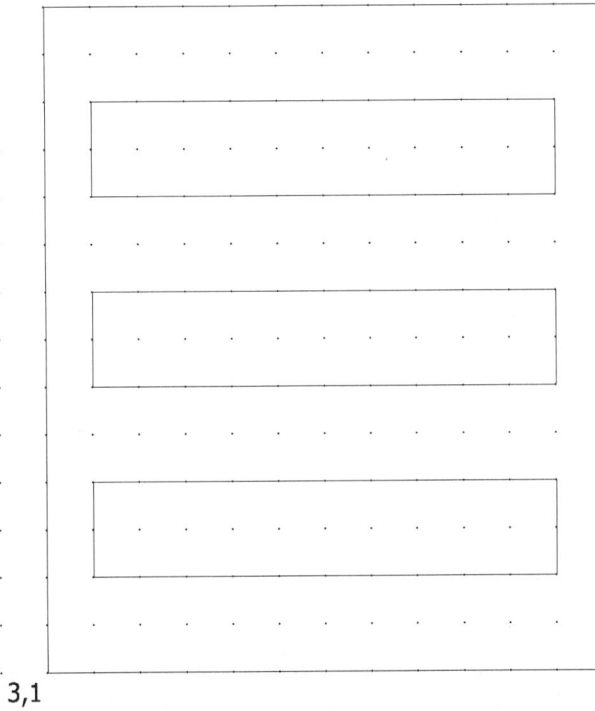

GRATE
Drawing 1-1

1.10   Drawing 1-2: Design

This design will give you further practice with the LINE command.

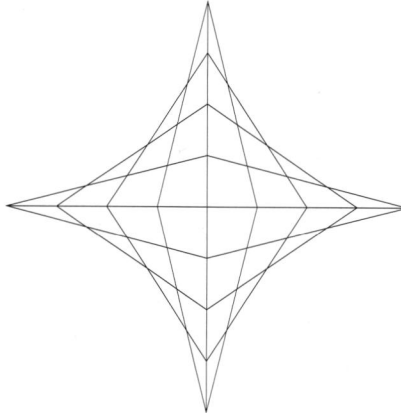

DRAWING SUGGESTIONS

- If you are beginning a new drawing, type or select "New..." and then check the Start Up dialog box to ensure that you Start from Scratch.
- Draw the horizontal and vertical lines first. Each is eight units long.
- Notice how the rest of the lines work—outside point on horizontal to inside point on vertical, then working in, or vice versa.
- You will want ORTHO off to do this drawing.
- Placing the bottom tip of the design at (6,0.5) as shown will keep your drawing well positioned on the grid.

REPEATING A COMMAND

Remember, you can repeat a command by pressing enter or the space bar at the Command: prompt. This will be useful in this drawing, since you have several sets of lines to draw.

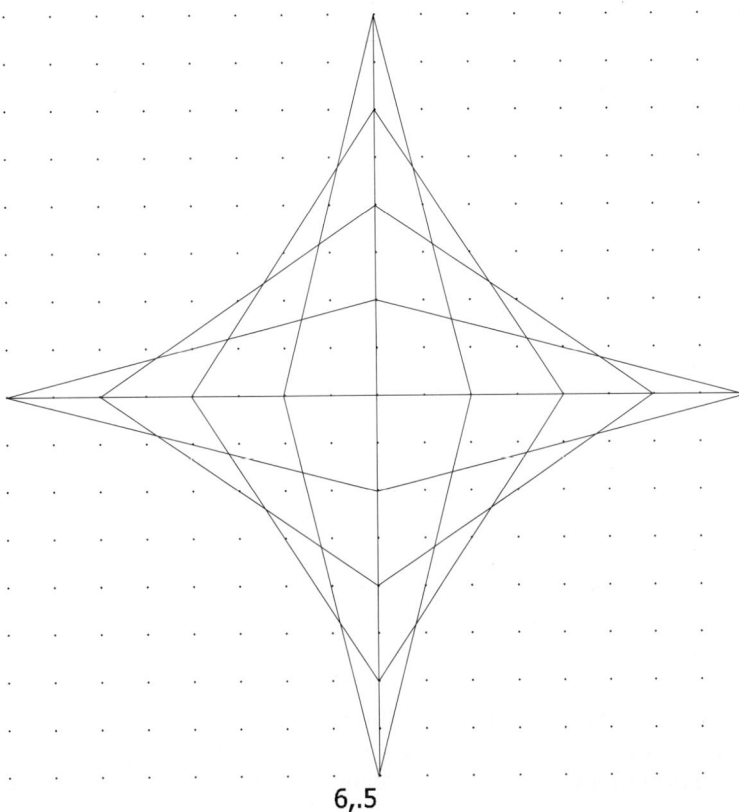

6,.5

DESIGN #1
Drawing 1-2

1.11 Drawing 1-3: Shim

This drawing will give you further practice in using the LINE command. In addition, it will give you practice in translating dimensions into distances on the screen. Note that the dimensions are only included for your information; they are not part of the drawing at this point. Your drawing will appear like the reference drawing that follows. Dimensioning is discussed in Chapter 8.

DRAWING SUGGESTIONS

- If you are beginning a new drawing, type or select "New..." and Start from Scratch.
- It is most important that you choose a starting point that will position the drawing so that it fits on your screen. If you begin with the bottom left-hand corner of the outside figure at the point (3,1), you should have no trouble.
- Read the dimensions carefully to see how the geometry of the drawing works. It is good practice to look over the dimensions before you begin drawing. Often the dimension for a particular line may be located on another side of the figure or may have to be extrapolated from other dimensions. It is not uncommon to misread, misinterpret, or miscalculate a dimension, so take your time.

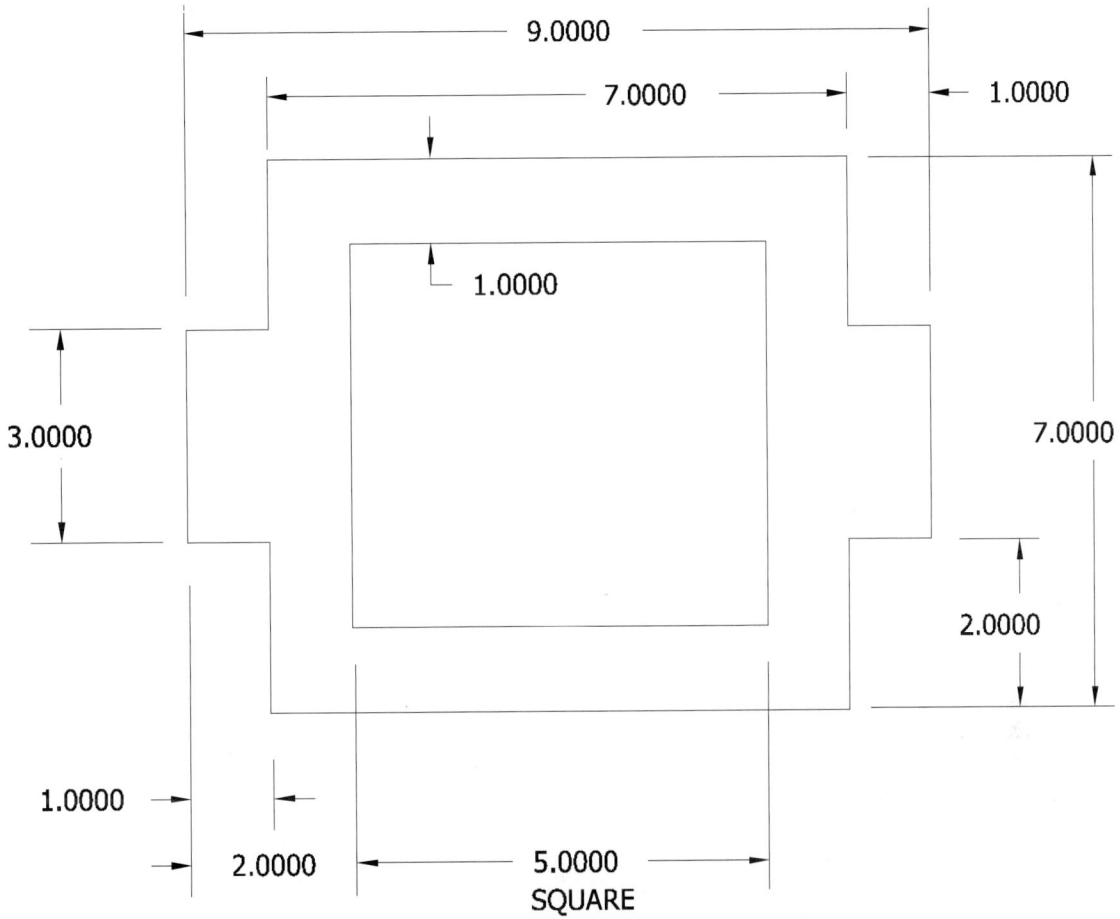

SHIM

Drawing 1-3

1.12   Drawing 1-4: Stamp

This drawing will give you practice in point selection. You can begin anywhere and use any of the point selection methods introduced in this chapter. We recommend that you try them all.

DRAWING SUGGESTIONS

- If you are beginning a new drawing, type or select "New..." and Start from Scratch.
- ORTHO should be off to do this drawing.
- The entire drawing can be done without leaving the LINE command if you wish.
- If you do leave LINE, remember that you can repeat LINE by pressing enter or the space bar, and then select the last point as a new start point by pressing enter or the space bar again.
- Plan to use point selection by typing, by pointing, and by direct distance entry. Make use of absolute, relative, and polar coordinates.

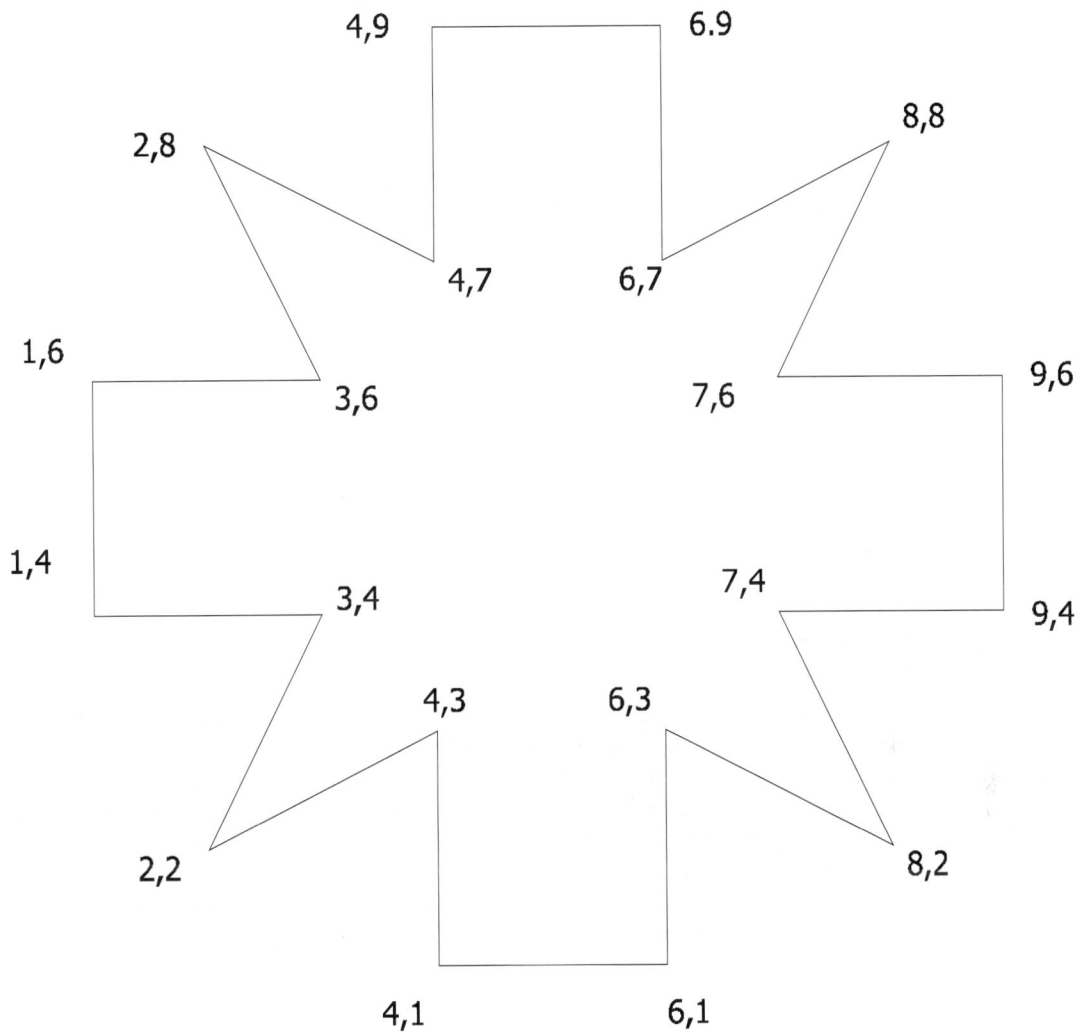

4,9   6.9

8,8

2,8

4,7   6,7

1,6

3,6   7,6   9,6

1,4

3,4   7,4   9,4

4,3   6,3

2,2   8,2

4,1   6,1

STAMP
Drawing 1-4

2

Circles and Drawing Aids

COMMANDS

CIRCLE	ERASE	OOPS	SNAP
DDRMODES	GRID	PLOT	UNITS
DIST	HELP	RECTANGLE	

OVERVIEW

This chapter is loaded with new material and techniques. Here you will begin to gain control of your drawing environment by changing the spacing of the grid and the snap and the units in which coordinates are displayed. You will add to your repertoire of objects by drawing circles with the CIRCLE command and rectangles with the RECTANGLE command. You will explore the many methods of object selection as you continue to learn editing procedures with the ERASE command. You will gain access to convenient HELP features and begin to learn AutoCAD's extensive plotting and printing procedures.

TASKS

2.1 Changing the GRID setting
2.2 Changing the SNAP setting
2.3 Changing UNITS
2.4 Drawing CIRCLES giving center point and radius
2.5 Drawing CIRCLES giving center point and diameter
2.6 Accessing AutoCAD HELP features
2.7 Using the ERASE command
2.8 Using the RECTANGLE command

2.9 Using the DIST command
2.10 Plotting or printing a drawing
2.11 Review material
2.12 WWW Exercise #2 (Optional)
2.13 Drawing 2-1: Aperture Wheel
2.14 Drawing 2-2: Roller
2.15 Drawing 2-3: Fan Bezel
2.16 Drawing 2-4: Switch Plate
2.17 Drawing 2-5: Gasket

2.1 Changing the GRID Setting

GENERAL PROCEDURE

1. Type "Grid".
2. Enter a new value.

When you begin a new drawing from scratch in AutoCAD 2000, the grid and snap are set with a spacing of 0.5000. In Chapter 1 all drawings were done without altering the grid and snap spacings from the default value. Usually you will want to change this to a value that reflects your application. You may want a 10-mile snap for a mapping project, or a 0.010-inch snap for a printed circuit diagram. The grid may match the snap setting or may be set independently.

⊕ To begin, open a new drawing by selecting the New tool from the Standard toolbar, and then selecting Start from Scratch and English units in the Start Up dialog box.

Once again, this ensures that you begin with the settings we have used in preparing this chapter.

⊕ Using F7 and F9, or clicking on the status bar, be sure that GRID and SNAP are both on.

⊕ Type "grid".

We will no longer remind you to press enter after typing a command or response to a prompt. Do not use the pull-down menu or toolbar yet. We will get to those procedures momentarily.

The command area prompt will appear like this, with options separated by slashes (/):

```
Specify grid spacing(X) or [ON/OFF/Snap/Aspect] <0.5000>:
```

You can ignore the options for now. The number <0.5000> shows the current setting. AutoCAD uses this format (<default>) in many command sequences to show you a current value or default setting. It usually comes at the end of a series of options. Pressing the enter key or space bar at this point will confirm the default setting.

⊕ In answer to the prompt, type "1" and watch what happens (of course you remembered to press enter).

The screen will change to show a one-unit grid.

⊕ Move the cursor around to observe the effects of the new grid setting.

The snap setting has not changed, so you still have access to all half-unit points, but the grid shows only single-unit increments.

⊕ Try other grid settings. Try 2, 0.25, and 0.125.

Remember that you can repeat the last command, GRID, by pressing enter or the space bar.

⊕ What happens when you try 0.05?

When you get too small (smaller than 0.109 on our screen), the grid becomes too dense to display, but the snap can still be set smaller.

⊕ Before going on to Task 2; 2 set the grid back to 0.5000.

2.2 Changing the SNAP Setting

GENERAL PROCEDURE

1. Select Drafting Settings... from the Tools pull-down menu, or right click on the Grid or Snap button and select Settings....
2. Enter a new snap value.
3. Click OK to exit the dialog box.

The process for changing the snap setting is the same as changing the grid. In fact, the two are similar enough to cause confusion. The grid is only a visual reference. It has no effect on selection of points. Snap is invisible, but it dramatically affects point selection. Grid and snap may or may not have the same setting.

Using the Drafting Settings Dialog Box

Snap may be changed using the SNAP command at the prompt, as we did with the GRID command in the last section. Both can also be changed in the Drafting Settings dialog box, as we will do in this task. The procedure is somewhat different, but the result is the same.

⊕ Type "ds" or open the Tools pull-down menu and click on "Drafting Settings...", as shown in Figure 2-1.

This will open the Drafting Settings dialog box shown in Figure 2-2. DSETTINGS is the command that calls up this dialog box, and "ds" is the command alias. Look at the dialog box. It contains some common features, including tabs, check boxes, radio buttons, and edit boxes.

Tabs

At the top of the dialog box you will see an arrangement that resembles a well-ordered set of three tabbed index cards with the words "Snap and Grid", "Polar Tracking", and "Object Snap" on the tabs. Tabbed dialog boxes are common in Windows programs. With this tabbed arrangement, a single dialog box can provide access to a large variety of related features. By clicking on a tab you can bring the related "index card" to the top of the "stack" so that is visible in front of the others. We will not need to access the Polar Tracking or Object Snap cards at this time.

⊕ If the Snap and Grid card is not on top, click its tab to bring it up.

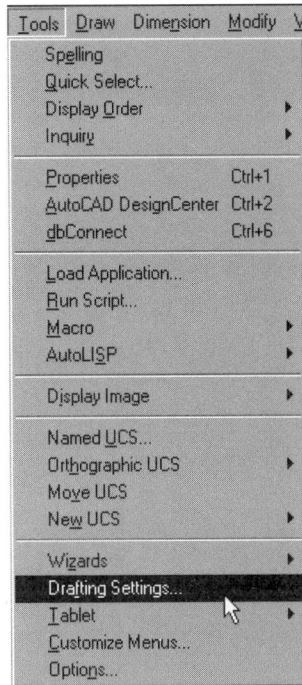

Figure 2-1

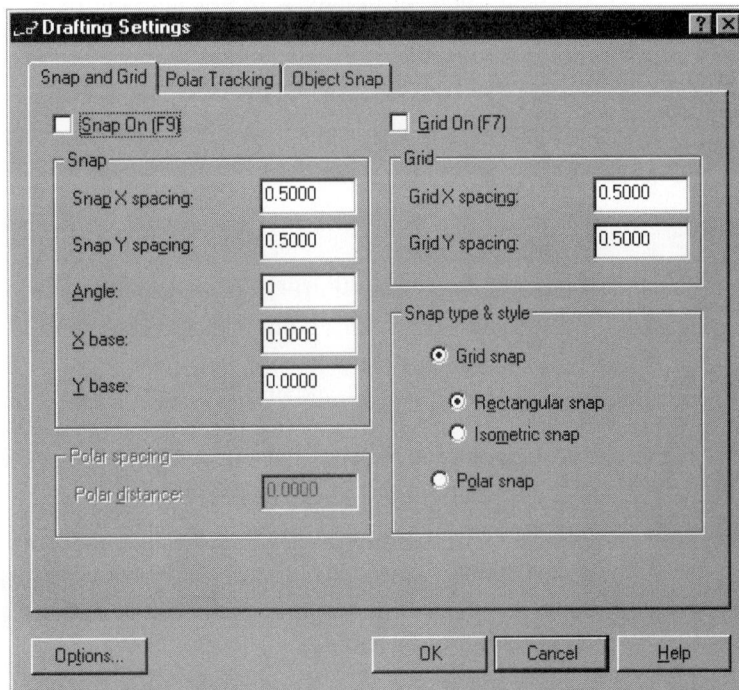

Figure 2-2

Check Boxes

Below the tabs you will see check boxes labeled "Snap on" and "Grid on". You can turn snap and grid on and off by moving the arrow inside the appropriate check box and pressing the pickbutton. A checked box is on, while an empty box is off. In your dialog box, check boxes should show that both Snap and Grid are on.

Panels

On the Snap and Grid card you will see four bordered and labeled areas. Most dialog boxes are divided into sections in this way. We will refer to these labeled sections as panels. The four panels here are Snap, Grid, Snap type & style, and Polar spacing. In this task we will look at the Snap and Grid panels only.

Edit Boxes

The snap and grid settings are shown in edit boxes, labeled Snap X spacing, Snap Y spacing, Grid X spacing, and Grid Y spacing. Edit boxes contain text or numerical information that can be edited as you would in a text editor. You can highlight the entire box to replace the text, or point anywhere inside to do partial editing.

To change the snap setting, do the following:

⊕ Move the arrow into the edit box labeled "Snap X spacing".

Note: The dialog box has places to set both *x* and *y* spacing. It is unlikely that you will want to have a grid or snap matrix with different horizontal and vertical increments, but the capacity is there if you do. Also notice that you can change the snap angle. Setting the snap angle to 45, for example, would turn your snap and grid at a 45-degree angle. When you alter the grid or snap angle, you may also want to designate *x* and *y* base points around which to rotate. This is the function of the *x* and *y* base point settings.

⊕ Double click to highlight the entire number 0.5000 in the Snap X spacing edit box.

⊕ Type "1" and press Enter.

Pressing enter at this point is like clicking on OK in the dialog box. It will take you out of the dialog box and back to the screen.

Snap is now set at 1 and grid is still at 0.5. This makes the snap setting larger than the grid setting. Move the cursor around the screen and you will see that you can only access half of the grid points. This type of arrangement is not too useful. Try some other settings.

Tip: Another way to open the Drafting settings dialog box is to right click while pointing at the Grid or Snap button on the status bar. This will open a short cut menu with On, Off, and Settings... options. Selecting Settings... will open the Drafting settings dialog box.

⊕ Open the dialog box again by right clicking on the Snap button on the status bar and then choosing Settings... from the short cut menu.

⊕ Change the snap x spacing to 0.25.

Move the cursor slowly and observe the coordinate display. This is a more efficient type of arrangement. With grid set "coarser" than snap, you can still pick exact points easily, but the grid is not so dense as to be distracting.

⊕ Set the snap to 0.05.

Remember what happened when you tried to set the grid to 0.05?

⊕ Move the cursor and watch the coordinate display.

Observe how the snap setting is reflected in the available coordinates. How small a snap will AutoCAD accept?

⊕ Try 0.005.

Move the cursor and observe the coordinate display.

⊕ Try 0.0005.

You could even try 0.0001, but this would be like turning snap off, since the coordinate display is registering four decimal places anyway. Unlike the grid, which is limited by the size of your screen, you can set snap to any value you like.

⊕ Finally, before you leave this task, set the snap back to 0.25 and leave the grid at 0.5.

Tip: If you wish to keep snap and grid the same, set the grid to "0" in the Drafting Settings dialog box, or enter the GRID command and then type "s", for the Snap option. The grid will then change to match the snap and will continue to change anytime you reset the snap. To free the grid, just give it its own value again using the GRID command or the dialog box.

2.3 Changing UNITS

GENERAL PROCEDURE

1. Type "Units", or select "Units..." from the Format menu.
2. Answer the prompts.

Pop-down lists and the Drawing Units dialog box

The Drawing Units dialog box makes use of pop down lists, another common dialog box feature. Lists give you quick access to settings, files, and other items that are organized as a list of options.

⊕ Type "Units" or select Units... from the Format menu.

This will call up the Drawing Units dialog box shown in Figure 2-3. This four-panel dialog box has five pop down lists for specifying various characteristics of linear and angular drawing units, and a Sample Output area at the bottom. Pop down lists show a current setting next to an arrow that is used

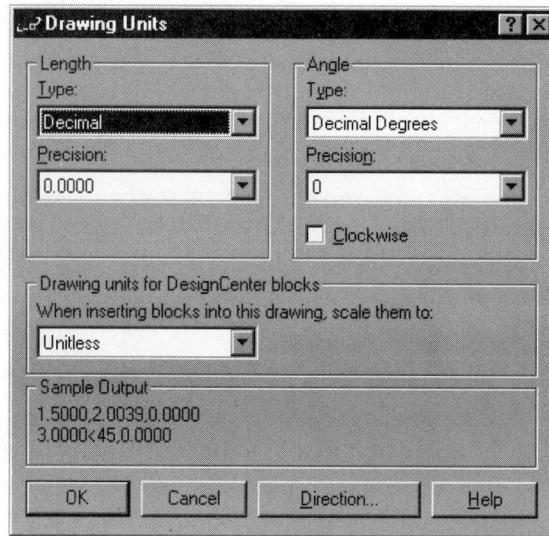

Figure 2-3

to open the list of other possibilities. Your dialog box should show that the current length type in your drawing is Decimal units precise to 0.0000 places, and Angle type is Decimal Degrees with 0 places.

⊕ Click on the arrow to the right of the word "Decimal", under Type in the Length panel of the dialog box.

A list will pop down with the following options:

> Architectural
> Decimal
> Engineering
> Fractional
> Scientific

Architectural units display feet and fractional inches $\left(1'-3\frac{1}{2}''\right)$, Engineering units display feet and decimal inches $(1'-3.50'')$, Fractional units display units in a mixed number format $\left(15\frac{1}{2}\right)$, Scientific units use exponential notation for the display of very large or very small numbers (1.55E+01). With the exception of Engineering and Architectural formats, these formats can be used with any basic unit of measurement. For example, decimal mode works for metric units as well as English units.

Through most of this book we will stick to decimal units. Obviously, if you are designing a house you will want architectural units. If you are building a bridge you may want engineering-style units. You might want scientific units if you are mapping subatomic particles.

Whatever your application, once you know how to change units, you can do so at any time. However, as a drawing practice you will want to choose appropriate units when you first begin work on a new drawing.

⊕ Click on Decimal, or click anywhere outside the list box to close the list without changing the setting.

Now we will change the precision setting to two-place decimals.

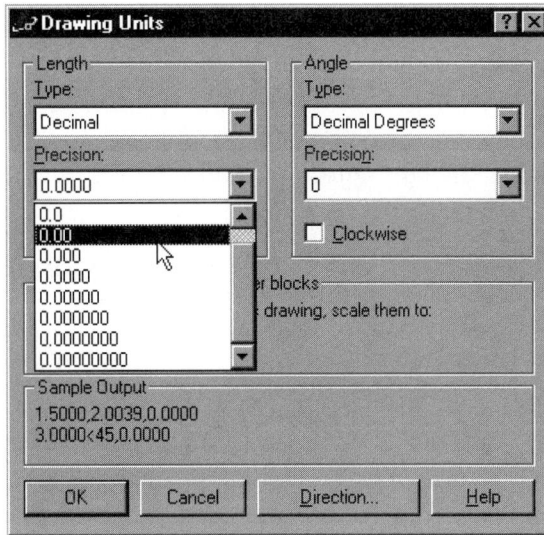

Figure 2-4

⊕ Click the arrow next to 0.0000 in the Precision list box in the Length panel.

This will open a list with options ranging from 0 to 0.00000000 as shown in Figure 2-4. Notice the scroll bars on the right of the list. These appear anytime the list is too large to be contained entirely within the box.

We will use two-place decimals because they are practical and more common than any other choice.

⊕ Run your cursor arrow down the list until 0.00 is highlighted, as shown in Figure 2-4.

⊕ Click on 0.00.

The list will close and 0.00 will replace 0.0000 as the current precision for units of length. Notice that the Sample Output has also changed to reflect the new setting.

The area to the right allows you to change the units in which angular measures, including polar coordinates, are displayed. If you open the angle type list you will see the following options:

```
Decimal Degrees
Deg/Min/Sec
Grads
Minutes
Seconds
```

The default system is standard decimal degrees with 0 decimal places, measured counterclockwise, with 0 being straight out to the right (3 o'clock), 90, straight up (12 o'clock), 180 to the left (9 o'clock), and 270 straight down (6 o'clock). We will leave these settings alone.

⊕ Check to see that you have two-place decimal units for length and zero-place decimal degree units for angles. Then click OK to close the dialog.

Tip: All dialog boxes can be moved on the screen. This is done by clicking in the gray title area at the top of the dialog box, holding down the pickbutton, and dragging the box across the screen.

2.4 Drawing Circles Giving Center Point and Radius

GENERAL PROCEDURE

1. Type "c", select Circle from the Draw menu, or select the Circle tool from the Draw toolbar.
2. Pick a center point.
3. Enter or show a radius value.

Circles can be drawn by giving AutoCAD a center point and a radius, a center point and a diameter, three points on the circle's circumference, two points that determine a diameter, two tangent points on other objects and a radius, or three tangent points. In this chapter we will use the first two options.

We will begin by drawing a circle with radius 3 and center at the point (6,5). Then we will draw two smaller circles centered at the same point. Later we will erase them using the ERASE command.

⊕ Grid should be set to 0.5, snap to 0.25, and units to two-place decimal.

⊕ Type "c", select Circle from the Draw menu, or select the Circle tool from the Draw toolbar, illustrated in Figure 2-5.

Figure 2-5

The prompt that follows will look like this:

```
Specify center point for circle or
[3P/2P/Ttr (tan tan radius)]/<Center point>:
```

⊕ Type coordinates or point to the center point of the circle you want to draw. In our case it will be the point (6,5).

AutoCAD assumes that a radius or diameter will follow and shows the following prompt:

```
Specify radius of circle or [Diameter]:
```

If we type or point to a value now, AutoCAD will take it as a radius, since that is the default.

⊕ Move your cursor and observe the rubber band and dragged circle.

⊕ If your coordinate display is not showing polar coordinates, click on it once or twice until you see something like "3.00 < 0, 0.00".

⊕ Press the pickbutton to show the radius end point at a distance of 3.00 from the center.

You should now have your first circle complete.

⊕ Draw two more circles using the same center point, radius method. They will be centered at (6,5) and have radii of 2.50 and 2.00.

The results are illustrated in Figure 2-6.

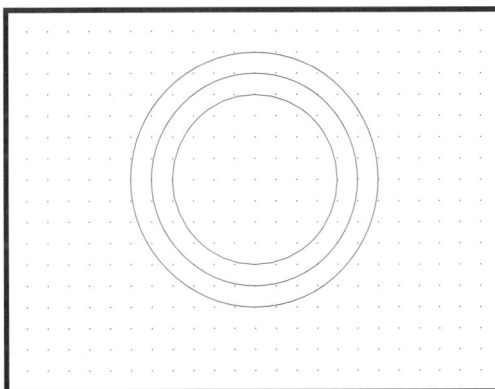

Figure 2-6

2.5   Drawing Circles Giving Center Point and Diameter

GENERAL PROCEDURE

1. Type "c", select Circle from the Draw menu, or select the Circle tool from the Draw toolbar.
2. Pick a center point.
3. Type "d".
4. Enter or show a diameter value.

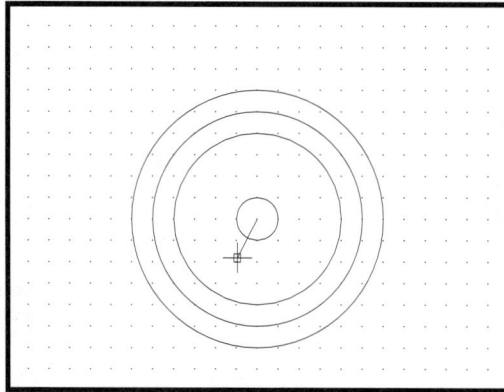

Figure 2-7

We will draw three more circles centered on (6,5) having diameters of 1, 1.5, and 2. Drawing circles this way is almost the same as the radius method, except you will not use the default, and you will see that the rubber band works differently.

⊞ Press enter or the space bar to repeat the CIRCLE command.

⊞ Indicate the center point (6,5) by typing coordinates or pointing.

⊞ Answer the prompt with a "d", for diameter.

  Notice that the cross hairs are now outside the circle you are dragging on the screen (see Figure 2-7). This is because AutoCAD is looking for a diameter, but the last point you gave was a center point. So the diameter is being measured from the center point out, twice the radius. Move the cursor around, in and out from the center point, to get a feel for this.

⊞ Point to a diameter of 1.00, or type "1".

  You should now have four circles.

⊞ Draw two more circles with diameters of 1.50 and 2.00.

  When you are done, your screen should look like Figure 2-8.

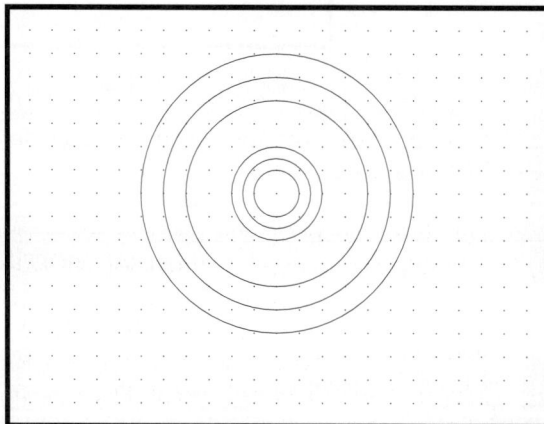

Figure 2-8

2 POINT

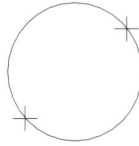

Pick two points.
Line between is used as
diameter to construct circle.

3 POINT

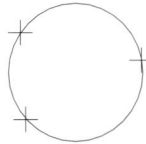

Pick three points.
Arc through all three is
completed to form circle.
Circle is visible on screen
after second point selection.

TANGENT, TANGENT, RADIUS

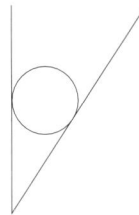

Select two objects on the
screen ("Tangent Specs").
Type or show radius length.
AutoCAD constructs the
circle that has the given
radius and is tangent to
both objects.

TANGENT, TANGENT, TANGENT

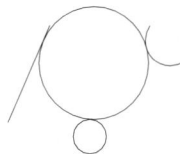

Select three objects on the
screen ("Tangent Specs").
Autocad constructs the circle
that is tangent to the three
objects.

Figure 2-9

Studying Figure 2-9 and using the HELP command, as discussed in the next task, will give you a good introduction to the remaining options in the CIRCLE command.

Tip: Here are two ways to stay heads-up and avoid going to the keyboard to type D for the diameter option. (1.) After entering the Circle command, press the right mouse button. This will call a short cut menu with the options Enter, Cancel, Diameter, Pan, and Zoom. Select Diameter. (2.) If you enter the CIRCLE command from the Draw pull-down menu and select one of the options on the submenu, some of the command steps will be automated. For example, if you select the Center, Diameter option, the command will behave as if Diameter is the default and you will not have to enter a "d".

2.6 Accessing AutoCAD HELP Features

> **GENERAL PROCEDURE**
>
> 1. Press F1 or open the Help menu and select AutoCAD Help Topics....
> 2. Click on the Index tab.
> 3. Type the name of a command or topic.
> 4. Highlight the item you want.
> 5. Press enter or click on Display.

The AutoCAD 2000 HELP command gives access to an extraordinary amount of information in a comprehensive library of AutoCAD references and information. The procedures for using HELP are standard Windows 98 procedures and access the Command Reference, the AutoCAD User's Guide, the AutoCAD Customization Guide, the AutoCAD Installation Guide, AutoCAD Visual LISP Help, AutoCAD VBA and ActiveX Help, and AutoCAD Express Tools Help. In this task we will focus on the use of the Index feature, which pulls information from all of the references, depending on the topic you select. For demonstration, we will look for further information on the CIRCLE command.

⊕ **To begin you should be at the command prompt.**

HELP is context sensitive, meaning that it will go directly to the AutoCAD Command Reference if you ask for help while in the middle of a command sequence. You should try this later.

⊕ **Press F1 or open the Help menu and select AutoCAD Help topics....**

Either method will open the AutoCAD Help dialog box shown in Figure 2-10. If the Contents tab is showing, you will see the list of available references.

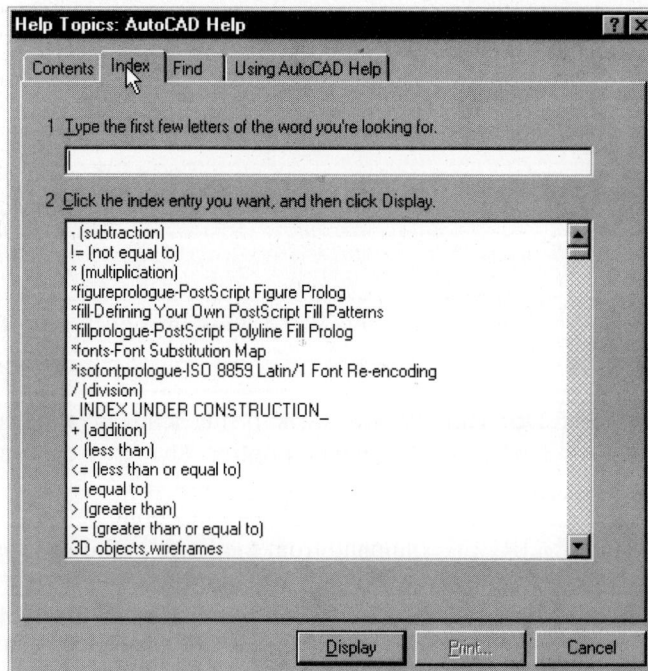

Figure 2-10

These contain the same information as the actual AutoCAD manuals, and you can browse through their contents as you would with the books. It is usually quicker to use the Index, however.

⊕   **If necessary, click on the Index tab.**

You should see the Index as shown in Figure 2-10. The list of topics is very long, so it is rare that you will use the scroll bar on the right. Most often you will type in a command or topic. The list will update as you type, so you may not need to type the complete word or command.

⊕   **Type "Cir".**

Do this slowly, one letter at a time, and you will see how the index follows along. When you have typed "cir" you will be at the Circle (Draw menu) options entry. Adding the rest of the letters "cle" will have no further effect.

The entry we want is the CIRCLE command entry, which is just below the Draw menu options.

⊕   **Double click on "CIRCLE command" or highlight it and then press enter or click on display.**

This will call up a second smaller dialog box with three options. We want the first option.

⊕   **Double click on "CIRCLE command" again, or press enter or click on display.**

AutoCAD will display the CIRCLE command page from the AutoCAD Command Reference, as shown in Figure 2-11. Links to additional information

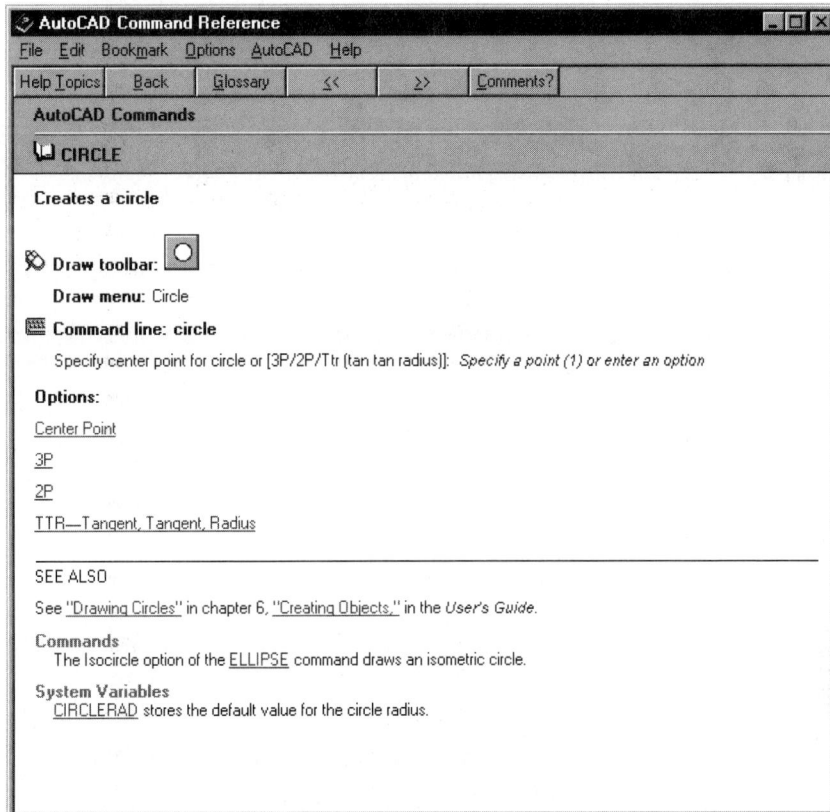

Figure 2-11

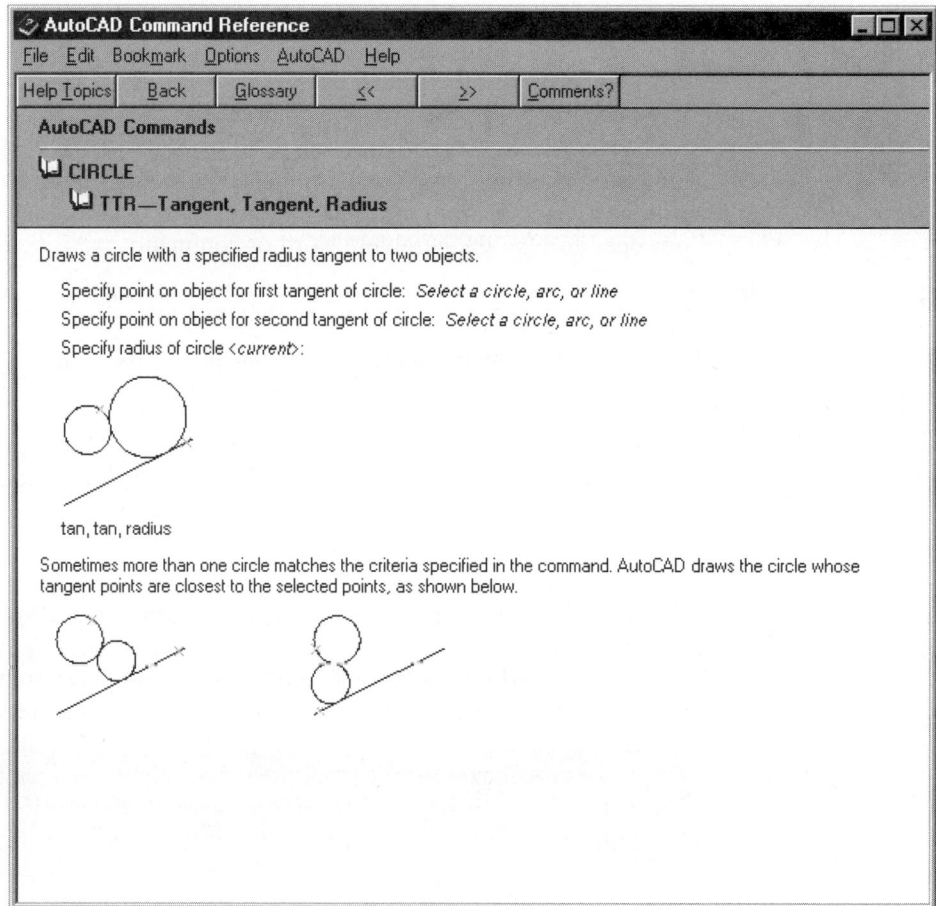

Figure 2-12

on items on this page is available for words underlined and shown in green.

⊕ Click on "TTR-Tangent, Tangent, Radius".

This will call up the page for the Tangent, Tangent, Radius option of the CIRCLE command, shown in Figure 2-12.

⊕ To exit HELP, click on the close button, the x in the upper right corner of the Help window.

This terminates the HELP command and brings you back to the command prompt. The HELP feature is a great resource. You are encouraged to access it at any time to expand your knowledge of AutoCAD 2000.

2.7 Using the ERASE Command

GENERAL PROCEDURE

1. Type "e" or select the Erase tool from the Modify toolbar.
2. Select objects.
3. Press enter to carry out the command.

    or

1. Select objects.
2. Type "e" or select the Erase tool from the Modify toolbar.

AutoCAD allows for many different methods of editing and even allows you to alter some of the basics of how edit commands work. Fundamentally, there are two different sequences for using most edit commands. These are called the Noun/Verb and the Verb/Noun methods.

In earlier versions of AutoCAD, most editing was carried out in a verb/noun sequence. That is, you would enter a command, such as ERASE (the verb), then select objects (the nouns), and press enter to carry out the command. This method is still effective, but AutoCAD now allows you to reverse the verb/noun sequence. You can use either method as long as "Noun/Verb" selection is enabled in your drawing.

In this task we will explore the traditional verb/noun sequence and then introduce the noun/verb or "pick first" method along with some of the many methods for selecting objects.

Verb/Noun Editing

⊕ To begin this task you should have the six circles on your screen, as shown previously in Figure 2-8.

    We will use verb/noun editing to erase the two outer circles.

⊕ Type "e" or select the Erase tool from the Modify toolbar, as shown in Figure 2-13.

    Erase can also be found on the Modify menu, but the other methods are more efficient.

Figure 2-13

The cross hairs will disappear, but the pickbox will still be on the screen and will move when you move your cursor.

Also notice the command area. It should be showing this prompt:

> Select objects:

This is a very common prompt. You will find it in all edit commands and many other commands as well.

⊕ Move your cursor so that the outer circle crosses the pickbox.

Tip: In many situations you may find it convenient or necessary to turn snap off (F9) while selecting objects, since this gives you more freedom of motion.

⊕ Press the pickbutton.

The circle will be highlighted (dotted). This is how AutoCAD indicates that an object has been selected for editing. It is not yet erased, however. You can go on and add more objects to the selection set and they, too, will become dotted.

⊕ Use the box to pick the second circle moving in toward the center.

It too should now be dotted.

⊕ Press enter, the space bar, or the right button on your pointing device to carry out the command.

This is typical of the verb/noun sequence in most edit commands. Once a command has been entered and a selection set defined, a press of the enter key is required to complete the command. At this point the two outer circles should be erased.

Tip: In Verb/Noun edit command procedures where the last step is to press enter to complete the command, it is good heads-up practice to use the right button on your mouse in place of the space bar or enter key. It will carry out your command in exactly the same way but is more convenient. There will be no intervening short cut menu.

Noun/Verb Editing

Now let's try the noun/verb sequence.

⊕ Type "u" to undo the ERASE and bring back the circles.

⊕ Use the pickbox to select the outer circle.

The circle will be highlighted, and your screen should now resemble Figure 2-14. Those little blue boxes are called "grips." They are part of Auto-CAD's autoediting system, which we will begin exploring in Chapter 3. For now you can ignore them.

⊕ Pick the second circle in the same fashion.

The second circle will also become dotted, and more grips will appear.

⊕ Type "e" or select the Erase tool from the Modify toolbar.

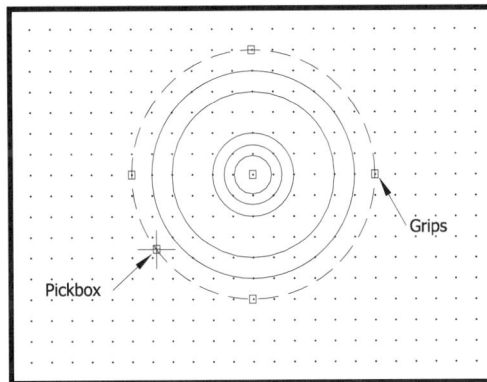

Figure 2-14

Your two outer circles will disappear as soon as you press enter or pick the tool. Note that in this sequence the right mouse button calls a short cut menu, so you should avoid it unless you have use for the options on the menu.

The two outer circles should now be gone. As you can see, there is not a lot of difference between the two sequences. One difference that is not immediately apparent is that there are numerous selection methods available in the verb/noun system that cannot be activated when you pick objects first. We will get to other object selection methods momentarily, but first try out the OOPS command.

OOPS!

⊕ Type "oops" and watch the screen.

If you have made a mistake in your erasure, you can get your selection set back by typing "oops". OOPS is to ERASE as REDO is to UNDO. You can use OOPS to undo an ERASE command, as long as you have not done another ERASE in the meantime. In other words, AutoCAD only saves your most recent ERASE selection set.

You can also use U to undo an ERASE, but notice the difference: U simply undoes the last command, whatever it might be; OOPS works specifically with ERASE to recall the last set of erased objects. If you have drawn other objects in the meantime, you can still use OOPS to recall a previously erased set. But if you tried to use U, you would have to backtrack, undoing any newly drawn objects along the way.

Other Object Selection Methods

You can select individual entities on the screen by pointing to them one by one, as we have done previously, but in complex drawings this will often be inefficient. AutoCAD offers a variety of other methods, all of which have application in specific drawing circumstances. In this exercise we will select circles by the "windowing" and "crossing" methods, by indicating "last" or "L", meaning the last entity drawn, and by indicating "previous" or "P" for the previously defined set. There are also

OBJECT SELECTION METHOD	DESCRIPTION	ITEMS SELECTED
(W) WINDOW	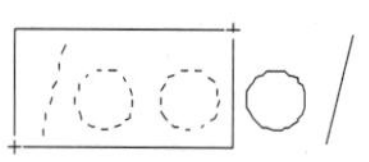	The entities within the box.
(C) CROSSING	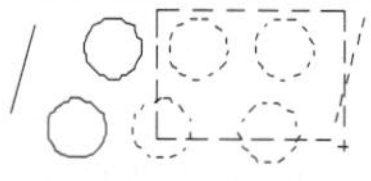	The entities crossed by or within the box.
(P) PREVIOUS	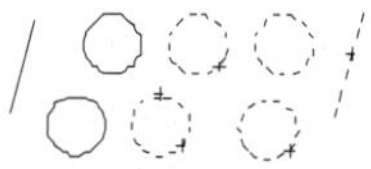	The entities that were previously picked.
(L) LAST		The entity that was drawn last.
(R) REMOVE	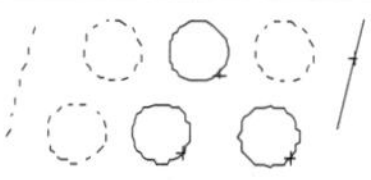	Removes entities from the items selected so they will not be part of the selected group.
(A) ADD	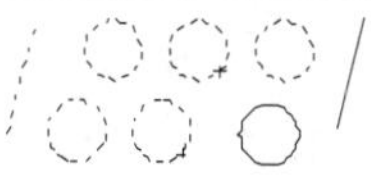	Adds entities that were removed and allows for more selections after the use of remove.
ALL		All the entities currently visible on the drawing.
(F) FENCE	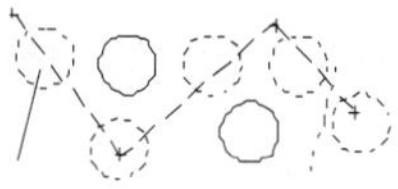	The entities crossed by the fence.
(WP) WPOLYGON	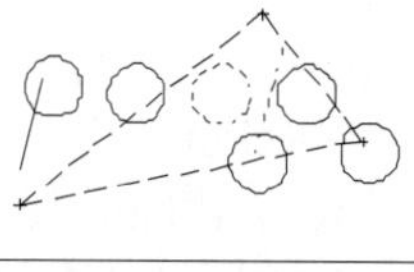	All the entities completely within the window of the polygon.
(CP) CPOLYGON	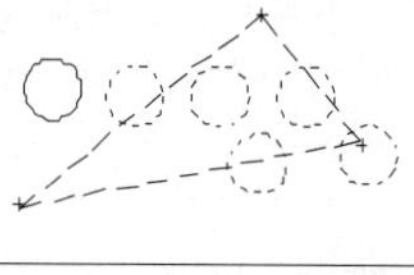	All the entities crossed by the polygon.

Figure 2-15

options to add or remove objects from the selection set and other variations on windowing and crossing. We suggest that you study Figure 2-15 to learn about other methods. The number of selection options available may seem a bit overwhelming at first, but time learning them will be well spent. These same options appear in many AutoCAD editing commands (MOVE, COPY, ARRAY, ROTATE, MIRROR) and should become part of your CAD vocabulary.

Selection by Window

The object selection window was demonstrated in Chapter 1. Now we will put it to use. Window and crossing selections, like individual object selection, can be initiated without entering a command. In other words, they are available for noun/verb selection. Whether you select objects first or enter a command first, you can force a window or crossing selection simply by picking points on the screen that are not on objects. AutoCAD will assume you want to select by windowing or crossing and will ask for a second point.

Let's try it. We will show AutoCAD that we want to erase all of the inner circles by throwing a temporary selection window around them. The window will be defined by two points moving left to right that serve as opposite corners of a rectangle. Only entities that lie completely within the window will be selected. See Figure 2-16.

⊕ Pick point 1 at the lower left of the screen, as shown. Any point in the neighborhood of (3.5,1) will do.

AutoCAD will prompt for another corner:

Specify opposite corner:

⊕ Pick point 2 at the upper right of the screen, as shown.

Any point in the neighborhood of (9.5,8.5) will do. To see the effect of the window, be sure that it crosses the outside circle, as in Figure 2-16.

⊕ Type "e" or select the Erase tool.

The inner circles should now be erased.

⊕ Type "oops" to retrieve the circles once more. Since ERASE was the last command, typing "U" or selecting the Undo tool will also work.

Selection by Crossing Window

Crossing is an alternative to windowing that is useful in many cases where a standard window selection could not be performed. The selection procedure is the

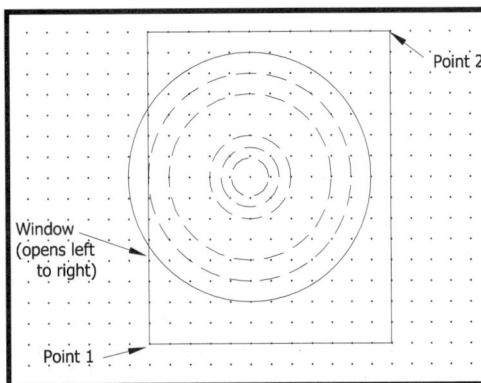

Figure 2-16

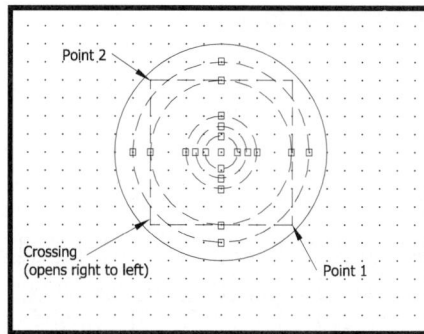

Point 2

Crossing
(opens right to left)

Point 1

Figure 2-17

same, but a crossing box opens to the left instead of to the right and all objects that cross the box will be chosen, not just those that lie completely inside the box.

We will use a crossing box to select the inside circles.

⊕ Pick point 1 close to (8.0,3.0), as in Figure 2-17.

AutoCAD prompts:

Specify opposite corner:

⊕ Pick a point near (4.0,7.0).

This point selection must be done carefully to demonstrate a crossing selection. Notice that the crossing box is shown with dashed lines, whereas the window box was shown with solid lines.

Also, notice how the circles are selected: those that cross and those that are completely contained within the crossing box, but not those that lie outside.

At this point we could enter the ERASE command to erase the circles, but instead we will demonstrate how to use the Esc key to cancel a selection set.

⊕ Press the Esc key on your keyboard.

This will cancel the selection set. The circles will no longer be highlighted, but you will see that the grips are still visible. To get rid of the grips you will need to cancel again.

⊕ Press Esc again.

The grips should now be gone as well.

Selecting the "Last" Entity

AutoCAD remembers the order in which new objects have been drawn during the course of a single drawing session. As long as you do not close the drawing, you can select the last drawn entity using the "last" option.

⊕ Type "e" or select the Erase tool.

Notice that there is no way to specify "last" before you enter a command. This option is only available as part of a command procedure. In other words, it only works in a verb/noun sequence.

⊕ Type "L".

> The inner circle should be highlighted.

⊕ Press enter to carry out the command.

> The inner circle should be erased.

Selecting the "Previous" Selection Set

The P or previous option works with the same procedure, but it selects the previous selection set rather than the last drawn entity. If the difference is not obvious to you now, don't worry: It will become clear as you work more with edit commands and selection sets.

Remove and Add

Together, the remove and add options form a switch in the object selection process. Under ordinary circumstances, whatever you select using any of the aforementioned options will be added to your selection set. By typing "r" at the "Select objects:" prompt you can switch over to a mode in which everything you pick is deselected or removed from the selection set. Then by typing "a" you can return to the usual mode of adding objects to the set.

Undoing a Selection

The ERASE command and other edit commands have an internal undo feature, similar to that found in the LINE command. By typing "u" at the "Select objects:" prompt you can undo your last selection without leaving the edit command you are in and without undoing previous selections. You can also type "u" several times to undo your most recent selections one by one. This allows you to back up one step at a time without having to cancel the command and start all over again.

ALL

"All" is a powerful option that should be used with care. By typing "all" at the "Select objects:" prompt you can select all objects currently visible in your drawing. If you use this with ERASE it will clear your screen.

Fence

Type "f" at the "Select objects:" prompt and AutoCAD will prompt for a series of "fence points." These points will define a series of line segments called a fence. Any entity that the fence crosses or touches will be selected. This is a very useful option in tight, complex areas.

WPolygon and CPolygon

Type "wp" for "window polygon" or "cp" for "crossing polygon" at the "Select objects:" prompt. AutoCAD will ask for a series of polygon points. These will become the vertices of an irregular polygon of as many sides as you like. Objects will be selected as in window and crossing selections. That is, a window polygon will select only objects that lie completely within the window. A crossing polygon will select objects inside and objects that cross the polygon.

Group

Using the GROUP command, you can define a set of objects as a named group. Once defined, a group may be selected as a unit using the group option and the group name. Groups are discussed in Chapter 10.

Other Options

If you hit any key other than the ones AutoCAD recognizes, at the "Select objects:" prompt you will see the following:

```
Expects a point
or
Window/Last/Crossing/Box/All/Fence/WPolygon/Cpolygon/Group/Add/
Remove/Multiple/Previous/Undo/AUto/SIngle
Select objects:
```

Along with the options already discussed, you will see Box, Multiple, AUto, and SIngle. These options mostly are used in programming customized applications. Look up the SELECT command in the AutoCAD Command Reference for additional information.

2.8 Using the RECTANGLE Command

```
                          GENERAL PROCEDURE

  1. Select the Rectangle tool from the Draw toolbar.
  2. Pick first corner point.
  3. Pick other corner point.
```

Now that you have created object selection windows, the RECTANGLE command will come naturally. Creating a rectangle in this way is just like creating an object selection window.

⊕ To prepare for this exercise, erase all objects from your screen.

⊕ Select the Rectangle tool from the Draw toolbar, as shown in Figure 2-18.

AutoCAD will prompt for a corner point:

```
Specify first corner point or
[Chamfer/Elevation/Fillet/Thickness/Width]:
```

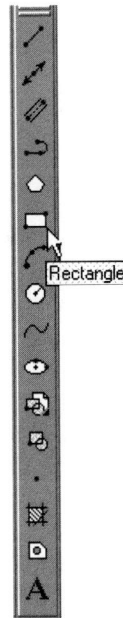

Figure 2-18

You can ignore the options for now and proceed with the defaults.

⊕ Pick (3.00,3.00) for the first corner point, as shown in Figure 2-19.

AutoCAD will prompt for another point:

```
Specify other corner point:
```

⊕ Pick (9.00, 6.00) for a second corner point, as shown in Figure 2-19.

As soon as you enter the second corner, AutoCAD draws a rectangle between the two corner points and returns you to the command prompt. This is a faster way to draw a rectangle than drawing it line by line. There are also some other advantages that we will examine in Chapter 3.

Leave the rectangle on your screen for the plotting demonstration in Task 2.10.

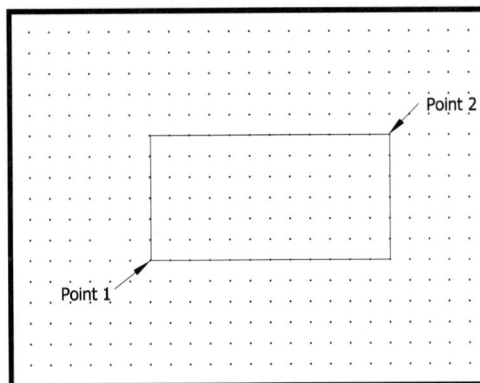

Figure 2-19

2.9 Using the DIST Command

GENERAL PROCEDURE

1. Select the Distance tool from the Standard toolbar.
2. Pick first point.
3. Pick second point.
4. Read information in command area.

The DIST command is one of AutoCAD's most useful inquiry commands. Inquiry commands give you information about your drawing or objects within it. DIST works like a simple LINE command procedure, but it gives you distances instead of actually drawing a line. Let us say that you need to know the distance from corner point 1 to corner point 2, the diagonal in the rectangle you just drew. Try this:

⊕ Select the Distance tool from the Standard toolbar, as shown in Figure 2-20.

AutoCAD will prompt you to pick a point:

Specify first point:

⊕ Pick (3,3) again.

Notice that AutoCAD gives you a rubber band, just as if you were drawing a line. You are also prompted for a second point:

Specify second point:

⊕ Pick (9,6) again.

You are returned to the command point and no line is drawn between the two points. But you should see something like this in the command prompt area:

Distance = 6.71 Angle in XY Plane = 27, Angle from XY Plane = 0
Delta X = 6.00, Delta Y = 3.00, Delta Z = 0.00

All of this information can be useful, depending on the situation. "Distance" gives the straight-line distance between the two selected points. "Angle in XY Plane" gives the angle that a line between the two points would make within the coordinate system in which 0 degrees represents a horizontal line out to the right. "Angle from XY Plane" is a 3D feature and will always be 0 in 2D drawings. "Delta X" is the horizontal displacement, which may be either positive or negative. Similarly, "Delta Y" is the vertical displacement.

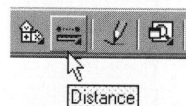

Figure 2-20

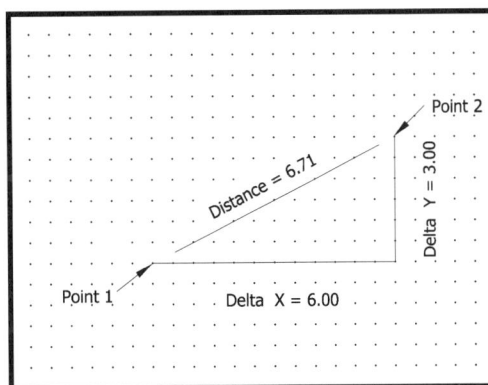

Figure 2-21

"Delta Z" is the displacement in the *z* direction. It will always be 0 until we begin to explore AutoCAD's 3D drawing capabilities in Chapter 12.

Compare what is on your screen with Figure 2-21.

2.10   Plotting or Printing a Drawing

GENERAL PROCEDURE

1. Select the Plot tool from the Standard toolbar, or select Plot... from the File menu.
2. Click on "Window...".
3. Pick two points to define a window.
4. See that "Scaled to Fit" is showing in the Scale list box.
5. Prepare printer or plotter.
6. Click on "OK".

AutoCAD 2000's printing and plotting capabilities are extensive, complex, and significantly different from previous versions of AutoCAD. In this book we will introduce you to them a little at a time. As usual we will try to keep you moving and get your drawing on paper as efficiently as possible. You will find discussions of plotting and printing in Chapters 2 through 8, before the review material and drawings in each chapter.

Plotting and printing in AutoCAD 2000 requires that you understand the relationships among model space, paper space, plot styles, page setups, and layouts. All of these concepts will be introduced as you need them. In this chapter, we will perform the simplest type of plot, going directly from your current model space objects to a sheet of drawing paper, changing only one or two plot settings. One of the difficulties is that different types of plotters and printers work somewhat differently. This introductory procedure assumes that you do not have to change devices or configuration details. It should work adequately for all plotters and printers and the drawings in this chapter. We will use a Window selection to define a plot area and observe how this affects the plot scale.

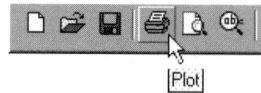

Figure 2-22

⊕ Select Plot... from the File menu, or the Plot tool from the Standard toolbar, as shown in Figure 2-22.

Either of these methods will call up the Plot dialog box illustrated in Figure 2-23. You will become very familiar with it as you work through this book. It is one of the most important working spaces in AutoCAD. It contains many options, but for now we are going to look at only two settings.

As you look over the Plot dialog you will see the following panels. At the top are two panels devoted to Layouts and Page Setups. These allow you to save plot configurations and to use them in other drawings. Below this there are two tabs, one for Plot Device and one for Plot Settings.

⊕ If Plot Settings is not on top, click the tab to bring it up.

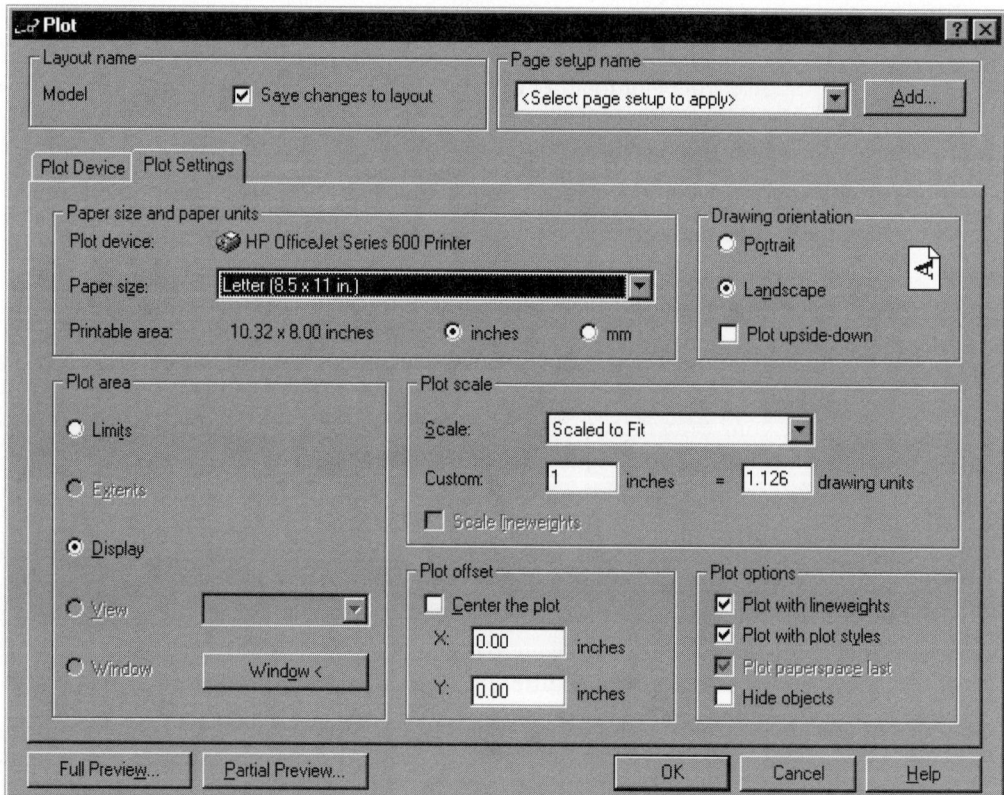

Figure 2-23

On the Plot Settings tab are panels for Paper size and paper units, Drawing orientation, Plot area, Plot scale, Plot offset, and Plot options.

Dialog Box Radio Buttons

Look at the panel labeled "Plot area" on the left. The options in the panel make use of radio buttons. Unlike check boxes, radio buttons are mutually exclusive. In a list of radio buttons, only one button can be on at a time. This list of radio buttons allows you to tell AutoCAD what part of your drawing you want to plot. Right now you will see that only Display and Limits are accessible. The Window option will become available after you have defined a window in the drawing. Windowing allows you to plot any portion of a drawing simply by defining the window. AutoCAD will base the size and placement of the plot on the window you define.

Before creating the plot area window, look at the Plot scale panel on the right of the dialog box. In the Scale list box, you should see the words "Scaled to fit". If your plot scale is configured as scaled to fit, as it should be by default, then AutoCAD will plot your drawing at maximum size based on paper size and the window you specify.

⊕ If for any reason "Scaled to fit" is not in the Scale list box, open the list and select it.

On the Custom line below Plot scale, you should see edit boxes with numbers something like 1 = 1.126. Right now the plot area is based on the outer limits of your grid. When you use a window to create a plot area that is somewhat smaller, these scale numbers will change automatically.

⊕ Click on "Window<" at the bottom of the Plot area panel.

The Plot dialog box will disappear temporarily, giving you access to the drawing. You will see the cross hairs, but the pickbox will be absent. AutoCAD will prompt for point selection:

Specify first corner:

⊕ Select the point (1.00,1.00), as shown in Figure 2-24.

AutoCAD will prompt:

Specify other corner:

⊕ Select the point (11.00,8.00), as shown in Figure 2-24.

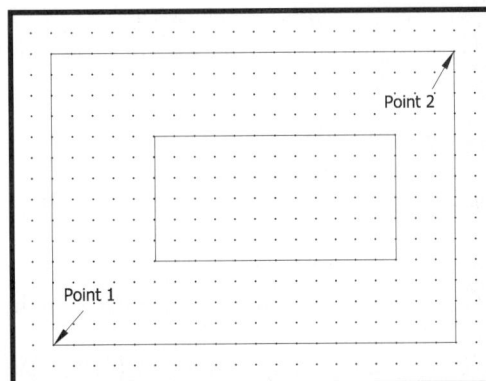

Figure 2-24

As soon as you have picked the second point, AutoCAD will display the Plot dialog box again. There will be two changes. First, the Window radio button will now be accessible. Second, the Custom scale ratio will change to something like 1 = .9533. We use the phrase "something like" because there may be minor variations depending on your plotter.

You are now ready to plot.

⊕ **If you want to plot or print the rectangle, prepare your plotter and then click on OK. Otherwise, click on Cancel.**

Clicking OK sends the drawing information out to be printed. You can sit back and watch the plotting device at work. If you need to cancel for any reason, click on the Cancel button.

For now, that's all there is to it. If your plot does not look perfect—if it is not centered on your drawing sheet, for example—don't worry, you will learn all you need to know about plotting in later chapters.

2.11   Review Material

Questions

1. Which is likely to have the smaller setting, GRID or SNAP? Why? What happens if the settings are reversed?
2. Why do some dialog box panels use check boxes while others use radio buttons?
3. How do you switch from decimal units to architectural units?
4. Where is 0 degrees located in AutoCAD's default units setup? Where is 270 degrees? Where is −45 degrees?
5. How do you enter the CIRCLE command?
6. Why does the rubber band touch the circumference of the circle when you are using the radius option, but not when you are using the diameter option?
7. How does AutoCAD know when you want a crossing selection instead of a window selection?
8. What is the difference between a "Last" selection and a "Previous" selection?
9. What is the difference between noun/verb and verb/noun editing?
10. How do you access the AutoCAD HELP index?

Drawing Problems

1. Leave the grid at .50 and set snap to .25.
2. Use the 3P option to draw a circle that passes through the points (2.25,4.25), (3.25,5.25), and (4.25,4.25).
3. Using the 2P option, draw a second circle with a diameter from (3.25,4.25) to (4.25,4.25).
4. Draw a third circle centered at (5.25,4.25) with a radius of 1.00.
5. Draw a fourth circle centered at (4.75,4.25) with a diameter of 1.00.

2.12   WWW Exercise #2 (Optional)

In this second voyage to the World Wide Web, we will show you how to change the default URL so that you don't have to type a long ugly address every time you go out to the Web. URL, by the way, stands for Uniform Resource Locator, and simply refers to a properly formatted Web address.

In this case, we suggest that you set your system up to go to the companion Web site for this book. The general procedure will work just as well with any other legitimate Web address. Whether you actually want to retain our Web site as the default, we encourage you to go there now, take the self-scoring review test, and try the Web project.

⊕   Type "inetlocation" at the command prompt.

INETLOCATION is a system variable that stores the name of the default URL. AutoCAD prompts:

```
Enter new value for inetlocation <c:\program files\....>:
```

Remember that the address within the arrows is the current default. This value will be replaced by the address you enter.

⊕   Type "www.prenhall.com/dixriley/".

The new value will be stored and AutoCAD will return you to the command prompt. Now all you need to do is enter the BROWSER command and press enter at the prompt.

⊕   Type "browser".

The AutoCAD prompt will show the new default URL:

```
Enter web location (URL)
<prenhall.com/dixriley/>:
```

⊕   Press enter to accept the default location.

Away you go. Good luck on the test.

2.13   Drawing 2-1: Aperture Wheel

This drawing will give you practice creating circles using the center point, radius method. Refer to the table below the drawing for radius sizes. With snap set at 0.25, some of the circles can be drawn by pointing and dragging. Other circles have radii that are not on a snap point. These circles can be drawn by typing in the radius.

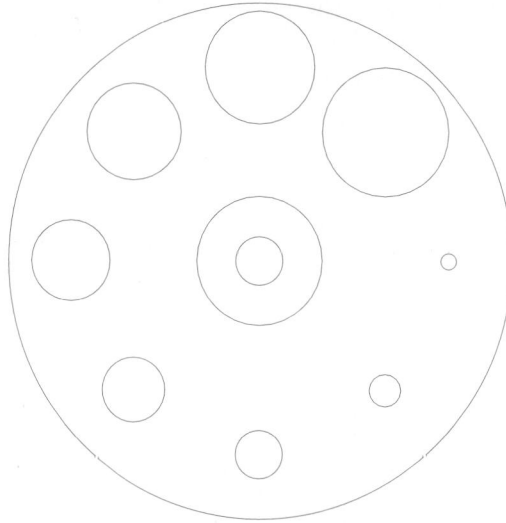

DRAWING SUGGESTIONS

GRID = 0.50
SNAP = 0.25

- A good sequence for doing this drawing would be to draw the outer circle first, followed by the two inner circles (h and c). These are all centered on the point (6.00,4.50). Then begin at circle a and work around clockwise, being sure to center each circle correctly.
- Notice that there are two circles c and two h. The two circles having the same letter are the same size.
- Remember, you may type any value you like and AutoCAD will give you a precise graphic image, but you cannot always show the exact point you want with a pointing device. Often it is more efficient to type a few values than to turn snap off or change its setting for a small number of objects.

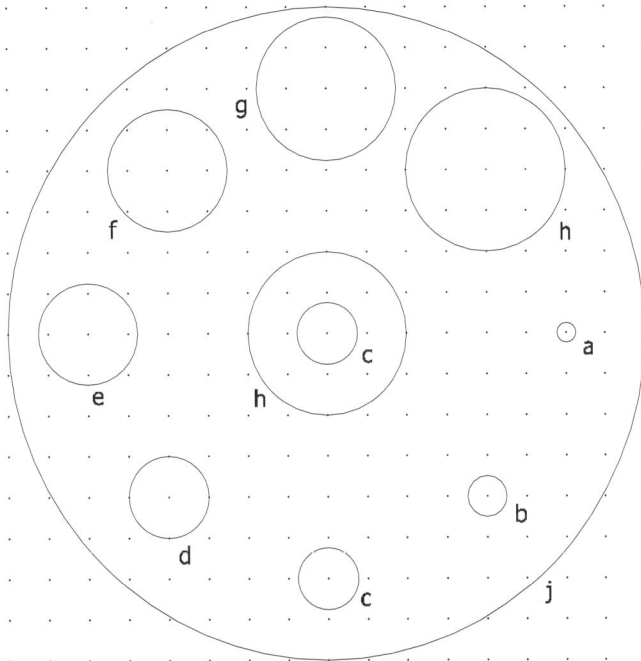

LETTER	a	b	c	d	e	f	g	h	j
RADIUS	.12	.25	.38	.50	.62	.75	.88	1.00	4.00

APERTURE WHEEL

Drawing 2-1

2.14 Drawing 2-2: Roller

This drawing will give you a chance to combine lines and circles and to use the center point, diameter method. It will also give you some experience with smaller objects, a denser grid, and a tighter snap spacing.

> *Tip:* Even though units are set to show only two decimal places, it is important to set the snap using three places (0.125) so that the grid is on a multiple of the snap (0.25 = 2 × 0.125). AutoCAD will show you rounded coordinate values, like 0.13, but will keep the graphics on target. Try setting snap to either 0.13 or 0.12 instead of 0.125, and you will see the problem for yourself.

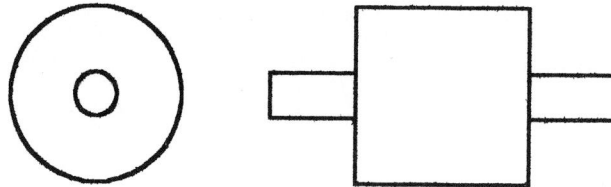

DRAWING SUGGESTIONS

GRID = 0.25
SNAP = 0.125

- The two views of the roller will appear fairly small on your screen, making the snap setting essential. Watch the coordinate display as you work and get used to the smaller range of motion.
- Choosing an efficient sequence will make this drawing much easier to do. Since the two views must line up properly, we suggest that you draw the front view first, with circles of diameter 0.25 and 1.00, and then use these circles to position the lines in the right side view.
- The circles in the front view should be centered in the neighborhood of (2.00,6.00). This will put the upper left-hand corner of the 1 × 1 square at around (5.50,6.50).

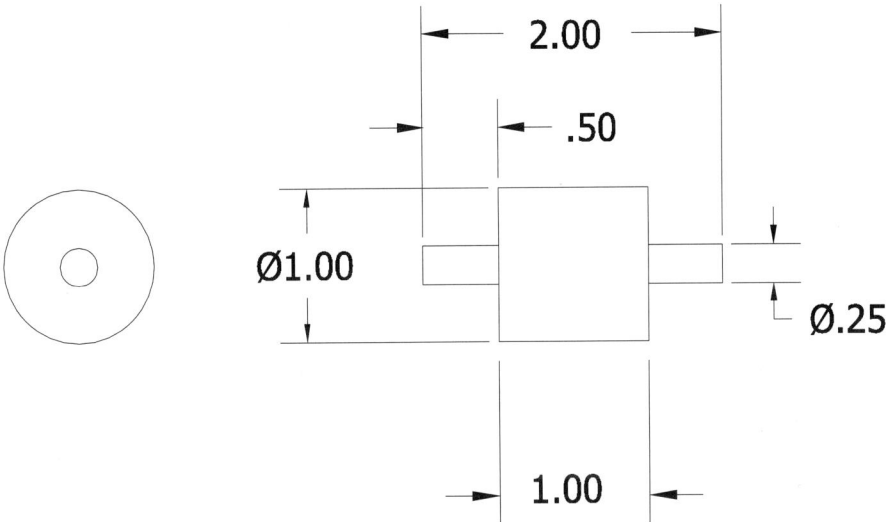

ROLLER

Drawing 2-2

2.15   Drawing 2-3: Fan Bezel

This drawing should be easy for you at this point. Set grid to 0.50 and snap to 0.25 as suggested, and everything will fall into place nicely.

DRAWING SUGGESTIONS

GRID = 0.50
SNAP = 0.25

- Notice that the outer figure is a 6 × 6 square and that you are given diameters for the circles.
- You should start with the lower left-hand corner of the square somewhere near the point (3.00,2.00) if you want to keep the drawing centered on your screen.
- Be careful to center the large inner circle at the center of the square.

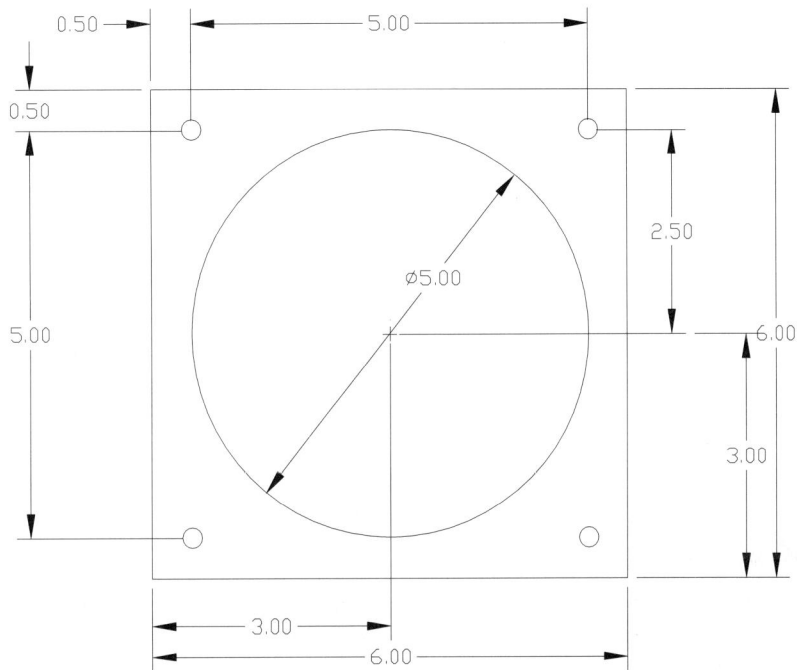

0.50   5.00
0.50
5.00   ⌀5.00   2.50   6.00
3.00
3.00   6.00

FAN BEZEL

Drawing 2-3

2.16   Drawing 2-4: Switch Plate

This drawing is similar to the last one, but the dimensions are more difficult, and a number of important points do not fall on the grid. The drawing will give you practice using grid and snap points and the coordinate display. Refer to the table below the drawing for dimensions of the circles, squares, and rectangles inside the 7×10 outer rectangle. The placement of these smaller figures is shown by the dimensions on the drawing itself.

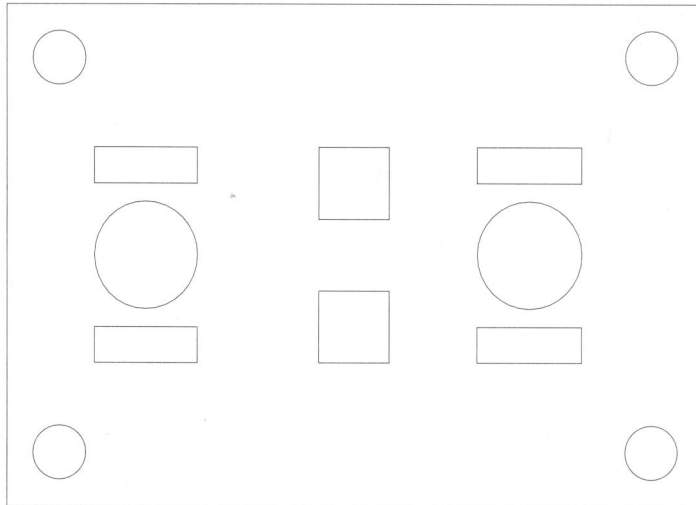

DRAWING SUGGESTIONS

GRID = 0.50
SNAP = 0.25

- Turn on ortho or polar snap to do this drawing.
- A starting point in the neighborhood of (1,1) will keep you well positioned on the screen.

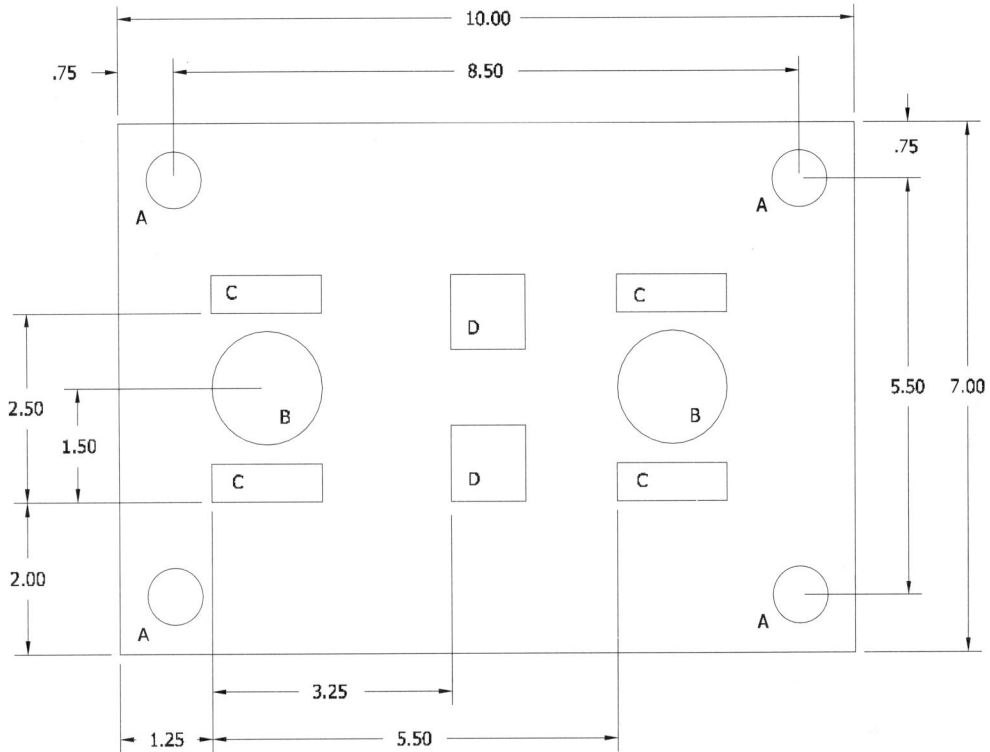

HOLE	SIZE
A	Ø.75
B	Ø1.50
C	.50 H x 1.50 W
D	1.00 SQ

SWITCH PLATE

Drawing 2-4

2.17   Drawing 2-5: Gasket

This drawing will give you practice creating simple lines and circles while utilizing the grid and snap. The circles in this drawing have a 0.50 diameter. With snap set at 0.25, the radii are on a snap point. These circles can be drawn easily by dragging the circle out to show the radius or by typing in the diameter.

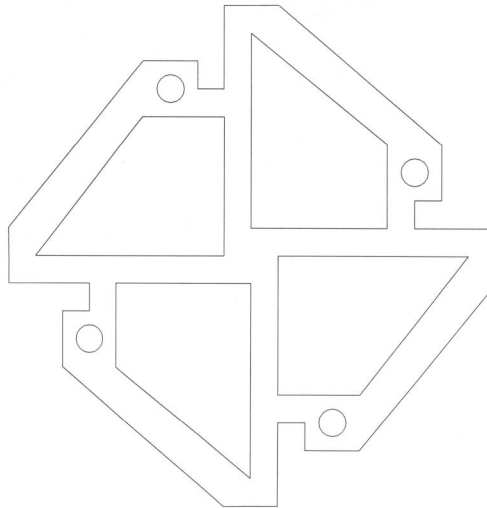

DRAWING SUGGESTIONS

GRID = 0.50
SNAP = 0.25

- A good sequence for doing this drawing would be to draw the outer lines first, followed by the inner line and then the circles.
- Notice that all end points of all lines fall on grid points; therefore, they are on a snap point.

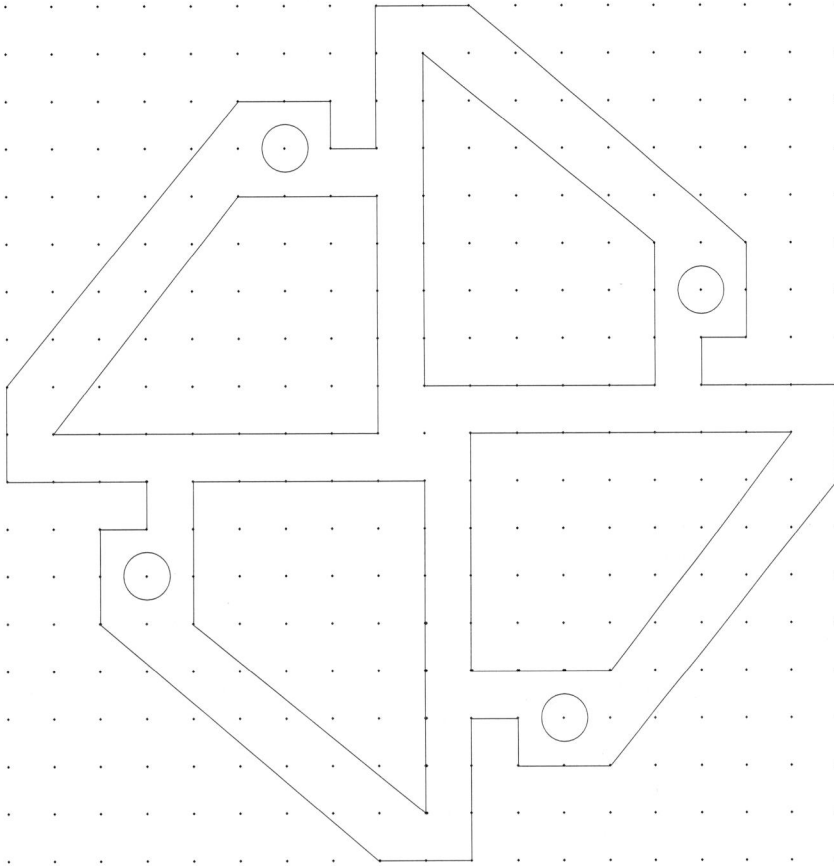

GASKET
Drawing 2-5

3

Layers, Colors, and Linetypes

COMMANDS

CHAMFER	LAYER	PAN	ZOOM
FILLET	LTSCALE	REGEN	

OVERVIEW

CAD is much more than a computerized way to do drafting. CAD programs have many powerful features that have no real correlation in manual drawing. Layering is a good example. Layers exist in the same space and the same drawing but can be set up and controlled individually, allowing for greater control, precision, and flexibility. In the first two chapters all of your drawings were done on a single layer called "0". In this chapter you will create and use three new layers, each with its own associated color and linetype.

The ZOOM command is another bit of CAD magic, allowing your drawings to accurately represent real world detail at the largest and smallest scales within the same drawing. In this chapter you will also learn to FILLET and CHAMFER the corners of previously drawn objects and to move between adjacent portions of a drawing with the PAN command. You will gain further control of the PLOT command by using partial and full previews. All of these new techniques will add considerably to the professionalism of your developing CAD technique.

TASKS

3.1 Creating New Layers

> **GENERAL PROCEDURE**
>
> 1. Select the Layer tool from the Object Properties toolbar or "Layer..." from the Format pull-down menu.
> 2. Click on "New".
> 3. Type in a layer name.
> 4. Repeat for other new layers.
> 5. Click on OK to leave the dialog box.

Layers allow you to treat specialized groups of entities in your drawing separately from other groups. For example, all of the dimensions in this book were drawn on a special dimension layer so that we could turn them on and off at will. We turned off the dimension layer to prepare the reference drawings for Chapters 1 through 7, which are shown without dimensions. When a layer is turned off, all the objects on that layer become invisible, though they are still part of the drawing database and can be recalled at any time. In this way, layers can be viewed, edited, manipulated, and plotted independently.

It is common practice to put dimensions on a separate layer, but there are many other uses of layers as well. Fundamentally, layers are used to separate colors and linetypes, and these, in turn, take on special significance depending on the drawing application. It is standard drafting practice, for example, to use small, evenly spaced dashes to represent objects or edges that would, in reality, be hidden from view. On a CAD system, these hidden lines can also be given their own color to make it easy for the designer to remember what layer he or she is working on.

In this book we will use a simple layering system, most of which will be presented in this chapter. You should remember that there are countless possibilities. AutoCAD allows as many as 256 different colors and as many layers as you like.

You should also be aware that linetypes and colors are not restricted to being associated with layers. It is possible to mix linetypes and colors on a single layer. But while this may be useful for certain applications, we do not recommend it at this point.

⊕ Open a new drawing using the Start from Scratch option to ensure that you are using the same defaults as those used in this chapter.

The Layer Properties Manager Dialog Box

The creation and specification of layers and layer properties in AutoCAD 2000 is handled through the Layer Properties Manager dialog box. This dialog box consists of a table of layers. Clicking in the appropriate row and column will change a setting or take you to another dialog where a setting may be changed.

⊕ Select the Layer tool from the Object Properties toolbar, as shown in Figure 3-1, or select "Layer..." from the Format pull-down menu.

Figure 3-1

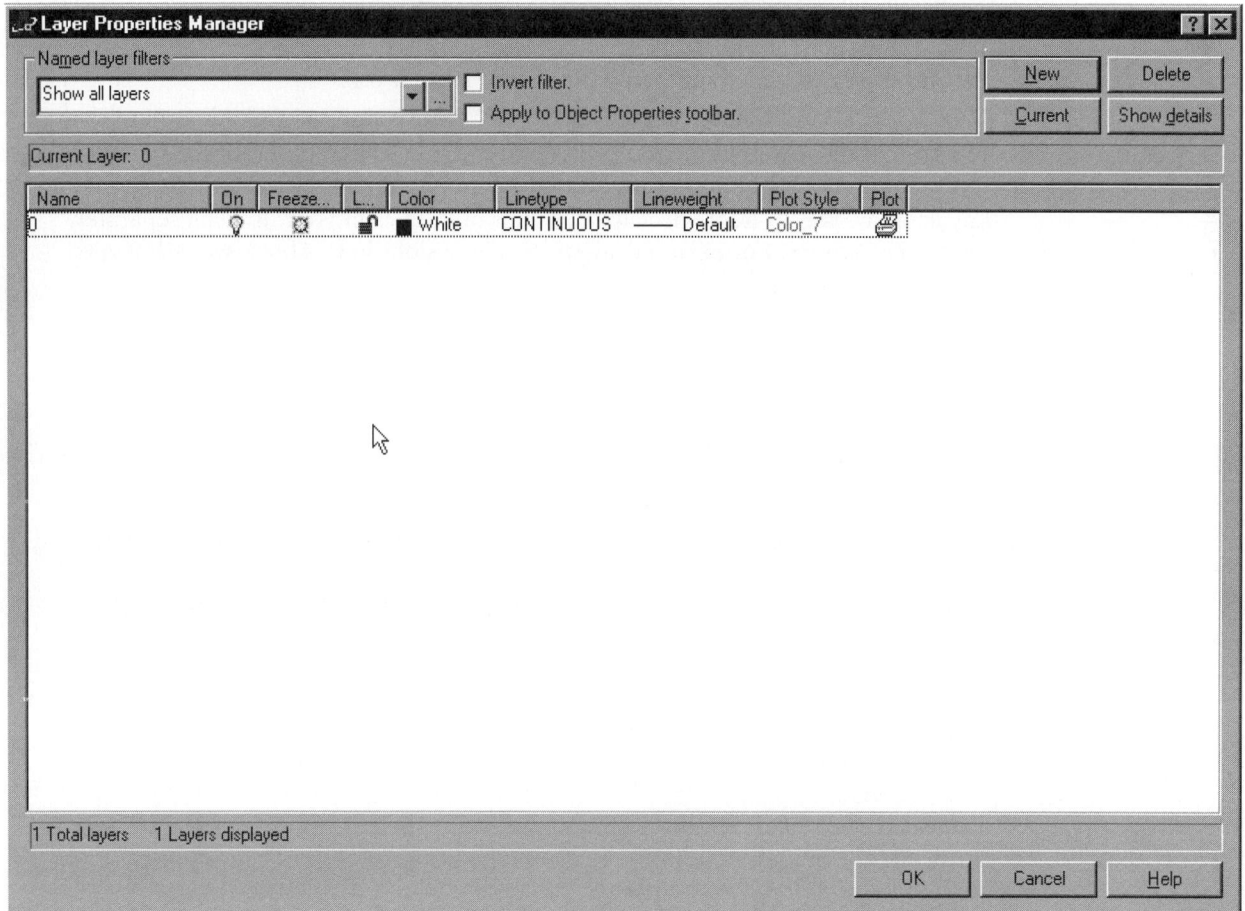

Figure 3-2

Either method will call the Layer Properties Manager dialog box illustrated in Figure 3-2. The large open space in the middle shows the names and properties of all layers defined in the current drawing. Layering systems can become very complex, and for this reason there is a system to limit or "filter" the layer names shown on the layer list. This is controlled by the box at the top left, which currently says "Show all layers". This is an unusual list box with the added feature of an ellipse button, which calls a Named Layers Filter dialog box. From this dialog you can specify features to use as filters. You could, for example, only show layers of a certain color. Since we will be working with a small set of layers, we will not need to do filtering.

In the layer name list window, you will see that "0" is the only defined layer. The icons on the line after the layer name show the current state of various properties of that layer. We will get to these shortly.

Now we will create three new layers. AutoCAD 2000 makes this easy.

⊕ Click on "New", to the right of the Named layers filter list.

A newly defined layer, "Layer1", will be created immediately and added to the layer name window. You will see that the new layer is given the characteristics of layer 0. We will alter these in Task 3.2. But first, we will give this layer a new name and then define three more layers.

Layer names may be long or short. We have chosen single-digit numbers as layer names because they are easy to type and we can match them to AutoCAD's color numbering sequence.

⊕ Type "1" for the layer name.

"Layer1" will change to simply "1". It is not necessary to press enter after typing the name.

⊕ Click on "New" again.

A second new layer will be added to the list. It will again have the default name "Layer1". Change it to "2".

⊕ Type "2" for the second layer name.

⊕ Click on "New" again.

⊕ Type "3" for the third layer name.

At this point your layer name list should show layers 0, 1, 2, and 3, all with identical properties.

3.2 Assigning Colors to Layers

GENERAL PROCEDURE

1. Select the Layers tool from the Object Properties toolbar, or select "Layer..." from the Format menu.
2. Click on the color icon on the row for the layer you want to change.
3. In the Color dialog box, select a color from the color chart or type a color name or number in the edit box.
4. Click on OK.

We now have four layers, but they are all pretty much the same. Obviously, we have more changes to make before our new layers will have useful identities.

Layer 0 has some special features, which will be discussed in Chapter 10. Because of these it is common practice to leave it defined the way it is. We will begin our changes on layer 1.

⊕ (If for any reason you have left the Layer Properties Manager dialog box, re-enter it by selecting the Layers tool from the Object properties toolbar or "Layers..." from the Format menu.)

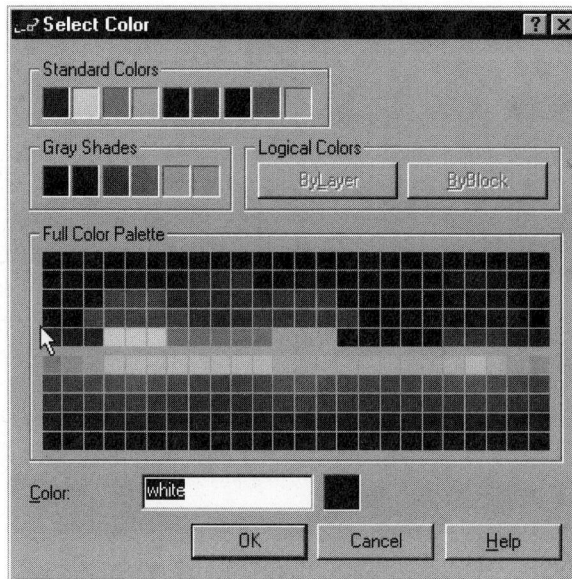

Figure 3-3

⊞ Move the cursor arrow to the layer 1 line and click on the white square under "Color".

Clicking on the white square in the color column of layer 1 will select layer 1 and call the Select Color dialog box illustrated in Figure 3-3. There are nine standard colors at the top, followed by gray shades and a palette of colors.

AutoCAD can display up to 256 different color shades. The nine standard colors shown at the top of the box are numbered 1 through 9 and are the same for all color monitors. Color numbers 10–249 are shown in the full color palette, and numbers 250–255 are the gray shades shown in between.

⊞ Select the red box, the first of the nine standard colors at the top of the box.

You should see the word red and the color red shown in the edit box at the bottom of the dialog. Note that you can also select colors by typing names or numbers directly in this edit box. Typing "red" or the number 1 (for color #1) is the same as selecting the red color box from the chart.

⊞ Click on OK.

You will now see that layer 1 is defined with the color red in the layer name list box.

Next we will assign the color yellow to layer 2.

⊞ Click on the white square under Color in the layer 2 line and assign the color yellow to layer 2 in the Select Color dialog box.

⊞ Click on OK.

⊞ Select layer 3 and set this layer to green.

Look at the layer list. You should now have the layers 0, 1, 2, and 3 defined with the colors white, red, yellow, and green.

3.3 Assigning Linetypes

GENERAL PROCEDURE

1. Select the Layers tool from the Object Properties toolbar or "Layer..." from the Format menu.
2. Click in the Linetype column of the layer you want to set.
3. In the Select Linetype dialog box, select a linetype. If necessary, load linetypes first.
4. Click on OK.
5. Click on OK again to exit the dialog box.

AutoCAD has a standard library of linetypes that can be assigned easily to layers. There are 45 standard types in addition to continuous lines. In addition to continuous lines, we will be using hidden and center lines. We will put hidden lines in yellow on layer 2 and center lines in green on layer 3.

The procedure for assigning linetypes is almost identical to the procedure for assigning colors, except that you will have to load linetypes into the drawing before they can be used.

⊕ (If for any reason you have left the Layer Properties Manager, re-enter it by selecting the Layer tool from the Object Properties toolbar.)

⊕ Click on "Continuous" in the Linetype column of the layer 2 line.

Note: Make sure that you actually click on the word "Continuous". If you click on one of the icons in the layer 2 line, you may turn the layer off or freeze it so that you cannot draw on it. These properties are discussed at the end of task 3.5.

This will select layer 2 and call up the Select Linetype dialog box illustrated in Figure 3-4. The box containing a list of loaded linetypes currently only

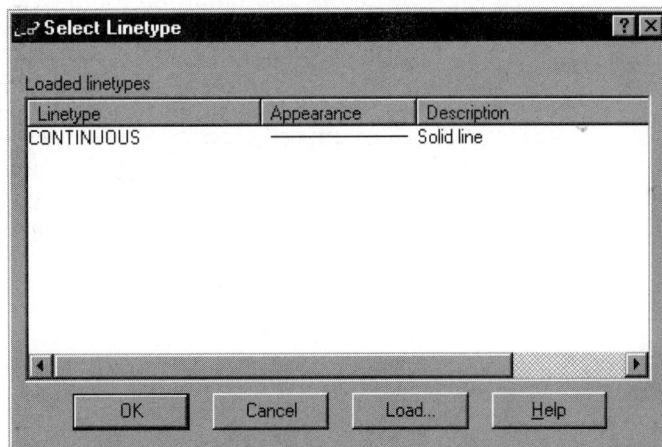

Figure 3-4

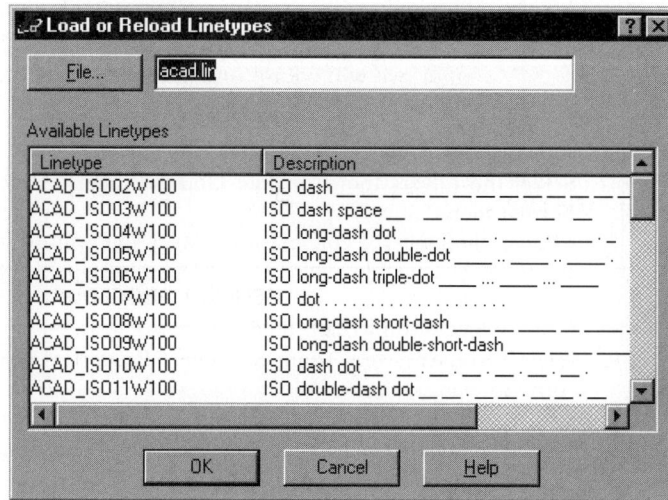

Figure 3-5

shows the continuous linetype. We can fix this by selecting the "Load..." button at the bottom of the dialog box.

⊕ Click on "Load...".

This will call a second dialog box, the Load or Reload Linetypes box illustrated in Figure 3-5. Here you can pick from the list of linetypes available from the standard "acad" file or from other files containing linetypes, if there are any on your system. You also have the option of loading all linetypes from any given file at once. The linetypes are then defined in your drawing, and you can assign a new linetype to a layer at any time. This makes things easier. It does, however, use up more memory.

For our purposes we will load only the hidden and center linetypes we are going to be using.

⊕ Scroll down until you see the Center linetype.

⊕ Click on "Center" in the Linetype column at the left.

⊕ Scroll down again until you see the "Hidden" linetype on the list.

⊕ Hold down the Ctrl key and click on "Hidden" in the Linetype column.

The Ctrl key lets you highlight two separated items in a list.

⊕ Click on OK to complete the loading process.

You should now see the center and hidden linetypes added to the list of loaded linetypes. Now that these are loaded, we can assign them to layers.

⊕ Click on "Hidden" in the linetype column.

⊕ Click on OK to close the box.

You should see that layer 2 now has the hidden linetype.

Next assign the center linetype to layer 3.

⊕ Click on "Continuous" in the linetype column of the layer 3 line.

⊕ In the Select Linetype dialog box, select the Center linetype.

⊕ Click on OK.

Examine your layer list again. It should show layer 2 with the hidden line-type and layer 3 with the center linetype. Before exiting the Layer Properties Manager, we will create one additional layer in order to demonstrate AutoCAD 2000's lineweight feature.

3.4 Assigning Lineweight

GENERAL PROCEDURE

1. Select the Layers tool from the Object Properties toolbar or "Layer..." from the Format menu.
2. Click in the Lineweight column of the layer you want to change.
3. In the Lineweight dialog box, select a lineweight.
4. Click on OK.
5. Click on OK again to exit the dialog box.

Lineweight is a new feature in AutoCAD 2000. It refers to the thickness of lines as they are displayed and plotted. All lines are initially given a default lineweight, which is .01 inches or .25 mm. Lineweights are assigned by layer and will be displayed only if the LWT button on the status bar is in the on position. In this task we will create a new layer and give it a much larger lineweight for demonstration purposes.

⊕ (If for any reason you have left the Layer Properties Manager dialog box, re-enter it by selecting the Layers tool from the Object Properties toolbar.)

First we will create a new layer, since we do not want to change our previous layers from the default lineweight setting.

⊕ If layer 3 is not highlighted, highlight it by pointing to the name "3" and pressing the pickbutton.

⊕ Click on the New button in the dialog box.

Notice that the new layer takes the characteristics of the previously highlighted layer. Our last action was to give layer 3 the center linetype, so your new layer should have green center lines and the other characteristics of layer 3.

⊕ Type "4" for the new layer name.

⊕ Click on "default" in the Lineweight column of layer 4.

This will open the Lineweight dialog box, shown in Figure 3-6. We will use a rather large lineweight to create a clear demonstration.

⊕ Scroll down until you see "1.00 mm" on the list.

⊕ Highlight the 1.00 mm line.

Below the list you will see that the original specification for this layer was the default and is now being changed to 1.00 mm.

⊕ Click on OK to return to the Layer Properties Manager.

It is now time to leave the dialog and see what we can do with our new layers.

⊕ Click on OK to exit Layer Properties Manager.

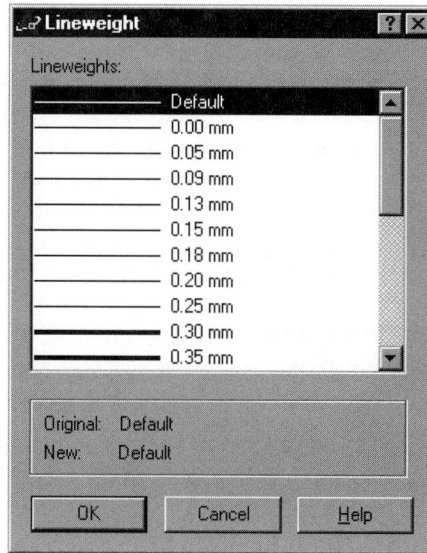

Figure 3-6

Note: Do not exit the dialog box by clicking the close button. Exit only by clicking OK. If you use the close button, or if you cancel the dialog, all of your changes, new layers, etc. will be lost.

Before proceeding, you should be back in your drawing window with your new layers defined in your drawing. To verify that you have successfully defined new layers, open the layer list on the Object Properties toolbar, as shown in Figure 3-7.

⊕ To open the layer list, click anywhere in the list box.
   Your list should resemble the one in Figure 3-7.

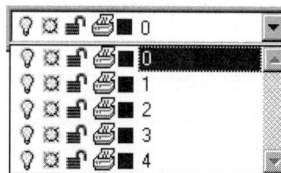

Figure 3-7

3.5 Changing the Current Layer

GENERAL PROCEDURE

1. Open the Layer list from the Object Properties toolbar.
2. Select a layer name.

or

1. Select the Make Object's Layer Current tool from the Object Properties toolbar.
2. Select an object on the layer you wish to make current.

In this task we will make each of your new layers current and draw objects on them. You will immediately see how much power you have added to your drawing by the addition of new layers, colors, linetypes, and lineweight.

To draw new entities on a layer, you must make it the currently active layer. Previously drawn objects on other layers that are turned on will be visible also and will be plotted, but new objects will go on the current layer.

There are two quick methods to establish the current layer. The first works the same as any dialog box pop down list. The second makes use of previously drawn objects. We will use the first method to draw the objects in Figure 3-8.

⊕ Click anywhere in the current layer list box on the Object Properties toolbar.

This will open the list, as shown in Figure 3-7.

⊕ Select Layer 1, by clicking on the layer name "1" in the pop down list.

Layer 1 will replace layer 0 as the current layer on the Object Properties toolbar.

⊕ Using the Rectangle command, draw the 6 × 6 square shown in Figure 3-8, with first corner at (3,2) and other corner at (9,8).

Your rectangle should show the red, continuous lines of layer 1.

⊕ Click anywhere in the Layer Control box on the Object Properties toolbar.

⊕ Click on the layer name "2".

Layer 2 will become the current layer.

⊕ With layer 2 current, draw the hidden circle in Figure 3-8, centered at (6,5) with radius 2.

Your circle should appear in yellow hidden lines.

⊕ Make layer 3 current and draw a horizontal center line from (2,5) to (10,5).

This line should appear as a green center line.

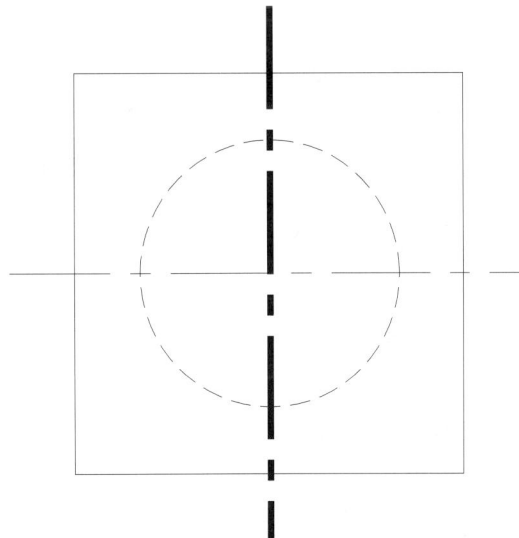

Figure 3-8

Figure 3-9

⊕   Click on the LWT button on the status line so that it is in the On position.

⊕   Make layer 4 current and draw a vertical line from (6,1) to (6,9).

This line should appear as a green center line with noticeable thickness.

⊕   Click the LWT button again to put it in the off position.

With LWT off, the lineweight of the horizontal center line will not be displayed.

Making an Object's Layer Current

Finally, we will use another method to make layer 1 current before moving on.

⊕   Select the Make Object's Layer Current tool from the Object Properties toolbar, as shown in Figure 3-9.

This tool allows us to make a layer current by selecting any object on that layer. AutoCAD will show this prompt:

```
Select object whose layer will become current:
```

⊕   Select the red rectangle drawn on layer 1.

Layer 1 will replace layer 4 in the current layer box.

Other Properties of Layers

There are several other properties that may be set in the Layer Properties Manager, or, more conveniently, in the Layer list box. These settings probably will not be useful to you until later on, but we introduce them briefly here for your information.

Layers can be turned on or off with the light bulb icon. On and off status affects only the visibility of objects on a layer. Objects on layers that are off are not visible or plotted, but are still in the drawing and are considered when the drawing is "regenerated." Regeneration is the process by which AutoCAD translates the precise numerical data that make up a drawing file database into the less precise values of screen graphics. Regeneration can be a slow process in large, complex drawings. As a result it may be useful not to regenerate all layers all the time. This is where the Freeze and Thaw options come in. Frozen layers are not only invisible but are ignored in regeneration. Thaw reverses this setting. Thawed layers will always be regenerated. Freeze and Thaw properties are set using the sun icon. Layers are thawed by default as indicated by the yellow sun.

The Lock and Unlock setting does not affect visibility but does affect availability of objects for editing. Objects on locked layers are visible but cannot be edited. Unlocking reverses this setting. This property is set with the lock icon.

Finally, layers may be set as plottable or not plottable using the printer icon. This will allow you to create a plot in which only objects on designated layers are plotted.

Deleting Layers

You can delete layers using the Delete button in the Layer Properties Manager dialog box. However, you cannot delete layers that have objects drawn on them. Also, you cannot delete the current layer or layer 0.

3.6 Editing Corners Using FILLET

GENERAL PROCEDURE

1. Type "f", select the Fillet tool from the Modify toolbar, or select Fillet from the Modify menu.
2. Type "r" for radius.
3. Enter a radius value.
4. Press Enter to repeat the FILLET command.
5. Select two lines that meet at a corner.

Now that you have a variety of linetypes to use, you can begin to do more realistic mechanical drawings. All you will need is the ability to create filleted (rounded) and chamfered (cut) corners. The two work similarly, and AutoCAD makes them easy. Fillets may also be created between circles and arcs, but the most common usage is the type of situation demonstrated here.

We will only be working with the square in this exercise, but instead of erasing the other objects, turn them off, as follows:

⊕ If you have not already done so, set Layer 1 as the current layer.

⊕ Open the layer list on the Object Properties toolbar, and click the light bulb icons on layers 2, 3, and 4 so that they turn from yellow to gray, indicating that they are off.

⊕ Click anywhere outside the list box to close it.

When you are done you should see only the square. The other objects are still in your drawing and may be recalled anytime simply by turning their layers on again.

We will use the square to practice fillets and chamfers.

⊕ Type "f" or select the Fillet tool from the Modify toolbar, as shown in Figure 3-10.

Fillet is also on the Modify menu, but it is near the bottom of a lengthy list, so the alias or the toolbar selection is quicker.

A prompt with options will appear as follows:

```
Current settings: Mode = TRIM, Radius = 0.50
Select first object or [Polyline/Radius/Trim]:
```

Figure 3-10

Polylines are discussed in Chapter 9, but we will have something to show you about this option in a moment. Trim mode is discussed at the end of this exercise.

The first thing you must do is determine the degree of rounding you want. Since fillets are really arcs, they can be defined by a radius.

⊕ Type "r".

AutoCAD prompts:

Enter fillet radius <0.50>:

The default is 0.50.

⊕ Type ".75" or show two points 0.75 units apart.

You have set 0.75 as the current fillet radius for this drawing. You can change it at any time. Changing will not affect previously drawn fillets.

⊕ Press Enter or the space bar to repeat FILLET.

The prompt is the same as before, but the radius value has changed:

```
Current settings: Mode = TRIM, Radius = 0.75
Select first object or [Polyline/Radius/Trim]:
```

You will notice that you have the pickbox on the screen now without the cross hairs.

⊕ Use the pickbox to select two lines that meet at any corner of your square.

Behold! A fillet! You did not even have to press Enter. AutoCAD knows that you are done after selecting two lines.

⊕ Press Enter or the space bar to repeat FILLET. Then fillet another corner.
⊕ Proceed to fillet all four corners.

When you are done, your screen should resemble Figure 3-11.

Trim Mode

Trim mode allows you to determine whether or not you want AutoCAD to remove square corners as it creates fillets and chamfers. Examples of fillets created with Trim mode on and off are shown in Figure 3-12. In most cases, you will want to

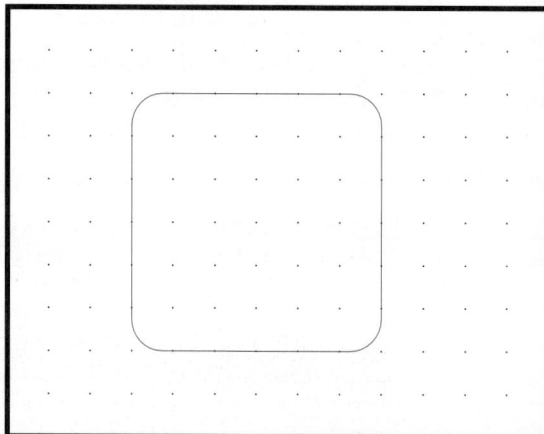

Figure 3-11

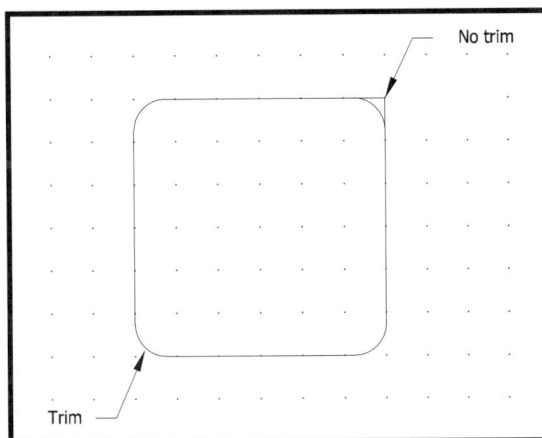

Figure 3-12

leave trim mode on. To turn it off, enter FILLET and type "t" for "Trim" and then "n" for "No Trim".

3.7   Editing Corners Using CHAMFER

GENERAL PROCEDURE

1. Select the Chamfer tool from the Modify toolbar, or select Chamfer from the Modify menu.
2. Type "d" for the "Distance" option.
3. Enter a chamfer distance.
4. Enter a second chamfer distance or press enter for an even chamfer.
5. Press Enter to repeat the CHAMFER command.
6. Select two lines that meet at a corner.

The CHAMFER command sequence is almost identical to the FILLET command, with the exception that chamfers may be uneven. That is, you may cut back farther on one side of a corner than on the other. To do this you must give AutoCAD two distances instead of one.

In this exercise will draw even chamfers on the four corners of the square. By using the Polyline option, we will chamfer all four corners at once. We will also take the opportunity to use a new cursor menu.

⊕   Select the Chamfer tool, as shown in Figure 3-13.

AutoCAD prompts:

```
(TRIM mode) Current chamfer Dist1 = 0.50, Dist2 = 0.50
Select first line or [Polyline/Distance/Angle/Trim/Method]:
```

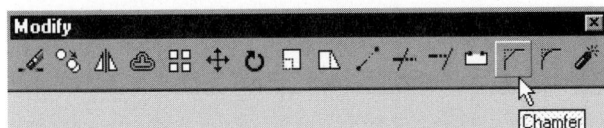

Figure 3-13

You can type a letter to select an option, but there is also a short cut menu.

⊕ Right click anywhere in the drawing area.

This will call a cursor menu with the Polyline, Distance, Angle, Trim, and Method options in the middle panel.

⊕ Select "Distance".

The next prompt will be

> Specify first chamfer distance <0.50>:

⊕ Type "1".

AutoCAD asks for another distance:

> Specify second chamfer distance <1.00>:

The first distance has become the default and most of the time it will be used. If you want an asymmetric chamfer, enter a different value for the second distance.

⊕ Press enter to accept the default, making the chamfer distances symmetrical.

⊕ Repeat the CHAMFER command.

At this point you could proceed to chamfer each corner of the square independently. However, if you drew the square using the RECTANGLE command you have a quicker option. The RECTANGLE command draws a polyline rectangle. Polylines are discussed in Chapter 9, but for now it is useful to know that a polyline is a single entity comprised of several lines and arcs. If you have drawn a closed polyline and specify the Polyline option in the CHAMFER or FILLET commands, AutoCAD will edit all corners of the object.

⊕ Type "p" or open the short cut menu and select Polyline.

AutoCAD prompts:

> Select 2D polyline:

⊕ Answer the prompt by pointing to any part of the square.

You should have four neat chamfers on your square, replacing the fillets from the previous task. Your screen should resemble Figure 3-14.

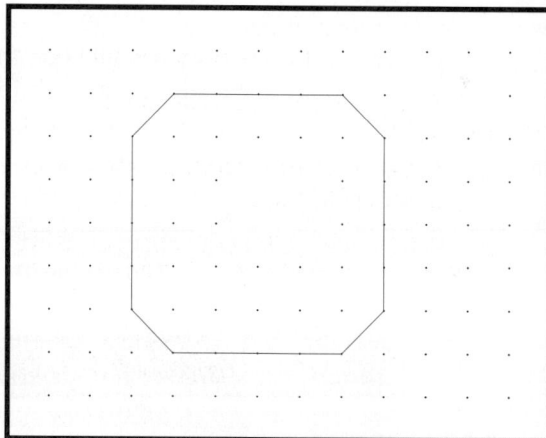

Figure 3-14

3.8 ZOOMing Window, Previous, and All

GENERAL PROCEDURE

1. Type "z" or select a Zoom tool from the Standard toolbar.
2. Enter a ZOOM method or magnification value.
3. Enter values or points, if necessary, depending on choice of method.

The capacity to zoom in and out of a drawing is one of the more impressive bene-
fits of working on a CAD system. When drawings get complex, it often becomes
necessary to work in detail on small portions of the drawing space. Especially with
a small monitor, the only way to do this is by making the detailed area larger on
the screen. This is done easily with the ZOOM command.

⊕ **You should have a square with chamfered corners on your screen
from the previous exercise.**

We will demonstrate zooming using the window, all, previous, and realtime options.

⊕ **Type "z" or select the Zoom Window tool from the Standard toolbar,
as illustrated in Figure 3-15.**

The prompt that follows includes the following options:

```
Specify corner of window, enter a scale factor (nX or nXP), or
[All/Center/Dynamic/Extents/Previous/Scale/Window] <realtime>:
```

If you have used the Zoom Window tool, the Window option will be entered automatically. As in ERASE and other edit commands, you can force
a window selection by typing "w" or selecting "Window". However, this is
unnecessary. The windowing action is automatically initiated if you pick a
point on the screen after entering ZOOM.

⊕ **Pick a point just below and to the left of the lower left-hand corner
of your square (point 1 in Figure 3-16).**

AutoCAD asks for another point:

```
Specify opposite corner:
```

You are being asked to define a window, just as in the ERASE command.
This window will be the basis for what AutoCAD displays next. Since you are
not going to make a window that exactly conforms to the screen size and
shape, AutoCAD will interpret the window this way: Everything in the window will be shown, plus whatever additional area is needed to fill the screen.
The center of the window will become the center of the new display.

Zoom Window

Figure 3-15

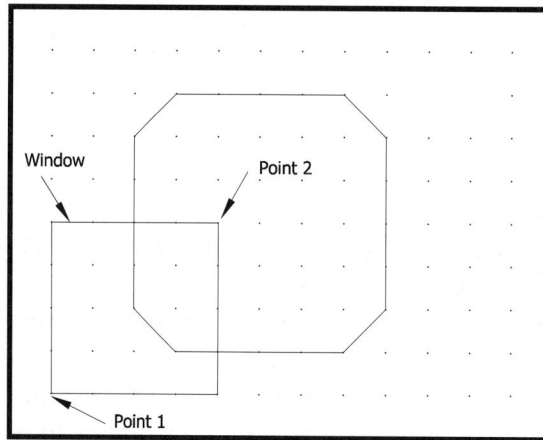

Figure 3-16

⊕   Pick a second point near the center of your square (point 2 in the figure).

The lower left corner of the square should now appear enlarged on your screen, as shown in Figure 3-17.

⊕   Using the same method, try zooming up further on the chamfered corner of the square. If snap is on, you may need to turn it off (F9).

Remember that you can repeat the ZOOM command by pressing Enter or the space bar.

At this point, most people cannot resist seeing how much magnification they can get by zooming repeatedly on the same corner or angle of a chamfer. Go ahead. After a couple of zooms the angle will not appear to change. An angle is the same angle no matter how close you get to it. But what happens to the spacing of the grid and snap as you move in?

When you are through experimenting with window zooming, try zooming to the previous display.

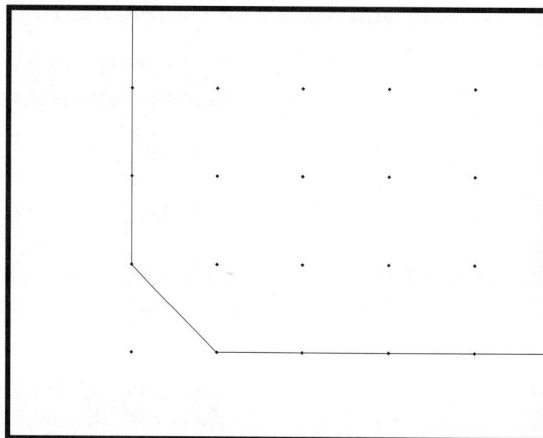

Figure 3-17

Figure 3-18

Zoom Previous

⊕ Press Enter to repeat the ZOOM command, or select the Zoom Previous tool, as shown in Figure 3-18.

⊕ If you repeated the command by pressing enter, type "p".

You should now see your previous display.

AutoCAD keeps track of up to 10 previous displays.

⊕ ZOOM "Previous" as many times as you can until you get a message that says

No previous display saved.

Zoom All

ZOOM All zooms out to display the whole drawing. It is useful when you have been working in a number of small areas of a drawing and are ready to view the whole scene. You do not want to have to wade through previous displays to find your way back. ZOOM All will take you there in one jump.

To see it work, you should be zoomed in on a portion of your display before executing ZOOM All.

⊕ Press Enter or type "z" to repeat the ZOOM command and zoom in on a window within your drawing.

⊕ Press Enter or type "z" to repeat ZOOM again.

⊕ Type "a" for the All option.

Note: The Zoom Window tool also has a flyout that includes tools for all of the ZOOM command options, including ZOOM All, as shown in Figure 3-19.

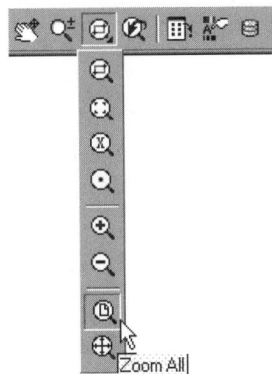

Figure 3-19

Flyouts are toolbar features that make additional tools available. Any tool button that has a small black triangle in one corner will open a flyout. To open a flyout, hold down the pickbutton while the arrow is on the tool. Then run down or across the flyout to the tool you want. When the tool button is "down," release the pickbutton.

3.9   Using Realtime ZOOM and PAN

GENERAL PROCEDURE

1. Pick the PAN Realtime or ZOOM Realtime tool from the Standard toolbar.
2. Use the cursor to move objects (PAN) or increase or decrease magnification (ZOOM).
3. Use enter or the space bar to exit the command.

Realtime ZOOM and PAN allow you to see changes in display and magnification dynamically as you make adjustments. As soon as you start to use ZOOM, you are likely to need PAN as well. While ZOOM allows you to magnify portions of your drawing, PAN allows you to shift the area you are viewing in any direction.

You also have the option of panning with the scroll bars at the edges of the drawing area, but the PAN command allows more flexibility. In particular, it allows diagonal motion. We will use the PAN Realtime tool first and then the ZOOM Realtime tool.

⊕   Type "p" or select the Pan Realtime tool from the Standard toolbar (as illustrated in Figure 3-20).

   With either method, you will see the PAN command cursor representing a hand with which you can move objects on the screen. When the mouse button is not depressed, the hand will move freely across the screen. When you move the mouse with the pickbutton held down, the complete drawing display will move along with the hand.

⊕   Move the hand near the middle of the screen without holding down the pickbutton.

⊕   Hold down the pickbutton and move the cursor diagonally up and to the right, as illustrated in Figure 3-21.

⊕   Release the pickbutton to complete the PAN procedure.

   Experiment with Realtime PAN, moving objects up, down, left, right, and diagonally. Watch the scroll bars respond as you PAN across the drawing area.

Figure 3-20

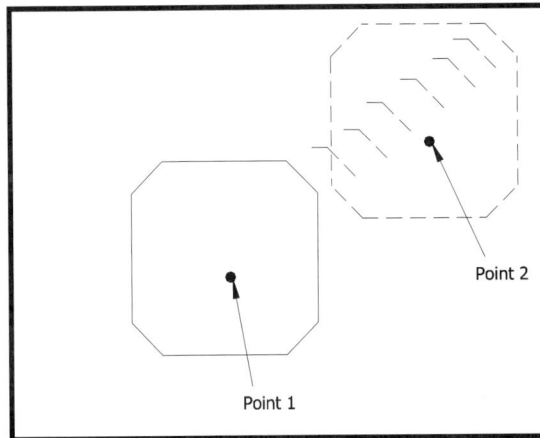

Figure 3-21

Realtime ZOOM

When you are in either the ZOOM or PAN command, you can access a short cut menu by right clicking anywhere on the screen. Try it.

✦ Without leaving PAN, press the right button on your mouse.

This will call up the short cut menu illustrated in Figure 3-22. This menu will allow you to switch quickly between realtime PAN and realtime ZOOM.

✦ Select Zoom from the short cut menu.

The menu will vanish and the realtime ZOOM cursor will appear. As illustrated in Figure 3-23, this represents a magnifying glass with a + sign above and a − sign below.

✦ Without pressing the pickbutton, move the zoom cursor near the bottom of the screen.

As with the PAN cursor, you will be able to move freely when the pickbutton is not held down.

✦ Press the pickbutton and move the cursor upward.

With the pickbutton down, upward motion will increase magnification, enlarging objects on the screen.

✦ Move up and down to see the effects of zoom cursor movement.

Release the pickbutton to complete the process. When you release the button you will not exit the command. This is important because it may take

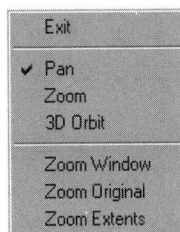

Exit
✔ Pan
Zoom
3D Orbit
Zoom Window
Zoom Original
Zoom Extents

Figure 3-22

Figure 3-23

several trips up or down the screen to indicate the amount of magnification you want. Moving the cursor halfway up the screen will produce a 100% magnification.

⊕ Continue to experiment with Realtime ZOOM and PAN until you feel comfortable.

⊕ To exit, press ESC, the space bar, or the enter key.

You can also right click to open the short cut menu and then select Exit.

Transparent Commands

If you have used the toolbar or the menu to enter the ZOOM and PAN commands, you may have noticed that they place an apostrophe and an underline before the name of the command. If you select the Pan tool, for example, you will see the following in the command area:

Command: '_pan

The apostrophe is a command modifier that makes the command transparent. This means that you can enter it in the middle of another command sequence, and when you are done you will still be in that sequence. For example, you can pan while drawing a line. This is a convenience if you already have selected the first point and then realize that the second point will be off the screen. A sample procedure using transparent PAN would go as follows:

1. Type "l" or select "Line".
2. Pick a first point.
3. Type "'p" (notice the apostrophe) or select the Pan tool.
4. Move the display as you wish.
5. Exit PAN.
6. Pick a second point to complete the line.

The underline character (_) you see after the apostrophe and before many commands that AutoCAD sends to the command line is added to commands in menu systems to ensure that AutoCAD interprets the commands in English. Foreign language versions of AutoCAD have their own command names but can still use menus developed in English, as long as the underline is there as a flag.

3.10   Using Plot Preview

GENERAL PROCEDURE

1. Type CTRL-P, select the Plot tool from the Standard toolbar, or select Plot from the File pull-down menu.
2. Change parameters as needed.
3. Select Partial or Full preview.

Plot preview is an essential tool in carrying out efficient plotting and printing. Plot configuration is complex, and the odds are good that you will waste time and paper by printing drawings directly without first previewing them on the screen. AutoCAD 2000 has new previewing tools that assist you in knowing exactly what to expect when your drawing reaches a sheet of drawing paper.

In this task we are still significantly limited in our use of plot settings, but learning to use the plot preview will make all of your future work with plotting and printing more effective. As in Chapter 2, we suggest that you work through this task now with the objects on your screen, and refer to it as necessary after you have done any of the drawings at the end of this chapter.

⊕ To begin this task you should have objects or a drawing on your screen ready to preview.

⊕ Type CTRL-P, or select the Plot tool from the Standard toolbar or Plot from the File menu.

This will open the Plot dialog box, familiar from the last chapter. The two preview options are at the bottom left of the dialog box. A partial preview will show you an outline of the effective plotting area in relation to the paper size but will not show an image of the plotted drawing. A full preview will display an image of the objects in your drawing on a sheet of drawing paper.

Note: We will address paper sizes in the next chapter. For now, we will assume that your plot configuration is correctly matched to the paper in your printer or plotter. If you do not get good results with this task, the problem may very well lie here.

Partial Preview

Partial previews are quick and should be accessed frequently as you specify plot settings that affect how paper will be used and oriented to print your drawing. Partial previews give you specific information on how your settings translate into areas on your drawing sheet. Full previews give you less detailed information, but let you see how your drawing will actually appear on paper.

We will look at a partial preview first.

⊕ Click on Partial Preview.

You will see a preview image similar to the one shown in Figure 3-24. The exact image will depend on your plotting device, so it may be different from the one shown here. The elements of the preview will be the same, however. The white rectangle represents your drawing paper. It may be oriented in landscape (horizontally) or portrait (vertically). Typically, printers are in portrait, and plotters in landscape. Below the preview image you will see the dimensions of this area listed as Paper size.

The blue dotted line rectangle inside the white area illustrates the printable plotting area. Its dimensions are listed as Printable area.

The area in blue cross hatching represents the effective plotting area, the size and shape of the area that AutoCAD can actually use given the shape and orientation of the drawing area in relation to the size and orientation of

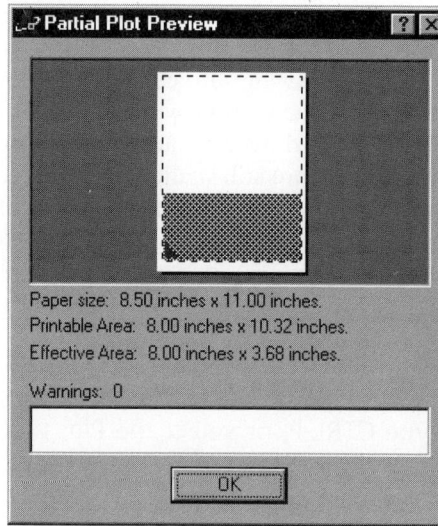

Figure 3-24

the paper. Its dimensions are listed as Effective area. The effective area is dependent on many things, as you will see. We will leave it as is for now and return to it later when you begin to alter the plot configuration.

In one corner of the preview image you will see a small red triangle. This is the rotation icon. It shows the corner of the plotting area where the plotter will begin plotting (the origin).

⊕ Click on OK to exit the preview box.

Full Preview

⊕ Click on the Full preview button.

The dialog box will disappear temporarily and you will see a preview image similar to the one in Figure 3-25. This image represents your drawing on paper as it is now configured for printing. The ZOOM Realtime cursor appears to allow you to zoom in or out on aspects of the preview. By clicking on the right button, you can access the zoom and pan pop-up list demonstrated earlier in this chapter. Panning and zooming in the preview has no effect on the plot parameters. You may want to experiment with this feature now.

⊕ When you are done experimenting with Zoom and Pan, press ESC or the enter key or space bar to return to the Plot dialog box.

This ends our initial preview of your drawing. In ordinary practice, if everything looked right in the preview you would move on to plot or print your drawing now by clicking on OK. In the chapters that follow, we will explore more features of the plot dialog box and will use full and partial plot previews extensively as we change plot parameters. For now, get used to using plot preview. If things are not coming out quite the way you want, you will be able to fix them soon.

⊕ Click OK to plot or print your drawing, or Cancel to exit without printing.

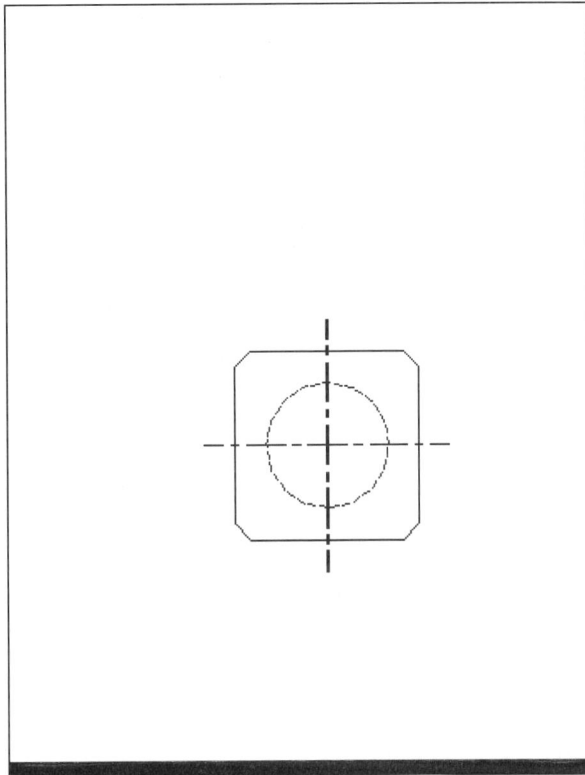

Figure 3-25

Using Print Preview

AutoCAD 2000 also has a Print preview tool on the Standard toolbar, as illustrated in Figure 3-26. This tool looks like the preview tool in other Windows applications and performs the same function as the Full preview option in the Plot dialog box. It will give you a quick look at your drawing positioned on a drawing sheet, but you will have to go to the Plot dialog if you want to make changes in plot configuration. Try it.

⊕ Click the Print preview tool, as illustrated in Figure 3-26.

You will see a full preview of your printed drawing, as shown previously in Figure 3-25.

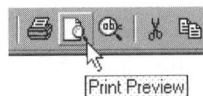

Figure 3-26

3.11 Review Material

Questions

1. What function(s) can be performed directly from the Layer list on the Object Properties toolbar? What functions can be performed from the Layer Properties Manager?
2. What linetype is always available when you start a drawing from scratch in AutoCAD? What must you do to access other linetypes?
3. How many colors are available in AutoCAD?
4. How many different layers does AutoCAD allow you to create?
5. Name three ways to change the current layer.
6. You have been working in the Layer Properties Manager, and when you return to your drawing you find that some objects are no longer visible. What happened?
7. Why is it often necessary to enter the FILLET and CHAMFER commands twice to create a single fillet or chamfer?
8. What is a transparent command? How do you make a command transparent when entering it at the command line?
9. What happens to the grid when you zoom way out on a drawing?
10. Name one limitation of scroll bars that the PAN command does not have.
11. What is the difference between a partial and a full plot preview?
12. What type of preview is created by the Print preview tool?

Drawing Problems

1. Make layer 3 current and draw a green center line cross with two perpendicular lines, each two units long and intersecting at their midpoints.
2. Make layer 2 current and draw a hidden line circle centered at the intersection of the cross drawn in step 1, with a diameter of two units.
3. Make layer 1 current and draw a red square two units on a side centered on the center of the circle. Its sides will run tangent to the circle.
4. Use a window to zoom in on the objects drawn in steps 1, 2, and 3.
5. Fillet each corner of the square with a 0.125 radius fillet.

3.12 WWW Exercise #3 (Optional)

This time out we will demonstrate the use of the Web toolbar. Your task is to open the toolbar, use the Browse the web tool to go to our Web site, take the test, and then do the Web project. The project for this chapter will take you deeper into the world of CAD on the internet. The WWW is full of interesting and informative CAD-related Web sites. There are sites maintained by professional journals, CAD newsgroups, CAD industry sites, sites with drawings that can be viewed and/or downloaded, sites with tutorials, sites with tips on CAD technique, sites with information on CAD-related software, not to mention Autodesk's own corporate Web site.

We start by opening the Web toolbar, using the toolbar short cut menu. This is the quickest way to open a toolbar.

⊕ Move the cursor so that the arrow is pointing anywhere inside of any of the currently visible toolbars.

⊕ With the arrow in this position, right click.

This will open the toolbars short cut menu, shown in Figure 3-27. This long menu includes 20 toolbar selections.

⊕ Move to the bottom of the list, using the arrow at the bottom if the complete menu does not fit on your screen.

⊕ Select "Web".

This will open the Web toolbar, shown in Figure 3-28.

⊕ Select the Browse the web tool, as shown.

The Web tool executes the BROWSER command and automatically enters the default URL.

⊕ (If you have not made our Web site the default, navigate to it from your default site, using the address: "www. prenhall.com/ bookbind/pubbooks/dix/".)

Away you go!

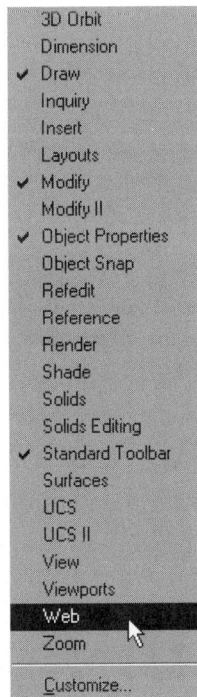

Figure 3-27

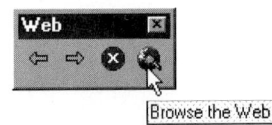

Figure 3-28

3.13   Drawing 3-1: Mounting Plate

This drawing will give you experience using center lines and chamfers. Since there are no hidden lines, you will have no need for layer 2, but we will continue to use the same numbering system for consistency. Draw the continuous lines in red on layer 1 and the center lines in green on layer 3.

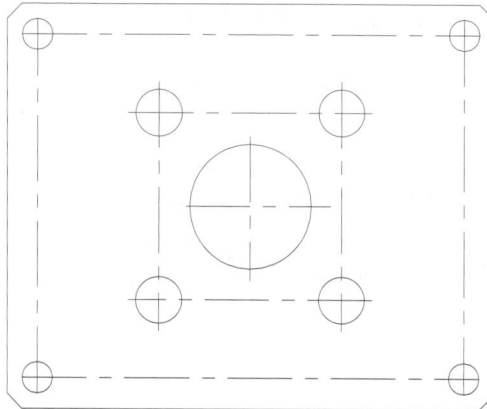

DRAWING SUGGESTIONS

GRID = 0.5
SNAP = 0.25
LTSCALE = 0.5

LTSCALE

The size of the individual dashes and spaces that make up center lines, hidden lines, and other linetypes is determined by a global setting called "LTSCALE". By default it is set to a factor of 1.00. In smaller drawings this setting will be too large and will cause some of the shorter lines to appear continuous regardless of what layer they are on.

To remedy this, change LTSCALE as follows:

1. Type "lts".
2. Enter a value.

For the drawings in this chapter use a setting of 0.50. See Figure 3-29 for some examples of the effect of changing LTSCALE.

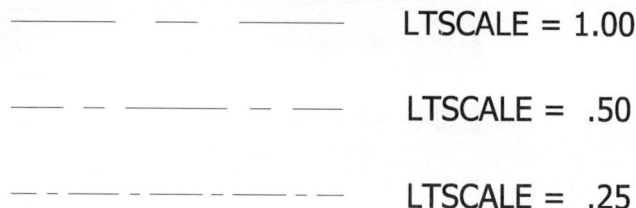

LTSCALE = 1.00

LTSCALE = .50

LTSCALE = .25

Figure 3-29

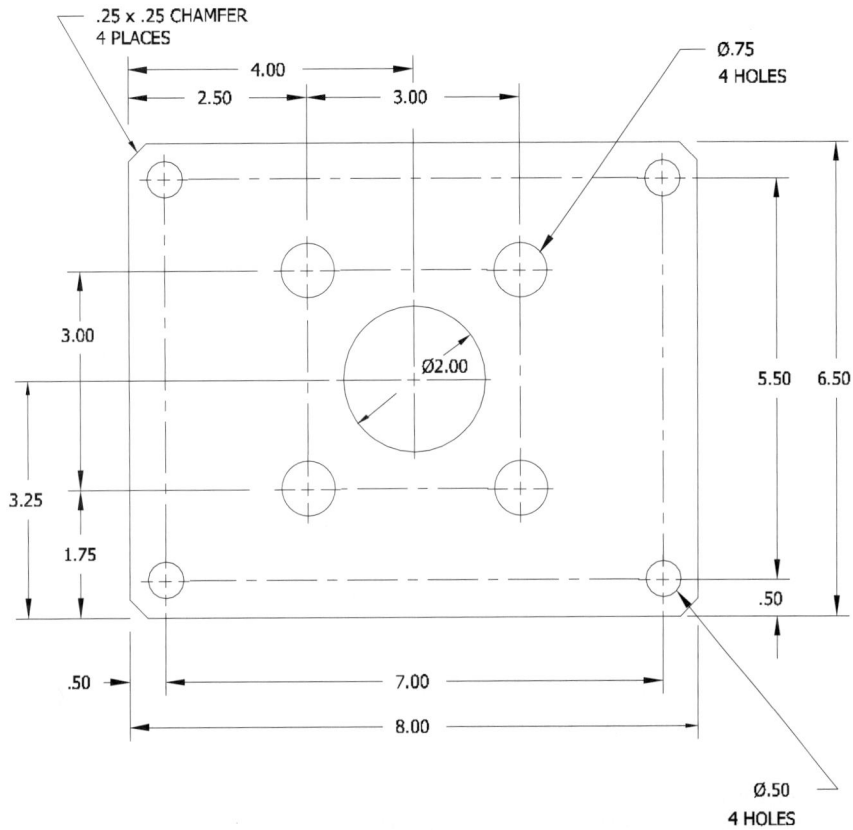

.25 x .25 CHAMFER
4 PLACES

Ø.75
4 HOLES

4.00

2.50   3.00

Ø.75
4 HOLES

3.00

Ø2.00

5.50   6.50

3.25

1.75

.50

.50

7.00

8.00

Ø.50
4 HOLES

MOUNTING PLATE

Drawing 3-1

3.14 Drawing 3-2: Stepped Shaft

This two-view drawing uses continuous lines, center lines, chamfers, and fillets. You may want to zoom in to enlarge the drawing space you are actually working in, and pan right and left to work on the two views.

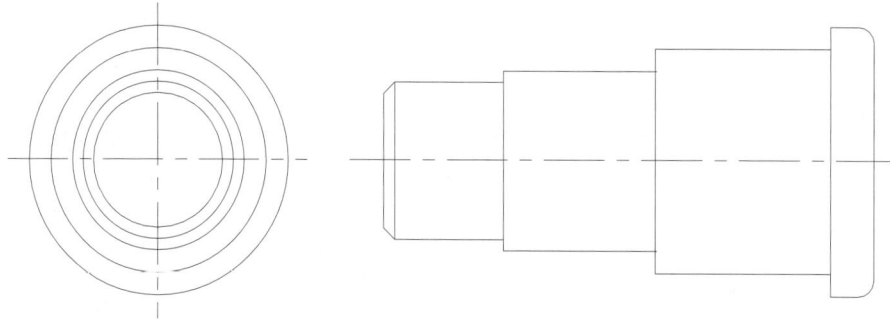

DRAWING SUGGESTIONS

GRID = 0.25
SNAP = 0.125
LTSCALE = 0.5

- Center the front view in the neighborhood of (2,5). Then the right side view will have a starting point at about (5,4.12), before the chamfer cuts this corner off.
- Draw the circles in the front view first, using the vertical dimensions from the side view for diameters. Save the inner circle until after you have drawn and chamfered the right side view.
- Draw a series of rectangles for the side view, lining them up with the circles of the front view. Then chamfer two corners of the leftmost rectangle and fillet two corners of the rightmost rectangle.
- Use the chamfer on the side view to line up the radius of the inner circle.
- Remember to set the current layer to 3 before drawing the center line through the side view.

.12 5 FILLET

.12 5 X .125
CHAMFER

Ø1.750   Ø2.000   Ø2.750   Ø3.25

1.375   1.75   2.00   .50

5.625 REF

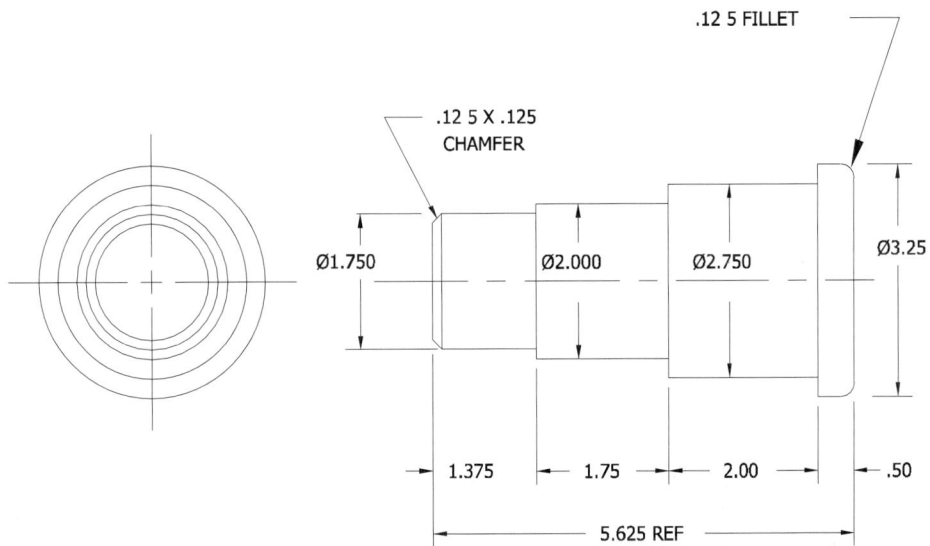

STEPPED SHAFT

Drawing 3-2

3.15   Drawing 3-3: Base Plate

This drawing uses continuous lines, hidden lines, center lines, and fillets. The side view should be quite easy once the front view is drawn. Remember to change layers when you want to change linetypes.

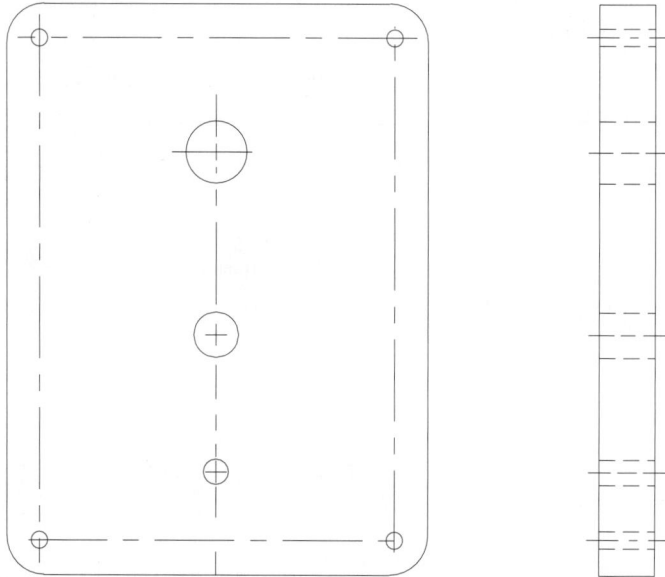

DRAWING SUGGESTIONS

GRID = 0.25
SNAP = 0.125
LTSCALE = 0.5

- Study the dimensions carefully and remember that every grid increment is 0.25, while snap points not on the grid are exactly halfway between grid points. The four circles at the corners are 0.38 (actually 0.375 rounded off) over and in from the corner points. This is three snap spaces ($0.375 = 3 \times 0.125$).
- Position the three circles along the center line of the rectangle carefully. Notice that dimensions are given from the center of the screw holes at top and bottom.
- Use the circle perimeters to line up the hidden lines on the side view, and the centers to line up the center lines.

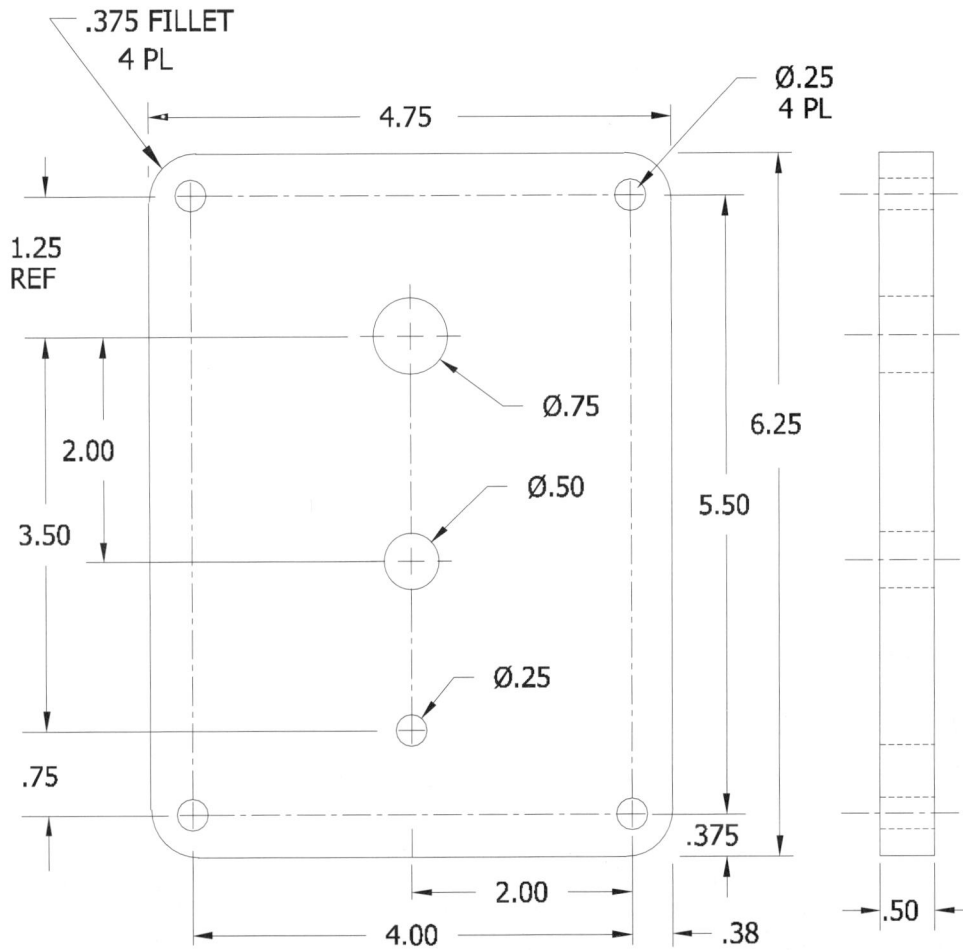

.375 FILLET
4 PL

Ø.25
4 PL

4.75

1.25
REF

Ø.75

2.00

6.25

Ø.50

5.50

3.50

Ø.25

.75

.375

2.00

4.00

.38

.50

BASE PLATE

Drawing 3-3

3.16   Drawing 3-4: Bushing

This drawing will give you practice with chamfers, layers, and zooming. Notice that because of the smaller dimensions here, we have recommended a smaller LTSCALE setting.

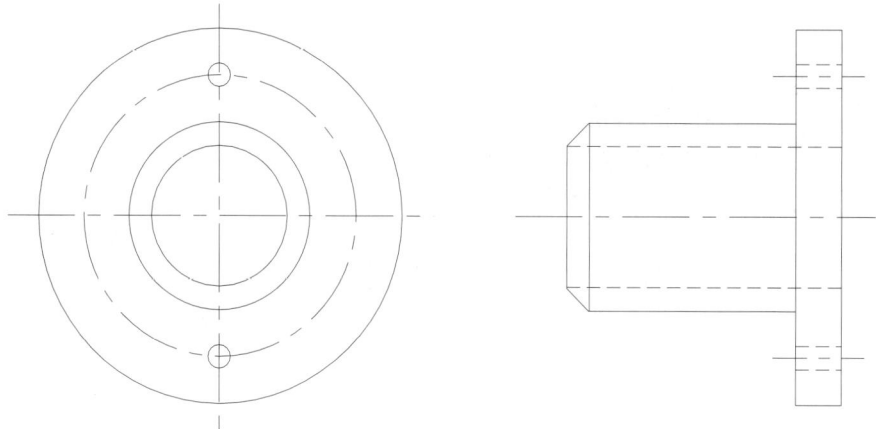

DRAWING SUGGESTIONS

GRID = 0.25
SNAP = 0.125
LTSCALE = 0.25

- Since this drawing will appear quite small on your screen, it would be a good idea to ZOOM in on the actual drawing space you are using and PAN if necessary.
- Notice that the two 0.25-diameter screw holes are 1.50 apart. This puts them squarely on grid points that you will have no trouble finding.

REGEN

When you zoom you may find that your circles turn into many-sided polygons. AutoCAD does this to save drawing regeneration time. These time savings are not noticeable now, but when you get into larger drawings they become significant. If you want to see a proper circle, type "Regen". This command will cause your drawing to be regenerated more precisely from the data you have given.

You may also notice that REGENs happen automatically when certain operations are performed, such as changing the LTSCALE setting after objects are already on the screen.

Ø.25 THRU
2 HOLES EQ SP
ON Ø1.50 B.C

.75 DIA
THRU

.25

Ø1.00

Ø2.00

1.50

.12 x .12 CHAMFER

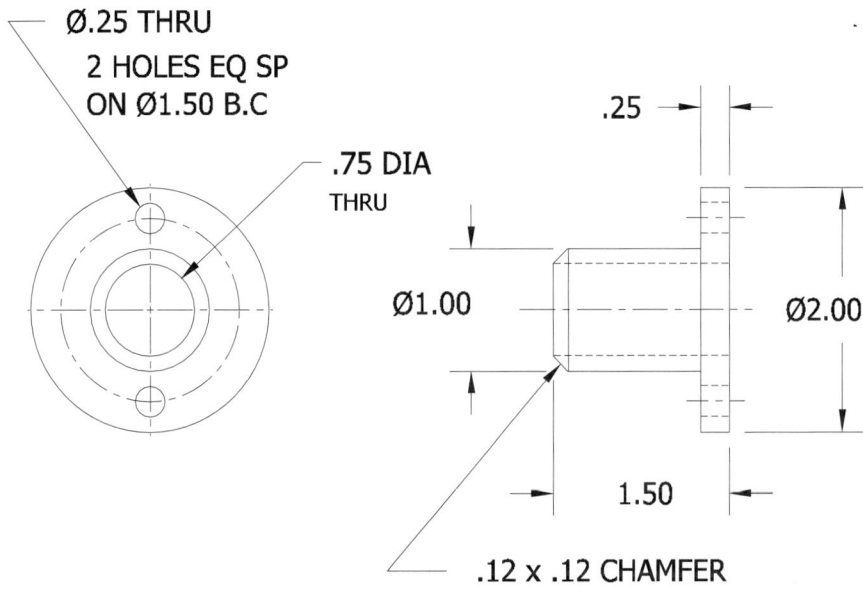

BUSHING
Drawing 3-4

3.17 Drawing 3-5: Half Block

This cinder block is the first project using architectural units in this book. Set units, grid, and snap as indicated, and everything will fall into place nicely.

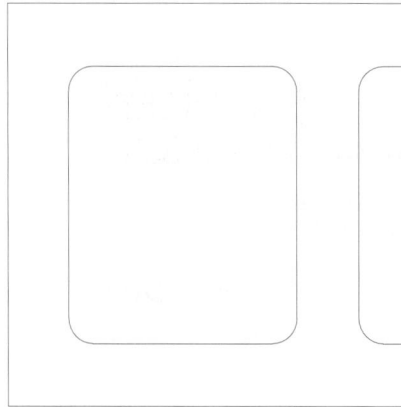

DRAWING SUGGESTIONS

$$\text{UNITS} = \text{Architectural}$$
$$\text{smallest fraction} = 4\left(\tfrac{1}{4}''\right)$$
$$\text{GRID} = \tfrac{1}{4}''$$
$$\text{SNAP} = \tfrac{1}{4}''$$

- Start with the lower left corner of the block at the point $(0'—1'', 0'—1'')$ to keep the drawing well placed on the display.
- Set the FILLET radius to $\tfrac{1}{2}''$ or 0.5. Notice that you can use decimal versions of fractions. The advantage is that they are easier to type.

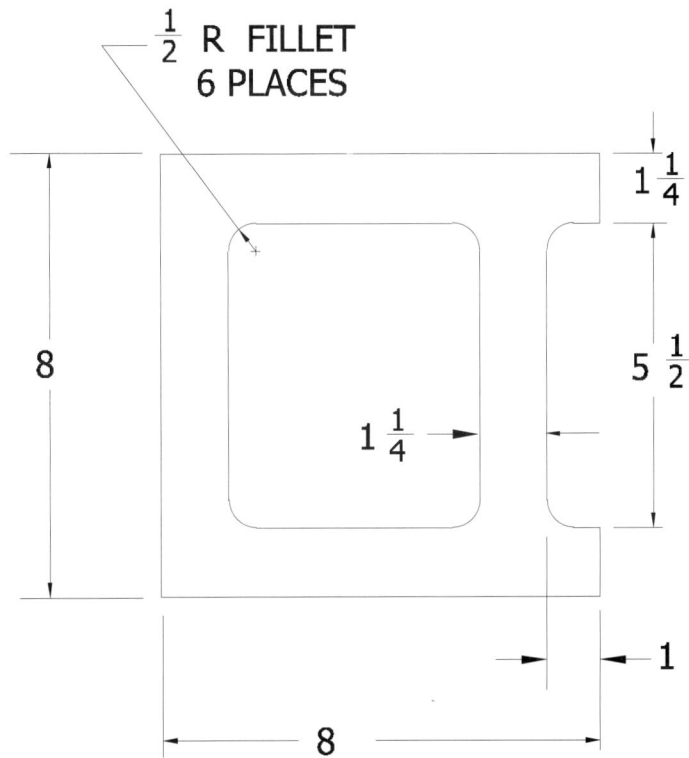

$\frac{1}{2}$ R FILLET
6 PLACES

$1\frac{1}{4}$

8

$5\frac{1}{2}$

$1\frac{1}{4}$

1

8

HALF BLOCK

Drawing 3-5

3.18   Drawing 3-6: Packing Flange

This drawing uses continuous lines, hidden lines, center lines, and fillets. The side view should be quite easy once the top view is drawn. Remember to change layers when you want to change linetypes.

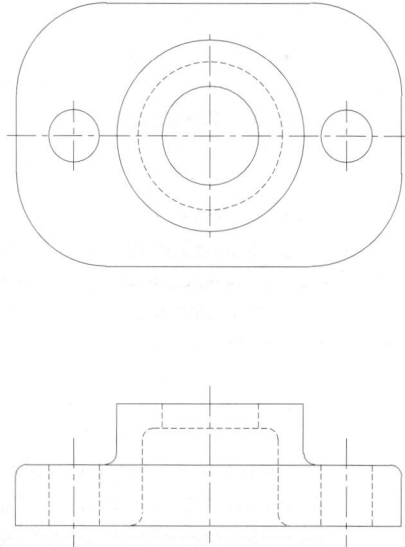

DRAWING SUGGESTIONS

UNITS = Fractional
GRID = $\frac{1}{4}$
SNAP = $\frac{1}{8}$
LTSCALE = 0.5

- Study the dimensions carefully and remember that every grid increment is $\frac{1}{4}$, while snap points not on the grid are exactly halfway between grid points. Notice that the units should be set to fractions.
- Begin by drawing the outline and then the three center lines in the top view. Then proceed by drawing all circles.
- The circles can be drawn using center and diameter. Position the center of the circle where the center lines cross and type in the diameter.
- Use the top view to line up all the lines on the side view.

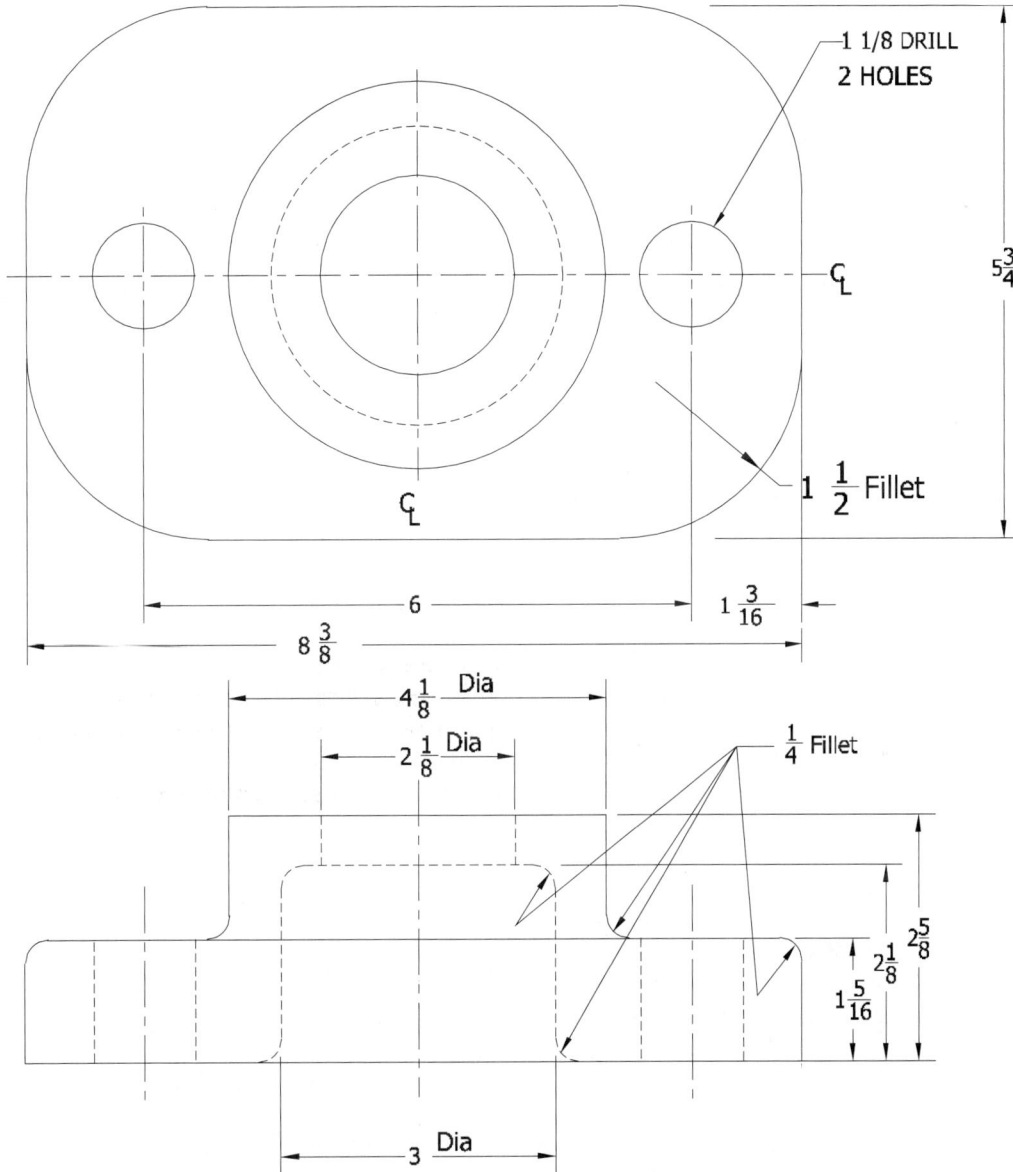

1 1/8 DRILL
2 HOLES

C_L

$5\frac{3}{4}$

$1\frac{1}{2}$ Fillet

C_L

6

$1\frac{3}{16}$

$8\frac{3}{8}$

$4\frac{1}{8}$ Dia

$2\frac{1}{8}$ Dia

$\frac{1}{4}$ Fillet

$2\frac{5}{8}$

$2\frac{1}{8}$

$1\frac{5}{16}$

3 Dia

PACKING FLANGE
Drawing 3-6

4

Template Drawings

COMMANDS

| ARRAY (rectangular) | COPY | LIMITS | MOVE |

OVERVIEW

In this chapter you will learn some real timesavers. If you have grown tired of defining the same three layers, along with units, grid, snap, and ltscale, for each new drawing, read on. You are about to learn how to use template drawings. With templates, you can begin each new drawing with whatever setup you want.

In addition, you will learn to reshape the grid using the LIMITS command and to COPY, MOVE, and ARRAY objects on the screen so that you do not have to draw the same thing twice. We will begin with LIMITS, since we will want to change the limits as part of defining your first template.

TASKS

4.1   Setting LIMITS

GENERAL PROCEDURE

1. Open a new drawing using the Advanced Setup Wizard.
2. Set up each unit type, using Next to move on after making changes.
3. Click Finish to exit the Advanced Setup dialog box.

or

1. Select "Drawing limits…" from the Format menu.
2. Enter a width.
3. Enter a length.
4. Exit the dialog box.

You have changed the density of the screen grid many times, but always within the same 12×9 space, which basically represents an A-size sheet of paper. Now you will learn how to change the shape by setting new limits to emulate other sheet sizes or any other space you want to represent. But first, a word about model space and paper space.

Model Space and Paper Space

Model space is an AutoCAD concept that refers to the imaginary space in which we create and edit objects. In model space, objects are always drawn full scale (1 screen unit = 1 unit of length in the real world). The alternative to model space is paper space, in which screen units represent units of length on a piece of drawing paper. You will encounter paper space when you begin to use AutoCAD 2000's layout features. A layout is like an overlay on your drawing in which you specify a sheet size and other paper-related options. Layouts also allow you to create multiple views of the same model space objects. To avoid confusion and keep your learning curve on track, however, we will avoid using layouts for the time being.

   In this exercise we will reshape our model space to emulate different drawing sheet sizes. This will not be necessary in later practice. With AutoCAD you can scale your drawing to fit any drawing sheet size when it comes time to plot. Model space limits should be determined by the size and shapes of objects in your drawing, not by the paper you are going to use when you plot.

The Advanced Setup Wizard

Limits can be set from within a drawing using the LIMITS command. When you are beginning a new drawing, however, a quick way is to use a drawing setup wizard, which will set up units at the same time. Wizards are standard Windows features that guide you through setup functions in all kinds of applications. We will use the Advanced Setup Wizard to begin this drawing and set 18×12 limits.

⊕   Start AutoCAD or begin a new drawing.

If the Create New Drawing dialog box is not showing, open the File menu and select New, or select the New tool from the Standard toolbar.

⊕ In the Create New Drawing dialog box click the Use a Wizard icon, the one on the right.

This will open the Select a Wizard box with the two options "Advanced Setup" and "Quick Setup".

⊕ Highlight Advanced Setup in the Select a Wizard box.

How do you like that, you are already into advanced options! The Quick Setup Wizard will also allow you to set limits, but does not allow for units setup.

⊕ Click on OK.

This will bring up the Advanced Setup dialog box illustrated in Figure 4-1. The list on the left shows you the steps the Wizard will take you through: Units, Angle, Angle Measure, Angle Direction, and Limits. The first four are familiar from the UNITS command. Limits is new. In the first four steps you will set up 2 place decimal units, 0 place angles measured in degrees, starting with 0 on the right horizontal and moving counterclockwise. Then you will set limits at 18×12.

⊕ If the Decimal radio button is not selected, select it.

⊕ Open the Precision box at the bottom right and select 0.00.

⊕ Click Next to move on to the next step, Angle units.

The wizard will show a second set of dialog box options. Here again you can choose an option for units and an option for precision.

⊕ Check to see that the Decimal degrees radio button is selected and that the precision is set to 0.

⊕ Click Next to move on to Angle Measure.

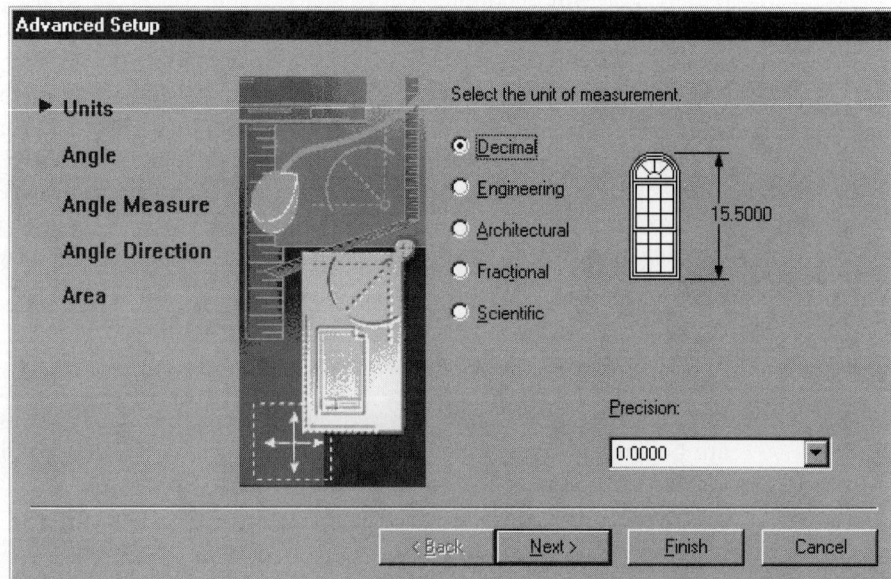

Figure 4-1

The only options here are the four points of the compass. This will allow you to determine which compass point is 0 degrees. East is the standard setting.

⊕ Check to see that the East radio button is selected, then click Next to move on to Angle Direction.

Here you have only two options, clockwise or counterclockwise. Counterclockwise is the usual AutoCAD direction for measuring and specifying angles.

⊕ Check to see that Counter-Clockwise is selected, then click Next to move on to Area.

This, at last, is where you set the limits of your new drawing, using the edit boxes and icon shown in Figure 4-2. The number in the width box should read 12.00. The number in the length box should show 9.00.

At the right you will see a preview image of a sheet of drawing paper with the 12 × 9 limits. We will change to an 18 × 12 area.

⊕ Double click in the Width box and type "18".
⊕ Double click in the Length box and type "12".

The width box and the preview image will show 18 × 12.

⊕ Click Finish to exit the Advanced Setup Wizard.

Upon returning to the drawing area you will see that the grid now covers your screen. To see the complete new area, however, you will need to ZOOM All.

⊕ Type "z" to enter the ZOOM command and then "a" for the "All" option.

Your screen should resemble Figure 4-3, showing an 18 × 12 grid.

After we are finished exploring the LIMITS command, we will create the other new settings we want and save this drawing as your B-size template.

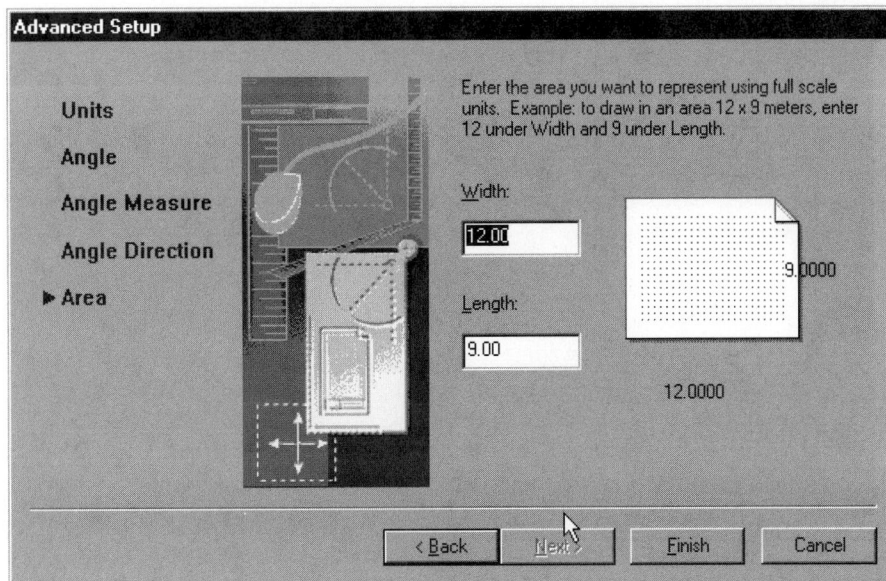

Figure 4-2

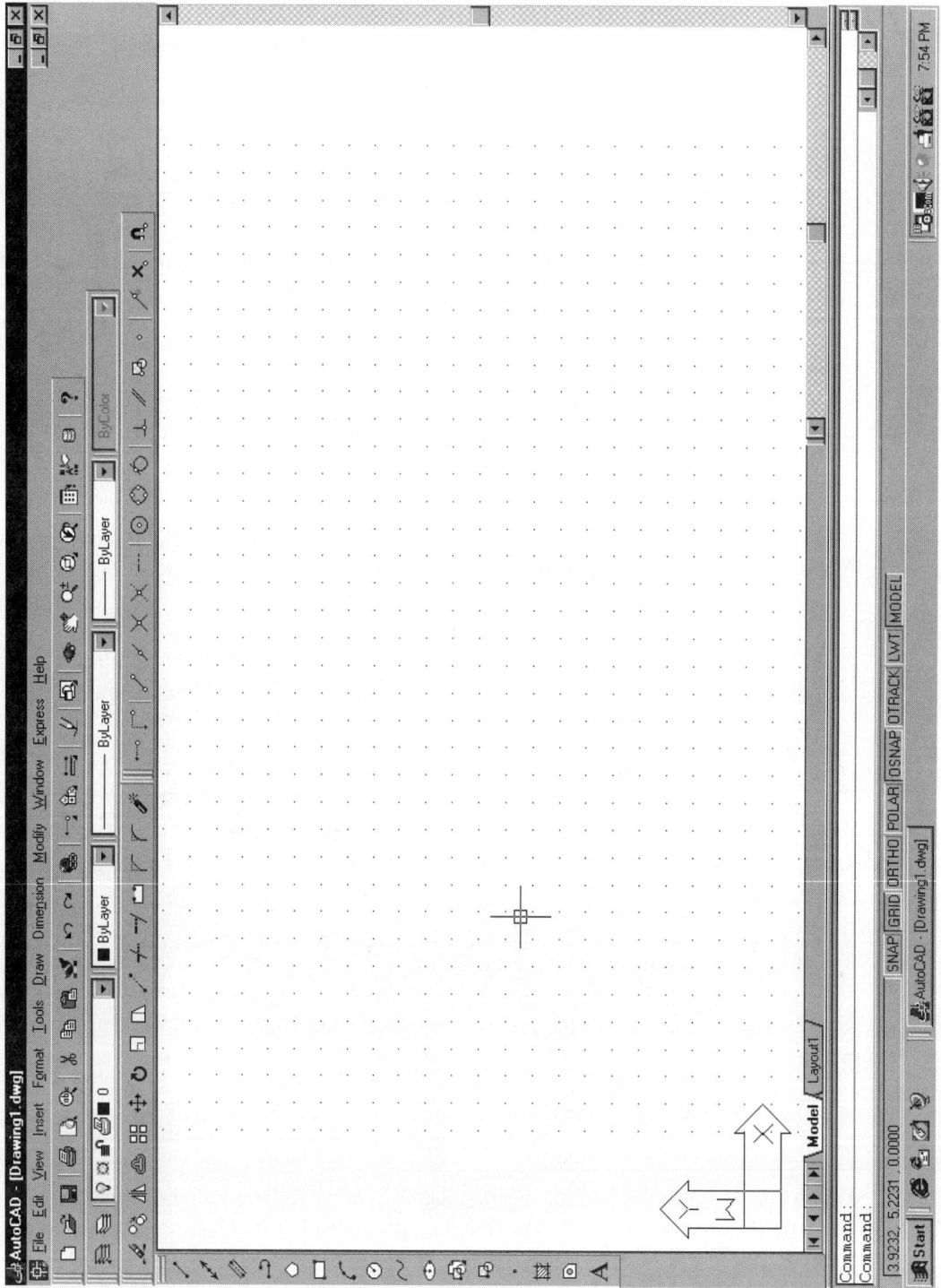

Figure 4-3

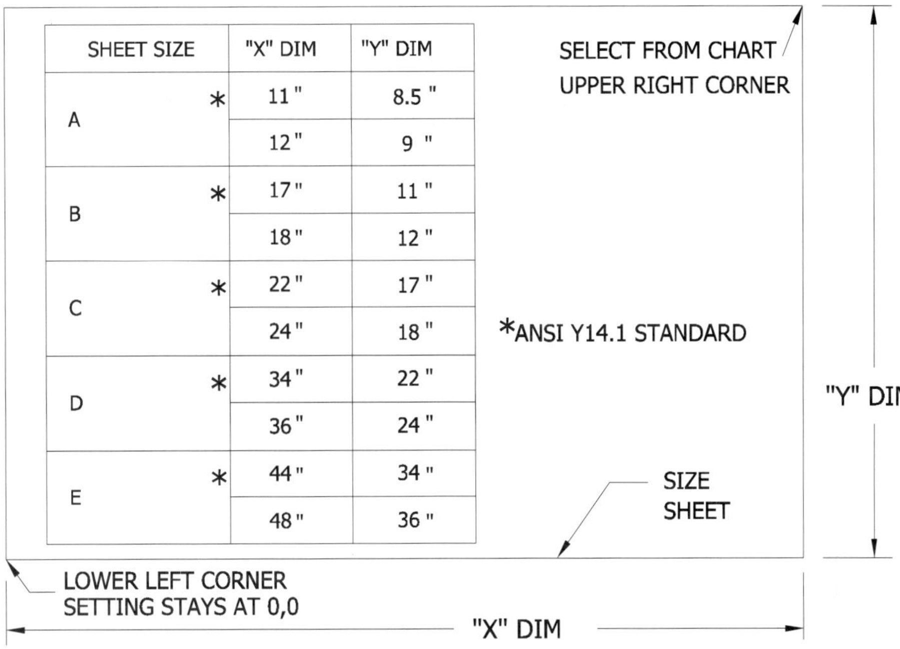

SHEET SIZE		"X" DIM	"Y" DIM
A	*	11 "	8.5 "
		12 "	9 "
B	*	17 "	11 "
		18 "	12 "
C	*	22 "	17 "
		24 "	18 "
D	*	34 "	22 "
		36 "	24 "
E	*	44 "	34 "
		48 "	36 "

SELECT FROM CHART
UPPER RIGHT CORNER

*ANSI Y14.1 STANDARD

"Y" DIM

SIZE
SHEET

LOWER LEFT CORNER
SETTING STAYS AT 0,0

"X" DIM

Figure 4-4

We suggest that you continue to experiment with setting limits and that you try out the Quick Setup Wizard, as well as the LIMITS command, described following. Try some of the possibilities listed in Figure 4-4, which is a table of sheet sizes. Notice that there are two sets of standards commonly in use. Sometimes the standard you use will be determined by your plotter. This is particularly true for the larger sheet sizes. Some plotters that plot on C-size paper, for example, will take a 24 × 18 inch sheet but not a 22 × 17.

The LIMITS command

The LIMITS command changes the grid area in the same way as the Advanced Setup Wizard, except that it is used after a drawing has already been opened and it uses coordinate values for the lower left and upper right corners of the grid in place of widths and lengths of the grid boundaries. To use LIMITS, follow this procedure:

1. Select "Drawing Limits" from the Format menu.
2. Type coordinates for the lower left corner—for example, "0,0".
3. Type coordinates for the upper right corner—for example, "18,12".

The Off and On options in the LIMITS command control what happens when you try to draw outside of the defined limits. With LIMITS off, nothing will happen. With LIMITS on, AutoCAD will not accept any attempt to begin an entity outside of limits. By default, LIMITS is off.

⊕   Use the LIMITS command to create a C size drawing area.

Remember to ZOOM all after changing limits.

⊕ Try at least one other limits setting.

⊕ When you are done experimenting, return LIMITS to (0,0) and (18,12), using the LIMITS command, and then ZOOM All.

You are now in the drawing that we will use for your template, so it is not necessary to begin a new drawing for the next section.

4.2 Creating a Template

GENERAL PROCEDURE

1. Define layers and change settings (grid, snap, units, limits, ltscale, etc.) as desired.
2. Save the drawing, giving it an appropriate name for a template.

To make your own template, so that new drawings will begin with the settings you want, all you have to do is create a drawing that has those settings and then tell AutoCAD that this is a drawing you want to use to define an initial drawing setup. The first part should be easy for you now, since you have been doing your own drawing setup for each new drawing in this book.

⊕ Make changes to the present drawing as follows:

GRID:	1.00 ON (F7)	COORD:	ON (F6)
SNAP:	0.25 ON (F9)	LTSCALE:	0.5
UNITS:	2-place decimal	LIMITS:	(0,0)(18,12)

Also, ensure that the Snap, Grid, and Model buttons on the status line are on, and that Ortho, Polar, Osnap, Otracking, and LWT are off.

⊕ Load all linetypes from the ACAD file using the following procedure.
1. Open the Linetype dialog box from the Format menu.
2. Click on Load... to open the Load dialog box.
3. Highlight the first linetype on the list.
4. Scroll down to the end of the list.
5. Hold down the shift key as you highlight the last linetype on the list.
6. With all linetypes highlighted, click on OK.
7. Click on OK in the Linetype dialog box.

⊕ Create layers and associated colors, linetypes, and settings to match those in Figure 4-5.

Remember that you can make changes to your template at any time. The layers called "text," "hatch," and "dim" will not be used until Chapters 7 and 8, in which we introduce text, hatch patterns, and dimensions to your drawings. But creating them now will save time and avoid confusion later.

At this point your drawing is on file and ready to be saved as a template, which is the focus of the next task.

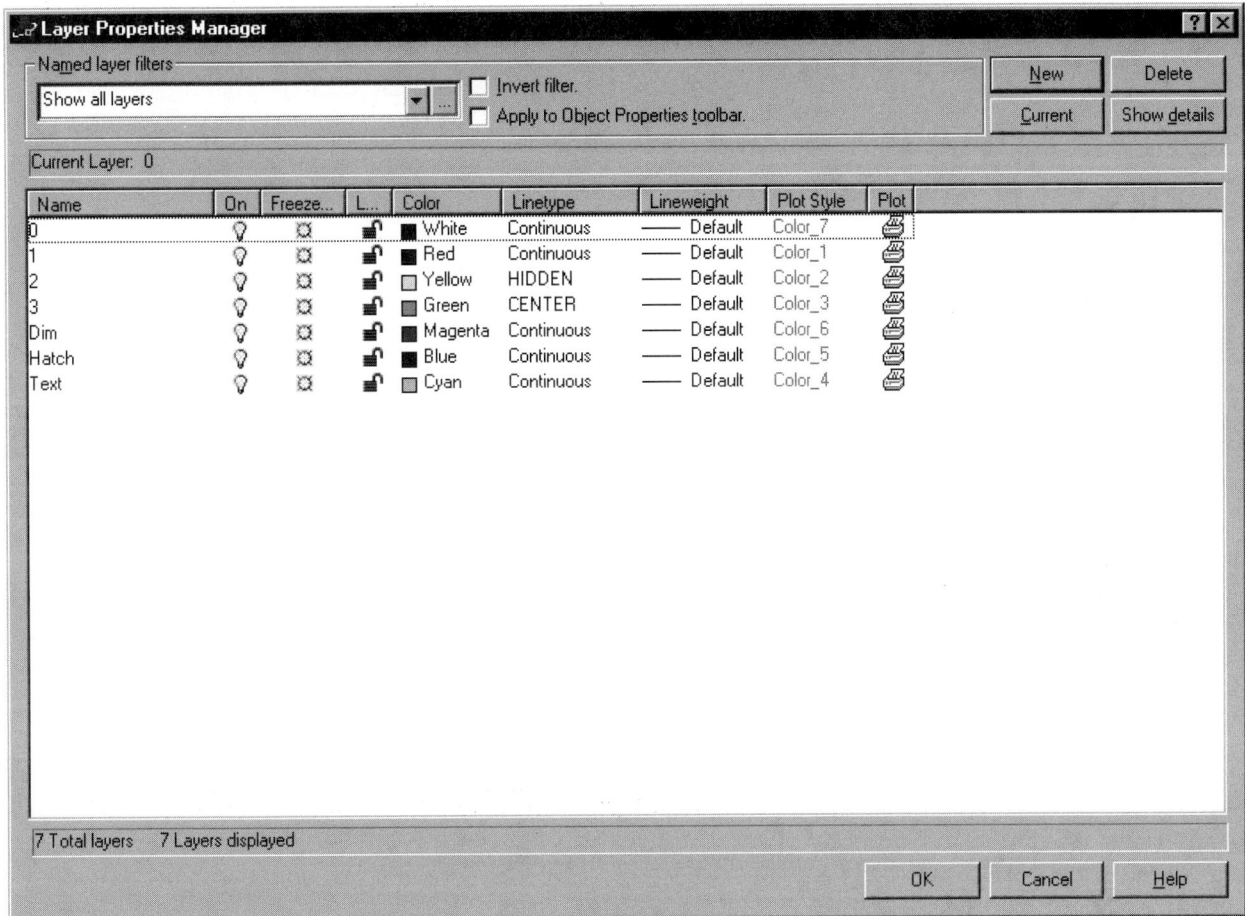

Figure 4-5

Note: Do not leave anything drawn on your screen or it will come up as part of the template each time you open a new drawing. For some applications this is quite useful. For now we want a blank template.

4.3 Saving a Template Drawing

GENERAL PROCEDURE

1. Select Save As... from the File menu.
2. Enter your template drawing name in the File Name edit box.
3. Select "AutoCAD Drawing Template File (*.dwt)" in the Save as type list box.
4. Click on Save.
5. Type a template description in the Template Description box.
6. Click on OK.

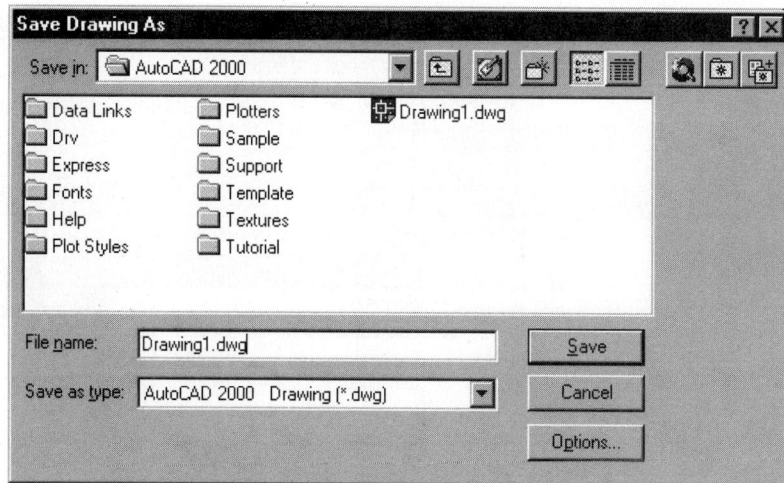

Figure 4-6

A drawing becomes a template when it is saved as a template. Template files are given a .dwt extension and placed in the template file folder.

⊕ To begin this task you should be in the drawing created in the last task. All the drawing changes should be made as described previously.

⊕ Open the File menu and select Save As....

This will call up the familiar Save Drawing As dialog box shown in Figure 4-6. The edit box in the middle holds the name of the current drawing. If you have not named the drawing, it will be called "Drawing1".

⊕ Double click in the File name box to highlight the drawing name.

⊕ Type "1B" for the new name.

Tip: Since template files are listed alphabetically in the file list, it is convenient to start your template file name with a number so that it appears before the Acad and Ansii standard templates that come with the AutoCAD software. Numbers precede letters in the alphanumeric sequence, so your numbered template file will appear at the top of the list and save you the trouble of scrolling down to find it.

Below the file name box is the Save as type box. This box will list options for saving the drawing. AutoCAD Drawing Template File is fourth on the list.

⊕ Highlight "AutoCAD Drawing Template File (*.dwt)", and click on it so that it shows up in the list box.

This will also open the Template file folder automatically. You will see that there are many templates already there. These are supplied by Auto-CAD and may be useful to you later. At this point it is more important to learn how to make your own.

Once your drawing name ("1B") is in the name box and the Save as type box shows AutoCAD Drawing Template File, you are ready to save.

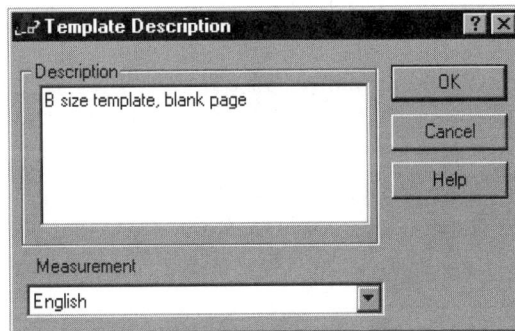

Figure 4-7

⊕ **Click on Save.**

This will call up a Template Description box, as illustrated in Figure 4-7. Here you can specify a description that will appear in the Create New Drawing dialog box whenever this template is used.

⊕ **Type "B size template, blank page".**

This will indicate that this is your B template and that there is no title block or other object drawn in the template.

⊕ **Click on OK.**

The task of creating the drawing template is now complete. All that remains is to create a new drawing using the template to see how it works.

⊕ **Open the File menu and select New, or pick the New tool from the standard toolbar.**

This will bring up the Create New Drawing dialog box. The Use a Wizard icon will be selected since you used it last. But now you want to start with the Use a Template option.

⊕ **Click on "Use a Template," the third option.**

The heading next to the icons will change to "Use a Template" and a list of available templates will appear in the list panel below. There will also be a preview area on the right.

Note: The AutoCAD software includes many standard templates that you will want to access soon. The templates consist of various standard sheet sizes, all with title blocks and borders. These are convenient. At this point, however, they will cause confusion because they are created in paper space and will automatically put you into a paper space layout. Also you will have no use for titles until we cover text in Chapter 7.

⊕ **Try highlighting several different templates, one after the other, and observe the images in the preview panel at the right.**

Your 1B template will show a blank box; Acad.dwt will show no box, because it contains AutoCAD default settings and is therefore the same as starting from scratch. Acadiso.dwt will also show no preview. It is similar to Acad.dwt except that limits are 420 × 290 and snap and grid are set to 10. All other templates will show borders and title blocks of various sizes and orientations. What will not be obvious is that all of these except the first three are created in paper space.

⊕ If 1B is not highlighted, highlight it now as the template you wish to use.

Notice the template description.

⊕ Click on OK to begin the drawing.

A new drawing will open with all the settings in 1B already in place.

4.4 Using the MOVE Command

GENERAL PROCEDURE

1. Type "m", select the Move tool from the Modify toolbar, or select Move from the Modify menu.
2. Define a selection set. (If noun/verb selection is enabled, you can reverse steps 1 and 2.)
3. Choose the base point of a displacement vector.
4. Choose a second point.

The ability to copy and move objects on the screen is one of the great advantages of working on a CAD system. It can be said that CAD is to drafting as word processing is to typing. Nowhere is this analogy more appropriate than in the cut-and-paste capacities that the COPY and MOVE commands give you.

⊕ Draw a circle with a radius of 1 near the center of the screen (9,6), as shown in Figure 4-8.

As discussed in Chapter 2, AutoCAD allows you to pick objects before or after entering an edit command. In this exercise we will use MOVE both ways, beginning with the verb/noun method. We will use the circle you have

Figure 4-8

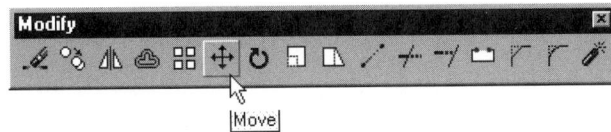

Figure 4-9

just drawn, but be aware that the selection set could include as many entities as you like and that a group of entities can be selected with a window or crossing box.

✛ Type "m", select Move from the Modify menu, or select the Move tool from the Modify toolbar, as shown in Figure 4-9.

You will be prompted to select objects to move.

✛ Point to the circle.

As in the ERASE command, your circle will become dotted.

In the command area, AutoCAD will tell you how many objects have been selected and prompt you to select more. When you are through selecting objects you will need to press Enter to move on.

✛ Right click to end object selection.

AutoCAD prompts:

```
Specify base point or displacement:
```

Most often you will show the movement by defining a vector that gives the distance and direction you want the object to be moved. To define movement with a vector, all AutoCAD needs is a distance and a direction. Therefore, the base point does not have to be on or near the object you are moving. Any point will do, as long as you can use it to show how you want your objects moved. This may seem strange at first, but it will soon become natural. Of course, you may choose a point on the object if you wish. With a circle, the center point may be convenient.

✛ Point to any location not too near the right edge of the screen.

AutoCAD will give you a rubber band from the point you have indicated and will ask for a second point:

```
Specify second point of displacement or
<use first point as displacement>:
```

As soon as you begin to move the cursor, you will see that AutoCAD also gives you a circle to drag so you can immediately see the effect of the movement you are indicating. An example of how this may look is shown in Figure 4-10. Let's say you want to move the circle 3.00 to the right. Watch the coordinate display and stretch the rubber band out until the display reads "3.00 < 0,0" (press F6 or double click on the coordinate display to get polar coordinates).

✛ Pick a point 3.00 to the right of your base point.

The rubber band and your original circle disappear, leaving you a circle in the new location.

Now, if ortho is on, turn it off (F8) and try a diagonal move.

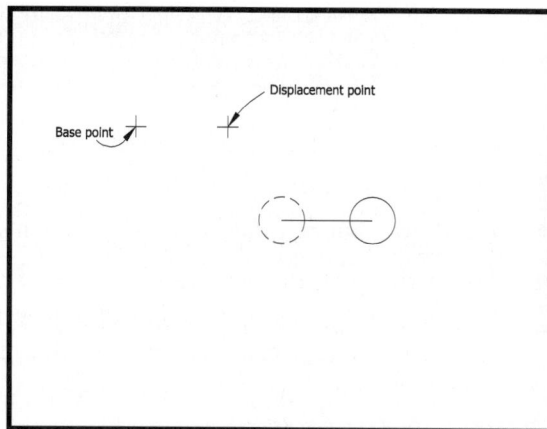

Figure 4-10

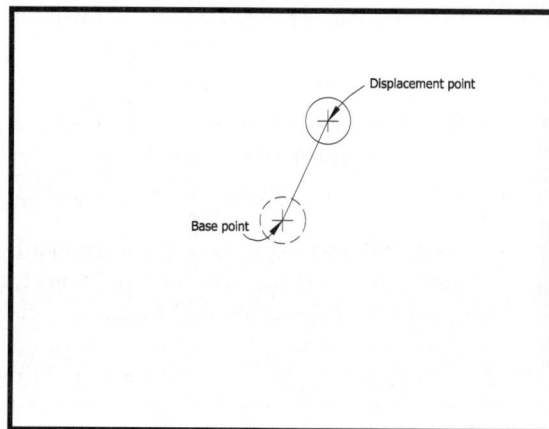

Figure 4-11

⊕ Type "m", or select the Move tool, or press the space bar to repeat the command.

AutoCAD follows with the "Select objects:" prompt.

⊕ Reselect the circle.

⊕ Right click to end the object selection process.

⊕ Select a base point.

⊕ Move the circle diagonally in any direction you like.

Figure 4-11 is an example of how this might look.

⊕ Try moving the circle back to the center of the screen.

It may help to choose the center point of the circle as a base point this time, and choose a point at or near the center of the grid for your second point.

Moving with Grips

You can use grips to perform numerous editing procedures without ever entering a command. This is probably the simplest of all editing methods, called autoediting. It does have some limitations, however. In particular, you can only select by pointing, windowing, or crossing.

⊕   Point to the circle.

The circle will become highlighted and grips will appear.

Notice that grips for a circle are placed at quadrants and at the center. In more involved editing procedures the choice of which grip or grips to use for editing is significant. In this exercise you will do fine with any of the grips.

⊕   Move the pickbox slowly over one of the grips.

If you do this carefully you will notice that the pickbox "locks onto" the grip as it moves over it. You will see this more clearly if snap is off (F9).

⊕   When the pickbox is locked on a grip, press the pickbutton.

The selected grip will become filled and change colors (from blue to red).

In the command area you will see this:

```
**STRETCH**
Specify stretch point or [Base point/Copy/Undo/eXit]:
```

Stretching is the first of a series of five autoediting modes that you can activate by selecting grips on objects. The word "stretch" has many meanings in AutoCAD, and they are not always what you would expect. We will explore the stretch autoediting mode and the STRETCH command in Chapter 6. For now, we will bypass stretch and use the MOVE mode.

AutoCAD 2000 has a convenient short cut menu for use in grip editing.

⊕   Click the right button on your mouse.

This will call up the short cut menu shown in Figure 4-12. It contains all of the grip edit modes plus several other options.

⊕   Select Move on the short cut menu.

The pop-up list will disappear and you will be in Move mode. Move the cursor and you will see a rubber band from the selected grip to the same position on a dragged circle. Notice that the prompt has changed to

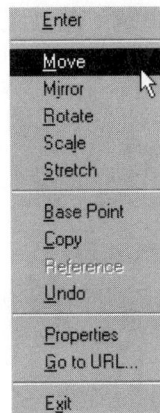

Figure 4-12

```
**MOVE**
Specify move point or [Base point/Copy/Undo/eXit]:
```

⊕ Pick a point anywhere on the screen.

The circle will move where you have pointed.

Moving by Typing a Displacement

There is one more way to use the MOVE command. Instead of showing AutoCAD a distance and direction, you can type a horizontal and vertical displacement. For example, to move the circle three units to the right and two units up, you would use the following procedure (there is no autoediting equivalent for this procedure):

1. Press Esc twice to remove grips.
2. Pick the circle.
3. Type "m" or select the Move tool.
4. Type "3, 2" in response to the prompt for base point or displacement.
5. Press Enter in response to the prompt for a second point.

4.5 Using the COPY Command

GENERAL PROCEDURE

1. Select the Copy Object tool from the Modify toolbar (not Copy to Clipboard, which is on the Standard toolbar).
2. Define a selection set (steps 1 and 2 can be reversed if noun/verb selection is enabled).
3. Choose a base point.
4. Choose a second point.

The COPY command works so much like the MOVE command that you should find it easy to learn at this point, and we will give you fewer instructions. The main difference is that the original object will not disappear when the second point of the displacement vector is given. There is the additional option of making multiple copies of the same object, which we will explore in a moment.

First, we suggest that you try making several copies of the circle in various positions on the screen. Try using both noun/verb and verb/noun sequences.

⊕ To initiate COPY, type "co", select Copy from the Modify menu, or select the Copy Object tool from the Modify toolbar, as shown in Figure 4-13.

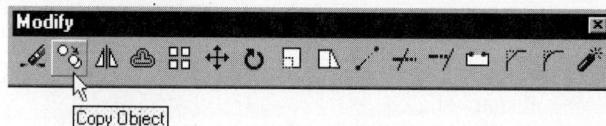

Figure 4-13

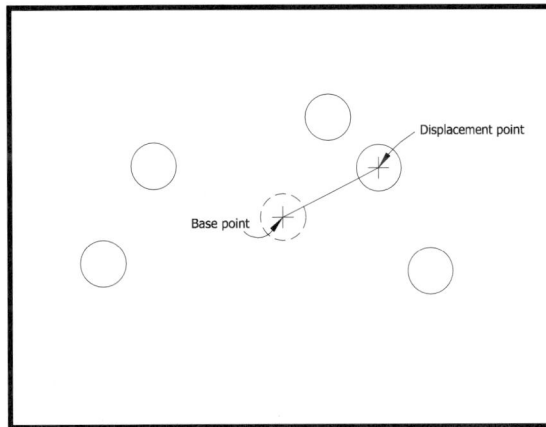

Figure 4-14

Notice that "c" is not an alias for COPY. Also notice that there is a Copy to Clipboard tool on the Standard toolbar that initiates the COPYCLIP command. This tool has a very different function. It is used to copy objects to the Windows 98 Clipboard and then into other applications or drawings. It has no effect on objects within your current drawing, other than to save them on the clipboard.

⊕   Make several copies of the circle at different points on the screen, as shown in Figure 4-14.

When you are satisfied that you know how to use the basic COPY command, move on to the Multiple copy option.

The Multiple Copy Option

This option allows you to show a series of vectors starting at the same base point, with AutoCAD placing copies of your selection set accordingly.

⊕   Select the Copy tool from the Modify toolbar.
⊕   Point to one of the circles on your screen.
⊕   Right click to end the selection process.
⊕   Type "m" for the Multiple option.
⊕   Show AutoCAD a base point.
⊕   Show AutoCAD a second point.

You will see a new copy of the circle. Notice also that the prompt to "Specify second point of displacement" has returned in the command area. AutoCAD is waiting for another vector, using the same base point as before.

⊕   Show AutoCAD another second point.
⊕   Show AutoCAD another second point.

Repeat as many times as you wish. If you get into this you may begin to feel like a magician pulling rings out of thin air and scattering them across the screen.

Copying with Grips

The grip editing system includes a variety of special techniques for creating multiple copies in all five modes. The function of the Copy option will differ depending on the grip edit mode. For now we will use the Copy option with the Move mode, which provides a short cut for the same kind of process you just executed with the COPY command.

Since you should have several circles on your screen now, we will take the opportunity to demonstrate how you can use grips on more than one object at a time. This can be very useful if your drawing contains two or more objects that maintain the same relationship with each other at different locations in your drawing.

⊕ Pick any two circles.

> The circles you pick should become highlighted, and grips should appear on both, as illustrated in Figure 4-15.

⊕ Pick any grip on either of the two highlighted circles.

> The grip should change colors. This time we will not use the pop-up menu. In the command area you will see the grip edit prompt for the Stretch mode:

> ```
> **STRETCH**
> Specify stretch point or [/Base point/Copy/Undo/eXit]:
> ```

⊕ Press the space bar.

> This will bring you to the MOVE mode prompt:

> ```
> **MOVE**
> Specify move point or [/Base point/Copy/Undo/eXit]:
> ```

⊕ Type "c" to initiate copying.

> The prompt will change to

> ```
> **MOVE (multiple)**
> Specify move point or [/Base point/Copy/Undo/eXit]:
> ```

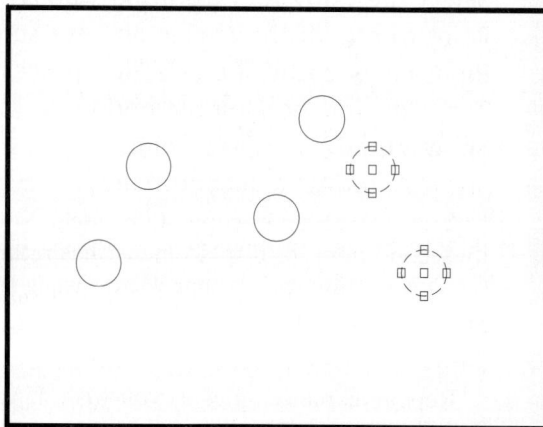

Figure 4-15

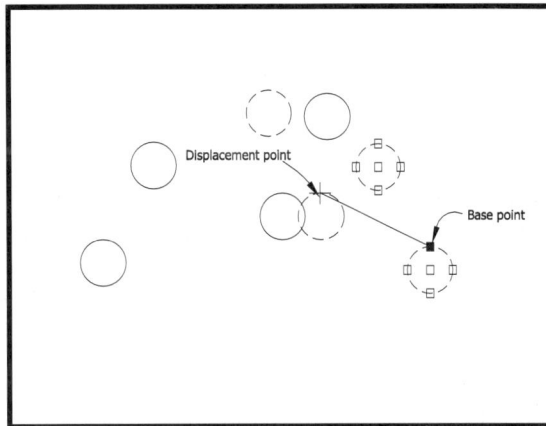

Figure 4-16

You will find that all copying in the grip editing system is multiple copying. Once in this mode AutoCAD will continue to create copies wherever you press the pickbutton until you exit by typing "x" or pressing the space bar.

⊕ Move the cursor and observe the two dragged circles.

⊕ Pick a point to create copies of the two highlighted circles, as illustrated in Figure 4-16.

⊕ Pick another point to create two more copies.

⊕ When you are through, press Enter or the space bar to exit the grip editing system.

⊕ Press Esc twice to remove grips.

4.6 Using the ARRAY Command—Rectangular Arrays

GENERAL PROCEDURE

1. Select the Array tool from the Modify toolbar or Array from the Modify menu.
2. Define a selection set. (Steps 1 and 2 can be reversed if noun/verb editing is enabled.)
3. Press Enter to end selection.
4. Type "r" for rectangular.
5. Enter the number of rows in the array.
6. Enter the number of columns.
7. Enter the distance between rows.
8. Enter the distance between columns.

The ARRAY command gives you a powerful alternative to simple copying. An array is the repetition of an image in matrix form. This command takes an object or group of objects and copies it a specific number of times in mathematically defined, evenly spaced locations.

There are two types of arrays. Rectangular arrays are linear and defined by rows and columns. Polar arrays are angular and based on the repetition of objects around the circumference of an arc or circle. The dots on the grid are an example of a rectangular array; the lines on any circular dial are an example of a polar array. Both types are common. We will explore rectangular arrays in this chapter and polar arrays in the next.

In preparation for this exercise, erase all the circles from your screen. This is a good opportunity to try the ERASE All option.

⊕ Type "e" or select the Erase tool from the Modify toolbar.
⊕ Type "all".
⊕ Press Enter.
⊕ Now draw a single circle, radius 0.5, centered at the point (2,2).
⊕ Type "Ar" or select Array from the Modify menu, or the Array tool from the Modify toolbar, as shown in Figure 4-17.

You will see the "Select objects" prompt.

⊕ Point to the circle.
⊕ Right click to end the selection process.

AutoCAD will ask which type of array you want:

```
Enter the type of array [Rectangular/Polar]<R>:
```

⊕ Type "r", or you can press Enter if R is the default.

AutoCAD will prompt you for the number of rows in the array.

```
Enter the number of rows (---) <1>:
```

The (---) is to remind you of what a row looks like (i.e., it is horizontal). The default is 1. So if you press Enter you will get a single row of circles. The number of circles in the row will depend, then, on the number of columns you specify. We will ask for three rows instead of just one.

⊕ Type "3".

AutoCAD now asks for the number of columns in the array:

```
Enter the number of columns (|||) <1>:
```

Using the same format (|||), AutoCAD reminds you that columns are vertical. The default is 1 again. What would an array with three rows and only one column look like?

We will construct a five-column array.

⊕ Type "5".

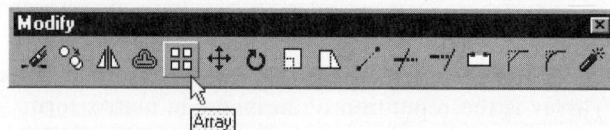

Figure 4-17

Now AutoCAD needs to know how far apart to place all these circles. There will be 15 of them in this example—three rows with five circles in each row. AutoCAD prompts

Enter the distance between rows or specify unit cell (---):

"Unit cell" means that you can respond by showing two corners of a window. The horizontal side of this window would give the space between columns; the vertical side would give the space between rows. You could do this exercise by showing a 1 × 1 window. We will use the more basic method of typing values for these distances. The distance between rows will be a vertical measure.

⊕ Type "1".

AutoCAD now asks for the horizontal distance between columns:

Specify the distance between columns (|||):

⊕ Type "1" again.

You should have a 3 × 5 array of circles, as shown in Figure 4-18.

Notice that AutoCAD builds arrays up and to the right. This is consistent with the coordinate system, which puts positive values to the right on the horizontal *x* axis, and upward on the vertical *y* axis. Negative values can be used to create arrays in other directions.

We will use the array now on your screen as the selection set to create another array. We will specify an array that has three rows and three columns, with 3.00 between rows and 5.00 between columns. This will keep our circles touching without overlapping.

⊕ Press Enter to repeat the ARRAY command.

⊕ Using a window, select the whole array of 15 circles.

⊕ Press Enter to end the selection process.

⊕ Type "r" or press enter.

⊕ Type "3" for the number of rows.

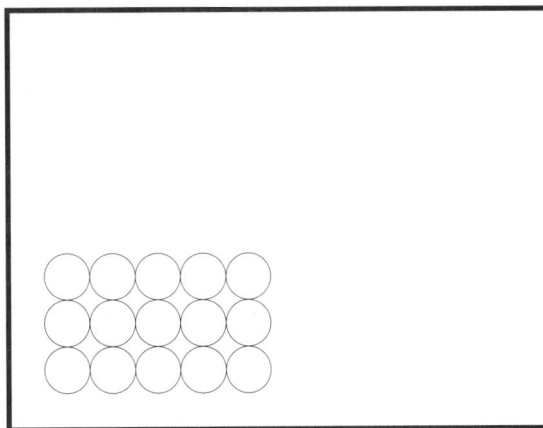

Figure 4-18

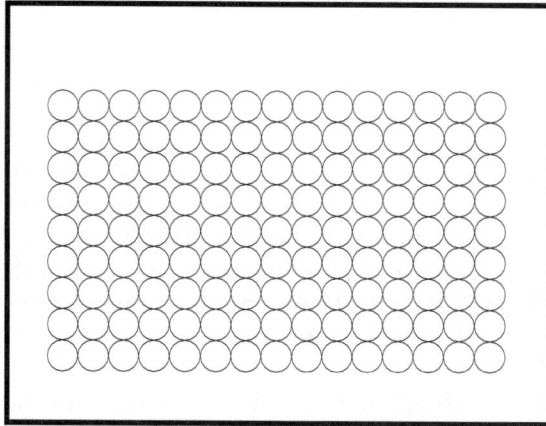

Figure 4-19

⊕   Type "3" for the number of columns.

⊕   Type "3" for the distance between rows.

⊕   Type "5" for the distance between columns.

You should have a screen full of circles, as in Figure 4-19.

When you are ready to move on, use the U command to undo the last two arrays.

⊕   Type "u" to undo the second array.

⊕   Type "u" again to undo the first array.

Now you should be back to your original circle centered at (2,2). Notice that the U command works nicely to undo an incorrectly drawn array quickly. This is good to know, because it is easy to make mistakes creating arrays. Be aware, however, that for other purposes the objects in an array are treated as separate entities, just as if you had drawn them one by one.

Try using some negative distances to create an array down and to the left.

⊕   First, use the MOVE command or grips to move your circle to the middle of the screen.

⊕   Select the Array tool.

⊕   Select the circle.

⊕   Right click to end the selection process.

⊕   Type "r" or press Enter.

⊕   Type "3" for the number of rows.

⊕   Type "3" for the number of columns.

⊕   Type "–2" for the distance between rows.

⊕   Type "–2" for the distance between columns.

Your array should be built down and to the left. The –2 distance between rows causes the array to be built going down. The –2 distance between columns causes the array to be built across to the left.

4.7   Changing Plot Settings

In the previous chapter you began using full and partial plot previews. In this chapter we will complete the exploration of many of the basic options in the Plot dialog box. There is a lot of information here, so walk through the material carefully and try out the options and previews as suggested. We have used no specific drawing for illustration. Now that you know how to use plot preview, you can observe the effects of changing plot parameters with any drawing you like and decide at any point whether you actually want to print out the results. We will continue to remind you to look at a plot preview after making changes. Plot previewing will save you a lot of time, paper, and will speed up your learning curve.

⊕   To begin this exploration, you should have a drawing or drawn objects on your screen so that you can observe the effects of various changes you will be making. The drawing you are in should use the 1B template so that Limits are set to 18 × 12.

⊕   Select Plot... from the File pull-down menu, or the Plot tool from the Standard toolbar.

> This will open up the Plot dialog box.

The Plot Device Tab

We will begin by looking into the Plot Device tab before we return to conclude the discussion of plot settings.

⊕   Click on the Plot Device tab.

> This will call the dialog box shown in Figure 4-20. The first area within this tab will show whatever plotter or printer is currently selected in your system and will probably be different from ours.

⊕   Click on the arrow at the right to open the plotter name list.

> The list you see will depend on your system and may include printers, plotters, and any faxing devices you have, along with AutoCAD 2000's DWF Classic and Eplot utilities, which may be used to send plotting information to the Internet.

The Add a Plotter Wizard

For a thorough exploration of AutoCAD 2000 plotting it will be important that you have at least one plotter available. If you have only a printer, you will probably be somewhat limited in the range of drawing sheets available. You may not have a B size option, for example. For the exercises in this book, you can use the DWF ePlot utility to simulate a plotter, or you can use the Add a Plotter Wizard to install one of the AutoCAD standard plotter drivers, even if you actually have no such plotter on your system. To add a plotter, follow this procedure:

1. Close the Plot dialog box.
2. From the File menu, select Plotter Manager....

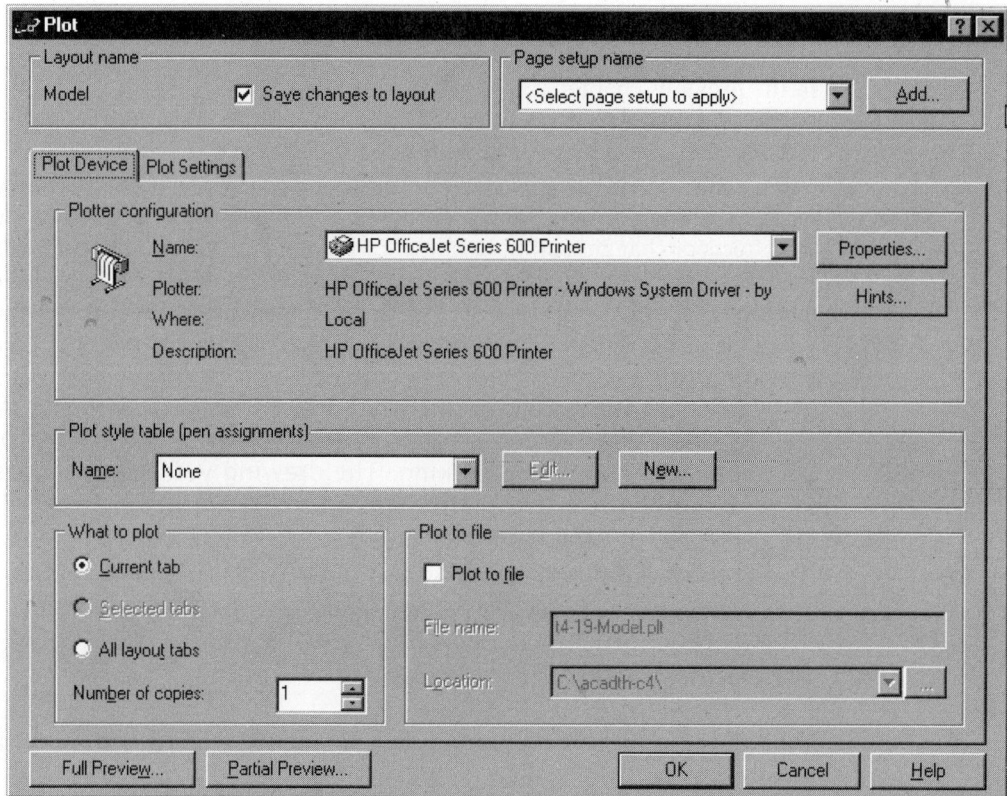

Figure 4-20

3. From the Plotters box, select the Add A Plotter Wizard....
4. Click Next on the Introduction page.
5. Check to see that My Computer is selected on the Add Plotter-Begin page, then click Next.
6. On the Plotter Model page, select a manufacturer and a model, then click Next.
7. Click Next on the Import Pcp or Pc2 page.
8. Click Next on the Ports page.
9. Click Next on the Plotter Name page.
10. Click Finish on the Finish page.

When the Wizard is done, the new plotting device will be added to your list of plotting devices.

⊕ If you have left the Plot dialog to install a plotter driver, re-enter it by selecting the plot tool from the Standard toolbar. Click the Plot Device tab if necessary, then open the list of plotting devices.

⊕ From the list of plotting devices, select a plotter or the DWF ePlot utility to simulate a plotter.

Note: Whenever you change plotting devices it is likely that you will see a Warning that says "The paper size in the layout is not supported by the selected plotting device. The layout will use the paper size specified by the plotting device." Click OK to move on.

Plot Styles

Below the Plotter Configuration panel of the Plot Device tab you will see the Plot Style table area. Most of the time you will not need to work with a plot style because plotters and printers are configured to produce colors, linetypes, and lineweights just as they appear on your screen. Plot styles come into play when you want to present your drawing in a manner different from the way you have drawn it. Plot styles essentially override the color, linetype, and lineweight setting of objects and layers in your drawing. This allows you to completely change the presentation of objects in your drawing without changing anything in the drawing itself. Since plot styles can be named and saved, you can use several different plot styles with a single drawing to create a variety of different presentations. Plot styles can also be saved and transferred from one drawing to another so that a wide variety of presentation styles may be quickly applied with a few clicks of the mouse and without actually changing the drawing. Plot styles offer a lot of power and flexibility, but can be ignored most of the time when you are creating your drawing in the way you want it to appear.

What to Plot

At the bottom left of the Plot Device dialog you will see a panel labeled "What to plot". The choices are Current tab, Selected tab, or All layout tabs. The tabs referred to are those at the bottom of your drawing area, to the left of the horizontal scroll bar, labeled "Model" and "Layout1". At this time we are making use of only the Model tab, which will also be the current tab as long as you are in model space. We will begin to use other layouts and layout tabs in Chapter 6. Once you have more than one tab active in your drawing you can choose to plot them one at a time or all at once using these options. You also have the option of printing multiple copies.

Plot to File

To the right of What to plot you will see the Plot to file panel. AutoCAD plot information may be sent to a plot file so that it can be plotted at a later time or sent to another site for plotting. Plots saved to a file are given the same name as the drawing but with a .plt extension.

We will now return to the Plot Settings tab to complete our exploration of the PLOT dialog box.

⊕ Click on the Plot Settings tab.

You should now have a plotter selected that will give you a number of paper size options.

⊕ From the Paper size list, below the plotter name list, select a B size drawing sheet.

The exact size will depend on the plotter you have selected. An ANSII B (17 × 11) sheet will be a common choice.

Drawing Orientation

There are basically two options for drawing orientation: Portrait, in which the short edge of the paper is across the bottom, and Landscape, in which the long edge is across the bottom. Portrait is typical of a letter or printed sheet of text, Landscape is typical of a drawing sheet. Your plotting device has a default orientation, but you can print either way using the radio buttons. Drawing orientation will obviously have a major impact on how the plotting area of the page is used, so be sure to check out the partial preview any time you switch orientations. Try this:

⊕ Do a partial preview to see how your current drawing orientation is interpreted.

⊕ Switch from Landscape to Portrait, or vice versa.

⊕ Do a second partial preview to see how drawing orientation changes the plot.

> *Tip:* On some plotters you will have a choice of different paper orientations. You may have an 11 × 17 and a 17 × 11 option, for example. In this case there should be a correlation between the paper you choose and the drawing orientation. If you are plotting in Landscape, select the 17 × 11, in Portrait, select the 11 × 17. Otherwise your paper setting will be 90° off from your drawing orientation and things will get confusing.

⊕ For this task, check to see that your drawing orientation is set to Landscape.

This will be the default for most plotters.

Plot Area

Look at the Plot area panel at the left of the Plot settings dialog. This is a crucial area of the dialog box that allows you to specify the portion of your drawing to be plotted. You have some familiarity with this from Chapter 2, where you plotted using a window selection. Other options include Limits, Extents, Display, and View. Changes here will have a significant impact on the effective plotting area. Be sure to use plot preview any time you make changes in these parameters.

The radio buttons on the left show the options for plotting area. "Limits", as you know, are specified using the LIMITS command or a setup Wizard. If you are using our standard B-size template, and the Limits radio button is selected, the plot area will be 18 × 12. "Extents" refers to the actual drawing area in which you have drawn objects. It may be larger or smaller than the limits of the drawing. "Display" will create a plot using whatever is actually on the screen. If you used the ZOOM command to enlarge a portion of the drawing before entering PLOT and then selected this option, AutoCAD would plot whatever is showing in your drawing window. "View" will be accessible only after you have defined named views in the drawing using the VIEW command (Chapter 11). "Window" will not be accessible until you define a window, as you have done previously in other drawings.

⊕   Try switching among Limits, Extents, Display, and Window selections and use plot preview to see the results. Use both partial and full previews to ensure that you clearly see what is happening.

    Whenever you make a change, also observe the changes in the boxes showing inches = drawing Units. Assuming that "Scaled to Fit" is checked, you will see significant changes in these scale ratios as AutoCAD adjusts scales according to the area it is being asked to plot.

Plot Scale

Plot scale has many options, but most of the time you will only need two very simple settings. In model space you will usually use Scaled to fit. In paper space you will use 1:1.

When you are plotting from model space you will use Scaled to fit since there may be no logical relation between model space units, which are determined by the real world size of objects, and the size of the paper you are using. The most important consideration will be fitting the drawing to the drawing sheet, which is best accomplished using the Scaled to fit option. If you have a need for a precise drawing unit to paper unit ratio, you can find many options on the Scale list, or type in a custom option. In all cases, the scale ration will be given with the paper unit first followed by the drawing unit. For example, 1:2 will mean that 1 inch on the drawing sheet will represent 2 drawing units.

⊕   Try changing the scale selection to 1:2 and observe the effect in a partial preview. Try other options if you like and then return to Scaled to fit.

Plot Offset

The Plot offset panel is at the bottom middle of the Plot Settings dialog. Plot offset determines the way the Plot area is positioned on the drawing sheet. Specifically, it determines where the plot origin is placed. To understand plot offset it is best to use Partial preview and observe the location of the red triangle that marks the plot origin. The default locates the origin point (0,0) at the lower left of the plotted area and determines other locations from there. If you enter a different offset specification, (2,3) for example, then the origin point of the drawing area will be positioned at this point instead and plot locations determined from there. This will have a dramatic effect on the placement of objects on paper.

    The other option in Plot offset is to Center the plot. In this case AutoCAD will position the drawing so that the center point of the plot area coincides with the center point of the drawing sheet. Try this:

⊕   Try various plot offset combinations, including Center the plot, and use plot preview to see the results.

Be sure to use partial previews and observe the red origin triangle to ensure that you clearly see what is happening.

Plot Options

This last area of the Plot settings tabs has four settings that can be turned on or off. Plot with lineweights determines whether lineweights that have been specified in your drawing will be used in plotting, or if all lines will be given the same default weight. This is just like the LWT button on the taskbar, but it is for plotting rather than screen display. Depending on your application, you may want to keep to the default lineweights in early drafts of a drawing and save the full lineweight plot for final versions.

Similarly, plot styles may be ignored in early drafts and turned on later when you want to create a specific presentation effect. Plot styles are essentially tables of plotting characteristics that can be defined, named, saved, and attached to objects or layers. They override layer specifications and can therefore be used to create very different plots of the same drawing.

Plot paperspace last will not be accessible until you have defined at least one paper space layout. We will continue to plot from model space for now, but later this option will cause your plotter to draw the model space objects in your drawing before it draws the titles, text, and annotation objects that may exist in your paper space layout.

Finally, the issue of hidden line removal is irrelevant until you are drawing in three dimensions. In 3D drawings it is possible to remove lines that are part of the object being plotted but would be hidden by other objects in the current view.

This completes our discussion of basic model space plotting options. With a little practice you should be able to plot any area of any drawing in model space and position it on any size drawing sheet so that it is well presented. In Chapter 5 we will take up the subject of page setups so that you can create different page setups for the same drawing and not have to redefine settings each time you switch from one setup to another.

4.8   Review Material

Questions

1. What command is automated through the first four steps of the Advanced Setup Wizard?
2. Name at least five settings that would typically be included in a Template drawing.
3. Where are template drawings stored in a standard AutoCAD file configuration? What extension is given to template file names?
4. What is the value of using a template drawing?
5. What is the main difference between the command procedure for MOVE and that for COPY?

6. What is the main limitation of grip editing?
7. What do you have to do to remove grips from an object once they are displayed?
8. How do you access the grip edit short cut menu?
9. Explain how arrays are a special form of copying.
10. What is a rectangular array? What is a polar array?
11. Why is it important to do a partial plot preview after changing plot area or plot offset?

Drawing Problems

1. Create a C-size drawing template using an ANSI standard sheet size, layers, and other settings as shown in this chapter. Start with your 1B template settings to make this process easier.
2. Open a drawing with your new C-size template and draw a circle with a two-unit radius centered at (11,8).
3. Using grips, make four copies of the circle, centered at (15,8), (11,12), (7,8), and (11,4).
4. Switch to layer 2 and draw a 1 × 1 square with lower left corner at (1,1).
5. Create a rectangular array of the square with 14 rows and 20 columns, one unit between rows, and one unit between columns.

4.9 WWW Exercise #4 (Optional)

At Chapter 4 of our companion Web site you will find a drawing project to complete and a new Web site to visit, in addition to the self-scoring chapter test. The drawing project will force you to use edit commands in place of drawing commands. The Web page you will visit is a part of the Autodesk Corporate Web site. Here you can find tips and other technical assistance direct from the makers of AutoCAD. The Autodesk site is extensive, so this time around we will provide the convenience of a hyperlink to take you directly to the AutoCAD 2000 tips page, instead of asking you to search down through the Web site hierarchy. So, when you are ready,

⊕ Make sure that you are connected to your Internet service provider.

⊕ Type "browser" or open the Web toolbar and select the Browse the Web tool.

⊕ If necessary, navigate to our companion Web site at "www.prenhall.com/dixriley".

Good Luck!

4.10   Drawing 4-1: Pattern

All the drawings in this chapter will use your 1B template. Do not expect, however, that you will never need to change settings. Layers will stay the same throughout this book, but limits will change from time to time, and grid and snap will change frequently.

   This drawing will give you practice using the COPY command. There are numerous ways in which the drawing can be done. The key is to try to take advantage of the repetition in the pattern by copying in an efficient manner. The following figures suggest one way it can be done.

(a)

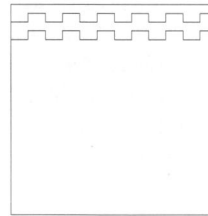

(b)

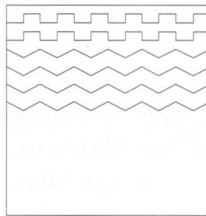

(c)

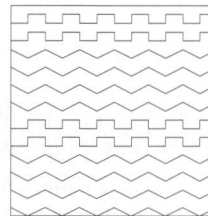

(d)

DRAWING SUGGESTIONS

GRID = 0.5
SNAP = 0.25

- Begin with a 6 × 6 square. Then draw the first set of lines as in Reference 4-1a.
- Copy the first set down 0.5 to produce Reference 4-1b.
- Draw the first set of V-shaped lines. Then use a multiple copy to produce Reference 4-1c.
- Finally, make a single copy of all the lines you have so far, using a window or crossing box for selection. (Be careful not to select the outside lines.) Watch the displacement carefully and you will produce Reference 4-1d, the completed drawing.

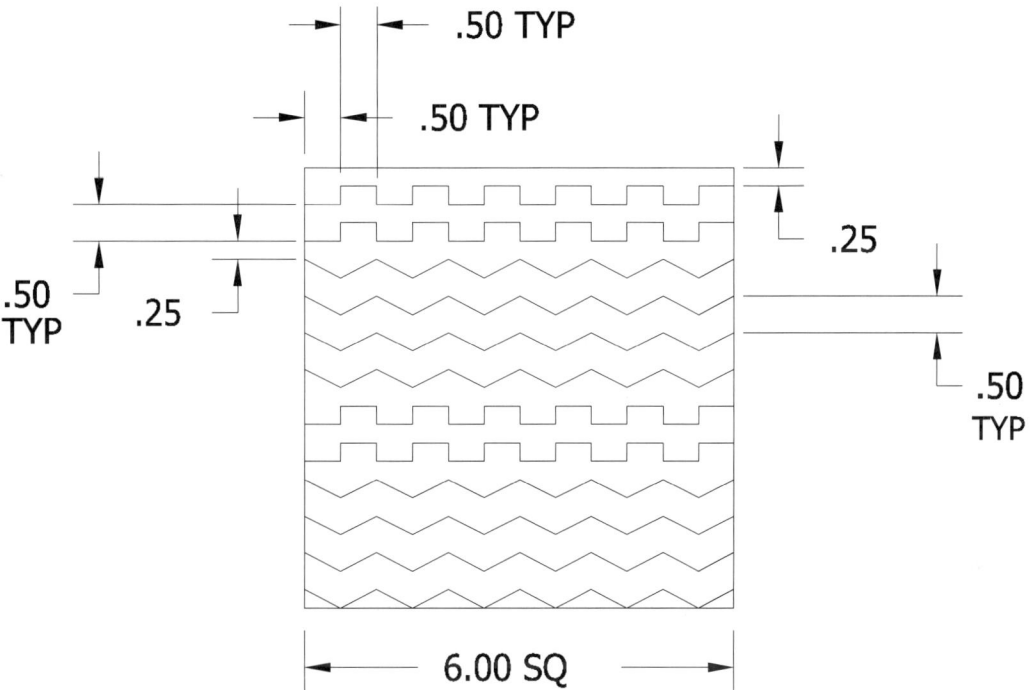

.50 TYP

.50 TYP

.25

.50
TYP

.25

.25

.50
TYP

6.00 SQ

PATTERN

Drawing 4-1

4.11   Drawing 4-2: Grill

This drawing should go very quickly if you use the ARRAY command.

DRAWING SUGGESTIONS

GRID = 0.5
SNAP = 0.25

- Begin with a 4.75 × 4.75 square.
- Move in 0.25 all around to create the inside square.
- Draw the rectangle in the lower left-hand corner first; then use the ARRAY command to create the rest.
- Also remember that you can undo a misplaced array using the U command.

.25
(TYP)

.25

.25
(TYP)

4.75

.25
(TYP)

1.75
(TYP)

.50   1.75   .25

4.75

GRILL
Drawing 4-2

4.12   Drawing 4-3: Weave

As you do this drawing, watch AutoCAD work for you and think about how long it would take to do by hand! The finished drawing will look like Reference 4-3. For clarity, the drawing shows only one cell of the array and its dimensions.

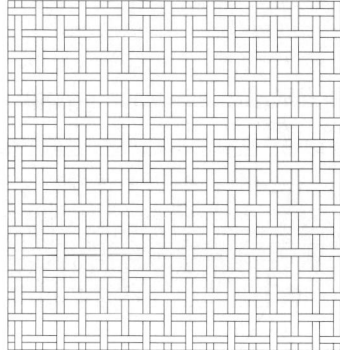

DRAWING SUGGESTIONS

GRID = 0.5
SNAP = 0.125

- Draw the 6 × 6 square; then zoom in on the lower left using a window. This will be the area shown in the lower left of the dimensioned drawing.
- Observe the dimensions and draw the line patterns for the lower left corner of the weave. You could use the COPY command in several places if you like, but the time gained will be minimal. Don't worry if you have to fuss with this a little to get it correct; once you've got it right the rest will be easy.
- Use ARRAY to repeat the lower left-hand cell in an 8 × 8 matrix.

If you get it wrong, use U and try again.

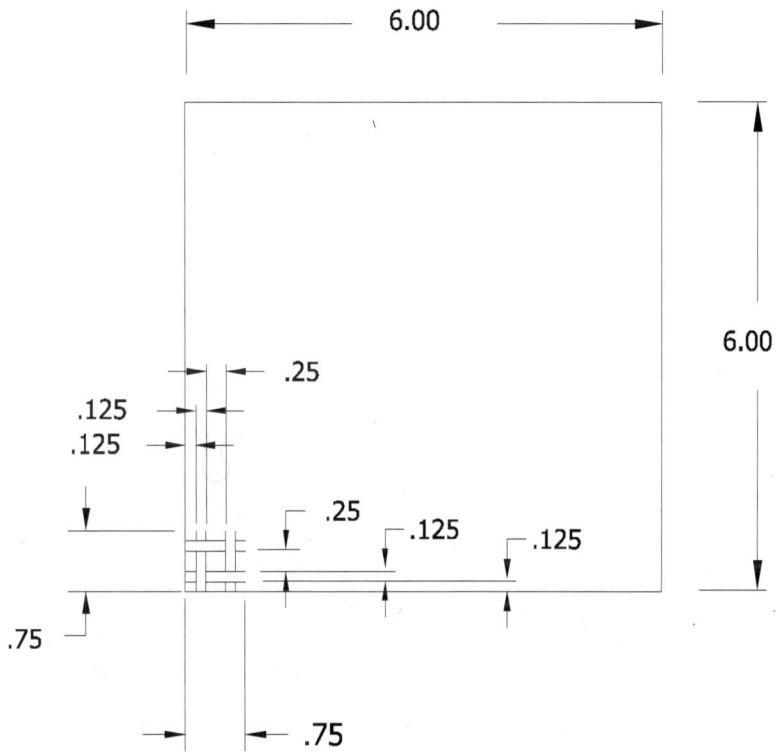

6.00

6.00

.25

.125

.125

.25

.125

.125

.75

.75

WEAVE

Drawing 4-3

4.13 Drawing 4-4: Test Bracket

This is a great drawing for practicing much of what you have learned up to this point. Notice the suggested snap, grid, ltscale, and limit settings, and use the AR-RAY command to draw the 25 circles on the front view.

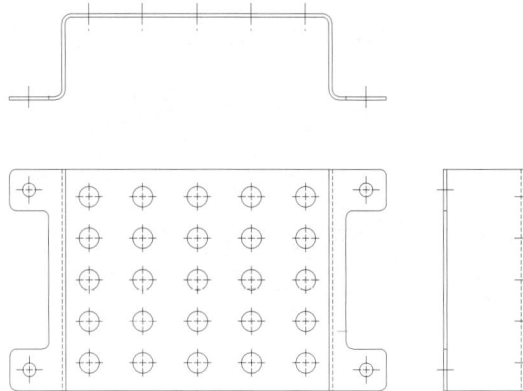

DRAWING SUGGESTIONS

GRID = 0.25   SNAP = 0.125
LTSCALE = 0.50   LIMITS = (0,0)(24,18)

- Be careful to draw all lines on the correct layers, according to their linetypes.
- Draw center lines through circles before copying or arraying them; otherwise you will have to go back and draw them on each individual circle or repeat the array process.
- A multiple copy will work nicely for the four 0.50-diameter holes. A rectangular array is definitely desirable for the twenty-five 0.75-diameter holes.

CREATING CENTER MARKS WITH THE DIMCEN SYSTEM VARIABLE

There is a simple way to create the center marks and center lines shown on all the circles in this drawing. It involves changing the value of a dimension variable called "dimcen" (dimension center). Dimensioning and dimension variables are discussed in Chapter 8, but if you would like to jump ahead, the following procedure will work nicely in this drawing.

1. Type "dimcen". The default setting for dimcen is 0.09, which will cause Auto-CAD to draw a simple cross as a center mark. Changing it to −.09 will tell AutoCAD to draw a cross that reaches across the circle.
2. Type "−.09".
3. After drawing your first circle, and before arraying it, type "dim". This will put you in the dimension command.
4. Type "cen", indicating that you want to draw a center mark. This is a very simple dimension feature.
5. Point to the circle.
6. Press the Esc key to quit the DIM command.

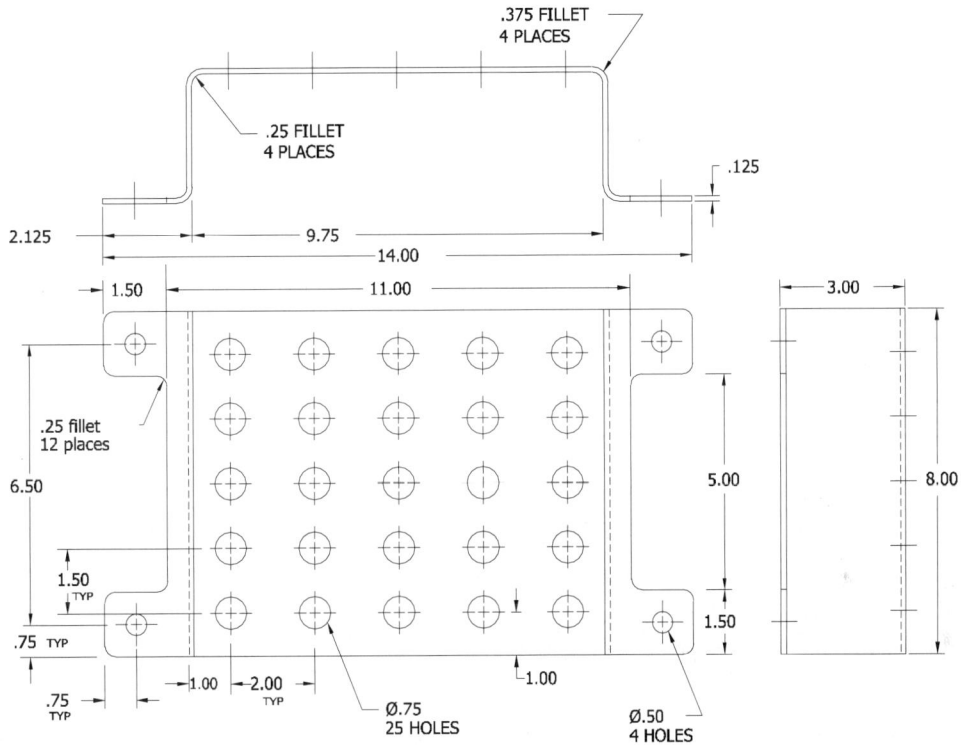

.375 FILLET
4 PLACES

.25 FILLET
4 PLACES

.125

2.125

9.75

14.00

1.50

11.00

3.00

.25 fillet
12 places

6.50

5.00

8.00

1.50
TYP

.75 TYP

1.50

1.00

.75
TYP

1.00

2.00
TYP

Ø.75
25 HOLES

Ø.50
4 HOLES

TEST BRACKET

Drawing 4-4

4.14 Drawing 4-5: Floor Framing

This architectural drawing will require changes in many features of your drawing setup. Pay close attention to the suggested settings.

DRAWING SUGGESTIONS

> UNITS = Architectural, smallest fraction = 1″
> LIMITS = 36″, 24″
> GRID = 1′
> SNAP = 2″
> LTSCALE = 12

- Be sure to use foot (′) and inch (″) symbols when setting limits, grid, and snap (but not ltscale).
- Begin by drawing the 20′ × 17′-10″ rectangle, with the lower left corner somewhere in the neighborhood of (4′,4′).
- Complete the left and right 2 × 10 joists by copying the vertical 17′-10″ lines 2″ in from each side. You may find it helpful to use the arrow keys when working with such small increments.
- Draw a 19′-8″ horizontal line 2″ up from the bottom and copy it 2″ higher to complete the double joists.
- Array the inner 2 × 10 in a 14″ row by 1-column array, with 16″ between rows.
- Set to layer 2 and draw the three 17′-4″ hidden lines down the center.

2 x 10 (2)

2 x 10 (2)

2X10-16"O.C.

2 x 10

2 x 10

2 x 10 (2)

17'-6"

17'-10"

20'-0"

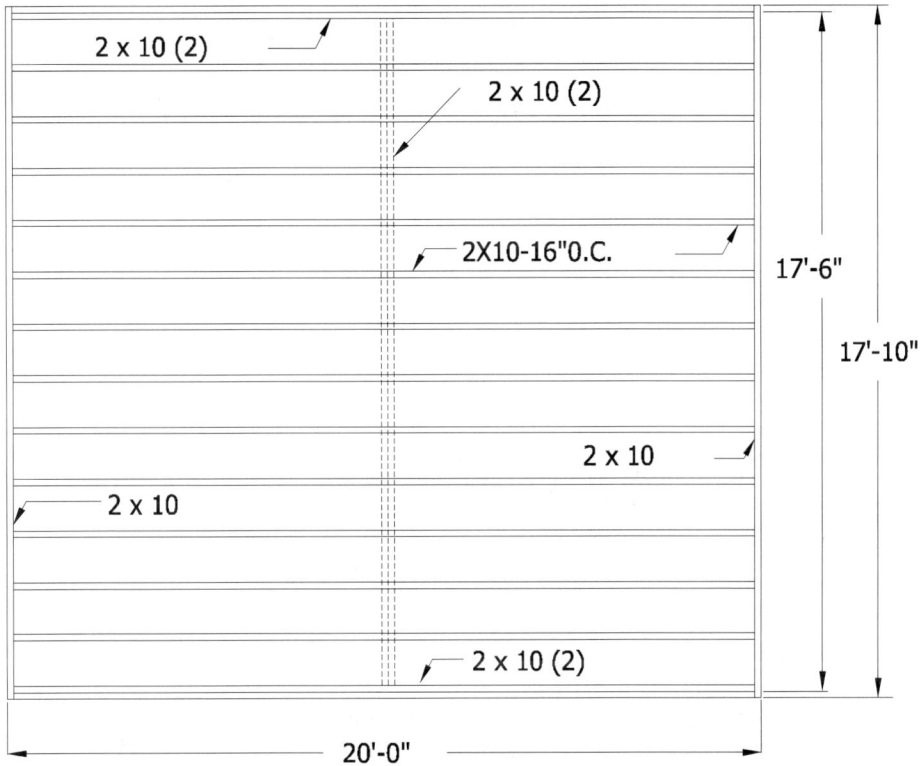

FLOOR FRAMING

Drawing 4-5

4.15   Drawing 4-6: Threaded Shaft

The finished drawing should be the top and front views without dimensions. Draw the circular view first. This will be the top view. Use the top view to line up the front view.

This drawing includes a typical application of rectangular array and copy commands.

DRAWING SUGGESTIONS

GRID = 1/4
SNAP = 1/8
LIMITS = (0,0)(18,12)
LTSCALE = 0.5

- Draw the circles in the top view and use these to line up the horizontal lines in the front view.
- Pay particular attention to the detail drawing when designing the acme screw thread. Draw the outline of the zig-zag shape on each side for one thread and then connect the lines, creating the full thread. Be sure the zig-zag on opposite sides is offset by one thread before drawing the angular lines.
- Now that one thread is created, a simple array will complete the whole shaft length.
- Complete the drawing by drawing shaft lines and the square shape at the top end.

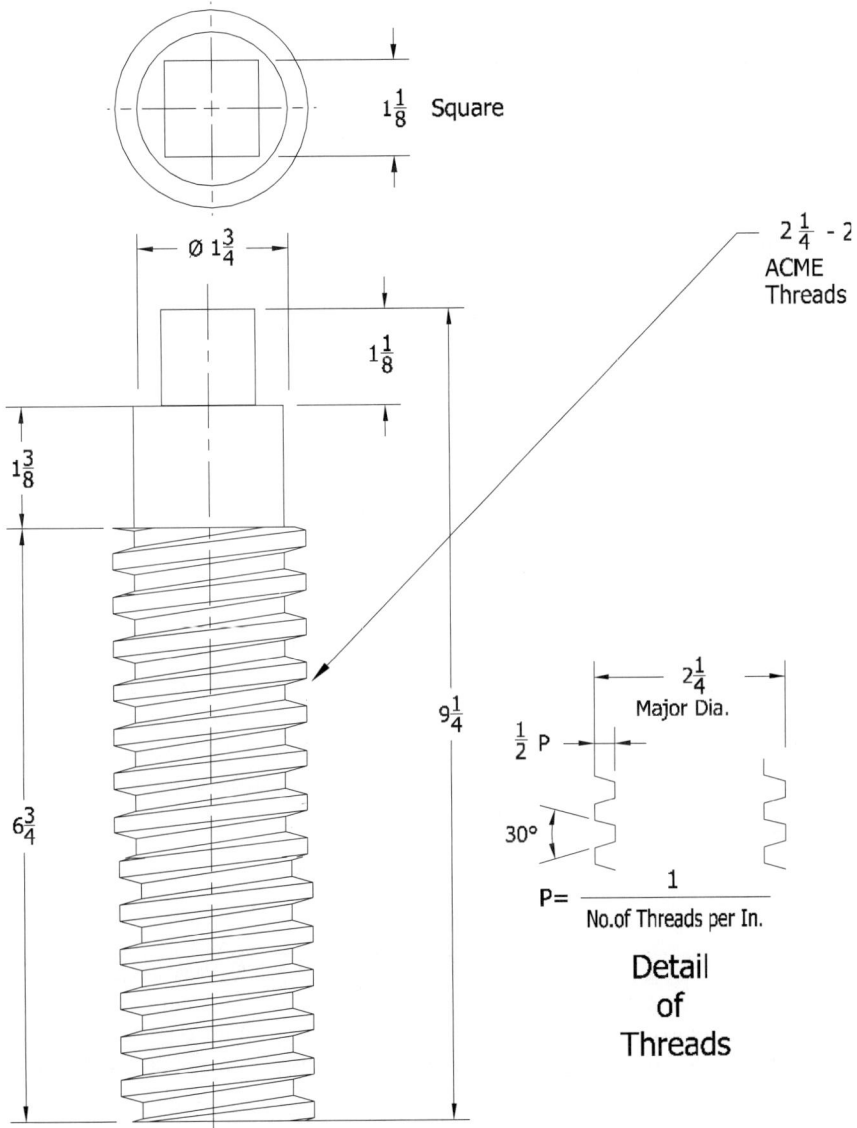

$1\frac{1}{8}$ Square

$\varnothing\,1\frac{3}{4}$

$1\frac{1}{8}$

$1\frac{3}{8}$

$6\frac{3}{4}$

$9\frac{1}{4}$

$2\frac{1}{4}$ - 2
ACME
Threads

$2\frac{1}{4}$
Major Dia.

$\frac{1}{2}$ P

30°

$$P=\frac{1}{\text{No.of Threads per In.}}$$

Detail
of
Threads

THREADED SHAFT
Drawing 4-6

5 Arcs and Polar Arrays

COMMANDS

ARC	ARRAY (polar)
MIRROR	ROTATE

OVERVIEW

So far, every drawing you have done has been composed of lines and circles. In this chapter you will learn a third major entity, the ARC. In addition, you will expand your ability to manipulate objects on the screen. You will learn to ROTATE objects and create their MIRROR images. You will learn to save Plot settings as named Page setups. But first, we will pick up where we left off in Chapter 4 by showing you how to create polar arrays.

TASKS

5.1 Creating polar arrays
5.2 Drawing arcs
5.3 Using the ROTATE command
5.4 Using polar tracking at any angle
5.5 Creating mirror images of objects on the screen
5.6 Creating page setups
5.7 Review Material
5.8 WWW Exercise #5 (Optional)
5.9 Drawing 5-1: Flanged Bushing
5.10 Drawing 5-2: Guide
5.11 Drawing 5-3: Dials
5.12 Drawing 5-4: Alignment Wheel
5.13 Drawing 5-5: Hearth
5.14 Drawing 5-6: Slotted Flange

5.1 Creating Polar Arrays

GENERAL PROCEDURE

1. Select the Array tool from the Modify toolbar, or select Array from the Modify menu.
2. Define a selection set. (Steps 1 and 2 can be reversed if noun/verb selection is enabled.)
3. Type "p" for "polar".
4. Pick a center point.
5. Enter the number of items to be in the array (or press Enter).
6. Enter the angle to fill (or 0).
7. Enter the angle between items.
8. Tell whether or not to rotate items.

The procedure for creating polar arrays is lengthy and requires some explanation. The first two steps are the same as in rectangular arrays. Step 3 is also the same, except that you respond with "p" instead of "r". From here on the steps will be new. First you will pick a center point, and then you will have several options for defining the array.

There are three qualities that define a polar array, but two are sufficient. A polar array is defined by two of the following: (1) a certain number of items, (2) an angle that these items span, and (3) an angle between each item and the next. However you define your polar array, you will have to tell AutoCAD whether or not to rotate the newly created objects as they are copied.

⊕   Begin a new drawing using the 1B template.

⊕   In preparation for this exercise, draw a vertical 1.00 line at the bottom center of the screen, near (9.00,2.00), as shown in Figure 5-1.

   We will use a 360-degree polar array to create Figure 5-2.

⊕   Type "Ar", select Array from the Modify menu, or select the Array tool from the Modify toolbar, as illustrated in Figure 5-3.

Figure 5-1

Figure 5-2

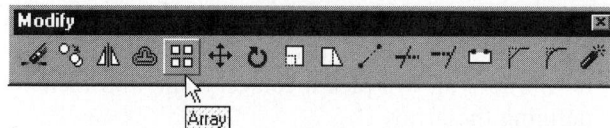

Array

Figure 5-3

⊕ Select the line.

So far, so good. Nothing new up to this point.

⊕ Type "p".

Now you have a prompt that looks like this:

> Specify center point of array:

Rectangular arrays are not determined by a center, so we did not encounter this prompt before. Polar arrays, however, are built by copying objects around the circumferences of circles or arcs, so we need a center to define one of these. We will also need to specify whether objects should be rotated as they are copied.

⊕ Pick a point directly above the line and somewhat below the center of the screen.

Something in the neighborhood of (9.00,4.50) will do. The next prompt is

> Enter the number of items in the array:

Remember that we have a choice of two out of three among number of items, angle to fill, and angle between items. This time we will give AutoCAD the first two.

⊕ Type "12".

Now that AutoCAD knows that we want 12 items, all it needs is either the angle to fill with these or the angle between the items. It will ask first for the angle to fill:

> Specify the angle to fill (+=ccw,-=cw) <360>:

The symbols in parentheses tell us that if we give a positive angle, the array will be constructed counterclockwise; if we give a negative angle, it will be constructed clockwise. Get used to this; it will come up frequently.

The default is 360 degrees, meaning an array that fills a complete circle. If we did not give AutoCAD an angle (that is, if we responded with a "0"), we would be prompted for the angle between. This time around we will give 360 as the angle to fill.

⊕ Press Enter to accept the default, a complete circle.

AutoCAD now has everything it needs, except that it doesn't know whether we want our lines to retain their vertical orientation or to be rotated along with the angular displacement as they are copied. AutoCAD prompts:

`Rotate arrayed objects [Yes/No] <Y>:`

Notice the default, which we will accept.

⊕ Press Enter or type "y".

Your screen should resemble Figure 5-2. Now let's try some of the other options. We will define an array that has 20 items placed 15 degrees apart and not rotated.

⊕ Type "U" to undo the first array.

⊕ Select the Array tool.

⊕ Select the line again.

⊕ Right click to end object selection.

⊕ Type "p".

⊕ Pick the same center point as before.

⊕ Type "20" for the number of items.

⊕ Type "0" for the angle to fill.

As mentioned, this response tells AutoCAD to issue a prompt for the angle between items:

`Angle between items (+=ccw,-=cw):`

The symbols in parentheses are familiar from the "angle to fill" prompt. Notice that there is no default angle here.

⊕ Type "15" for the angle between items.

All that remains is to tell AutoCAD not to rotate the lines as they are copied.

⊕ Type "n".

Your screen should now resemble Figure 5-4.

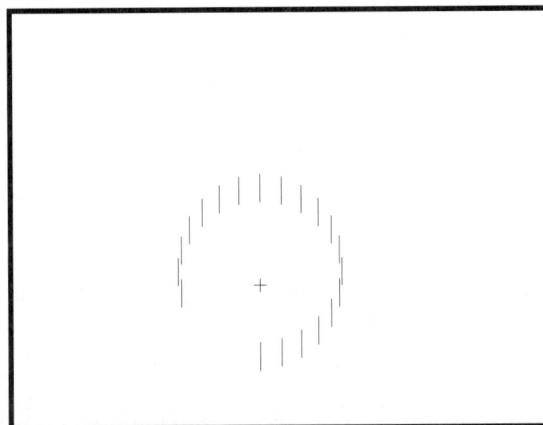

Figure 5-4

Figure 5-5

Try one more and then you will be on your own with polar arrays. For this one, define an array that fills 270 degrees moving clockwise and has 30 degrees between each angle, as in Figure 5-5.

⊕ Undo the last array.

⊕ Repeat the first four steps, up to the "number of items" prompt.

⊕ Press Enter to skip the "Number of items" prompt.

This tells AutoCAD to issue the other two prompts instead.

⊕ Type "−270" for the angle to fill.

What will the negative angle do?

⊕ Type "30" for the angle between.

⊕ Press Enter to rotate items as they are copied.

Your screen should resemble Figure 5-5.

This ends our discussion of polar arrays. With the options AutoCAD gives you, there are many possibilities that you may want to try out. As always, we encourage experimentation. When you are satisfied, erase everything on the screen in preparation for learning the ARC command.

5.2 Drawing Arcs

GENERAL PROCEDURE

1. Type "a", select the Arc tool from the Draw toolbar, or select Arc from the Draw menu.
2. Type or show where to start the arc, where to end it, and what circle it is a portion of, using any of the 11 available methods.

Learning AutoCAD's ARC command is an exercise in geometry. In this section we will give you a firm foundation for understanding and drawing arcs so that you will not be confused by all the options that are available. The information we give you will be more than enough to do the drawings in this chapter and most drawings you will encounter elsewhere. Refer to the AutoCAD Command Reference and the chart at the end of this section (Figure 5-8) if you need additional information.

AutoCAD gives you eight distinct ways to draw arcs, eleven if you count variations in order. With so many choices, some generalizations will be helpful.

First, notice that every option requires you to specify three pieces of information: where to begin the arc, where to end it, and what circle it is theoretically a part of. To get a handle on the range of options, look at the list of options from the Arc submenu.

⊕ Open the Draw menu and select Arc to open the cascading submenu illustrated in Figure 5-6.

Notice that the options in the third panel (Center, Start, End etc.) are simply reordered versions of those in the second panel (Start, Center, End, etc.). This is how we end up with eleven options instead of eight.

More important, "start" is always included. In every option, a starting point must be specified, though it does not have to be the first point given.

The options arise from the different ways you can specify the end and the circle from which the arc is cut. The end may be shown as an actual point (all End options) or inferred from a specified angle or length of chord (all Angle and Length options).

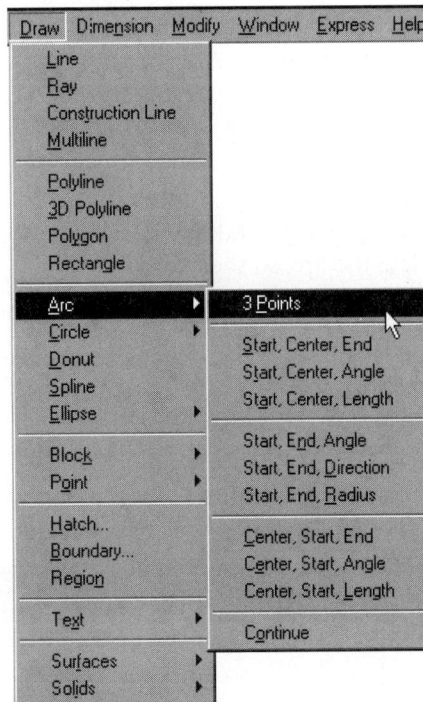

Figure 5-6

The circle that the arc is part of may be specified directly by its center point (all Center options) or inferred from other information, such as a radius length (Radius options), an angle between two given points (Angle options), or a tangent direction (the Start, End, Direction, and Continue options).

With this framework in mind, we will begin by drawing an arc using the simplest method, which is also the default, the three-points option. The geometric key to this method is that any three points not on the same line determine a circle or an arc of a circle. AutoCAD uses this in the CIRCLE command (the 3P option) as well as in the ARC command.

⊕ Type "a" or select the Arc tool from the Draw toolbar, as shown in Figure 5-7.

AutoCAD's response will be this prompt:

`Specify start point of arc or [Center]:`

Accepting the default by specifying a point will leave open all those options in which the start point is specified first.

If you instead type a "c", AutoCAD will prompt for a center point and follow with those options that begin with a center.

⊕ Select a starting point near the center of the screen.

AutoCAD prompts:

`Specify second point of arc or [Center/End]:`

We will continue to follow the default three-point sequence by specifying a second point. You may want to refer to the chart (Figure 5-8) as you draw this arc.

⊕ Select any point one or two units away from the previous point. Exact coordinates are not important.

Once AutoCAD has two points, it gives you an arc to drag. By moving the cursor slowly in a circle and in and out, you can see the range of what the third point will produce.

AutoCAD also knows now that you have to provide an end point to complete the arc, so the prompt has only one option:

`Specify end point of arc:`

Any point you select will do, as long as it produces an arc that fits on the screen.

⊕ Pick an end point.

As you can see, three-point arcs are easy to draw. It is much like drawing a line, except that you have to specify three points instead of two. In practice, however, you do not always have three points to use this way. This necessi-

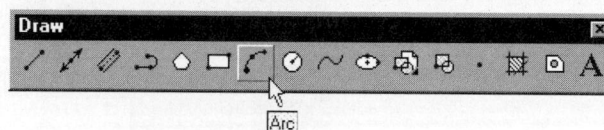

Figure 5-7

tates the broad range of options in the ARC command. The dimensions you are given and the objects already drawn will determine what options are useful to you.

Next, we will create an arc using the start, center, end method, the second option illustrated in Figure 5-8.

⊕ Type "U" to undo the three-point arc.

⊕ Type "a" or select the Arc tool.

⊕ Select a point near the center of the screen as a start point.

The prompt that follows is the same as for the three-point option, but we will not use the default this time:

```
Specify second point of arc or [Center/End]:
```

We will choose the Center option.

Tip: If you choose options from the Draw menu, you will find some steps automated. If you select "Start,Center,End", for example, the "c" will be entered automatically.

⊕ Type "c", if necessary.

This tells AutoCAD that we want to specify a center point next, so we see this prompt:

```
Specify center point of arc:
```

⊕ Select any point roughly one to three units away from the start point.

The circle from which the arc is to be cut is now clearly determined. All that is left is to specify how much of the circle to take, which can be done in one of three ways, as the prompt indicates:

```
Specify end point of arc or [Angle/chord Length]:
```

We will specify an end point by typing coordinates or pointing. But first, move the cursor slowly in a circle and in and out to see how the method works. As before, there is an arc to drag, and now there is a radial direction rubber band as well. If you pick a point anywhere along this rubber band, AutoCAD will assume that you want the point where it crosses the circumference of the circle.

Note: Here, as in the polar arrays in this chapter, AutoCAD is building arcs counterclockwise, consistent with its coordinate system.

⊕ Select an end point to complete the arc.

We will draw one more arc, using the start, center, angle method, before going on. This method has some peculiarities in the use of the rubber band that are typical of the ARC command and can be confusing. An example of how the start, center, angle method may look is shown in Figure 5-8.

⊕ Type "u" to undo the last arc.

TYPE	APPEARANCE	DESCRIPTION
3-point	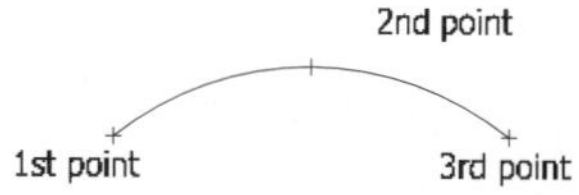 2nd point / 1st point / 3rd point	Clockwise or counterclockwise
S,C,E (start, center, end)	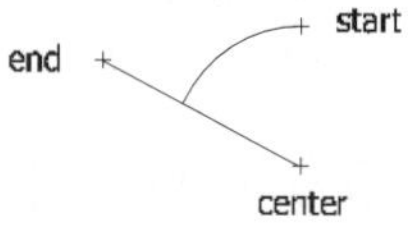 end / start / center	Counterclockwise Radial rubber band indicates angle only, length is insignificant
S,C,A (start, center, angle)	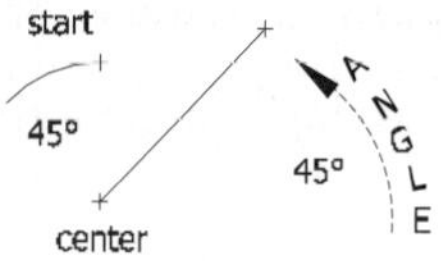 start / 45° / center / ANGLE / 45°	+ angle = CCW - angle = CW Rubber band shows angle only, starting from horizontal
S,C,L (start, center, length of chord)	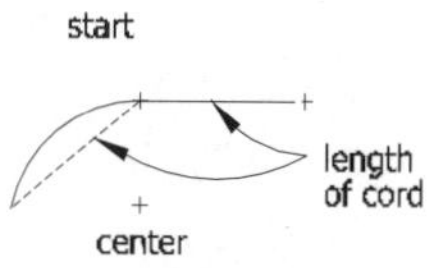 start / length of cord / center	Counterclockwise "Chord" rubber band shows length of chord only, direction is insignificant
S,E,A (start, end, angle)	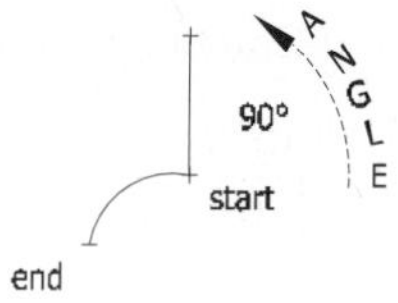 90° / start / end / ANGLE	+ angle = CCW - angle = CW Rubber band shows angle only, starting from horizontal
S,E,R (start, end, radius)	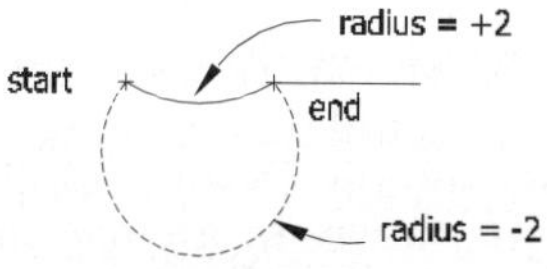 radius = +2 / start / end / radius = -2	Counterclockwise + radius = minor arc - radius = major arc Rubber band shows + radius values only, For - radius (type value)
S,E,D (start, end, direction)	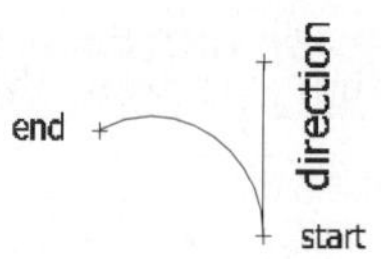 end / direction / start	Direction of rubber band is a line tangent to the arc being constructed and runs through the start point
CONTIN: (continuous from line)	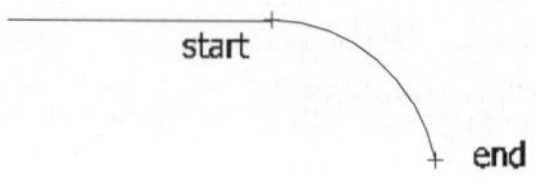 start / end	Arc begins at end point of previous line or arc and is tangent to it; Rubber band is a chord from start point to end point

Figure 5-8

⊕ Type "a" or select the Arc tool.

AutoCAD will ask for a center or start point:

Specify start point of arc or [Center]:

⊕ Pick a start point near the center of the screen.

AutoCAD prompts:

Specify second point of arc or [Center/End]:

⊕ Type "c".

AutoCAD prompts for a center point:

Specify center point of arc:

⊕ Pick a center point one to three units below the start point.

AutoCAD will prompt, as before,

Specify end point of arc or [Angle/chord Length]:

⊕ Type "a" to indicate that you will specify an angle.

You can type an angle specification or show an angle on the screen. Notice that the rubber band now shows an angle only; its length is insignificant. The indicated angle is being measured from the horizontal, but the actual arc begins at the start point and continues counterclockwise, as illustrated in Figure 5-8. The prompt reads

Specify included angle:

⊕ Type "45" or show an angle of 45 degrees.

(Remember, you can use F6 to change to polar coordinates that will show the angle.)

Now that you have tried three of the basic methods for constructing an arc, we strongly suggest that you study the chart in Figure 5-8 and then try out the other options. The notes in the right-hand column will serve as a guide to what to look for.

The differences in the use of the rubber band from one option to the next can be confusing. You should understand, for instance, that in some cases the linear rubber band is only significant as a distance indicator; its angle is of no importance and is ignored by AutoCAD. In other cases it is just the reverse; the length of the rubber band is irrelevant, while its angle of rotation is important.

> **Tip:** One additional trick you should try out as you experiment with arcs is as follows: If you press Enter or the space bar at the "Specify start point [Center]:" prompt, AutoCAD will use the end point of the last line or arc you drew as the new starting point and construct an arc tangent to it. This is the same as the Continue option on the pull-down menu.

This completes the present discussion of the ARC command. Constructing arcs, as you may have realized, can be tricky. Another option that is available and often useful is to draw a complete circle and then use the TRIM or BREAK commands to cut out the arc you want. BREAK and TRIM are introduced in the next chapter.

5.3　Using the ROTATE Command

GENERAL PROCEDURE

1. Select Rotate from the Modify menu, or select the Rotate tool from the Modify toolbar.
2. Define the selection set. (Steps 1 and 2 can be reversed if noun/verb selection is enabled.)
3. Pick a base point.
4. Indicate an angle of rotation.

ROTATE is a fairly straightforward command, and it has some uses that might not be apparent immediately. For example, it frequently is easier to draw an object in a horizontal or vertical position and then ROTATE it rather than drawing it in a diagonal position.

In addition to the ROTATE command, there is a rotate mode in the grip edit system, which we will introduce later in this section.

⊕　In preparation for this exercise, clear your screen and draw a three-point arc using the points (8,4), (11.5,2), and (15,4), as in Figure 5-9.

We will begin by rotating the arc to the position shown in Figure 5-10.

⊕　Select the arc.

⊕　Type "Ro", select Rotate from the Modify menu, or select the Rotate tool from the Modify toolbar, as shown in Figure 5-11.

You will be prompted for a base point:

Specify base point:

This will be the point around which the object is rotated. The results of the rotation, therefore, are dramatically affected by your choice of base point. We will choose a point at the left tip of the arc.

⊕　Point to the left tip of the arc.

Figure 5-9

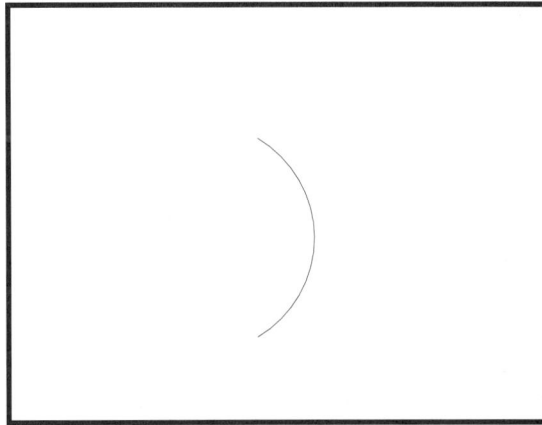

Figure 5-10

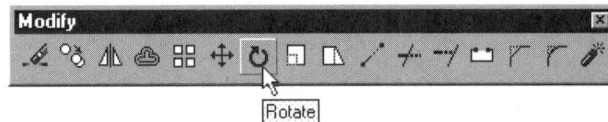

Figure 5-11

The prompt that follows looks like this:

Specify rotation angle or [Reference]:

The default method is used to indicate a rotation angle directly. The object will be rotated through the angle specified and the original object will be deleted.

Move the cursor in a circle and you will see that you have a copy of the object to drag into place visually. If ortho or snap are on, turn them off to see the complete range of rotation.

⊕ Type "90" or point to a rotation of 90 degrees (use F6 if your coordinate display is not showing polar coordinates).

The results should resemble Figure 5-10.

Notice that when specifying the rotation angle directly like this, the original orientation of the selected object is taken to be 0 degrees. The rotation is figured counterclockwise from there. However, there may be times when you want to refer to the coordinate system in specifying rotation. This is the purpose of the "Reference" option. To use it, all you need to do is specify the present orientation of the object relative to the coordinate system, and then tell AutoCAD the orientation you want it to have after rotation. Look at Figure 5-12. To rotate the arc as shown, you either can indicate a rotation of −45 degrees or tell AutoCAD that it is presently oriented to 90 degrees and you want it rotated to 45 degrees. Try this method for practice.

⊕ Repeat the ROTATE command.

⊕ Select the arc.

⊕ Right click to end selection.

⊕ Choose a base point at the lower tip of the arc.

⊕ Type "r".

AutoCAD will prompt for a reference angle:

> Specify the reference angle <0>:

⊕ Type "90".

AutoCAD prompts:

> Specify the new angle:

⊕ Type "45".

Your arc should now resemble the solid arc in Figure 5-12.

Rotating with Grips

Rotating with grips is simple, and there is a useful option for copying, but your choice of object selection methods is limited, as always, to pointing and windowing. Try this:

⊕ Pick the arc.

The arc will become highlighted and grips will appear.

⊕ Pick the center grip.

⊕ Right click to open the grip short cut menu.

⊕ Select Rotate.

Move your cursor in a circle and you will see the arc rotating around the grip at the center of the arc.

⊕ Now type "b" or right click again and select Base point from the menu.

Base point will allow you to pick a base point other than the selected grip.

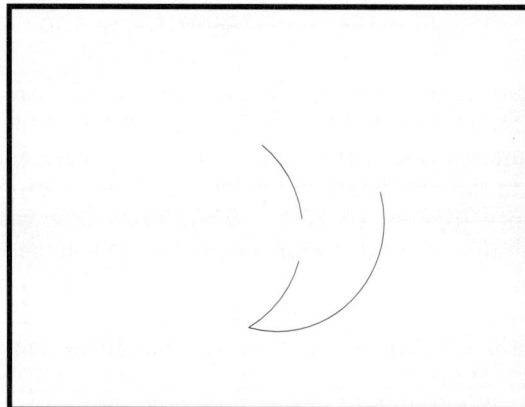

Figure 5-12

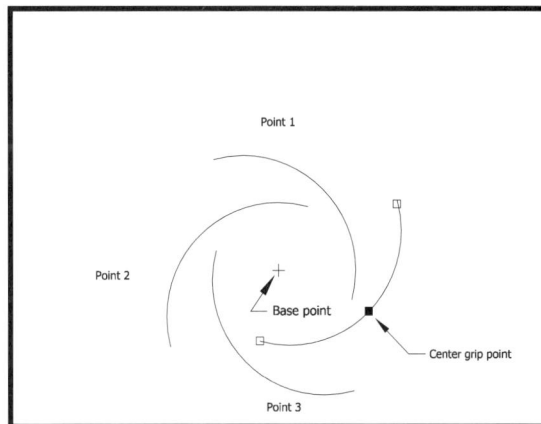

Figure 5-13

⊕ Pick a base point above and to the left of the grip, as shown in Figure 5-13.

Move your cursor in circles again. You will see the arc rotating around the new base point.

⊕ Type "c" or open the short cut menu and select Copy.

Notice the Command area prompt, which indicates that you are now in a rotate and multiple copy mode.

⊕ Pick a point showing a rotation angle of 90 degrees, as illustrated by the top arc in Figure 5-13.

⊕ Pick a second point showing a rotation angle of 180 degrees, as illustrated by the arc at the left in the figure.

⊕ Pick point 3 at 270 degrees to complete the design shown in Figure 5-13.

⊕ Press enter or the space bar to exit the grip edit mode.

This capacity to create rotated copies is very useful, as you will find when you do the drawings at the end of this chapter.

5.4   Using Polar Tracking at any Angle

You may have noticed that using Ortho or Polar Tracking to force or snap to the 90-, 180-, and 270-degree angles in the last exercise would make the process more efficient. In AutoCAD 2000 you can extend this concept to include angular increments other than the standard 90° orthogonal angles. This feature combined with the Rotate Copy technique will facilitate the creation of rotated copies at regular angles. As an example, we will use this process to create Figure 5-14.

⊕ To begin this task, Erase or Undo all but one arc on your screen.

⊕ Move the arc to the center of your screen.

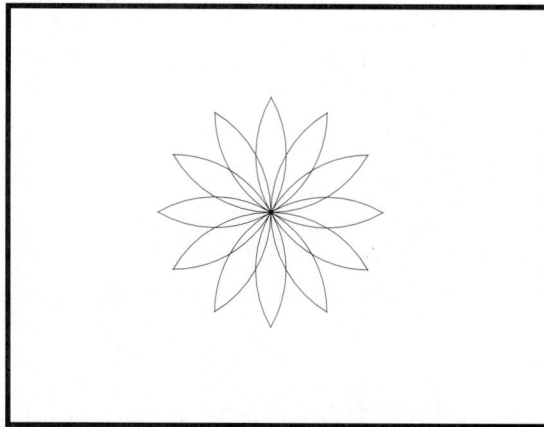

Figure 5-14

We are going to rotate and copy this arc as before, but first we will set Polar Tracking to track at 30° angles. This is done in the Drafting Settings dialog box.

⊕ Left click on the Polar button on the status bar so that Polar tracking is on.

⊕ Right click on the same Polar button.

This will open a small short cut menu with three options: On, Off, and Settings.... On and off are not very useful since you can turn the Polar button on and off more quickly by left clicking. But Settings... will open the Drafting Settings dialog box with the Polar Tracking tab selected.

⊕ Select Settings....

You will see the Drafting Settings dialog box as shown in Figure 5-15. This is the same dialog box used to specify Snap and Grid settings, but now the Polar Tracking tab is selected. In the next chapter we will use the third tab, Object Snap.

If you are using AutoCAD default settings, the increment angle will be 90°. Otherwise, you will see whatever increment was set last in your Auto-CAD system.

⊕ Open the Increment angle pop down list.

Notice the standard selections, from 90 at the top to 5 at the bottom. Notice also that you can add custom angles by checking the Additional angles box, clicking on New, and typing in a new value.

⊕ Select 30 from the list.

30 will replace 90 as the current increment angle. We will not use the other two panels yet. The first panel sets the relationship between Object Snap Tracking settings and Polar Tracking. This will be covered in Chapter 6. The second panel gives you the option of measuring angles from the last line segment drawn instead of measuring from the 0 point of the screen coordinate system (absolute).

⊕ With 30 showing as the current increment angle, click on OK.

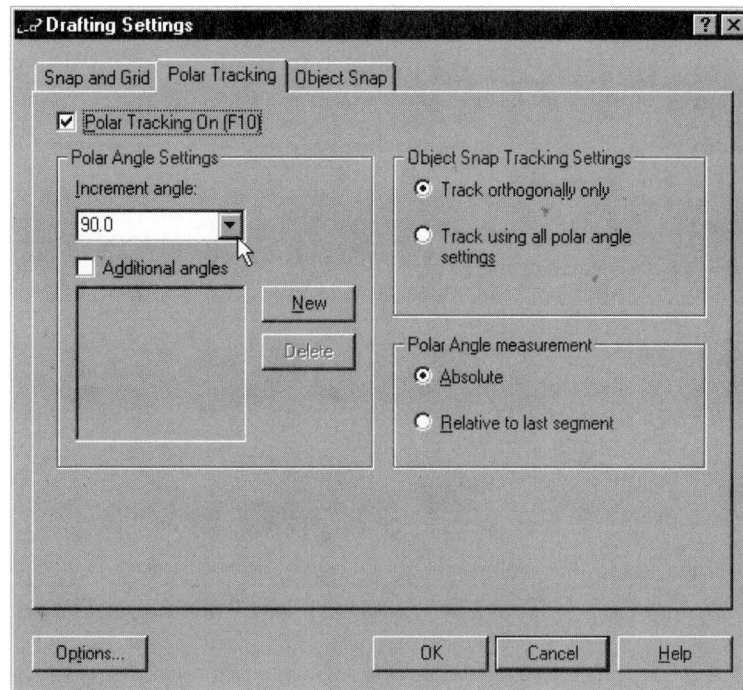

Figure 5-15

⊕ Select the arc.

⊕ Click on the grip in the center of the arc.

⊕ Right click to open the grip short cut menu.

⊕ Select Rotate.

⊕ Slowly move the cursor in a wide circle around the selected grip.

   You will see that Polar Tracking now tracks and snaps to every 30° angular increment.

⊕ Right click to open the short cut menu again.

⊕ Select Copy.

⊕ Carefully create a copy at every 30° angle until you have created a design similar to Figure 5-14.

   If your design is not exactly like ours, in particular if the ends of the arcs overlap or do not meet, it is because you have used an arc that is not the same as the one we used.

5.5 Creating Mirror Images of Objects on the Screen

GENERAL PROCEDURE

1. Select Mirror from the Draw menu, or the Mirror tool from the Modify toolbar.
2. Define a selection set. (Steps 1 and 2 can be reversed if noun/verb selection is enabled.)
3. Point to two ends of a mirror line.
4. Indicate whether or not to delete the original object.

There are two main differences between the command procedures for Mirror and Rotate. First, to mirror an object you will have to define a mirror line; second, you will have an opportunity to indicate whether you want to retain the original object or delete it. In the Rotate sequence the original is always deleted.

There is also a mirror mode in the grip edit system, which we will explore later in this section.

⊕ To begin this exercise, Erase or Undo all but one arc on your screen.

⊕ Rotate the arc and move it so that you have a bowl-shaped arc placed left of the center of your screen, as in Figure 5-16.

⊕ Keep Polar tracking on to do this exercise.

⊕ Select the arc.

⊕ Type "Mi", select Mirror from the Draw menu, or select the Mirror tool from the Modify toolbar, as shown in Figure 5-17.

Now AutoCAD will ask you for the first point of a mirror line:

Specify first point of mirror line:

A mirror line is just what you would expect; the line serves as the "mirror," and all points on your original object will be reflected across the line at an equal distance and opposite orientation.

We will show a mirror line even with the top of the arc, so that the end points of the mirror images will be touching.

⊕ Select a point even with the left end point of the arc, as in Figure 5-18.

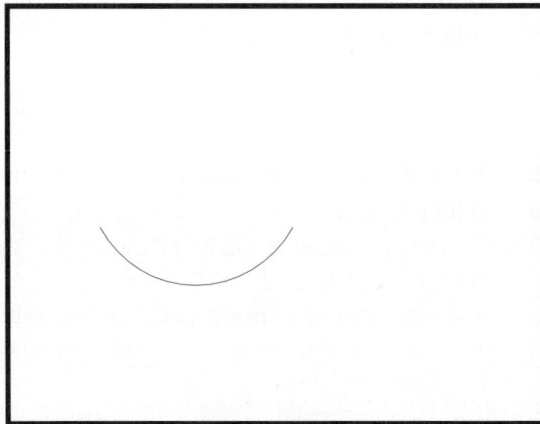

Figure 5-16

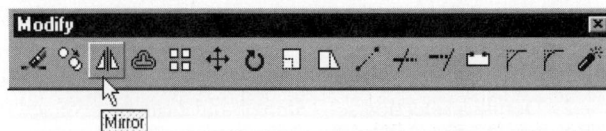

Figure 5-17

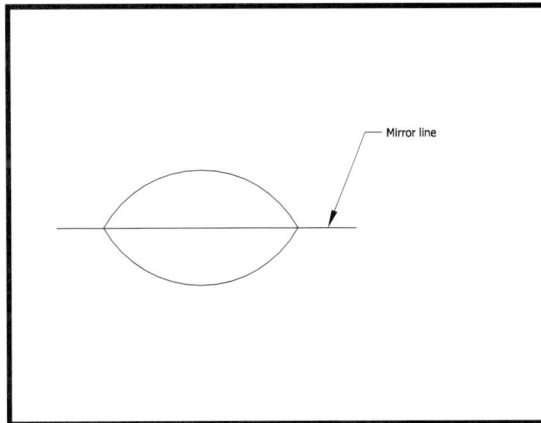

Figure 5-18

You are prompted to show the other end point of the mirror line:

Specify second point of mirror line:

The length of the mirror line is not important. All that matters is its orientation. Move the cursor slowly in a circle, and you will see an inverted copy of the arc moving with you to show the different mirror images that are possible, given the first point you have specified.

We will select a point at 0 degrees from the first point, so that the mirror image will be directly above the original arc and touching at the end points, as in Figure 5-18.

⊕ Select a point directly to the right (0 degrees) of the first point.

The dragged object will disappear until you answer the next prompt, which asks if you want to delete the original object or not.

Delete source objects [Yes/No]? <N>:

This time around we will not delete the original.

⊕ Press Enter to retain the old object.

Your screen will look like Figure 5-18, without the mirror line in the middle. Now let's repeat the process, deleting the original this time and using a different mirror line.

⊕ Repeat the MIRROR command.

⊕ Select the original (lower) arc.

⊕ Right click to end selection.

We will create a mirror image above the last one by choosing a mirror line slightly above the two arcs, as in Figure 5-19.

⊕ Select a first point of the mirror line slightly above and to the left of the figure.

⊕ Select a second point directly to the right of the first point.

⊕ Type "y", indicating that you want the source object, the lower arc, deleted.

Your screen should now resemble Figure 5-20.

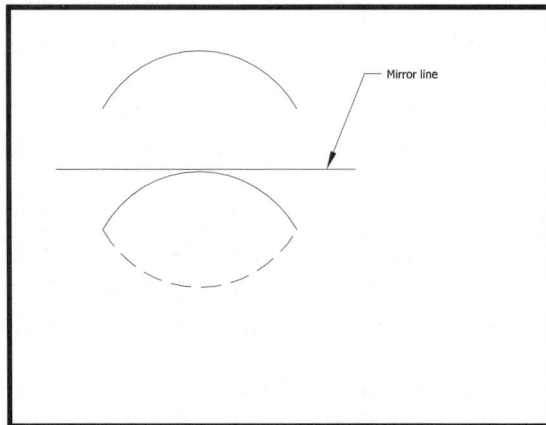

Figure 5-19

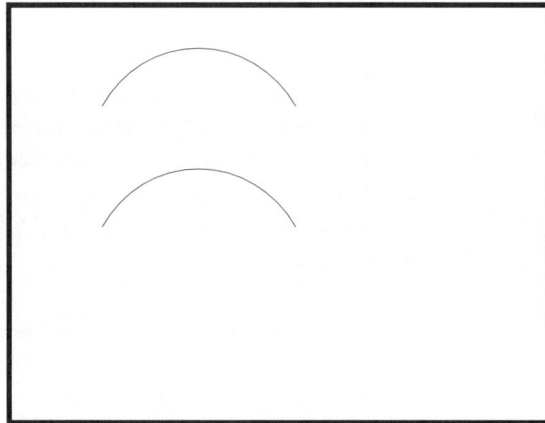

Figure 5-20

Mirroring with Grips

The Mirror grip edit mode works exactly like the rotate mode, except that the rubber band will show you a mirror line instead of a rotation angle. The option to retain or delete the original is obtained through the copy option, just as in the Rotate mode. Try it.

⊕   Select the two arcs on your screen by pointing or windowing.

   The arcs will be highlighted and grips will be showing.

⊕   Pick any of the grips.

⊕   Right click and then select Mirror from the short cut menu.

   Move the cursor and observe the dragged mirror images of the arcs. Notice that the rubber band operates as a mirror line, just as in the Mirror command.

⊕   Type "b" or right click again and select Base point.

This frees you from the selected grip and allows you to create a mirror line from any point on the screen. Notice the "Specify base point:" prompt in the command area.

⊕ Type "c" or right click and select Copy from the short cut menu.

As in the Rotate mode, this is how you retain the original in a grip edit mirroring sequence.

⊕ Pick a base point slightly below the arcs.

⊕ Pick a second point to the right of the first.

Your screen should resemble Figure 5-21.

⊕ Press enter or the space bar to exit grip edit mode.

We suggest that you complete this exercise by using the Mirror grip edit mode with the copy option to create Figure 5-22.

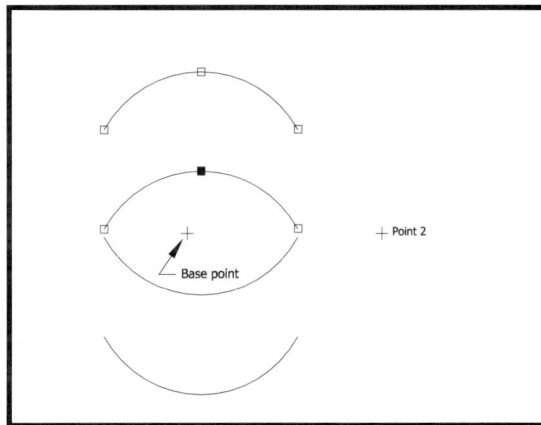

Figure 5-21

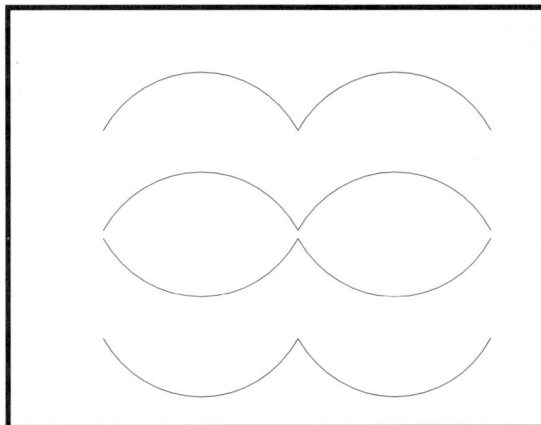

Figure 5-22

5.6 Creating Page Setups

GENERAL PROCEDURE

1. Select the Plot tool from the Standard toolbar.
2. Make changes in Plot settings.
3. Click on Add... to open the User Defined Page Setups dialog box.
4. Enter a name for the page setup.
5. Click OK.

In this chapter and the next you will move to another level in your exploration of AutoCAD 2000 plotting. So far we have confined ourselves to plot configurations tied directly to objects visible in your model space drawing area. In the last chapter we went through many of the remaining options of the PLOT dialog box. In this chapter we will continue to plot from model space, but will introduce the concept and technique of Page Setups. With page setups you can name and save different plot configurations so that one drawing may produce several different page setups. We will define two simple page setups. You will not need to learn any new options, but all of the options you have learned so far can be saved and reused as part of a page setup.

⊕ To begin this task you should be in an AutoCAD 2000 drawing using the 1B template.

Any drawing will do. We will continue using the objects drawn in Task 5.5.

The Page Setup Dialog Box

A page setup is nothing more than a group of plot settings, like the ones you have been specifying since Chapter 2. The only difference is that you will give the configuration a name and save it on a list of setups. Once named, the plot settings can be restored by selecting the name and can even be exported to other drawings.

  You can define a page setup from the Plot dialog box or from the Page Setup dialog box, accessible from the File menu. There is little difference between the two dialogs. One important difference, however, is that Page Setup does not have preview options. For this reason alone, we will continue to use the Plot dialog box.

⊕ Select the Plot tool from the Standard toolbar.

  You should now be in the familiar Plot dialog box with the Plot settings tab on top. We will make a few changes in parameters and then give this page setup a name.

  We will create a portrait setup and a landscape setup. Besides the difference in orientation the only difference in settings between the two will be that the portrait setup will be centered, while the landscape setup will be plotted from the origin. Remember, however, that everything from sheet size to the plotter you are using can be included in a page setup.

⊕ Open the paper size list and select an A size (8.50 × 11.00) sheet.

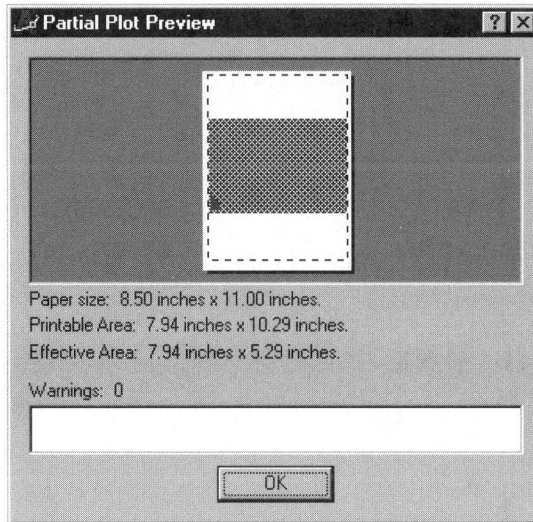

Figure 5-23

⊕ Click on the Portrait radio button in the Drawing Orientation panel.

⊕ Select Limits in the Plot area panel.

⊕ Select Center the plot.

⊕ Do a partial preview.

You should see a preview similar to the one in Figure 5-23, showing that the drawing will be plotted in a reduced area in the middle of the portrait-oriented page. Pause a minute to make sure you understand why the preview looks this way. Assuming you are using the objects drawn in this chapter, or another drawing using the 1B template, you have model space limits set to 18×12. You are plotting to an 8.5×11 sheet of paper. The 18×12 limits have been positioned in portrait orientation, placed across the effective area of the drawing sheet, scaled to fit, and centered on the paper.

Now we will name this page setup.

⊕ Click on the Add... button at the upper right of the dialog box next to the Page setup name box.

This will open the User Defined Page Setups box shown in Figure 5-24.

⊕ Type "Portrait setup" as the page setup name.

⊕ Click on OK.

This will bring you back to the Plot dialog. "Portrait setup" will now be entered in the Page setup name box. That's all there is to it. The Portrait page setup is now part of the current drawing.

Next we will define a landscape page setup and put it on the list as well. The only difference in this setup will be that it is in landscape orientation and plotted from the origin rather than centered.

⊕ Click on the Landscape radio button in the Drawing Orientation panel.

⊕ Deselect Center the plot.

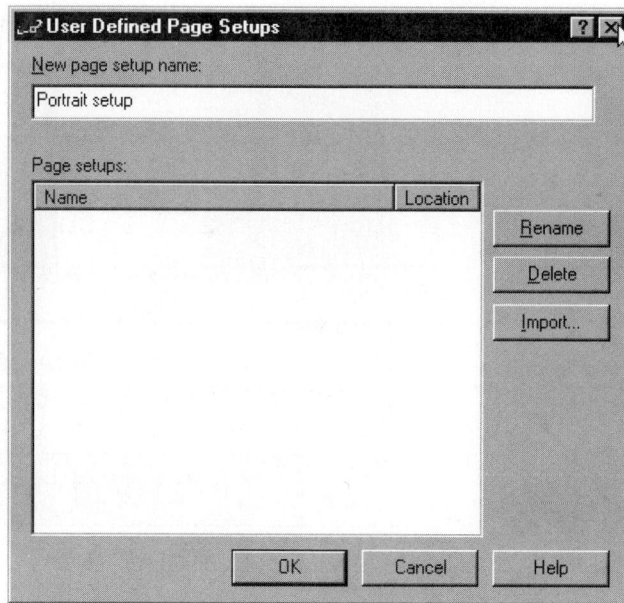

Figure 5-24

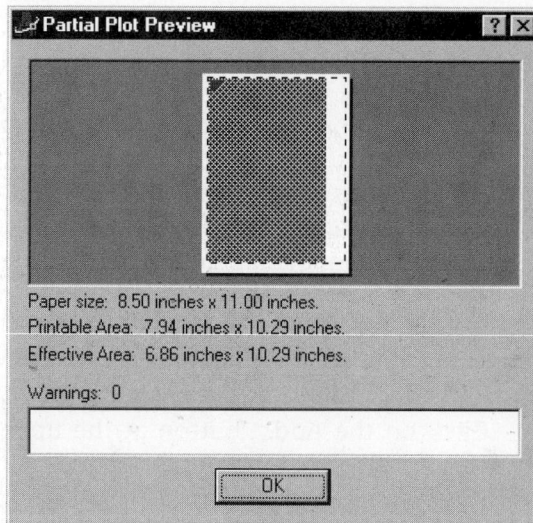

Figure 5-25

⊕ Do a partial preview.

You should see a preview similar to the one in Figure 5-25, showing that the drawing will be plotted from the corner of the landscape-oriented page. Notice that the image of the page stays in the portrait position even though the plot will be a landscape plot. This is because the sheet size is 8.5 × 11. If we wanted to rotate this image to the horizontal, we would need to select an 11 × 8.5 sheet. So now you have the 18 × 12 limits aligned with the left edge of the page, positioned at the origin of the effective area, and scaled to fit. Let's give this setup a name.

⊕ Click on the Add... button again.

⊕ Type "Landscape setup" in the User Defined Page Setups box.

⊕ Click on OK.

Back in the Plot dialog again you will see that "Landscape setup" has been entered as the current page setup. You should now restore the portrait settings.

⊕ Open the list and select "Portrait setup".

Your portrait settings, including the portrait radio button and center the plot, will be restored.

⊕ Click on Full preview.

You should see a preview similar to Figure 5-26.

⊕ Press Esc to return to the dialog box.

⊕ Open the list again and select "Landscape setup".

Your landscape settings will be restored.

⊕ Click on Full preview.

You should see a preview similar to Figure 5-27. Notice that AutoCAD 2000 turns the paper image to landscape orientation in the full preview.

This is a simple demonstration, but remember that everything from sheet size to the plotter you are using can be included in a named page setup.

Figure 5-26

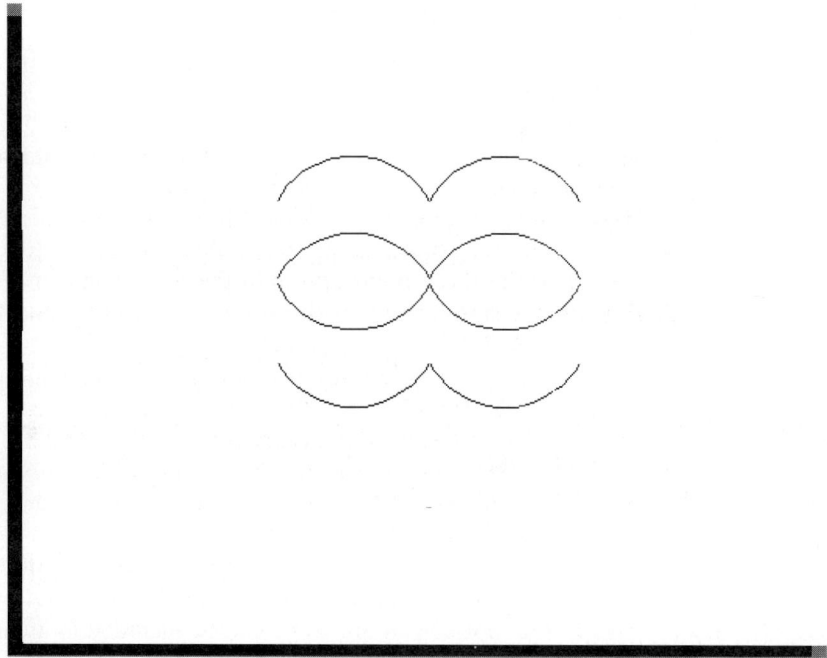

Figure 5-27

Importing Page Setups

A powerful feature of page setups is that they can be exchanged between drawings using the PSETUPIN command. This is accomplished by importing page setups from a known drawing into the current drawing. The procedure is as follows:

1. From a drawing into which you would like to import a page setup, type "psetupin" at the command line.
2. In the Select File box enter the name and path of the drawing file from which you would like to import a page setup, or open the folder containing the file and select the file name.
3. In the Import user defined page setups box, select the name of the page setup you want to import.
4. Enter the Plot or Page Setup dialog box and open the Page setup name list. The imported page setup should be there.

> **Note:** Page setups are defined in either model space or paper space as part of a layout. If you have created a page setup in model space and then go into a paper space layout, you will not see it on your list. Also if you define a page setup as part of a layout, you will not see it if you begin a plot from model space.

5.7 Review Material

Questions

1. What factors define a polar array? How many are needed to define an array?
2. What factors define an arc? How many are needed for any single method?
3. How would you use Polar Tracking instead of Polar ARRAY to create Figure 5-5?
4. What is the difference between the three-point option in the CIRCLE command and the three-point option in the ARC command?
5. Explain the significance of the rubber band in the Start, Center, Angle and the Start, End, Direction methods.
6. How would you use the reference option to rotate a line from 60° to 90°? How would you accomplish the same rotation without using reference?
7. What is the purpose of the base point option in the grip edit Rotate mode?
8. Why does Mirror require a mirror line where Rotate only requires a single point?
9. How do you create a landscape plot if your printer prints in portrait orientation?
10. What would happen if a drawing created with our 1B template were printing with a 1-to-1 scale on an A-size printer? What feature of the Plot Configuration dialog box would you use to find out if you weren't sure?

Drawing Problems

1. Draw an arc starting at (10,6) and passing through (12,6.5) and (14,6).
2. Create a mirrored copy of the arc across the horizontal line passing through (10,6).
3. Rotate the pair of arcs from step 2 45° around the point (9,6).
4. Create a mirrored copy of the pair of arcs mirrored across a vertical line passing through (9,6).
5. Create mirrored copies of both pairs of arcs mirrored across a horizontal line passing through (9,6).
6. Erase any three of the four pairs of arcs on your screen and re-create them using a polar array.

5.8 WWW Exercise #5 (Optional)

In addition to the self-scoring test, Chapter 5 of our companion Web site will give you another challenge to draw an object using a limited number of objects and edit commands. We will also give you links to two new CAD-related Web sites. So, when you are ready,

⊕ Make sure that you are connected to your Internet service provider.
⊕ Type "browser" or open the Web toolbar and select the Browse the Web tool.
⊕ If necessary, navigate to our companion Web site at "www.prenhall.com/dixriley".
Bon voyage!

5.9   Drawing 5-1: Flanged Bushing

This drawing makes use of a polar array to draw eight screw holes in a circle. It also reviews the use of layers and linetypes. Please save this drawing as noted below.

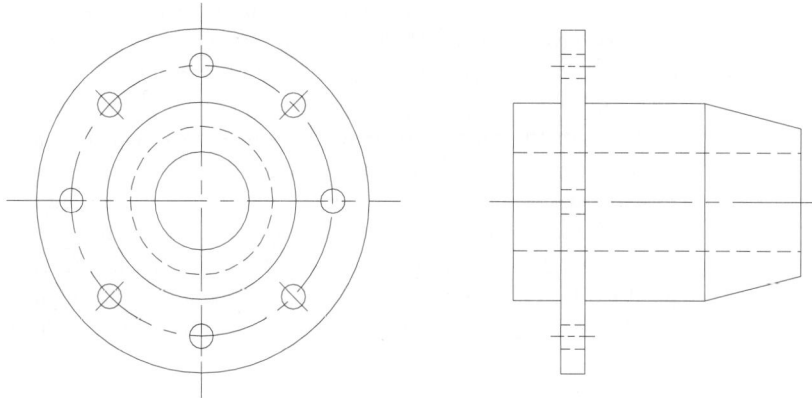

DRAWING SUGGESTIONS

GRID = 0.25
SNAP = 0.25
LTSCALE = 0.50
LIMITS = (0,0)(12,9)

- Draw the concentric circles first, using dimensions from both views. Remember to change layers as needed.
- Once you have drawn the 2.75-diameter bolt circle, use it to locate one of the bolt holes. Any of the circles at a quadrant point (0, 90, 180, or 270 degrees) will do.
- Draw a center line across the bolt hole, and then array the hole and the center line 360 degrees. Be sure to rotate the objects as they are copied; otherwise, you will get strange results from your center lines.

SAVE THIS DRAWING

This drawing will be used in Chapter 6 to demonstrate AutoCAD 2000 drawing layouts, paper space, and the use of multiple viewports. It is important that you save the drawing so that you can use it to learn these important plotting techniques.

Ø.25
8 HOLES EQ SP
ON 2.75 DIA B.C.

.50

.25

Ø3.50

Ø2.00

Ø1.50

Ø1.00

Save This Drawing
(use in chapter 6)

1.00

3.25

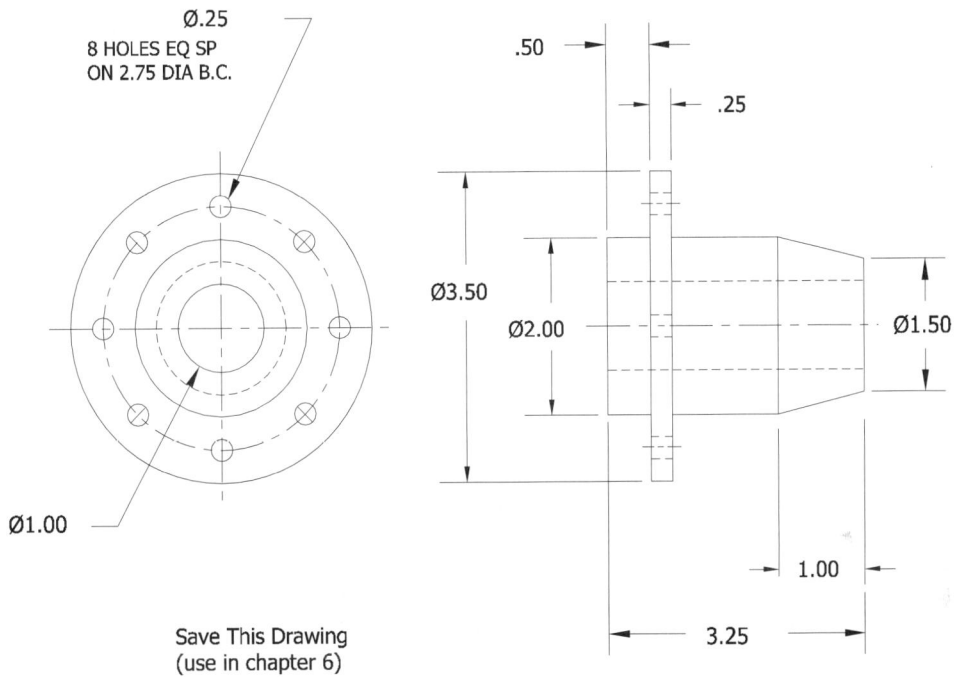

FLANGED BUSHING

Drawing 5-1

5.10   Drawing 5-2: Guide

There are six arcs in this drawing, and while some of them could be drawn as fillets, we suggest that you use the ARC command for practice. By drawing arcs you will also avoid a common problem with fillets. Since fillets are designed to round intersections at corners, creating a fillet in the middle of a line will erase part of that line unless you turn Trim mode off. This would affect the center line on the left side of the front view of this drawing, for example.

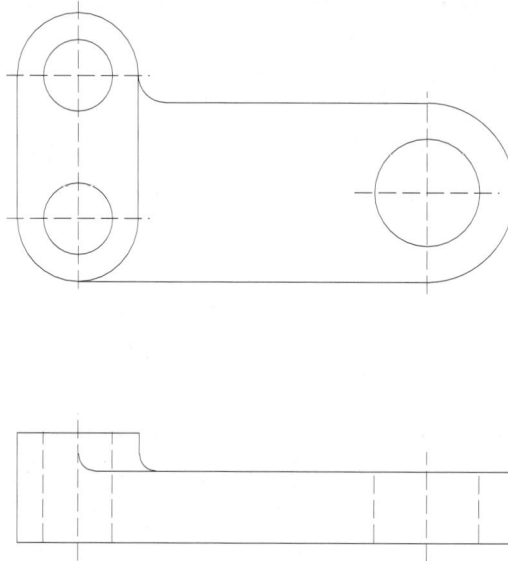

DRAWING SUGGESTIONS

GRID = 0.25
SNAP = 0.125
LTSCALE = 0.50
LIMITS = (0,0)(12,9)

- The three large arcs in the top view all can be drawn easily using Start, Center, End.
- The smaller 0.375 arc in the top view could be drawn by filleting the top arc with the horizontal line to its right. However, we suggest you try an arc giving start, center, end or start, center, angle. Note that you can easily locate the center by moving 0.375 to the right of the end point of the upper arc.
- The same method will work to draw the 0.25 arc in the front view. Begin by dropping a line down 0.25 from the horizontal line. Start your arc at the end of this line, and move 0.25 to the right to locate its center. Then the end will simply be 0.25 down from the center (or you could specify an angle of 90 degrees).
- Similarly, the arc at the center line can be drawn from a start point 0.25 up from the horizontal. It will have a radius of 0.25 and make an angle of 90 degrees.

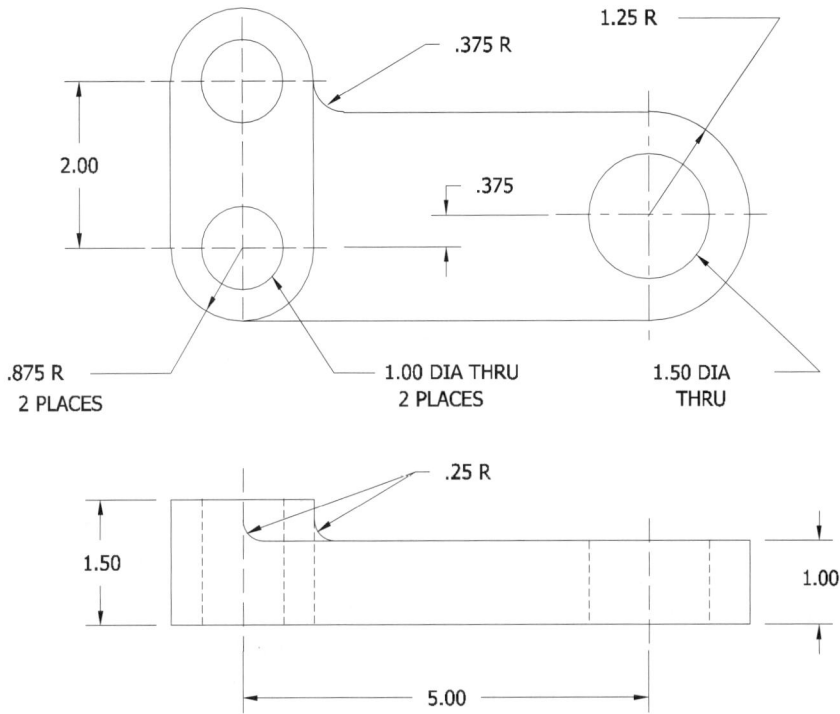

.375 R

1.25 R

2.00

.375

.875 R
2 PLACES

1.00 DIA THRU
2 PLACES

1.50 DIA
THRU

.25 R

1.50

1.00

5.00

GUIDE
Drawing 5-2

5.11   Drawing 5-3: Dials

This is a relatively simple drawing that will give you some good practice with polar arrays and the ROTATE and COPY commands.

Notice that the needle drawn at the top of the next page is only for reference; the actual drawing includes only the plate and the three dials with their needles.

DRAWING SUGGESTIONS

GRID = 0.25
SNAP = 0.125
LTSCALE = 0.50
LIMITS = (0,0)(18,12)

- After drawing the outer rectangle and screw holes, draw the leftmost dial, including the needle. Draw a 0.50 vertical line at the top and array it to the left (counterclockwise—a positive angle) and to the right (negative) to create the 11 larger lines on the dial. Question: How many lines in each of these left and right arrays do you need in order to end up with 11?
- Draw a .25 line on top of the .50 line at the top of the dial. Then use right and left arrays with a Last selection to create the 40 small markings. How many lines in these two arrays?
- Complete the first dial and then use a multiple copy to produce two more dials at the center and right of your screen. Be sure to use a window to select the entire dial.
- Finally, use the ROTATE command to rotate the needles as indicated on the new dials. Use a window to select the needle, and rotate it around the center of the dial.

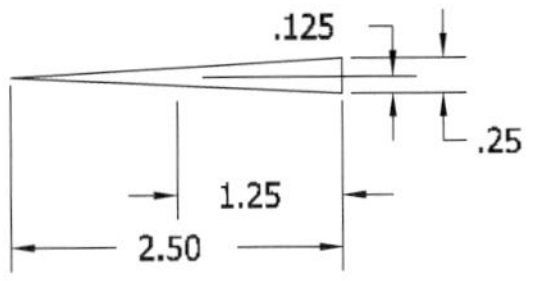

.125

.25

1.25

2.50

Detail of pointer

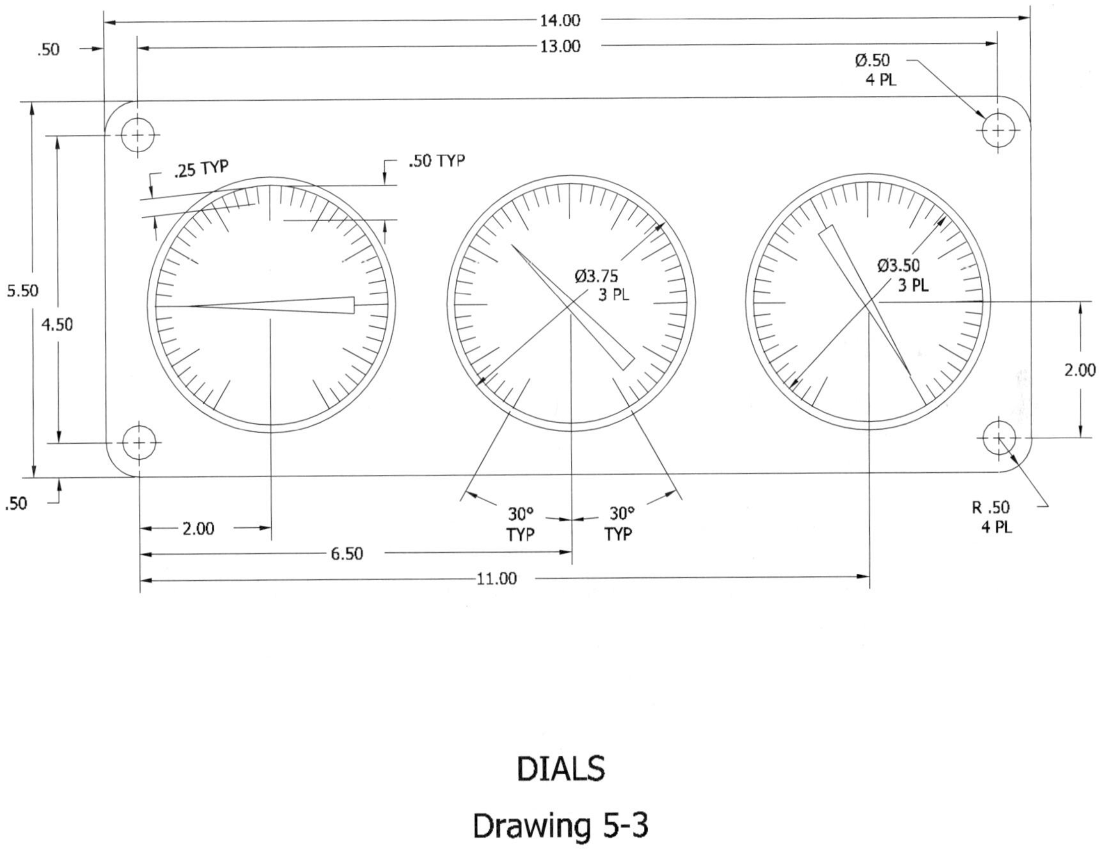

14.00

13.00

Ø.50
4 PL

.50

.25 TYP

.50 TYP

5.50

4.50

Ø3.75
3 PL

Ø3.50
3 PL

2.00

.50

2.00

30°
TYP

30°
TYP

R .50
4 PL

6.50

11.00

DIALS

Drawing 5-3

5.12   Drawing 5-4: Alignment Wheel

This drawing shows a typical use of the MIRROR command. Carefully mirroring sides of the symmetrical front view will save you from duplicating some of your drawing efforts. Notice that you will need a small snap setting to draw the vertical lines at the chamfer.

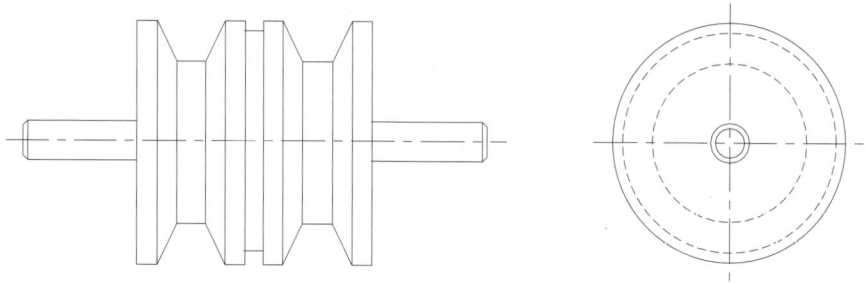

DRAWING SUGGESTIONS

GRID = 0.25
SNAP = 0.125
LTSCALE = 0.50
LIMITS = (0,0)(12,9)

- There are numerous ways to use Mirror in drawing the front view. As the reference shows, there is top–bottom symmetry as well as left–right symmetry. The exercise for you is to choose an efficient mirroring sequence.
- Whatever sequence you use, consider the importance of creating the chamfer and the vertical line at the chamfer before this part of the object is mirrored.
- Once the front view is drawn, the right side view will be easy. Remember to change layers for center and hidden lines and to line up the small inner circle with the chamfer.

(ORTHO ON)

MIRROR LINES

REFERENCE

.25

2.875

.375

.25

27° REF

.06 X 45° CHAMFER
BOTH ENDS

Ø2.00

Ø3.00

Ø2.75

Ø.50

.25

1.375

3.00

1.50

6.00

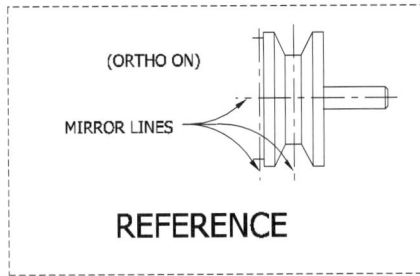

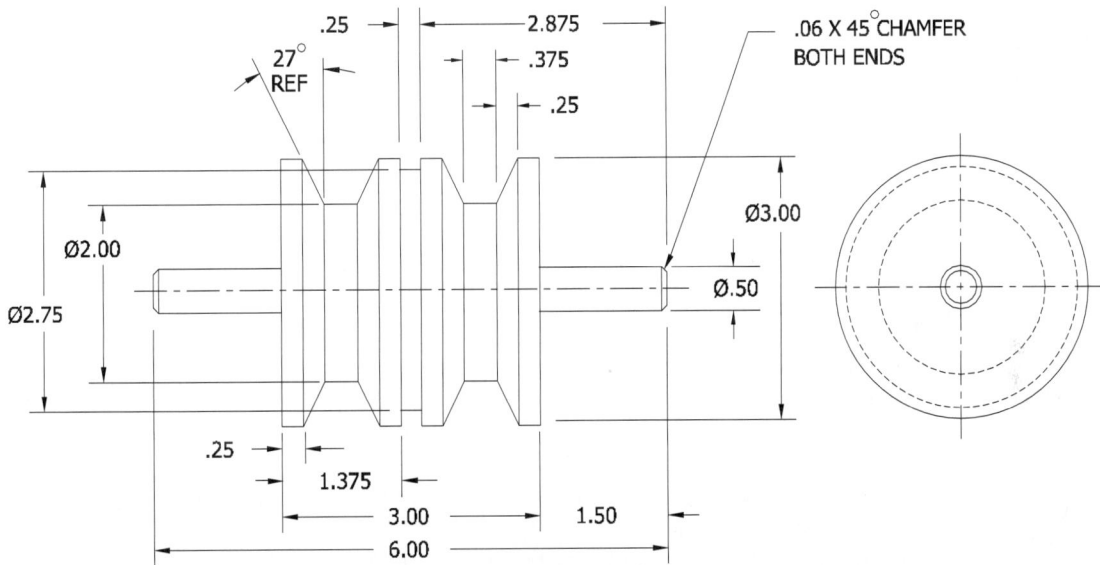

ALIGNMENT WHEEL
Drawing 5-4

5.13   Drawing 5-5: Hearth

Once you have completed this architectural drawing as it is shown, you might want to experiment with filling in a pattern of firebrick in the center of the hearth. The drawing itself is not complicated, but little errors will become very noticeable when you try to make the row of 4 × 8 bricks across the bottom fit with the arc of bricks across the top, so work carefully.

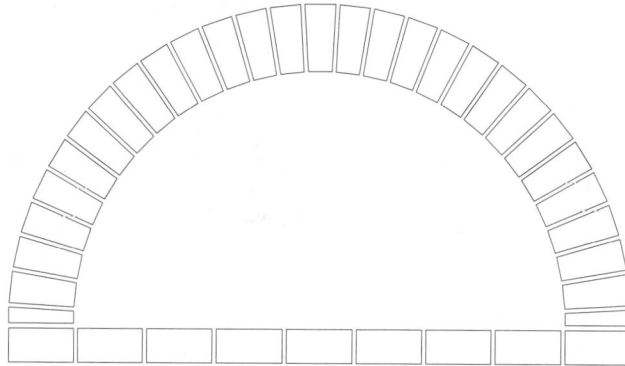

DRAWING SUGGESTIONS

UNITS = Architectural
                    Smallest fraction = 8 (1/8″)
LIMITS = (0,0) (12′,9′)
GRID = 1′
SNAP = 1/8″

- Zoom in to draw the wedge-shaped brick indicated by the arrow on the right of the dimensioned drawing. Draw half of the brick only and mirror it across the center line as shown. (Notice that the center line is for reference only.) It is very important that you use Mirror so that you can erase half of the brick later.
- Array the brick in a 29-item, 180-degree polar array.
- Erase the bottom halves of the end bricks at each end.
- Draw a new horizontal bottom line on each of the two end bricks.
- Draw a 4 × 8 brick directly below the half brick at the left end.
- Array the 4 × 8 brick in a one-row, nine-column array, with 8.5″ between columns.

R3'-2"

R2'-6"

2-3/4"

3-3/4"

8"

1/2

Erase bottom half of end bricks
after array

4" x 8" Bricks
1/2" Mortar between bricks

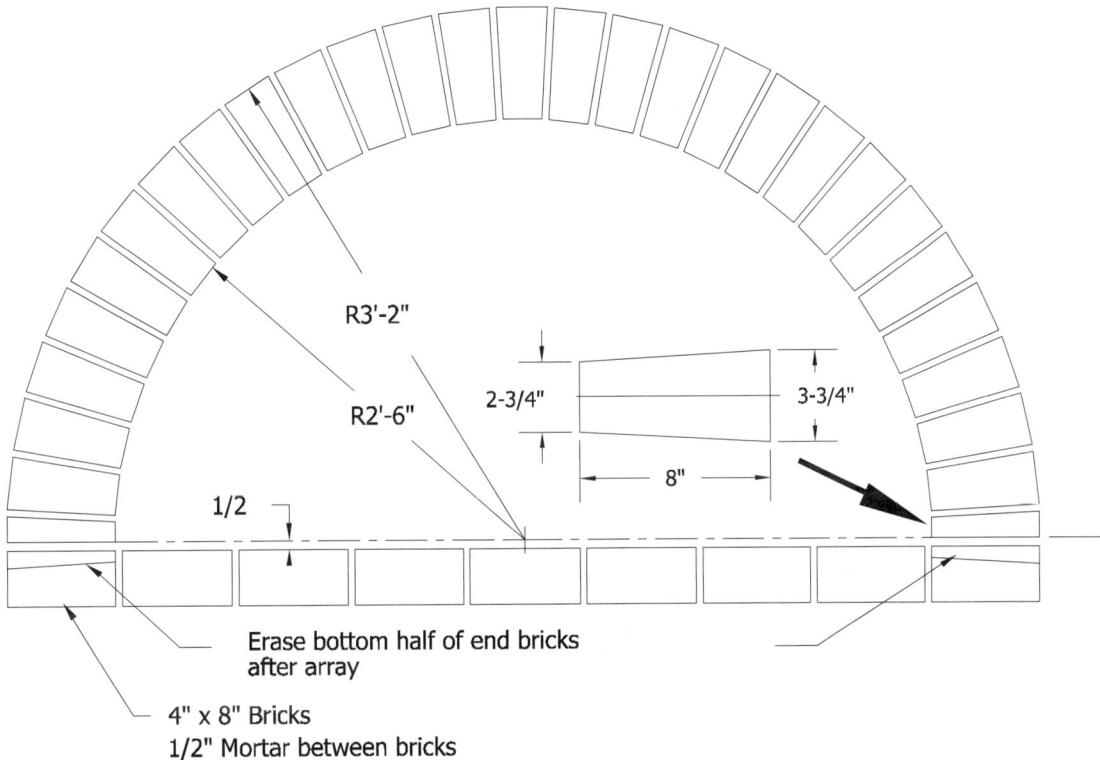

Drawing Compliments   of Thomas Casey

HEARTH

Drawing 5-5

5.14 Drawing 5-6: Slotted Flange

This drawing includes a typical application of polar arrays and arcs. The finished drawing should consist of the top view and front view. The center lines and outline of the large circle in the top view are shown in the reference drawing. Use the three-dimensional view as a reference to draw the 2D top and front views.

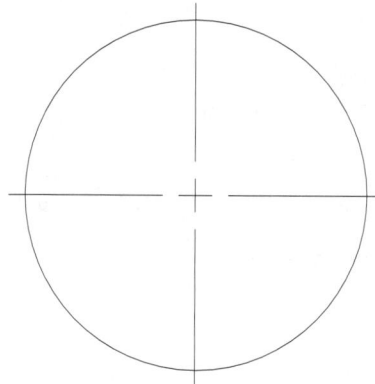

Location of Top View

Location of Front View

DRAWING SUGGESTIONS

- Begin by drawing the circles in the top view. Use the circles to line up the vertical lines in the front view.
- The small arcs in the slots can be drawn on a center line and rotated and copied into place using grips.
- A quick method for drawing the vertical lines in the front view is to use a quadrant object snap beginning from all the circles in the top view to make guide lines.

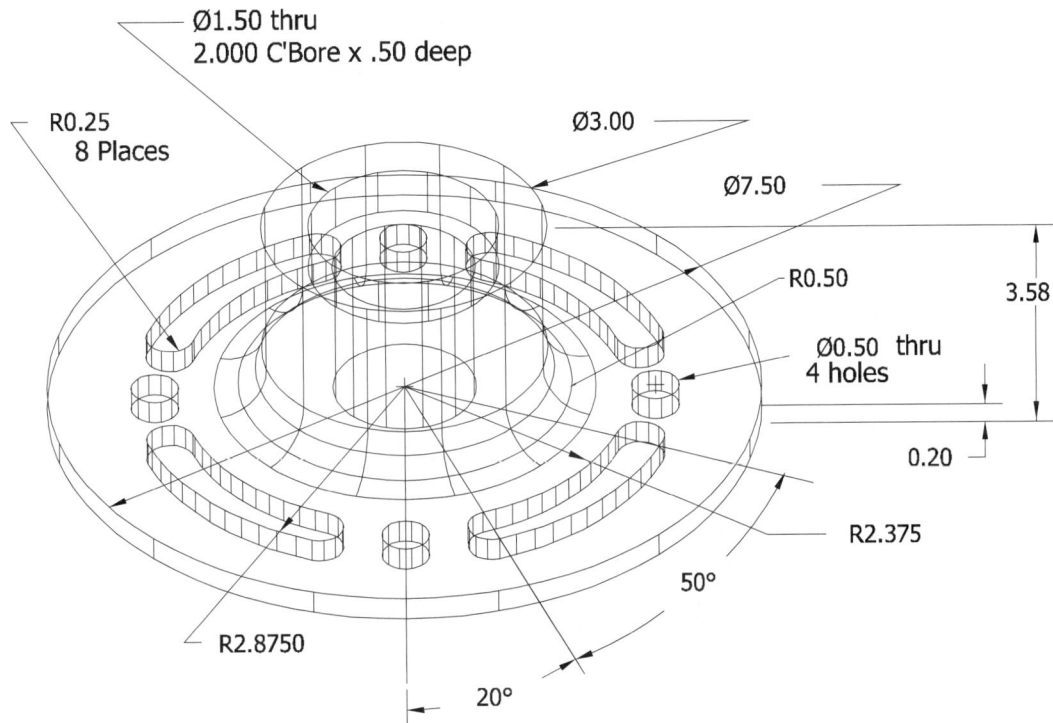

Ø1.50 thru
2.000 C'Bore x .50 deep

R0.25
8 Places

Ø3.00

Ø7.50

R0.50

Ø0.50 thru
4 holes

3.58

0.20

R2.375

50°

R2.8750

20°

SLOTTED FLANGE
Drawing 5-6

6 Object Snap

COMMANDS

BREAK	LENGTHEN	STRETCH
EXTEND	OSNAP	TRIM
	OFFSET	

OVERVIEW

This chapter completes the introduction to basic 2D drafting and editing techniques and brings you to a very significant plateau in your developing AutoCAD technique. The techniques you will have learned in Part I will be the basis for everything you do in more complex two- and three-dimensional drawings.

In this chapter you will begin to use AutoCAD 2000's very powerful Object Snap and Object Tracking features. These will take you to a new level of accuracy and efficiency as a CAD operator. You will also learn to BREAK entities on the screen into pieces so that they may be manipulated or erased separately, to shorten objects at intersections with other objects using the TRIM command, or to lengthen them with the EXTEND and LENGTHEN commands. Finally, you move into the world of paper space as you begin to use AutoCAD 2000's layout and multiple viewport system.

TASKS

6.1 Selecting points with object snap (Single-Point Override)
6.2 Selecting points with OSNAP (Running Mode)
6.3 Object Snap Tracking
6.4 Using the OFFSET command
6.5 BREAKing previously drawn objects
6.6 Shortening objects with the TRIM command
6.7 Extending objects with the EXTEND command
6.8 Using STRETCH to alter objects connected to other objects
6.9 Changing lengths with the LENGTHEN command
6.10 Creating plot layouts
6.11 Review Material
6.12 WWW Exercise #6 (Optional)
6.13 Drawing 6-1: Bike Tire
6.14 Drawing 6-2: Archimedes Spiral
6.15 Drawing 6-3: Spiral Designs
6.16 Drawing 6-4: Grooved Hub
6.17 Drawing 6-5: Cap Iron
6.18 Drawing 6-6: Deck Framing
6.19 Drawing 6-7: Tool Block

6.1 Selecting Points with Object Snap (Single-Point Override)

GENERAL PROCEDURE

1. Enter a drawing command, such as LINE, CIRCLE, or ARC.
2. Right click while holding down the CTRL key.
3. Select an object snap mode from the short cut menu.
4. Point to a previously drawn object.

or

1. Enter a drawing command, such as LINE, CIRCLE, or ARC.
2. Select an object snap mode from the object snap toolbar.
3. Point to a previously drawn object.

Some of the drawings in the last two chapters have pushed the limits of what you can accomplish accurately on a CAD system with incremental snap alone. Object snap is a related tool that works in a very different manner. Instead of snapping to points defined by the coordinate system, it snaps to geometrically specifiable points on objects that you already have drawn. There are thirteen different varieties of object snap, and each may be used as a one-time option for selecting a point (single-point override) or turned on to affect all point selection (running object snap). In this task we will introduce the single-point method and then move on to the running mode in the next task.

Let's say you want to begin a new line at the end point of one that is already on the screen. If you are lucky, the end point may be on a snap point, but it is just as likely not to be. Turning snap off and moving the cursor to the apparent end point may appear to work, but when you zoom in you probably will find that you have missed the point. Using object snap is the only precise way, and it is as precise as you could want. Let's try it.

⊕   The Osnap button and the Snap button should be *off* for this exercise.

⊕   To prepare for this exercise, draw a 6 × 6 box with a circle inside, as in Figure 6-1.

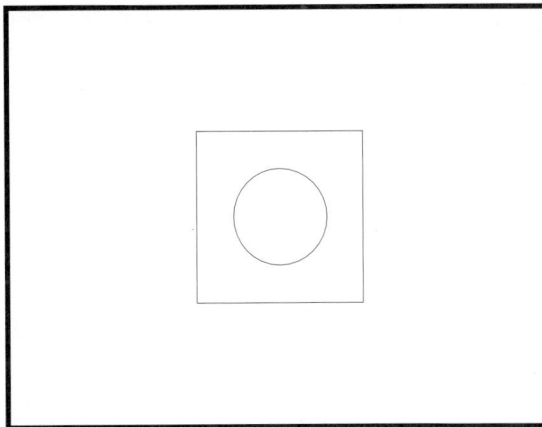

Figure 6-1

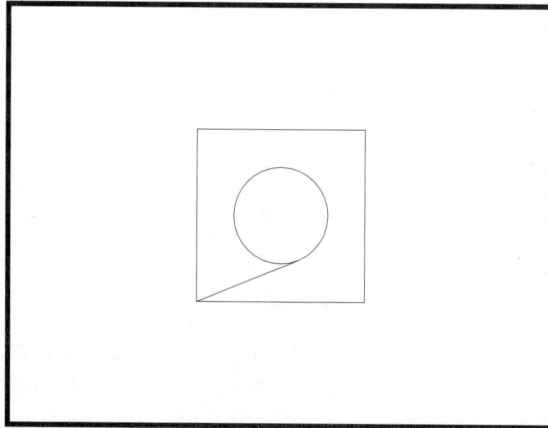

Figure 6-2

Exact sizes and locations are not important; however, the circle should be centered within the square.

⊕ Now enter the LINE command (type "L" or select the Line tool).

We are going to draw a line from the lower left corner of the square to a point on a line tangent to the circle, as shown in Figure 6-2. This task would be extremely difficult without object snap. The corner is easy to locate, since you probably have drawn it on snap, but the tangent may not be.

We will use an end point object snap to locate the corner and a tangent object snap to locate the tangent point. When AutoCAD asks for a point, you can select an object snap mode from the object snap short cut menu.

⊕ At the "Specify first point:" prompt, instead of specifying a point, hold down the Shift or Ctrl key and press the right button on your mouse.

This will open the short cut menu illustrated in Figure 6-3.

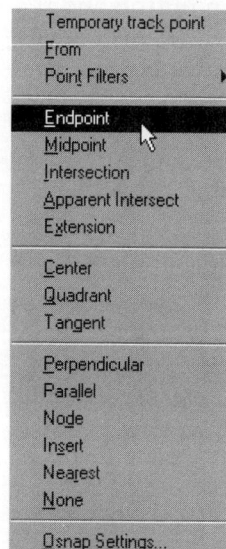

Figure 6-3

⊕   Select "Endpoint".

This tells AutoCAD that you are going to select the start point of the line by using an end point object snap rather than by direct pointing or entering coordinates.

Now that AutoCAD knows that we want to begin at the end point of a previously drawn entity, it needs to know which one.

⊕   Move the cursor near the lower left corner of the square.

When you are close to the corner, AutoCAD will recognize the end point of the lines there and indicate this with a yellow box surrounding the end point. This object snap symbol is called a marker. There are different-shaped markers for each type of object snap. If you let the cursor rest here for a moment, a tooltip-like label will appear, naming the type of object that has been recognized, as shown in Figure 6-4. This label is called a snap-tip. Also notice that if the cross hairs are inside the marker, they will lock onto the end point. This action can be turned on or off and is called the magnet setting. You do not have to be locked on to the end point, however. As long as the end point marker is showing, the end point will be selected.

⊕   With the end point object snap marker showing, press the pickbutton.

The yellow end point box and the snap-tip will disappear, and there will be a rubber band stretching from the lower left corner of the square to the cursor position. In the command area you will see the Specify next point prompt.

We will use a tangent object snap to select the second point.

⊕   At the "Specify next point or [Undo]:" prompt, select "Tangent" from the short cut menu (shift + right click).

⊕   Move the cursor to the right and position the cross hairs so that they are near the lower right side of the circle.

When you approach the tangent area, you will see the yellow tangent marker, as shown in Figure 6-5. Here again, if you let the cursor rest you will see a snap-tip.

⊕   With the tangent marker showing, press the pickbutton.

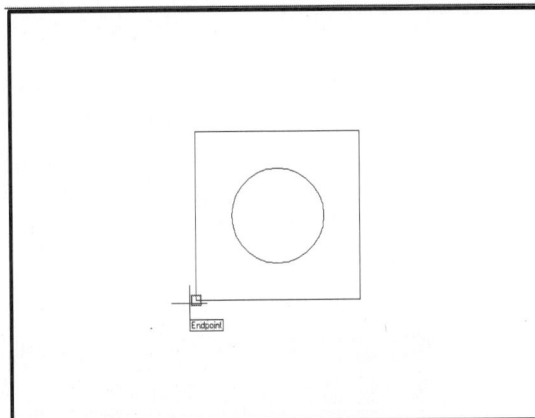

Figure 6-4

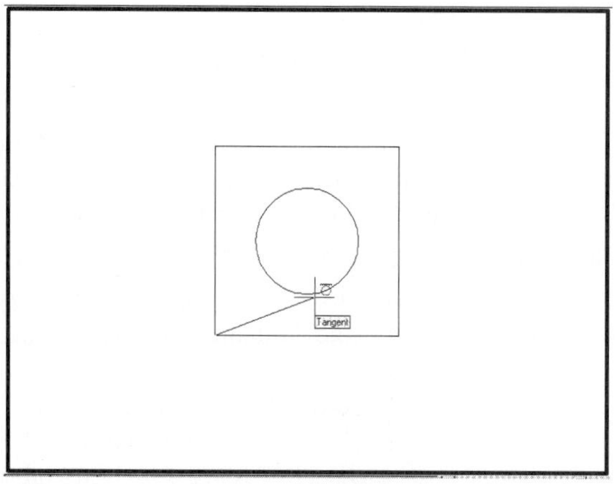

Figure 6-5

AutoCAD will locate the tangent point and draw the line. Notice the power of being able to precisely locate the tangent point in this way.

⊕ Press Enter to exit the LINE command.

Your screen should now resemble Figure 6-2.

We will repeat the process now, but start from the midpoint of the bottom side of the square instead of its end point. Also, this time we will use the object snap toolbar instead of the short cut menu. Object snap is so important a feature that you may find yourself leaving this toolbar open much of the time.

⊕ Move the cursor over any toolbar on your screen and right click to open the toolbar short cut menu.

⊕ Select "Object snap".

This will open the Object snap toolbar shown in Figure 6-6.

⊕ Move the toolbar anywhere out of the way, or dock it along one side.

⊕ Enter the LINE command.

⊕ At the prompt for a point, select the Snap to Midpoint tool from the toolbar.

All of the Osnap modes have fairly obvious icons. Snap to Midpoint is the second tool in the second panel.

⊕ Position the aperture anywhere along the bottom side of the square so that a yellow triangle, the snap to midpoint marker, appears at the midpoint of the line.

⊕ Press the pickbutton.

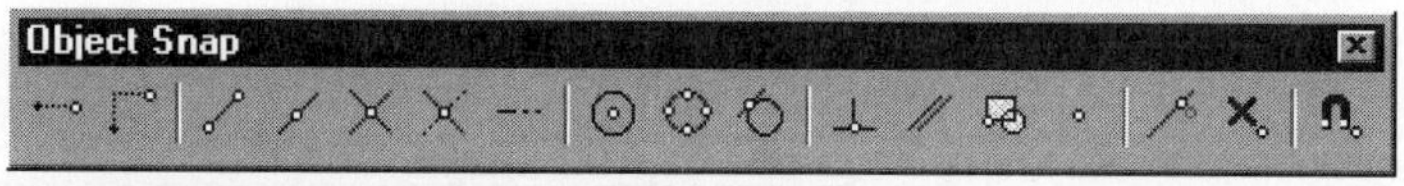

Figure 6-6

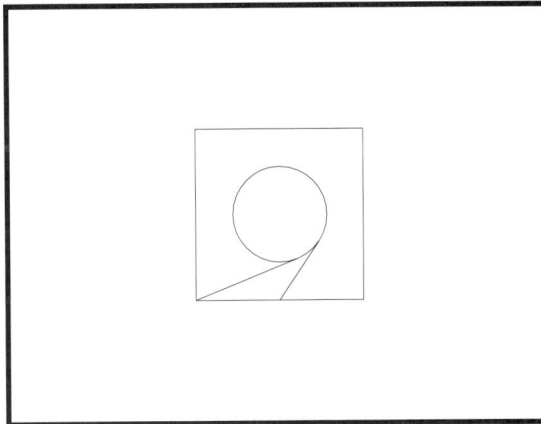

Figure 6-7

⊕   At the prompt for a second point, select the Snap to Tangent tool from the toolbar.

Snap to tangent is the third tool in the third panel.

⊕   Position the aperture along the right side of the circle so that the tangent symbol appears and then press the pickbutton.

⊕   Press Enter or the space bar to exit the LINE command.

At this point your screen should resemble Figure 6-7.

That's all there is to it. Remember the steps: (1) Enter a command; (2) when AutoCAD asks for a point, specify an object snap mode; (3) position the cross hairs near an object to which the mode can be applied and let AutoCAD find the point.

Note: Both the short cut menu and the toolbar are efficient methods of specifying a single-point object snap. But you can also type the name of any object snap method when AutoCAD asks for a point. All modes have aliases that are the first three letters of the mode, "end" for endpoint, "tan" for tangent, etc.

6.2   Selecting Points with OSNAP (Running Mode)

GENERAL PROCEDURE

1. Select object snap modes from the Drafting Settings dialog box.
2. Click the Osnap button on the status bar so that it is on.
3. Enter drawing commands.
4. If there is more than one object snap choice in the area, cycle through using the tab key.

So far we have been using object snap one point at a time. Since object snap is not constantly in use for most applications, this single-point method is common.

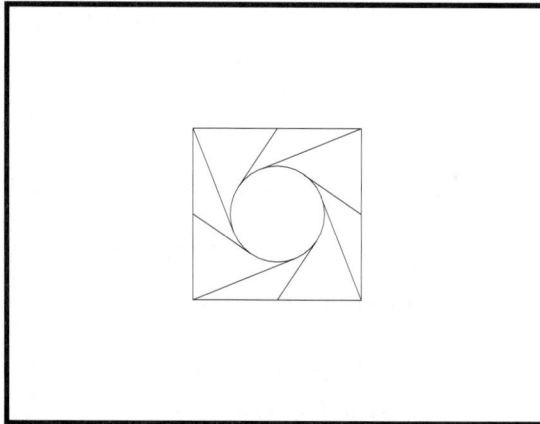

Figure 6-8

But often you will find that you are going to be using one or a number of object snap types repeatedly and will not need to select many points without them. In this case you can keep object snap modes on so that they affect all point selection. This is called running object snap. We will use this method to complete the drawing shown in Figure 6-8. Notice how each line is drawn from a midpoint or corner to a tangent point on the circle. This is easily done with running object snaps.

⊕ Click the Osnap button on the status bar so that it is on.

When the Osnap button is on, you will be in running object snap mode. The modes that will be in effect depend on the AutoCAD default settings, or whatever settings were last selected. To change settings or see what settings are on, we open the Drafting Settings dialog box. You used this dialog box in Chapter 2.

⊕ Right click on the status bar Osnap button.

This will open a small short cut menu with three options: On, Off, and Settings.... On and off are redundant since you can turn Osnap on and off more easily by left clicking as usual. But Settings is very useful.

⊕ Select Settings....

⊕ This will open the Drafting Settings dialog box with the Object Snap tab on top, as shown in Figure 6-9.

You will find a description of all of the object snap modes on the chart in Figure 6-10, but for now we will be using three: Midpoint, Intersection, and Tangent. Midpoint and tangent you already know. Intersection snaps to the point where two entities meet or cross. We will use intersect instead of end point to select the remaining three corners of the square. Endpoint could be used instead.

⊕ Select Midpoint, Intersection, and Tangent, and deselect any other modes that are checked.

When you are done, your dialog box should resemble Figure 6-9. Notice that Object Snap On (F3) is checked at the top of the box, and Object Snap Tracking On (F11) is *not* checked. We will save Object Snap Tracking for Task 6.3.

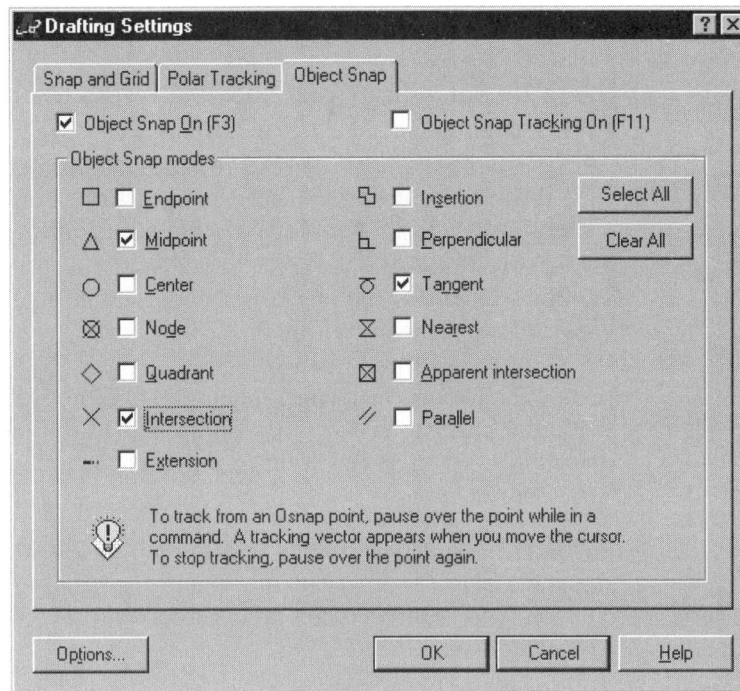

Figure 6-9

✦ Click OK.

✦ Enter the LINE command.

✦ Position the aperture so that the lower right corner is within the box.

A yellow X, the intersection marker, will appear.

✦ With the intersection marker showing, press the pickbutton.

AutoCAD will select the intersection of the bottom and the right sides and give you the rubber band and the prompt for the next point.

✦ Move the cross hairs up and along the right side of the circle until the tangent marker appears.

✦ With the tangent marker showing, press the pickbutton.

AutoCAD will construct a new tangent from the lower right corner to the circle.

✦ Press the space bar to complete the command sequence.

✦ Press the space bar again to repeat LINE so you can begin with a new start point.

We will continue to move counterclockwise around the circle. This should begin to be easy now.

✦ Position the aperture along the right side of the square so that the midpoint triangle marker appears.

✦ With the midpoint marker showing, press the pickbutton.

AutoCAD snaps to the midpoint of the side.

⊕ Move up along the upper right side of the circle so that the tangent marker appears.

⊕ With the tangent marker showing, press the pickbutton.

⊕ Press the space bar to exit LINE.

⊕ Press the space bar again to repeat LINE and continue around the circle drawing tangents like this: upper right corner to top of circle, top side midpoint to top left of circle, upper left corner to left side, left side midpoint to lower left side.

Remember that running osnap modes should give you both speed and accuracy, so push yourself a little to see how quickly you can complete the figure.

Your screen should now resemble Figure 6-8. Before going on you should study the Object Snap chart, Figure 6-10. Before you can effectively analyze situations and look for opportunities to use object snap and object snap tracking, you will need to have a good acquaintance with all of the object snap modes.

Tip: Occasionally you may encounter a situation where there are several possible object snap points in a tight area. If AutoCAD does not recognize the one you want, you can cycle through all choices by pressing the tab key repeatedly.

6.3 Object Snap Tracking

GENERAL PROCEDURE

1. Select object snap modes from the Drafting Settings dialog box.
2. Click the OTRACK button on the status bar so that it is on.
3. Enter drawing commands.
4. To acquire a point for tracking, position the cursor so that the Osnap marker appears, but do not click.
5. Use the temporary construction lines that AutoCAD draws from this "acquired point".

Object Snap tracking is a new AutoCAD 2000 system that creates temporary construction lines from designated object snap points. Once you are in a Draw command, such as LINE, any object snap point that can be identified in an active object snap mode can be "acquired". An acquired point is highlighted with a yellow cross. Once a point is acquired, object snap tracking will automatically throw out temporary construction lines from this point. Construction lines are dotted lines like those used by Polar tracking. They extend to the edge of the display and are drawn along the horizontal and vertical from the acquired point, or along polar tracking angles. Try this:

⊕ To begin this task the Osnap button should be on with the Endpoint mode in effect; all other modes from the last exercise should be turned off.

TYPE	APPEARANCE	DESCRIPTION
CENter	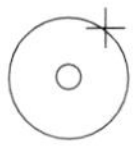	Snaps to the center of an arc, circle, ellipse, or elliptical arc.
ENDpoint		Snaps to the closest endpoint of an arc, elliptical arc, line, mline, polyline, ray, or to the closest corner of a trace, solid or 3D face.
INSertion	(See Chapter 10)	Snaps to the insertion point of a block, attribute, shape or text.
INTersection		Snaps to crossing or meeting point of arcs, lines, circles, ellipses, elliptical arcs, mlines, polylines, rays, splines, or xlines.
APParent Inter	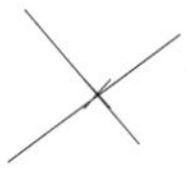	Snaps to apparent crossing or meeting point of arcs, lines, circles, ellipses, elliptical arcs, mlines, polylines, rays, splines, or xlines. If apparent intersection and intersection are on at the same time, varying results may occur.
MIDpoint	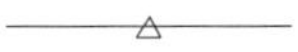	Snaps to the midpoint of an arc, circle, ellipse, elliptical arc, line, mline, polyline, solid, spline, or xline.
NEArest		Snaps to the nearest point on an arc, circle, ellipse, elliptical arc, line, mline point, polyline, spline or xline.
NODe		Snaps to a point object.
PERpendicular	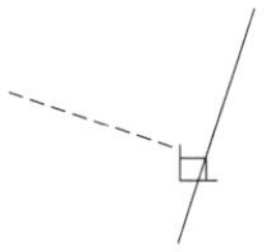	Snaps to a point on an arc, circle, ellipse, elliptical arc, line, mline, ray, solid, spline or xline.
QUAdrant	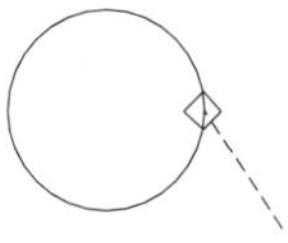	Snaps to nearest quadrant point of an arc, circle ellipse, or elliptical arc. 0, 90, 180, or 270 degrees
QUIck	(Modifies other modes)	Snaps to the first snap point found. Quick must be used in conjunction with other objects snap modes.
TANgent	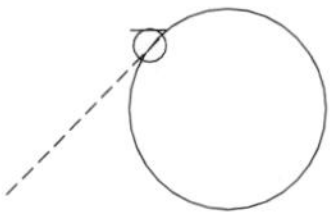	Snaps to the tangent of an arc, circle ellipse, or elliptical arc.
EXTension	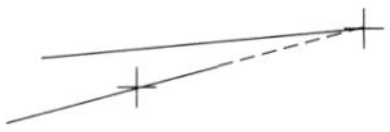	Snaps to the extension point of an object. Establish an extension path by moving the cursor over the endpoint of an object. A marker is placed on the endpoint. While the endpoint is marked, the cursor snaps to the extension path of the endpoint.
PARallel	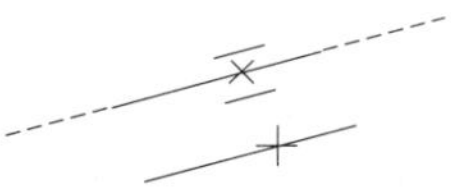	Snaps to an extension parallel with an object. When the cursor is moved over the endpoint of an object, the endpoint is marked and the cursor snaps to the parallel alignment path to that object. The alignment path is calculated from the current "from point" of the command.

Figure 6-10

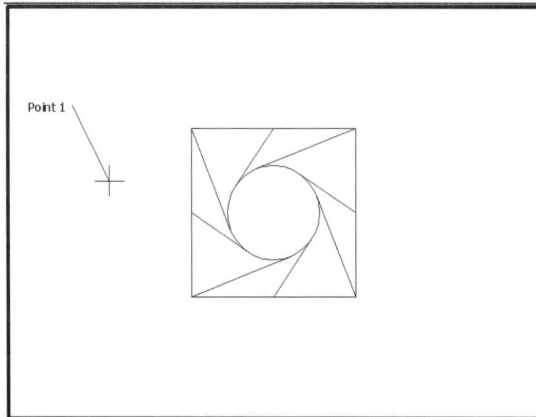

Figure 6-11

As a reminder:
1. Right Click on the Osnap button.
2. Select Settings....
3. Check Endpoint, and uncheck everything else.
4. Click on OK.

⊕ Click the Otrack button on the status bar so that it is in the on position.
⊕ Enter the LINE command.
⊕ Select a first point to the left of the square and circle even with the top of the square, as shown by Point 1 in Figure 6-11.

Point Acquisition

To take the next step, you will need to learn a new technique called point acquisition. Before a point can be used for object snap tracking it must be acquired, which is a form of selection. To acquire a point, move the cursor over it so that the object snap marker shows and pause for about a second without clicking. Try it.

⊕ Move the cursor over the lower left corner of the square, Point 2 in Figure 6-12, so that the end point marker appears.

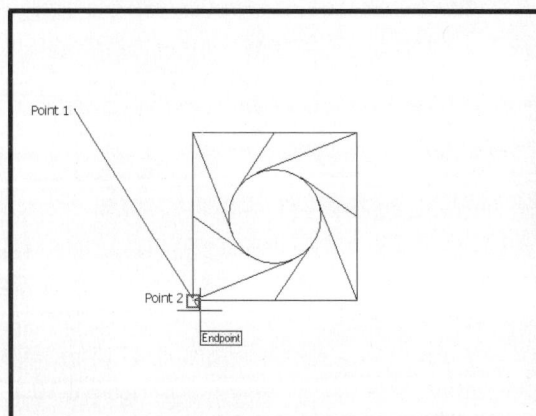

Figure 6-12

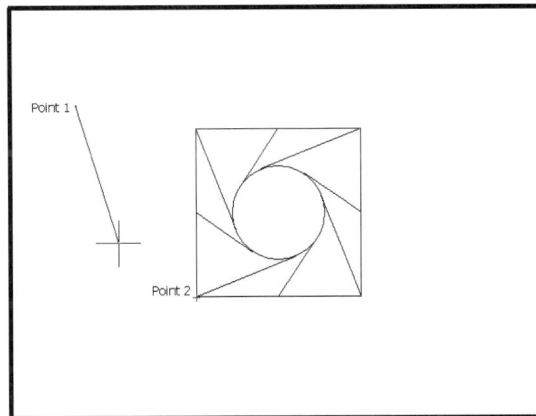

Figure 6-13

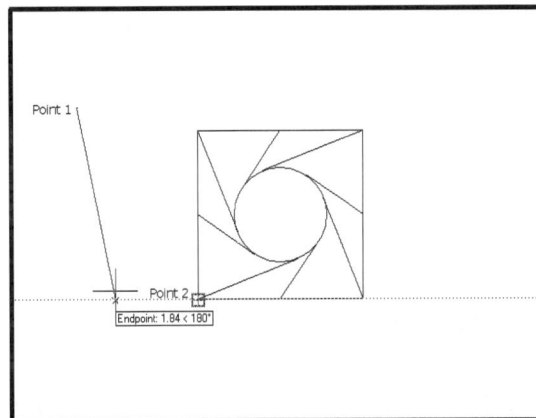

Figure 6-14

⊕ Pause...

⊕ Now move the cursor away from the corner.

If you have done this correctly, a small yellow cross will appear at the corner intersection, as shown in Figure 6-13, indicating that this point has been acquired for object snap tracking. (Repeating this procedure over the same point will remove the cross.)

⊕ Move the cursor to a position left of Point 2 and even with the horizontal lower side of the square, as shown in Figure 6-14.

You will see a construction line and a tracking tip like those in Figure 6-14.

⊕ Now move the cursor over and down to a position even with and below the vertical left side of the square, as shown in Figure 6-15.

You will see a different construction line and tracking tip, like those in Figure 6-15.

These construction lines are interesting, but they do not accomplish a great deal since your square is probably constructed on grid snap points anyway. So

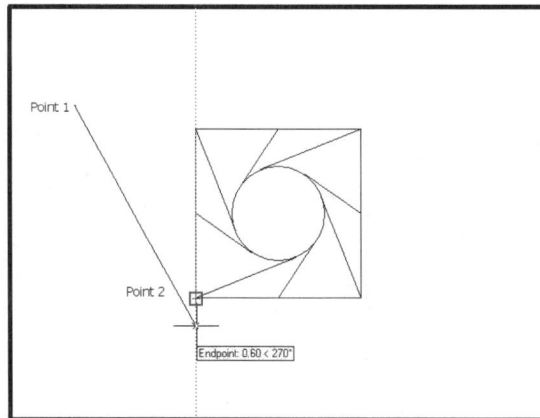

Figure 6-15

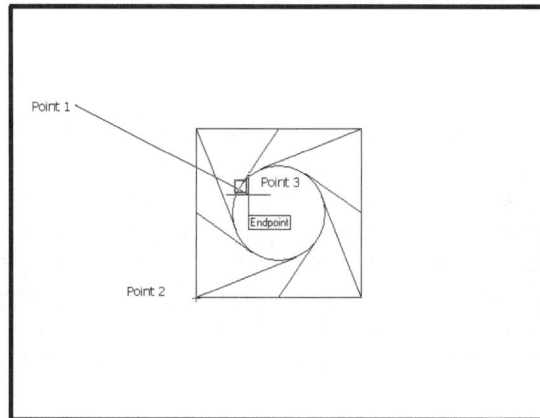

Figure 6-16

let's try something more difficult and a lot more interesting. Here we will use two acquired points to locate a point that currently is not specifiable either in object snap or incremental snap.

⊕ Move the cursor up and acquire Point 3, as shown in Figure 6-16.

Point 3 is the end point of the line drawn from the midpoint of the top side of the square to a point tangent to the circle. You should now have two acquired points, with two yellow crosses showing, one at Point 2 and one at Point 3.

⊕ Move the cursor slowly up along the left side of the square.

You are looking for Point 4, the point where the vertical tracking line from point A intersects the horizontal tracking line from point B. When you near it your screen should resemble Figure 6-17. Notice the double tracking tip "Endpoint: <90, Endpoint: <180".

⊕ With the double tracking tip and the two tracking lines showing, press the pickbutton.

A line will be drawn from Point 1 to Point 4.

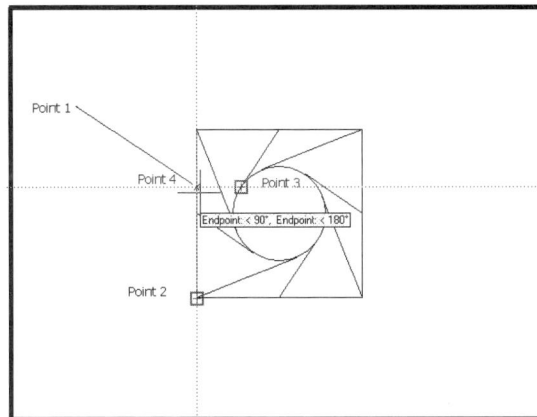

Figure 6-17

Before going on, we need to turn off the running osnap to endpoint mode.

⊕   Click the Osnap button or press F3 to turn off running Osnap modes.

If you have followed this exercise closely, you have already increased greatly the power of your understanding of CAD technique. You will find many opportunities to use Object Snap and Object Snap Tracking from now on.

Next we will move on to a very powerful editing command called OFFSET. Before leaving Object Snap, be sure that you have studied the chart in Figure 6-10, which shows examples of all the Object Snap modes.

6.4   Using the OFFSET Command (Creating Parallel Objects with OFFSET)

GENERAL PROCEDURE

1. Select the Offset tool from the Modify toolbar.
2. Type or show an offset distance.
3. Select object to offset.
4. Show which side to offset.

OFFSET is one of the most powerful editing commands in AutoCAD. With the combination of Object Snap and the OFFSET command you can become completely free of incremental snap and grid points. Any point in the drawing space can be precisely located. Essentially, OFFSET creates parallel copies of lines, circles, arcs, or polylines. You will find a number of typical applications in the drawings at the end of this chapter. In this brief exercise we will perform an offset operation to draw some lines through points that would be very difficult to locate without OFFSET.

Figure 6-18

⊕ Select Offset from the Modify menu, or the Offset tool from the Modify toolbar, as shown in Figure 6-18.

AutoCAD prompts:

```
Specify offset distance or [Through]:
```

There are three methods. You can type a distance, show a distance with two points, or pick a point that you want the new copy to run through (the through option). We will type a distance.

⊕ Type ".258".

We have chosen this rather odd number to make the point that this command can help you locate positions that would be difficult to find otherwise. AutoCAD prompts for an object:

```
Select object to offset or <exit>:
```

⊕ Type "l" for last, or select the diagonal line drawn in the last exercise.

AutoCAD now needs to know whether to create the offset image above or below the line:

```
Specify point on side to offset:
```

⊕ Pick a point anywhere below the line.

Your screen should now resemble Figure 6-19. AutoCAD continues to prompt for objects to offset using the same offset distance. You can continue to create offset objects at the same offset distance by pointing and clicking.

⊕ Pick the line just created.

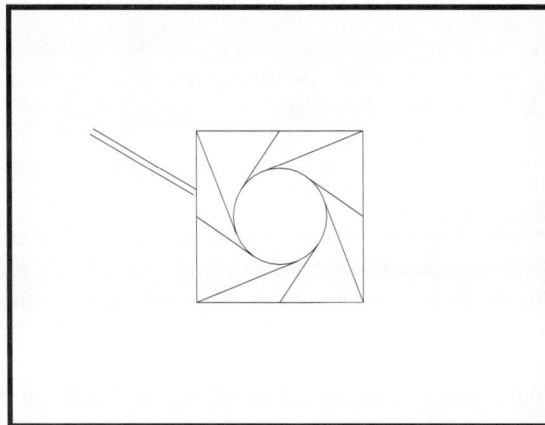

Figure 6-19

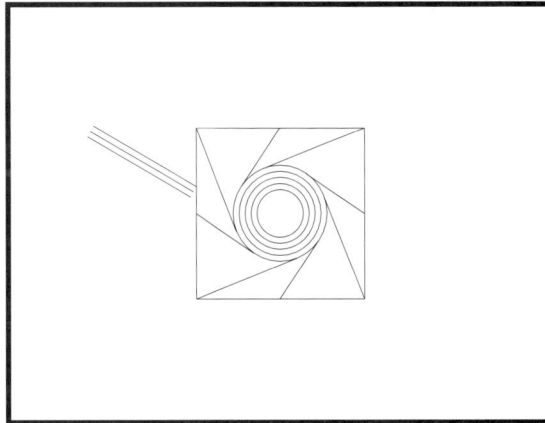

Figure 6-20

⊕ Pick any point below the line.

A second offset line will be added, as shown in Figure 6-20. As long as you stay within the OFFSET command you can select any object to offset using the same offset distance.

⊕ Pick the circle in the square.

⊕ Pick any point inside the circle.

An offset circle will be added, as shown in Figure 6-20.

⊕ Continue pointing and clicking to create additional offset circles, as shown in Figure 6-20.

⊕ Press Enter to exit the OFFSET command.

When you exit OFFSET, the offset distance will be retained as the default, so you can return to the command and continue using the same distance.

Next we will turn to five useful commands that allow you to shorten and lengthen objects.

6.5 BREAKing Previously Drawn Objects

GENERAL PROCEDURE

1. Type "Br", select Break from the Modify menu, or select the Break tool from the Modify toolbar.
2. Select an object to be broken.
3. Show the first point of the break.
4. Show the second point of the break.

The BREAK command allows you to break an object on the screen into two entities, or to cut a segment out of the middle or off the end. The command sequence is similar for all options. The action taken will depend on the points you select for

Figure 6-21

breaking. BREAK works on lines, circles, arcs, and polylines (polylines are discussed in Chapter 9).

⊕ In preparation for this section, clear your screen of objects left over from previous tasks and draw a 5.0 horizontal line across the middle of your screen, as in Figure 6-21.

Exact lengths and coordinates are not important. Also, be sure to turn off object snap.

AutoCAD allows for four different ways to break an object, depending on whether the point you use to select the object is also to be considered a break point. You can break an object at one point or at two points, and you have the choice of using your object selection point as a break point.

We begin by breaking the line you have just drawn into two independent lines using a single break point, which is also the point used to select the line.

⊕ Type "br", select the Break tool from the Modify menu, or select the Break tool from the Modify toolbar, as shown in Figure 6-22.

Be aware that the noun/verb or pick first sequence does not work with BREAK.

AutoCAD will prompt you to select an object to break:

Select object:

You may select an object in any of the usual ways, but notice that you can only break one object at a time. If you try to select more—with a window, for

Figure 6-22

example—AutoCAD will highlight only one. Because of this you will best indicate the object you want to break by pointing to it.

Tip: Object snap modes work well in edit commands such as BREAK. If you wish to break a line at its midpoint, for example, you can use the midpoint object snap mode to select the line and the break point.

⊕   Select the line by picking any point near its middle. (The exact point is not critical; if it were, we would use a midpoint object snap.)

The line has now been selected for breaking, and since there can be only one object, you do not have to press Enter to end the selection process, as you often do in other editing commands. AutoCAD will prompt as follows:

Specify second break point or [First point]:

When you are selecting an object by pointing, AutoCAD will assume that the point you use for selection is also the first point of the break. It will be most efficient, therefore, if you do select the object with a break point. Then you can proceed by selecting the second point immediately. If not, type "f" and you will be prompted for the first break point, as the bracketed option tells you.

Having selected the object and the first break point, we now want to select a point that will break the object in two without erasing anything. To do this, simply pick the same point again.

⊕   Point to the same point that you just used to select the line, or type "@".

The "@" symbol is shorthand for the last point entered.

The break is complete. To demonstrate that the line is really two lines now, we will select the right half of it for our next break.

⊕   Press Enter or the space bar to repeat the BREAK command.

⊕   Point to the line on the right side of the last break.

The right side of the line should be highlighted, as in Figure 6-23. Clearly, the original line is now being treated as two separate entities.

Figure 6-23

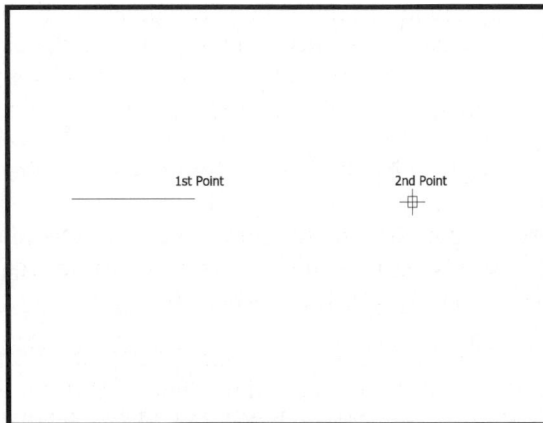

Figure 6-24

    We will shorten the end of this dotted section of the line. Assume that the point you just used to select the object is the point where you want it to end; now all you need to do is to select a second point anywhere beyond the right end of the line.

⊕   Select a second point beyond the right end of the line.

    Your line should now be shortened, as in Figure 6-24.

Next we will cut a piece out of the middle of the left side.

⊕   Press Enter or the space bar to repeat BREAK.

⊕   Select the left side of the original line with a point toward the left end.

    We want to cut a piece out of the middle of the left side, so the next point needs to be to the right of the first point, but still toward the middle of the left-hand line.

    Note: It is not necessary that the second point be on the line at all. It could be above or below it, as in Figure 6-25. AutoCAD will break the line along

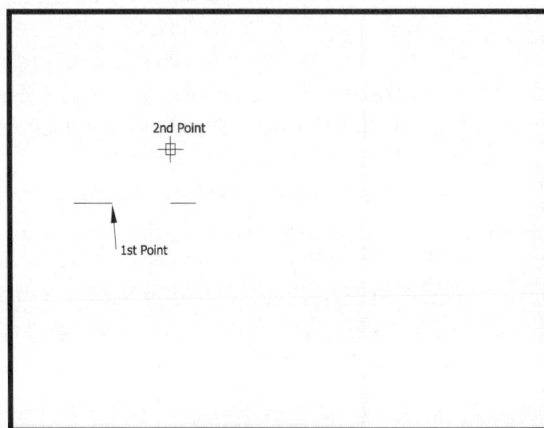

Figure 6-25

a perpendicular between the point we choose and the line we are breaking. The same system would apply if we were breaking a polyline. An arc or a circle would be broken along a line between the selected point and the center of the arc or circle.

⊕ Select a second point on or off the line, somewhat to the right of the first point.

Your line should now have a piece cut out, as in Figure 6-25. Notice that there are now three lines on the screen, one to the left and two shorter lines to the right of the last break.

BREAK is a useful command, but there are times when it is cumbersome to shorten objects one at a time. The TRIM command has some limitations that BREAK does not have, but it is much more efficient in situations where you want to shorten objects at intersections.

6.6 Shortening Objects with the TRIM Command

GENERAL PROCEDURE

1. Type "Tr" or select Trim from the Modify menu or the Trim tool from the Modify toolbar.
2. Select a cutting edge or edges.
3. Right click to end the cutting edge selection process.
4. Select object to trim.
5. Select other objects to trim.
6. Press Enter to return to "Command" prompt.

The TRIM command works wonders in many situations where you want to shorten objects at their intersections with other objects. It will work with lines, circles, arcs, and polylines (see Chapter 9). The only limitation is that you must have at least two objects and they must cross or meet. If you are not trimming to an intersection, use BREAK.

⊕ In preparation for exploring TRIM, clear your screen and then draw two horizontal lines crossing a circle, as in Figure 6-26. Exact locations and sizes are not important.

First we will use the TRIM command to go from Figure 6-26 to Figure 6-27.

⊕ Type "Tr" or select Trim from the Modify menu or the Trim tool from the Modify toolbar, as shown in Figure 6-28.

The first thing AutoCAD will want you to specify is at least one cutting edge. A cutting edge is an entity you want to use to trim another entity. That is, you want the trimmed entity to end at its intersection with the cutting edge.

```
Current settings: Projection=UCS, Edge=None
Select cutting edges...
Select objects:
```

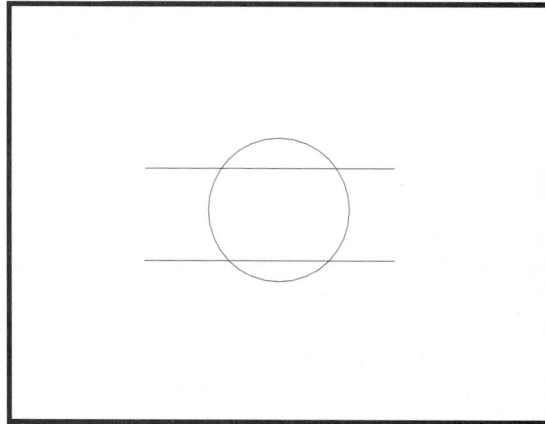

Figure 6-26

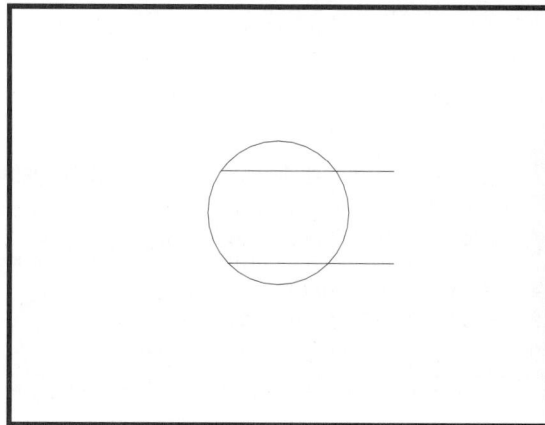

Figure 6-27

Figure 6-28

The current settings are relevant to 3D drawing and need not concern you at this point. (For your information, Projection and Edge refer to system variables that determine the way AutoCAD will interpret boundaries and intersections in 3D space.) The second line reminds you that you are selecting edges first—the objects you want to trim will be selected later. The option of selecting more than one edge is a useful one, as we will demonstrate shortly.

For now we will select the circle as an edge and use it to trim the upper line.

⊹   Point to the circle.

The circle becomes dotted and will remain so until you leave the TRIM command. AutoCAD will prompt for more objects until you indicate that you are through selecting edges.

⊕ **Right click to end the selection of cutting edges.**

You will be prompted for an object to trim:

`Select object to trim or [Project/Edge/Undo]:`

We will trim off the segment of the upper line that lies outside the circle on the left. The important thing is to point to the part of the object you want to remove, as shown in Figure 6-27.

⊕ **Point to the upper line to the left of where it crosses the circle.**

The line is trimmed immediately, but the circle is still dotted, and AutoCAD continues to prompt for more objects to trim. Note how this differs from the BREAK command, in which you could only break one object at a time.

Also notice that you have an undo option, so that if the trim does not turn out the way you wanted, you can back up without having to leave the command and start over.

⊕ **Point to the lower line to the left of where it crosses the circle.**

Now you have trimmed both lines.

⊕ **Press Enter or the space bar to end the TRIM operation.**

Your screen should resemble Figure 6-27.

This has been a very simple trimming process, but more complex trimming is just as easy. The key is that you can select as many edges as you like and that an entity may be selected as both an edge and an object to trim, as we will demonstrate.

⊕ **Repeat the TRIM command.**

⊕ **Select both lines and the circle as cutting edges.**

This can be done with a window or with a crossing box.

⊕ **Right click or press the space bar to end the selection of edges.**

⊕ **Point to each of the remaining two line segments that lie outside the circle on the right, and to the top and bottom arcs of the circle to produce the band-aid-shaped object in Figure 6-29.**

⊕ **Press Enter to exit the TRIM command.**

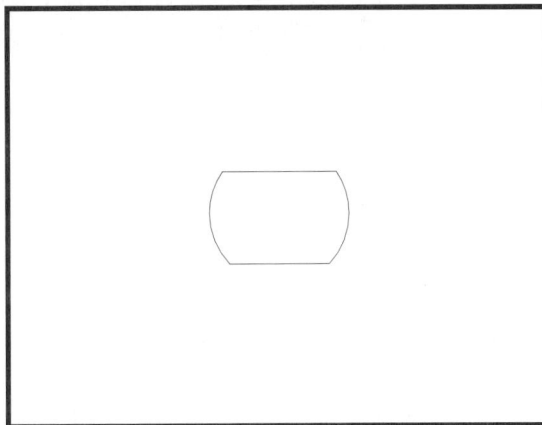

Figure 6-29

6.7 Extending Objects with the EXTEND Command

GENERAL PROCEDURE

1. Type "Ex" or select Extend from the Modify menu or the Extend tool from the Modify toolbar.
2. Select a boundary or boundaries.
3. Press Enter to end the boundary selection process.
4. Select object to extend.
5. Select other objects to extend.
6. Press Enter to return to the command prompt.

If you compare the procedures of the EXTEND command and the TRIM command, you will notice a remarkable similarity. Just substitute the word "boundary" for "cutting edge" and the word "extend" for "trim" and you've got it. These two commands are conceptually related and are so efficient that it is sometimes good practice to draw a temporary cutting edge or boundary on your screen and erase it after trimming or extending.

⊕ Leave Figure 6-29, the band aid, on your screen and draw a vertical line to the right of it, as in Figure 6-30.

We will use this line as a boundary to which to extend the two horizontal lines, as in Figure 6-31.

⊕ Type "Ex" or select Extend from the Modify menu or the Extend tool from the Modify toolbar, as shown in Figure 6-32.

You will be prompted for objects to serve as boundaries:

```
Current settings: Projection=UCS, Edge=None
Select boundary edges...
Select objects:
```

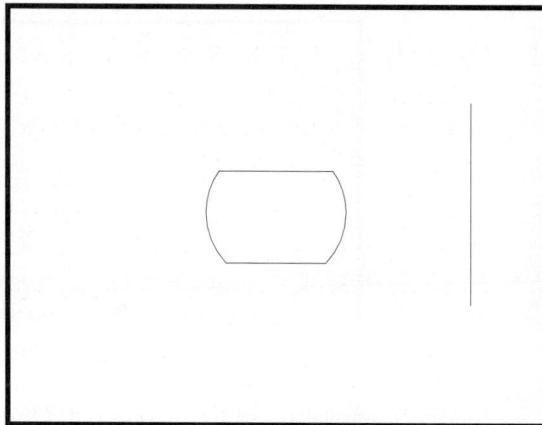

Figure 6-30

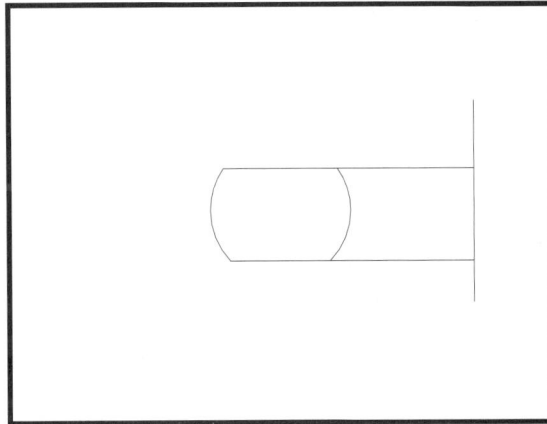

Figure 6-31

Figure 6-32

Look familiar? As with the TRIM command, any of the usual selection methods will work. For our purposes, simply point to the vertical line.

⊕ Point to the vertical line on the right.

You will be prompted for more boundary objects until you exit object selection.

⊕ Right click or press the space bar to end the selection of boundaries.

AutoCAD now asks for objects to extend:

    Select object to extend or [Project/Edge/Undo]:

⊕ Point to the right half of one of the two horizontal lines.

Notice that you have to point to the line on the side closer to the selected boundary. Otherwise AutoCAD will look to the left instead of the right and give you the following message:

    Object does not intersect an Edge

Note also that you only can select objects to extend by pointing. Windowing, crossing, or last selections will not work. Also be aware that arcs and polylines can be extended in the same manner as lines.

⊕ Point to the right half of the other horizontal line. Both lines should be extended to the vertical line.

Your screen should resemble Figure 6-31.

⊕ Press the space bar to exit the EXTEND command.

6.8 Using STRETCH to Alter Objects Connected to Other Objects

---

GENERAL PROCEDURE

1. Type "S" or select the Stretch tool from the Modify toolbar or select Stretch from the Modify menu.
2. Select objects to stretch, using at least one window or crossing selection.
3. Press Enter to end selection.
4. Show the first point of stretch displacement.
5. Show the second point of stretch displacement.

The STRETCH command is a phenomenal timesaver in special circumstances in which you want to move objects without disrupting their connections to other objects. Often STRETCH can take the place of a whole series of moves, trims, breaks, and extends. It is commonly used in such applications as moving doors or windows within walls without having to redraw the walls.

The term "stretch" must be understood to have a special meaning in AutoCAD. When a typical stretch is performed, some objects are lengthened, while others are shortened, and others are simply moved.

There is also a stretch mode in the grip edit system, as we have seen previously. We will take a look at it later in this section.

First, we will do a simple stretch on the objects you have already drawn on your screen. This will give you a good basic understanding of the STRETCH command. Further experimentation on your own is recommended.

⊹ Type "S" or select Stretch from the Modify menu or select the Stretch tool from the Modify toolbar, illustrated in Figure 6-33.

AutoCAD will prompt for objects to stretch in the following manner:

```
Select objects to stretch by crossing-window
or crossing-polygon...
```

This prompt reminds you of a unique quality of the STRETCH command procedure. You must include at least one crossing-window or crossing-polygon selection in your selection set. Beyond that you can include other selection types as well. This ensures that you will include all the objects in an intersection in the stretch procedure. If this is not your intent, you probably should be using a different modifying command.

⊹ Point to the first corner of a crossing box, as shown by point 1 (P1) in Figure 6-34.

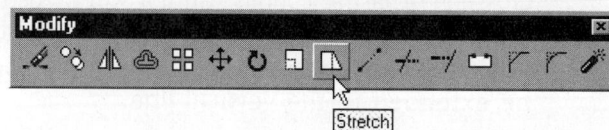

Figure 6-33

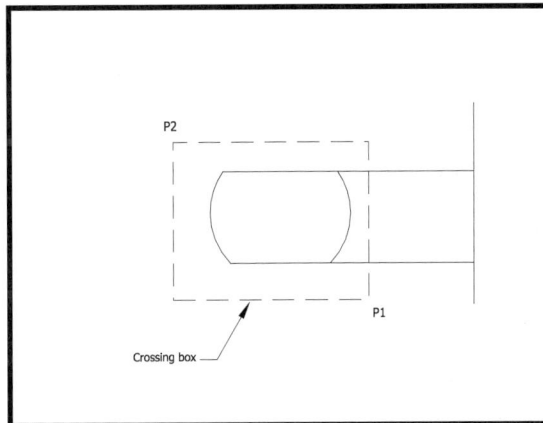

Figure 6-34

AutoCAD will prompt for a second corner:

Specify opposite corner:

✛ Point to a second corner, as shown by point 2 (P2) in the figure.

AutoCAD will continue to prompt for objects, so we need to show that we are through selecting.

✛ Right click or press the space bar to end the selection process.

Now you will need to show the degree and direction of stretch you want. In effect, you will be showing AutoCAD how far to move the objects that are completely within the box. Objects that cross the box will be extended or shrunk so that they remain connected to the objects that move.

The prompt sequence for this action is the same as the sequence for a move:

Specify base point or displacement:

✛ Pick any point near the middle of the screen, leaving room to indicate a horizontal displacement to the right, as illustrated in Figure 6-35.

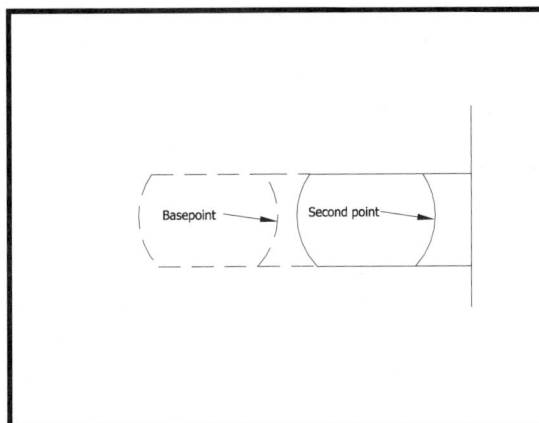

Figure 6-35

AutoCAD prompts:

> Specify second point of displacement:

⊕ Pick a second point to the right of the first, as shown in Figure 6-35.

Having ortho on will ensure a horizontal move (F8).

The arcs will be moved to the right and the horizontal lines will be shrunk as shown. Notice that nothing here is literally being stretched. The arcs are being moved and the lines are being compressed. This is one of the ways STRETCH can be used.

⊕ Try performing another stretch like the one illustrated in Figures 6-36 and 6-37.

Here the lines are being lengthened, while one arc moves and the other stays put, so that the original band aid is indeed stretched.

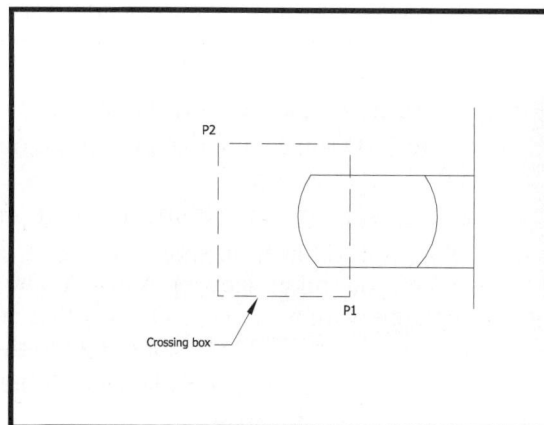

Figure 6-36

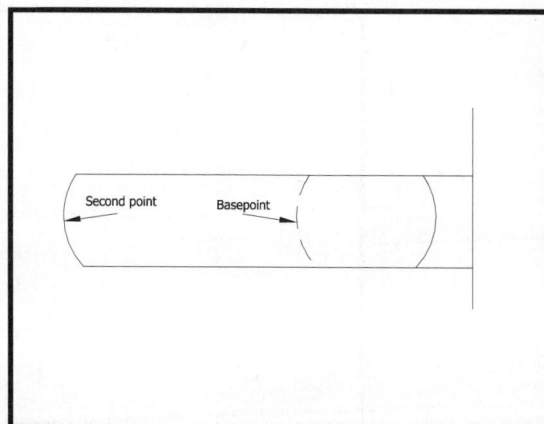

Figure 6-37

Stretching with Grips

Stretching with grips is a simple operation and is best reserved for simple stretches. Stretches like the ones you have just performed with the STRETCH command are possible in grip editing, but they require careful selection of multiple grips. The results are not always what you expect, and it takes more time to complete the process. The type of stretch that works best with grips is illustrated in the following exercise.

⊕ Pick the lower horizontal line.

The line will be highlighted and grips will appear.

⊕ Pick the vertical line.

Now both lines should appear with grips, as in Figure 6-38. We will use one grip on the horizontal line and one on the vertical line to create Figure 6-39.

⊕ Pick the grip at the right end of the horizontal line.

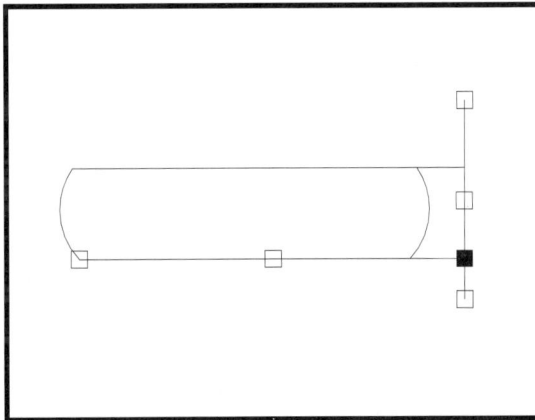

Figure 6-38

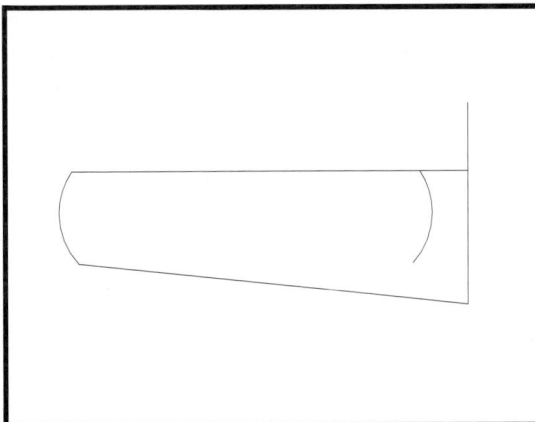

Figure 6-39

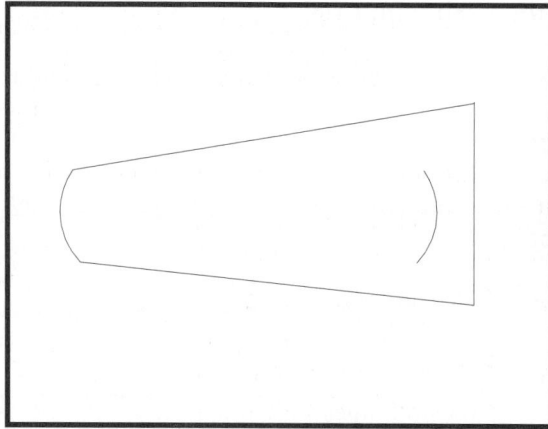

Figure 6-40

As soon as you press the pickbutton, the autoedit system puts you into STRETCH mode and the grip will change color.

In the command area you will see the following:

```
**STRETCH**
Specify stretch point or [Base point/Copy/Undo/eXit]:
```

We will stretch the line to end at the lower end point of the vertical line.

⊕ **Move the cross hairs slowly downward and observe the screen.**

If ortho is off, you will see two rubber bands. One represents the line you are stretching, and the other connects the cross hairs to the grip you are manipulating.

⊕ **Pick the grip at the bottom of the vertical line.**

Your screen should resemble Figure 6-39. Notice how the grip on the vertical line works like an object snap point.

⊕ **Try one more grip stretch to create Figure 6-40. Stretch the end point of the upper line just as you did the lower.**

In the next task you will learn the LENGTHEN command—one more edit command for changing the lengths of lines and arcs.

6.9 Changing Lengths with the LENGTHEN Command

GENERAL PROCEDURE

1. Select the Lengthen tool from the Modify toolbar or select Lengthen from the Modify menu.
2. Type initials to specify a length option.
3. If necessary, type a value.
4. Select an object to lengthen.
5. Select another object or press enter to exit the command.

Figure 6-41

The LENGTHEN command can be used to lengthen or shorten lines, polylines, and arcs using four different methods. In this exercise we will use two methods to manipulate further the objects in Figure 6-40. We will begin by lengthening and then shortening the vertical line at the right of the figure.

⊕ Select Lengthen from the Modify menu, or the Lengthen tool from the Modify toolbar, illustrated in Figure 6-41.

The prompt that follows shows the different lengthening methods:

Select an object or [DElta/Percent/Total/DYnamic]:

Delta lengthens an object by a specified amount, Percent by a percent of the current length. Total changes the current length to a specified value, and Dynamic allows you to change length by cursor movement. If you select an object at this prompt, its current length will be reported in the command area. We will work with Delta and Dynamic.

⊕ Type "de" for the delta option.

AutoCAD prompts:

Enter Delta length or [Angle] <0.00>:

Angle will allow you to lengthen an arc by a specified angle. To change a linear length, type in a value. A positive value will cause objects to be lengthened, while a negative value will cause shortening.

⊕ Type "1".

AutoCAD prompts you to select an object:

Select an object to change or [Undo]:

⊕ Pick a selection point on the upper half of the vertical line.

The object will be lengthened by one unit upward, as shown in Figure 6-42. AutoCAD will continue to prompt for objects. You can select any line, arc,

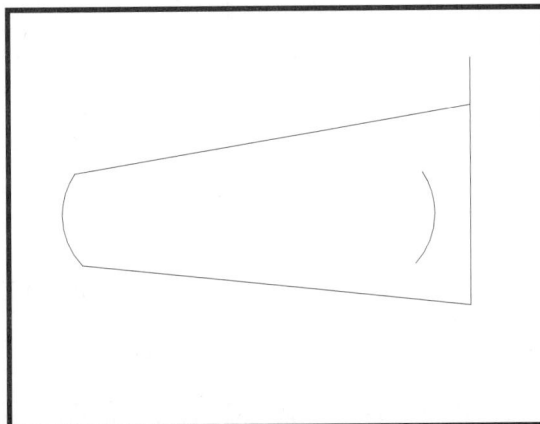

Figure 6-42

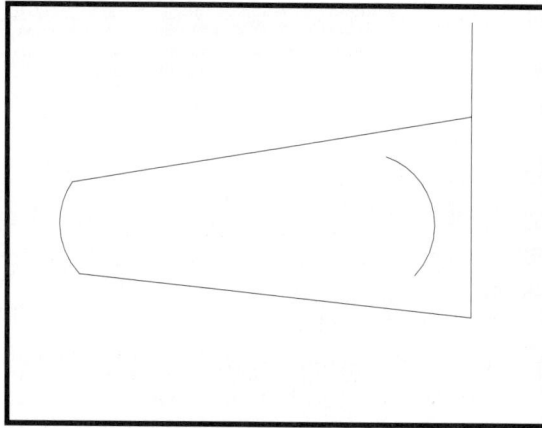

Figure 6-43

or polyline. Also, you can pick the same line again to add another one-unit length. Try it.

⊕ Pick another point on the upper half of the vertical line.

The object will be lengthened again.

Now try lengthening the arc in the middle of the figure.

⊕ Pick a point on the upper half of the arc.

The arc will be lengthened by one unit along a circular path, as shown in Figure 6-43.

Now try the Dynamic option.

⊕ Press enter or the space bar to exit LENGTHEN.

⊕ Press enter or the space bar again to repeat the command.

⊕ Type "dy" for the Dynamic option.

You are prompted to select objects.

⊕ Select the angled line at the top of the drawing, choosing a point on the right half of the line.

AutoCAD will show a rubber band and will lengthen or shorten the selected line dynamically as you move the cursor.

⊕ Move the cursor back and forth on the screen to get a feel for how the rubber band and cross hairs work in this command option.

⊕ Select any point and observe the resulting change.

⊕ Type "u" to undo the change.

You may wish to continue experimenting with LENGTHEN. We encourage you to try out the percent and total options, to use positive and negative values, and to select arcs and lines to observe the results.

In the next task you will take a giant leap in plotting technique as you begin to use paper space, multiple layouts, and multiple viewports within layouts.

6.10   Creating Plot Layouts

GENERAL PROCEDURE

1. Right click a layout tab and select "New layout".
2. Define or select a page setup.
3. Create paper space viewports.
4. Switch to model space to position or edit objects in the drawing.
5. Switch to paper space to plot.
6. Type or select "Plot".
7. Preview plot, change parameters, and execute plotting as usual.

Up until now we have plotted everything directly from model space. Plotting from model space has its uses, particularly in the early stages of a design process. But when your focus shifts from modeling issues to presentation issues, paper space layouts have much more to offer. The separation of model space and paper space in AutoCAD 2000 allows you to focus entirely on modeling and real world dimensions when you are drawing, and then shift your focus to paper output issues when you plot. On the drafting board, all drawings are committed to paper from the start. People doing manual drafting are inevitably conscious of scale, paper size, and rotation from start to finish. When draftspeople first begin using CAD systems, they still tend to think in terms of the final hard copy their plotter will produce even as they are creating lines on the screen. The AutoCAD 2000 plotting system takes full advantage of the powers of a CAD system, allowing us to ignore scale and other drawing paper issues entirely, if we wish, until it is time to plot.

In addition, the paper space world will allow us to create multiple views of the same objects without copying or redrawing them, and to plot these viewports simultaneously. In this task we will create two layouts of Drawing 5-1, the "Flanged Bushing" from the last chapter. The first will contain only one viewport. The second will be used to demonstrate some basic principles of working with multiple viewports. You can work through the exercise with whatever objects or drawing you have on your screen, but the illustrations will make more sense if you use Drawing 5-1 as shown. One word of caution: Drawing 5-1 was created on a 12 × 9 grid. If your drawing is on a different scale you will get different results.

Opening Layout1

⊕ To begin this exercise you should have on your screen a drawing you want to plot showing some close-up views.

   We have used Drawing 5-1, shown in Figure 6-44, for illustration.

⊕ Before leaving model space, turn off the grid (F7).

   Layouts have their own grid, so if you leave the model space grid on you will see overlapping grids that are very confusing.

⊕ Click the Layout1 tab at the bottom of the drawing area.

   This may call up the Page Setup dialog box discussed in Chapter 4 automatically. If so, you can ignore it for now. We will return to it for the next layout.

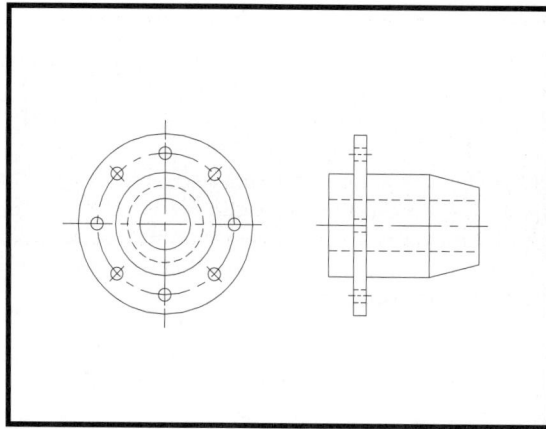

Figure 6-44

✦ If necessary, close the Page Setup dialog box.

Once the dialog box is closed you should see an image similar to the one in Figure 6-45. This is a simple one-viewport layout. AutoCAD has automatically created a single viewport determined by the extents of your drawing. Paper space viewports are sometimes called floating viewports because they can be moved and reshaped. They are somewhat like windows from paper space into model space. Try this:

✦ Select the viewport border, just as you would select any AutoCAD object.

Floating viewports are, in fact, AutoCAD objects and are treated and stored as such. You can move them, stretch them, copy them, and erase them. Editing the viewport will not affect the model space objects within the viewport. When a viewport is selected the border will be highlighted and grips will be shown at each corner.

✦ Type "e" or select the Erase tool from the Modify toolbar.

This will eliminate the viewport and leave you with the image of a blank sheet of paper. Without a viewport you have no view of model space.

✦ Undo the Erase to bring the viewport back.

✦ Now try to select any of the objects within the viewport.

You will find that you cannot. As long as you are in paper space, model space objects are not accessible. To gain access to model space objects while in a layout view, you must work in model space inside a selected viewport. In AutoCAD 2000 this is easily done by double clicking inside a viewport.

✦ Double click anywhere within the viewport.

Two things will happen. The border of the viewport will taken on a bold outline and the Paper button on the status bar will switch to Model, indicating that you are now in model space. You will also notice that the MSPACE command has been entered at the command prompt. Notice the difference between working within a viewport in a layout and switching into model

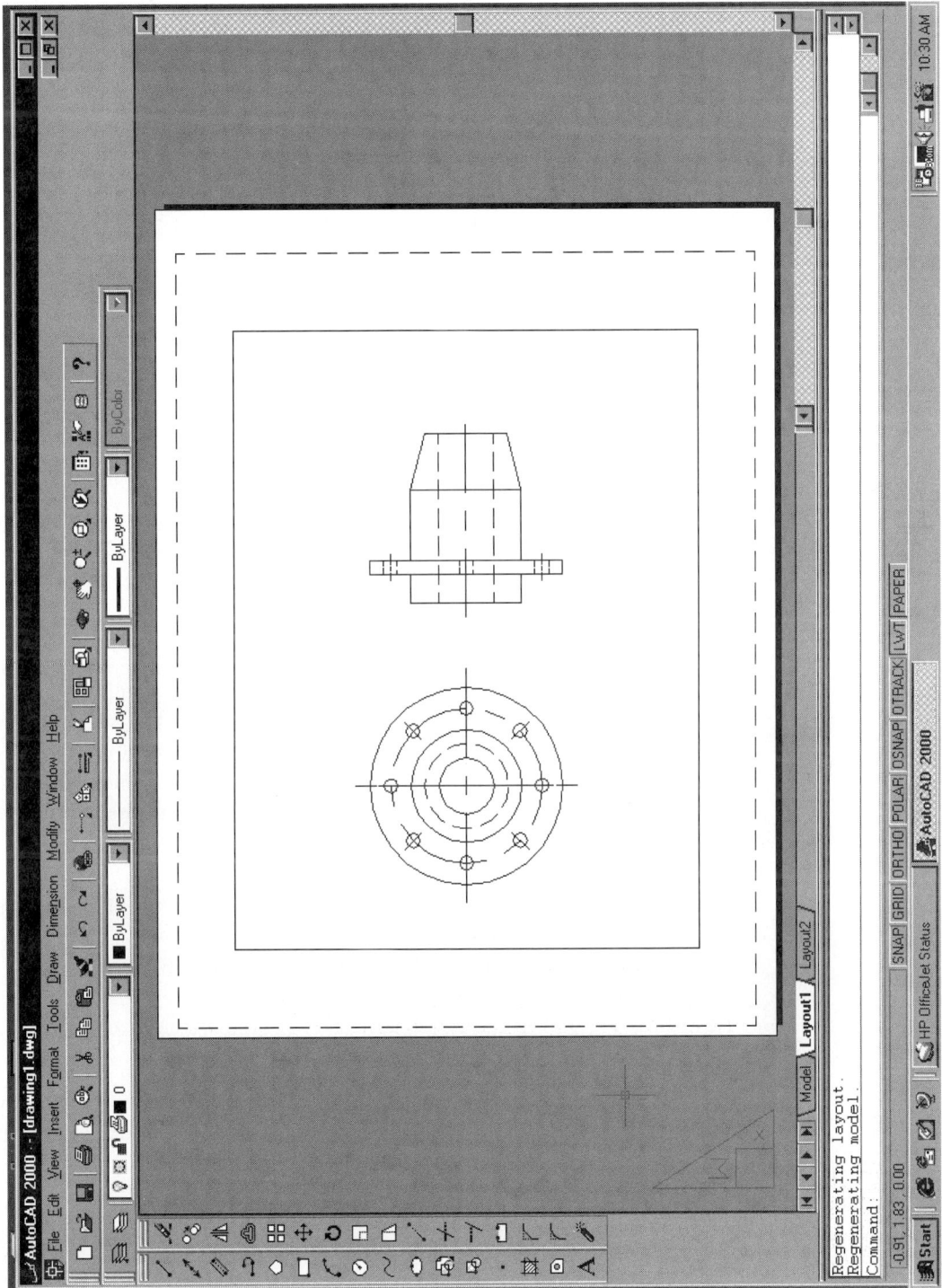

Figure 6-45

space by clicking on the model tab. If you click on the model tab, the layout will disappear and you will be back in the familiar model space drawing area.

⊕ **Try selecting objects in your viewport again.**

Model space objects are now available for editing or positioning within the viewport. While in the model space of a viewport, you cannot select any objects drawn in paper space, including the viewport border.

⊕ **Try selecting the viewport border.**

You will not have access to this paper space object.

⊕ **Double click anywhere outside the viewport border.**

This will return you to paper space.

Next we will create a more complex layout.

Creating a New Layout

Layouts are saved automatically and assigned to tabs. You can create new layouts and layout tabs, and you can delete any layout tab. You cannot delete the model tab. There are several ways to create a new layout. The simplest is to use the layout short cut menu. You probably already have Layout1 and Layout2 tabs, so we will create a Layout3 tab and rename it.

⊕ **Right click on the Layout1 or Layout2 tab.**

This will open a short cut menu with the following options: New layout, which creates a new tab; From template, which creates a new layout from a layout template; Delete, which deletes the currently selected layout; Rename, to rename the selected layout tab; Move or Copy, which can be used to copy a layout or change the order of tabs; and Select all layouts, which allows all layouts to be sent to the plotter at once. The bottom panel of the menu gives convenient access to the Page Setup and Plot dialog boxes.

⊕ **Select New layout from the short cut menu.**

A Layout3 tab will be added (if you have no Layout2, then Layout2 will be added instead).

⊕ **Right click on the Layout3 tab to open the short cut menu again.**

⊕ **Select Rename.**

A simple Rename Layout dialog box will appear as shown in Figure 6-46.

⊕ **Type "3view" and click OK.**

The name on the Layout3 tab will change to "3view". We will enter this layout, change some page setup specifications, and create three floating viewports.

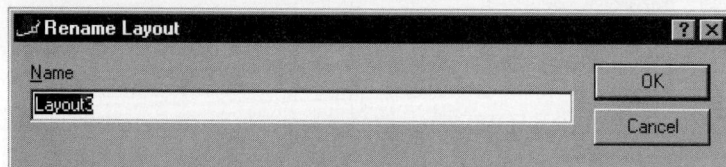

Figure 6-46

⊕ Select the 3view tab.

Your system may be set so that the Page Setup dialog box will appear automatically when you enter a new layout. If not, you should open Page Setup now, using the short cut menu.

⊕ If necessary, open the short cut menu and select Page Setup.

You can also open Page Setup from the File pull-down menu. As mentioned in the last chapter, the Page Setup dialog box is almost identical to the Plot dialog, without the preview buttons. Page setup is part of defining a layout for plotting, just as it is part of defining a plot from model space. In this case we will use a D size drawing sheet for illustration. If you do not have a D size plotter we recommend that you use AutoCAD's ePlot driver, which is designed to create electronic plots that can be sent out over the Internet or a local network. If you prefer to use a different size paper you will have to make adjustments as you go along. Using A size, for example, most specifications can be divided by four. We will include A size specifications at critical points in case you have don't have access to a D size plotter or want to use a printer.

⊕ Select the Plot Device tab from the Page Setup dialog box.
⊕ Select a plotting device that has a D size sheet option (DWF ePlot is recommended).
⊕ Select the Plot Settings tab.
⊕ Select an ANSI D (34 × 22).
⊕ If necessary, check Landscape.
⊕ Click OK to exit Page Setup.

Whatever size viewport AutoCAD 2000 has created will be okay, since we will erase it anyway.

⊕ Select the floating viewport and type "e" of select the Erase tool.

You are now looking at a blank sheet of paper in paper space once again. Take a moment to explore the limits of this drawing sheet.

⊕ Turn on the paper space grid (F7 or the Grid button on the status bar).
⊕ Turn incremental snap on (F9 or the Snap button on the status bar).
⊕ Move the cursor over the lower left corner of the paper grid and locate (0,0).

This will be the origin of the plot, indicated by the corner of the dashed border that shows the effective drawing area.

⊕ Move the cursor to the upper right corner of the effective drawing area.

This will be less than the limits of the grid. The exact point will depend on your plotter. With the AutoCAD 2000 DWF ePlot driver and D size paper, it will be (33.50,20.50).

Your screen is now truly representative of a drawing sheet. The plot will be made 1-to-1, with one paper space screen unit equaling 1 inch on the drawing sheet. There is little reason to do it any other way, since the whole point of paper space is to emulate the paper on the screen.

Now it is time to create viewports.

⊕   Type "Mv" or open the View menu, select Viewports, and then 1 Viewport.

Either of these methods will enter the MVIEW command. AutoCAD prompts:

```
Specify corner of viewport or
[ON/OFF/Fit/Hideplot/Lock/Object/Polygonal/Restore/2/3/4] <Fit>:
```

We will deal only with the specify corner option in this exercise. With this option you create a viewport just as you would a selection window.

⊕   Pick point (1.00,1.00) at the lower left of your screen, as shown in Figure 6-47.

If you are not using D size paper you will do fine by making your viewports resemble ours in size, shape, and location.

⊕   Pick an opposite corner, as shown in Figure 6-47. This will be (20,13) on a D size sheet.

Your screen will be redrawn with the drawing extents at maximum scale centered within the viewport.

Now we will create a second viewport to the right of the first.

⊕   Repeat MVIEW.

⊕   Pick point (24.00,1.00), as shown in Figure 6-47.

⊕   Pick point (32.00,13.00), as shown.

You have now created a second viewport. Notice that the images in the two viewports are drawn at different scales. Each is drawn to fit within its viewport. This can create problems later when you add dimension and text. You will want to maintain control over the scale of objects within viewports and have a clear knowledge of the relationships among scales in different viewports. For this we use the ZOOM scale feature of the ZOOM command. We will create different zoom magnifications inside the two viewports.

⊕   Double click inside the left viewport.

This takes you into model space within the left viewport. We are going to zoom so that the two-view drawing is in a precise and known scale relation to paper space.

⊕   Type "z" to enter the ZOOM command.

Notice the ZOOM command prompt:

```
 Specify corner of window, enter a scale factor (nX or nXP), or
[All/Center/Dynamic/Extents/Previous/Scale/Window] <real time>:
```

In this task we will use two new options, the paper space scale factor option (nXP) and the Center option.

⊕   Type "2xp" (on A size paper divide these factors by four, so you will use .5xp).

This will create only a slight change in the left viewport. "XP" means "times paper." It allows you to zoom relative to paper space units. If you zoom 1xp, then a model space unit will take on the size of a current paper space unit, which in turn equals 1 inch of drawing paper. We zoomed 2xp. This will mean that one unit in the viewport will equal two paper space units, or 2 inches on paper. We now have a precise relationship between model

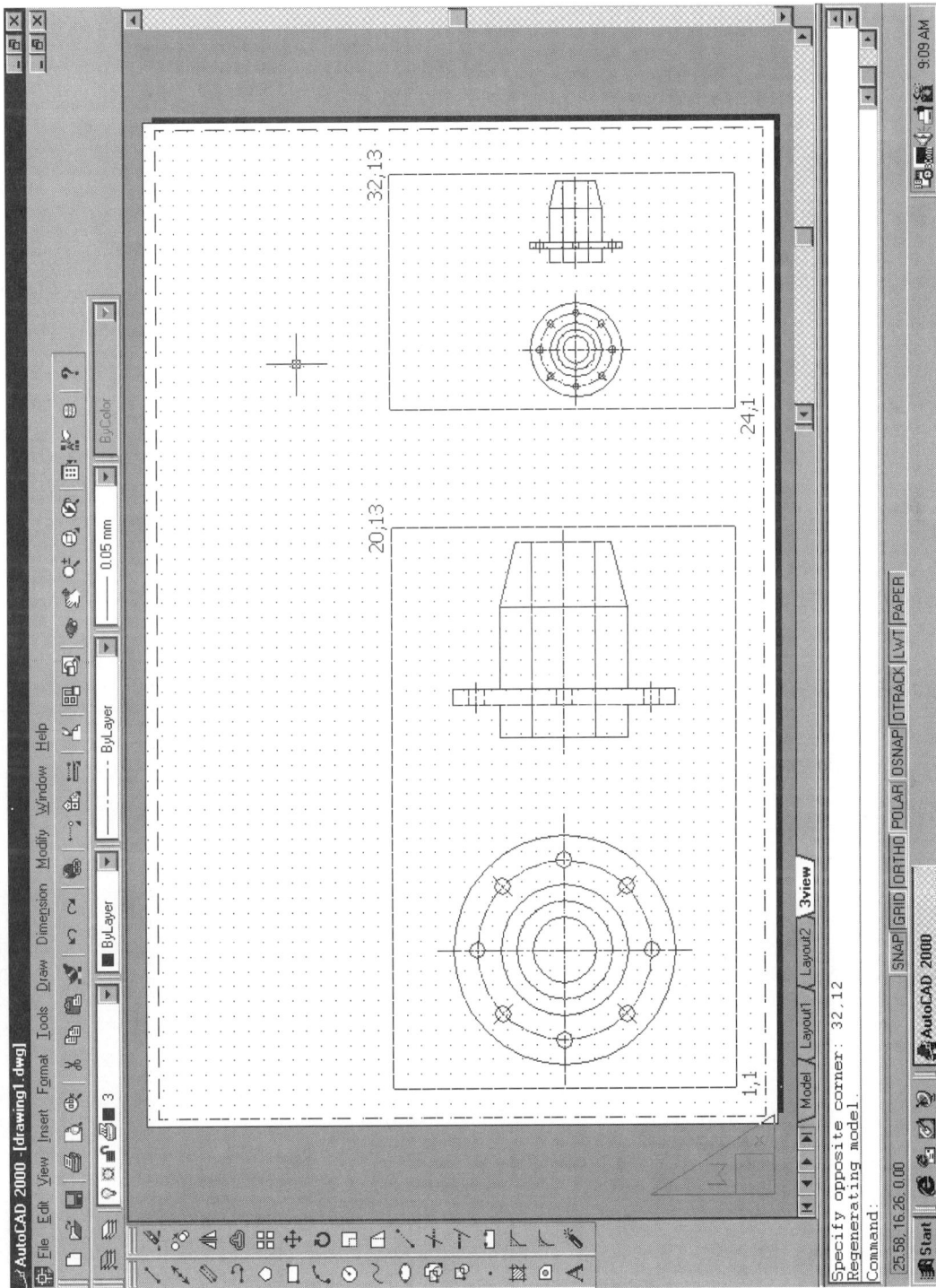

Figure 6-47

space and paper space in this viewport. The change in presentation size is trivial, but the change in terms of understanding and control is great.

Now we will set an XP zoom factor in the right viewport so that we control not only the model space/paper space scale relations, but the scale relations among viewports as well.

⊕ Click inside the right viewport to make it active.

You are already in model space, so double clicking is unnecessary.

⊕ Re-enter the ZOOM command.

In the right viewport we are going to show a close-up image of the right side view. To accomplish this we need a larger zoom factor and we need to be centered on the right side view.

⊕ Type "c" for the Center option.

AutoCAD asks you to specify a center point.

⊕ Pick a point on the center line near the center of the flange.

Look at Figure 6-48. The point you select will become the center point of the right viewport when AutoCAD zooms in.

Auto prompts:

```
Enter magnification or height<3.00>:
```

Accepting the default would simply center the image in the viewport. We will specify an XP value here.

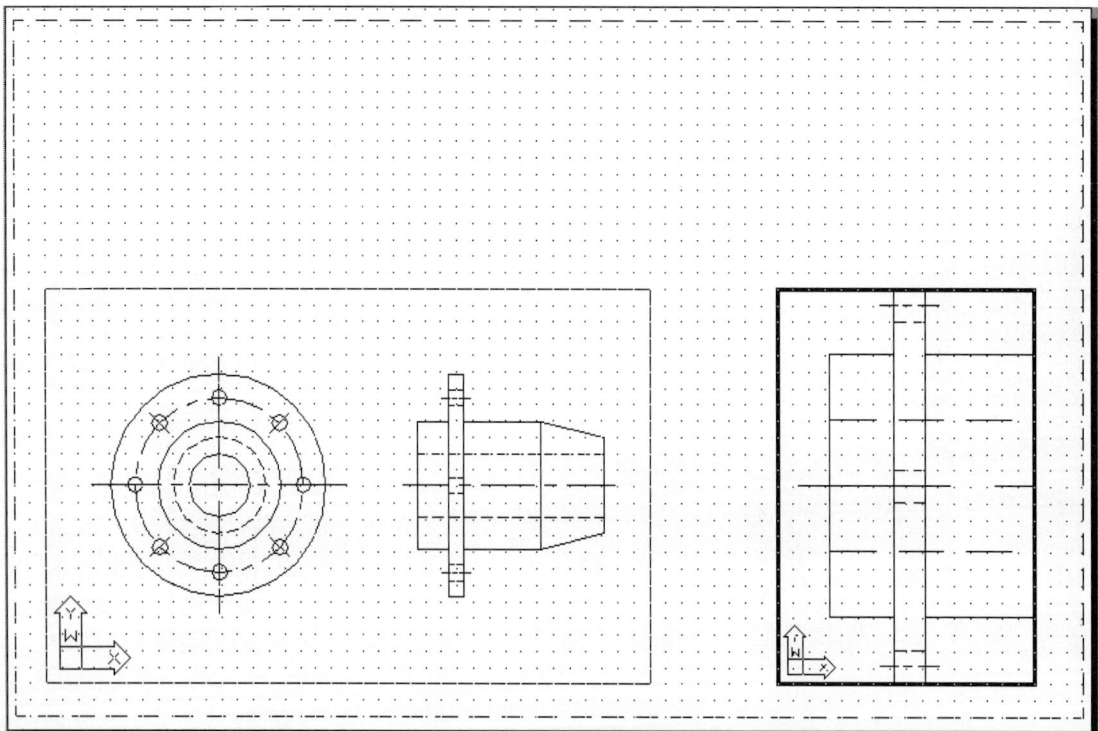

Figure 6-48

⊕ Type "4xp".

Your right viewport will be redrawn to resemble the one in Figure 6-48. In this enlarged image one model space unit equals 4 inches in the drawing sheet (1 = 1 on A size).

Tip: You may wish to pan slightly to the left or right to position the image in the viewport. Notice that you can use the scroll bars to pan inside the active viewport without losing horizontal or vertical alignment.

Now that you have the technique, we will create one more enlargement, focusing on one of the circle of holes in the flange.

⊕ Double click anywhere outside the two viewports to return to paper space.

⊕ Re-enter the MVIEW command.

⊕ Pick point (1.00,14.00).

⊕ Pick point (9.00,20.00).

⊕ Enter model space in the new viewport and zoom in, centering on the hole at the bottom of the flange, at 6 times paper in the new viewport.

This is tricky and will require the use of a Center or Quadrant object snap. Remember that you can access a single-point object snap by holding down Shift, right clicking, and then selecting from the Osnap short cut menu.

⊕ Open the View menu and select Regen All to regenerate the display and create truer circles.

Your screen should resemble Figure 6-49.

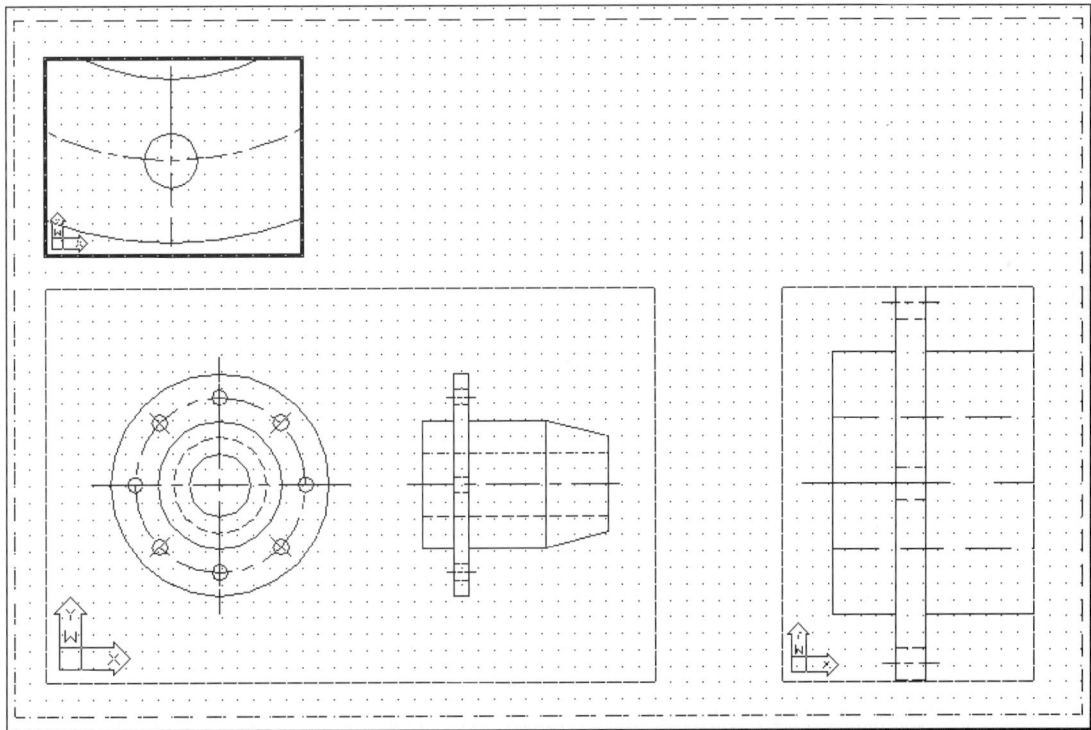

Figure 6-49

⊕   Before proceeding to plot, try a print preview to ensure that you are ready.
Select the Print preview tool from the Standard toolbar.

This full preview should look very much like the layout image. This is the beauty of the AutoCAD 2000 plotting system. You have a great deal of control and the ability to assess exactly what your paper output will be before you actually plot the drawing.

Plotting the Multiple-View Drawing

Now we are ready to plot. Plotting a multiple-viewport drawing is no different from plotting from a single view. But now that you have two or three different layouts as well as model space, you need to make sure the layout or layouts you want to plot are selected before you enter the Plot dialog.

> **Tip:** The selection controls for layout tabs are the same as those in Microsoft Office and other Windows applications. To Select two or more adjacent tabs, use Shift-Left click. To select individual layout tabs that are separated by other layout tabs, use Ctrl-Left click.

⊕   **With the 3view tab selected, select the Plot tool from the Standard toolbar, or right click on the 3view layout tab and select Plot... from the short cut menu.**

At this point you should have no need to adjust settings within the Plot dialog box since you have already made adjustments to the page setup and the plotting device. Notice that Layout is the default for Plot area.

⊕   **Prepare your plotter. (Make sure you use the right size paper.)**

⊕   **Click OK.**

> **Important:** *If you have been working with Drawing 5-1, be sure to save it with its multiple-viewport "3view" layout before leaving this chapter, because we will return to this it in Chapter 8 to explore scaling dimensions between model space and paper space.*

6.11   Review Material

Questions

1. Why is it important to keep Object Snap turned off when you are not using it? What are two simple ways to turn running Osnap on and off?
2. At what point in a command procedure would you use an object snap single-point override? How would you signal the AutoCAD program that you want to use an object snap?
3. How do you access the Object Snap short cut menu?
4. What is an acquired point? How do you acquire a point? How do you eliminate an acquired point?

5. How do you use BREAK to shorten a line at one end? When would you use this procedure instead of the TRIM command? How would you accomplish the same thing with LENGTHEN?
6. You have selected a line to extend and a boundary to extend it to, but Auto-CAD gives you a message that says "Object does not intersect an Edge". What happened?
7. What selection method is always required when you use the STRETCH command?
8. Why is it usual practice to plot 1 to 1 in paper space?
9. Why do we use the Zoom XP option when zooming in floating model space viewports?
10. How is CAD different from manual drafting with regard to issues of scaling and paper size?

Drawing Problems

1. Draw a line from (6,2) to (11,6). Draw a second line perpendicular to the first starting at (6,6).
2. Break the first line at its intersection with the second.
3. There are now three lines on the screen. Draw a circle centered at their intersection and passing through the midpoint of the line going up and to the right of the intersection.
4. Trim all the lines to the circumference of the circle.
5. Erase what is left of the line to the right of the intersection and trim the portion of the circle to the left, between the two remaining lines.

6.12   WWW Exercise #6 (Optional)

You will conclude Part I of your exploration of online CAD with two more Web sites that serve as launching pads with links to many other AutoCAD and CAD-related Web sites. In addition, we offer a challenge to create a design using object snap and a limited number of commands.

As you go, here is yet another way to access the Web without disrupting your AutoCAD 2000 drawing session. You already know, from previous chapters, how to configure AutoCAD so that AutoCAD's BROWSER command will take you directly to a default Web site without leaving your drawing session. Another way to get to frequently accessed pages quickly is to add them to your list of Favorites in your system's browser. With Windows 98, you can usually open your browser from a taskbar icon without closing or minimizing your current application (Auto-CAD 2000). Assuming, for example, that you have Windows 98 and Microsoft Internet Explorer 4.0 installed on your computer, the following procedure will allow you to open your browser and add our companion Web site to your list of favorites.

⊞   Connect to your Internet service provider.
⊞   Select the Launch Internet Explorer Browser button from the Windows 98 taskbar, as shown in Figure 6-50.

Figure 6-50

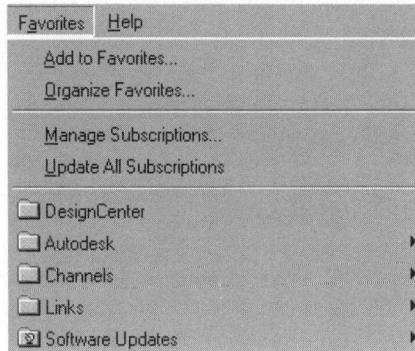

Figure 6-51

You will now be at your browser's home page, or whatever has been set as the default home page for your system.

⊞ Type in the address "www.prenhall.com/dixriley".

This will take you to our companion Web site. Before you proceed to Chapter 6, add our page to your Favorites list so you will not need to type in the address in the future.

⊞ Select Favorites from the Internet Explorer menu bar, as shown in Figure 6-51.

Use the menu selection, not the Favorites folder icon. The folder does not give you the Add option.

⊞ Select Add to Favorites... from the menu.

This will open an Add to Favorites dialog box, as shown in Figure 6-52.

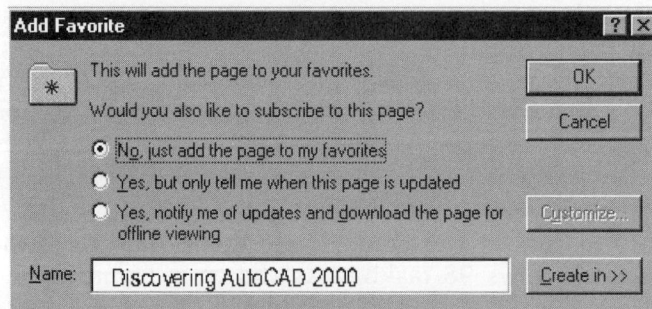

Figure 6-52

⊕ Check to see that the "No, just add the page to my favorites" radio button is selected.

⊕ Click OK to exit the dialog box.

From now on you can access the site with a few easy clicks. All you will need to do is the following:

1. Make sure you are connected to your Internet service provider.
2. Open your browser from the Windows 98 taskbar.
3. Open either the Favorites pull-down menu, or the Favorites folder icon.
4. Select *Discovering AutoCAD 2000* from the list of favorites.

Enjoy your visit.

6.13   Drawing 6-1: Bike Tire

This drawing can be done very quickly with the tools you now have. It makes use of one object snap, three trims, and a polar array. Be sure to set the limits large, as suggested.

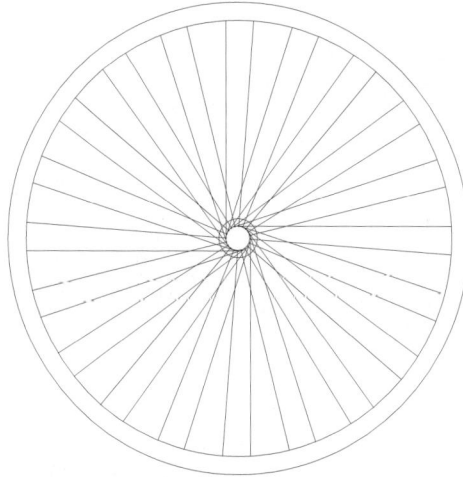

DRAWING SUGGESTIONS

GRID = 1.00
SNAP = 0.25
LIMITS = (0,0)(48,36)

- Begin by drawing the 1.25, 2.50, 24.00, and 26.00 diameter circles centered on the same point near the middle of your display.
- Draw line (a) using a Quadrant object snap to find the first point on the inside circle. The second point can be anywhere outside the 24 circle at 0 degrees from the first point. The exact length of the line is insignificant since you will trim it back to the circle.
- Draw line (b) from the center of the circles to a second point anywhere outside the 24 circle at an angle of 14 degrees. Use the coordinate display or polar tracking to construct this angle. This line also will be trimmed.
- Trim lines (a) and (b) using the 24 circle as a cutting edge.
- Trim the other end of line (b) using the 1.25 circle as a cutting edge.
- Construct a polar array, selecting lines (a) and (b). There are 20 items in the array, and they are rotated as they are copied.

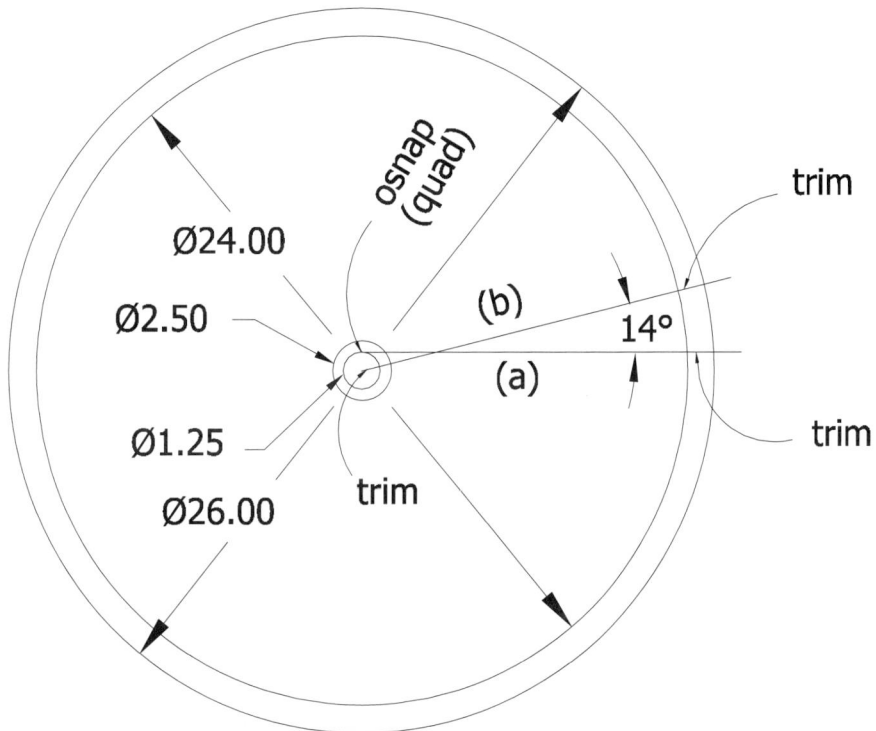

BIKE TIRE

Drawing 6-1

6.14   Drawing 6-2: Archimedes Spiral

This drawing and the next go together as an exercise you should find interesting and enjoyable. These are not technical drawings, but they will give you valuable experience with important CAD commands. You will be creating a spiral using a radial grid of circles and lines as a guide. Once the spiral is done, you will use it to create the designs in the next drawing, 6-3, "Spiral Designs."

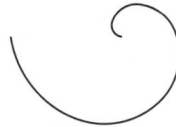

DRAWING SUGGESTIONS

GRID = 0.5   SNAP = 0.25
LIMITS = (0,0)(18,12)   LTSCALE = 0.5

- The alternating continuous and hidden lines work as a drawing aid. If you use different colors and layers, they will be more helpful. Since all circles are offset .50, you can draw one continuous and one hidden circle, then use the OFFSET command to create all the others.
- Begin by drawing one of the continuous circles on layer 0, centered near the middle of your display, then offset all the other continuous circles.
- Draw the continuous horizontal line across the middle of your six circles and then array it in a three-item polar array.
- Set to layer 2, draw one of the hidden circles, then offset the other hidden circles.
- Draw a vertical hidden line and array it as you did the horizontal continuous line.
- Set to layer 1 for the spiral itself.
- Turn on a running object snap to Intersection mode and construct a series of three-point arcs. Be sure to turn off any other modes that may get in your way. Start points and end points will be on continuous line intersections; second points always will fall on hidden line intersections.
- When the spiral is complete, turn off layers 0 and 2. There should be nothing left on your screen but the spiral itself. Save it or go on to Drawing 6-3.

GROUPING OBJECTS

Here is a good opportunity to use the GROUP command. GROUP is discussed more fully in Chapter 10, but you will find it useful here. GROUP defines a collection of objects as a single entity so that they may be selected and modified as a unit. The spiral you have just drawn will be used in the next drawing, and it will be easier to manipulate if you GROUP it. For more information, see Chapter 10.

1. Type "g".
2. In the Object Grouping dialog box, type "Spiral" for a group name.
3. Click on "New<".
4. Select the six arcs with a window.
5. Right click to end selection.
6. Click on OK.

The spiral can now be selected, moved, rotated, and copied as a single entity.

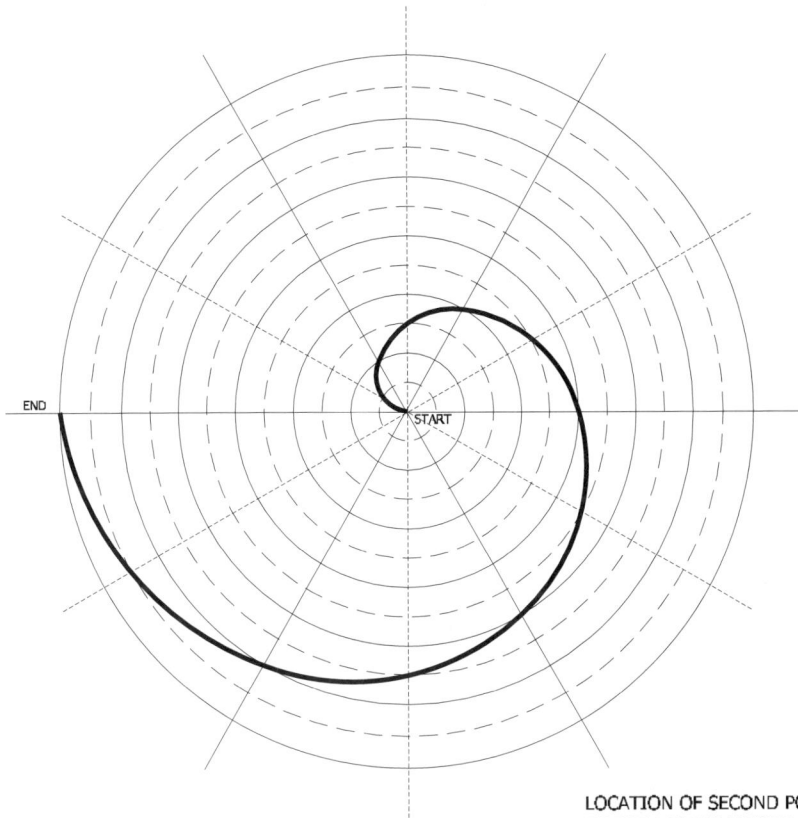

LOCATION OF SECOND POINT
OF EACH ARC IS WHERE
HIDDEN LINES INTERSECT

SOLID CIRCLE RADII	HIDDEN CIRCLE RADII
0.50	0.25
1.00	0.75
1.50	1.25
2.00	1.75
2.50	2.25
3.00	2.75

NOTE: THIS DRAWING IS USED
ON DRAWING 6-3

SAVE THIS DRAWING!

ARCHIMEDES SPIRAL

Drawing 6-2

6.15   Drawing 6-3: Spiral Designs

These designs are different from other drawings in this book. There are no dimensions, and you will use only edit commands now that the spiral is drawn. Below the designs is a list of the edit commands you will need. Don't be too concerned with precision. Some of your designs may come out slightly different from ours. When this happens, try to analyze the differences.

DRAWING SUGGESTIONS

$$\text{LIMITS} = (0,0)(34,24)$$

These large limits will be necessary if you wish to draw all of these designs on the screen at once.

In some of the designs and in Drawing 6-4 you will need to rotate a copy of the spiral and keep the original in place. You can accomplish this by using the grip edit rotate procedure with the copy option. Setting up Polar snap to track at various angles may also be useful.

HOW TO ROTATE AN OBJECT AND RETAIN THE ORIGINAL USING GRIP EDIT

1. Select the spiral.
2. Pick the grip around which you want to rotate, or any of the grips if you are not going to use the grip as a base point for rotation.
3. Right click and select Rotate from the short cut menu.
4. Right click and type "b" or select Base point from the short cut menu, if the design needs a base point not on a grip. In this exercise the base point you choose for rotation will depend on the design you are trying to create.
5. Right click and type "c" or select Copy from the short cut menu.
6. Show the rotation angle(s).
7. Press the space bar to exit the grip edit system.

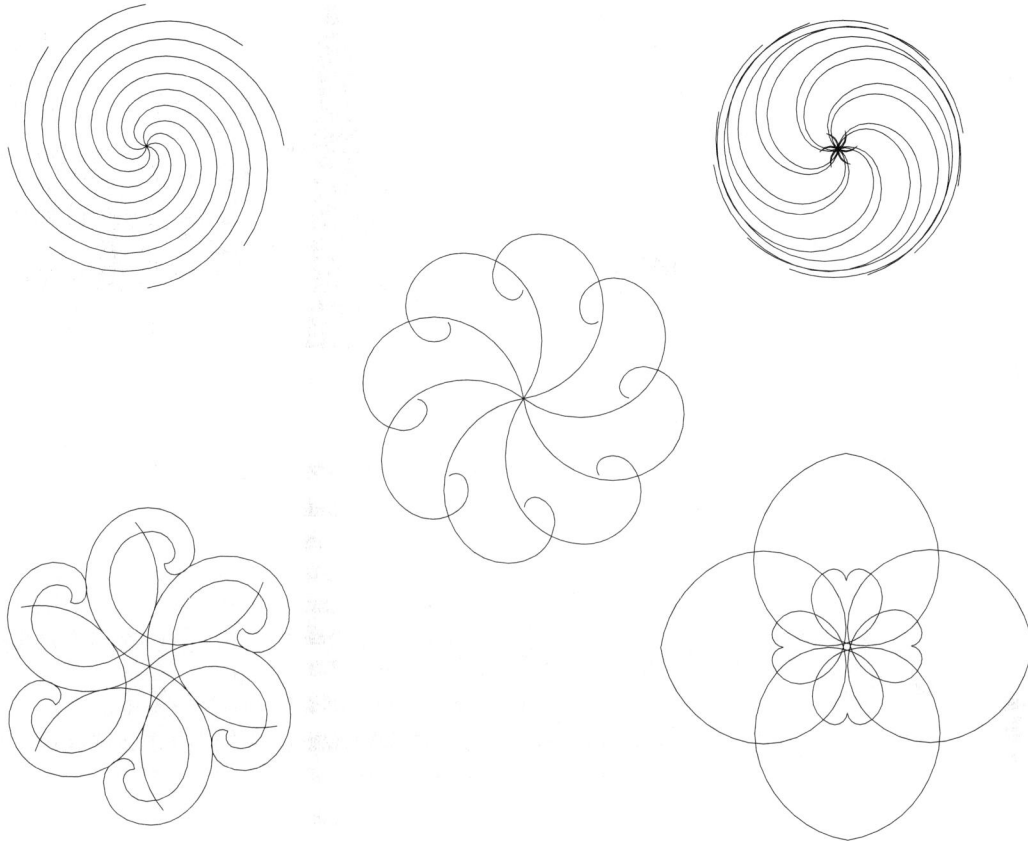

SPIRAL DESIGNS

(Make from Drawing 6-2)

Drawing 6-3

6.16   Drawing 6-4: Grooved Hub

This drawing includes a typical application of the rotation technique just discussed. The hidden lines in the front view must be rotated 120 degrees and a copy retained in the original position. There are also good opportunities to use MIRROR, Object Snap, Object Snap tracking, and TRIM.

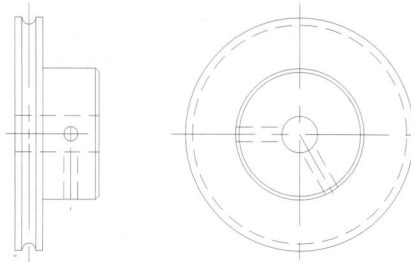

DRAWING SUGGESTIONS

GRID = 0.5   SNAP = 0.0625

LIMITS = (0,0)(12,9)   LTSCALE = 1

- Draw the circles in the front view and use these to line up the horizontal lines in the left side view. This is a good opportunity to use Object Snap tracking. By acquiring the quadrant of a circle in the front view, you can track along the horizontal construction lines to the left side view.
- There are several different planes of symmetry in the left side view, which suggests the use of mirroring. We leave it up to you to choose an efficient sequence.
- A quick method for drawing the horizontal hidden lines in the left side view is to acquire the upper and lower quadrants points of the 0.625-diameter circle in the front view to track horizontal construction lines. Draw the lines in the left side view longer than actual length and then use TRIM to erase the excess on both sides of the left side view.
- The same method can be used to draw the two horizontal hidden lines in the front view. A slightly different method that does not use object tracking is to Snap lines directly to the top and bottom quadrants of the 0.25-diameter circle in the left side view as a guide and draw them all the way through the front view. Then trim to the 2.25-diameter circle and the 0.62-diameter circle.
- Once these hidden lines are drawn, rotate them, retaining a copy in the original position.

CREATING THE MULTIPLE-VIEW LAYOUT

Use this drawing to create the multiple-view layout shown below the dimensioned drawing. This three-view layout is very similar to the one created in Task 6.10. Exact dimensions of the viewports are not given. You should create them depending on the paper size you wish to use. What should remain consistent is the scale relationships among the three viewports. On an A sheet, for example, if the largest viewport is zoomed .5xp, then the left close up is 1.0xp and the top close-up is 1.5xp. These ratios will have to be adjusted for other sheet sizes.

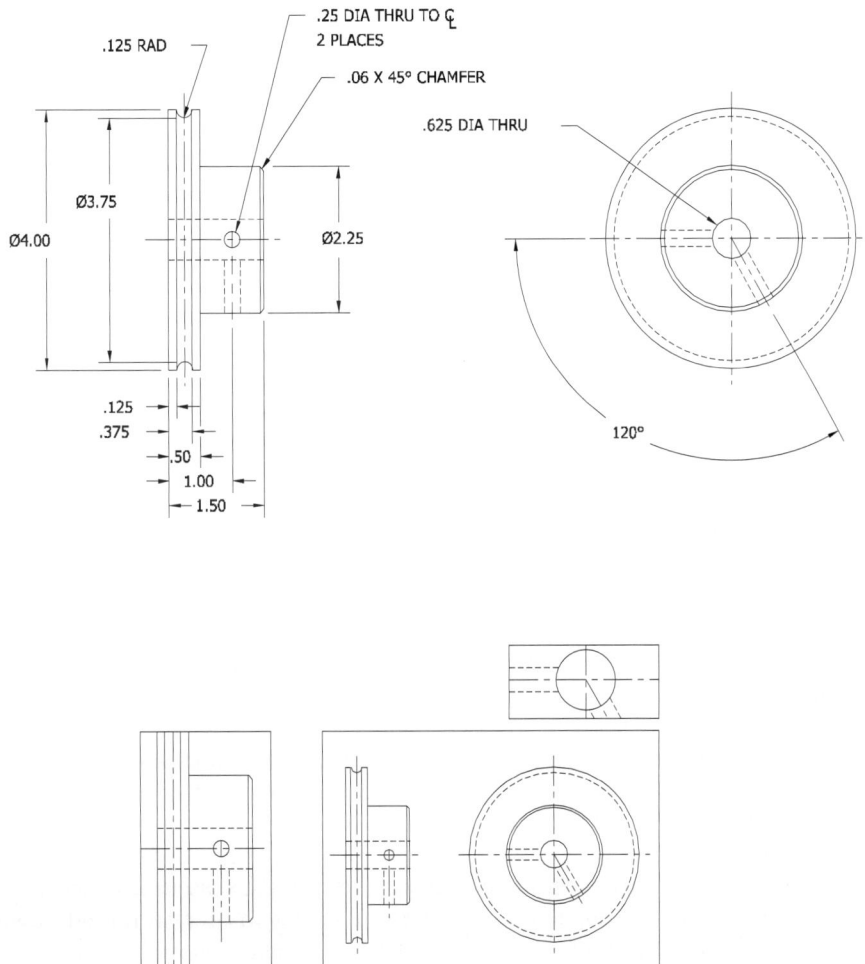

.125 RAD

.25 DIA THRU TO ℄
2 PLACES

.06 X 45° CHAMFER

.625 DIA THRU

Ø3.75

Ø4.00

Ø2.25

120°

.125
.375
.50
1.00
1.50

GROOVED HUB

Drawing 6-4

6.17   Drawing 6-5: Cap Iron

This drawing is of a type of blade used in a wood plane. When wood is planed, the cap iron causes it to curl up out of the plane so that it does not jam. There are several good applications for the TRIM command here.

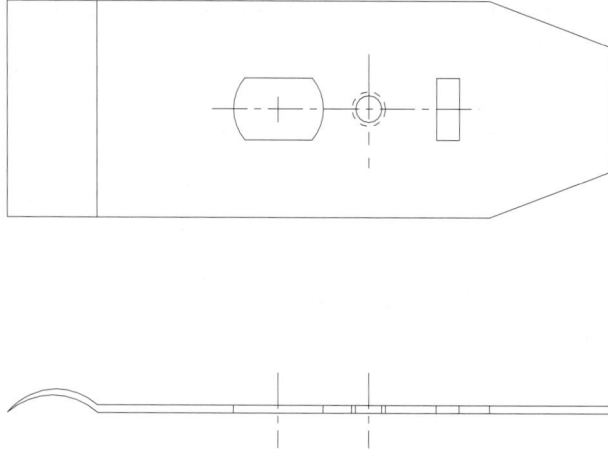

DRAWING SUGGESTIONS

GRID = 1.00
SNAP = 0.25
LIMITS = (0,0)(18,12)
LTSCALE = 0.25

- The circle with a hidden line outside a continuous line represents a tapped hole. The dimension is given to the hidden line; the continuous inner line is drawn with a slightly smaller radius that is not specified.
- The figure near the center of the top view that has two arcs with 0.38 radii can be drawn exactly the same way as the band aid discussed earlier in this chapter. Draw a circle and two horizontal lines and then trim it all down.
- The small 0.54 and 0.58 arcs in the front view can be drawn using Start,End,Radius.
- The small vertical hidden lines in the front view can be drawn using techniques introduced in the last drawing. Draw lines down from snap points on the figures in the top view and then trim them, or use Object snap tracking to create lines with excess length and then trim them. For the tapped hole and the arced opening in the middle, use the right and left quadrant points of the arcs and circle as acquired points or snap points.

CAP IRON

Drawing 6-5

6.18   Drawing 6-6: Deck Framing

This architectural drawing may take some time, although there is nothing in it you have not done before. Notice that some of the settings are quite different from our 1B template, so be sure to adjust them before beginning.

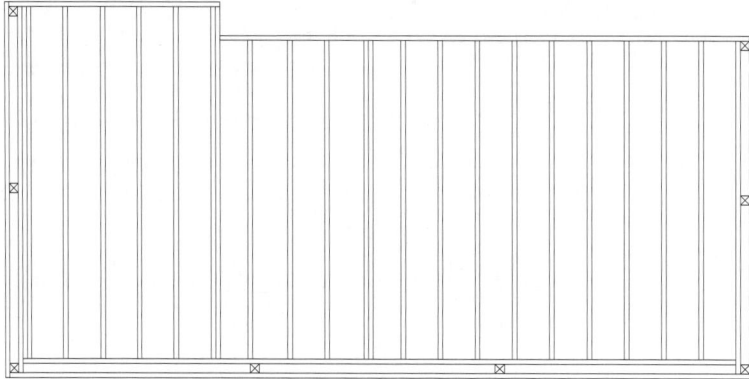

DRAWING SUGGESTIONS

UNITS = Architectural
            Smallest fraction = 1
LIMITS = (0′,0′)(48′,36′)
GRID = 1′
SNAP = 2″

- Whatever order you choose for doing this drawing, we suggest that you make ample use of COPY, ARRAY, OFFSET, and TRIM.
- Keep ortho on, except to draw the lines across the middle of the squares, representing upright posts.
- With snap set at 2″ it is easy copy lines 2″ apart, as you will be doing frequently to draw the 2 × 80 studs.
- You may need to turn snap off when you are selecting lines to copy, but be sure to turn it on again to specify displacements.
- Notice that you can use ARRAY effectively, but that there are three separate arrays. They are all 16" on center, but the double boards in several places make it inadvisable to do a single array of studs all the way across the deck. What you can do, however, is to draw, copy, and array all the "vertical" studs at the maximum length first and then go back and trim them to their various actual lengths using the "horizontal" boards as cutting edges.

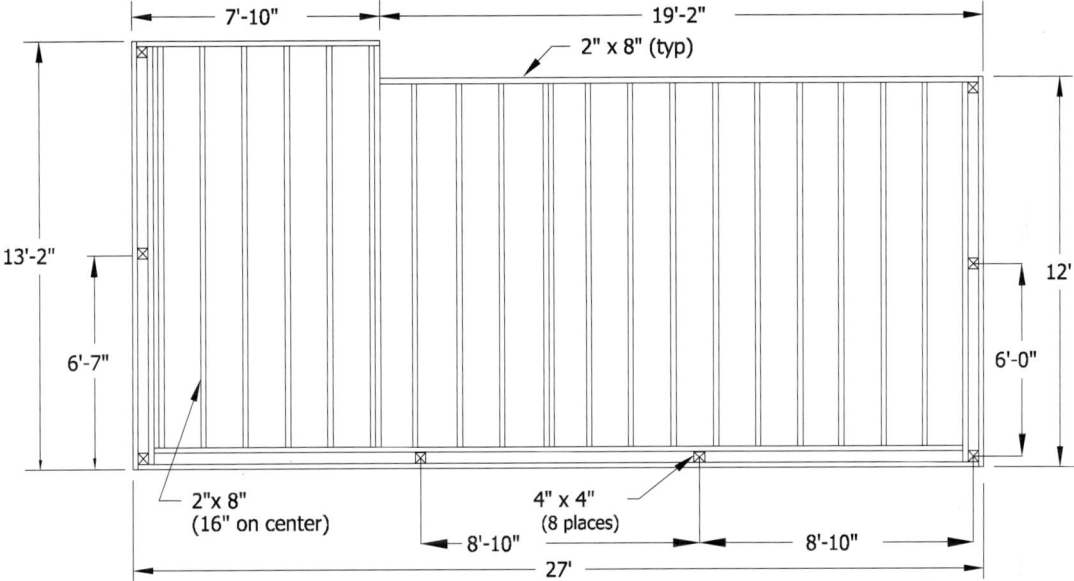

7'-10"

19'-2"

2" x 8" (typ)

13'-2"

12'

6'-7"

6'-0"

2"x 8"
(16" on center)

4" x 4"
(8 places)

8'-10"

8'-10"

27'

DECK FRAMING

Drawing 6-6

6.19   Drawing 6-7: Tool Block

In this drawing you will need to take information from a three-dimensional drawing and develop it into a three-view drawing. The finished drawing should be composed of the Top View, Front View, and Side View. The reference drawing shows a portion of each view to be developed. You are to complete these views.

Location of
Top View

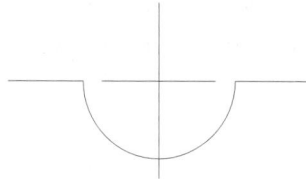

Location of
Front View

Location of
Side View

DRAWING SUGGESTIONS

- Begin by drawing the top view. Use the top view to line up the front view and side view.
- The slot with the angular lines must be drawn in the front view before the other views. These lines can then be lined up with the top and side view and used as guides to draw the hidden lines.
- Be sure to include all the necessary hidden lines and center lines in each view.

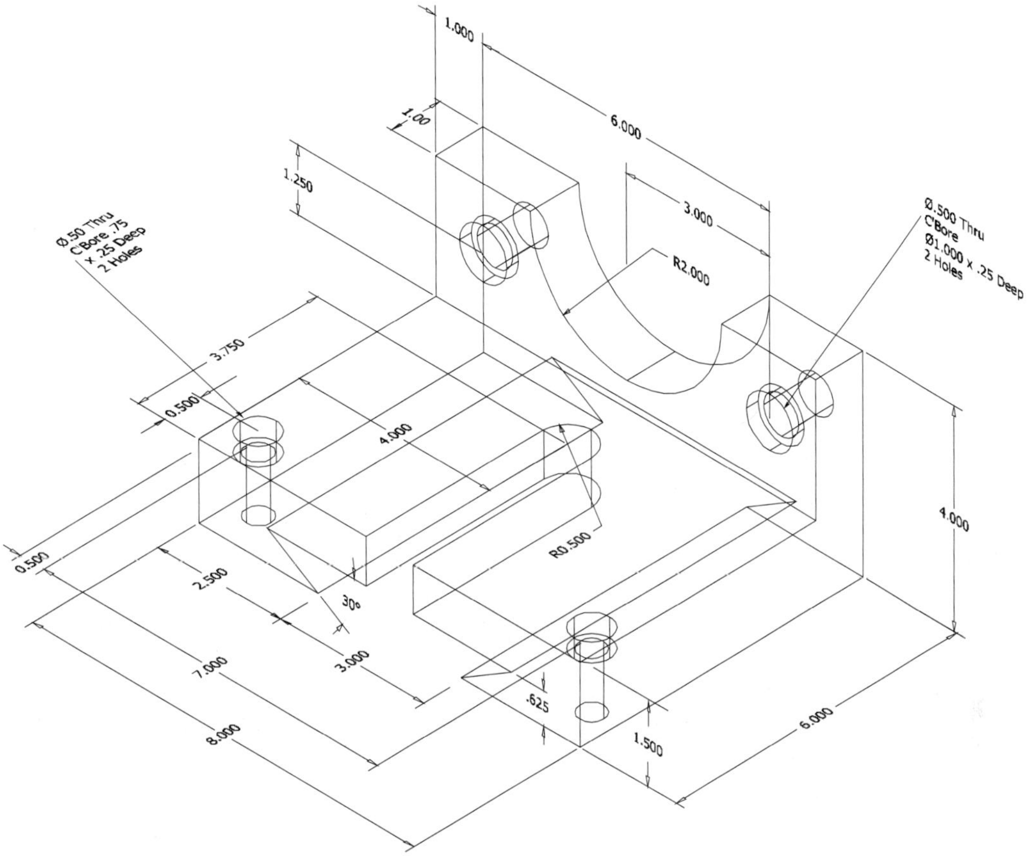

1.000

1.00

1.250

6.000

3.000

R2.000

Ø.50 Thru
C'Bore .75
× .25 Deep
2 Holes

Ø.500 Thru
C'Bore
Ø1.000 × .25 Deep
2 Holes

3.750

0.500

4.000

R0.500

4.000

0.500

2.500

30°

7.000

3.000

.625

8.000

1.500

6.000

TOOL BLOCK

Drawing 6-7

PART II

TEXT, DIMENSIONS, AND OTHER COMPLEX ENTITIES

7 Text

COMMANDS

CHANGE	DDEDIT	DTEXT	SCALE	TEXT
CHPROP	DDEMODES	MATCHPROP	SPELL	
DDCHPROP	DDMODIFY	MTEXT	STYLE	

OVERVIEW

This chapter begins Part II of the book. Part I focused on basic 2D entities such as lines, circles, and arcs. In the next five chapters you will be learning to draw a number of AutoCAD entities that are constructed as groups of lines, circles, and arcs. Text, dimensions, polylines, and blocks are all entities made up of basic 2D entities, but you will not have to treat them line by line, arc by arc. Also in Part II, you will continue to learn AutoCAD editing and plotting features.

Right now it's time to add text to your drawings. In this chapter you will learn to find your way around AutoCAD 2000's DTEXT and MTEXT commands. In addition, you will learn many new editing commands that are often used with text but that are equally important for editing other objects.

TASKS

7.1 Entering left-justified text using DTEXT
7.2 Using other text justification options
7.3 Entering text on an angle and text using character codes
7.4 Entering multiline text using MTEXT
7.5 Editing text with DDEDIT
7.6 Modifying text with PROPERTIES
7.7 Using the SPELL command
7.8 Changing fonts and styles
7.9 Changing properties with MATCHPROP
7.10 SCALEing previously drawn entities
7.11 Review Material
7.12 WWW Exercise #7 (Optional)
7.13 Drawing 7-1: Title Block
7.14 Drawing 7-2: Gauges
7.15 Drawing 7-3: Stamping
7.16 Drawing 7-4: Control Panel
7.17 Drawing 7-5: Tower

7.1 Entering Left-Justified Text Using DTEXT

GENERAL PROCEDURE

1. Open the Draw menu, highlight Text, and select single-line text.
2. Pick a start point.
3. Answer prompts regarding height and rotation.
4. Enter text on one line and press enter.
5. Enter text on other lines or press enter to exit the command.

AutoCAD 2000 provides two commands for entering text in a drawing. DTEXT (also called TEXT in AutoCAD 2000) allows you to enter single lines of text and displays them as you type. You can backspace through lines to make corrections if you do not leave the command. MTEXT allows you to type multiple lines of text in a dialog box and then positions them in a windowed area in your drawing. Both commands have numerous options for placing text and a variety of fonts to use and styles that can be created from them. In the first three tasks we will focus on the basic placement features of the DTEXT command, sticking with the standard style and font.

> **Note:** An older command called TEXT has been eliminated from Auto-CAD 2000. If you type "Text" at the command prompt, you will get the DTEXT command; if you type the alias "t", you will get the MTEXT command. If you see references to TEXT in AutoCAD documentation, you can assume the reference is to DTEXT.

⊕ To prepare for this exercise, open a new drawing using the B template and draw a 4.00 horizontal line beginning at (1,1). Then create a six-row by one-column array with 2.00 between rows, as shown in Figure 7-1.

Figure 7-1

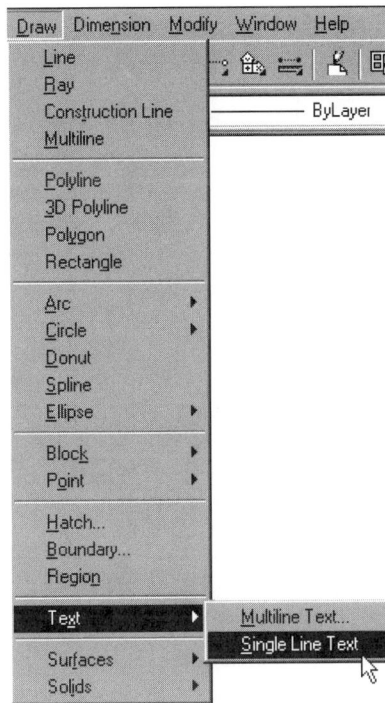

Figure 7-2

These lines are for orientation in this exercise only; they are not essential for drawing text.

⊹ Type "dt" or open the Draw menu, highlight Text, and then select single-line text, as shown in Figure 7-2.

There is a text tool on the Draw toolbar, but it enters the MTEXT command.

Either of these methods will enter the DTEXT command, and you will see a prompt with three options in the command area:

```
Current text style: "STANDARD" Text height: 0.20
Specify start point of text or [Justify/Style]:
```

"Style" will be explored in Task 7.8. In this task we will be looking at different options for placing text in a drawing. These are all considered text justification methods and will be listed if you choose the "Justify" option at the command prompt.

First we will use the default method by picking a start point. This will give us left-justified text, inserted left to right from the point we pick.

⊹ Pick a start point at the left end of the upper line.

Look at the prompt that follows and be sure that you do not attempt to enter text yet:

```
Specify height <0.20>:
```

This gives you the opportunity to set the text height. The number you type specifies the height of uppercase letters in the units you have specified for the current drawing. For now we will accept the default height.

⊕ **Press Enter to accept the default height (0.20).**

The prompt that follows allows you to place text in a rotated position.

                    `Specify rotation angle of text <0>:`

The default of 0 degrees orients text in the usual horizontal manner. Other angles can be specified by typing a degree number relative to the polar coordinate system or by showing a point. If you show a point, it will be taken as the second point of a baseline along which the text string will be placed. For now we will stick to horizontal text.

⊕ **Press Enter to accept the default angle (0).**

Now, at last, it is time to enter the text itself. AutoCAD prompts

                              `Enter text:`

Notice also that a small text cursor has appeared at the start point on your screen. Move your cross hairs away from this point and you will see the cursor clearly. This shows where the first letter you type will be placed. For our text we will type the word "Left", identifying this as an example of left-justified text. Watch the screen as you type and you will see dynamic text at work.

⊕ **Type "Left" and press Enter.**

(Remember, you cannot use the space bar in place of the enter key when entering text.) Notice that the text cursor jumps down below the line when you hit Enter. Also notice that you are given a second "Enter text:" prompt in the command area.

⊕ **Type "Justified" and press Enter.**

The text cursor jumps down again and another "Enter text:" prompt appears. This is how DTEXT allows for easy entry of multiple lines of text directly on the screen in a drawing. To exit the command, you need to press Enter at the prompt.

⊕ **Press Enter to exit DTEXT.**

This completes the process and returns you to the command prompt.

   Figure 7-3 shows the left-justified text you have just drawn, along with the other options as we will demonstrate them in the rest of this exercise.

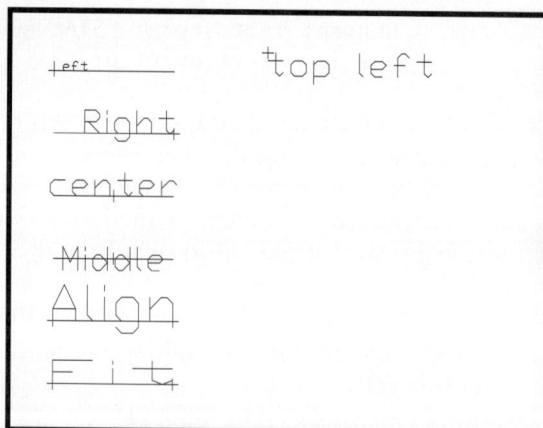

Figure 7-3

Before proceeding with other text justification options, we will demonstrate two additional features of DTEXT.

⊕ **Press Enter to repeat the DTEXT command.**

If you press Enter again at this point instead of showing a new start point or selecting a justification option, you will go right back to the "Enter text:" prompt as if you had never left the command. Try it.

⊕ **Press Enter.**

You will see the "Enter text:" prompt in the command area and the text box will reappear on the screen just below the word "Justification".

⊕ **Type "Text" and press Enter.**

At this point you will still be in the DTEXT command with the "Text:" prompt showing. You could press Enter to exit the command or continue typing lines. Instead try this:

⊕ **Move the cross hairs to any part of the screen and press the pickbutton.**

The text box will move to whatever point you have selected. This means that you can type text in several areas of the screen without ever leaving DTEXT, as long as the text is the same height, angle, and style. You do not even have to press Enter before you move the text box. Try it again.

⊕ **Move the cross hairs once again and press the pickbutton.**

The text cursor will move wherever you want.

⊕ **Type "here" in the new spot.**

⊕ **Move the text box again and type "and there".**

Now, before leaving DTEXT, use the backspace feature to erase the last two lines.

⊕ **Backspace through "and there" and "here".**

This demonstrates how you can backspace dynamically through text created in DTEXT even if the text is in different areas. However, this only works before you exit the command.

⊕ **Press Enter again to exit the command.**

Once you have left DTEXT, there are other ways to edit text, which we will explore in Tasks 7.5 and 7.6.

7.2 Using Other Text Justification Options

GENERAL PROCEDURE

1. Type "dt" or Open the Draw menu, highlight Text, and select single-line text.
2. Choose a justification option.
3. Pick a start point.
4. Answer prompts regarding height and rotation.
5. Enter text.

We will now proceed to try out some of the other text placement options, beginning with right-justified text, as shown on the second line of Figure 7-3. We will also specify a change in height.

Right-Justified Text

Right-justified text is constructed from an end point backing up, right to left.

⊕ Repeat the DTEXT command.

You will see the same prompt as before.

⊕ Type "r" for right-justified text.

Now AutoCAD prompts for an end point instead of a start point:

> Specify right endpoint of text baseline:

We will choose the right end of the second line.

⊕ Point to the right end of the second line.

This time we will change the height to 0.50. Notice that AutoCAD gives you a rubber band from the end point. It can be used to specify height and rotation angle by pointing, if you like.

⊕ Type ".5" or show a height of 0.50 by pointing.

⊕ Press Enter to retain 0 degrees of rotation.

You are now prompted to enter text.

⊕ Type "Right" and press Enter.

Here you should notice an important fact about the DTEXT command. Initially, DTEXT ignores your justification choice, entering the letters you type from left to right as usual. The justification will be carried out only when you exit the command.

At this point you should have the word "Right" showing to the right of the second line. Watch what happens when you press Enter a second time to exit the command.

⊕ Press Enter.

The text will jump to the left, onto the line. Your screen should now include the second line of text in right-justified position, as shown in Figure 7-3.

Centered Text

Centered text is justified from the bottom center of the text.

⊕ Repeat the DTEXT command.

⊕ Type "c".

AutoCAD prompts

> Specify center point of text:

⊕ Point to the midpoint of the third line.

⊕ Press Enter to retain the current height, which is now set to 0.50.

⊕ Press Enter to retain 0 degrees of rotation.

⊕ Type "Center" and press Enter.

Notice again how the letters are displayed on the screen in the usual left-to-right manner.

⊕ Press Enter again to complete the command.

The word "Center" should now be centered, as shown in Figure 7-3.

Middle Text

Middle text is justified from the middle of the text both horizontally and vertically, rather than from the bottom center.

⊕ Repeat DTEXT.

⊕ Type "m".

AutoCAD prompts

Specify middle point of text:

⊕ Point to the midpoint of the fourth line.

⊕ Press Enter to retain the current height of 0.50.

⊕ Press Enter to retain 0 degrees of rotation.

⊕ Type "Middle" and press Enter.

⊕ Press Enter again to complete the command.

Notice the difference between center and middle. Center refers to the midpoint of the baseline below the text. Middle refers to the middle of the text itself, so that the line now runs through the text.

Aligned Text

Aligned text is placed between two specified points. The height of the text is calculated proportional to the distance between the two points, and the text is drawn along the line between the two points.

⊕ Repeat DTEXT.

⊕ Type "a".

AutoCAD prompts

Specify first endpoint of text baseline:

⊕ Point to the left end of the fifth line.

AutoCAD prompts for another point:

Specify second endpoint of text baseline:

⊕ Point to the right end of the fifth line.

Notice that there is no prompt for height. AutoCAD will calculate a height based on the space between the points you chose. There is also no prompt for an angle, because the angle between your two points (in this case 0) will be used. You could position text at an angle using this option.

⊕ Type "Align" and press enter.

⊕ Press Enter again to complete the command.

Notice that the text jumps in size and placement to fill the line.

Text Drawn to Fit between Two Points

The Fit option is similar to the Aligned option, except that the specified text height is retained.

⊕ Repeat DTEXT.

⊕ Type "f".

You will be prompted for two points, as in the "align" option.

⊕ Point to the left end of the sixth line.

⊕ Point to the right end of the sixth line.

⊕ Press Enter to retain the current height.

As in the align option, there will be no prompt for an angle of rotation.

⊕ Type "Fit" and press Enter.

⊕ Press Enter again to complete the command.

This time the text will be stretched horizontally to fill the line without a change in height. This is the difference between fit and align. In the align option, text height is determined by the width you show. With fit, the specified height is retained and the text is stretched or compressed to fill the given space.

Other Justification Options

Before proceeding to the next task, take a moment to look at the list of justification options. The options will be listed on the command line if you enter DTEXT and type "J". The command line prompt looks like this:

```
[Align/Fit/Center/Middle/Right/TL/TC/TR/ML/MC/MR/BL/BC/BR]:
```

The letter options are spelled out in the chart shown in Figure 7-4. We already have explored the first five plus the default Left option. For the others, study the figure. As shown on the chart, T is for top, M is for middle, and B is for bottom. L, C, and R stand for left, center, and right. Notice that it is not necessary to type "J" and see the list before entering the option. Just enter DTEXT and then the one or two letters of the option. Let's try one.

⊕ Repeat DTEXT and then type "tl" for the "Top Left" option.

AutoCAD will ask you to "Specify top-left point of text". As shown in Figure 7-4, top left refers to the highest potential text point at the left of the word.

⊕ Pick a top left point, as shown in Figure 7-3 above the words "top left".

⊕ Press Enter twice to accept the height and rotation angle settings and arrive at the "Text:" prompt.

⊕ Type "top left" and press Enter.

⊕ Press Enter again to complete the command.

TEXT JUSTIFICATION	
START POINT TYPE ABBREVIATION	TEXT POSITION +INDICATES START POINT or PICK POINT
A	ALIGN+
F	+FIT+
C	CENTER
M	MIDDLE
R	RIGHT+
TL	+TOP LEFT
TC	TOP CENTER
TR	TOP RIGHT+
ML	+MIDDLE LEFT
MC	MIDDLE+CENTER
MR	MIDDLE RIGHT+
BL	BOTTOM LEFT
BC	BOTTOM CENTER
BR	BOTTOM RIGHT+

Figure 7-4

As before, the text will jump into top-left-justified position when you exit the command. Your screen should now resemble Figure 7-3.

7.3 Entering Text on an Angle and Text Using Character Codes

GENERAL PROCEDURE

1. Enter the DTEXT command.
2. Specify justification option, start point, and text height.
3. Specify a rotation angle.
4. Enter text, including character codes as needed.

We have already seen how you can use DTEXT to enter multiple lines of text. In this task we will explore this further by entering several lines on an angle, adding

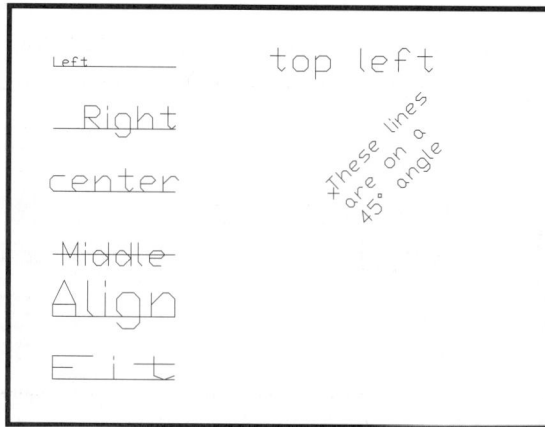

Figure 7-5

special character symbols along the way. We will create three lines of left-justified text, one below the other and all rotated 45 degrees, as shown in Figure 7-5.

⊕ Repeat the DTEXT command.

You will see the familiar prompt:

Specify start point of text or [Justify/Style]:

⊕ Pick a starting point near (12.00,8.00), as shown by the mark next to the word "These" in Figure 7-5.

⊕ Type ".3" to specify a smaller text size.

⊕ Type "45" or show an angle of 45 degrees.

Notice that the text box is shown at the specified angle.

⊕ Type "These lines" and press Enter.

The text will be drawn on the screen at a 45-degree angle, and you will be returned to the "Enter text:" prompt. Notice that the text box on the screen is still at the specified angle.

⊕ Type "are on a" and press Enter.

You should be at the "Enter text:" prompt.

The Degree Symbol and Other Special Characters

The next line contains a degree symbol. Since you do not have this character on your keyboard, AutoCAD provides a special method for drawing it. Type the text with the %% signs just as shown following and then study Figure 7-6, which lists other special characters that can be drawn in the same way.

⊕ Type "45%%d angle" and press Enter.

DTEXT will initially type the character code directly to the screen, just as you have typed it. When you exit the command, the character code will be translated and redrawn. Watch.

Control Codes and Special Characters	
Type at Text Prompt	Text on Drawing
%%O OVERSCORE	OVERSCORE
%%U UNDERSCORE	UNDERSCORE
180%%D	180°
2.00 %%P.01	2.00 ±.01
%%C4.00	Ø4.00

Figure 7-6

⊕   Press Enter again to complete the command sequence.
     Your screen should now resemble Figure 7-5.

7.4   Entering Multiline Text Using MTEXT

GENERAL PROCEDURE

1. Type "t", select the Text tool from the Draw toolbar, or Open the Draw menu, highlight Text, and select multiline text.
2. Specify options.
3. Pick an insertion point.
4. Pick a second corner.
5. Type text in the dialog box.
6. Click on OK.

The MTEXT command allows you to create multiline text in a dialog box and position it within a defined window in your drawing. Like DTEXT, MTEXT has nine options for text justification and its own set of character codes.

We begin by creating a simple left-justified block of text.

⊕   Type "t" or select the Multiline Text tool from the Draw toolbar, as shown in Figure 7-7.

Figure 7-7

You will see the following prompt in the command area:

```
MTEXT Current text style: STANDARD Text height: 0.20
Specify first corner:
```

We will discuss options momentarily, after you see how the command works.

Fundamentally, MTEXT lets you define the width of a group of text lines that you will create in a dialog box. When the text is entered using MTEXT, AutoCAD formats it to conform to the specified width and justification method and draws the text on your screen. The width can be defined in several ways. The default method for specifying a width is to draw a window on the screen. This can be misleading. MTEXT does not attempt to place the complete text inside the window, but only within its width. The first point of the window becomes the insertion point of the text. How AutoCAD uses this insertion point depends on the justification option. The second window point defines the width and the text flow direction (that is, whether the text lines should be drawn above or below, to the left or right of the insertion point). Exactly how this is interpreted is also dependent on the justification option.

⊕ **Pick an insertion point near the middle of your drawing area, in the neighborhood of (9.00,6.00).**

AutoCAD will begin a window at the selected point and give you a new prompt:

```
Specify opposite corner or [Height/Justify/Line spacing/
Rotation/Style/Width]:
```

We will continue with the default options by picking a second corner. For purposes of demonstration we suggest a window 3.00 wide, drawn down and to the right.

⊕ **Pick a second point 3.00 to the right and about 1.00 below the first point.**

As soon as you pick the opposite corner, AutoCAD will open the Multiline Text Editor dialog box with the Character tab showing, as illustrated in Figure 7-8. The most important feature of this dialog box is the editing area. When you enter text in this area, the text will wrap around as it will be drawn in your drawing, according to the width you have specified.

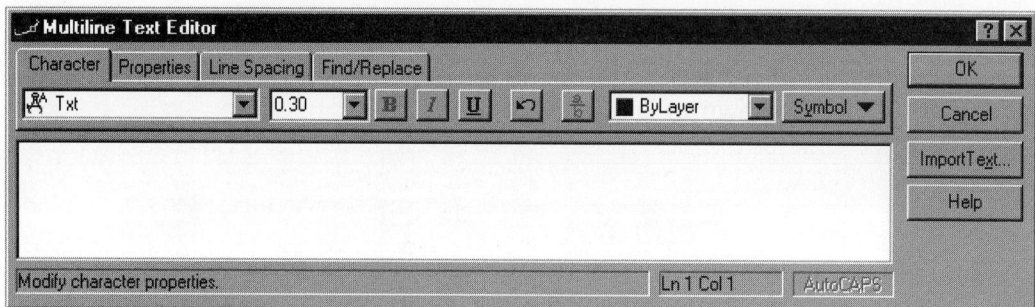

Figure 7-8

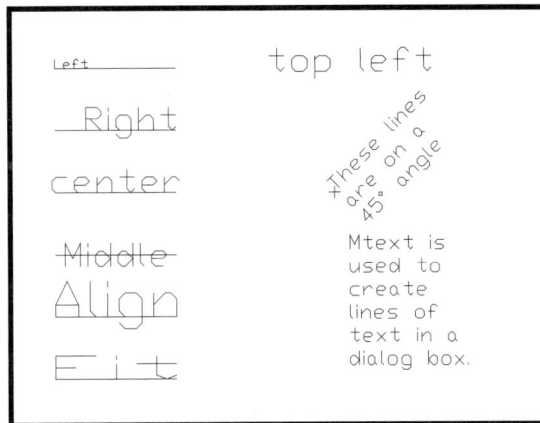

Figure 7-9

Notice that the dialog box also has Properties, Line spacing, and Find and Replace tabs. Mtext properties include text style, justification, width, and rotation. These can also be set at the command line, as indicated by the previous prompt. Line spacing is either single, 1.5, or double. Find and Replace works in your drawing as it would in a text editor.

Tip: Notice also that there is a Symbol button in this dialog box. If you select this button, a short list of symbols will drop down, including the degree symbol, the plus or minus symbol, and the diameter symbol. Selecting from this list will save you from typing the %% characters.

⊕   Type "Mtext is used to create lines of text in a dialog box."
⊕   Click on "OK" to leave the dialog box.

You will be returned to the drawing window and the new text will be added, as shown in Figure 7-9. Notice that the text you typed has been wrapped around to fit within the 3.00 width window; the 0.30 height of the text has been retained and the 1.00 height of the text window you defined has been ignored.

We will explore other Mtext justification options as an editing procedure using DDMODIFY. But first, we will do some simple text editing with DDEDIT.

7.5   Editing Text with DDEDIT

GENERAL PROCEDURE
1. Open the Modify menu and select Text. 2. Select text to edit. 3. Edit text in the Edit text dialog box. 4. Click on OK.

There are several ways to modify text that already exists in your drawing. You can change wording and spelling as well as properties such as layer, style, and justification. For simple changes in text, use the DDEDIT command, accessed from the Modify menu; for property changes, use the Properties manager, discussed in Task 7.6.

In this task we will do some simple DDEDIT text editing. In Task 7.6 we will use the property modification powers of the PROPERTIES command to show different justification options of MTEXT paragraphs.

⊞ Open the Modify menu and select Text.

There is also an Edit Text tool that you can access by opening the Modify II toolbar. Regardless of how you enter the command, AutoCAD will prompt you to select an object for editing:

> Select an annotation object or [Undo]:

Annotation objects will include all objects that have text, including text, dimensions, and attributes. Dimensions are the subject of Chapter 8. Attributes are discussed in Chapter 10.

We will select one line of the angled text.

⊞ Select the words "These lines" by clicking on any of the letters.

As soon as you select the text, it will appear in a small edit box, as illustrated in Figure 7-10. This is the DDEDIT dialog box for text created with DTEXT. If you had selected text created with MTEXT, you would be in the Multline Text Editor. We will demonstrate momentarily. Now add the word "three" to the middle of this line.

⊞ Move the dialog box arrow to the center of the text in the edit box, between "These" and "lines", and press the pickbutton.

The text should no longer be highlighted, and a flashing cursor should be present, indicating where text will be added if you begin typing.

⊞ Type the word "three" and add a space so that the line reads "These three lines".

⊞ Click on "OK".

The dialog box will disappear and your text will be redrawn with the word "three" added, as shown in Figure 7-11.

Now let's try it with the text you created in MTEXT. The first difference you will notice is that since MTEXT creates multiple lines of text as a group, you cannot select a single line of text. When you click, the whole set of lines will be selected.

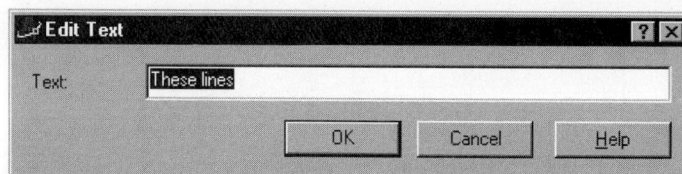

Figure 7-10

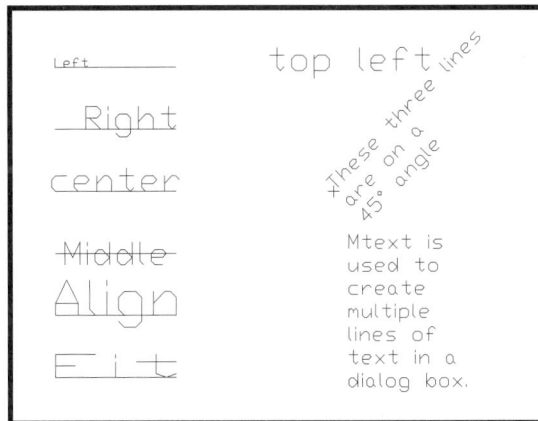

Figure 7-11

DDEDIT repeats automatically, so you should have the following prompt in the command area before proceeding:

```
Select an annotation object or [Undo]:
```

If not, repeat DDEDIT.

⊕ Select the text beginning with "Mtext is".

This will call up the Multiline Text Editor, with the chosen paragraph showing in the edit area.

⊕ Move the screen cursor to the second line, after "create", and press the pickbutton.

You should now have a flashing cursor on the line after "create".

⊕ Add "multiple" so that the paragraph will read "Mtext is used to create multiple lines of text in a dialog box."

⊕ Click on "OK".

You will return to the drawing window, with the new text added and reformatted as shown in Figure 7-11. That's it for DDEDIT. Next we will explore PROPERTIES along with more MTEXT placement options.

7.6 Modifying Text with PROPERTIES

GENERAL PROCEDURE

1. Select Properties... from the Modify menu.
2. Select text to modify (steps 1 and 2 can be reversed if noun/verb editing is enabled in your drawing).
3. Use the Properties dialog box to specify property changes.
4. Click on OK.

PROPERTIES is one of several commands that can be used to change properties of objects in a drawing. It is used with many other kinds of objects besides text. In this exercise you will learn how to use PROPERTIES and at the same time explore the MTEXT justification options. Justification is one of the properties you will be able to modify, and this will be an efficient way to explore the options without having to input new text. We will begin this task with a look at the Properties dialog box and end it with a summary of MTEXT placement options.

⊕   Draw a 3.00 line just above the MTEXT paragraph, as shown in Figure 7-12.

This line is only for reference. It should begin at the same snap point that was used as the insertion point for the text. The left end of the line will show the insertion point, and the length will show the width of the paragraph. We have used the point (9.00,6.00) and the 3.00 width.

⊕   Select Properties... from the Modify menu.

⊕   Select the paragraph beginning with "Mtext is".

⊕   Press Enter to end object selection.

You should now see the Properties dialog box illustrated in Figure 7-13. Take a look at it. This dialog is different from any we have encoutered. In the top edit box you will see "Mtext". This indicates the type of object you have selected. If you had chosen multiple objects you could select from a pop down list opening from this box.

Below are all the properties that can be modified for the object you have chosen. The list will be different for different types of objects, but many properties, such as layer, color, etc., are standard. The two tabs, Alphabetic and Categorized, will show the same list in different orders.

⊕   If necessary, select the Categorized tab, as shown in Figure 7-13.

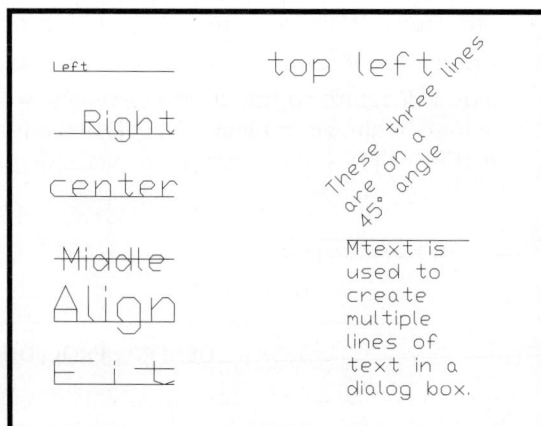

Figure 7-12

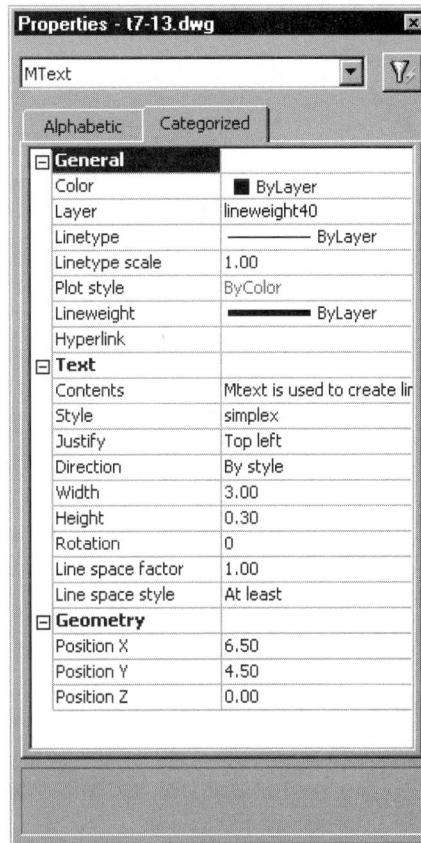

Figure 7-13

We are going to make a change in text justification, but first notice that there is also an option here to change text content. This is an alternative to the DDEDIT command. If you select "Content", an ellipsis button will appear in the right column. Clicking this would open the Multiline Text Editor. For DTEXT objects, content editing is done directly in the right column.

⊕ Look over the list and then select "Justify".

When Justify is selected a list arrow will appear in the right column, next to "Top left".

⊕ Click on the arrow.

This will open a list box with a list of nine justification options, as shown in Figure 7-14. The list should look familiar to you since it includes some of the same choices as the text justification options introduced previously for DTEXT. The difference is that here you will place and justify multiple lines of text as a group.

Figure 7-14

Notice that the current justification is Top Left. We will change it to Top Center, the second option on the list.

⊕ Click on "TopCenter".

The list box will close, and "TopCenter" should now be shown in the Justify edit box. You will also see that the change is immediately reflected in your drawing even while the dialog box is still open.

⊕ Click the close button to exit the Properties dialog.

Notice that in this case it is safe to close the dialog box. There is no OK button and changes are reflected immediately. You can close without losing any changes.

Your text will be redrawn as shown in Figure 7-15. The paragraph will now be in centered format, centered in the original insertion window. You may wish to continue with other justification options. Also, study Figure 7-16, which illustrates Mtext justification options.

Before you go, remember that all AutoCAD objects can be modified using this Properties dialog box.

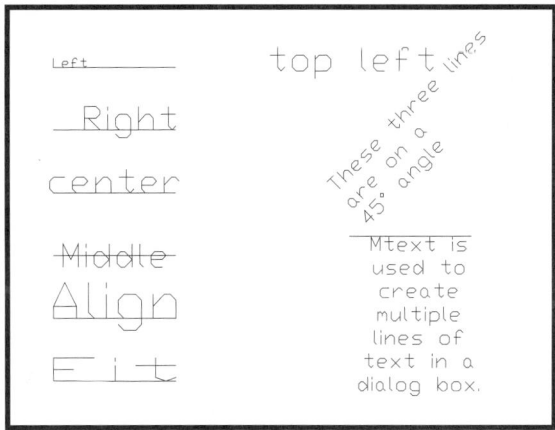

Figure 7-15

Figure 7-16

7.7   Using the SPELL Command

GENERAL PROCEDURE

1. Select Spelling from the Tools menu.
2. Select objects.
3. Press enter to end selection.
4. Use the dialog box to ignore, change, or add words the spell checker does not recognize.

AutoCAD's SPELL command is simple to use and will be very familiar to anyone who has used spell checkers in word processing programs. We will use SPELL to check the spelling of all the text we have drawn so far.

⊕   **Type "sp" or select Spelling from the Tools menu.**

You will see a "Select objects:" prompt on the command line. At this point you could point to individual objects. Any object may be selected, although no checking will be done if you select a line, for example.

For our purposes we will use an "All" option to check all the spelling in the drawing.

⊕   **Type "all".**

AutoCAD will continue to prompt for object selection until you press Enter.

⊕   **Press Enter to end object selection.**

This will bring you to the Check Spelling dialog box shown in Figure 7-17. If you have followed the exercise so far and not misspelled any words along the way, you will see "Mtext" in the Current word box and "Text" as a suggest-

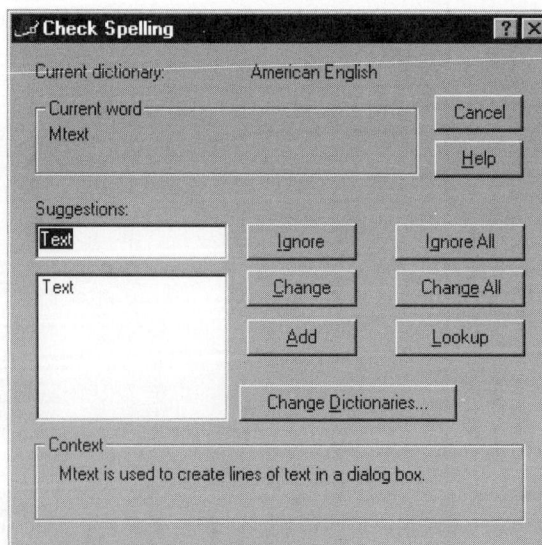

Figure 7-17

ed correction. We will ignore this change, but before you leave SPELL, look at what is available: You can ignore a word the checker does not recognize, or change it. You can change a single instance of a word, or change all instances in the currently selected text. You can add a word to a customized dictionary or you can change to another dictionary.

⊕ Click on "Ignore".

If your drawing does not contain other spelling irregularities, you should now see an AutoCAD message that says

Spelling check complete.

⊕ Click on "OK" to end the spell check.

If you have made any corrections in spelling, they will be incorporated into your drawing at this point.

7.8 Changing Fonts and Styles

GENERAL PROCEDURE

1. Select Text Style... from the Format menu.
2. Change settings in the Text Style dialog box. Specify height, width, and font.
3. Click on New.
4. Type in a name for the new style.
5. Click on OK.
6. Click on Close.

By default, the current text style in any AutoCAD drawing is one called "STANDARD". It is a specific form of a font called "txt" that comes with the software. All the text you have entered so far has been drawn with the standard style of the "txt" font.

Changing fonts is a simple matter. However, there is room for confusion in the use of the words "style" and "font." Fonts are the basic patterns of character and symbol shapes that can be used with the DTEXT and MTEXT commands. Styles are variations in the size, orientation, and spacing of the characters in those fonts. It is possible to create your own fonts, but for most of us this is an esoteric activity. In contrast, creating your own styles is easy and practical.

We will begin by creating a variation of the STANDARD style you have been using.

⊕ Type "st" or select Text Style... from the Format menu.

Either method will open the Text Style dialog box shown in Figure 7-18. You will probably see STANDARD listed in the Style name box. However, it is possible that there will be other styles listed. In this case you should open the list with the arrow on the right and select STANDARD, the AutoCAD default style. We will create our own variation of the STANDARD style and call it "VERTICAL". It will use the same "txt" character font but will be drawn down the display instead of across.

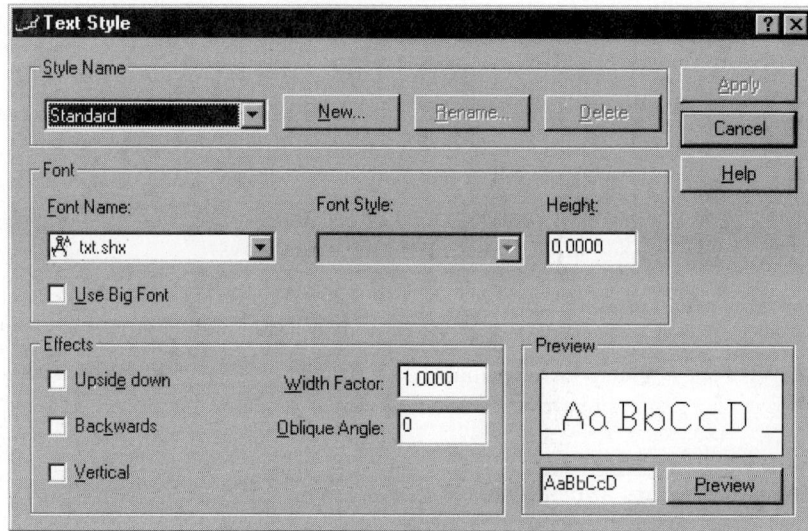

Figure 7-18

⊕ Click in the "Vertical" check box.

We will also give this style a fixed height and a width factor. Notice that the current height is 0.00. This does not mean that your characters will be drawn 0.00 units high. It means that there will be no fixed height, so you will be able to specify a height whenever you use this style. STANDARD currently has no fixed height, so VERTICAL has inherited this setting. Try giving our new "VERTICAL" style a fixed height.

⊕ Double click in the Height edit box and then type ".5".

⊕ Double click in the Width Factor box and type "2".

⊕ Click on "New".

AutoCAD opens a smaller dialog box that asks for a name for the new text style.

⊕ Type "vertical".

⊕ Click on OK.

This brings you back to the Text Style dialog box, with the new style listed in the style name area.

⊕ Click on Close to exit the Text Style dialog.

The new VERTICAL style is now current. To see it in action you will need to enter some text.

⊕ Type "dt" or open the Draw menu, highlight Text, and then highlight Single Line text.

⊕ Pick a start point, as shown by the placement of the letter "V" in Figure 7-19.

Notice that you are not prompted for a height because the current style has height fixed at 0.50.

⊕ Press Enter to retain 270 degrees of rotation.

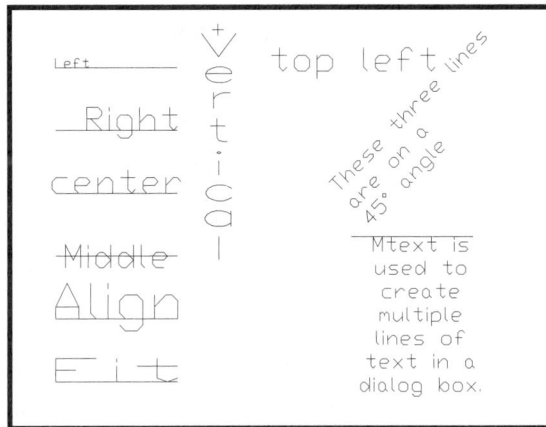

Figure 7-19

⊕   Type "Vertical".
⊕   Press Enter to end the line.

Before going on, notice that the DTEXT text placement box has moved up to begin a new column of text next to the word "vertical."

⊕   Press Enter to exit DTEXT.

Your screen should resemble Figure 7-19.

There are now two text styles in the current drawing. Both use the txt font. Next we will create a third style using a different font and some of the other style options.

⊕   Type "st" or select Text Style... from the Format menu.
⊕   Open the Font name list by clicking on the arrow.
⊕   Scroll to "Romand.shx" and stop.

Romand stands for "Roman Duplex", an AutoCAD font.

⊕   Click on "romand.shx" to place it in the font name box.
⊕   Click in the Vertical box to remove the check.
⊕   Set the text height to 0.00.
⊕   Set the width factor to 1.
⊕   Set Obliquing angle to 45.

This will cause your text to be slanted 45 degrees to the right. For a left slant, you would type a negative number.

⊕   Click on New to give the style a name.
⊕   In the New text style dialog box, give the style the name "Slanted".
⊕   Click on OK to close the New Text Style box.
⊕   Click on Close to exit the Text Style box.

Now enter some text to see how this slanted Roman Duplex style looks.

⊕   Enter the DTEXT command and answer the prompts to draw the words "Roman Duplex" with a 0.50 height, as shown in Figure 7-20.

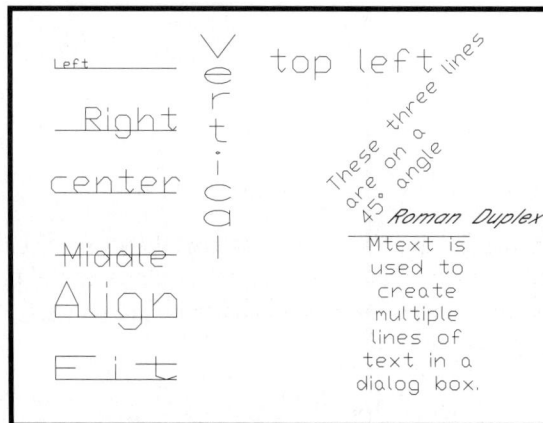

Figure 7-20

Switching the Current Style

All new text is created in the current style. The style of previously drawn text can be changed, as we will show later. Once you have a number of styles defined in a drawing, you can switch from one to another by using the Style option of the DTEXT and MTEXT commands or by selecting a text style from the Text Style dialog box.

> **Note:** If you change the definition of a text style, all text previously drawn in that style will be regenerated with the new style specifications.

7.9 Changing Properties with MATCHPROP

GENERAL PROCEDURE

1. Select the Match Properties tool from the Standard toolbar, or Match Properties from the Modify menu.
2. Select a source object with properties you wish to transfer to another object.
3. If necessary, specify properties you wish to match.
4. Select destination objects.
5. Press enter to end object selection.

MATCHPROP is a very efficient command, that lets you match all or some of the properties of an object to those of another object. Properties that can be transferred from one object to another, or to many others, include layer, linetype, color, and linetype scale. These settings are common to all AutoCAD entities. Other

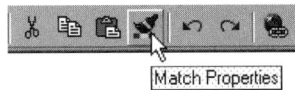

Figure 7-21

properties that only relate to specific types of entities are thickness, text style, dimension style, and hatch style. In all cases the procedure is the same.

Here we will use MATCHPROP to change some previously drawn text to the new "Third" style.

⊕ Select the Match Properties tool from the Standard toolbar, as shown in Figure 7-21.

You can also type "ma" or select Match Properties from the Modify menu.

AutoCAD will prompt:

```
Select Source Object:
```

You can have many destination objects but only one source object.

⊕ Select the text "Roman Duplex", drawn in the last task in the Slanted style.

AutoCAD switches to the Match Properties cursor, shown in Figure 7-22, and displays a list of active settings, and prompts:

```
Current active settings: Color Layer Ltype Ltscale
   Lineweight Thickness
PlotStyle Text Dim Hatch
Select destination object(s) or [Settings]:
```

At this point you can limit the settings you want to match by typing "s" for settings, or you can select destination objects, in which case all properties will be matched.

⊕ Type "s".

This opens the Property Settings dialog box, shown in Figure 7-23. The Basic properties panel shows properties that can be changed and the settings that will be used based on the source object you have selected.

At the bottom you will see Dimension, Text, and Hatch in the Special Properties panel. These refer to dimension, text, and hatch styles that have been defined in your drawing. If any of these is deselected, then Match Properties will ignore style definitions and will only match the basic properties checked.

⊕ Click on OK to exit the dialog.

AutoCAD returns to the screen with the same prompt as before.

⊕ Select the words "Align" and "Vertical".

These two words will be redrawn in the Slanted style, as shown in Figure 7-24.

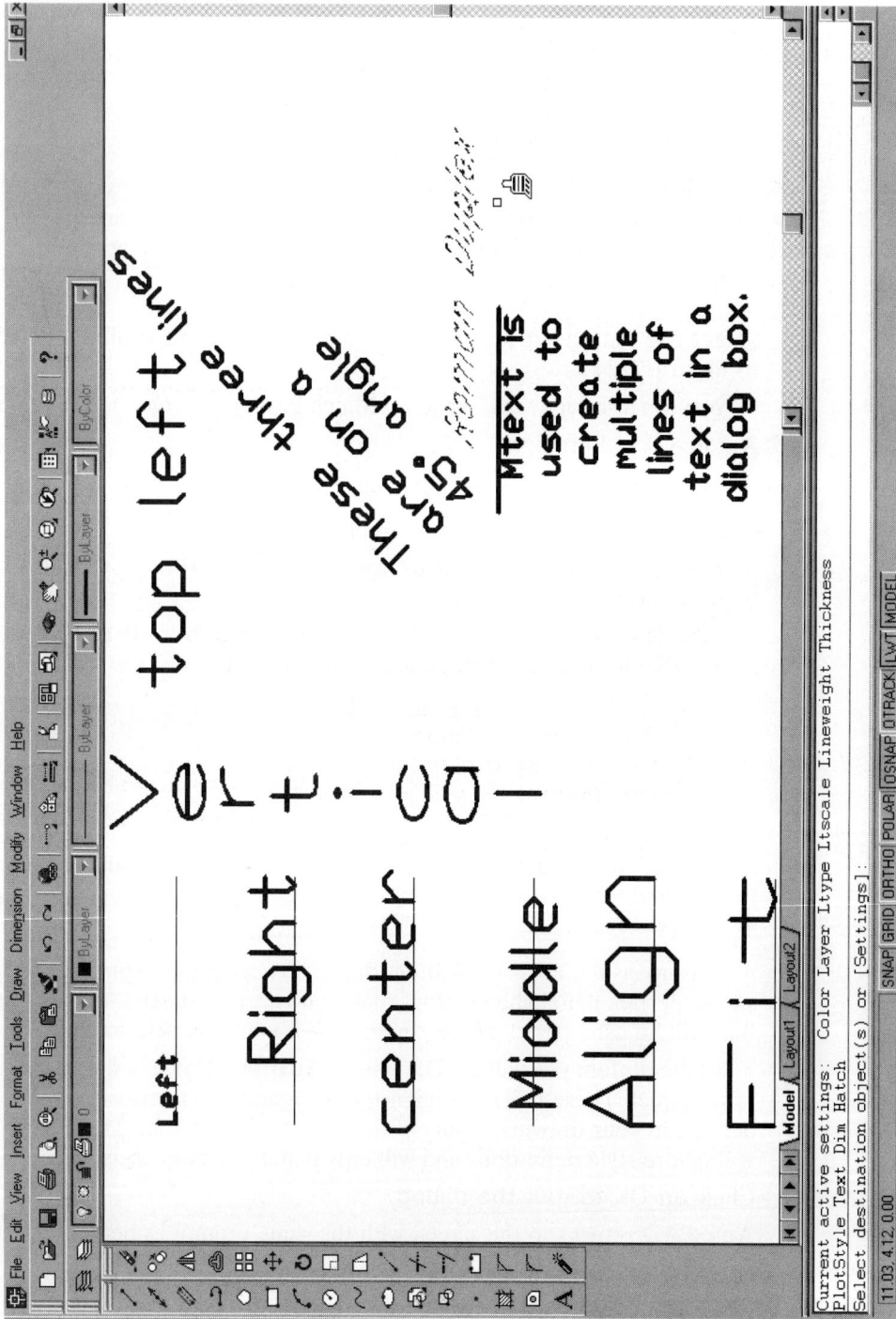

Left

Right

center

Middle

Align

Fit

top left

These three
are on a
45° angle

Roman Simplex

Mtext is
used to
create
multiple
lines of
text in a
dialog box.

Vertical

Current active settings: Color Layer Ltype Ltscale Lineweight Thickness
PlotStyle Text Dim Hatch
Select destination object(s) or [Settings]:

Figure 7-22

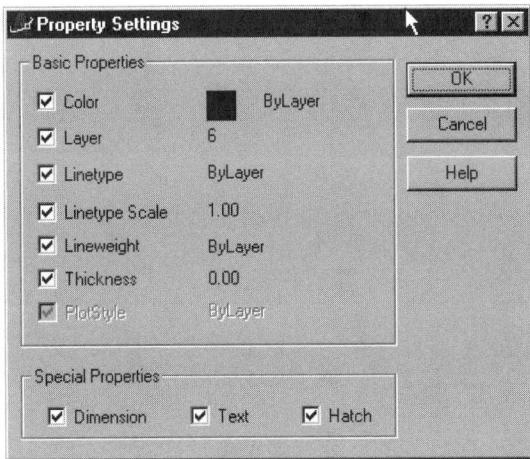

Figure 7-23

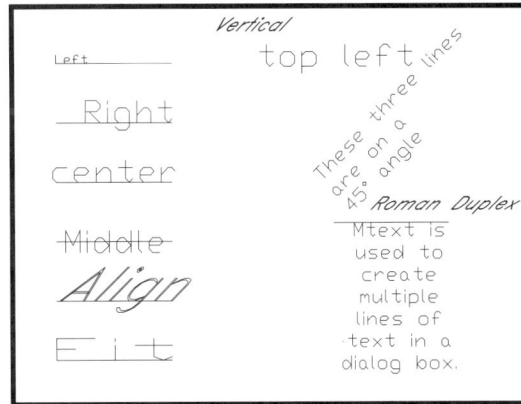

Figure 7-24

The CHANGE command

The CHANGE command is an older AutoCAD command that has been largely replaced by other editing commands. CHANGE works at the command line and allows you to modify all of the basic text properties, including insertion point, style, height, rotation angle, and text content. You can select as many objects as you like and CHANGE will cycle through them. In addition, CHANGE can be used to alter the end points of lines and the size of circles. With lines, CHANGE will perform a function similar to the EXTEND command, but without the necessity of defining an extension boundary. CHANGE will cause circles to be redrawn so that they pass through a designated "change point." The effects of change points on lines and circles are shown in Figure 7-25. Notice in particular the way lines will react to a change point with ortho on.

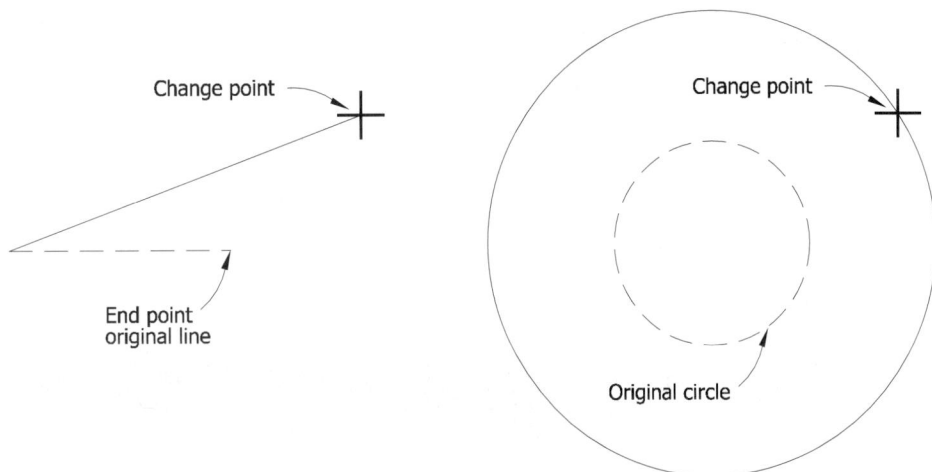

Figure 7-25

7.10 SCALEing Previously Drawn Entities

```
                        GENERAL PROCEDURE

 1.  Select the Scale tool from Modify toolbar.
 2.  Select objects (steps 1 and 2 can be reversed if noun/verb editing is enabled).
 3.  Pick a base point.
 4.  Enter a scale factor.
```

Any object or group of objects can be scaled up or down using the SCALE command or the grip edit scale mode. In this exercise we will practice scaling some of the text and lines that you have drawn on your screen. Remember, however, that there is no special relationship between SCALE and text and that other types of entities can be scaled just as easily.

⊕ Select the Scale tool from Modify toolbar, as shown in Figure 7-26.

You can also type "sc" or select Scale from the Modify menu.

AutoCAD will prompt you to select objects.

⊕ Use a crossing box (right to left) to select the set of six lines and text drawn in Task 7.1.

⊕ Press Enter to end selection.

You will be prompted to pick a base point:

    Specify base point:

The concept of a base point in scaling is critical. Imagine for a moment that you are looking at a square and you want to shrink it using a scale-down procedure. All the sides will be shrunk the same amount, but how do you want this to happen? Should the lower left corner stay in place and the whole square shrink toward it? Or should everything shrink toward the center? Or toward some other point on or off the square (see Figure 7-27)? This is what you will tell AutoCAD when you pick a base point.

⊕ Pick a base point at the left end of the bottom line of the selected set (shown as Base point in Figure 7-28).

AutoCAD now needs to know how much to shrink or enlarge the objects you have selected:

    Specify scale factor or [Reference]:

We will get to the reference method in a moment. When you enter a scale factor, all lengths, heights, and diameters in your set will be multiplied by that

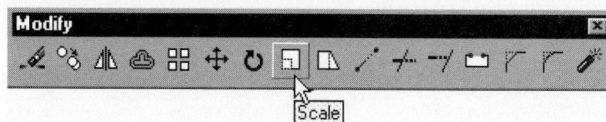

Figure 7-26

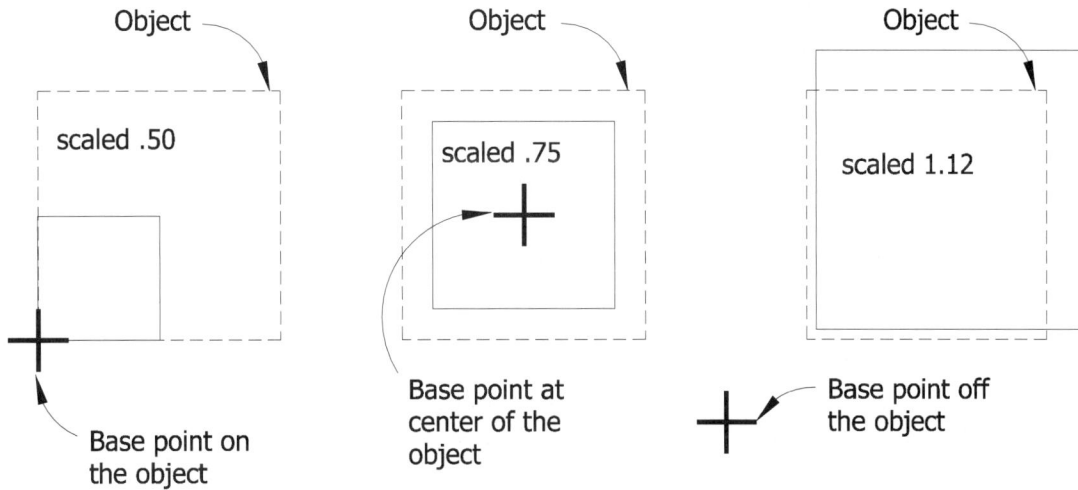

Object

scaled .50

Base point on
the object

Object

scaled .75

Base point at
center of the
object

Object

scaled 1.12

Base point off
the object

Figure 7-27

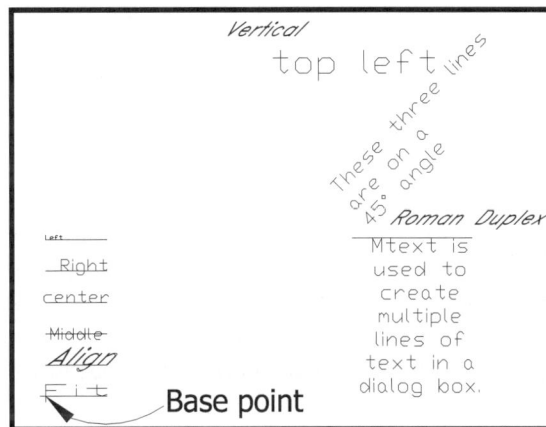

Vertical

top left *lines*

These three lines are on a 45° angle

Roman Duplex

Mtext is
used to
create
multiple
lines of
text in a
dialog box.

Left

Right

center

Middle

Align

Fit

Base point

Figure 7-28

factor and redrawn accordingly. Scale factors are based on a unit of 1. If you enter .5, objects will be reduced to half their original size. If you enter 2, objects will become twice as large.

⊕ Type ".5" and press Enter.

Your screen should now resemble Figure 7-28.

SCALEing by Reference

This option can save you from doing the arithmetic to figure out scale factors. It is useful when you have a given length and you know how large you want that length to become after the scaling is done. For example, we know that the lines we just scaled are now 2.00. Let's say that we want to scale them again to become 2.33 long (a scale factor of 1.165, but who wants to stop and figure that out?). This could be done using the following procedure:

1. Enter the SCALE command.
2. Select the lines.
3. Pick a base point.
4. Type "r" or select "reference".
5. Type "2" for the reference length.
6. Type "2.33" for the new length.

> **Note:** You can also perform reference scaling by pointing. In the preceding procedure, you could point to the ends of the 2.00 line for the reference length and then show a 2.33 line for the new length.

Scaling with Grips

Scaling with grips is very similar to scaling with the SCALE command. To illustrate this, try using grips to return the text you just scaled back to its original size.

Use a window or crossing box to select the six lines and the text drawn in Task 7.1 again.

There will be a large number of grips on the screen, three on each line and two on most of the text entities. Some of these will overlap or duplicate each other.

⊕ Pick the grip at the lower left corner of the word "Fit," the same point used as a base point in the last scaling procedure.

⊕ Right click to open the short cut menu and then select Scale.

⊕ Move the cursor slowly and observe the dragged image.

AutoCAD will use the selected grip point as the base point for scaling unless you specify that you want to pick a different base point.

Notice that you also have a reference option as in the SCALE command. Unlike the SCALE command, you also have an option to make copies of your objects at different scales.

As in SCALE, the default method is used to specify a scale factor by pointing or typing.

⊕ Type "2" or show a length of 2.00.

Your text will return to its original size, and your screen will resemble Figure 7-24 again.

⊕ Press Esc twice to clear grips.

> **Note:** Grips can be used to edit text in the usual grip edit modes of moving, copying, rotating, mirroring, and scaling. The stretch mode works the same as moving. Grips cannot be used to reword, respell, or change text properties.

7.11 Review Material

Questions

1. What is the main difference between DTEXT and MTEXT?
2. You have drawn two lines of text using DTEXT and have left the command to do some editing. You discover that a third line of text should have been en-

tered with the first two lines. What procedure will allow you to add the third line of text efficiently so that it is spaced and aligned with the first two, as if you had never left DTEXT?

3. What is the difference between center-justified text and middle-justified text?
4. What is the purpose of "%%" in text entry?
5. In the MTEXT command, what information does AutoCAD take from the two corners of the rectangle you specify before entering text? What else is needed to predict how AutoCAD will interpret these point selections?
6. What aspect of text can be changed with DDEDIT? What aspects of text can be changed with PROPERTIES? What is the purpose of MATCHPROP?
7. How do you check all the spelling in your drawing at once?
8. What is the difference between a font and a style?
9. What can happen if you choose the wrong base point when using the SCALE command?
10. How would you use SCALE to change a 3.00 line to 2.75? How could you use LENGTHEN (Chapter 6) to do the same thing?

Drawing Problems

1. Draw a 6 × 6 square. Draw the word "Top", on top of the square, 0.4 units high, centered on the midpoint of the top side of the square.
2. Draw the word "Left", 0.4 units high, centered on the left side of the square.
3. Draw the word "Right", 0.4 units high, centered on the right side of the square.
4. Draw the word "Bottom", 0.4 units high, below the square so that the top of the text is centered on the midpoint of the bottom side of the square.
5. Draw the words "This is the middle", inside the square, 0.4 units high, so that the complete text wraps around within a 2-unit width and is centered on the center point of square.

7.12   WWW Exercise #7 (Optional)

In Chapter 7 of our companion Web site we will ask you to explore the Web and bring back information on an important innovator in the field of architecture. We will define your task and give you two links to get you started. We will also give you another design challenge and, as always, the self-scoring test for this chapter. So, when you are ready,

⊕   Make sure that you are connected to your Internet service provider.

⊕   Type "browser", open the Web toolbar, and select the Browse the Web tool, or open your system browser from the Windows 98 taskbar.

⊕   If necessary, navigate to our companion Web site at "www.prenhall.com/dixriley/".

　　Happy hunting!

7.13   Drawing 7-1: Title Block

This title block will give you practice in using a variety of text styles and sizes. You may want to save it and use it as a title block for future drawings. In Chapter 10 we will show you how to insert one drawing into another, so you will be able to incorporate this title block into any drawing.

QTY REQ'D	D E S C R I P T I O N		P A R T N O.	I T E M NO.
	BILL OF MATERIALS			
UNLESS OTHERWISE SPECIFIED DIMENSIONS ARE IN INCHES	DRAWN BY: *Your Name*	DATE	**CSA INC.**	
REMOVE ALL BURRS & BREAK SHARP EDGES	APPROVED BY:			
TOLERANCES FRACTIONS ± 1/64 DECIMALS ANGLES ± 0'–15' XX ± .01 XXX ± .005	ISSUED:		DRAWING TITLE:	
MATERIAL:	FINISH:	SIZE **C**	CODE IDENT NO. 38178	DRAWING NO.	REV.
		SCALE:	DATE:	SHEET	OF

DRAWING SUGGESTIONS

$$GRID = 1$$
$$SNAP = 0.0625$$

- Make ample use of TRIM as you draw the line patterns of the title block. Take your time and make sure that at least the major divisions are in place before you start entering text into the boxes.
- Set to the "text" layer before entering text.
- Use DTEXT with all the STANDARD, 0.09, left-justified text. This will allow you to do all of these in one command sequence, moving the cursor from one box to the next and entering the text as you go.
- Remember that once you have defined a style, you can make it current in the DTEXT command. This will save you from having to restyle more than necessary.
- Use "%%D" for the degree symbol and "%%P" for the plus or minus symbol.

ALL TEXT UNLESS OTHERWISE NOTED IS:
Font (SIMPLEX)
Height (.09)
Left justified

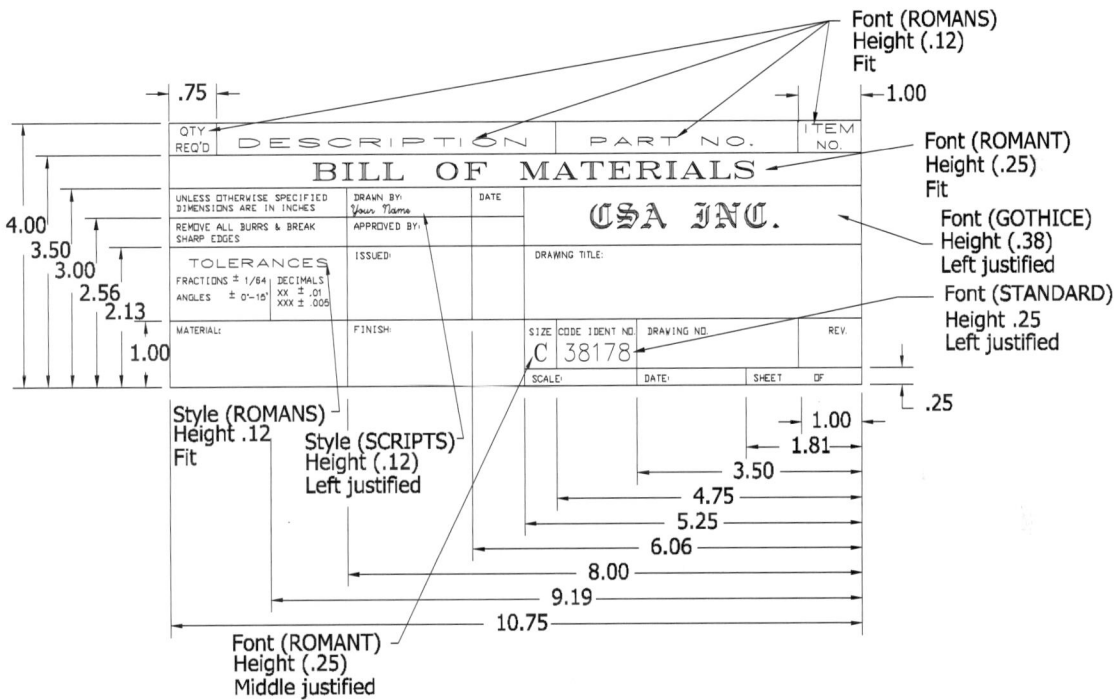

Font (ROMANS)
Height (.12)
Fit

Font (ROMANT)
Height (.25)
Fit

Font (GOTHICE)
Height (.38)
Left justified

Font (STANDARD)
Height .25
Left justified

QTY REQ'D	DESCRIPTION	PART NO.	ITEM NO.

BILL OF MATERIALS

| UNLESS OTHERWISE SPECIFIED DIMENSIONS ARE IN INCHES | DRAWN BY: Your Name | DATE |
| REMOVE ALL BURRS & BREAK SHARP EDGES | APPROVED BY: |

CSA INC.

| TOLERANCES | ISSUED: | DRAWING TITLE: |
FRACTIONS ± 1/64 DECIMALS
ANGLES   ± 0'-16' XX ± .01
                   XXX ± .005

| MATERIAL: | FINISH: | SIZE CODE IDENT NO. | DRAWING NO. | REV. |

C 38178

| SCALE: | DATE: | SHEET | OF |

.75
1.00
4.00
3.50
3.00
2.56
2.13
1.00
.25

1.00
1.81
3.50
4.75
5.25
6.06
8.00
9.19
10.75

Style (ROMANS)
Height .12
Fit

Style (SCRIPTS)
Height (.12)
Left justified

Font (ROMANT)
Height (.25)
Middle justified

TITLE BLOCK

Drawing 7-1

7.14 Drawing 7-2: Gauges

This drawing will teach you some typical uses of the SCALE and DDEDIT commands. Some of the techniques used will not be obvious, so read the suggestions carefully.

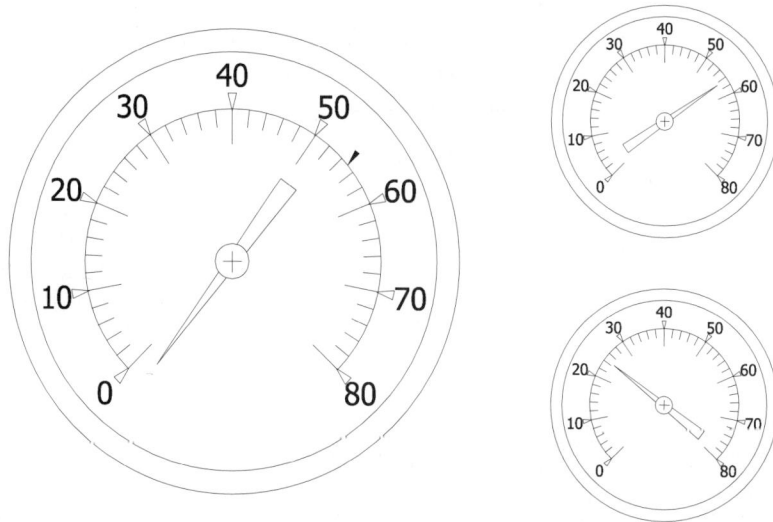

DRAWING SUGGESTIONS

GRID = 0.5
SNAP = 0.125

- Draw three concentric circles at diameters of 5.0, 4.5, and 3.0. The bottom of the 3.0 circle can be trimmed later.
- Zoom in to draw the arrow-shaped tick at the top of the 3.0 circle. Then draw the 0.50 vertical line directly below it and the number "40" (middle-justified text) above it.
- These three objects can be arrayed to the left and right around the perimeter of the 3.0 circle using angles of +135 and −135 as shown.
- Use DDEDIT to change the arrayed numbers into 0, 10, 20, 30, etc. You can do all of these without leaving the command.
- Draw the 0.25 vertical tick directly on top of the 0.50 mark at top center and array it left and right. There will be 20 marks each way.
- Draw the needle horizontally across the middle of the dial.
- Make two copies of the dial; use SCALE to scale them down as shown. Then move them into their correct positions.
- Rotate the three needles into positions as shown.

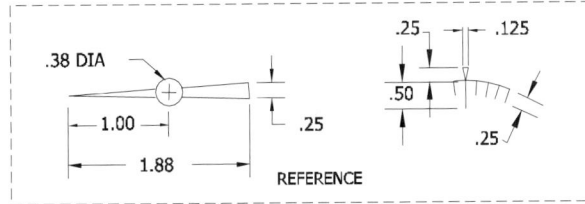

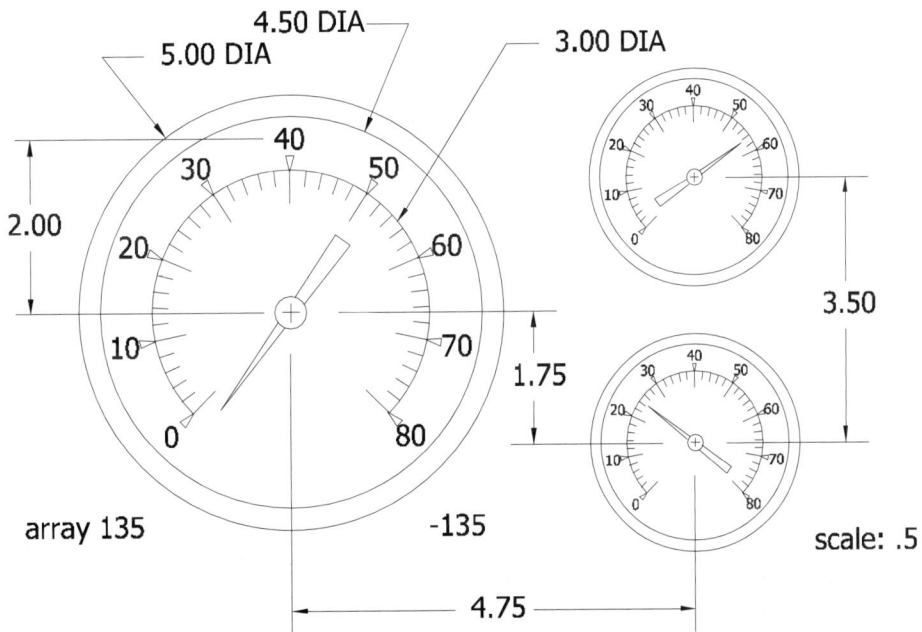

.38 DIA

1.00

1.88

.25

REFERENCE

.25   .125

.50

.25

4.50 DIA
5.00 DIA   3.00 DIA

40
30   50
20   60
10   70
0   80

2.00

1.75

3.50

array 135   -135   scale: .5

4.75

GAUGES
Drawing 7-2

7.15   Drawing 7-3: Stamping

This drawing is trickier than it appears. There are many ways that it can be done. The way we have chosen not only works well but makes use of a number of the commands and techniques you have learned in the last two chapters. Notice that a change in limits is needed to take advantage of some of the suggestions.

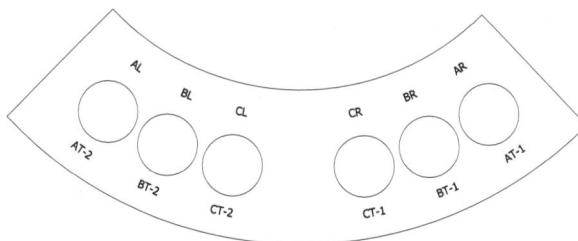

DRAWING SUGGESTIONS

GRID = 0.50
SNAP = 0.25
LIMITS = (0,0) (24,18)

- Draw two circles, radius 10.25 and 6.50, centered at about (13,15). These will be trimmed later.
- Draw a vertical line down from the center point to the outer circle. We will copy and rotate this line to form the ends of the stamping.
- Use the rotate, copy mode of the grip edit system to create copies of the line rotated 45 degrees and −45 degrees (coordinate display will show 315 degrees).
- Trim the lines and the circles to form the outline of the stamping.
- Draw a 1.50-diameter circle in the center of the stamping, 8.50 down from (13,15). Draw middle-justified text, "AR", 7.25 down, and "AT-1" down 9.75 from (13,15).
- Follow the procedure given in the next subsection to create offset copies of the circle and text; then use DDEDIT to modfiy all text to agree with the drawing.

GRIP COPY MODES WITH OFFSET SNAP LOCATIONS

Here is a good opportunity to try out another grip edit feature. If you hold down the shift key while picking multiple copy points, AutoCAD will be constrained to place copies only at points offset from each other the same distance as your first two points. For example, try this:

1. Select the circle and the text.
2. Select any grip to initiate grip editing.
3. Select Rotate from the short cut menu.
4. Type "b" or select Base point from the short cut menu.
5. Pick the center of the stamping (13,15) as the base point.
6. Type "c" or select Copy from the short cut menu.
7. Hold down Shift and move the cursor to rotate a copy 11 degrees from the original.
8. Keep holding down the shift key as you move the cursor to create other copies. All copies will be offset 11 degrees.

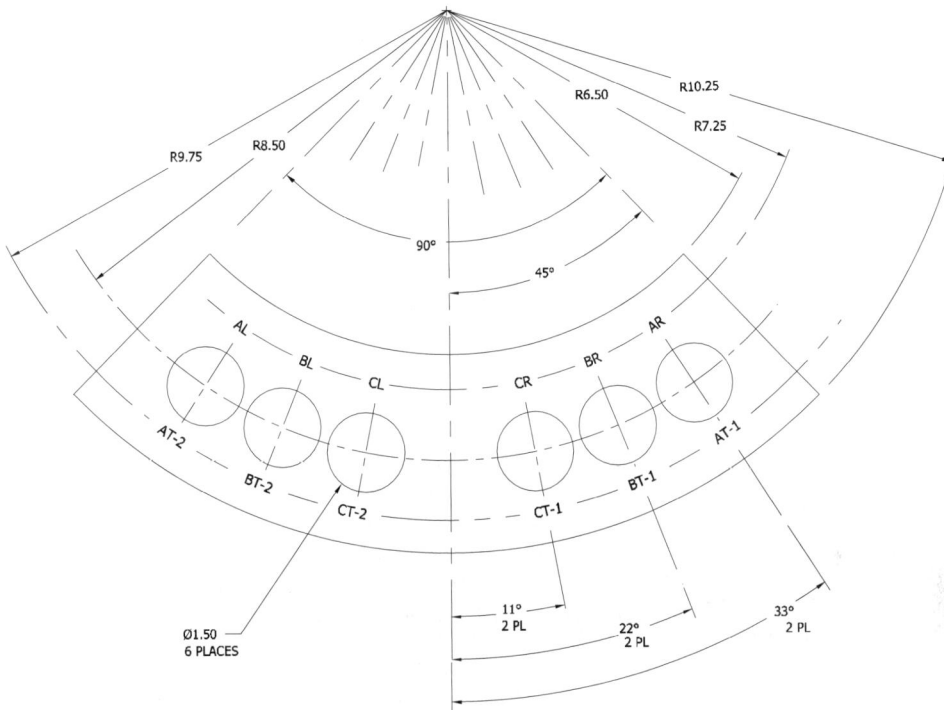

STAMPING
Drawing 7-3

7.16   Drawing 7-4: Control Panel

Done correctly, this drawing will give you a good feel for the power of the commands you now have available to you. Be sure to take advantage of combinations of ARRAY and DDEDIT as described. Also, read the suggestion on moving the origin before you begin. Moving the origin in this drawing will make it easier to read the dimensions, which are given in ordinate form measured from the (0,0) point at the lower left corner of the object.

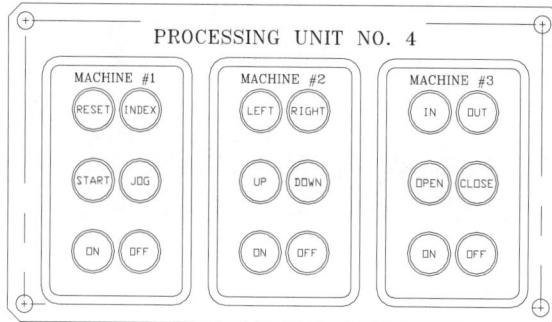

DRAWING SUGGESTIONS

GRID = 0.50
SNAP = 0.0625

- After drawing the chamfered outer rectangle, draw the double outline of the left button box, and fillet the corners. Notice the different fillet radii.
- Draw the "on" button with its text at the bottom left of the box. Then array it 2 × 3 for the other buttons in the box.
- Use DDEDIT to change the lower right button text to "off" and draw the MACHINE # text at the top of the box.
- ARRAY the box 1 × 3 to create the other boxes.
- Use DDEDIT to change text for other buttons and machine numbers as shown.

MOVING THE ORIGIN WITH THE UCS COMMAND

The dimensions of this drawing are shown in ordinate form, measured from a single point of origin in the lower left-hand corner. In effect, this establishes a new coordinate origin. If we move our origin to match this point, then we will be able to read dimension values directly from the coordinate display. This could be done by setting the lower left-hand limits to (−1, −1). But it may be done more efficiently using the UCS command to establish a User Coordinate System with the origin at a point you specify. User Coordinate Systems are discussed in depth in Chapter 12. For now, here is a simple procedure:

1. Type "ucs".
2. Type "o" for the "Origin" option.
3. Point to the new origin.

That's all there is to it. Move your cursor to the new origin and watch the coordinate display. It should show "0.00,0.00,0.00", and all values will be measured from there.

PROCESSING UNIT NO. 4

ROMANT
.38 high

Ø.50
4 holes

CHAMFER
.25 x .25
4 places

.50 rad
12 places

7.25

MACHINE #1

MACHINE #2

MACHINE #3

ROMANC
.25 high

Ø1.13
18 places

Ø1.25
18 places

.25 rad
12 places

.75

MONO
.20 high

RESET	INDEX
START	JOG
ON	OFF

LEFT	RIGHT
UP	DOWN
ON	OFF

IN	OUT
OPEN	CLOSE
ON	OFF

0   1.00   3.19   5.38   5.88   8.06   10.25   10.75   12.94   15.13

9.00   8.50   7.94   7.50   6.94   6.00   4.00   2.00   .50   0

0   .50   1.25   2.50   3.88   5.13   6.13   7.38   8.75   10.00   11.00   12.25   13.63   14.88   15.50   16.13

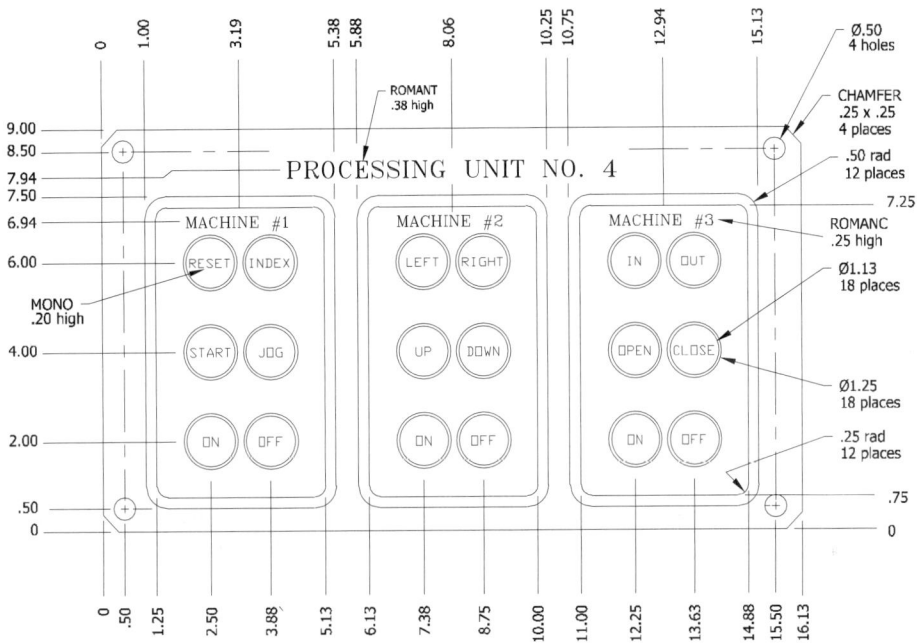

CONTROL PANEL
Drawing 7-4

7.17 Drawing 7-5: Tower

This architectural drawing will take some time, and you will utilize many commands that you have learned in this and previous chapters. Notice that the settings are quite different from our standard template, so be sure to change them before beginning.

DRAWING SUGGESTIONS

UNITS = Architectural
                Smallest fraction = 1
GRID = 10′
SNAP = 1′

- This drawing can be transfered, using the proper scale, from the book to your AutoCAD. You can use the scale provided on the drawing or use an architectural scale with the setting of 1/32″ = 1′. Either transfer method will produce similar results.
- Whatever order you choose for doing this drawing, we suggest that you make ample use of COPY, ARRAY, TRIM, and OFFSET.
- Keep ortho on, except to draw lines at an angle.
- With snap set at 1/16, it is easy to copy and array lines and shapes, as you will be doing frequently to reproduce the many rectangular shapes.
- You may need to turn snap off when you are selecting lines to copy, but be sure to turn it on again to specify displacements.
- Notice that you can use polar ARRAY effectively to draw the text in a circle and then use DDEDIT to change the text. Choose a text font that is similar to that shown (we used Dutch 801 Rm BT).

TOWER
Drawing 7-5

Scale

0   10   20   30   40   50

This drawing curtesy of Matt Rose

8 Dimensions

COMMANDS

BHATCH	DIMANGULAR	DIMLINEAR	PROPERTIES
BPOLY	DIMBASELINE	DIMOVERRIDE	QDIM
DDIM	DIMCONTINUE	DIMSTYLE	QLEADER
DIMALIGNED	DIMEDIT	DIMTEDIT	

OVERVIEW

The ability to dimension your drawings and add crosshatch patterns will greatly enhance the professional appearance and utility of your work. AutoCAD 2000's dimensioning features form a complex system of commands, subcommands, and variables that automatically measure objects and draw dimension text and extension lines. With AutoCAD's dimensioning tools and variables, you can create dimensions in a wide variety of formats, and these formats can be saved as styles. The time saved through not having to draw each dimension object line by line is among the most significant advantages of CAD. AutoCAD 2000 even has a new command, QDIM, which can be used to create multiple dimension objects at once.

TASKS

8.1 Creating and saving a dimension style
8.2 Drawing linear dimensions
8.3 Drawing multiple linear dimensions—QDIM
8.4 Drawing ordinate dimensions
8.5 Drawing angular dimensions
8.6 Dimensioning arcs and circles
8.7 Dimensioning with leaders
8.8 Changing and overriding dimension variables
8.9 Changing dimension text with DIMEDIT, DIMTEDIT, and PROPERTIES
8.10 Using the BHATCH command
8.11 Scaling dimensions between paper space and model space
8.12 Review Material
8.13 WWW Exercise #8 (Optional)
8.14 Drawing 8-1: Tool Block
8.15 Drawing 8-2: Flanged Wheel
8.16 Drawing 8-3: Shower Head
8.17 Drawing 8-4: Nose Adapter
8.18 Drawing 8-5: Plot Plan
8.19 Drawing 8-6: Panel
8.20 Drawing 8-7: Angle Support

8.1   Creating and Saving a Dimension Style

> **GENERAL PROCEDURE**
>
> 1. Type "d", select Style... from the Dimension menu, or select the Dimension style tool from the Dimension toolbar.
> 2. Click on New....
> 3. Give your new dimension style a name.
> 4. Click on OK to exit Create New Dimension Style dialog.
> 5. Select settings for Lines and Arrows, Text, Fit, Primary Units, Alternate Units, and Tolerances.
> 6. Click on OK to exit.

Dimensioning in AutoCAD 2000 is highly automated and very easy compared to manual dimensioning. To achieve a high degree of automation while still allowing for the broad range of flexibility required to cover all dimension styles, the AutoCAD dimensioning system is necessarily complex. In the exercises that follow we will guide you through the system, show you some of what is available, and give you a good foundation for understanding how to get what you want out of AutoCAD dimensioning. We will create a basic dimension style and use it to draw standard dimensions and tolerances. We will leave it to you to explore the many variations that are possible.

In AutoCAD 2000 it is best to begin by naming and defining a dimension style. A dimension style is a set of dimension variable settings that control the text and geometry of all types of AutoCAD dimensions. In older versions of AutoCAD, the default styles for most dimensions would use the drawing units set through the Units Control dialog box or the UNITS command. Now dimension units must be set separately. We recommend that you create the new dimension style in your template drawing and save it. Then you will not have to make these changes again when you start new drawings.

⊕   **To begin this exercise, open the 1B template drawing.**

Remember to look for this file in the Template folder and that it will have a .tmp file extension. We will make changes in dimension style settings in the template drawing so that all dimensions showing distances will be presented with two decimal places and angular dimensions will have no decimals. This will become the default dimension setting in any drawing created using the 1B template.

⊕   **Type "d", select Dimension style from the Format menu, or select Style from the Dimension menu, or open the Dimension toolbar and select the Dimension Style tool (see Figure 8-1).**

Figure 8-1

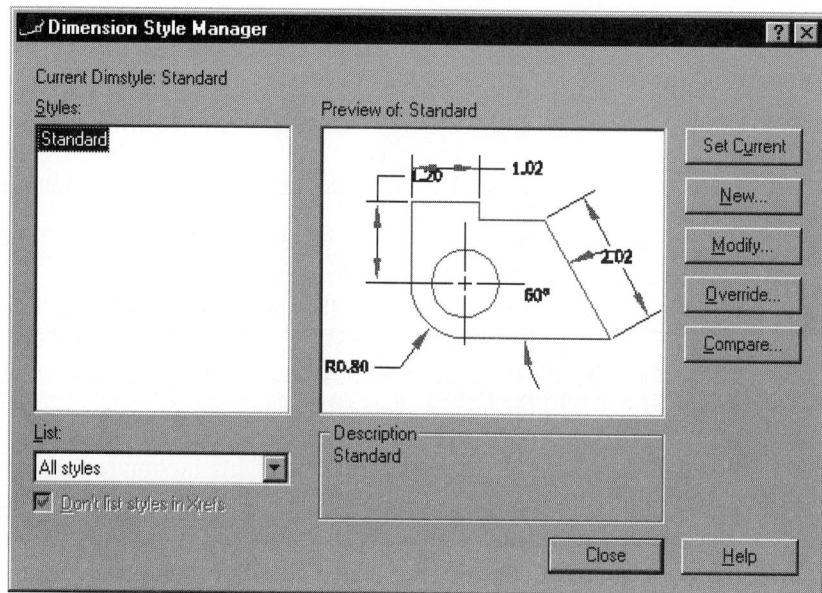

Figure 8-2

Tip: Dimensioning is a good example of a case where you may want to open a toolbar and leave it open for a while. Since dimensioning is often saved for last in a drawing and may be done all at once, bringing up the toolbar and keeping it on your screen while you dimension may be most efficient.

Any of the preceding methods will call the Dimension Style Manager shown in Figure 8-2. You will see that the current dimension style is called "Standard". Among other things, the AutoCAD Standard dimension style uses four-place decimals in all dimensions, including angular dimensions.

To the right of the Styles box is a preview image that will show you many of the Standard settings. The preview image will be updated immediately anytime you make a change in a dimension setting.

To the right of the preview is a set of five buttons, the second of which is New....

⊕ Click on the New... button.

This will open the small Create New Dimension style dialog box shown in Figure 8-3.

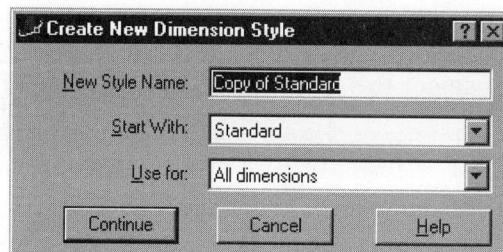

Figure 8-3

⊕ Double click in the New Style Name: edit box to highlight the word "Standard".

Note that the new style is based on the current Standard style. It will start with all of the Standard settings. Anything we don't change will be the same as in the Standard style.

⊕ Type "1B".

Any name will do. We chose this one to go with the template file name.

⊕ Click on Continue... .

This will create the new dimension style and take us into the New Dimension Style dialog box, shown in Figure 8-4. Here there are six tabbed cards that will allow us to make many changes in dimension Lines and Arrows, Text, Fit, Primary Units, Alternate Units, and Tolerance.

⊕ Click on the Primary Units tab.

This will bring up the Primary Units card, as shown in Figure 8-5. There are adjustments available for linear and angular units. The lists under Units and Angles are similar to the lists used in the Drawing Units dialog box. In the Linear dimension panel, Units format should show "Decimal" and in the Angular dimensions panel Units format should show "Decimal Degrees". If for any reason these are not showing in your box, you should make these changes now. For our purposes all we need to change is the number of decimal places showing in the Dimension Precision box. By default it will be 0.0000. We will change it to 0.00.

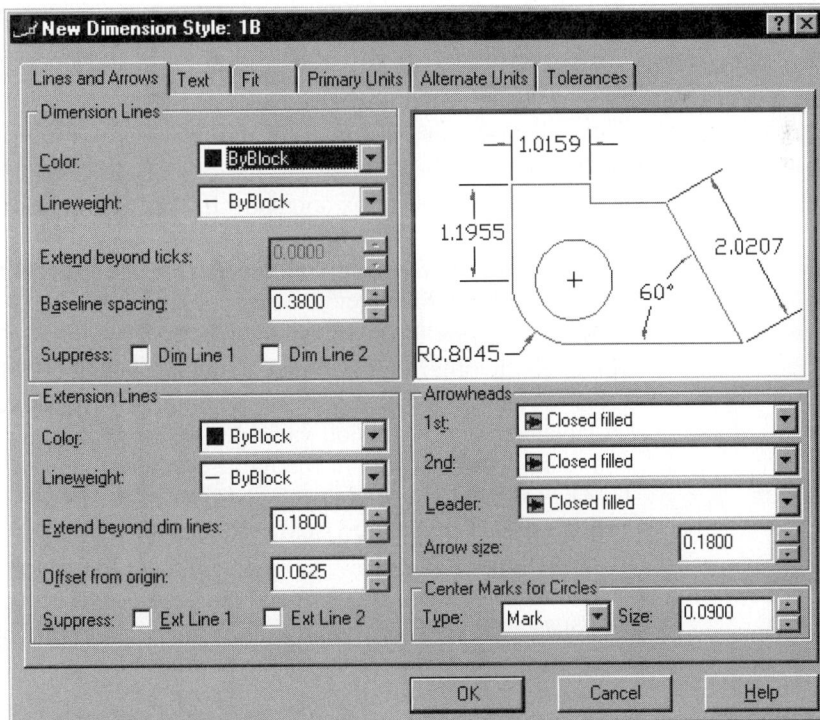

Figure 8-4

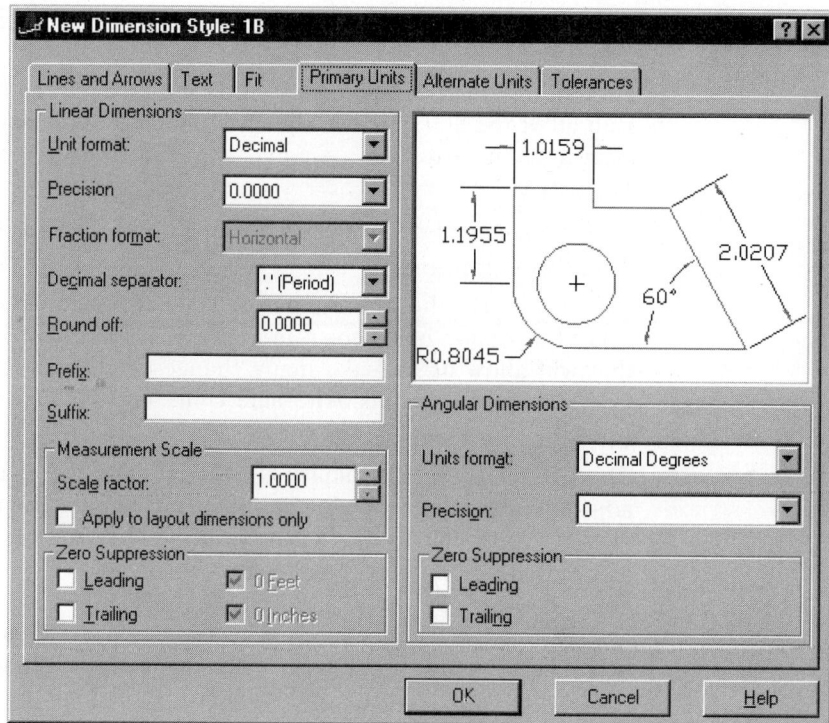

Figure 8-5

⊞ Click on the arrow to the right of the Precision box in the Linear dimensions panel.

This will open a list of precision settings ranging from 0 to 0.00000000.

⊞ Click on 0.00.

This will close the list box and show 0.00 as the selected precision. Notice the change in the preview image, which now shows two place decimals. At this point we are ready to complete this part of the procedure by returning to the Dimension Style Manager.

Before leaving the New Dimension Style dialog box, we recommend that you open the other tabs and take a look at the large variety of dimension features that can be adjusted. Each of the many options changes a dimension variable setting. Dimension variables have names and can be changed at the command line by typing in the name and entering a new value, but in Auto-CAD 2000 the dialog box makes the process much easier and the preview images give you immediate visual feedback.

In the Lines and Arrows tab you will find options for changing the size and positioning of dimension geometry. In Text you will be able to adjust the look and placement of dimension text. This tab includes the option of selecting different text styles previously defined in the drawing. In Fit you will be able to tell AutoCAD how to manage situations where there is a tight fit creating some ambiguity about how dimension geometry and text should be arranged. Primary Units, as you know, lets you specify the units in which dimensions are displayed. Alternate Units offers the capacity to include a secondary unit specification along with the primary dimension unit. A common use for this feature would be to give dimensions in both inches and centimeters, for example. Tolerances are added to dimension specifications to give the range of acceptable values in, for example, a machining process. The Tolerance tab gives several options for how tolerances are displayed.

⊕ Click on OK to exit the New Dimension Style dialog box.

Back in the Dimension Style Manager dialog you will see that 1B has been added to the list of styles. At this point you should have at least the Standard and 1B dimension styles defined in your drawing. 1B should be selected. The preview image shows the selected style.

Note: When a dimension style is selected in the Dimension Style Manager it is not necessarily the current style in the drawing. To make a style current you also need to click the Set Current button. You can tell which style is current by looking at the Override button. It will be accessible when the current style is selected and grayed out otherwise. This also indicates that you can temporarily override settings in the current style only.

⊕ Click on Set Current to set 1B as the current dimension style.

⊕ Click on Close to exit the Dimension Styles dialog box.

⊕ Save template drawing 1B.

⊕ Select New and open a new drawing using the 1B template.

If the new drawing is opened with the 1B template, the 1B dimension style will be current for the next task.

8.2 Drawing Linear Dimensions

> **GENERAL PROCEDURE**
>
> 1. Select Linear from the Dimension menu, or select the Linear Dimension tool from the Dimension toolbar.
> 2. Select an object or show two extension line origins.
> 3. Show the dimension line location.

AutoCAD 2000 has many commands and features that aid in the drawing of dimensions, as evidenced by the fact that there is an entire pull-down menu for dimensioning only. In this exercise you will create some basic linear dimensions in the now-current 1B style.

⊕ To prepare for this exercise, draw a triangle (ours is 3.00, 4.00, 5.00) and a line (6.00) above the middle of the display, as shown in Figure 8-6.

Exact sizes and locations are not critical. We will begin by adding dimensions to the triangle.

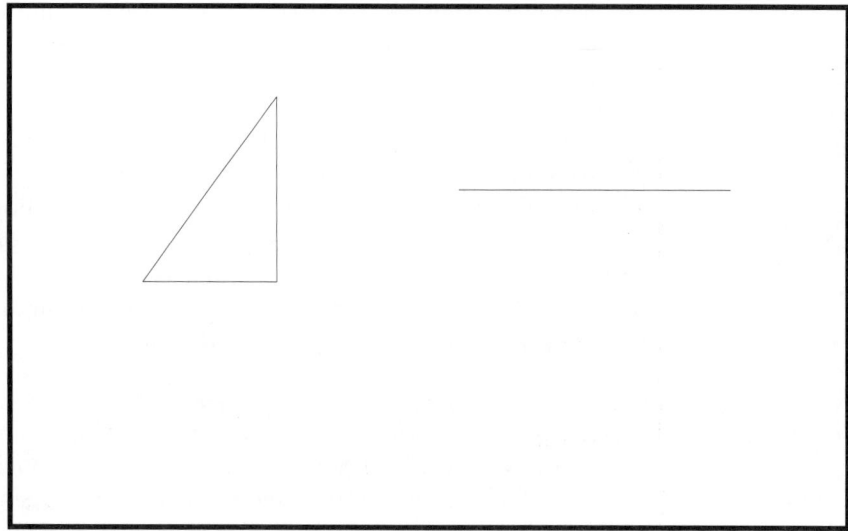

Figure 8-6

The dimensioning commands are streamlined and efficient. Their full names, however, are all rather long. They all begin with "dim" and are followed by the name of a type of dimension (for example, DIMLINEAR, DIMALIGNED, and DIMANGULAR). Use the Dimensioning menu or the Dimensioning toolbar to avoid typing these names.

We begin by placing a linear dimension below the base of the triangle.

⊕   Select Linear from the Dimension menu, or select the Linear Dimension tool from the Dimension toolbar, as shown in Figure 8-7.

This will initiate the DIMLINEAR command, with the following prompt appearing in the command area:

Specify first extension line origin or <select object>:

There are two ways to proceed at this point. One is to show where the extension lines should begin, and the other is to select the object you want to dimension and let AutoCAD position the extension lines. In most simple applications the latter method is faster.

⊕   Press Enter to indicate that you will select an object.

AutoCAD will replace the cross hairs with a pickbox and prompt for your selection:

Select object to dimension:

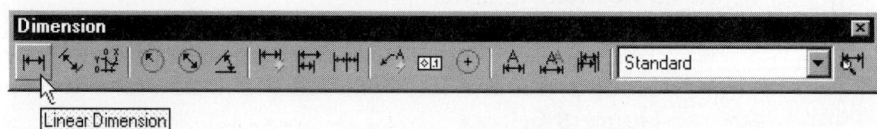

Figure 8-7

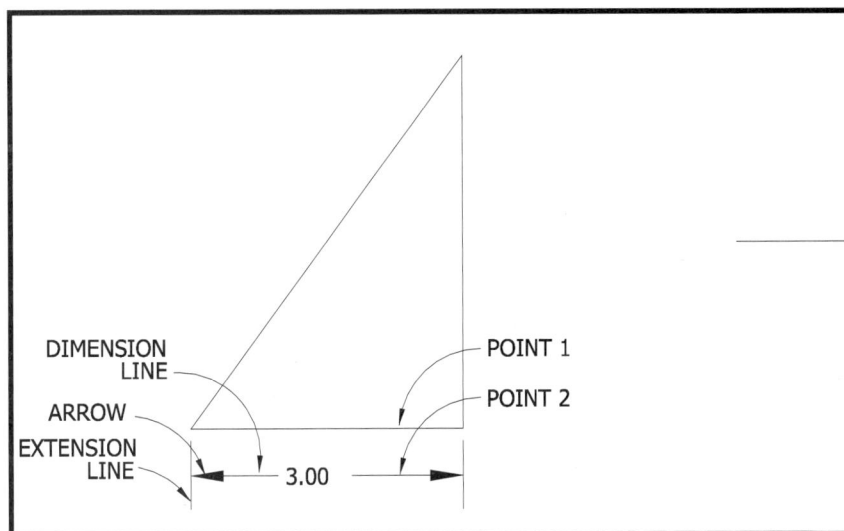

Figure 8-8

⊕ Select the horizontal line at the bottom of the triangle, as shown by point 1 in Figure 8-8.

AutoCAD immediately creates a dimension, including extension lines, dimension line, and text, that you can drag out away from the selected line. AutoCAD will place the dimension line and text where you indicate but will keep the text centered between the extension lines. The prompt is as follows:

```
Specify dimension line location or
[MText/Text/Angle/Horizontal/Vertical/Rotated]:
```

In the default sequence, you will simply show the location of the dimension. If you wish to alter the text content, you can do so using the "Mtext" or "Text" options, or you can change it later with a command called DIMEDIT. "Angle", "Horizontal", and "Vertical" allow you to specify the orientation of the text. Horizontal text is the default for linear text. "Rotated" allows you to rotate the complete dimension so that the extension lines move out at an angle from the object being dimensioned (text remains horizontal).

Note: If the dimension variable "dimsho" is set to 0 (off), you will not be given an image of the dimension to drag into place. The default setting is 1 (on), so this should not be a problem. If, however, it has been changed in your drawing, type "dimsho" and then "1" to turn it on again.

⊕ Pick a location about 0.50 below the triangle, as shown by point 2 in Figure 8-8.

Bravo! You have completed your first dimension. (Notice that our figure and others in this chapter are shown zoomed in on the relevant object for the sake of clarity. You may zoom or not as you like.)

At this point, take a good look at the dimension you have just drawn to see what it consists of. As in Figure 8-8, you should see the following components: two extension lines, two "arrows," a dimension line on each side of the text, and the text itself.

Notice also that AutoCAD has automatically placed the extension line origins a short distance away from the triangle base (you may need to zoom in to see this). This distance is controlled by a dimension variable called "dimexo", which can be changed in the Modify Dimension Style dialog, Lines and Arrows tab in the Extension lines panel. The setting is called Offset from origin.

Next, we will place a vertical dimension on the right side of the triangle. You will see that DIMLINEAR handles both horizontal and vertical dimensions.

⊕ Repeat the DIMLINEAR command.

You will be prompted for extension line origins as before:

> Specify first extension line origin or <select object>:

This time we will show the extension line origins manually.

⊕ Pick the right-angle corner at the lower right of the triangle, point 1 in Figure 8-9. AutoCAD will prompt for a second point:

> Specify second extension line origin:

Even though you are manually specifying extension line origins, it is not necessary to show the exact point where you want the line to start. AutoCAD will automatically set the dimension lines slightly away from the line as before, according to the setting of the dimexo dimension variable.

⊕ Pick the top intersection of the triangle, point 2 in Figure 8-9.

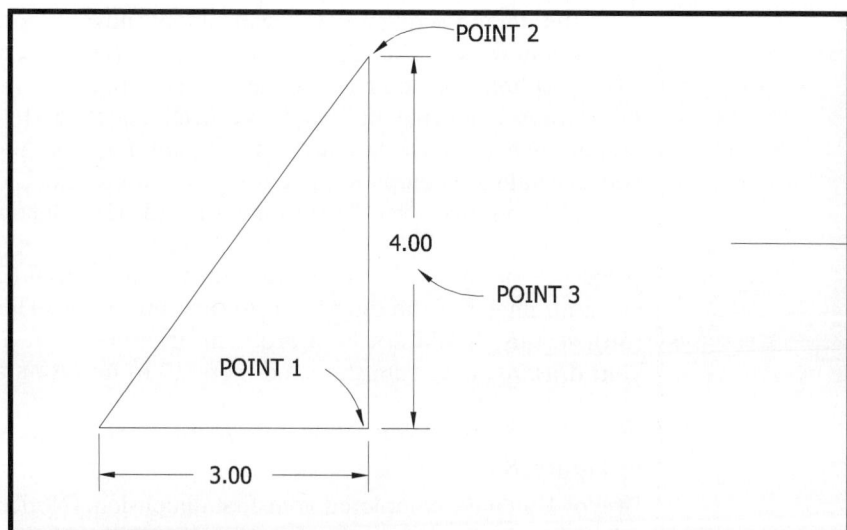

Figure 8-9

From here on, the procedure will be the same as before. You should have a dimension to drag into place, and the following prompt:

```
Specify dimension line location or
[Mtext/Text/Angle/Horizontal/Vertical/Rotated]:
```

⊕ Pick a point 0.50 to the right of the triangle, point 3 in Figure 8-9.

Your screen should now include the vertical dimension, as shown in Figure 8-9.

Now let's place a dimension on the diagonal side of the triangle. For this we will need the DIMALIGNED command.

⊕ Select Aligned from the Dimension menu, or the Aligned Dimension tool from the Dimension toolbar, as shown in Figure 8-10.

⊕ Press Enter, indicating that you will select an object.

AutoCAD will give you the pickbox and prompt you to select an object to dimension.

⊕ Select the hypotenuse of the triangle.

⊕ Pick a point approximately 0.50 above and to the left of the line.

Your screen should resemble Figure 8-11. Notice that AutoCAD retains horizontal text in aligned and vertical dimensions as the default.

Figure 8-10

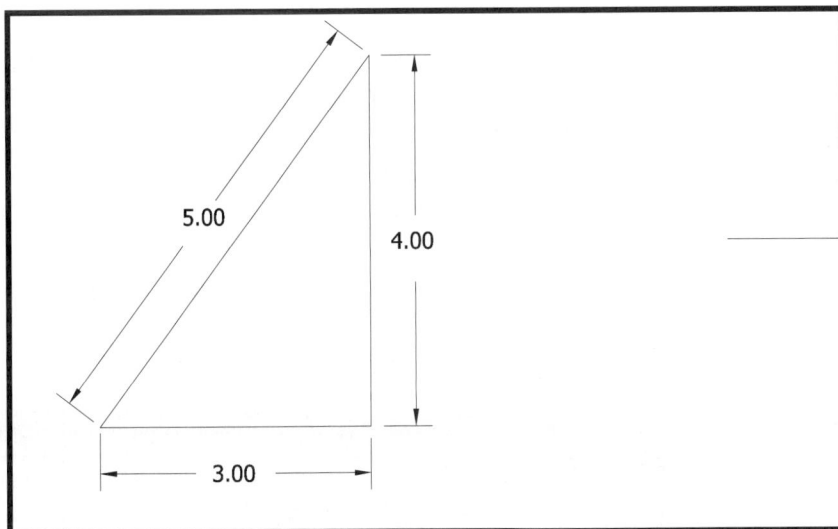

Figure 8-11

8.3 Drawing Multiple Linear Dimensions—QDIM

GENERAL PROCEDURE

1. Select QDIM from the Dimension menu or the Quick Dimension tool from the Dimension toolbar.
2. Select objects to dimension (steps 1 and 2 can be reversed if noun/verb editing is enabled).
3. Specify a multiple dimension type.
4. Show dimension line location.

QDIM is a miracle-working new AutoCAD 2000 command that automates the creation of certain types of multiple dimension formats. With this command you can create a whole series of related dimensions with a few mouse clicks. To introduce QDIM we will create a continuous dimension series dimensioning the bottom of the triangle, the space between the triangle and the line, and the length of the line itself. Then we will edit the series to show several points along the line. Finally we will change the dimensions on the line from a continuous series to a baseline series. In later tasks we will return to QDIM to create other types of multiple dimension sets.

⊕ To begin this task, erase the dimension from the bottom of the triangle.

Notice that you can select the complete dimension, including extension lines, dimension lines, text, and arrows with a single pick. The dimension is, like text and other objects in Part II of this book, a complex object, made up of many simple objects.

⊕ Select the bottom of the triangle and the 6.00 line to the right of the triangle.

Noun/verb editing allows you to select objects before entering QDIM. Your selected lines will be highlighted and have grips showing.

⊕ Select QDIM from the Dimension menu, or the Quick Dimension tool from the Dimension toolbar, as shown in Figure 8-12.

AutoCAD prompts:

```
Specify dimension line position, or
[Continuous/Staggered/Baseline/Ordinate/Radius/Diameter/
    datumPoint/Edit] <Continuous>:
```

The options here are various forms of multiple dimensions. Continuous, staggered, baseline, and ordinate are all linear styles. Radius and Diameter are

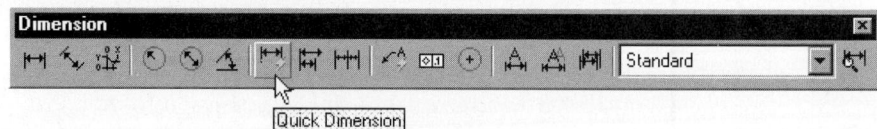

Figure 8-12

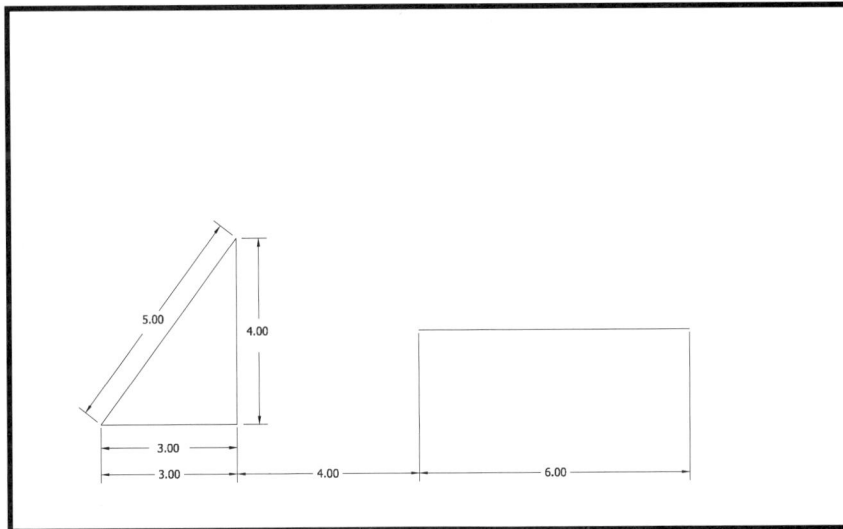

Figure 8-13

for dimensioning circles and arcs. Datum Point is used to change the point from which a set of linear dimensions is measured, and Edit has several functions we will explore in a moment.

Continuous dimensions are the AutoCAD default, but this may have changed if someone else has used QDIM on your system, since the last option used is retained as the default.

⊕ If necessary, type "c" for the Continuous option.

Continuous dimensions are positioned end to end, as shown in Figure 8-13. AutoCAD creates three linear dimensions at once, and positions them end to end.

⊕ Select a point about 1.0 unit below the triangle, as shown in Figure 8-13.

Next we will edit the dimension on the right, so that the line length is measured to several different lengths.

⊕ Repeat QDIM.

⊕ Select the dimension at the right, below the 6.00 line.

Notice that this dimension can be selected independently. The three continuous dimensions just created are separate objects, even though they were created simultaneously.

Note: The objects selected for the QDIM command can be dimensions or objects to be dimensioned. If you select objects, QDIM will create new dimensions for these objects; if you select dimensions, QDIM will edit or re-create these dimensions depending on the options you select.

⊕ Right click to end object selection.

AutoCAD will give you a single dimension to drag into place. If you pick a point now the selected 6.00 dimension will be re-created at the point you choose. We will do something more interesting.

⊕ Type "e" for the Edit option.

QDIM prompts:

```
Indicate dimension point to remove, or [Add/eXit] <eXit>:
```

We will add dimension points.

⊕ Type "a" for the Add option.

Small white x's are added at the end points of the line. These indicate the current dimension points. The prompt changes slightly.

```
Indicate dimension point to Add, or [Remove/eXit] <eXit>:
```

⊕ Pick point 1, as shown in Figure 8-14.

This point is 2 units from the left end point of the line. QDIM continues to prompt for points.

⊕ Pick point 2, as shown in Figure 8-14.

This point is 2 units from the right end point of the line.

⊕ Press enter or the space bar to end point selection.

QDIM now divides the single 6.00 dimension into a series of three continuous 2.00 dimensions. But we are not done yet. We will choose to draw these three dimensions in Baseline format.

⊕ Type "b" for the Baseline option.

QDIM immediately switches the three dragged dimensions to a baseline form.

⊕ Pick a point so that the top, shortest, dimension of the three is positioned about 1.00 below the line.

⊕ Press enter or the space bar to exit QDIM.

Your screen will be redrawn with three baseline dimensions as shown in Figure 8-14. We will have more to say about this powerful command as we go along. In the next task we will use it to create ordinate dimensions.

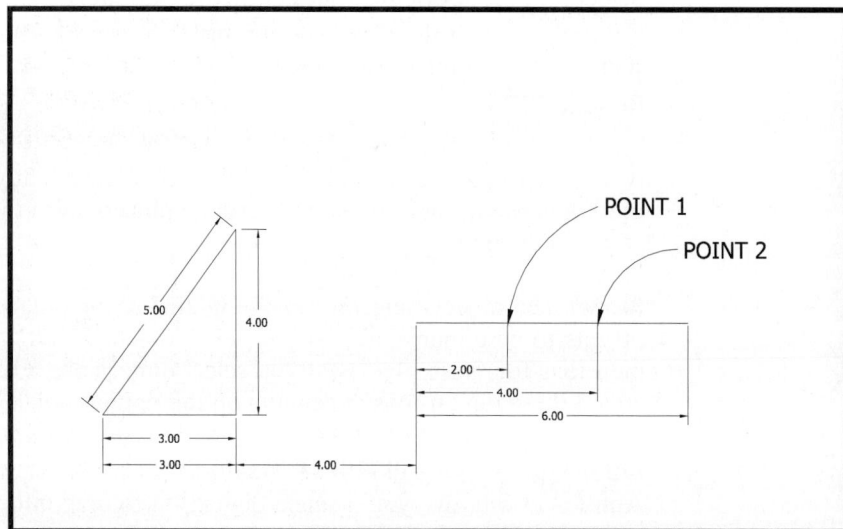

Figure 8-14

DIMBASELINE and DIMCONTINUE

Baseline and Continuous format dimensions can also be created one at a time using individual commands. The following general procedure is used with these commands.

1. Draw an initial linear dimension.
2. Select Baseline or Continue from the Dimension menu or the Baseline Dimension or Continue Dimension tool from the Dimension toolbar.
3. Pick a second extension line origin.
4. Pick another second extension line origin.
5. Press Enter to exit the command.

8.4   Drawing Ordinate Dimensions

GENERAL PROCEDURE

1. Define a coordinate system with the origin at the corner of the object to be dimensioned.
2. Select Ordinate from the Dimension menu or the Ordinate tool from the Dimension toolbar.
3. Select a location to be dimensioned.
4. Pick a leader end point.
5. Press Enter or change dimension text.

Ordinate dimensions are another way to specify linear dimensions. They are used to show multiple horizontal and vertical distances from a single point or the corner of an object. Since these fall readily into a coordinate system, it is efficient to show these dimensions as the x and y displacements from a single point of origin. There are two ways to create ordinate dimensions in AutoCAD 2000. AutoCAD will ordinarily specify points based on the point (0,0) on your screen. Using QDIM you can specify a new Datum Point that will serve as the origin for a set of ordinate dimensions. Using DIMORDINATE, it will be necessary to temporarily move the origin of the coordinate system to the point from which you want dimensions to be specified. In this task we will demonstrate both.

QDIM and the Datum Point Option

⊕   To prepare for this exercise, add a 4.00 vertical line up from the left end point of the 6.00 horizontal line, as shown in Figure 8-15.

We will use ordinate dimensions to specify a series of horizontal and vertical distances from the intersection of the two lines. First, we will use QDIM to add ordinate dimensions along the new vertical line. Then we will use DIMORDINATE to add ordinate dimensions to the horizontal line.

⊕   Enter the QDIM command.

⊕   Select the vertical line.

⊕   Right click to end object selection.

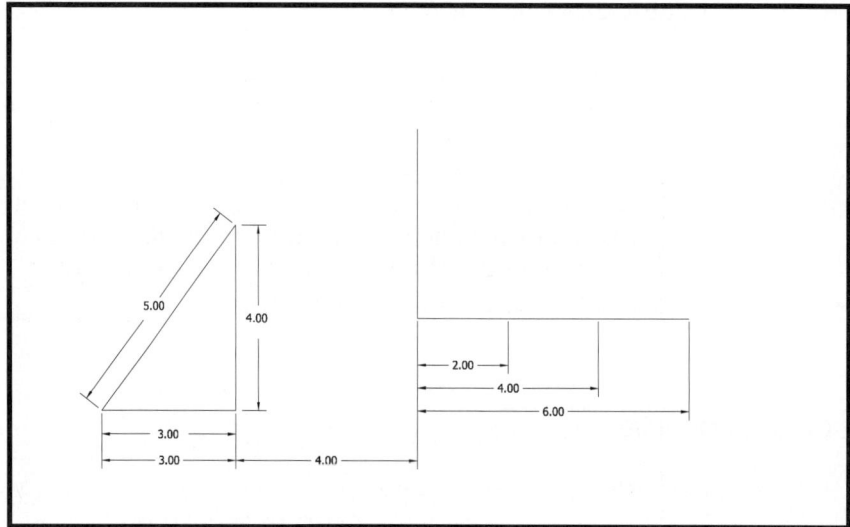

Figure 8-15

⊞ Type "o" for the Ordinate option.

⊞ Select a point about 1.00 unit to the left of the line, as shown in Figure 8-16.

The two dimensions you see will be at the ends of the line and will show the *Y* value of each end point. Whether in QDIM or in DIMORDINATE, AutoCAD 2000 will automatically choose the *X* or *Y* value depending on the object you choose and the position of the leaders relative to the dimensioned points. Since the values you see are measured from the origin at the lower left

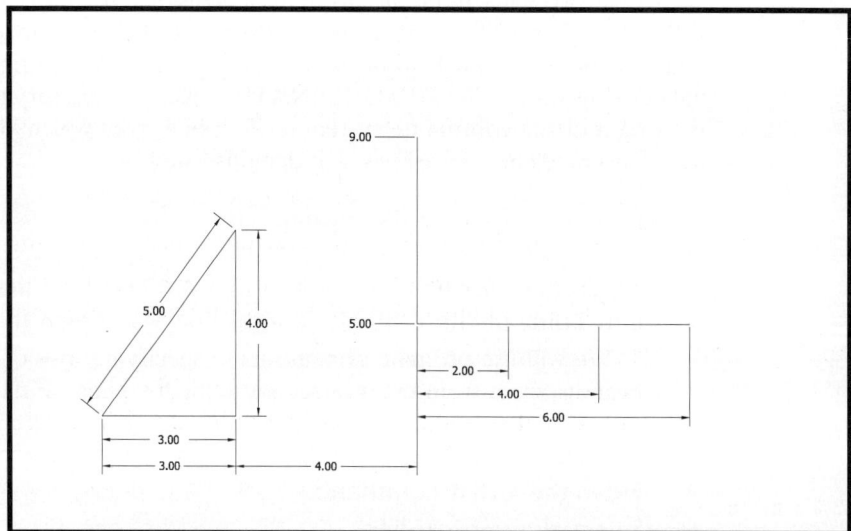

Figure 8-16

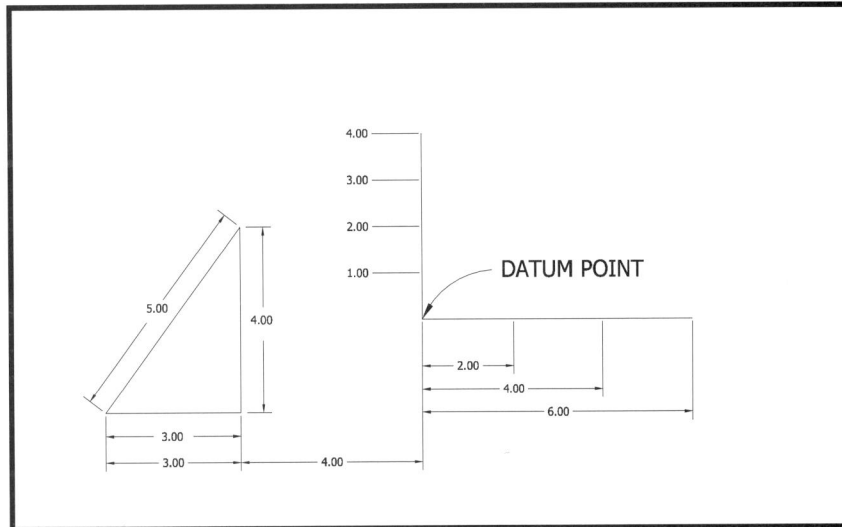

Figure 8-17

corner of the grid, they are not particularly useful. A more common use would be to measure points from the intersection of the two lines. This method was used to dimension Drawing 7-4, the Control Panel, in the last chapter, for example. To complete this set of dimensions, we will go back into QDIM, select a new Datum Point, and add and remove dimension points as shown in Figure 8-17.

⊕ Repeat QDIM.

⊕ Select the bottom ordinate dimension.

⊕ Select the top ordinate dimension.

   Notice that these need to be selected separately.

⊕ Right click to end geometry selection.

⊕ Type "p" for the Datum Point option.

   Notice the uppercase P in the option; if you type "d" you will get the Diameter option instead. QDIM prompts:

Select new datum point:

⊕ Select the intersection of the two lines, as shown in Figure 8-17.

   The new datum point is now established. We will add three new dimension points, and remove one before leaving QDIM.

⊕ Type "e" for the edit option.

   Even though remove may be the default edit option, you cannot have less than two dimension points in QDIM, so you will need to add first.

⊕ Type "a" to add points.

⊕ Add points 1.00, 2.00, and 3.00 up from the bottom of the line.

   As you add points, they will be marked by x's.

⊕ Type "r" to remove points.

⊕ Remove the point at the intersection of the two lines.

⊕ Press enter or the space bar to end point selection.

⊕ Pick a point about 1.00 unit to the left of the vertical line, as before.

Your screen will resemble Figure 8-17. Next we will dimension the horizontal line using the DIMORDINATE command.

DIMORDINATE and the UCS command

We will use DIMORDINATE to create a series of ordinate dimensions above the horizontal 6.00 line. This method requires you to create a new origin for the coordinate system using the UCS command. User Coordinate Systems are crucial in 3D drawing and are explored in depth in Chapter 12. Although DIMORDINATE will only create one dimension at a time, it does have some advantages over the QDIM system. To begin with you will not have to go back and edit the dimension to add and remove points. Additionally, you will be able to automatically create a variety of leader shapes.

⊕ Open the Tools menu and select Move UCS.

This selection executes the UCS command and automates the entry of the Move option. Specifying a new coordinate system by moving the point of origin is the simplest of many options in the UCS command. AutoCAD prompts

Specify new origin point or [Zdepth]<0,0,0>:

⊕ Pick the intersection of the two lines.

If you move your cursor to the intersection and watch the coordinate display, you will see that this point is now read as (0.00,0.00,0.00). If your user coordinate system icon is on and set to move to the origin, it will move to the new point.

⊕ Select Ordinate from the Dimension menu, or select the Ordinate Dimension tool from the Dimension toolbar, as shown in Figure 8-18.

AutoCAD prompts

Specify feature location:

In actuality, all you will do is show AutoCAD a point and then an end point for a leader. Depending on where the end point is located relative to the first point, AutoCAD will show dimension text for either an x or a y displacement from the origin of the current coordinate system.

⊕ Pick a point along the 6.00 line, 1.00 to the right of the intersection, as shown in Figure 8-19.

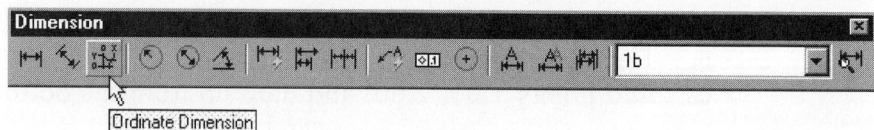

Figure 8-18

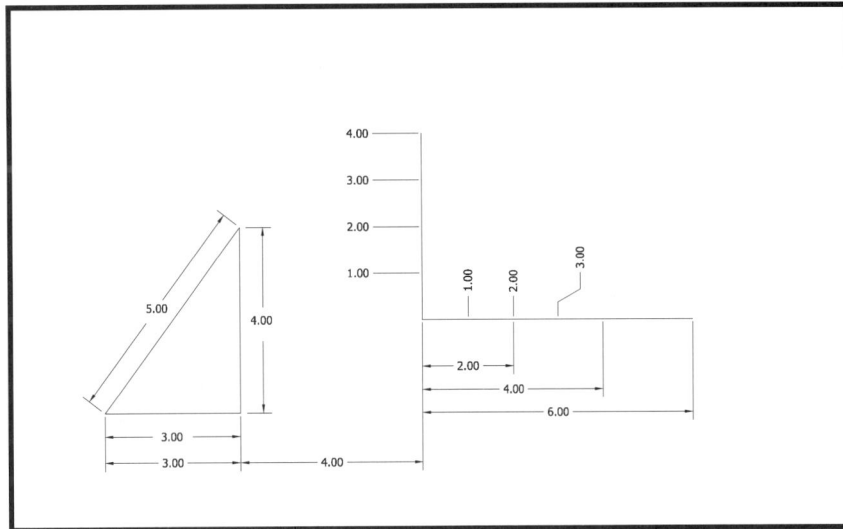

Figure 8-19

AutoCAD prompts

```
Specify leader endpoint or [Xdatum/Ydatum/Mtext/Text]:
```

You can manually indicate whether you want the *x* or *y* coordinate by typing "x" or "y". However, if you choose the end point correctly, AutoCAD will pick the right coordinate automatically. You can also provide your own text, but that would defeat the purpose of setting up a coordinate system that will give you the distances from the intersection of the two lines.

⊕ Pick an end point 0.5 above the line, as shown in Figure 8-19.

Your screen should now include the 1.00 ordinate dimension shown in Figure 8-19.

⊕ Repeat DIMORDINATE and add the second ordinate dimension at a point 2.00 from the origin.

⊕ Repeat DIMORDINATE once more.

⊕ Pick a point on the line 3.00 from the origin.

⊕ Move your cursor left and right to see some of the leader shapes that DIMORDINATE will create depending on the end point of the leader.

⊕ Pick an end point slightly to the right of the dimensioned point to create a broken leader similar to the one in Figure 8-19.

When you are done, you should return to the world coordinate system. This is the default coordinate system and the one we have been using all along.

⊕ Type "Ucs" or open the Tools menu and highlight "UCS".

⊕ Type "w", or select World from the UCS submenu.

This will return the origin to its original position at the lower left of your screen.

8.5 Drawing Angular Dimensions

GENERAL PROCEDURE

1. Select Angular from the Dimension menu or the Angular Dimension tool from the Dimension toolbar.
2. Select two lines that form an angle.
3. Pick a dimension location.

Angular dimensioning works much like linear dimensioning, except that you will be prompted to select objects that form an angle. AutoCAD will compute an angle based on the geometry that you select (two lines, an arc, part of a circle, or a vertex and two points) and construct extension lines, a dimension arc, and text specifying the angle. There is no angular option in the QDIM command.

For this exercise we will return to the triangle and add angular dimensions to two of the angles, as shown in Figure 8-21.

⊕ Select Angular from the Dimension menu or the Angular Dimension tool from the Dimension toolbar, as shown in Figure 8-20.

The first prompt will be

Select arc, circle, line, or <specify vertex>:

The prompt shows that you can use DIMANGULAR to dimension angles formed by arcs and portions of circles as well as angles formed by lines. If you press Enter, you can specify an angle manually by picking its vertex and a point on each side of the angle. We will begin by picking lines, the most common procedure in angular dimensioning.

⊕ Select the base of the triangle.

You will be prompted for another line:

Select second line:

⊕ Select the hypotenuse.

As in linear dimensioning, AutoCAD now shows you the dimension lines and lets you drag them into place. The prompt asks for a dimension arc location and also allows you the option of changing the text or the text angle.

Specify dimension arc line location or [Mtext/Text/Angle]:

Figure 8-20

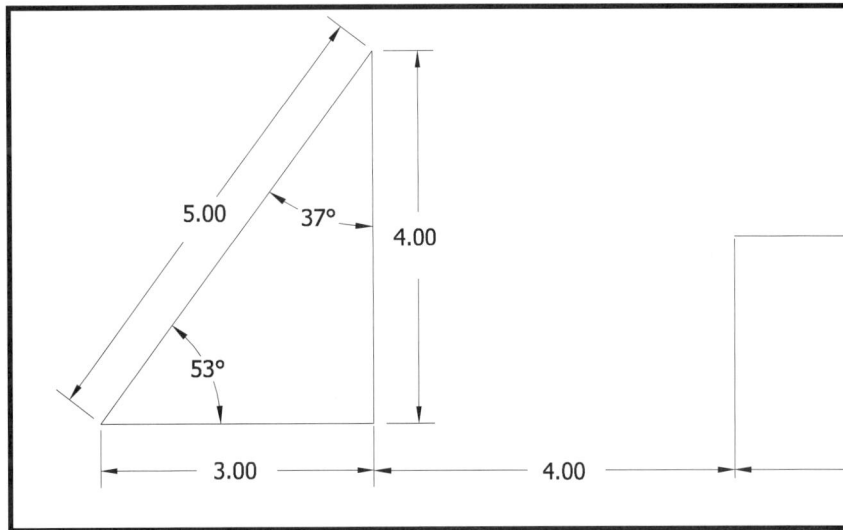

Figure 8-21

✛ Move the cursor around to see how the dimension may be placed and then pick a point between the two selected lines, as shown in Figure 8-21.

The lower left angle of your triangle should now be dimensioned, as in Figure 8-21. Notice that the degree symbol is added by default in angular dimension text.

We will dimension the upper angle by specifying its vertex.

✛ Repeat DIMANGULAR.

✛ Press Enter.

AutoCAD prompts for an angle vertex.

✛ Point to the vertex of the angle at the top of the triangle.

AutoCAD prompts

    Specify first angle endpoint:

✛ Pick a point along the hypotenuse.

To be precise, this should be a snap point. The most dependable one will be the lower left corner of the triangle.

AutoCAD prompts

    Specify second angle endpoint:

✛ Pick any point along the vertical side of the triangle.

There should be many snap points on the vertical line, so you should have no problem.

✛ Move the cursor slowly up and down within the triangle.

Notice how AutoCAD places the arrows outside the angle when you approach the vertex and things get crowded. Also notice that if you move outside the angle, AutoCAD switches to the outer angle.

✛ Pick a location for the dimension arc, as shown in Figure 8-21.

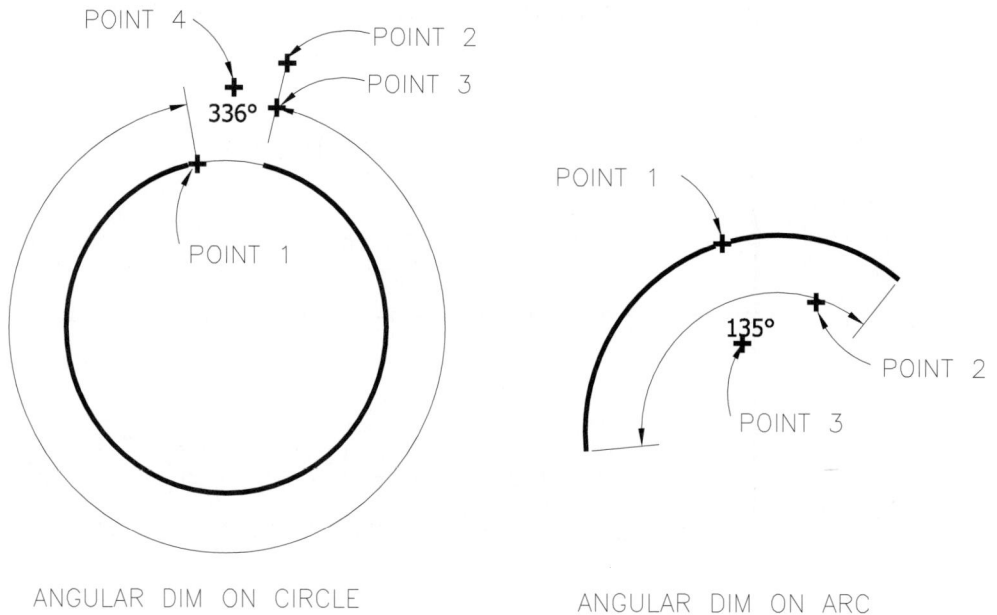

ANGULAR DIM ON CIRCLE   ANGULAR DIM ON ARC

Figure 8-22

Angular Dimensions on Arcs and Circles

You can also place angular dimensions on arcs and circles. In both cases AutoCAD will construct extension lines and a dimension arc. When you dimension an arc with an angular dimension, the center of the arc becomes the vertex of the dimension angle, and the end points of the arc become the start points of the extension lines. In a circle the same format is used, but the dimension line origins are determined by the point used to select the circle and a second point, which AutoCAD prompts you to select. These options are illustrated in Figure 8-22.

8.6 Dimensioning Arcs and Circles

GENERAL PROCEDURE

1. Select Radius or Diameter from the Dimension menu, or select the Radius Dimension or Diameter Dimension tool from the Dimension toolbar.
2. Pick the arc or circle at the point where you want the dimension line of leader to start.
3. Type text or press Enter.
4. Pick a leader line end point location.

The basic process for dimensioning circles and arcs is as simple as those we have already covered. It can get tricky, however, when AutoCAD does not place the dimension where you want it. Text placement can be controlled by adjusting dimension variables. In this exercise we will create a center mark and some diame-

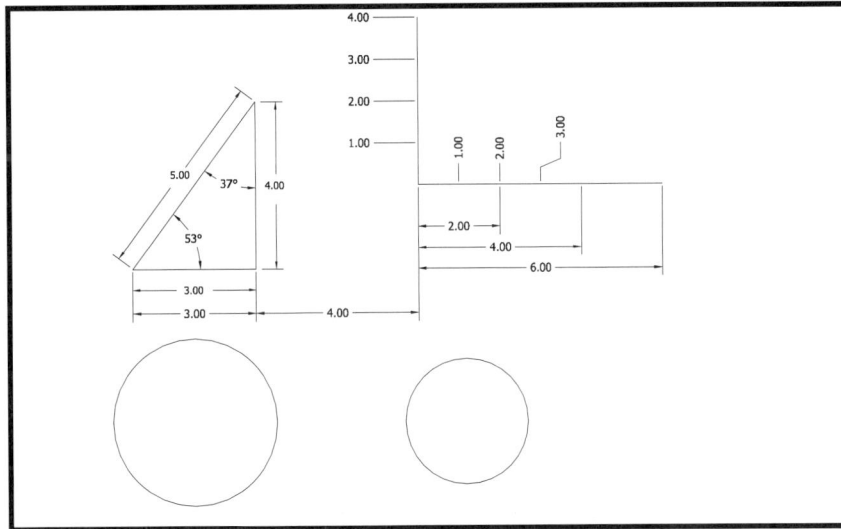

Figure 8-23

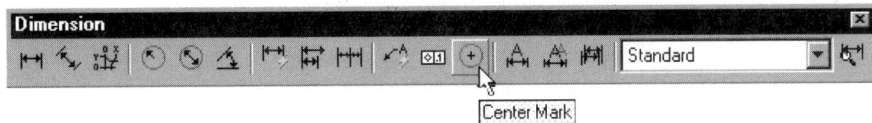

Figure 8-24

ter and radius dimensions. Then we will return to the QDIM command to see how multiple circles can be dimensioned at once.

⊕ To prepare for this exercise, draw two circles at the bottom of your screen, as shown in Figure 8-23.

The circles we have used have radii of 2.00 and 1.50.

⊕ Select Center Mark from the Dimension menu or the Center Mark tool from the Dimension toolbar, as shown in Figure 8-24.

Center marks are the simplest of all dimension features to create and are created automatically as part of some radius and diameter dimensions.

AutoCAD prompts

    Select arc or circle:

⊕ Select the smaller circle.

A center mark will be drawn in the 1.50 circle, as shown in Figure 8-25. The standard center mark is a small cross. The size of the cross can be changed in a small panel at the bottom right of the Lines and Arrows tab of the Modify Dimension Style dialog box. Here you also have a choice of standard continuous lines or broken center lines to form the mark.

Now we will add the diameter dimension shown on the larger circle in Figure 8-25.

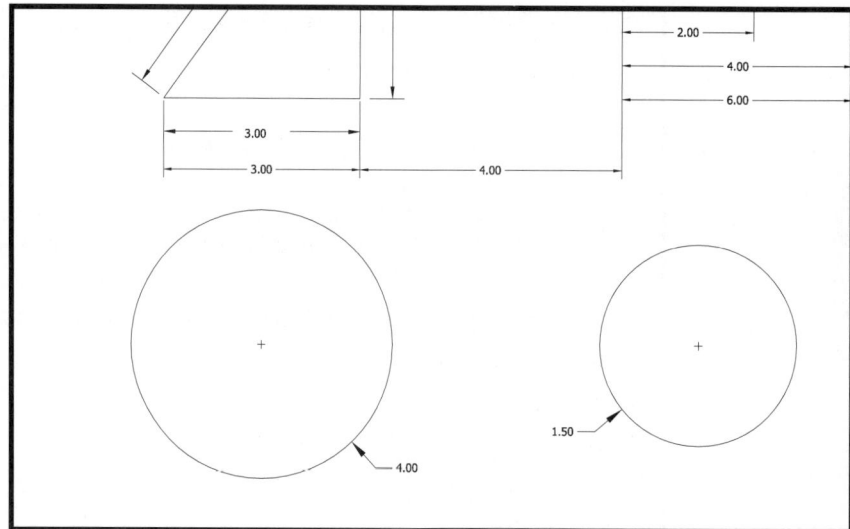

Figure 8-25

⊕ Select Diameter from the Dimension menu or the Diameter Dimension tool from the Dimension toolbar.

AutoCAD will prompt

<pre>   Select arc or circle:</pre>

⊕ Select the larger circle.

AutoCAD will show a diameter dimension and ask for Dimension line location with the following prompt:

<pre>   Specify dimension line location or [Mtext/Text/Angle]:</pre>

The Text and Angle options allow you to change the dimension text or put it at an angle. If you move your cursor around, you will see that you can position the dimension line anywhere around the circle.

⊕ Pick a dimension position so that your screen resembles Figure 8-25.

Notice that the diameter symbol prefix is added automatically by default.

Radius Dimensions

The procedures for radius dimensioning are exactly the same as those for diameter dimensions and the results look the same. The only differences will be the radius value of the text and the use of R for radius in place of the diameter symbol.

We will draw a radius dimension on the smaller circle.

⊕ Select Radius from the Dimension menu or the Radius Dimension tool from the Dimension toolbar.

⊕ Select the 1.50 (smaller) circle.

⊕ Move the cursor outside and around the circle.

⊕ Pick a point to complete the dimension, as shown in Figure 8-25.

The "R" for radius is added automatically.

Dimensioning Circles and Arcs with QDIM

Multiple radius or diameter dimensions can be created with QDIM. When this technique is used, all leaders will be created at the same angle. Try this:

⊕ Select QDIM from the Dimension menu, or the QDIM tool from the dimension toolbar.

⊕ Select both circles.

⊕ Right click to end object selection.

⊕ Type "r" for the radius option.

QDIM prompts

```
Specify dimension line position, or
[Continuous/Staggered/Baseline/Ordinate/Radius/Diameter/
    datumPoint/Edit] <Radius>:
```

⊕ Specify a line position by picking a point, as shown in Figure 8-26.

Radius dimensions will be added to both circles as shown in Figure 8-26. The diameter option works in exactly the same way.

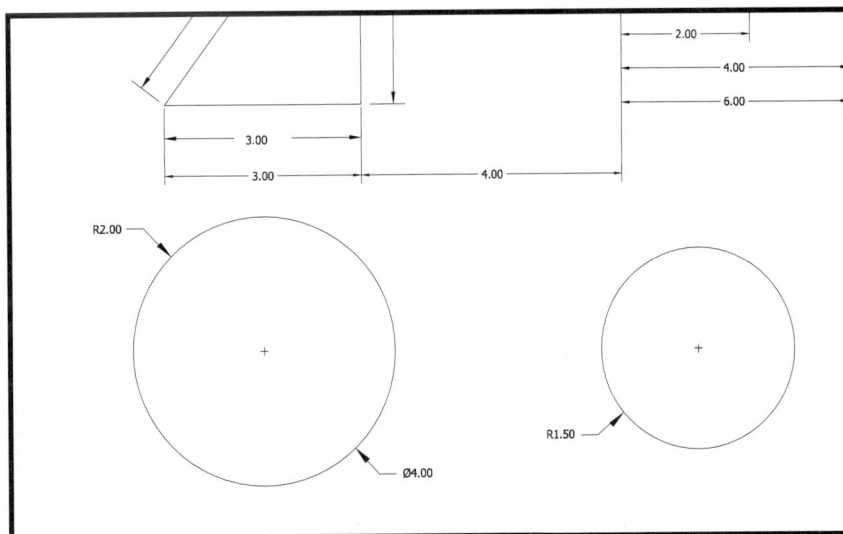

Figure 8-26

8.7   Dimensioning with Leaders

GENERAL PROCEDURE

1. Select Leader from the Dimension menu or the Leader tool from Dimension toolbar.
2. Select a start point.
3. Select an end point.
4. Select another end point.
5. Type dimension text.

Radius and diameter dimensions, along with ordinate dimensions, make use of leaders to connect dimension text to the object being dimensioned. Leaders can also be created independently to attach annotation to all kinds of objects. They may be used to dimension objects in crowded areas of a drawing. Unlike other dimension formats, in which you select an object or show a length, a leader is simply a line or series of lines with an arrow at the end to connect an object to its annotation. Because of this, when you create a dimension with a leader, AutoCAD does not recognize and measure any selected object or distance. You will need to know the dimension text you want to use before you begin.

AutoCAD 2000 has a new command called QLEADER, which organizes leader options into a single tabbed dialog box. In this exercise we will use QLEADER to create two leaders with associated text. One will be as simple as we can make it and the other will be more complex.

⊕   Select Leader from the Dimension menu, or select the Quick Leader tool from the Dimension toolbar, as shown in Figure 8-27.

AutoCAD will prompt you for a point:

```
Specify first leader point, or [Settings]<Settings>:
```

Usually you will want the leader arrow to start on the object, not offset, as an extension line would be. Often this will require the use of an object snap.

⊕   Hold down shift and right click your mouse to open the object snap short cut menu.

⊕   Select Nearest from the fourth panel of the menu.

The Nearest object snap specifies that you want to snap to the nearest point on whatever object you select. If you have not used the object snap mode before, take a moment to get familiar with it. As you move around the screen, you will see the Nearest snaptool whenever the cross hairs approach an object.

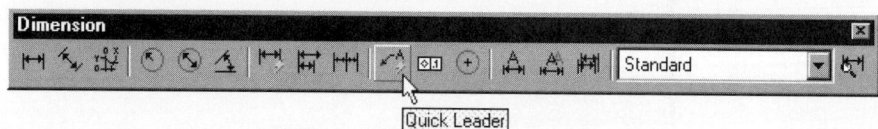

Figure 8-27

If you allow the cross hairs to rest on a point, the Nearest tooltip label will appear as well.

⊞ Position the cross hairs so that the upper right side of the 1.50-radius circle crosses the aperture, and press the pickbutton.

The leader will be snapped to the circle and a rubber band will appear extending to the cross hairs. AutoCAD will prompt for a second point:

Specify next point:

⊞ Pick a second point for the leader, up and to the right of the first point, as shown on the smaller circle in Figure 8-28.

QLEADER will prompt for another point. This allows you to create broken leaders made up of a series of line segments.

⊞ Press Enter to indicate that you are ready to create the annotation.

Leader text is created as MTEXT. AutoCAD prompts

Specify text width <2.00>:

You are being asked to specify text width as in the MTEXT command. The width is the width of the complete annotation, not of the character size.

⊞ Press enter or the space bar to accept the default text width.

You are prompted to enter text:

Enter first line of annotation text <Mtext>:

⊞ Type "3.00 DIA" and press Enter.

QLEADER prompts for additional lines of text:

Enter next line of annotation text:

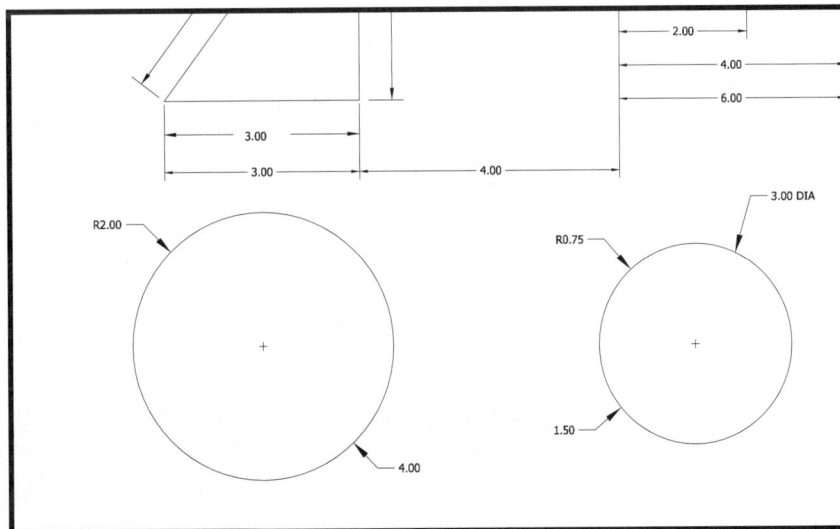

Figure 8-28

If you continue entering text, it will be added beneath the first line in MTEXT paragraph form.

Tip: Since text created in the QLEADER command is created as Mtext, it can be edited using all the tools available for Mtext, including the PROP-ERTIES command, DDEDIT, and the Mtext dialog box.

⊕ Press Enter (not the space bar, since you are entering text) to com-plete the command.

The annotated leader illustrated on the smaller circle in Figure 8-28 should be added to your drawing. If you look closely, you will notice that a short hori-zontal line segment is added automatically to "connect" the text to the leader.

Next we will use the Leader Settings dialog box to create a more complex spline curved leader attached to three lines of Mtext.

⊕ Repeat QLEADER.

⊕ Press enter or the space bar to open the Leader Settings dialog box, shown in Figure 8-29.

There are three tabs in this dialog. Annotation allows you to switch from Mtext to other types of annotation, which we will not explore at this point. The Leader Line and Arrow tab gives you options for changing the look and style of the leader and arrow. Attachment gives you options for attaching the leader to different points on the annotation text. These options are similar to the Mtext justification options.

⊕ Select the Leader Line and Arrow tab, as shown in Figure 8-29.

⊕ Select Spline in the Leader Line panel.

⊕ Open the Arrowhead options list and select "Open 30".

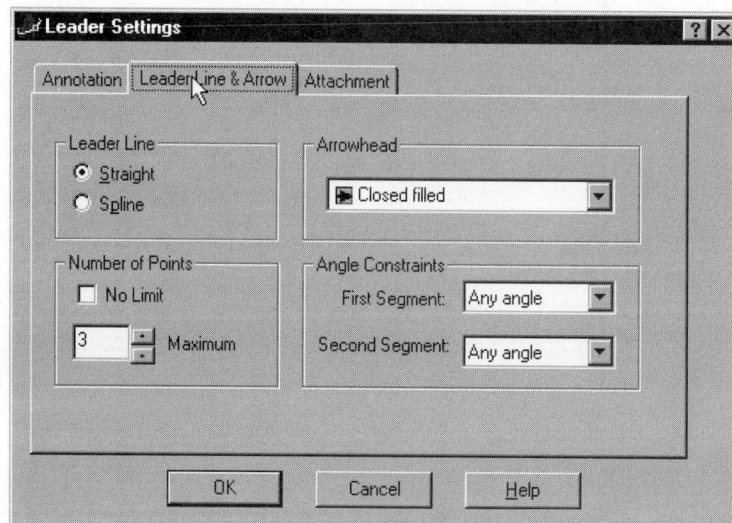

Figure 8-29

⊕   Switch to the Attachment tab.

⊕   In the list of radio buttons under "Text on right side", select "Middle of multi-line text".

⊕   Click on OK.

You should now be out of the dialog box and back to the prompt

```
Specify first leader point, or [Settings]<Settings>:
```

⊕   Open the Object Snap short cut menu and select Nearest from the short cut menu again.

⊕   Pick a leader start point on the upper right side of the larger, 2.00-radius circle.

⊕   Pick a second point for the leader about 45 degrees and 1.00 unit up and to the right of the first point.

⊕   Move the cursor slowly around the second point.

You will see that the line now bends and curves to the new point you are about to select.

⊕   Pick the third point slightly above and to the right of the second to create a curved leader similar to the one in Figure 8-30.

⊕   Press Enter to end the leader at this point.

QLEADER will now prompt for an annotation text width as before.

⊕   Type "3" and press Enter.

QLEADER prompts for text.

⊕   Type "This circle" and press Enter.

⊕   Type "is 4.00 inches" and press Enter.

⊕   Type "in diameter" and press Enter.

⊕   Press Enter to complete the command.

Your screen should now resemble Figure 8-30.

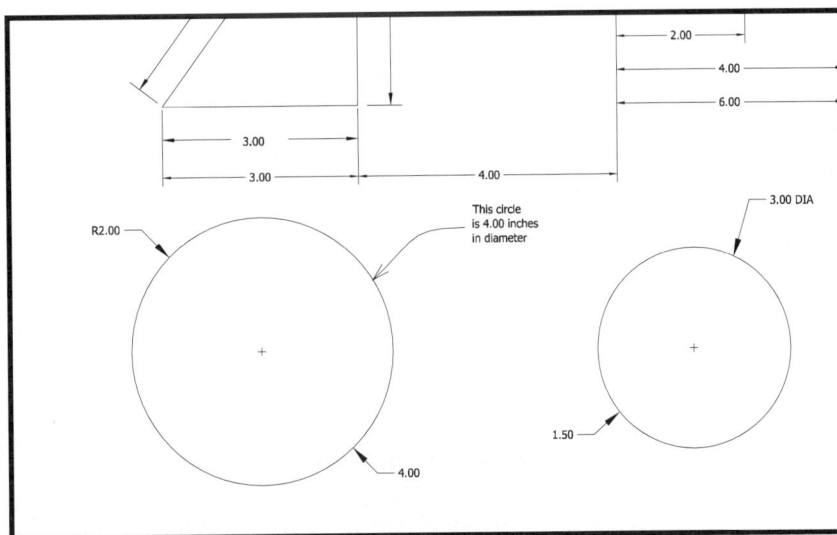

Figure 8-30

8.8 Changing and Overriding Dimension Variables

GENERAL PROCEDURE

1. Select "Override" from the Dimension menu.
2. Type a dimension variable name.
3. Type a new value.
4. Select dimensions to alter.

As you know from Task 8.1, you can save and restore dimension styles using the Dimension Style dialog box. When a new style is created and becomes current, all subsequent dimensions will be drawn using the new style. Sometimes, however, you may not want to create a whole new style in order to draw one or two dimensions that are slightly different from the others in your drawing. Or you may want to create a new style and apply it to some previously drawn dimensions. The first case is handled using a dimension override, the DIMOVERRIDE command. The second is done by changing dimension variables and then using the "apply" option in the DIMSTYLE command. We will demonstrate both, beginning with an override, and then look at a complete listing of all the dimension variables and their current settings.

⊕ Select Override from the Dimension menu.

AutoCAD prompts

```
Enter dimension variable name to override or
[Clear overrides]:
```

We can create some easily visible changes by altering the scale of a dimension using the dimscale variable.

⊕ Type "dimscale".

AutoCAD prompts for a new value and gives you the current value

```
Enter new value for dimension variable <1.00>:
```

⊕ Type "2".

AutoCAD continues to prompt for variables to override so that we can change more than one at a time.

⊕ Press Enter or the space bar.

Now that we have provided a new temporary dimension scale, we need to select dimensions that we want to show this scale. You will see the Select Objects prompt. We can use all of our usual selection methods here, including windowing and the all option. In this case we will change one dimension only.

⊕ Select the 3.00 linear dimension at the base of the triangle.

⊕ Press Enter to end object selection.

You will see that the 3.00 dimension text is redrawn twice as large, as shown in Figure 8-31. This alteration in dimension style is a one-time-only override. The change in dimscale has not been retained in memory, and any new di-

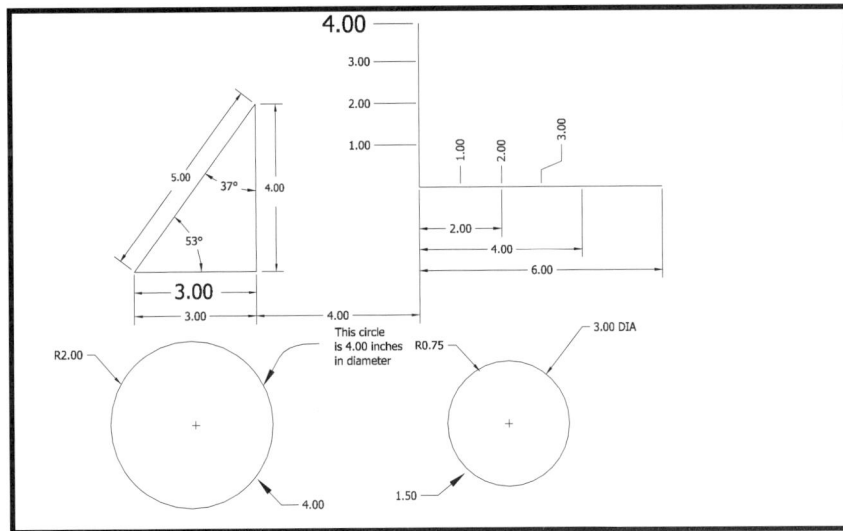

Figure 8-31

mensions drawn would have dimscale of 1.00. To make a more permanent change in style, we could go to the Dimension Style dialog box as before. Changes made in this way, however, will be applied to all dimensions previously drawn in the current dimension style. By changing a dimension variable at the command line, we can also gain the option of applying the change to selected dimensions only.

To change a variable at the command line, just type its name and then enter the new value.

⊕ Type "dimscale".

AutoCAD prompts

        Enter new value for DIMSCALE <1.00>:

⊕ Type "2".

This brings you back to the command prompt. The variable has been changed in the current dimension style, as you would see by opening the Dimension Style dialog box or by creating a new dimension. Now you need to update selected dimensions with the changed variable.

⊕ Select Update from the Dimension menu, or the Dimension Update tool from the Dimension toolbar, as shown in Figure 8-32.

These selections actually enter the –DIMSTYLE command. The minus sign in front of the command specifies that it is the command line version, not the

Figure 8-32

dialog box. In the command area you will see a list variables that have been changed and then a prompt with options for other types of changes.

```
Current dimension overrides:
DIMSCALE 2.00
Enter a dimension style option
[Save/Restore/STatus/Variables/Apply/?] <Restore>:
```

Do not be confused by the use of the word "override" here. There is a difference between one-time overrides like the one we did using the DIMOVERRIDE command, and running overrides like this one, which are retained in the current style until the style is restored to its original configuration.

We will use the "apply" option to apply the change in dimscale to one of our previously drawn dimensions.

⊕ Type "a".

AutoCAD needs to know which dimensions we want to apply the change to:

```
Select objects:
```

⊕ Select the 4.00 top ordinate dimension.

⊕ Press Enter to end object selection.

The 4.00 dimension text will be enlarged as shown in Figure 8-31.

While we are on the –DIMSTYLE command, use it to look at a list of all the dimension variables and their current settings. Setting dimension variables is easy, but the sheer number (67 in AutoCAD 2000) can be overwhelming. The dimension variable chart (Figure 8-33) will show you some of the most commonly used variables. You don't need to know all of them because in AutoCAD 2000 you have the great advantage of being able to see previews of most dimension variables in the Dimension Style dialog boxes.

⊕ Repeat -DIMSTYLE.

⊕ Type "st".

You will see 67 variables listed with their current settings and a phrase describing the effect of each setting. You will have to scroll to see the whole list.

Finally, before moving on, use the "restore" option to remove the change in dimscale.

⊕ Type "r", or press Enter, since Restore is the default option.

AutoCAD prompts

```
Enter a dimension style name, [?] or <select dimension>:
```

⊕ Type "1b" or the name of your current dimension style.

This will restore the original values of the 1B dimension style. To return altered dimensions to these original style settings, use Update from the Dimension menu, or the Update Dimension tool from the toolbar again.

COMMONLY USED DIMENSION VARIABLES					
Variable	Default Value	Appearance	DESCRIPTION	New Value	Appearance
dimaso	on	All parts of dim are one entity	Associative dimensioning	off	All parts of dim are separate entities
dimscale	1.00	⊢—2.00—⊣	Changes size of text & arrows, not value	2.00	⊢—2.00—⊣
dimasz	.18	▶	Sets arrow size	.38	▶
dimcen	.09	(+)	Center mark size and appearance	−.09	⊕
dimdli	.38		Spacing between continued dimension lines	.50	
dimexe	.18		Extension above dimension line	.25	
dimexo	0.06		Extension line origin offset	.12	
dimtp	0.00	1.50	Sets plus tolerance	.01	$1.50^{+0.01}_{-0.00}$
dimtm	0.00	1.50	Sets minus tolerance	.02	$1.50^{+0.00}_{-0.02}$
dimtol	off	1.50	Generate dimension tolerances (dimtp & dimtm must be set) (dimtol & dimlim cannot both be on)	on	$1.50^{+0.01}_{-0.02}$
dimlim	off	1.50	Generate dimension limits (dimtp & dimtm must be set) (dimtol & dimlim cannot both be on)	on	1.51 1.48
dimtad	off	⊢— 1.50 —⊣	Places text above the dimension line	on	1.50
dimtxt	.18	1.50	Sets height of text	.38	1.50
dimtsz	.18	⊢— 1.50 —⊣	Sets tick marks & tick height	.25	1.50
dimtih	on	1.50	Sets angle of text When off rotates text to the angle of the dimension	off	1.50
dimtix	off	Ø0.71 (+)	Forces the text to inside of circles and arcs. Linear and angular dimensions are placed inside if there is sufficient room	on	(Ø0.71)

Figure 8-33

8.9 Changing Dimension Text with DIMEDIT, DIMTEDIT, and PROPERTIES

Dimensions can be edited in many of the same ways that other objects are edited. They can be moved, copied, stretched, rotated, trimmed, extended, etc. There are three commands that can be used to change text placement or text content. DIMEDIT allows you to add text to current dimension text, DIMTEDIT allows you to adjust dimension placement, and PROPERTIES can be used to change dimension variables or text content. Try these quick demonstrations.

Figure 8-34

The DIMEDIT Command

⊕ Type "Dimedit" or select the Dimension Edit tool from the Dimension toolbar, as shown in Figure 8-34.

AutoCAD prompts with options:

```
Enter type of dimension editing [Home/New/Rotate/Oblique]
<Home>:
```

Home, Rotate, and Oblique are placement and orientation options; New refers to new text content.

⊕ Type "n" for New.

AutoCAD opens the Multiline Text Editor and waits for you to enter text. You will see two arrows in the edit box (< >). Whatever you type will be added to the existing dimension text. If you type to the left of the arrows, you will add text to the left; if you type to the right, text will be added to the right.

We will change the 5.00 aligned dimension to read "5.00 mm".

⊕ Click on the right side of <> so that the flashing cursor moves to the right.

⊕ Type "mm".

The text will appear in the edit box.

⊕ Click on "OK" or press Enter to return to the drawing.

AutoCAD prompts for objects to receive the new text:

$$\text{Select Objects:}$$

⊕ Select the 5.00 aligned dimension on the hypotenuse of the triangle.

⊕ Press Enter to end object selection.

The text will be redrawn, as shown in Figure 8-35. This command is very convenient when you want to add text to a dimension without re-creating the dimension.

The DIMTEDIT Command

DIMTEDIT is used to edit dimension text placement. It works on the whole dimension object, as if you had re-entered a dimension command at the point where you are asked to pick a dimension text location.

⊕ Type "dimtedit" or select the Dimension Text Edit tool from the Dimension toolbar.

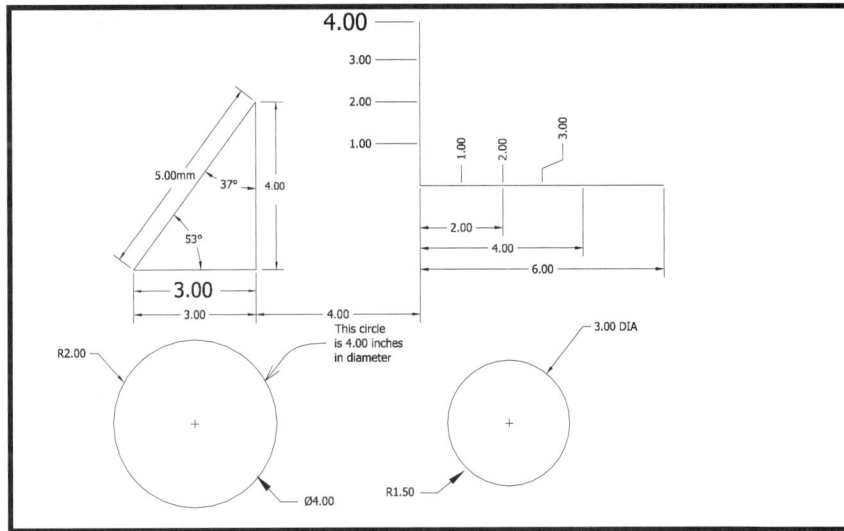

Figure 8-35

AutoCAD prompts

Select dimension:

⊞ Select the radius dimension on the 1.50 circle.

AutoCAD "frees up" the selected dimension and lets you drag it into a new position. The prompt is

Specify new location for dimension text or
[Left/Right/Center/Home/Angle]:

The options here are as follows: Left moves the dimension text to the left within the dimension line; Right to the right; Center places text in the center of the dimension line; Home returns the text to the standard "home" position, which is often also the center position; Angle lets you rotate the dimension text in place without changing the rest of the dimension geometry. The default action is to drag the dimension and extension lines and point to a new location for the dimension text.

⊞ Pick a new location for the dimension text.

PROPERTIES Command and the Dimension Edit Short Cut Menu

The PROPERTIES command gives you direct, dialog box access to many dimension variables, including text content. The PROPERTIES command can be opened from the Modify menu, or by selecting objects first and then right clicking to open an editing short cut menu. This short cut menu also provides another way to access DIMTEDIT functions, along with other edit options. Try this:

⊞ Pick the lower baseline dimension on the 6.00 line.
⊞ With this line selected, right click your mouse.

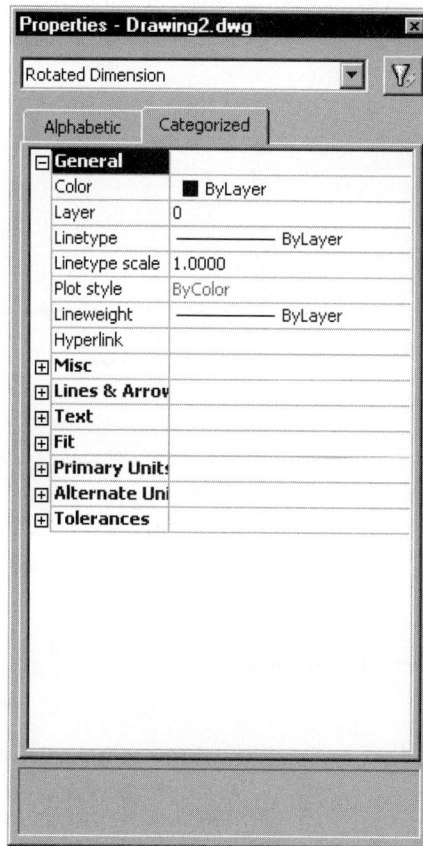

Figure 8-36

This will open a short cut menu with options for editing the selected object. The exact options shown on this short cut menu will depend on the object(s) selected. If you choose only dimension objects, you will have options to change Dimension Text position, dimension unit precision, and Dimension style, along with other standard edit commands including Erase, Move, Copy, Scale, and Rotate. At the bottom of the menu you will see Properties....

⊕ Select Properties from the short cut menu.

This will open the Properties manager, as shown in Figure 8-36. With the Categories tab selected, you will notice that the headings at the bottom of the list, Lines and Arrows, Text, Fit, etc. match the tabs in the Dimension Style dialog box. So here is yet another way to modify dimension variables.

⊕ With the Categories tab selected, click the + sign next to Text.

This opens the list of text-related dimension features that can be modified.

⊕ Scroll down the list to Text override.

This selection is at the bottom of the list.

⊕ Click twice in the box to the right of "Text override".

⊕ Type "6.00 inches".

Your screen will be redrawn with the dimension text shown in Figure 8-37.

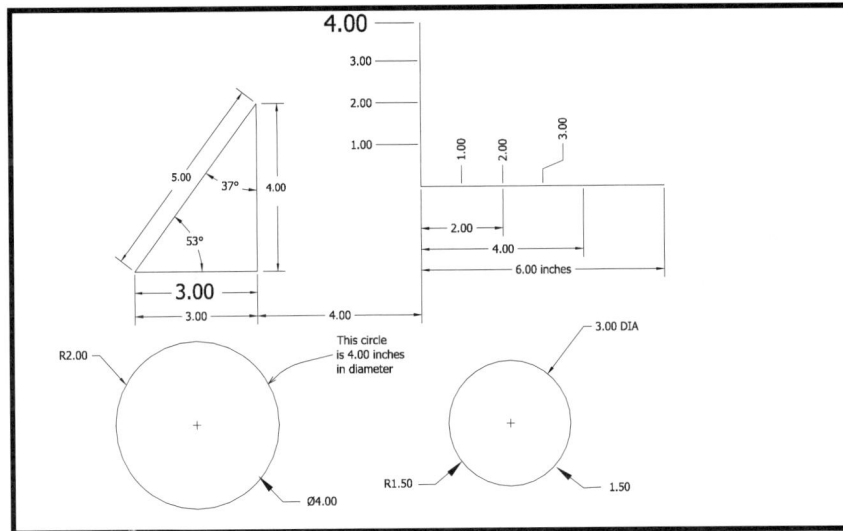

Figure 8-37

8.10 Using the BHATCH Command

<table>
<tr><td>

GENERAL PROCEDURE

1. Select Hatch from the Draw menu or the Hatch tool from the Draw menu.
2. Select a pattern.
3. Define style parameters.
4. Define boundaries of object to be hatched.

</td></tr>
</table>

Automated hatching is another immense timesaver. AutoCAD 2000 includes two commands for use in cross hatching. Of the two, BHATCH and HATCH, BHATCH is more powerful and easier to use. BHATCH differs from HATCH in that it automatically defines the nearest boundary surrounding a point you have specified. The HATCH command requires you to specify manually each segment of the boundary. In other words, with BHATCH you can point to the area you want to hatch and AutoCAD will go looking for its boundaries, whereas with HATCH you select the boundaries and AutoCAD hatches what's inside. The other big difference is that BHATCH creates associated hatch patterns. Associated hatching changes when the boundaries around it change. Nonassociated hatching is completely independent of the geometry that contains it.

⊞ To prepare for this exercise, clear your screen of all previously drawn objects and then draw three rectangles, one inside the other, with the word "TEXT" at the center, as shown in Figure 8-38.

⊞ Select Hatch from the Draw menu, or the Hatch tool on the Draw toolbar, as shown in Figure 8-39.

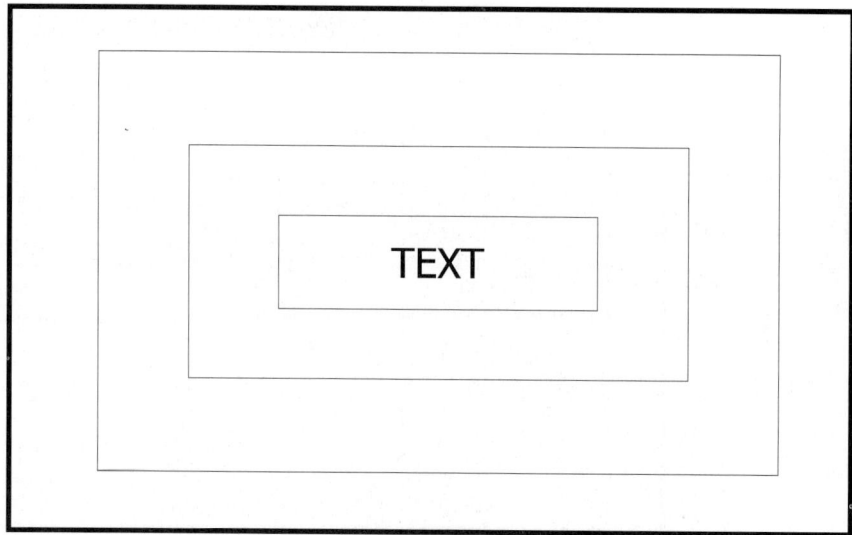

Figure 8-38

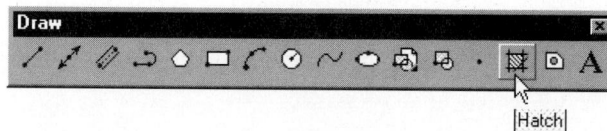

Figure 8-39

Both of these methods initiate the BHATCH command, which calls the Boundary Hatch dialog box shown in Figure 8-40. The Quick tab gives you access to AutoCAD's library of over fifty standard hatch patterns. The Advanced tab provides more options for the way AutoCAD finds boundaries, creates boundaries, and handles objects within boundaries.

At the top of the Quick tabbed card, you will see the Type box. Before we can hatch anything we need to specify a hatch pattern. Later we will show AutoCAD what we wish to hatch using the Pick Points button on the right.

The Pattern type currently shown in the image box is a predefined pattern. Before we look at predefined patterns we will create a simple user-defined pattern of straight lines on a 45-degree angle.

⊕ Click on the arrow to the right of "Predefined".

This opens a list including Predefined, User-defined, and Custom patterns.

⊕ Select User-defined.

When you select a user-defined pattern, the swatch box, which shows an example of the pattern, will change to show a set of horizontal lines. To create our user-defined pattern, we will specify an angle and a spacing.

⊕ Double click in the Angle edit box, and then type "45".

⊕ Double click in the Spacing edit box, and then type ".5".

Next we need to show AutoCAD where to place the hatching. To the right in the dialog box is a set of buttons with icons. The first two options are "Pick Points" and "Select Objects". Using the "Pick Points" option, you can have AutoCAD locate a boundary when you point to the area inside it.

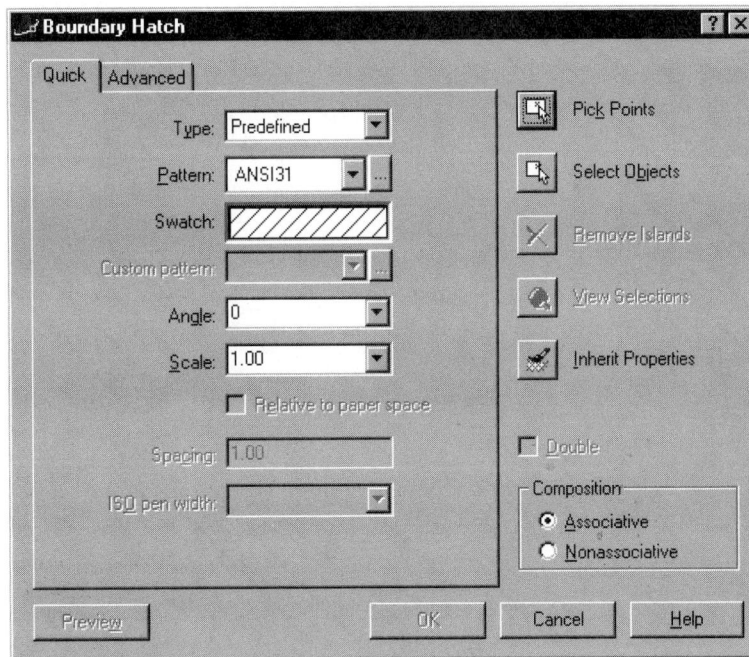

Figure 8-40

The "Select Objects" option can be used to create boundaries in the way that the older HATCH command works, by selecting entities that lie along the boundaries.

⊕ Click on "Pick Points".

The dialog box will disappear temporarily and you will be prompted as follows:

                    Select internal point:

⊕ Pick a point inside the largest, outer rectangle but outside the smaller rectangles.

AutoCAD displays these messages, though you may have to press F2 to see them:

                    Selecting everything...
                    Selecting everything visible...
                    Analyzing the selected data...
                    Analyzing internal islands...

In a large drawing this process can be time consuming because the program searches all visible entities to locate the appropriate boundary. When the process is complete, all of the rectangles and the text will be highlighted. It will happen very quickly in this case.

AutoCAD continues to prompt for internal points so that you can define multiple boundaries. Let's return to the dialog box and see what we've done so far.

⊕ Press Enter to end internal point selection.

The dialog box will reappear. You may not have noticed, but several of the options that were "grayed out" before are now accessible. We will make use

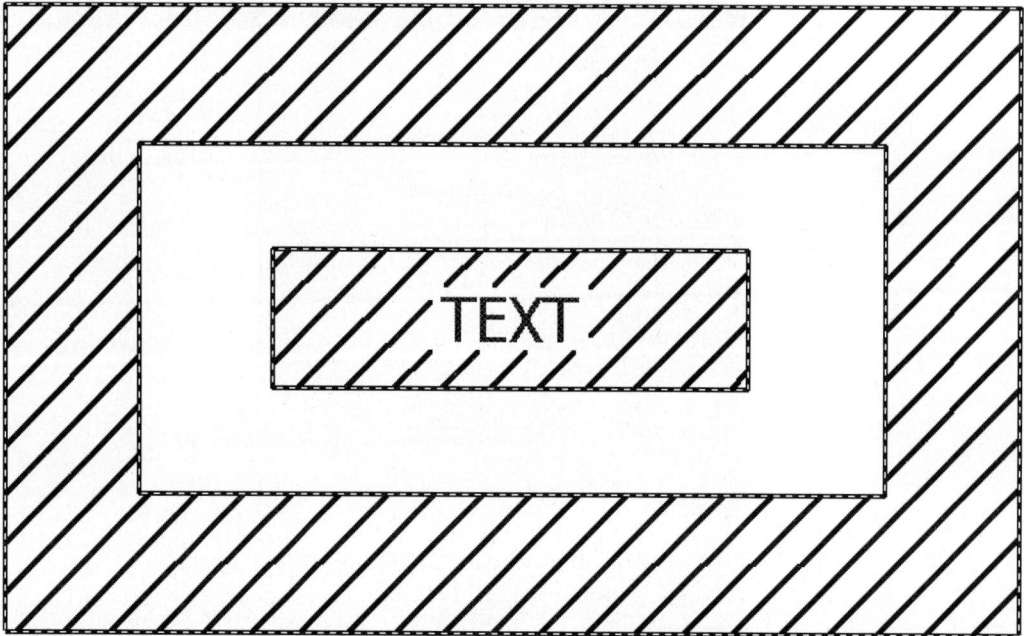

Figure 8-41

of the "Preview" button at the bottom left of the dialog box. Preview allows us to see what has been specified without leaving the command, so that we can continue to adjust the hatching until we are satisfied.

⊕ Click on Preview.

Your screen should resemble Figure 8-41. Notice the way the command has recognized and treated internal boundaries. Boundaries are hatched or left clear in alternating fashion, beginning with the outermost boundary and working inward. This demonstrates the "normal" style of hatching. We will explore the effect of the other styles by looking at the Advanced tab. Before going on, also notice that BHATCH has recognized the text as well as the other interior boundaries.

⊕ Hit enter or right click to return to the Boundary Hatch dialog box.

⊕ Click on the Advanced tab.

This Advanced card is shown in Figure 8-42. In the Island Detection Style panel you will see that there are three basic options that determine how BHATCH will treat interior boundaries. "Normal" is the current style. "Normal" hatches alternate areas moving inward, "Outer" hatches only the outer area, and "Ignore" hatches through all interior boundaries. You can see the same effects in your own drawing, if you like, by clicking the Preview button after changing from the "Normal" style to either of the other styles. Of course, the three styles are indistinguishable if you do not have boundaries within boundaries to hatch.

⊕ When you are done experimenting, select "Normal" style hatching again and return to the Quick tab.

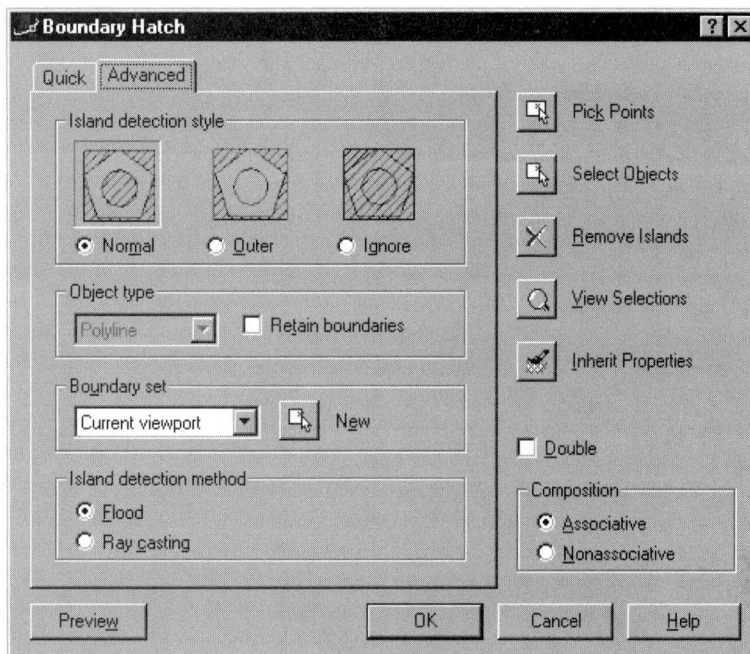

Figure 8-42

Now let's take a look at some of the fancier stored hatch patterns that Auto-CAD provides.

⊕ Click on the arrow to the right of "User-Defined" and select "Predefined".

⊕ Now click on either the ellipsis button or the Swatch.

This opens the Hatch Pattern Palette, as shown in Figure 8-43. This Palette contains AutoCAD's library of predefined hatch patterns. They are shown in tabbed dialog box fashion with four tabs. The first three contain images of patterns. The Custom tab is empty unless you have created and saved your own custom patterns. To produce the hatched image in Figure 8-44, we chose the Escher pattern.

⊕ Select the Other Predefined tab.

⊕ Scroll down the list until you come to "Escher".

⊕ Select "Escher".

⊕ Click on Okay to exit the Pattern Palette.

To produce the figure we also used a larger scale in this hatching.

⊕ Click the arrow in the Scale list box to open the list of scale factors and select 1.50.

⊕ Double click in the "Angle:" edit box and type "0".

⊕ Click the Preview button.

Your screen should resemble Figure 8-44, but remember this is still just the preview.

⊕ Hit enter or right click to return to the dialog box.

⊕ Click on OK to exit BHATCH and confirm the hatching.

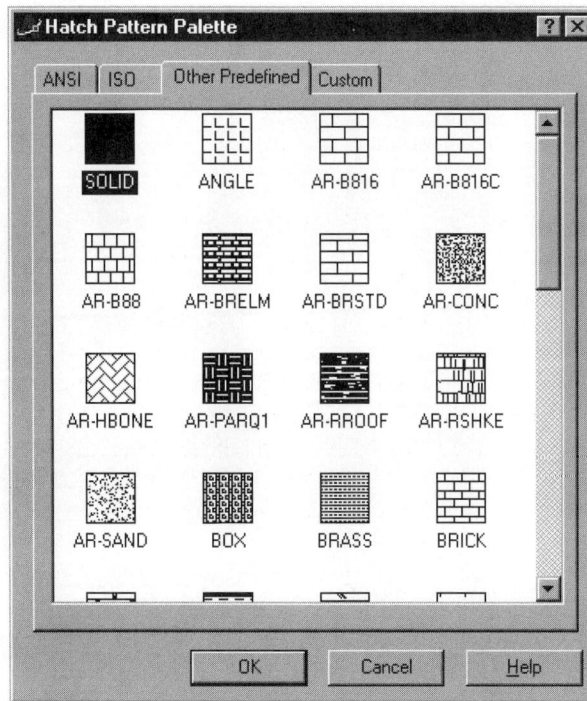

Figure 8-43

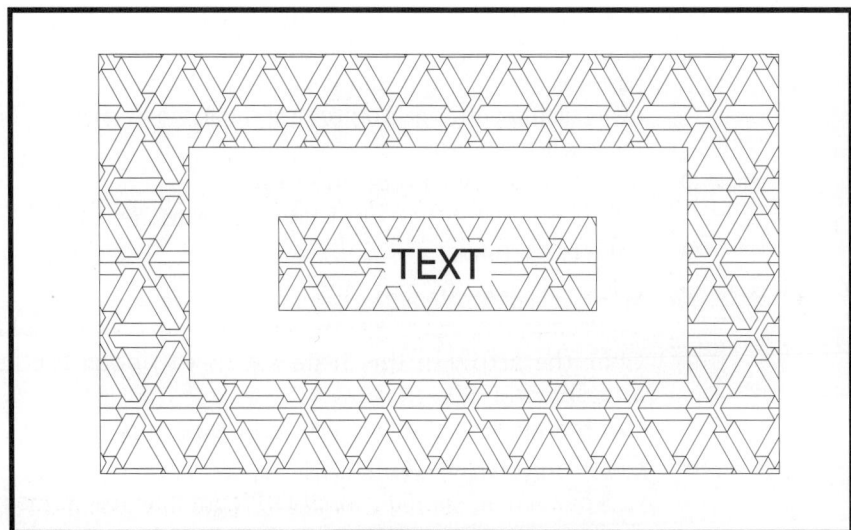

Figure 8-44

Other Advanced Options and the BPOLY Command

There are a number of worthwhile options and techniques that we have not explored in this exercise. Some of these options are available from the Advanced tab. For your information we offer the following notes:

1. When AutoCAD locates a boundary, it temporarily creates a polyline entity that completely outlines the boundaried area. A polyline (Chapter 9) is a single entity, which may be comprised of many straight and curved line segments. By default, the temporary polyline borders used by BHATCH are deleted after hatching is drawn. They may be retained for other uses, however, by checking the Retain Boundaries box in the Object type panel of the Advanced tab.
2. Using the BPOLY command, the same procedures that are used to create polyline hatch boundaries can be used to create polyline outlines independent of any hatching operation. BPOLY calls a Boundary Creation dialog box similar to the Advanced tab, but with no intervening steps through the BHATCH dialogs.
3. In very complex drawings it may be efficient to limit the number of entities AutoCAD needs to consider when looking for boundaries. This can be done using the New option in the Boundary Set panel. The boundary set does not need to be precise. By including all the entities in one portion of a drawing, for example, you could still substantially reduce the magnitude of AutoCAD's task. To specify a boundary set, click on New and then select objects.

8.11 Scaling Dimensions between Paper Space and Model Space

GENERAL PROCEDURE

1. Use ZOOM XP to set scale in viewports.
2. Set Dimtxt variable to a desirable text size.
3. Set Dimscale variable to 0.
4. Create dimensions in model space.

In Chapter 6 you learned how to create multiple-viewport layouts. Now that you will be adding text and dimensions to your drawings you will discover numerous scaling problems that arise when you are working with multiple viewports. The ZOOM XP feature introduced in Chapter 6 allows you to create precise scale relationships between model space images and paper space units. Other issues arise in annotating and dimensioning that have not been addressed yet. We will begin by illustrating some of the problems.

> **Important:** This task begins with the "3view" multiple-viewport layout of Drawing 5-1 created in Chapter 6. Hopefully, you have saved this layout and can open it now. If not, you have two choices: You can download a similar drawing from Chapter 8 of our companion Web site, or you can create a new

layout of any drawing. If you create a new layout, use 12×9 limits in model space and D size limits in the paper space layout. Then create three viewports. The zoom scale factors within the viewports should be as follows: a large viewport with a 2XP zoom factor, a smaller viewport with a 4XP zoom factor, and a still smaller viewport with a 6XP zoom factor. See Chapter 6, Task 6.10 for details.

⊕ To begin this task, open Drawing 5-1 and click the "3view" layout tab.

Draw Text in Paper Space

There are certain basic principles that are useful in adding text and dimensions to a multiple-view layout in paper space. The first is that most text should be created in paper space. To see why, try entering some text in paper space and model space as follows.

⊕ Type "Dt" or select Text and then Single Line text from the Draw menu.
⊕ Pick a start point outside any of the viewports. Our text begins about 3 units over the right side of the left viewport, as shown in Figure 8-45.
⊕ Type "1" for a text height of one unit.

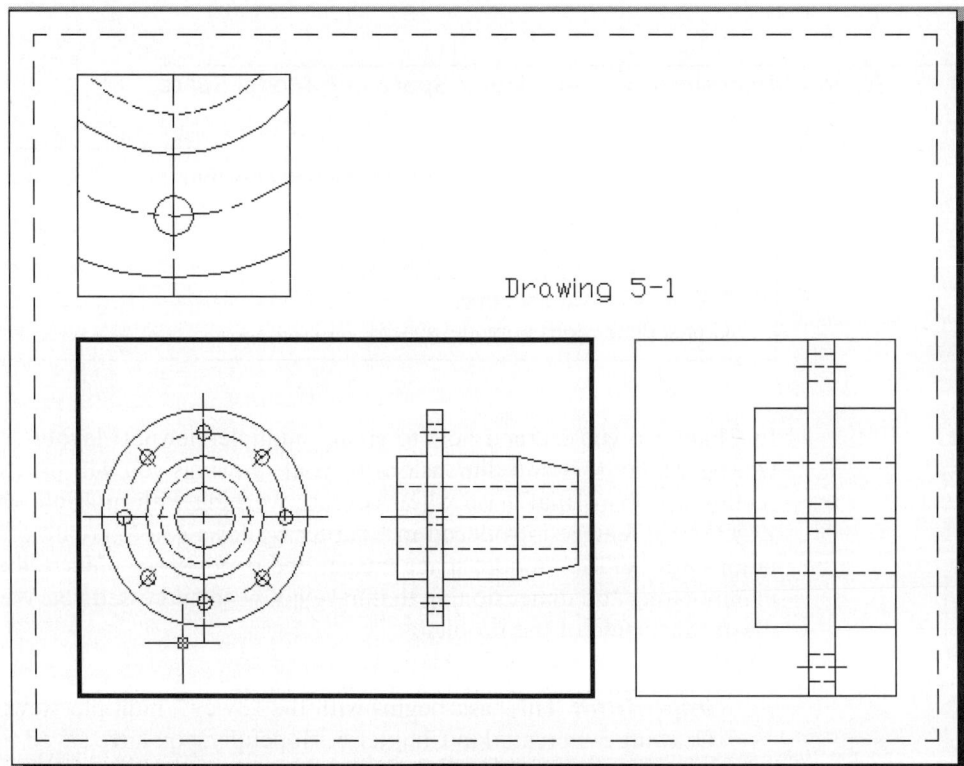

Figure 8-45

This assumes that you are using the D-size paper space limits from Chapter 6. If not, you will have to adjust for your own settings. On A size paper the text height will be about .25.

Note: This exercise assumes that the variable Dimscale is initially set to 1 and that Dimtxt is set to 0.18. These are default settings. If they have been changed in your drawing, you will not get the exact results shown here. To change the settings, type the variable name and enter the default value. Also, we assume that your current text style has a height setting of 0, meaning that it is variable. This is a default setting as well.

⊕ Press Enter for 0 rotation.
⊕ Type "Drawing 5-1".
⊕ Press Enter twice.
   Your screen should have text added, as shown in Figure 8-45.
⊕ Double click in the lower left, largest viewport to enter model space in this viewport.
⊕ Type "Dt" or select Text and then Single Line text from the Draw menu.
⊕ Pick a start point below the top view in the viewport, as shown in Figure 8-46.

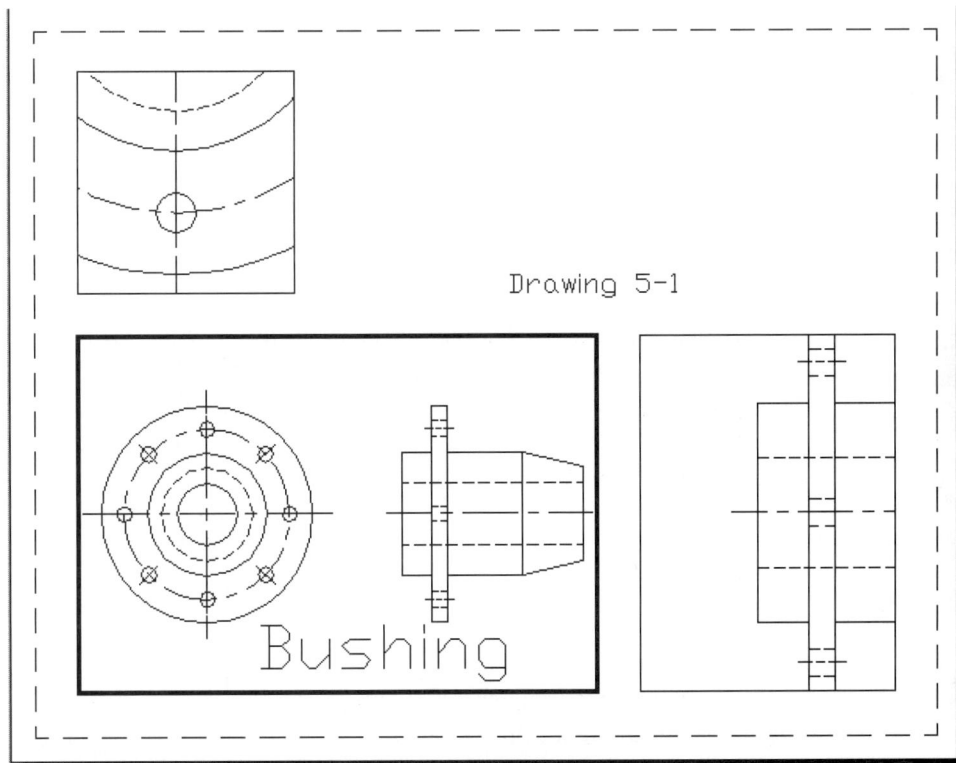

Figure 8-46

⊕ Press Enter to retain a height of 1.00 units.
⊕ Press Enter for 0 rotation.
⊕ Type "Bushing".
　　Your screen should resemble Figure 8-46.

What has happened here? Why is "Bushing" drawn twice as big as "Drawing 5-1"? Do you remember the zoom XP scale factor we used in this viewport? This viewport is enlarged by two times paper space. So any text you draw inside it will be enlarged by a factor of 2 as well. If you want, try drawing text in either of the other two viewports. You will find that text in the right viewport is magnified four times the paper space size and text in the uppermost viewport is magnified six times.

You could compensate for these enlargements by dividing text height by factors of 2, 4, and 6, but that would be cumbersome. Furthermore, if you decided to change the zoom factor at a later date, you would have to re-create any text drawn within the altered viewport. Otherwise, your text sizes in the overall drawing would become inconsistent. For this reason, it is recommended that text be drawn in paper space and kept consistent with paper space units.

Dimension Model Space Objects in Model Space

When it comes to dimensions, however, the rule is just the opposite. Dimensions should be kept in model space with the objects they refer to. The main reason is that dimensions in AutoCAD are associative. They will change when the objects they document are changed. This is true if they are in the same space. It will not be true if a model space object is dimensioned in paper space.

The rule is simple, but it requires some manipulation of variables to maintain consistency in dimension text size. As we proceed, we will also encounter some layering problems.

⊕ Make the "dim" layer current.
⊕ Make the large, lower left viewport active.
⊕ Select Linear from the Dimension menu.
⊕ Pick the top of the bushing cylinder in the right side view for the first extension line origin, as shown in Figure 8-47.
⊕ Pick the bottom of the cylinder for the second extension line origin.
⊕ Pick a dimension line location to the left of the object, as shown.
⊕ Press Enter to accept the dimension text (2.00).
⊕ If necessary, make the right viewport active and scroll so that the complete dimension text shows in both viewports.
　　Your screen should resemble Figure 8-47.

There are two things to notice: The dimension looks fine in the larger viewport, but it is duplicated in the enlargement on the right at twice the size. This illustrates our two main problems: We want all our dimensions to appear the same size, and we do not want dimensions intended for one viewport to appear in others. The first problem is a scaling issue, whereas the second involves layering. We will pursue scaling first and layer control in the next section.

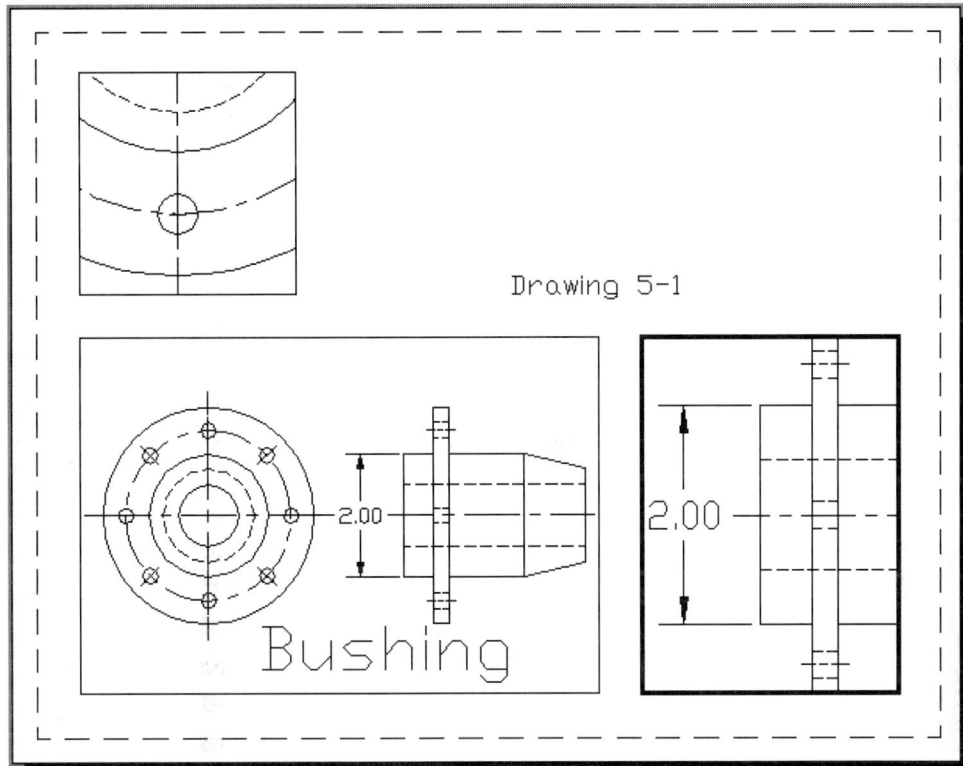

Figure 8-47

To get more of a flavor of what's going on, try one more dimension.

⊕ Make the small upper viewport active.
⊕ Select Radius from the Dimension menu.
⊕ Select the circle in the upper viewport.
⊕ Try to pick a dimension line location that allows you to see the dimension text clearly.
⊕ Look at the size of the dimension.

　Obviously, it is way too big.

⊕ Press Esc to cancel the command.

In fact, the dimension shown in the upper viewport was three times as big as the dimension in the central viewport and twice as big as the duplicate dimension in the right viewport. As you may have guessed, the dimensions in each viewport are being magnified just as the text was previously. The default dimension text size, set to 0.18 by the dimtxt variable, is being doubled (two times paper size) to 0.36 in the central viewport. So the text "2.00" has a height of 0.36 units in that viewport. But in the right viewport it has a height of 0.72 units (4 × .18). The radial dimension in the upper viewport had a height of 1.08 units, or six times the dimtxt setting.

AutoCAD has a simple fix for this problem. When the variable dimscale is set to 0 instead of the default value of 1 or some other explicit scaling factor, dimension text in viewports is adjusted according to the model space to paper space zoom factor. With this setting, dimensions in all viewports can be maintained at the same desirable size.

For our purposes, let's say we are satisfied with the 0.36 size we see in the central viewport. To achieve this size in all viewports simultaneously, we will need to set dimscale to 0 and dimtxt to 0.36.

⊕ Type "dimtxt".

AutoCAD shows you the current value and asks for a new value.

⊕ Type ".36".

⊕ Type "dimscale".

⊕ Type "0".

Now let's try drawing the radial dimension in the upper viewport again.

⊕ Select Radius from the Dimension menu.

⊕ Select the circle in the upper viewport.

⊕ Position the dimension, as shown in Figure 8-48.

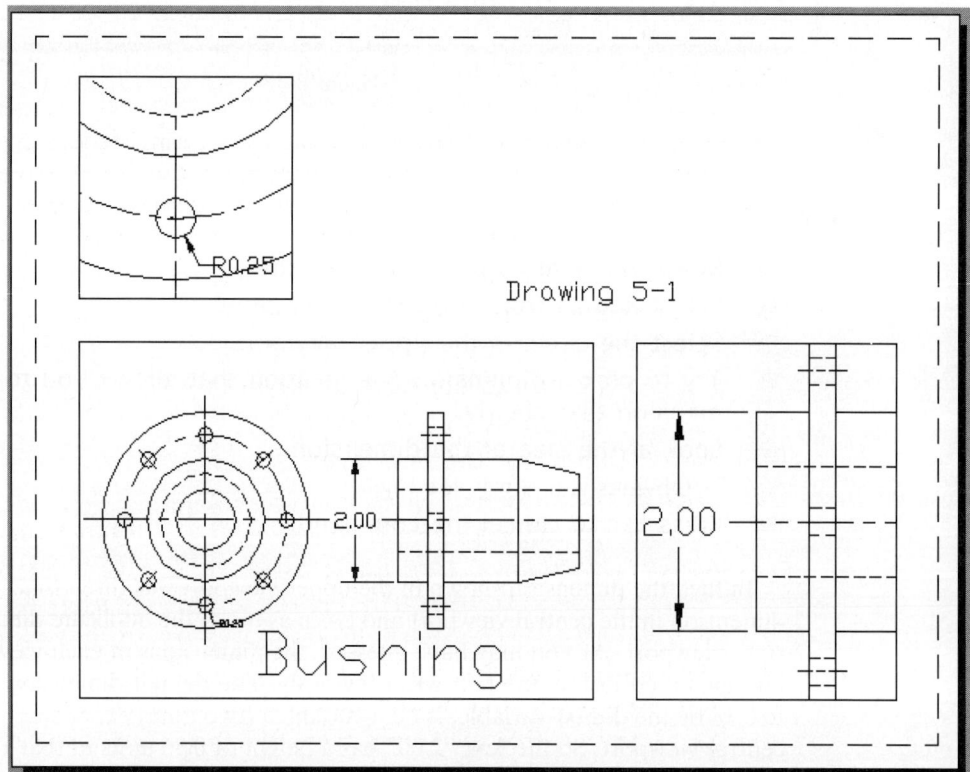

Figure 8-48

Wonderful, except that now we have a tiny duplicate of the radial dimension showing in the central viewport. This is another example of the layering problem, which we will explore next.

Manipulating Layer Visibility in Multiple Viewports

The duplicate dimensions in your drawing are just one example of the need to control layer visibility separately in different viewports. This can be done using the VPLAYER command or the Active Viewport Freeze feature of the Layer Properties Manager.

Our goal will be to make dimensions intended for the central viewport invisible in other viewports and vice versa. To accomplish this, we need at least two dimension layers. If you wanted independent dimensions in all three viewports, you would need three layers.

⊕   Make the upper viewport active.

⊕   Select the Layer tool from the Object Properties toolbar.

⊕   Click on New.

⊕   Type "Dim-u" (for dimensions in the upper viewport).

⊕   Click in the color column of the Dim-u layer to open the Set Color dialog.

⊕   Give Dim-u color number 4, cyan.

This should be the same color as your regular DIM layer.

⊕   Click on OK to return to the main dialog.

⊕   Click on OK to exit the dialog box.

Now that we have two dimension layers, we can freeze dimensions in the viewports where they are not wanted. But first we must move some of the previously drawn dimensions to the newly created layer and then make the viewport where we want to freeze the dimensions current.

⊕   Select the radial dimension.

⊕   Right click to open the short cut menu.

⊕   Select Properties from the short cut menu.

⊕   Click in the box to the right of "Layer".

⊕   Click on the arrow to open the layer list.

⊕   Select "Dim-u" for the new layer.

⊕   Click on Close to exit the Properties dialog.

Now the 2.00 diameter dimension and the 0.25 radial dimension are on different layers, although they appear the same. We need to freeze DIM in the right viewport and freeze DIM-U in the central viewport. This is most easily done in the Layer Properties Manager.

⊕   Click in the central viewport to make it active.

⊕   Click the Layer tool on the Object Properties toolbar.

⊕   Scroll to the right until you see the Active Viewport Freeze column, as shown in Figure 8-49.

⊕   Click the Active Viewport Freeze icon in the Dim-u layer row.

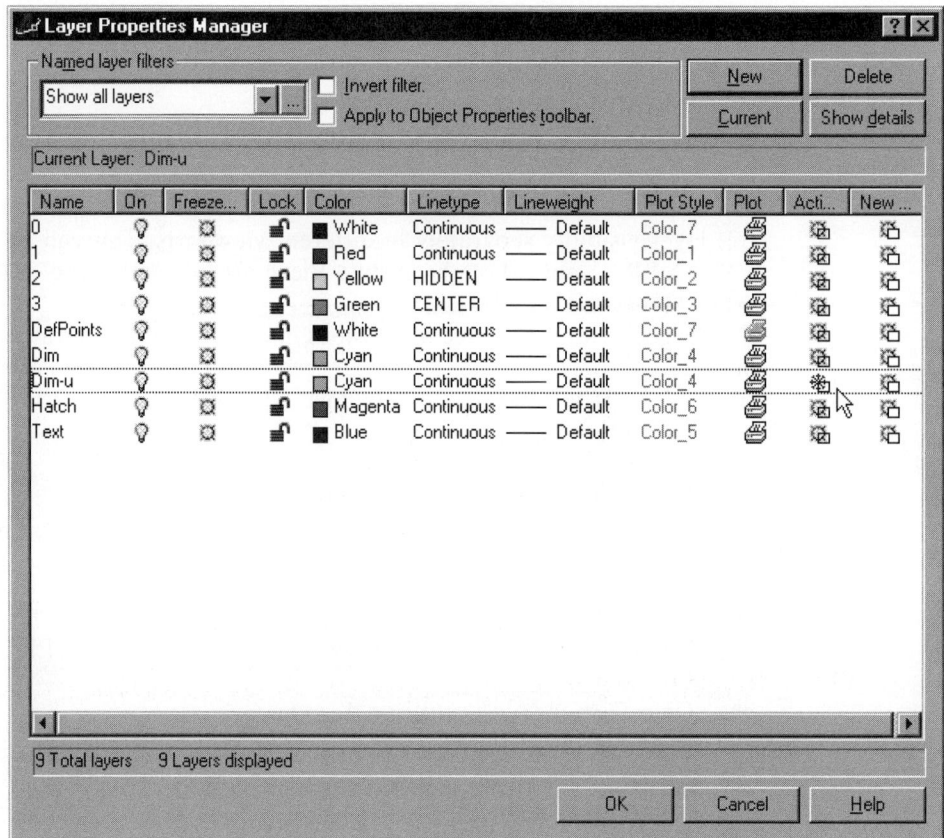

Figure 8-49

Since the central viewport is active, this will freeze the Dim-u layer in that viewport, so that it will not be seen or plotted.

⊞ Click OK to exit the Layer Properties Manager.

The radial dimension will remain visible in the small upper viewport, but will not be visible in the central viewport, as shown in Figure 8-50.

Now we need to repeat this process once more to remove the 2.00 dimension from the right viewport.

⊞ Click in the right viewport to make it active.

⊞ Open the Layer Properties Manager.

⊞ Scroll to the Active Viewport Freeze column.

⊞ Freeze the Dim layer.

⊞ Click OK to exit the dialog.

Dim is now frozen in the right viewport, but still visible in the central viewport, as shown in Figure 8-51.

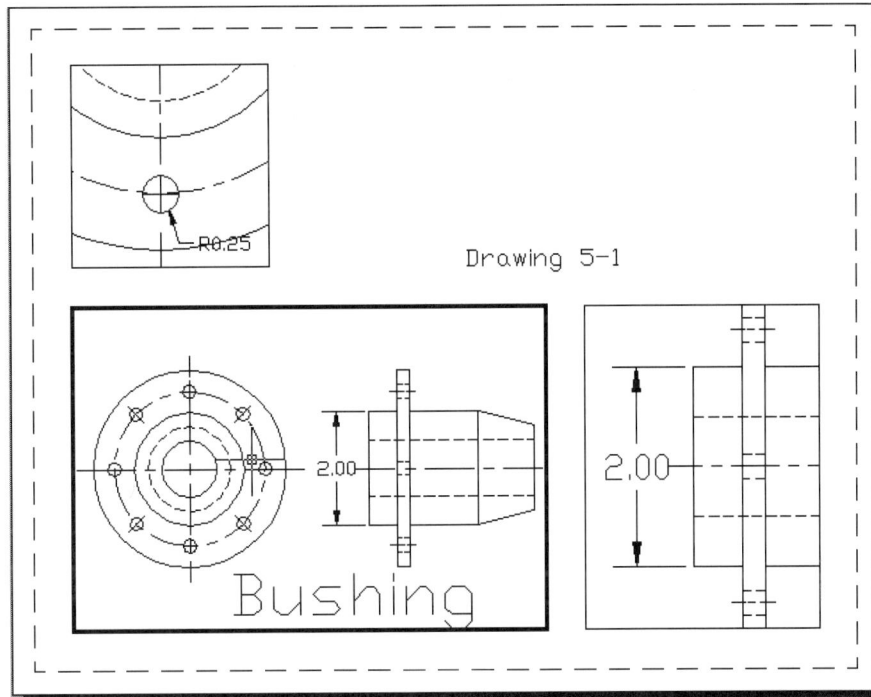

Figure 8-50

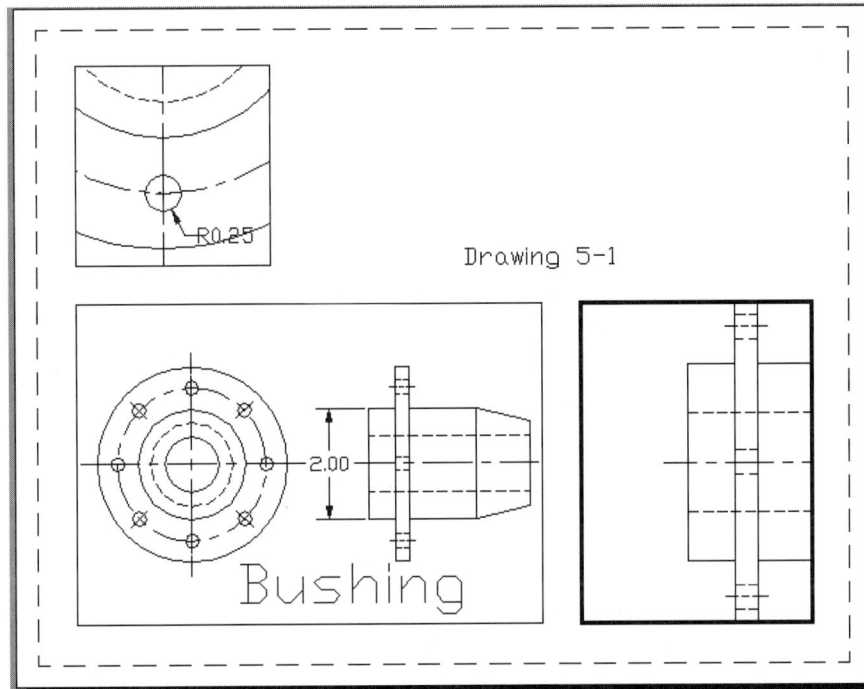

Figure 8-51

Turning Viewport Borders Off

We have used the borders of our viewports as part of our plotted drawing in this drawing layout. Frequently, you will want to turn them off. In a typical three-view drawing, for example, you do not draw borders around the three views.

In multiple-viewport paper space drawings the visibility of viewport borders is easily controlled by putting the viewports on a separate layer and then turning the layer off before plotting. You can make a "border" layer, for example, and make it current while you create viewports. Or you can use PROPERTIES to move viewports to the border layer later.

8.12 Review Material

Questions

1. You are working in a drawing with units set to architectural, but when you begin dimensioning, AutoCAD provides four-place decimal units. What is the problem? What do you need to do so that your dimensioning units match your drawing units?
2. Describe at least one way to change the size of the arrowheads in the dimensions of a drawing.
3. What changes can be made with the Edit option of the QDIM command?
4. What types of changes to dimension objects can be made with DIMEDIT, DIMTEDIT, and PROPERTIES?
5. What is a "nearest" object snap, and why is it important when dimensioning with leaders?
6. Why is it useful to move the origin of the coordinate system in order to make good use of ordinate dimensioning? What option to this is available in the QDIM command?
7. You have created a number of dimensions in a drawing and wish to change some of them to a new dimension style. Assuming you have already created the new dimension style, what procedure will allow you to update some of your previously drawn dimensions? What item on the Dimension menu executes this command?
8. What is the difference between HATCH and BHATCH?
9. Why is it important to dimension in model space?
10. In what circumstances would it be necessary to use the Active Viewport Freeze feature of the Layer Properties Manager rather than just turning layers on and off?

Drawing Problems

1. Create a new dimension style called "Dim-2". Dim-2 will use architectural units with 1/2″ precision for all units except angles, which will use two-place decimals. Text in Dim-2 will be 0.5 units high.
2. Draw an isosceles triangle with vertexes at (4,3), (14,3), and (9,11). Draw a 2″ circle centered at the center of the triangle.

3. Dimension the base and one side of the triangle using the Dim-2 dimension style.

4. Add a diameter dimension to the circle and change a dimension variable so that the circle will be dimensioned with a diameter line drawn inside the circle.

5. Add an angle dimension to one of the base angles of the triangle. Make sure that the dimension is placed outside of the triangle.

6. Hatch the area inside the triangle and outside the circle using a predefined crosshatch pattern.

8.13 WWW Exercise #8 (Optional)

In Chapter 8 of our companion Web site we will challenge you to find information on a great innovator in the fields of graphic arts whose name has come up in this chapter. We will give you links to get you started and then send you on your way. We will also offer you another design challenge and, as always, the self-scoring test for this chapter. So, when you are ready,

⊞ Make sure that you are connected to your Internet service provider.

⊞ Type "browser", open the Web toolbar, and select the Browse the Web tool, or open your system browser from the Windows 98 taskbar.

⊞ If necessary, navigate to our companion Web site at "www.prenhall.com/dixriley".

Happy Hunting!

8.14   Drawing 8-1: Tool Block

In this drawing the dimensions should work well without editing. The hatch is a simple user-defined pattern used to indicate that the front and right views are sectioned views.

DRAWING SUGGESTIONS

> GRID = 1.0
> SNAP = 0.125
> HATCH line spacing = 0.125

- As a general rule, complete the drawing first, including all cross hatching, and then add dimensions and text at the end.
- Place all hatching on the hatch layer. When hatching is complete, set to the dim layer and turn the hatch layer off so that hatch lines will not interfere when you select lines for dimensioning.
- The section lines in this drawing can be easily drawn as leaders. Set the dimension arrow size to 0.38 first. Check to see that ortho is on; then begin the leader at the tip of the arrow, and make a right angle as shown. After picking the other end point of the leader, press Enter to bring up the "First line of annotation" prompt. Type a space and press Enter so you will have no text. Press enter again to exit.
- You will need to set the dimtix variable ("dimension outside align" in the Properties dialog) to "on" in order to place the 3.25-diameter dimension at the center of the circle in the top view, and "off" to create the leader style diameter dimension in the front section.
- Remember, multiple lines of text can be drawn with the QLEADER command and may be specified to be centered on the Leader.

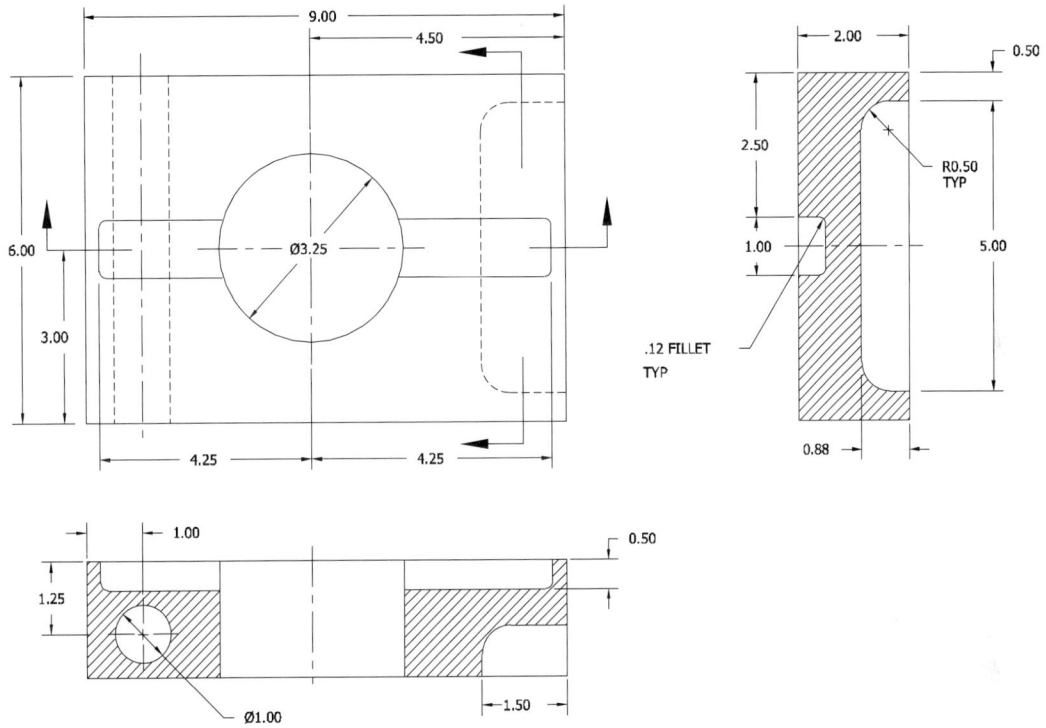

TOOL BLOCK
Drawing 8-1

8.15   Drawing 8-2: Flanged Wheel

Most of the objects in this drawing are straightforward. The keyway is easily done using the TRIM command. If necessary, use DIMTEDIT or grips to move the diameter dimension, as shown in the reference.

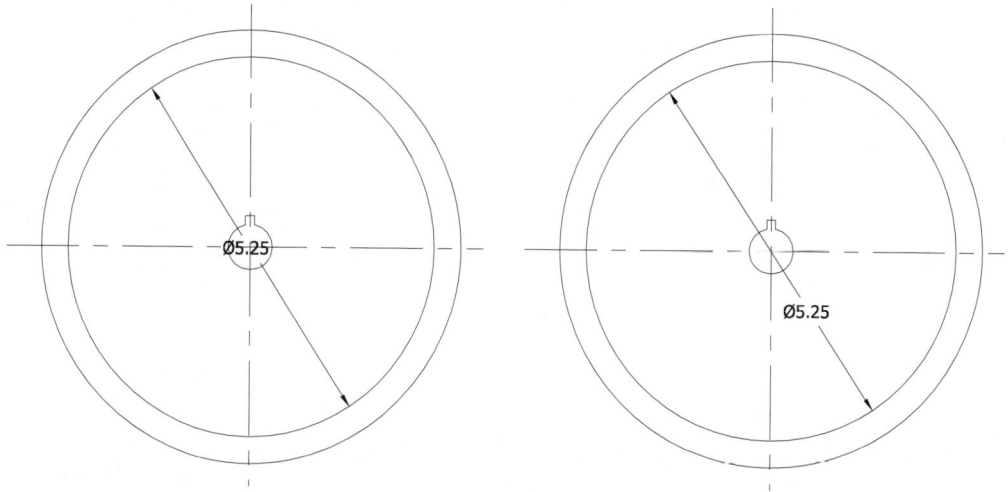

DRAWING SUGGESTIONS

GRID = 0.25
SNAP = 0.0625
HATCH line spacing = 0.50

- You will need a 0.0625 snap to draw the keyway. Draw a 0.125 × 0.125 square at the top of the 0.63-diameter circle. Drop the vertical lines down into the circle so they may be used to TRIM the circle. TRIM the circle and the vertical lines, using a window to select both as cutting edges.
- Remember to set to layer "hatch" before hatching, layer "text" before adding text, and layer "dim" before dimensioning.

1.00   2.00

Ø6.00

R1.00

5.00

KEYWAY
.12 W X .12 H

Ø5.25

Ø0.62

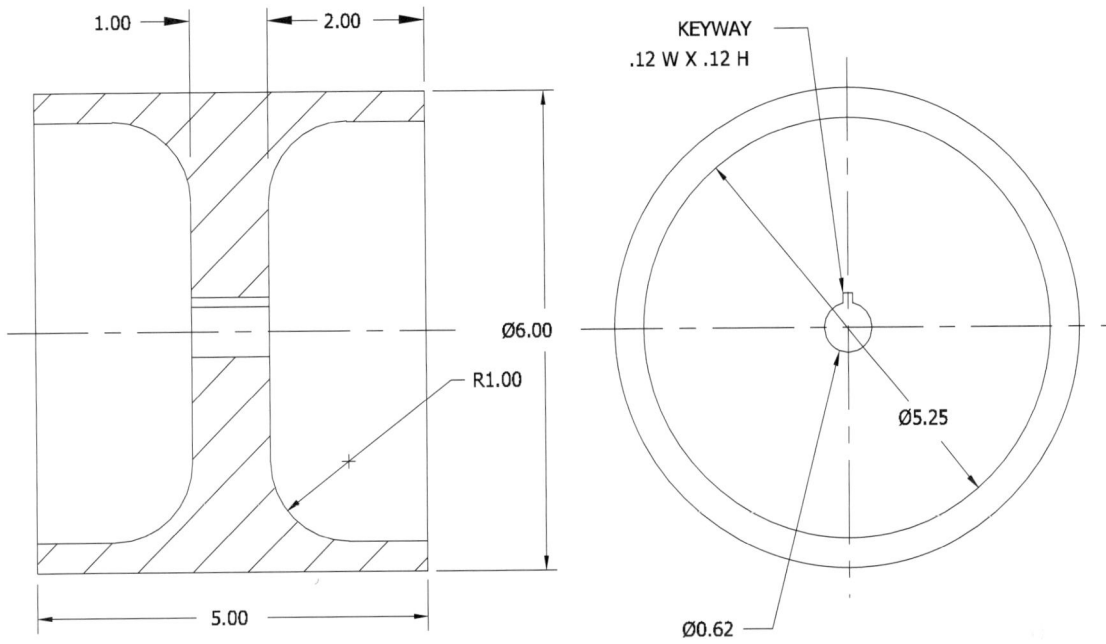

FLANGED WHEEL

Drawing 8-2

8.16   Drawing 8-3: Shower Head

This drawing makes use of the procedures for hatching and dimensioning you learned in the last two drawings. In addition, it uses an angular dimension, baseline dimensions, leaders, and "%%c" for the diameter symbol.

DRAWING SUGGESTIONS

> GRID = 0.50
> SNAP = 0.125
> HATCH line spacing = 0.25

- You can save some time on this drawing by using MIRROR to create half of the right side view. Notice, however, that you cannot hatch before mirroring, because the mirror command will reverse the angle of the hatch lines.
- To achieve the angular dimension at the bottom of the right side view, you will need to draw the vertical line coming down on the right. Select this line and the angular line at the right end of the shower head, and the angular extension will be drawn automatically. Add the text "2 PL" using the DIMEDIT command.
- Notice that the diameter symbols in the vertical dimensions at each end of the right side view are not automatic. Use %%c to add the diameter symbol to the text.

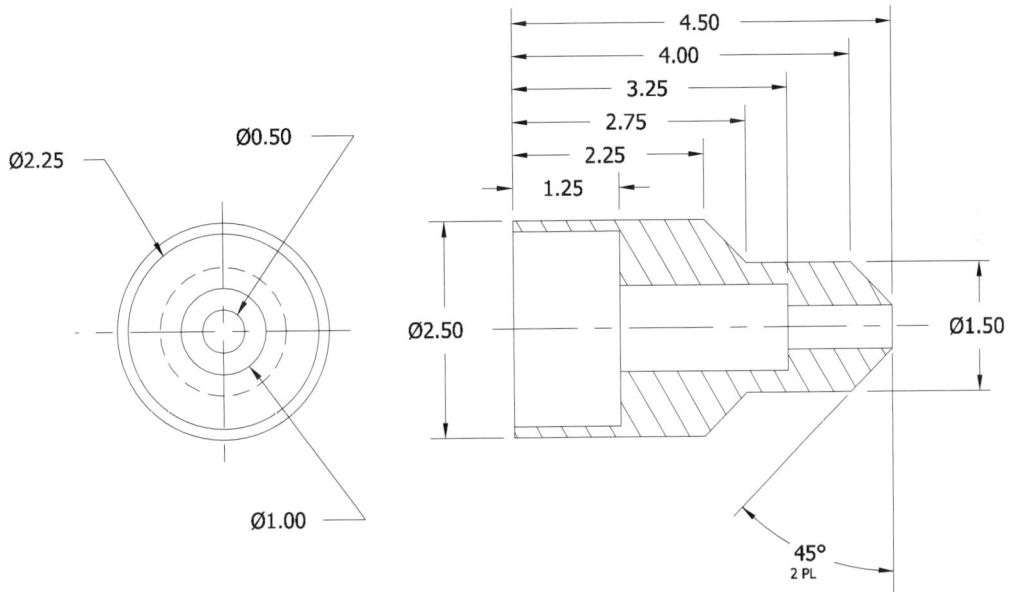

Ø2.25

Ø0.50

Ø1.00

4.50

4.00

3.25

2.75

2.25

1.25

Ø2.50

Ø1.50

45°
2 PL

SHOWER HEAD

Drawing 8-3

8.17   Drawing 8-4: Nose Adapter

Make ample use of ZOOM to work on the details of this drawing. Notice that the limits are set larger than usual, and the snap is rather fine by comparison.

DRAWING SUGGESTIONS

LIMITS = (0,0) (36,24)
GRID = 0.50
SNAP = 0.125
HATCH line spacing = 0.25

- You will need a 0.125 snap to draw the thread representation shown in the reference. Understand that this is nothing more than a standard representation for screw threads; it does not show actual dimensions. Zoom in close to draw it, and you should have no trouble.
- This drawing includes two examples of "simplified drafting" practice. The thread representation is one, and the other is the way in which the counterbores are drawn in the front view. A precise rendering of these holes would show an ellipse, since the slant of the object dictates that they break through on an angle. However, to show these ellipses in the front view would make the drawing more confusing and less useful. Simplified representation is preferable in such cases.

(thread representation)

30°
TYP

0.125

Reference

2.75

1.625

0.50

30°

Ø6.00
REF

Ø11.00

6.00 PITCH DIA
12 THREADS PER INCH

(SEE REFERENCE)

.25 DIA THRU
C'BORE .50 DIA X .625 DEEP
4 HOLES EQ SP AS SHOWN

Ø8.00

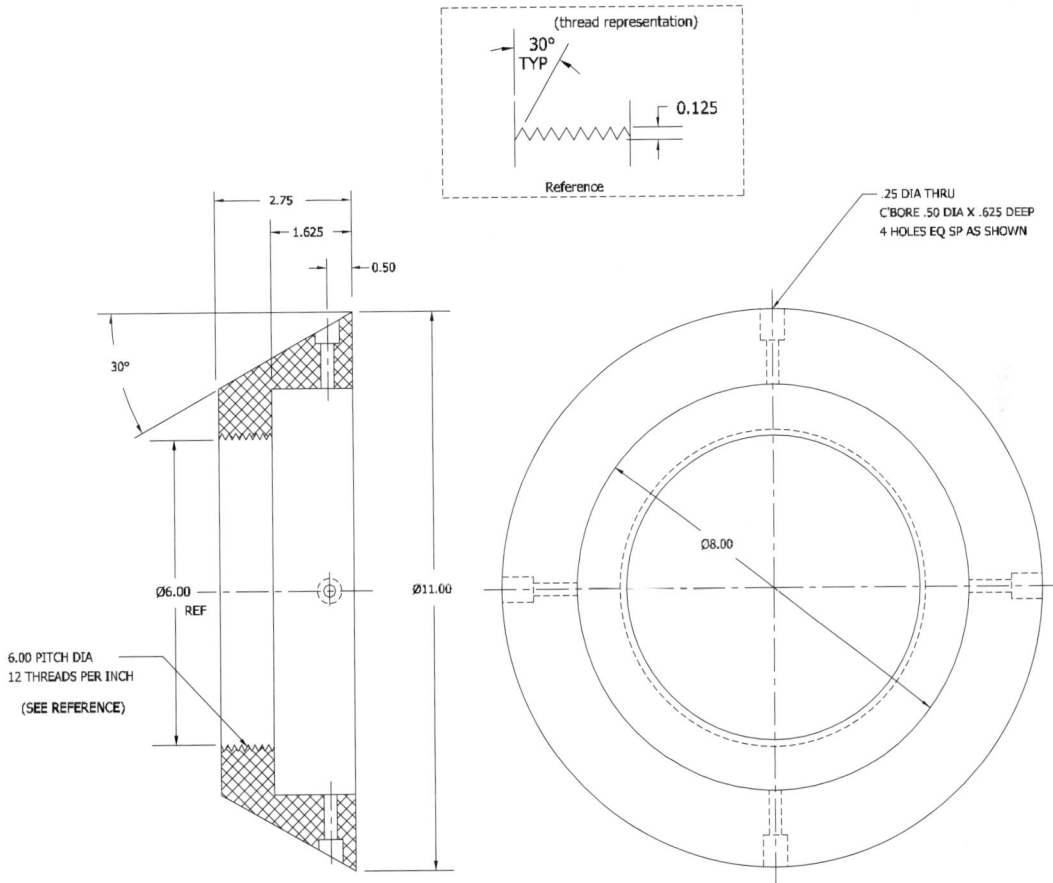

NOSE ADAPTOR
Drawing 8-4

8.18 Drawing 8-5: Plot Plan

This architectural drawing makes use of three hatch patterns and several dimension variable changes. Be sure to make these settings as shown.

DRAWING SUGGESTIONS

GRID = 10′
SNAP = 1′
LIMITS = 180′, 120′
LTSCALE = 2′

- The "trees" shown here are symbols for oaks, willows, and evergreens.
- BHATCH will open a space around text inside a defined boundary; however, sometimes you will want more white space than BHATCH leaves. The simple solution is to draw a rectangle around the text area as an inner boundary. If the BHATCH style is set to "Normal" it will stop hatching at the inner boundary. Later you can erase the box, leaving an island of white space around the text.

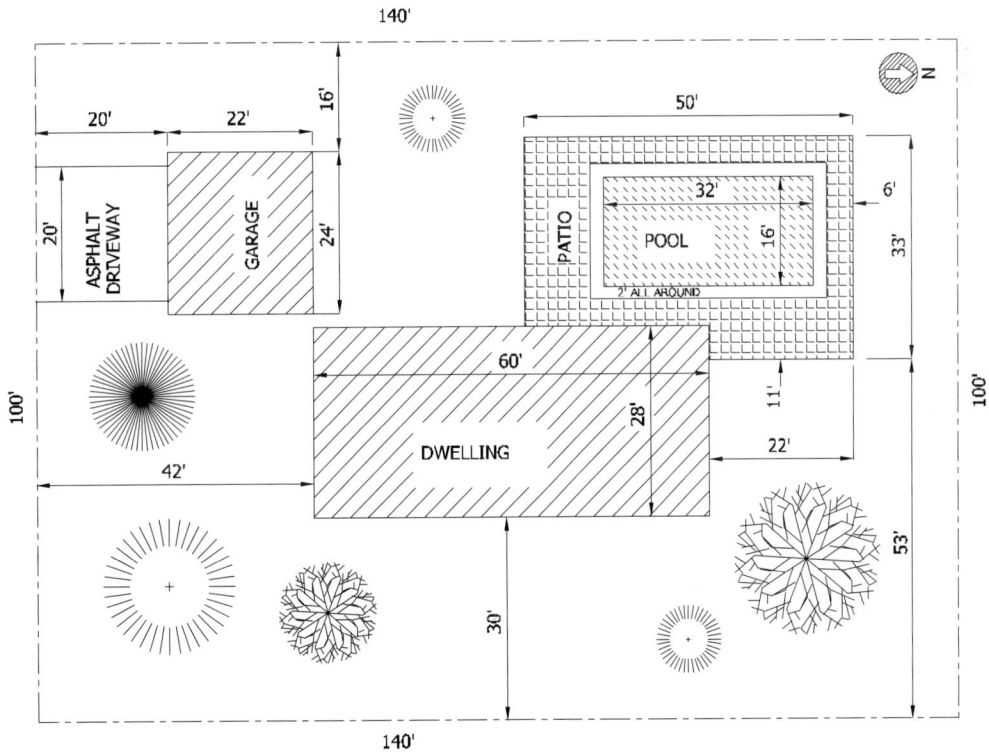

REFERENCE

EXAMPLE OF TREES
draw a pattern in
a circle as shown
and array.

Limits = 180',120'
Ltscale = 2'
Text height = 2'
Hatch = U,45°,2'
Hatch = Angle,0°,8'
Hatch = Dash,45°,8'

DIMVAR SETTINGS
dimasz = 2'
dimtxt = 2'
dimtad = on
dimtih = off

PLOT PLAN

Drawing 8-5

8.19   Drawing 8-6: Panel

This drawing is primarily an exercise in using ordinate dimensions. Both the drawing of the objects and the adding of dimensions will be facilitated dramatically by this powerful feature.

DRAWING SUGGESTIONS

GRID = 0.50
SNAP = 0.125
UNITS = three-place decimal

- After setting grid, snap, and units, create a new user coordinate system with the origin moved in and up about one unit each way. This technique was introduced in Task 8.6. For reference, here is the procedure:
  1. Select Move UCS from the Tools menu.
  2. Pick a new origin point.
- From here on all of the objects in the drawing can be easily placed using the x and y displacements exactly as they are shown in the drawing.
- When objects have been placed, switch to the dim layer and begin dimensioning using the ordinate dimension feature. You should be able to move along quickly, but be careful to keep dimensions on each side of the panel lined up. That is, the leader end points should end along the same vertical or horizontal line.

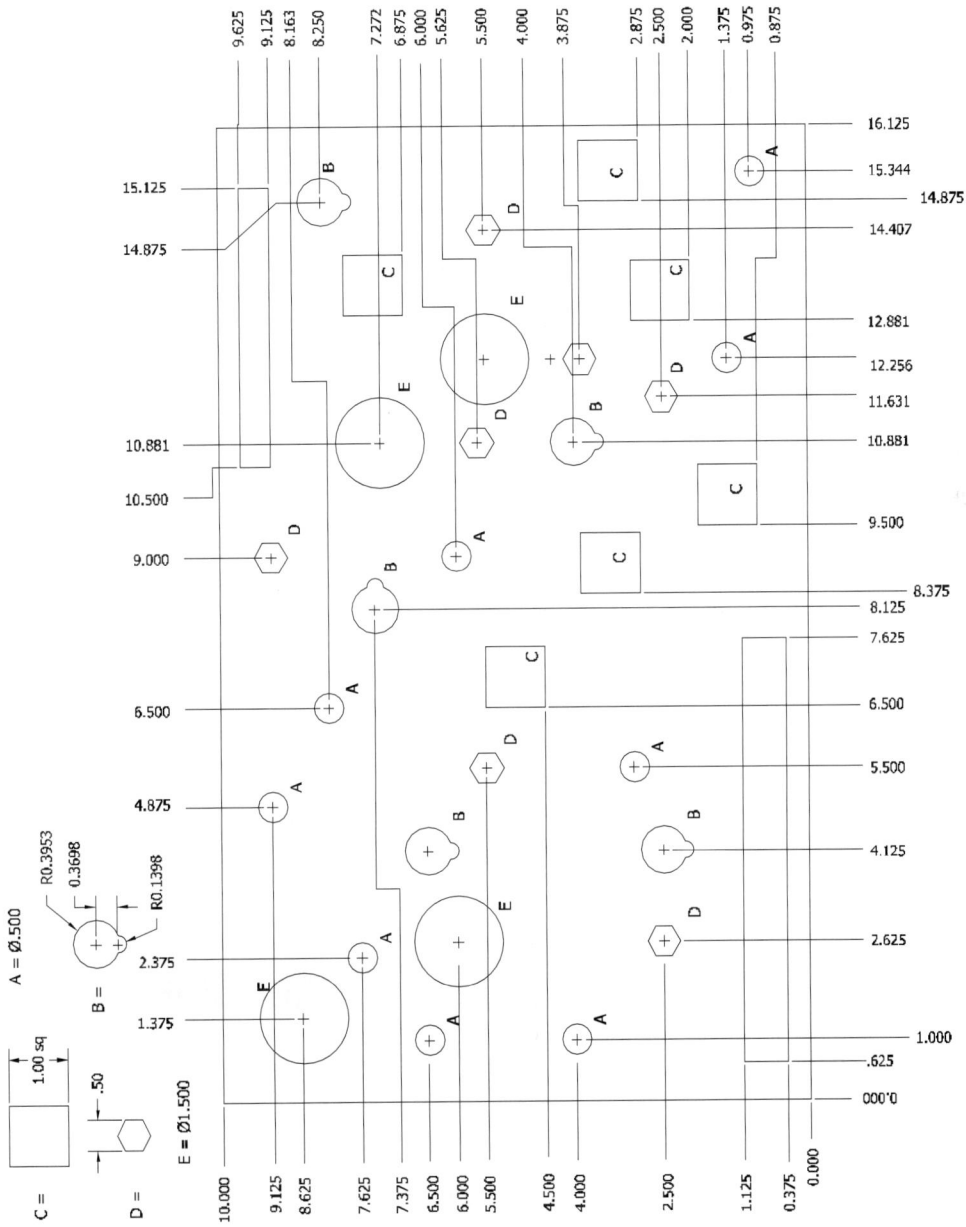

PANEL
DRAWING 8-6

8.20 Drawing 8-7: Angle Support

In this drawing you are expected to use the 3D view to create three orthographic views. Draw a Front View, Top View, and Side View. The Front and Top Views will be drawn showing all necessary hidden lines, and the Right Side View will be drawn in full section. The finished multiview drawing should be fully dimensioned.

Top View

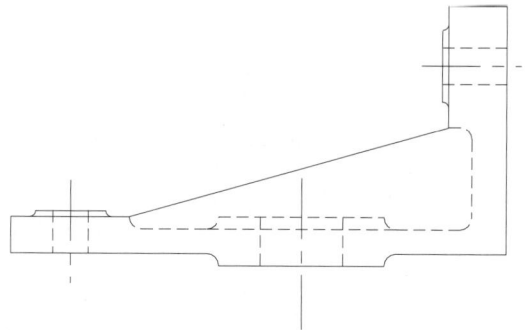

Front View   # Right Side View

DRAWING SUGGESTIONS

- Start this drawing by laying out the top view. Use the top view to line up the front view and side view.
- Use the illustration of the Right Side View when planning out the full section. Convert the hidden lines to solid lines, and use BHATCH to create cross hatching.
- Complete the Right Side View in full section using the ANSI31 hatch pattern.
- Be sure to include all the necessary hidden lines and center lines in each view.

Right Side View

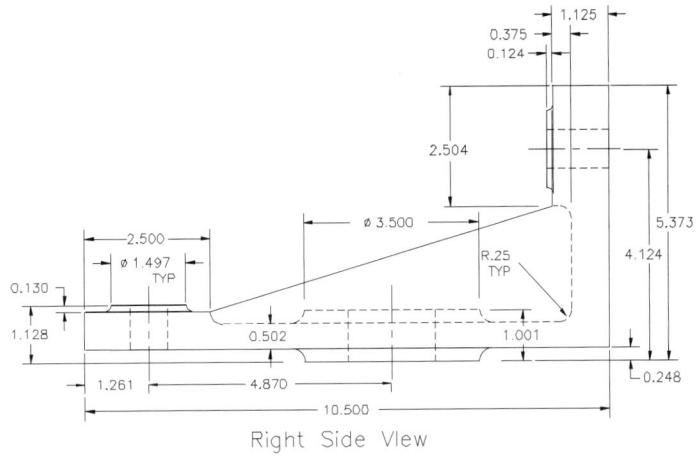

ANGLE SUPPORT
Drawing 8-7

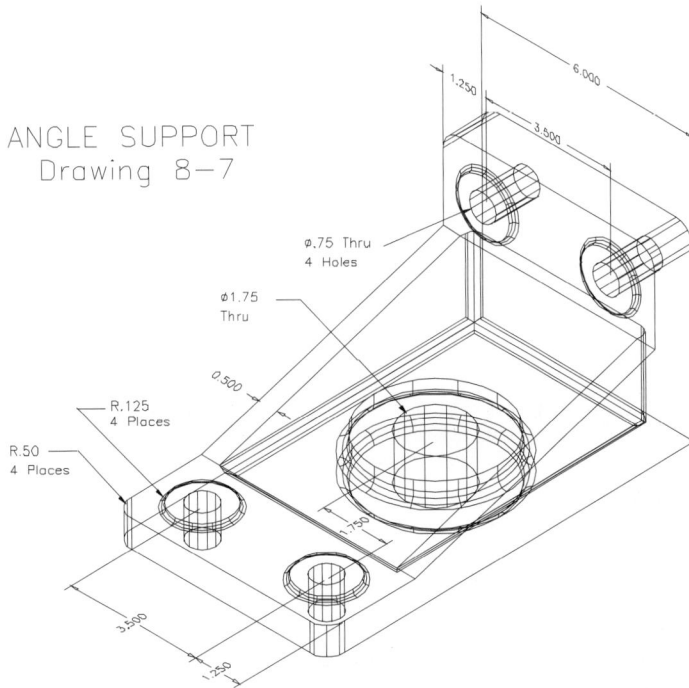

9 **Polylines**

COMMANDS

DONUT	MLINE	PLINE	SKETCH
FILL	MLSTYLE	POINT	SOLID
MLEDIT	PEDIT	POLYGON	SPLINE

OVERVIEW

This chapter should be fun. As you can see by the preceding list, you will be learning a large number of new commands. You will see new things happening on your screen with each command. The commands in this chapter are used to create special entities, some of which cannot be drawn any other way. All of them are complex objects made up of lines, circles, and arcs (like the text, dimensions, and hatch patterns discussed in the previous chapter), but they are stored and treated as singular entities. Some of them, such as polygons and donuts, are familiar geometric figures, while others, like polylines, are peculiar to CAD.

TASKS

9.1 Drawing POLYGONs

GENERAL PROCEDURE

1. Select the Polygon tool from the Draw toolbar or select Polygon from the Draw menu.
2. Type the number of sides.
3. Pick a center point.
4. Indicate "Inscribed" or "Circumscribed".
5. Show the radius of the circle.

Among the most interesting and flexible of the entities you can create in Auto-CAD is the polyline. In this chapter we will begin with two regularly shaped polyline entities, polygons and donuts. These entities have their own special commands, separate from the general PLINE command (Tasks 9.4 and 9.5), but are created as polylines and can be edited just as any other polyline would be.

Polygons with any number of sides can be drawn using the POLYGON command. (Rectangles can be drawn by showing two corners using the RECTANG command, which draws polyline rectangles.) In the default sequence, AutoCAD will construct a polygon based on the number of sides, the center point, and a radius. Optionally, the "edge" method allows you to specify the number of sides and the length and position of one side (see Figure 9-1).

⊕   Select Polygon from the Draw menu, or select the Polygon tool from the Draw toolbar, as shown in Figure 9-2.

AutoCAD's first prompt will be for the number of sides:

```
Enter number of sides <4>:
```

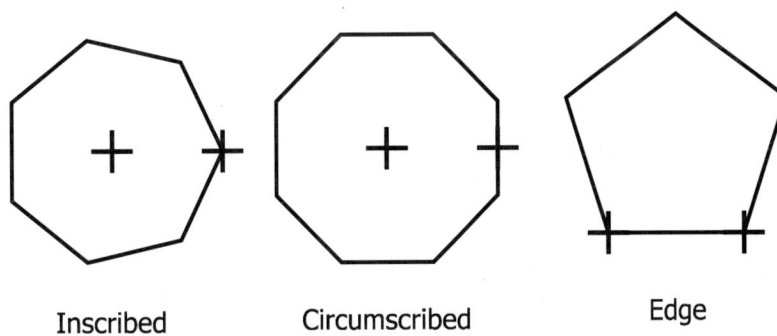

Inscribed   Circumscribed   Edge

Figure 9-1

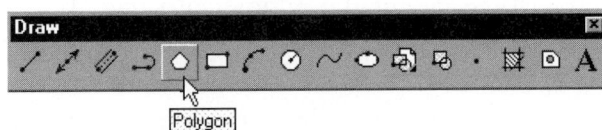

Figure 9-2

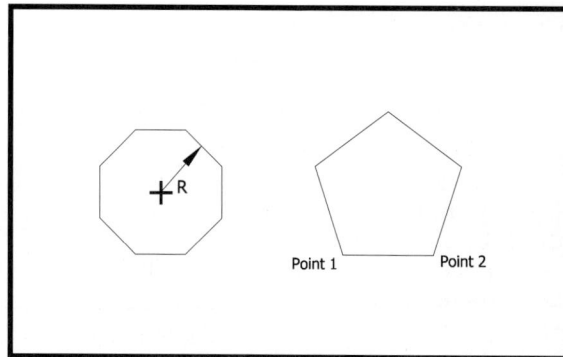

Figure 9-3

⊕ Type "8".

Now you are prompted to show either a center point or the first point of one edge:

> Specify center of polygon or [Edge]:

⊕ Pick a center point, as shown by the center mark on the left in Figure 9-3.

From here the size of the polygon can be specified in one of two ways, as shown in Figure 9-1. The radius of a circle will be given and the polygon drawn either inside or outside the imaginary circle. Notice that in the case of the "inscribed" polygon, the radius is measured from the center to a vertex, while in the "circumscribed" polygon it is measured from the center to the midpoint of a side. You can tell AutoCAD which you want by typing "i" or "c".

> Enter an option [Inscribed in circle/Circumscribed about circle] <I>:

The default is currently "inscribed". We will use the "circumscribed" method instead.

⊕ Type "c".

Now you will be prompted to show a radius of this imaginary circle (that is, a line from the center to a midpoint of a side).

> Specify radius of circle:

⊕ Show a radius similar to the one in Figure 9-3.

We leave it to you to try out the "inscribed" option. We will draw one more polygon, using the "edge" method.

⊕ Press Enter or the space bar to repeat the POLYGON command.

⊕ Type "5" for the number of sides.

⊕ Type "e".

AutoCAD will issue a different series of prompts:

> Specify first endpoint of edge:

⊕ Pick Point 1, as shown on the right in Figure 9-3.

AutoCAD prompts

> Specify second endpoint of edge:

⊕ Pick a second point as shown.

Your screen should resemble Figure 9-3.

9.2 Drawing DONUTs

> **GENERAL PROCEDURE**
>
> 1. Select Donut from the Draw menu.
> 2. Type or show an inside diameter.
> 3. Type or show an outside diameter.
> 4. Pick a center point.
> 5. Pick another center point.
> 6. Press Enter to exit the command.

The DONUT command is logical and easy to use. You show inside and outside diameters and then draw as many donut-shaped objects of the specified size as you like.

⊕ Clear your display of polygons before continuing.

⊕ Select Donut from the Draw menu.

AutoCAD prompts

> Specify inside diameter of donut <0.50>:

We will change the inside diameter to 1.00.

⊕ Type "1".

AutoCAD prompts

> Specify outside diameter of donut <1.00>:

We will change the outside diameter to 2.00.

⊕ Type "2".

AutoCAD gives you a donut to drag into place and prompts

> Specify center of donut or [exit]:

⊕ Pick any point.

A donut will be drawn around the point you chose, as shown by the "fat" donuts in Figure 9-4. (If your donut is not filled, see Task 9.3.)

AutoCAD stays in the DONUT command, allowing you to continue drawing donuts.

⊕ Pick a second center point.

⊕ Pick a third center point.

You should now have three "fat" donuts on your screen as shown.

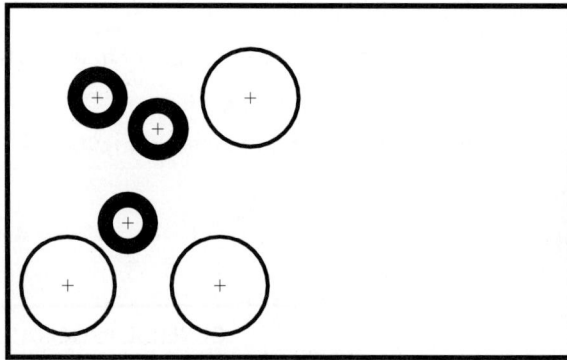

Figure 9-4

⊕ Press Enter or the space bar to exit the DONUT command.

Now draw the "thin" donuts in the figure.

⊕ Repeat DONUT.

⊕ Change the inside diameter to 3.00 and the outer diameter to 3.25.

⊕ Draw three or four "thin" donuts, as shown in Figure 9-4.

When you are done, leave the donuts on the screen so that you can see how they are affected by the FILL command.

9.3   Using the FILL Command

GENERAL PROCEDURE

1. Type "Fill".
2. Type "on" or "off".
3. Type or select "Regen".

Donuts, wide polylines (Tasks 9.4 and 9.5), and 2D solids (Task 9.7) are all affected by FILL. With FILL on, these entities are displayed and plotted as solid filled objects. With FILL off, only the outer boundaries are displayed (donuts are shown with radial lines between the inner and outer circles). Since filled objects are slower to regenerate than outlined ones, you may want to set FILL off as you are working on a drawing and turn it on when you are ready to print or plot.

⊕ For this exercise you should have at least one donut on your screen from Task 9.2.

⊕ Type "fill".

AutoCAD prompts

                    Enter Mode [ON/OFF] <ON>:

⊕ Type "off".

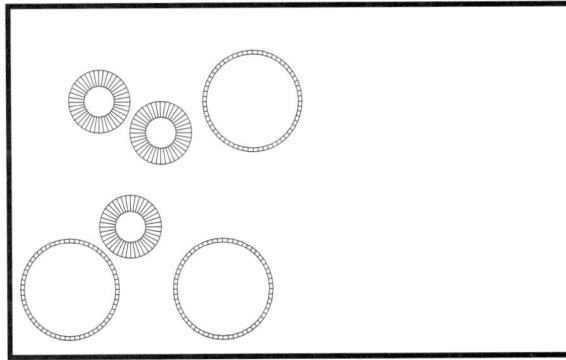

Figure 9-5

You will not see any immediate change in your display when you do this. To see the effect, you will have to regenerate your drawing.

⊕ Type "re" or select Regen from the View menu.

Your screen will be regenerated with FILL off and will resemble Figure 9-5. Many of the special entities that we will be discussing in the remainder of this chapter can be filled, so we encourage you to continue to experiment with FILL as you go along.

9.4 Drawing Straight Polyline Segments

GENERAL PROCEDURE

1. Select Polyline from the Draw menu, or select the Polyline tool from the Draw toolbar.
2. Pick a start point.
3. Type or select width, halfwidth, or other options.
4. Pick other points.

In the last two chapters you saw how text, dimensions, and hatch patterns are all created as complex entities that can be selected and treated as single objects. In the next chapter you will see how to create groups and blocks from separate entities. In this chapter we are focusing on the polyline. You have already drawn several polylines without going through the PLINE command. Donuts and polygons both are drawn as polylines and therefore can be edited using the same edit commands that work on other polylines. You can, for instance, fillet all the corners of a polygon at once. Using the PLINE command itself, you can draw anything from a simple line to a series of lines and arcs with varying widths. Most important, polylines can be edited using many of the ordinary edit commands as well as a set of specialized editing procedures found in the PEDIT command.

We will begin by creating a simple polyline rectangle. The process will be much like drawing a rectangular outline with the LINE command, but the result will be a single object rather than four distinct line segments.

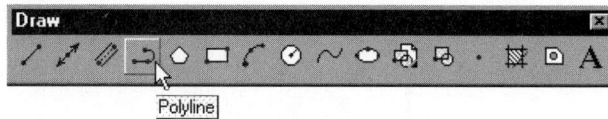

Figure 9-6

⊕ Clear your display of donuts before continuing.

⊕ Select Polyline from the Draw menu, or the Polyline tool from the Draw toolbar, as shown in Figure 9-6.

AutoCAD begins with a prompt for a starting point, as in the LINE command:

Specify start point:

⊕ Pick a start point, similar to P1 in Figure 9-7.

From here the PLINE prompt sequence becomes more complicated:

Current line width is 0.00
Specify next point or [Arc/Close/Halfwidth/Length/Undo/Width]:

The prompt begins by giving you the current line width, left from any previous use of the PLINE command.

Then the prompt offers options in the usual format. "Arc" will lead you into another set of options that deal with drawing polyline arcs. We will save polyline arcs for Task 9.5. "Close" works as in the LINE command to connect the last end point in a sequence to the original starting point. We will get to the other options momentarily.

This time around we will draw a series of 0 width segments, just as we would in the LINE command.

⊕ Pick an end point, similar to P2 in Figure 9-7.

AutoCAD will draw the segment and repeat the prompt.

⊕ Pick another end point, P3 in Figure 9-7.

⊕ Pick another end point, P4 in Figure 9-7.

⊕ Type "c" for "Close" to complete the rectangle, as shown in Figure 9-7.

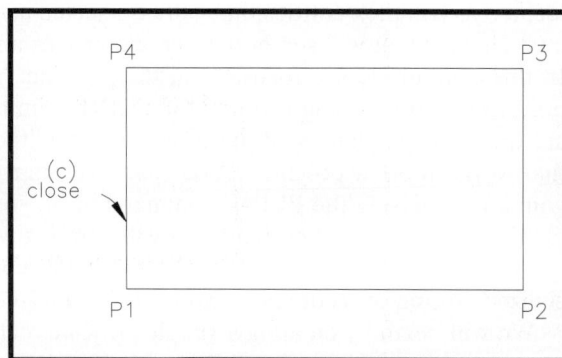

Figure 9-7

The Close option is very important in drawing closed polylines. AutoCAD will recognize the polyline as a closed object only if you use the close option.

⊕ Now select the rectangle by pointing to any of its sides.

You will see that the entire rectangle is selected, rather than just the side you pointed to. This means, for example, that you can FILLET or CHAMFER all four corners of the rectangle at once. Try it if you like, using the following procedure:

1. Select the Fillet tool from the Modify toolbar.
2. Type "r".
3. Specify a radius.
4. Repeat the FILLET command.
5. Type "p" or select "Polyline" to indicate that you want to fillet an entire polyline.
6. Select the rectangle.

Note: If a corner is left without a fillet, it is probably because you did not use the close option when you completed the rectangle.

Now let's create a rectangle with wider lines.

⊕ Enter the PLINE command.

⊕ Pick a starting point, as shown by P1 in Figure 9-8.

AutoCAD prompts

```
Specify next point or [Arc/Close/Halfwidth/Length/Undo/Width]:
```

This time we need to make use of the "Width" option.

⊕ Type "w".

AutoCAD will respond with

```
Specify starting width <0.00>:
```

You will be prompted for two widths, a starting width and an ending width. This makes it possible to draw tapered lines. For this exercise, our lines will have the same starting and ending width.

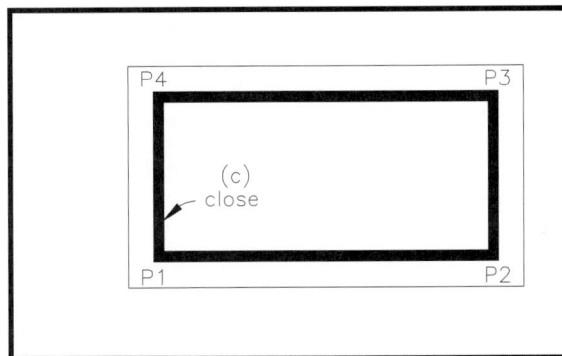

Figure 9-8

Note: The "halfwidth" option differs from "width" only in that the width of the line to be drawn is measured from the center out. With either option you can specify by showing a width rather than typing a value.

⊕ Type ".25".
AutoCAD prompts

> Specify ending width <0.25>

Notice that the starting width has become the default for the ending width. To draw a polyline of uniform width, we accept this default.

⊕ Press Enter or the space bar to keep the starting width and ending width the same.
AutoCAD returns to the previous prompt:

> Specify next point or [Arc/Close/Halfwidth/Length/Undo/Width]:

⊕ Pick an end point, as shown by P2 in Figure 9-8.
⊕ Continue picking points P3 and P4 to draw a second rectangle, as shown in Figure 9-8.
⊕ Use the Close option to draw the last side.

When the object is complete, AutoCAD will create joined corners. If you do not close the last side, the lower left corner will overlap rather than join. Notice also that once a polyline has been given width, it will be affected by the FILL setting.

The only options we have not discussed in this exercise are "Length" and "Undo". "Length" allows you to type or show a value and then draws a segment of that length starting from the end point of the previous segment and continuing in the same direction (if the last segment was an arc, the length will be drawn tangent to the arc). "Undo" undoes the last segment, just as in LINE.

In the next task we will draw some pline arc segments.

9.5 Drawing Polyline Arc Segments

GENERAL PROCEDURE

1. Enter the PLINE command.
2. Pick a start point.
3. Specify a width.
4. Type "a" or select "arc".
5. Type or select options or pick an end point.

A word of caution: Because of the flexibility and power of the PLINE command, it is tempting to think of polylines as always having weird shapes, tapered lines, and strange sequences of lines and arcs. Books tend to perpetuate this by consistently giving peculiar examples to show the range of what is possible with polylines. This

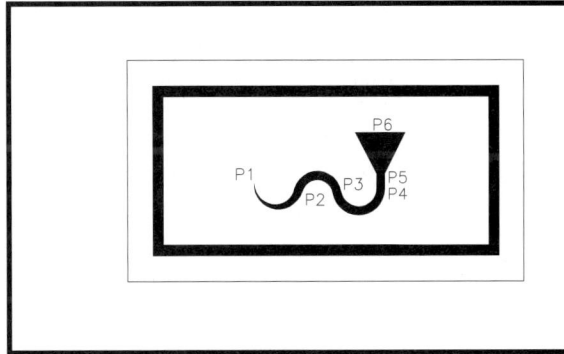

Figure 9-9

is useful but misleading. Remember, polylines are practical entities even for relatively simple applications such as the rectangles drawn in Task 9.4.

Having said that, we will proceed to add our own bit of strangeness to the lore of the polyline. We will draw a polyline with three arc segments and one tapered straight line segment, as shown in Figure 9-9. We call this thing a "goosenecked funnel." You may have seen something like it at your local garage.

⊕ Select Polyline from the Draw menu, or select the Polyline tool from the Draw toolbar.

⊕ Pick a new start point, as shown by P1 in Figure 9-9.

⊕ Type "w" to set new widths.

⊕ Type "0" for the starting width.

⊕ Type ".5" for the ending width.

⊕ Type "a" for the Arc option.

This will bring up the arc prompt, which looks like this:

```
Specify end point of arc or
[Angle/CEnter/CLose/Direction/Halfwidth/Line/Radius/
Second pt/Undo/Width]:
```

Let's look at this prompt for a moment. To begin with, there are four options that are familiar from the previous prompt. "CLose", "Halfwidth", "Undo", and "Width" all function exactly as they would in drawing straight polyline segments. The "Line" option returns you to the previous prompt so that you can continue drawing straight line segments after drawing arc segments.

The other options, "Angle", "CEnter", "Direction", "Radius", "Second pt", and "Endpoint of arc", allow you to specify arcs in ways similar to the ARC command. One difference is that AutoCAD assumes that the arc you want will be tangent to the last polyline segment entered. This is often not the case. The "center" and "direction" options let you override this assumption where necessary, or you can begin with a short line segment to establish direction before entering the arc prompt.

⊕ Pick an end point to the right, as shown by P2 in Figure 9-9, to complete the first arc segment.

Tip: If you did not follow the order shown in the figures and drew your previous rectangle clockwise, or if you have drawn other polylines in the meantime, you may find that the arc does not curve downward, as shown in Figure 9-9. This is because AutoCAD starts arcs tangent to the last polyline segment drawn. Fix this by using the Direction option. Type "d" and then point straight down. Now you can pick an end point to the right as shown.

AutoCAD prompts again:

```
Specify end point of arc or
[Angle/CEnter/CLose/Direction/Halfwidth/Line/Radius/
Second pt/Undo/Width]:
```

For the remaining two arc segments, retain a uniform width of 0.50.

⊕ Enter points P3 and P4 to draw the remaining two arc segments as shown.

Now we will draw two straight line segments to complete the polyline.

⊕ Type "L" (this takes you back to the original prompt).

⊕ Pick P5 straight up about 1.00 as shown.

⊕ Type "w" or select "width".

⊕ Press Enter to retain 0.50 as the starting width.

⊕ Type "3" for the ending width.

⊕ Pick an end point up about 2.00 as shown by P6.

⊕ Press Enter or the space bar to exit the command.

Your screen should resemble Figure 9-9.

9.6 Editing Polylines with PEDIT

GENERAL PROCEDURE

1. Select Polyline from the Modify menu.
2. Select a polyline.
3. Type or select a PEDIT option.
4. Follow the prompts.

The PEDIT command provides a subsystem of special editing capabilities that work only on polylines. We will not attempt to have you use all of them; some you may never need. Most important is that you be aware of the possibilities so that when you find yourself in a situation calling for a PEDIT procedure you will know what to look for. After executing the following task, study Figure 9-12, the PEDIT chart. For further information see the *AutoCAD User's Guide*.

We will perform two edits on the polylines already drawn.

⊕ **Open the Modify menu and select Polyline.**

This executes the PEDIT command. There is also an Edit Polyline tool on the Modify II toolbar, or you can type the alias "pe". You will be prompted to select a polyline:

> Select polyline:

⊕ **Select the outer 0-width polyline rectangle drawn in Task 9.4.**

Notice that PEDIT works on only one object at a time and that selected polylines do not become dotted. You are prompted as follows:

> Enter an option [Open/Join/Width/Edit vertex/
> Fit/Spline/Decurve/Ltype gen/Undo]:

"Open" will be replaced by "Close" if your polyline has not been closed. "Undo" and "eXit" are self-explanatory. Other options are illustrated in Figure 9-12. "Edit vertex" brings up the subset of options shown on the right side of the chart. When you do vertex editing, AutoCAD will mark one vertex at a time with an x. You can move the x to other vertices by pressing Enter, typing "n", or selecting "Next".

Now we will edit the selected polyline by changing its width.

⊕ **Type "w" for the Width option.**

This option allows you to set a new uniform width for an entire polyline. All tapering and variation is removed when this edit is performed.

AutoCAD prompts

> Specify new width for all segments:

⊕ **Type ".25".**

Your screen will be redrawn to resemble Figure 9-10.

Figure 9-10

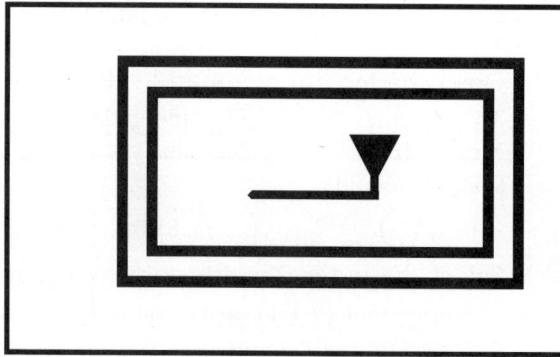

Figure 9-11

The prompt will be returned and the polyline is still selected so that you can continue shaping it with other PEDIT options.

⊕ Press Enter or the space bar to exit PEDIT.

⊕ Press Enter or the space bar to repeat PEDIT.

This exiting and re-entering is necessary in order to select another polyline to edit.

⊕ Select the "gooseneck funnel" polyline.

This time we'll try out the "Decurve" option. Decurve straightens all curves within the selected polyline.

⊕ Type "d".

Your screen will resemble Figure 9-11.

To complete this exercise, we suggest that you try some of the other editing options. In particular, you will get interesting results from "Fit" and "Spline". Be sure to study the PEDIT chart (Figure 9-12) before going on to the next task.

9.7 Drawing 2D SOLIDs

GENERAL PROCEDURE

1. Open the Draw toolbar, highlight Surfaces, and select 2D Solid.
2. Pick a first point.
3. Pick a second point.
4. Pick a third point.
5. Pick a fourth point or press Enter to draw a triangular section.
6. Pick another third point or press Enter to exit the command.

SOLID allows you to draw rectangular and triangular solid-filled shapes in two dimensions by specifying points that become corners or vertices. There is no relation between the 2D solid command and 3D solid modeling, which is the subject of Chapter 14.

There is a trick to using SOLID for rectangular sections involving the order in which you enter points. If you enter them in the wrong order, you will get the bow

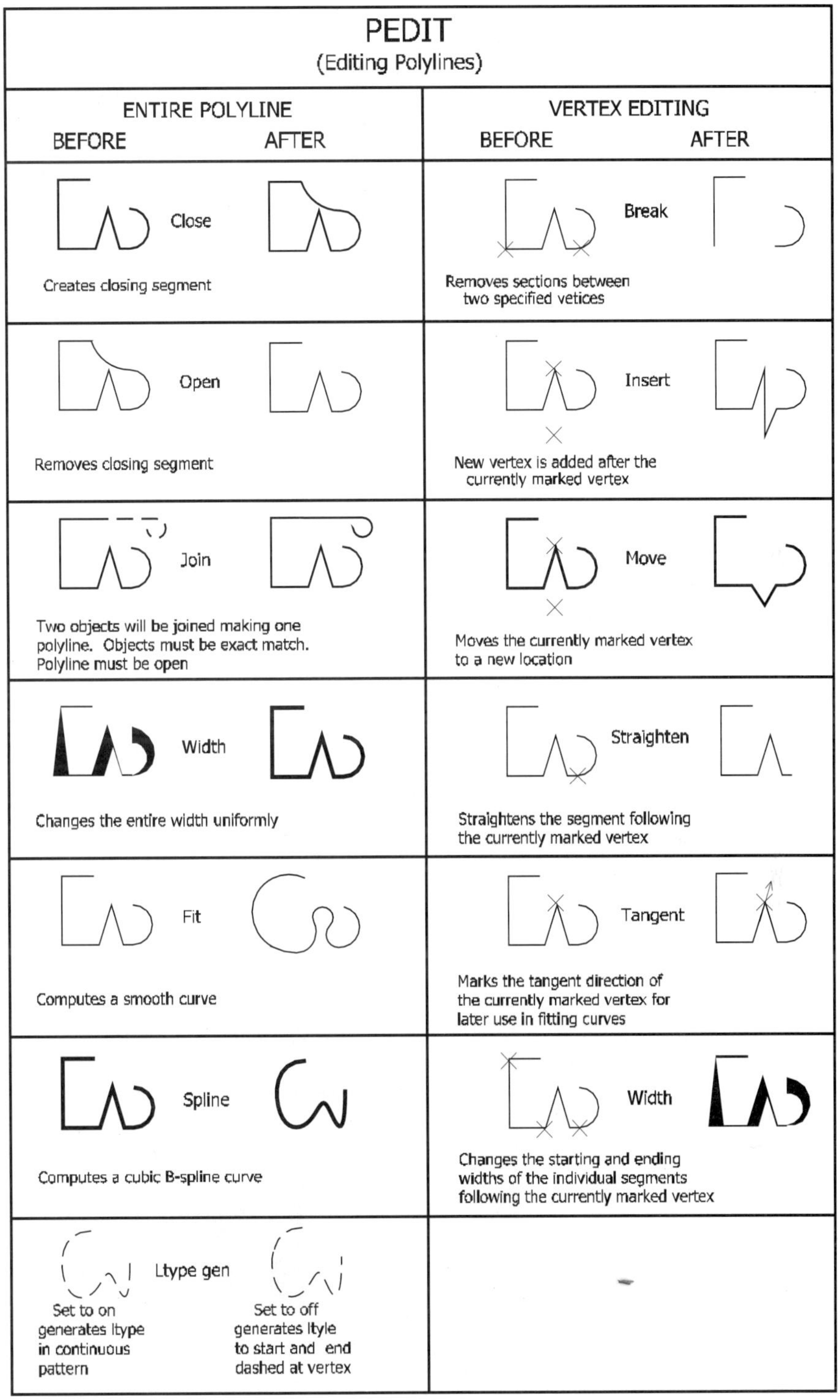

PEDIT
(Editing Polylines)

ENTIRE POLYLINE		VERTEX EDITING	
BEFORE	AFTER	BEFORE	AFTER

Close
Creates closing segment

Break
Removes sections between two specified vetices

Open
Removes closing segment

Insert
New vertex is added after the currently marked vertex

Join
Two objects will be joined making one polyline. Objects must be exact match. Polyline must be open

Move
Moves the currently marked vertex to a new location

Width
Changes the entire width uniformly

Straighten
Straightens the segment following the currently marked vertex

Fit
Computes a smooth curve

Tangent
Marks the tangent direction of the currently marked vertex for later use in fitting curves

Spline
Computes a cubic B-spline curve

Width
Changes the starting and ending widths of the individual segments following the currently marked vertex

Ltype gen
Set to on generates ltype in continuous pattern

Set to off generates ltype to start and end dashed at vertex

Figure 9-12

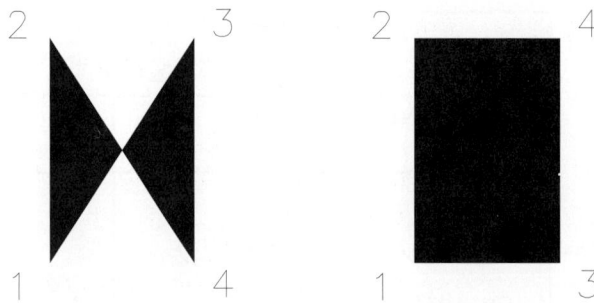

Figure 9-13

tie effect shown in Figure 9-13. It is natural to enter points in a rectangle by moving around the perimeter. However, AutoCAD solids are drawn with edges between point 1 and point 3 and between point 2 and point 4, so you need to be careful about the order in which you pick points.

⊕ To begin this task, clear the screen of polylines left over from Task 9.6.

⊕ FILL and ORTHO should be on for this exercise. We will begin with a rectangular solid.

⊕ Open the Draw menu, highlight Surfaces, and select 2D Solid.
There is also a 2D Solid tool on the Surfaces toolbar, or you can type the alias "so".
AutoCAD will prompt for a series of points, beginning with

Specify first point:

⊕ Pick a point similar to P1 in Figure 9-14.
In AutoCAD 2000, the SOLID command uses no rubber band or other visual feedback. You will simply see the next prompt:

Specify second point:

⊕ Pick a point similar to P2.
These first two points will become the end points of one side of a rectangular solid. AutoCAD prompts

Specify third point:

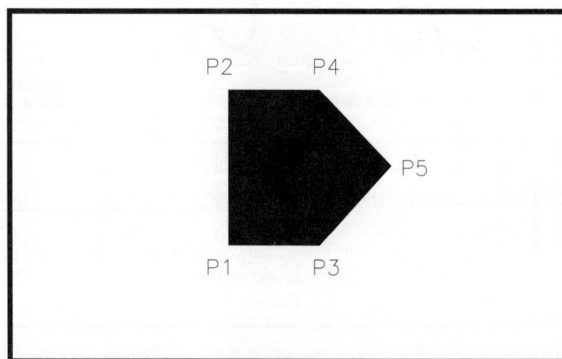

Figure 9-14

⊕ Pick a point similar to P3.

Remember that an edge will be drawn between point 1 and point 3. Auto-CAD prompts

Specify fourth point:

⊕ Pick a point similar to P4 in Figure 9-14.

When the fourth point is entered, AutoCAD will draw a solid rectangle and continue to prompt for points.

Specify third point:

If you continue entering points, the previous points 3 and 4 will become points 1 and 2 of the new section. You can draw a triangular section by picking a third point and then pressing Enter in response to the prompt for a fourth point. This also means that you will need to press Enter twice when you want to exit SOLID. We will draw a triangular solid before exiting.

⊕ Turn ortho off and pick a point similar to P5 in Figure 9-14.

⊕ Press Enter in response to the "Fourth point:" prompt.

Your screen should resemble Figure 9-14.

⊕ Press Enter again to exit the command.

9.8 Drawing and Editing Multilines

GENERAL PROCEDURE

1. Select Multiline from the Draw menu, or select the Multiline tool from the Draw toolbar.
2. Pick a start point.
3. Pick a next point.
4. Pick another to point, or press Enter to exit the command.

Multilines are groups of parallel lines with various forms of intersections and end caps. Each individual line is called an element, and you can have up to 16 elements in a single multiline style. Drawing multilines is about as simple as drawing lines. The complexity comes in defining multiline styles and in editing intersections. In this task we will draw standard multilines, create a new style, and edit the intersection of two multilines.

⊕ To begin this exercise, clear the screen of solids or other objects left from previous exercises.

First, we will draw some standard multilines.

⊕ Type "ml", select Multiline from the Draw menu, or select the Multiline tool from the Draw toolbar, as shown in Figure 9-15.

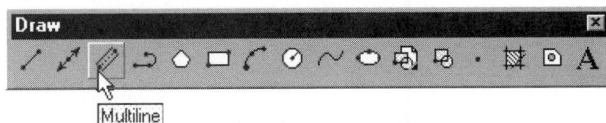

Figure 9-15

AutoCAD will issue the following prompt:

```
Current settings: Justification = Top, Scale = 1.00,
Style = STANDARD
Specify start point or [Justification/Scale/STyle]:
```

If you stick with the default option, you will see that the MLINE sequence is exactly like drawing a line. "Justification" refers to the way elements are positioned in relation to the points you pick on the screen. The default justification is "Top". This means that the top element of the multiline will be positioned at the cross hairs when you pick points. Try it, and we will discuss the other options later.

⊕ Pick a start point similar to P1 in Figure 9-16.

AutoCAD gives you a standard, two-element multiline to drag and prompts for another point:

```
Specify next point:
```

Move the cursor and notice how the cross hairs continue to connect with the top element. The other two options for justification are "Zero" and "Bottom". Zero lines up in the middle of the elements, at the zero point or origin. You will understand this better after we create a new style. Bottom lines up on the bottom element.

⊕ Pick a second point similar to P2 in Figure 9-16.

Exact lengths and angles are not important. Move the cursor around and notice how AutoCAD adjusts the corner to maintain parallel line elements.

AutoCAD has added an undo option now that you have one multiline segment complete.

```
Specify next point or [Undo]:
```

⊕ Pick P3, as in Figure 9-16.

Once you have two complete multiline segments, AutoCAD adds a close option:

```
Specify next point or [Close/Undo]:
```

⊕ Pick P4, as in Figure 9-16.

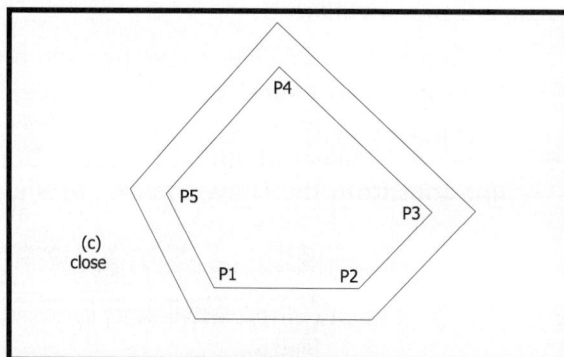

Figure 9-16

⊕　Pick P5, as in Figure 9-16.

⊕　Type "c" to close and complete the figure.

Creating Multiline Styles

The real power of multilines comes when you learn to create your own multiline style. This is done through the Multiline Styles dialog box, called by the ML-STYLE command.

⊕　Select "Multiline Style..." from the Format menu.

This will call the dialog box shown in Figure 9-17. Standard is the name of the current multiline style, which, as we have seen, includes two continuous line elements. We will begin by adding a new style to the list of multiline styles and then adding a third element to the new style.

⊕　Double click in the Name edit box.

Standard should be highlighted.

⊕　Type "new".

⊕　Click on "add" to add New to the style list.

New should now be showing in the Current style box.

⊕　Select "Element Properties...".

This calls the Element Properties dialog box shown in Figure 9-18. First look at the elements box. It shows that there are now only two elements: One is offset 0.5 above the origin point of the multiline (0.0) and the other is offset −0.5, or 0.5 below the origin. Standard multilines have a zero point between the two lines, but since the default justification is top, the cross hairs line up

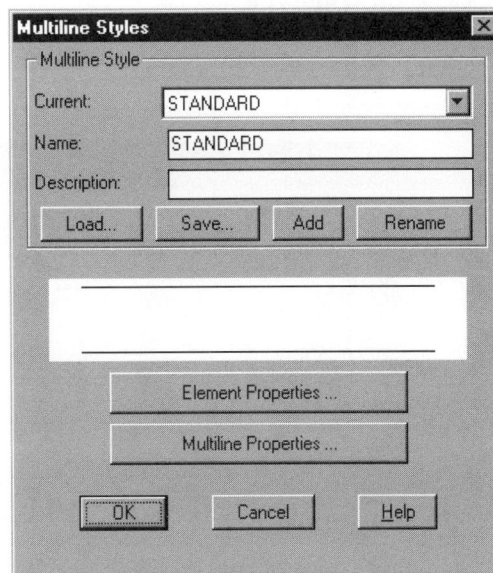

Figure 9-17

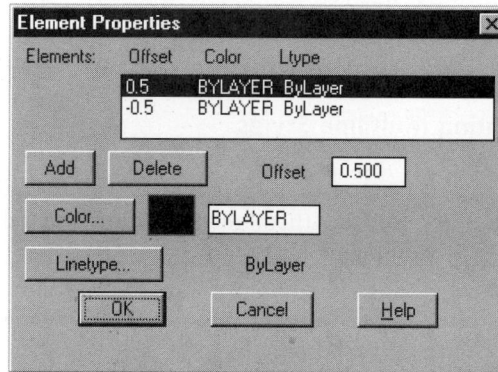

Figure 9-18

on the top element. With zero justification they would line up at 0.0. With Bottom justification they would line up on the −0.5 element.

⊕ Click on "Add".

This is how we begin to add a new element. As soon as you click "Add", a third element is added to the box. Notice that it is offset 0.0. In other words, it is right on the zero line between the two offset lines. For this style we will leave it there. If we needed to offset it, we would type a new offset number in the offset box.

Next, notice that all three elements are listed as having BYLAYER color and linetype. This means that the color and linetype will be determined by whatever layer the multiline is drawn on. We will change the linetype of our newly added middle element. This element should be highlighted. If it is not, click on it to highlight it before proceeding.

⊕ Click on "Linetype...".

This calls the "Select Linetype" dialog box shown in Figure 9-19. This box contains all the loaded linetypes in your drawing. From past exercises, you

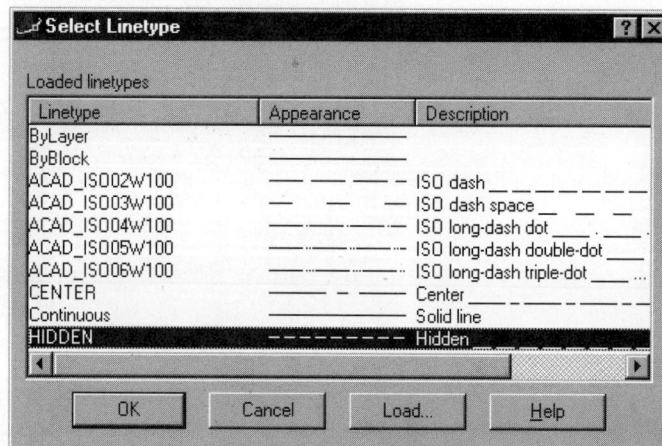

Figure 9-19

should at least have the hidden and center linetypes loaded, so we will use one of these. (If for any reason your template drawing does not have the HIDDEN linetype or if you want to use a linetype that is not loaded, select "Load..." from this dialog box and load them now.)

⊕ Run down the list until you see "HIDDEN".

⊕ Select "HIDDEN".

⊕ Click on OK.

Notice that the element at 0.0 now has the HIDDEN linetype style.

⊕ Click on OK again.

When you return to the Multiline Styles dialog box, you should see that the middle element has been added to the image box but is shown as a continuous line. The image box shows elements by position but does not show color or linetype.

Now let's look at the Multiline Properties dialog box.

⊕ Click on "Multiline Properties...".

This calls up the dialog box shown in Figure 9-20. This box controls the way joints and ends of multilines are treated. The variety of options is shown in Figure 9-21. For our purposes it will not be necessary to add joints or end caps at this point.

⊕ Click on OK or Cancel to exit the Multiline Properties box.

⊕ Click on Save to save the new style.

This will call a Save Multiline Style dialog box.

⊕ Click on Save to save the new style in the ACAD file.

Once your style has been named, defined, and saved and is the current style, you are ready to leave the box and draw some new multilines.

⊕ Click on OK to exit the dialog box.

⊕ Select the Multiline tool from the Draw toolbar.

⊕ Pick two points to draw the horizontal multiline shown in Figure 9-22.

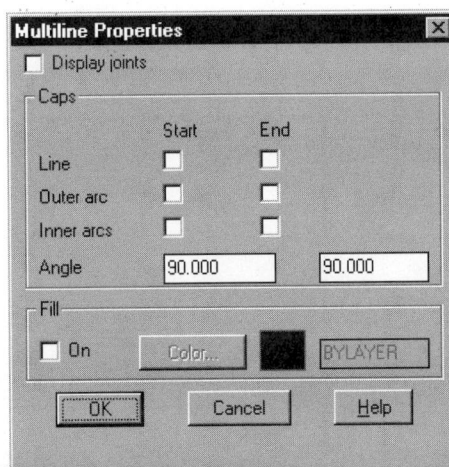

Figure 9-20

DISPLAY JOINTS (Multiline Properties)	
BEFORE	AFTER
Display Joints Off	Display Joints On
End Cap Line Off	End Cap Line On
End Cap Outer Arc Off	End Cap Outer Arc On
End Cap Inner Arcs Off	End Cap Inner Arcs On
End Cap Angle Off	End Cap Angle On

Figure 9-21

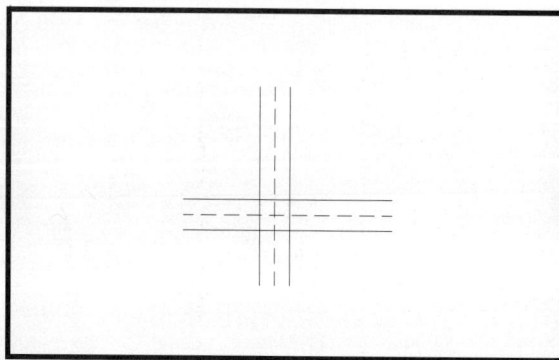

Figure 9-22

⊕ Press Enter to exit the MLINE command.

⊕ Repeat MLINE and pick two more points to draw the vertical multi-line shown in Figure 9-22.

Editing Multiline Intersections

Multilines can be modified using many of the same edit commands that are used with other entities. In addition, there is a special MLEDIT command for editing the intersection of two multilines. The possibilities will be easy to see since the dialog box illustrates the options using a figure similar to the one you have just drawn.

⊕ Select Multiline from Modify menu.

There is also a Multiline Edit tool on the Modify II toolbar. These selections call the Multiline Edit Tools dialog box shown in Figure 9-23. When you select any of the 12 images in the box, the name of that type of edit will be shown at the lower left corner of the box. Since the figure on your screen is similar to the one used in these image boxes, what you see is pretty much what you will get when you perform any of these edits.

⊕ Click on the top left image box.

As you see, this choice is called a Closed Cross.

⊕ Click on OK.

Now you will need to select the two multilines to edit.

⊕ Pick the vertical multiline.

The order in which you pick is clearly significant with this and many other of the multiline edits. In this case the second multiline selected does not change and will appear to "cross over" the first.

⊕ Pick the horizontal multiline.

Your screen should resemble Figure 9-24.

With up to 16 elements, 256 colors, 58 standard linetypes, plus the different end-cap forms and the various types of intersection edits, the possibilities for creating multiline styles are substantial. We encourage you to experiment before going on.

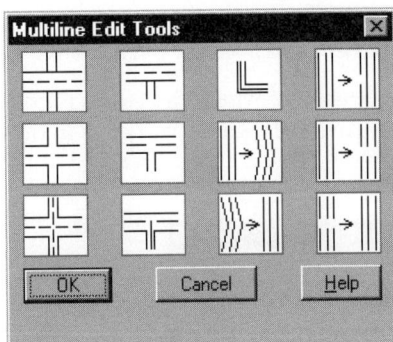

Figure 9-23

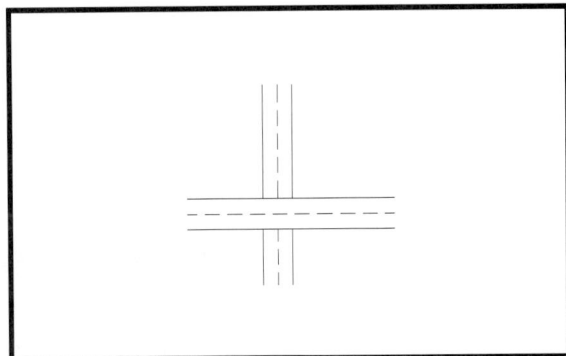

Figure 9-24

9.9 Drawing SPLINEs

GENERAL PROCEDURE

1. Select the Spline tool from the Draw toolbar.
2. Pick points.
3. Close or specify start and end tangent directions.

A Spline is a smooth curve passing through a specified set of points. In AutoCAD 2000, Splines are created in a precise mathematical form called NURBS (nonuniform rational B-spline). Splines can be drawn with varying degrees of tolerance, meaning the degree to which the curve is constrained by the defined points. With zero tolerance the curve will pass through all points. With higher degrees of tolerance, the curve will tend toward, but not necessarily pass through each point. In addition to tolerance and the set of points needed to define a spline, tangent directions are needed for the starting and ending portions of the curve. From Chapter 8, you will recall that dimension leaders may be drawn as splines. Polylines may be converted to spline curves. Splines may be used to create any smooth curve that can be defined by a set of control points. In this task we will use SPLINE to draw a curve surrounding the multilines drawn in Task 9.8.

⊕ Select the Spline tool from the Draw toolbar, as shown in Figure 9-25.

AutoCAD prompts

```
Specify first point or [Object]:
```

⊕ Pick a point roughly 1.00 unit to the left of the top element of the horizontal multiline, P1 as shown in Figure 9-26.

AutoCAD will prompt for a next point and will continue to prompt for points until you press enter.

⊕ Pick a second point about 1.00 unit above the left side of the horizontal multiline, P2 as shown in Figure 9-26.

As soon as you have two points, AutoCAD will show a spline that will drag with your cursor as you select a third point. The prompt will also change to add two options.

```
Specify next point or [Close/Fit tolerance] <start tangent>:
```

The Fit tolerance option determines the degree to which the curve is constrained by the selected points, as discussed previously. Close works as in oth-

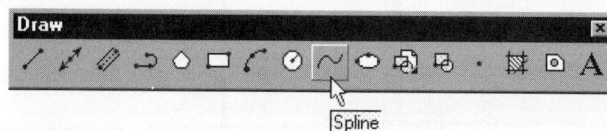

Figure 9-25

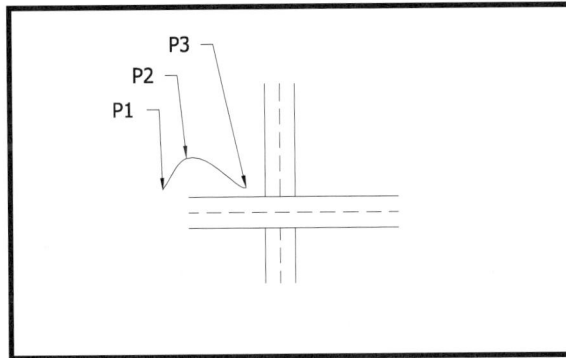

Figure 9-26

er commands to create a closed object. If the object is closed there is no need for tangent specifications. Otherwise, the start and end directions need to be specified when point selection is complete.

⊕ Pick a third point, P3 as shown in Figure 9-26.

From here on you are on your own as you continue entering points to surround the multilines. We have made no attempt to specify precise points. We used about 16 points to go all the way around without crossing the multilines, as shown in Figure 9-27. The exact number of points you choose is not important for this task.

⊕ Continue selecting points to surround the multilines without touching them.

⊕ After you reach and pick a point similar to P16 in Figure 9-27, press enter or the space bar.

This indicates that you are through specifying points. We left the spline open to demonstrate the tangent specifications. When you press enter, the cursor will be attached to the start point, P1 again, and the prompt will be

                    Specify start tangent:

⊕ Pick a point above P1.

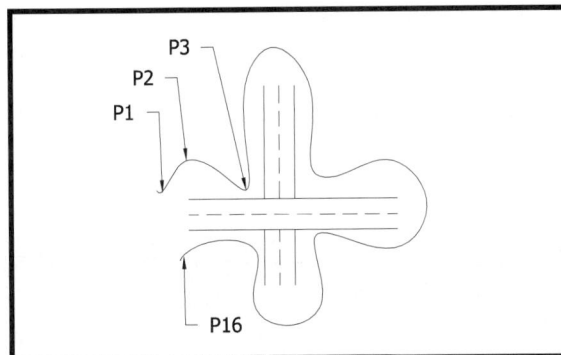

Figure 9-27

⊕   The cursor will now be attached to P16 again and the prompt will be

Specify end tangent:

⊕   Pick a point below P16.

Your screen will resemble Figure 9-27.

Editing Splines

Splines can be edited in the usual ways but also have their own edit command SPLINEDIT. Since splines are defined by sets of points, one useful option is to use grips to move grip points. The SPLINEDIT command gives you additional options including the option to change the tolerance, to add fit points for greater definition, or to delete unecessary points. An open spline can be closed, or the start and end tangent directions can be changed. To access SPLINEDIT, select Spline from the Modify menu.

9.10   Using the SKETCH Command

GENERAL PROCEDURE

1. Type "Sketch".
2. Type an increment.
3. Pick a start point (pen down).
4. Move cursor to sketch lines.
5. Pick an end point (pen up).
6. Record, exit, quit, or erase.

The SKETCH command allows you to draw freehand lines. We include it here though it is not used in any of the drawings that follow. SKETCH creates a polyline made up of many very short line segments. You control the coarseness of the sketch by specifying the length of the individual segment. Sketched polylines take up a large amount of memory, so they should be used sparingly.

The key to SKETCH is becoming familiar with its pen-up, pen-down action. Also, get used to the idea that SKETCHed lines are not part of the drawing until you "record" them or exit the SKETCH command.

⊕   Type "Sketch".

AutoCAD prompts

Record increment <0.10>:

This will allow you to decide how fine or coarse you want your lines to be. Remember also that AutoCAD will continue to observe your snap. If you want a small, flexible record increment, turn snap off.

⊕   Press Enter to accept .10 as the record increment.

You will see the following prompt:

```
Sketch. Pen eXit Quit Record Erase Connect.
```

We will discuss these options in a moment. They will make more sense after you have done some sketching.

⊕ **To begin sketching, choose any point on your screen and press the pickbutton once.**

This puts your imaginary sketching pen down.

⊕ **Move the cursor and watch the lines that appear on the screen.**

⊕ **Press the pickbutton again.**

This picks your imaginary pen up again, resulting in an end point. If you move the cursor again, no new lines will be drawn.

⊕ **Press the pickbutton once again and move the cursor.**

The pen is down and you can continue sketching from a new start point.

Now look at the other options:

```
Sketch. Pen eXit Quit Record Erase Connect.
```

"P" picks the imaginary pen up and down, but the pickbutton is more convenient. "X" records the lines you have drawn and exits the command. "Q" exits without recording. "R" records without exiting. "E" allows you to erase some of the lines you have sketched in the last sequence. The action of this erase option is interesting, and you should try it. "C" connects you to the point where you last picked up your pen. "." draws a straight line from the point where you left off to the current position of the cross hairs.

⊕ **Press the pickbutton again to pick the pen up.**

⊕ **When you are done sketching, press Enter or the space bar to exit the command.**

Exiting the command will also record the sketched polyline. You will see a message similar to this:

```
2 polylines with 186 edges recorded
```

9.11 Drawing POINTs

GENERAL PROCEDURE

1. Select the Point tool from the Draw toolbar.
2. Pick a point.

On the surface this is the simplest DRAW command in AutoCAD. However, if you look at Figure 9-28, you will see figures that were drawn with the POINT command that do not look like ordinary points. This capability adds a bit of power and complexity to the otherwise simple POINT command.

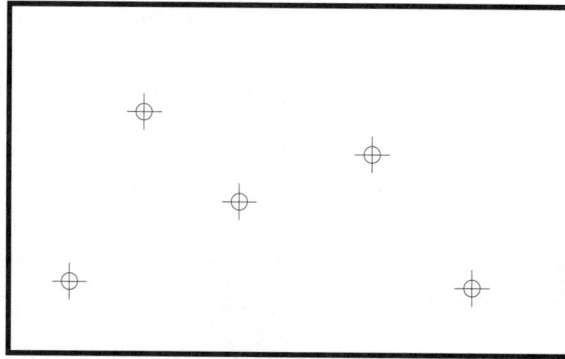

Figure 9-28

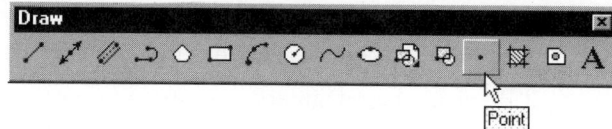

Figure 9-29

⊕ Erase objects from previous exercises.

⊕ Turn off the grid (F7).

⊕ Select the Point tool from the Draw toolbar, as shown in Figure 9-29.

You can also type "po" or select Point from the Draw menu.

⊕ Pick a point anywhere on the screen.

AutoCAD will place a point at the specified location and prompt for more points. Look closely and you will see the point you have drawn. Besides those odd instances in which you may need to draw tiny dots like this, points can also serve as object snap "nodes." See the OSNAP chart, Figure 6-10 in Chapter 6.

But what about those circles and crosses in Figure 9-28? AutoCAD 2000 has 18 other simple forms that can be drawn as points. Before we change the point form, we need to see our options.

⊕ Select Point Style from the Format menu.

AutoCAD displays a Point Style dialog box with an icon menu, as shown in Figure 9-30. It shows you graphic images of your choices. You can pick any of the point styles shown by pointing. You can also change the size of points using the Point Size edit box.

⊕ Pick the style in the middle of the second row.

⊕ Click on OK to exit the dialog box.

⊕ Select the Point tool from the Draw toolbar.

⊕ Pick a point anywhere on your screen.

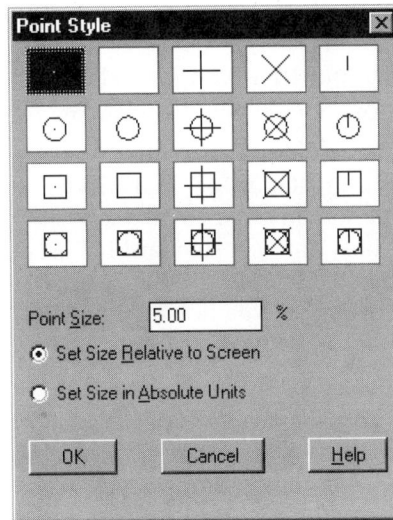

Figure 9-30

AutoCAD will draw a point in the chosen style, as shown in Figure 9-30.

If you have selected the POINT command from the toolbar, AutoCAD will continue to draw points wherever you pick them until you exit the command. If you have entered POINT from the command line, or selected Single Point from the Modify menu, you will have to repeat it to draw more points.

⊕ Repeat POINT, if necessary, and pick another point.

Draw a few more points, or return to the dialog box to try another style.

⊕ If necessary, cancel the POINT command.

9.12   Making and Viewing Slides

GENERAL PROCEDURE

1. Type "Mslide" or "Vslide".
2. Type or select the name of a .sld file.

We end this chapter with slides. Slides are not objects like the other entities in this chapter. They are simply "snapshots" of AutoCAD displays that are saved in a reduced format so they can be loaded quickly. They cannot be plotted or edited, but they are often used in developing business presentations that can be shown on a computer screen.

Slides are easily created using MSLIDE. Once created they can be displayed using the VSLIDE command. Since slides resemble drawings, it is important to understand the primary difference: Slides cannot be edited, added to, or changed in any way.

To create a slide of your present display, follow this procedure:

⊕ **To begin this task you should have some objects on your screen.**

Any objects will do, including the points from Task 9.8.

⊕ **Type "Mslide".**

MSLIDE stands for "make slide." It creates a slide from your current screen display. When the command is entered, you will see a Create Slide File dialog box. This is a standard file list box, listing files that have a .sld extension. When the box opens, the cursor will be blinking in the File Name edit box so that you can type in a name for the slide you want to create.

⊕ **Type a name for the file, like "9-1".**

⊕ **Press Enter or Click on Save.**

It's that simple. Your display will be saved as a file with a .sld extension. To see that it is really there, you must first alter your screen in some way and then load the file using VSLIDE.

⊕ **Erase the objects from your screen.**

⊕ **Type "Vslide".**

You will see another standard file list dialog box. This one will be titled "Select Slide File".

⊕ **Type or select the name of the file you just created with MSLIDE.**

⊕ **Press Enter or click on OK.**

Your slide will appear.

⊕ **Try to select any of the objects that appear in your slide.**

You will find that you cannot. Slides cannot be altered. However, It is possible to draw new objects while a slide is showing on your screen. These are not part of the slide but are part of your current drawing. If you REDRAW the screen, the newly drawn objects will remain and the slide will disappear.

⊕ **To clear the slide from your screen, type "r" or select Redraw from the View menu.**

Most slide applications use a series of slides, exactly as you would in a photographic slide show. This process can be automated and timed using a special kind of file called a script file. There are a number of commands used in the making of a script file, including SCRIPT, DELAY, RESUME, and RSCRIPT, in addition to MSLIDE and VSLIDE. See the *AutoCAD User's Guide* for further information if your goals include the use of slide presentations.

9.13 Review Material

Questions

1. If you wanted to draw a polygon around the outside of a circle so that its sides were tangent to the circle, what option of the POLYGON command would you use?

2. Halfwidth is to width as radius is to diameter. Explain.
3. Why does PLINE prompt for two different widths?
4. Why is it important to use the Close option when drawing closed polygons using the PLINE command?
5. How does AutoCAD decide in which direction to draw a polyline arc?
6. You are drawing a rectangular 2D Solid 2 units high by 4 units wide. Your first point is at (2,2) and your second point is at (2,4). Assuming you want to move to the right, where should points 3 and 4 be? List them in order.
7. What is an AutoCAD slide? How is it different from a drawing?
8. Where is the zero point in a standard AutoCAD multiline?
9. What properties make up a multiline style definition?
10. When is it necessary to use the MLEDIT command?
11. Describe the difference between a Spline curve constructed with a 0 tolerance and one with a 0.5 tolerance.
12. For what reason is it advisable to use the SKETCH command sparingly?

Drawing Problems

1. Draw a regular six-sided polygon centered at (9,6) with a circumscribed radius of 3.0 units. The top and bottom sides should be horizontal.
2. Fillet all corners of the hexagon with a single execution of the FILLET command, giving a radius of 0.25 units.
3. Give the sides of the hexagon a uniform width of 0.25 units.
4. Draw a STANDARD two-element multiline justified to its zero point from the midpoint of one angled side of the hexagon to the midpoint of the diagonally opposite side.
5. Draw a second multiline in the same manner, using the other two angled sides so that the two multilines cross.
6. Edit the intersection of the two multilines to create an "Open Cross" intersection.

9.14   WWW Exercise #9 (Optional)

In Chapter 9 of our companion Web site we will challenge you to find information on one of the twentieth century's greatest architects. We will give you two links to get you started and then you are on your own. We will also offer you another design challenge and the self-scoring test for this chapter. When you are ready,

⊕   Make sure that you are connected to your Internet service provider.
⊕   Type "browser", open the Web toolbar, and select the Browse the Web tool, or open your system browser from the Windows 98 taskbar.
⊕   If necessary, navigate to our companion Web site at "www.prenhall.com/dixriley".

9.15   Drawing 9-1: Backgammon Board

This drawing should go very quickly. It is a good warm-up and will give you practice with MLINE, PLINE, and SOLID. Remember that the dimensions are always part of your drawing now, unless otherwise indicated.

DRAWING SUGGESTIONS

GRID = 1.00
SNAP = 0.125

- First create the multiline line style for the frame with three elements 0.25, 0.00, and −0.50 and joints on as shown. Then draw the 15.50 × 17.50 multiline frame.
- Draw a 0-width 15.50 × 13.50 polyline rectangle and then OFFSET it 0.125 to the inside. The inner polyline is actually 0.25 wide; but it is drawn on center, so the offset must be half the width.
- Enter the PEDIT command and change the width of the inner polyline to 0.25. This will give you your wide filled border.
- Draw the four triangles at the left of the board and then array them across. The filled triangles are drawn with the SOLID command; the others are just outlines drawn with LINE or PLINE. (Notice that you cannot draw some solids filled and others not filled.)
- The dimensions in this drawing are straightforward and should give you no trouble. Remember to set to layer "dim" before dimensioning.

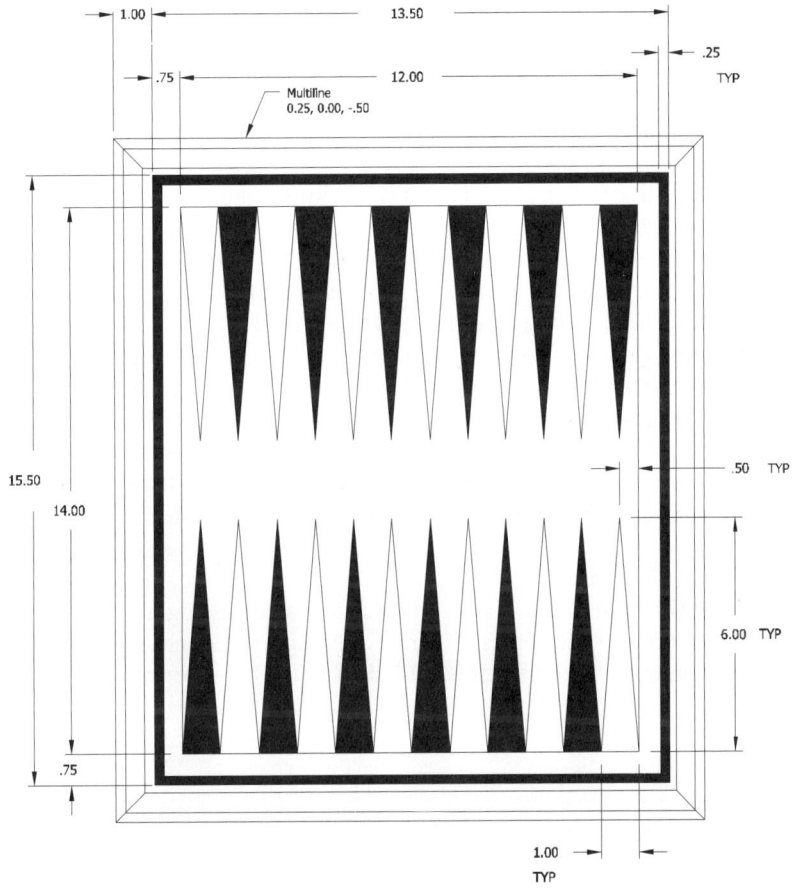

BACKGAMMON BOARD

Drawing 9-1

9.16 Drawing 9-2: Dart Board

Although this drawing may seem to resemble the previous one, it is quite a bit more complex and is drawn in an entirely different way. Using SOLID to create the filled areas here would be impractical because of the arc-shaped edges. We suggest you use DONUTs and TRIM them along the radial lines.

DRAWING SUGGESTIONS

> LIMITS = (0,0) (24,18)
> GRID = 1.00
> SNAP = 0.125

- The filled inner circle is a donut with 0 inner and 0.62 outer diameters.
- The second circle is a simple 1.50-diameter circle. From here, draw a series of donuts. The outside diameter of one will become the inside diameter of the next. The 13.00- and 17.00-diameter outer circles must be drawn as circles rather than donuts so they will not be filled.
- Draw a radius line from the center to one of the quadrants of the outer circle and array it around the circle.
- You may find it easier and quicker to turn fill off before trimming the donuts. Also, use layers to keep the donuts separated visually by color.
- To TRIM the donuts, select the radial lines as cutting edges. This is easily done using a very small crossing box around the center point of the board. Otherwise you will have to pick each line individually in the area between the 13.00 and 17.00 circle.
- Draw the number 5 at the top of the board using a "middle" text position and a rotation of 2 degrees. Array it around the circle and then use the DDEDIT command to change the copied fives to the other numbers shown.

DIAMETERS

Ø.62
Ø1.50
Ø7.50
Ø8.25
Ø13.00
Ø17.00

DART BOARD

Drawing 9-2

9.17   Drawing 9-3: Printed Circuit Board

This drawing uses donuts, solids, and polylines. Also notice the ordinate dimensions.

DRAWING SUGGESTIONS

> UNITS = 4-place decimal
> LIMITS = (0,0) (18,12)
> GRID = 0.5000
> SNAP = 0.1250

- Because this drawing uses ordinate dimensions, moving the 0 point of the grid using the UCS command will make the placement of figures very easy.
- The 26 rectangular tabs at the bottom can be drawn as polylines or solids.
- After placing the donuts according to the dimensions, draw the connections to them using polyline arcs and line segments. These will be simple polylines of uniform 0.03125 halfwidth. The triangular tabs will be added later.
- Remember, AutoCAD begins all polyline arcs tangent to the last segment drawn. Often this is not what you want. One way to correct this is to begin with a line segment that establishes the direction for the arc. The line segment can be extremely short and still accomplish your purpose. Thus many of these polylines will consist of a line segment, followed by an arc, followed by another line segment.
- There are two sizes of the triangular tabs, one on top of the rectangular tabs and one at each donut. Draw one of each size in place and then use multiple COPY, MOVE, and ROTATE commands to create all the others.

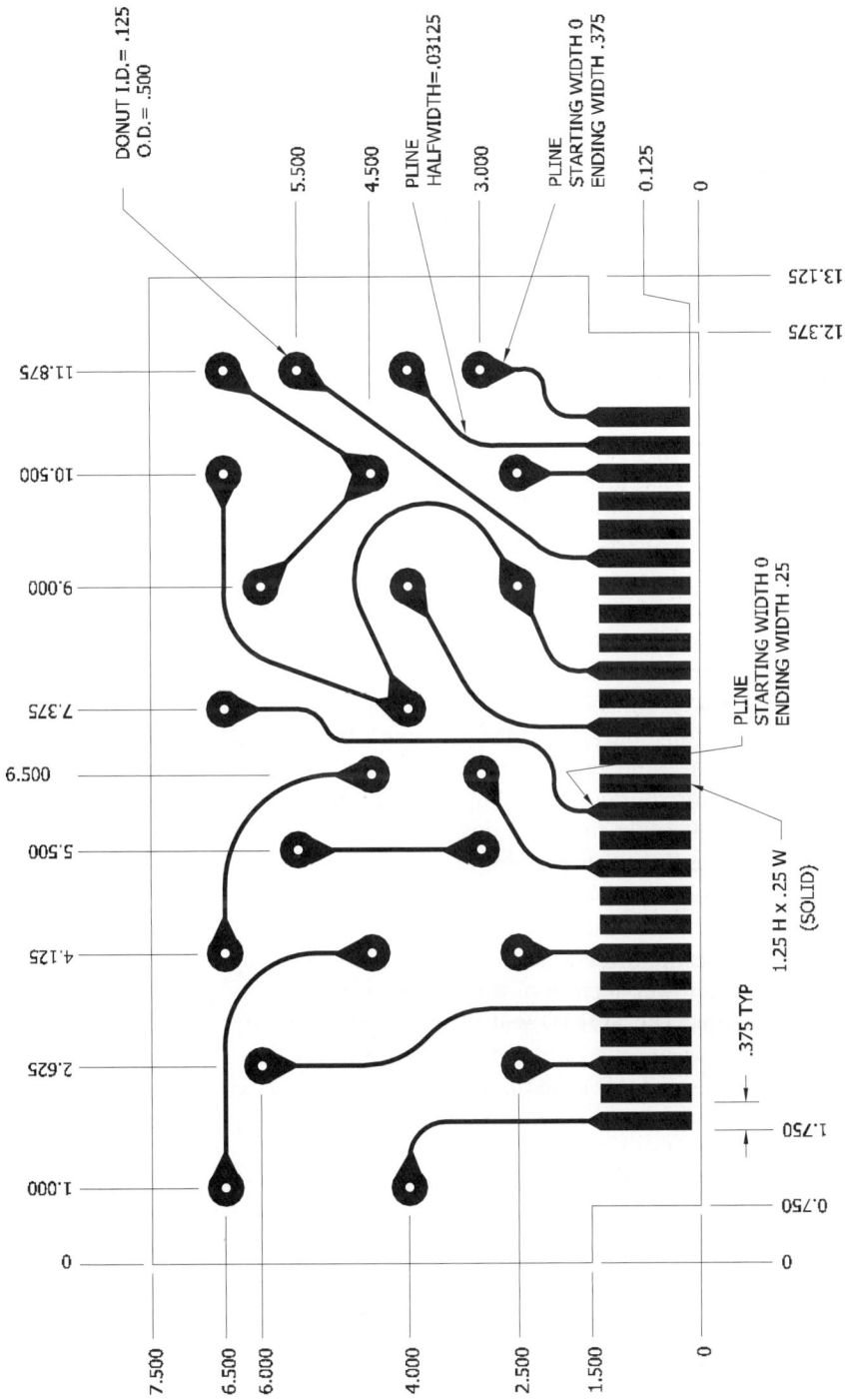

PRINTED CIRCUIT BOARD

DRAWING 9-3

DONUT I.D. = .125
O.D. = .500

5.500

4.500

PLINE
HALFWIDTH=.03125

3.000

PLINE
STARTING WIDTH 0
ENDING WIDTH .375

0.125

0

13.125

12.375

11.875

10.500

9.000

7.375

6.500

5.500

4.125

2.625

1.000

0

PLINE
STARTING WIDTH 0
ENDING WIDTH .25

1.25 H x .25 W
(SOLID)

.375 TYP

1.750

0.750

7.500

6.500

6.000

4.000

2.500

1.500

0

9.18   Drawing 9-4: Carbide Tip Saw Blade

This is a nice drawing that will require the creation of an odd shape combining a DONUT and a 2D SOLID that can be filled to form the carbide tips. There is also an opportunity to use temporary tracking points.

DRAWING SUGGESTIONS

GRID = 1.00
SNAP = 0.125

- After drawing the 7.25-diameter circle, draw a vertical line 1.50 over from the center line. This line will become the left side of the detailed "cut."
- Enter the LINE command and then use object snap and object snap tracking to acquire a point at the intersection of the line and the circle. Still in the LINE command, type "tt" or select Temporary track point from the osnap short cut menu and pick a temporary tracking point 0.58 below the intersection. Draw the horizontal center line running through the track point and out to the right.
- OFFSET the vertical center line 0.16 to the right of the 0.58 line, then change its layer to Layer 3, to make it a center line.
- Use the center lines to draw the 0.16-radius semicircular arc.
- From the right end point of the arc, draw a line extending upward at 80 degrees. The dimension is given as 10 degrees from the vertical, but the coordinate display will show 80 degrees from the horizontal.
- OFFSET this line 0.06 to the right and left to create the lines for the left and right sides of the carbide tip.
- Draw a horizontal line 0.12 up from the center line. You can use a temporary track point again to locate this point.
- TRIM the line with the sides of the carbide tip and create 0.06-radius fillets right and left.
- Draw the 3.68-radius circle to locate the outside of the tip.
- To fill the tip, draw a DONUT with 0 inside diameter and .12 outside diameter in the lower section of the tip and a quadilateral 2D SOLID to fill the rest of the tip. (The SOLID will have four straight edges and, technically, will only approximate the outer edge). Fill should be on.
- BREAK and TRIM the three 80-degree lines, leaving three extension lines for use in dimensioning. Then copy the whole area up to the right for the detail. When you start working on the detail, SCALE it up 2.00.
- In the original view, erase the extension lines and then array the cut and carbide tip around the circle. TRIM the 7.25 circle out of the new cuts and tips.
- Be sure to type in your own values as you dimension the detail, since it has been scaled.

10°

.12

.06

.58

.16 R

.06 R

SCALE: 2/1

Use donut & solid commands
to fill in carbide tips

.12

1.50

3.68 RAD

7.25 DIA

.62 DIA

2.00

.25 DIA

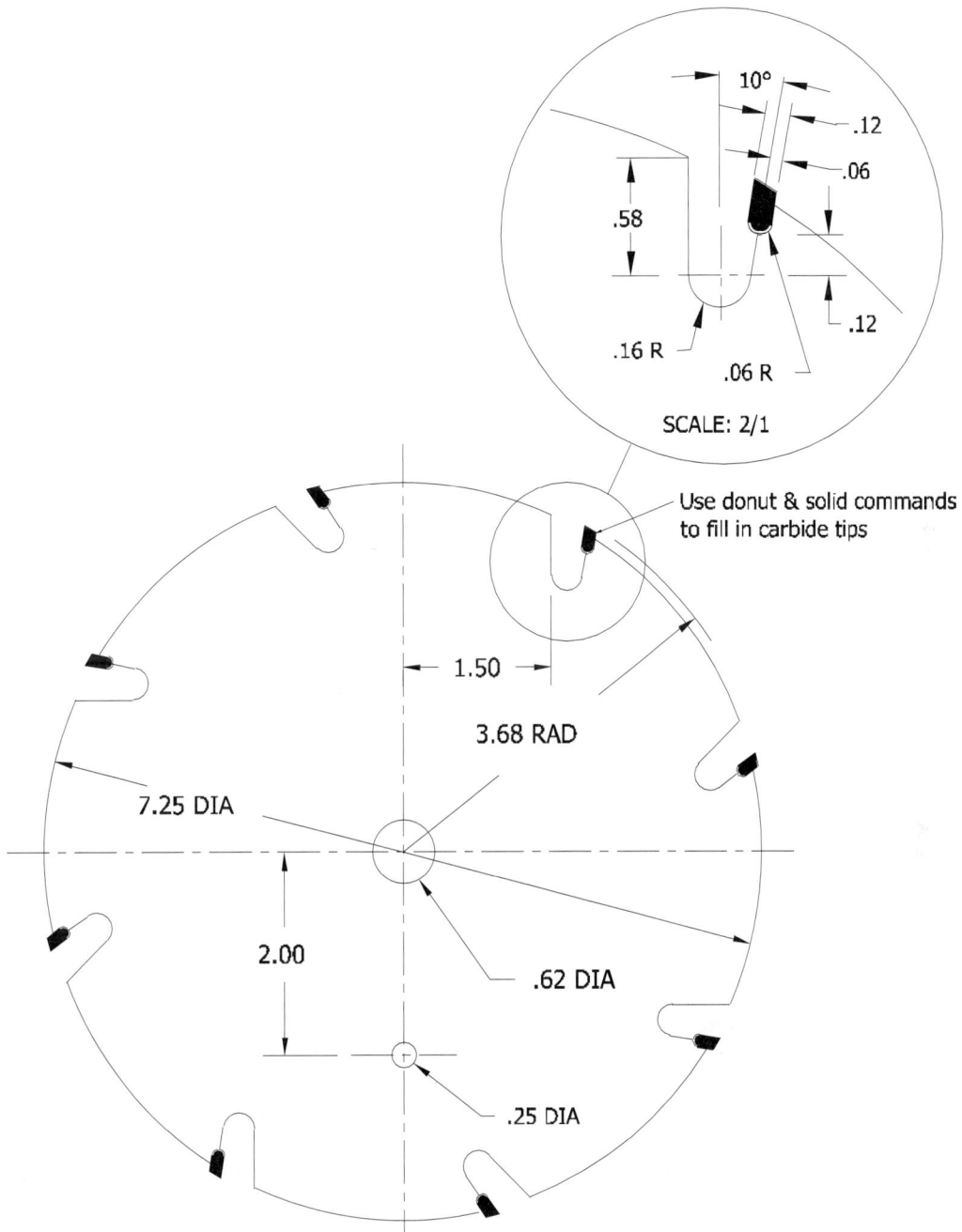

CARBIDE TIP SAW BLADE

Drawing 9-4

9.19   Drawing 9-5: Gazebo

This architectural drawing makes extensive use of both the POLYGON command and the OFFSET command.

DRAWING SUGGESTIONS

> UNITS = Architectural
> GRID = 19
> SNAP = 20
> LIMITS = (0',0') (48',36')

- All radii except the 6″ polygon are given from the center point to the midpoint of a side. In other words, the 6″ polygon will be "inscribed," while all the others will be "circumscribed."
- Notice that all polygon radii dimensions are given to the outside of the 2″ × 4″. OFFSET to the inside to create the parallel polygon for the inside of the board.
- Create radial studs by drawing a line from the midpoint of one side of a polygon to the midpoint of the side of another, or the midpoint of one to the vertex of another as shown; then offset 1″ each side and erase the original. Array around the center point.
- TRIM lines and polygons at vertices.
- You can make effective use of MIRROR in the elevation.

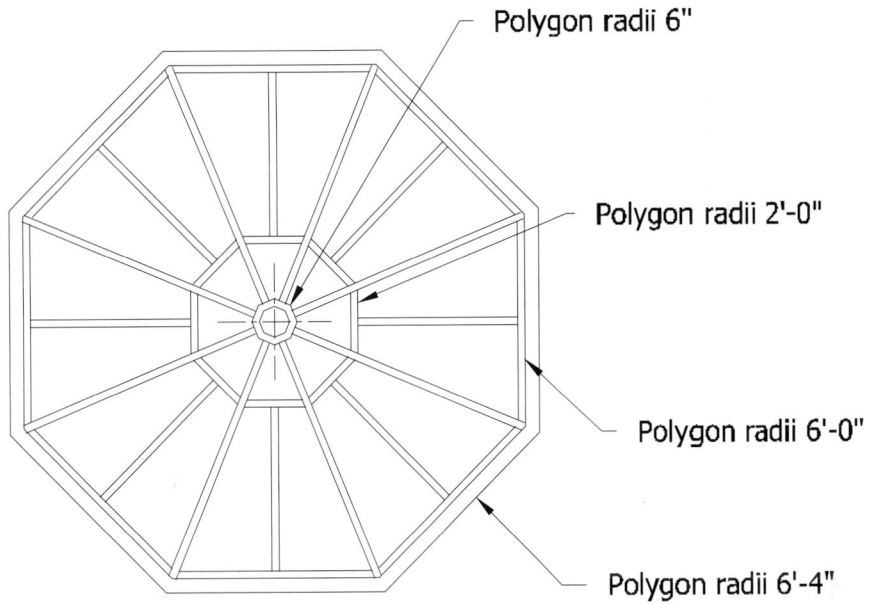

Polygon radii 6"

Polygon radii 2'-0"

Polygon radii 6'-0"

Polygon radii 6'-4"

ROOF FRAMING

4'

1'-2"

4"

4"
(TYP)

8"
(TYP)

6"

2'-4"

8'

2'-6"

4"

4"

4" THK CONCRETE SLAB

All lumber 2" x 4" unless otherwise noted

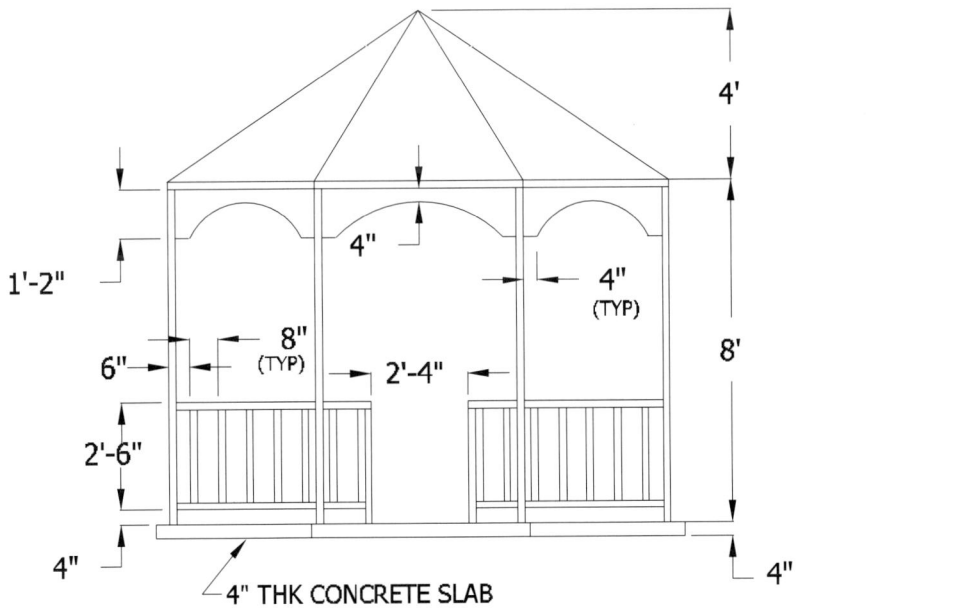

FRONT ELEVATION

GAZEBO
Drawing 9-5

9.20   Drawing 9-6: Frame

This drawing will give you practice using the MLINE command. The object is to draw the Front, Left Side, and Top Views. Position the views as indicated in the reference drawing. Although at first glance this drawing appears to be easy, it is somewhat complex, so proceed with caution. There are numerous ways in which the drawing can be done, but we suggest you take advantage of the MLINE command to draw each view. The drawing will be fully dimensioned, and all hidden lines will be shown.

Top

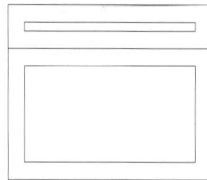

Left Side   Front

DRAWING SUGGESTIONS

- Begin by setting the MLINE command to a spacing of 1/2″.
- Draw the Left Side view first using the MLINE command and use the "C" to close the lines. Notice that the hidden lines are not shown in the reference drawing. You are to provide all hidden lines.
- Use the Left Side view to line up the front view, making sure you use the MLINE command.
- Finally, draw the Top View using the Front View for alignment.

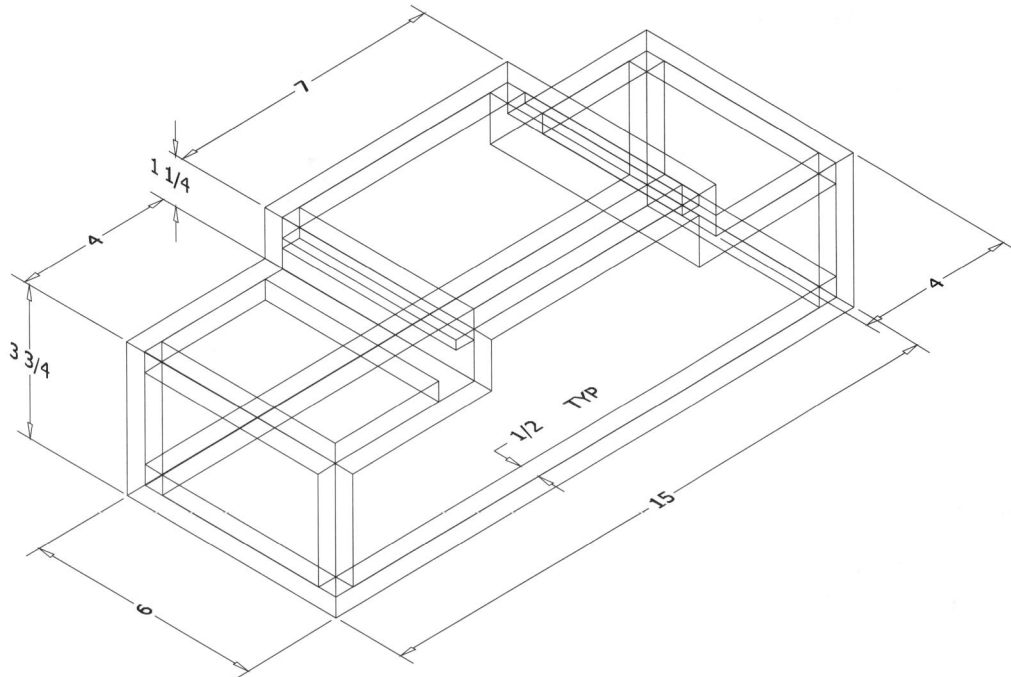

FRAME

Drawing 9-6

Blocks, Xrefs, and the AutoCAD DesignCenter

COMMANDS

ADCENTER	ATTEXT	GROUP	XCLIP
ATTDEF	BLOCK	INSERT	XREF
ATTDISP	COPYCLIP	WBLOCK	
ATTEDITT	EXPLODE	XATTACH	

OVERVIEW

One of the main goals of efficient CAD technique is to eliminate duplication of effort. This begins with the use of commands like COPY and ARRAY, which duplicate previously drawn objects, and extends outward to projects in which elements of a drawing created on one workstation may be reused in another drawing at a distant site linked through a network or the Internet.

In this chapter you will learn many of the tools necessary to achieve this level of efficiency. To begin, you will learn to create "groups" and "blocks." A group is simply a set of objects that can be selected, named, and manipulated collectively. A block is a set of objects defined as a single entity and saved so that it can be scaled and inserted repeatedly and potentially passed on to other drawings. Blocks become part of the content of a drawing that can be browsed, viewed, and manipulated within and between drawings using the new AutoCAD DesignCenter. The DesignCenter and other functions, including the Windows clipboard, allow AutoCAD objects to be shared with other drawings and applications. Finally, in this chapter we will introduce you to block "attributes." An attribute is an item of information attached to a block, such as a part number or price, that is stored along with the block definition. All the information stored in attributes can be extracted from a drawing into a spread sheet or database program and used to produce itemized reports.

TASKS

10.1 Creating GROUPs

GENERAL PROCEDURE

1. Type "G" or select Object Group... from the Tools menu.
2. Type a name.
3. Click on "New".
4. Select objects to be included in the group definition.
5. Press Enter to end object selection.
6. Click on OK to exit the dialog.

The simplest way to create a complex entity from previously drawn entities is to group them into a unit with the GROUP command. Groups are given names and can be selected for all editing processes if they are defined as selectable.

In this exercise we will form groups from objects that also will be used later to define blocks. In this way you will get a feel for the different functions of these two methods of creating collections of objects. You will be creating simple symbols for a computer, monitor, digitizer, and keyboard. Once created, these may also be inserted into Drawing 10-1.

⊕ Begin by making the following changes in the drawing setup:

1. Set to layer 0 (the reason for doing this is discussed in the Note following this list).
2. Change to architectural units, with precision = $0'-0''$.
3. Set GRID = $1'$.
4. Set SNAP = $1''$.
5. Set LIMITS = $(0',0')$ $(48',36')$.

Note: Blocks created on layer 0 will be inserted on the current layer. Blocks created on any other layer will stay on the layer on which they are created. Inserting blocks is discussed in Task 10.3.

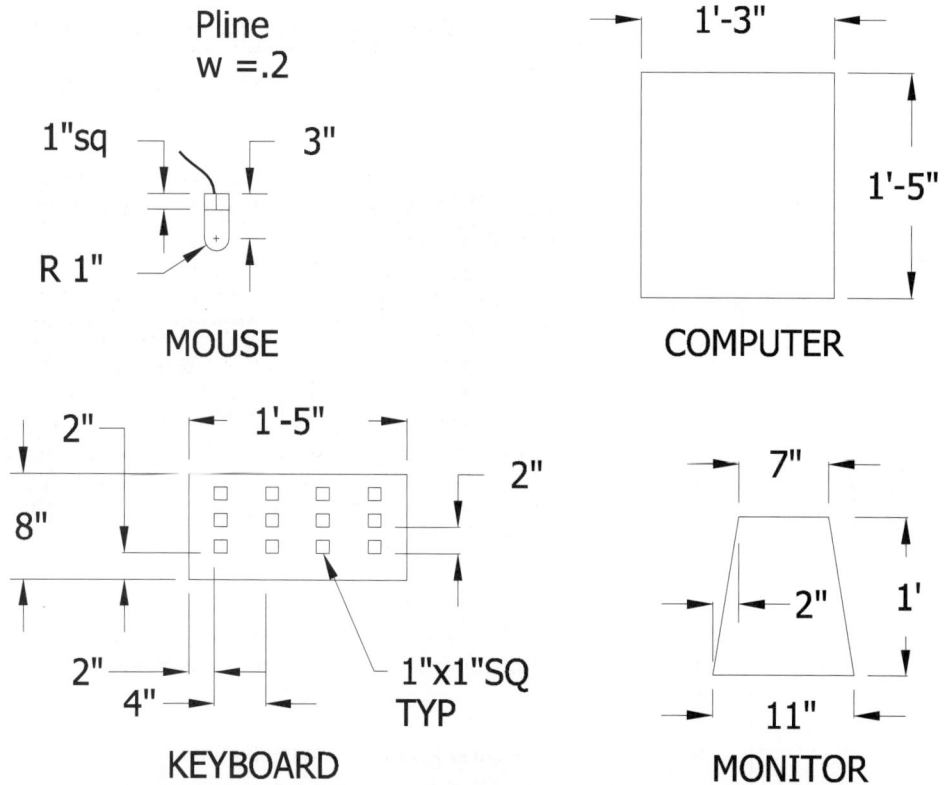

Pline
w =.2

1"sq   3"

R 1"

MOUSE

1'-3"

1'-5"

COMPUTER

2"   1'-5"

8"   2"

2"

4"

1"x1"SQ
TYP

KEYBOARD

7"

2"   1'

11"

MONITOR

Figure 10-1

⊕ Zoom into an area approximately 12′ × 9′.

⊕ Draw the four objects in Figure 10-1.

Draw the geometry only; the text and dimensions in the figure are for your reference only and should not be on your screen.

We will define the "keyboard" as a group.

⊕ Type "g".

This will call the Object Grouping dialog box shown in Figure 10-2. At the top of the box is the Group Name list box. It will be empty now since there are no groups defined in this drawing. Below that is the Group Identification area, with edit boxes for entering a group name and a group description. The flashing cursor bar should be in the group name box so that you can enter a name. Our first group will be the set of rectangles you have drawn as a symbol for a keyboard.

⊕ Type "keyboard" in the Group Name edit box.

Now look at the Create Group panel. The three boxes here are "New <", "Selectable", and "Unnamed". To create a group, you must indicate that it is a new group. But first, you need to be sure that the group will be defined as selectable, if that is your intention, as it most often will be. Unnamed groups are usually groups that have been created by copying named groups. In these cases AutoCAD assigns names beginning with *A and followed by a number.

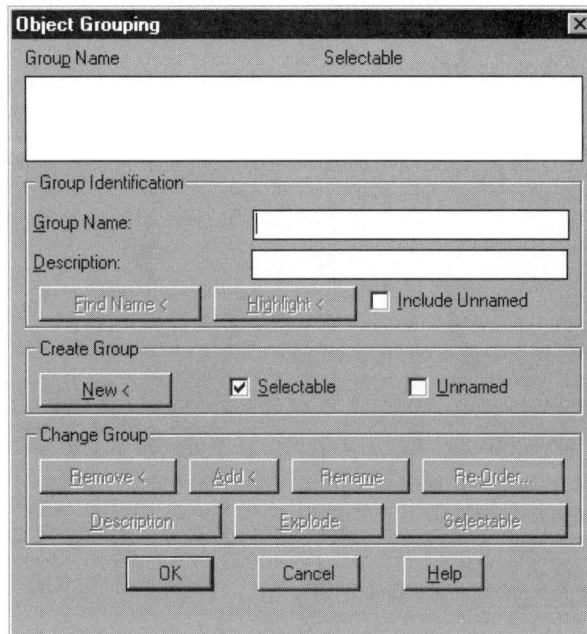

Figure 10-2

⊕ Be sure that "Selectable" is checked.

⊕ Click on "New <" in the Create Group panel.

At this point the dialog box will disappear to give you access to objects in your drawing. You will see a "Select Objects:" prompt at the command line.

⊕ Select the keyboard outer rectangles and small rectangles using a window.

⊕ Press Enter to end object selection.

This will bring back the dialog box. "KEYBOARD" should now be in the list box, with a "Yes" to the right indicating that it is a selectable group.

⊕ Click on OK to exit the dialog box.

The keyboard is now defined in the drawing as a selectable group. To see that this is so, try selecting it.

⊕ Position the pickbox anywhere on the "Keyboard" and press the pickbutton.

You will see from the highlights and blue grip boxes that the complete group is selected. That is all you need to do with groups at this point. Groups are useful for copying and manipulating groups of objects that tend to stay to-gether. The following notes will help you to go further with groups if you wish.

1. If you click on "Find Name" and then select any object that is part of group, AutoCAD will show you the name (or names) of the group (or groups) that the object belongs to.

2. Unnamed groups are only included in the Group Name list if Include Un-named is checked.

3. In editing commands you can select a group by pointing or by typing "g" at the Select Objects prompt and then typing the name of the group.
4. If the PICKSTYLE variable is set to 0 (default value is 1), you will only be able to select groups by typing their names, not by pointing.

Concerning the Change Group area of the dialog box:

1. Remove and Add allow you to remove or add individual objects of a previously defined group.
2. The objects in a group have a defined order, which can be changed using the Group Order dialog box. Select "Re-Order..." in the Object Grouping dialog box.
3. You can change the description of a previously defined group by highlighting the name on the group list, typing or editing the description, and then clicking on Description.
4. You can delete a group definition by highlighting its name on the group list and then clicking on Explode.
5. To switch the selectability status of a defined group between yes and no, use the Selectable box at the bottom right of the dialog box.

10.2   Creating BLOCKs

GENERAL PROCEDURE

1. Type "b", select the Make Block tool from the Draw toolbar, or open the Draw menu, highlight Block, and then select Make....
2. Type a name.
3. Pick an insertion point.
4. Select objects to be included in the block definition.

Blocks have more features than groups. Blocks can be stored as part of an individual drawing or as separate drawings. They can be inserted into the drawing in which they were created, or into other drawings, and can be scaled as they are inserted. In general, the most useful blocks are those that will be used repeatedly in many drawings and therefore can become part of a library of predrawn objects used by you and others. In mechanical drawing, for instance, you may want a set of screws drawn to standard sizes that can be called out anytime. Or, if you are doing architectural drawing, you might find a library of doors and windows useful.

In this chapter we are creating a set of simple symbols for some of the tools we know you will be using no matter what kind of CAD you are doing—namely, computers, monitors, keyboards, digitizers, plotters, and printers. We define them as blocks, insert them, and assemble them into a workstation. Later we will define the complete workstation as a block and insert workstations into an architectural drawing called "CAD ROOM."

⊕   Type "B", select the Make Block tool from the Draw toolbar, as shown in Figure 10-3, or open the Draw menu, highlight Block, and then select Make.

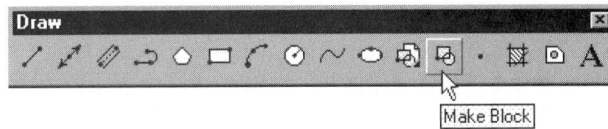

Figure 10-3

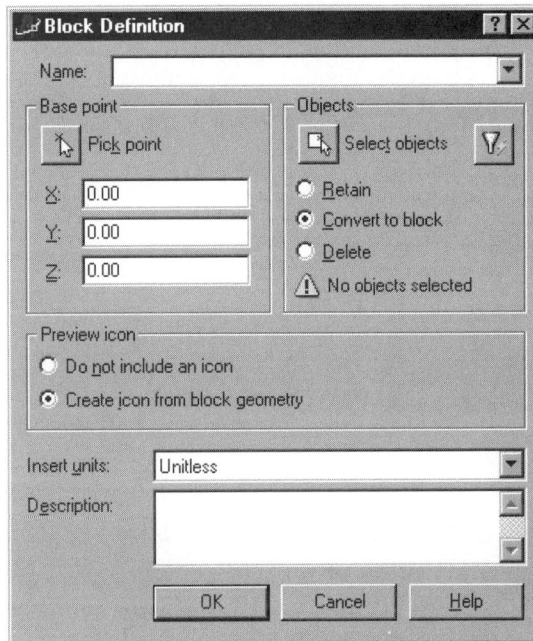

Figure 10-4

These methods execute the BMAKE command and open the Block Definition dialog box shown in Figure 10-4. BMAKE is a newer command. BLOCK, the old command, serves the same purpose but operates from the command line.

⊕ Type "computer" in the Block name box.

Next, choose object to define the block.

⊕ Click on the Select Objects button.

The dialog box disappears, giving access to objects in the drawing.

⊕ Use a window to select the computer rectangle.

AutoCAD continues to prompt for object selection.

⊕ Right click to end object selection.

This brings you back to the dialog box.

Blocks are intended to be inserted into drawings, so any block definition needs to include an insertion base point. Insertion points and insertion base points are critical in the whole matter of using blocks. The insertion base point is the point on

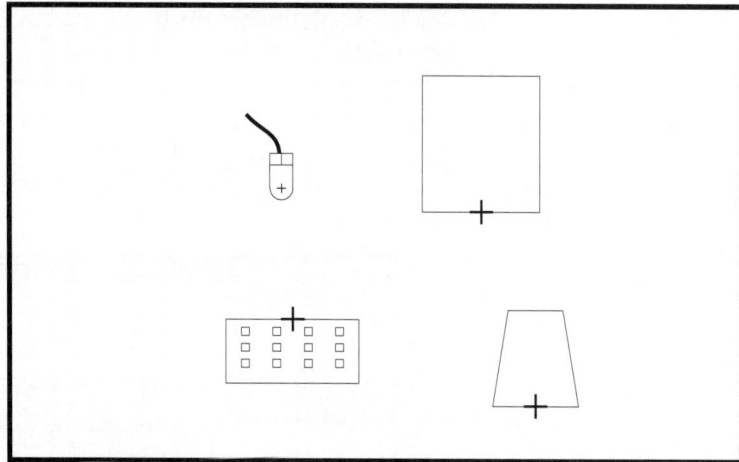

Figure 10-5

the block that will be at the intersection of the cross hairs when you insert the block. Therefore, when defining a block, try to anticipate the point on the block you would most likely use to position the block on the screen. If you do not define an insertion base point, AutoCAD will use the origin of the coordinate system, which may be quite inconvenient.

⊕ Click on the Pick point icon.
⊕ Use a midpoint object snap to pick the middle of the bottom line of the computer as the insertion point, as shown in Figure 10-5.

When creating blocks you have three choices regarding what happens to objects included in the block definition, shown by the three radio buttons in the Objects panel. Objects may be retained in the drawing separate from the block definition, converted to an instance of the new block, or deleted from the screen. In all instances the object data is retained in the drawing database as the block definition.

A common practice is to create a number of blocks, one after the other, and then assemble them at the end. To facilitate this method, check the Delete radio button. With this setting, newly defined blocks will be erased from the screen automatically. They can be retrieved using OOPS if necessary (but not U, as this would undo the block definition).

⊕ Click the Delete radio button.

The block definition is complete.

⊕ Click on OK to exit the dialog.

You have created a "computer" block definition. The computer has vanished from your screen but may be inserted using the INSERT command, which we will turn to momentarily. Now repeat the BMAKE process to make a "keyboard" block.

⊕ Repeat BMAKE.
⊕ Type "keyboard" in the Block name box.

⊕ Click on the Select Objects button.

⊕ Select the keyboard.

Since you have already defined the keyboard as a selectable group, one pick should select the whole thing. In the command area AutoCAD will show how many individual objects are in the selection set, and also that there is one group in the set. The group definition of the keyboard will now become part of the block definition.

⊕ Press Enter to end selection.

⊕ Click the Pick point button.

⊕ Pick the midpoint of the top line of the keyboard as the insertion base point.

⊕ Repeat the blocking process two more times to create "monitor" and "mouse" blocks, with insertion base points as shown in Figure 10-5.

When you are done, your screen should be blank. At this point your four block definitions are stored in your drawing base. In the next task we will insert them into your current drawing to create a computer workstation assembly. Before going on, take a look at these other commands that are useful in working with blocks. Many of them will be used in the tasks that follow.

Command	Usage
BASE	Allows you to specify a base insertion point for an entire drawing. The base point will be used when the drawing is inserted in other drawings.
DBLIST	Displays information for all entities in the current drawing database. Information includes type of entity and layer. Additional information depends on the type of entity. For blocks, it includes insertion point, X scale, Y scale, rotation, and attribute values.
EXPLODE	Reverses an instance of a block so that objects that have been combined in the block definition are redrawn as individual objects. Exploding a block reference has no effect on the block definition.
LIST	Lists information about a single block or entity. Information listed is the same as that in DBLIST, but for the selected entity only.
MINSERT	Multiple Insert. Allows you to insert arrays of blocks. MINSERT arrays take up less memory than ARRAYs of INSERTed blocks.
PURGE	Deletes unused blocks, layers, linetypes, shapes, or text styles from a drawing.
WBLOCK	Saves a block to a separate file so that it can be inserted in other drawings. Does not save unused blocks or layers, and therefore can be used to reduce drawing file size.

10.3 INSERTing Blocks into the Current Drawing

GENERAL PROCEDURE

1. Type "i" , select Block... from the Insert menu, or select the Insert Block tool from the Draw toolbar.
2. Type or select a block name.
3. Pick an insertion point.
4. Answer prompts for horizontal and vertical scale and for rotation angle.

The INSERT command is used to bring block references into a drawing. Here you begin to distinguish between block definitions, which are not visible and reside in the database of a drawing, and block references, which are instances of a block definition inserted into a drawing. The four block definitions you created in Task 10.1 are now part of the drawing database and can be inserted in this drawing anywhere you like. In this task we will focus on inserting into the current drawing. In the next we will explore sharing blocks between drawings.

Among other things, these procedures are useful in creating assembly drawings. You will find that assembling blocks can be done efficiently using appropriate OSNAP modes to place objects in precise relation to one another. Assembly drawing will be the focus of the drawing tasks at the end of this chapter.

In this task we will insert the computer, monitor, keyboard, and digitizer back into the drawing to create the "workstation" assembly shown in Figure 10-6. We will also discuss other options for drawing file management, including the use of complete drawings as blocks or as "external references."

⊕ If you are still on layer 0, switch to layer 1.

⊕ Type "i", select "Block" from the Insert menu, or select the Insert Block tool from the Draw toolbar, as shown in Figure 10-7.

This will bring up the Insert dialog box shown in Figure 10-8. In addition to the block Name list box at the top of the dialog, there are several scaling options. The options allow you to scale and rotate the block as you insert it. This

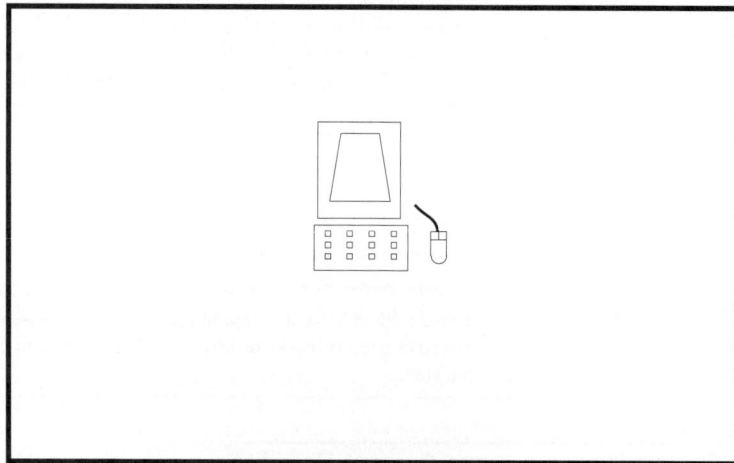

Figure 10-6

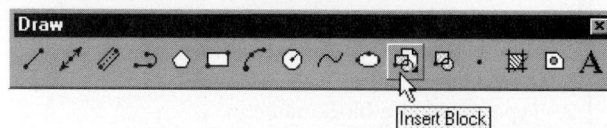

Figure 10-7

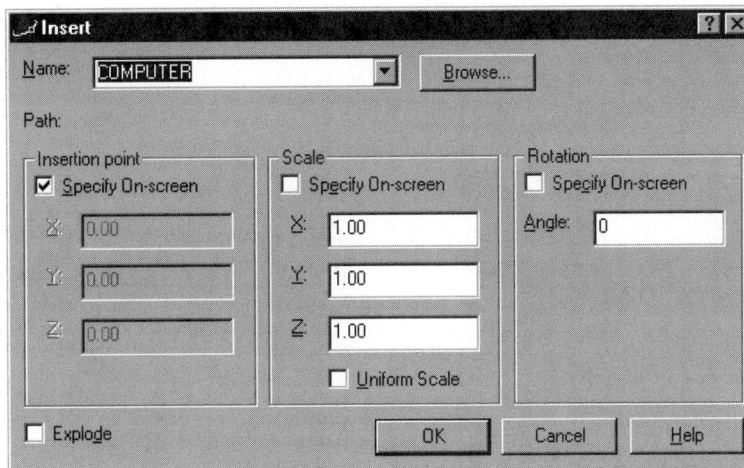

Figure 10-8

vastly increases the flexibility and power of the blocking system. The issue of scaling becomes particularly important when you move between drawings. What will happen when you insert a 20-foot object into a drawing that has $12'' \times 9''$ limits? We shall see in Task 10.4.

Unlike the SCALE command, which automatically scales both horizontally and vertically, blocks can be stretched or shrunk in either direction independently as you insert them. You can type an X scale factor or specify both an X and a Y factor at once by showing two corners of a window using the Corner option. Z is reserved for 3D applications. Uniform will scale X, Y, and Z uniformly.

Now is a good time to see that your block definitions are still in your database, even though they are no longer on the screen.

⊕ Click on the arrow in the Name list box.

You should see a list like this:

> COMPUTER
> KEYBOARD
> MONITOR
> MOUSE

⊕ Select COMPUTER from the list.

⊕ Click on OK to exit the dialog and begin inserting the block.

From here on you will follow prompts from the command line. AutoCAD now needs to know where to insert the computer, and you will see this prompt:

> Specify insertion point or
> [Scale/X/Y/Z/Rotate/PScale/PX/PY/PZ/PRotate]:

Notice that AutoCAD gives you a block to drag into place and that it is positioned with the block's insertion base point at the intersection of the cross hairs. The options provide the same scaling functions as the dialog box. The P options are for previewing as you insert.

⊕ Pick a point near the middle of the screen, as shown in Figure 10-6.

Notice that the block is inserted on layer 1 even though it was created on layer 0. Remember that *this only works with blocks drawn on layer 0*. Blocks drawn on other layers stay on the layer they were drawn on when they are inserted.

Now let's add a monitor.

⊕ Repeat the INSERT command.

Notice that the last block inserted becomes the default block name in the Block name box. This facilitates procedures in which you insert the same block in several different places in a drawing.

⊕ Select "MONITOR" from the Name list.

⊕ Click on OK.

⊕ Pick an insertion point 2 or 3 inches above the insertion point of the computer, as shown in Figure 10-6.

You should have the monitor sitting on top of the computer and be back at the "command" prompt. We will insert the keyboard, as shown in Figure 10-6.

⊕ Repeat INSERT.

⊕ Select "KEYBOARD" from the Name list.

⊕ Click OK.

⊕ Pick an insertion point 1 or 2 inches below the computer, as shown in Figure 10-6.

You should now have the keyboard in place.

⊕ Repeat INSERT once more and place the mouse block to the right of the other blocks as shown in Figure 10-6.

Congratulations, you have completed your first assembly. Now that you are familiar with BMAKE and INSERT, you have the primary tools needed to create and utilize a symbol library on your own computer. In the next two tasks we will explore moving blocks between drawings and moving drawn objects between applications using the Windows clipboard.

10.4 Using the Windows Clipboard

GENERAL PROCEDURE

1. Select the Cut to Clipboard or Copy to Clipboard tool from the Standard toolbar.
2. Select objects (steps 1 and 2 can be reversed).
3. Open another drawing or a different Windows application.
4. Type Ctrl-V or select "Paste" in that drawing or application.

The Windows clipboard makes it very easy to copy objects from one AutoCAD drawing to another or into other Windows applications. You will use the Copy to Clipboard and Cut to Clipboard tools from the Standard toolbar, which activate the COPYCLIP and COPYCUT commands. Cut will remove the selected objects from your AutoCAD drawing, while Copy will leave them. When you send blocks to an AutoCAD drawing via the Clipboard, they will be defined as blocks in the new drawing as well. Block names and definitions are maintained, but there is no option to scale as there is when you INSERT blocks.

In this task we will open a new drawing and copy the assembled workstation into it. The steps would be the same to copy the objects into another Windows application. The procedure is very simple and will work with any Windows application that supports Windows OLE (Object Linking and Embedding).

⊕ To begin this task you should have the assembled blocks on your screen, resembling Figure 10-6.

⊕ Select the Copy to Clipboard tool from the Standard toolbar, as shown in Figure 10-9.

AutoCAD prompts for object selection.

⊕ Using a window selection, select all of the objects in the computer workstation assembled in the last task.

⊕ Press Enter to end object selection.

AutoCAD will save the selected objects to the clipboard. Nothing will happen on your screen, but the selected objects are stored and could be pasted back into this drawing, another AutoCAD drawing, or another Windows application. Next we will open a new drawing.

⊕ Select the New tool from the Standard toolbar and open a new drawing using the 1B template.

For sake of clarity we will use the AutoCAD default drawing names, calling the original drawing "Drawing1" and the new drawing "Drawing2". In AutoCAD 2000 you can have multiple drawings open in a single AutoCAD session. Drawing2 will now be open in the drawing area with Drawing1 also open in the background.

⊕ In the new drawing (Drawing2), select the Paste from Clipboard tool from the Standard toolbar.

AutoCAD prompts for an insertion point and gives you an image to drag into place. You will see a very large image of the keyboard and mouse, as shown in Figure 10-10. Actually, the whole workstation is there, but the computer and monitor are off the screen. Why are they so large? It is because the scale of this drawing is very different from the one the objects were drawn in. The original drawing has been set up with architectural units and limits so that it may be used in Drawing 10-1, the Cad Room. In the new drawing, based on the 1B template, the 18×12 units are being interpreted as inches, so the keyboard is coming in at 17", covering most of the grid. Without the scaling capacity of the INSERT command, you have no control over this interpretation.

Figure 10-9

Figure 10-10

⊕ Pick an insertion point at the lower left of your grid, as shown in Figure 10-10.

That's all there is to it. It is equally simple to paste text and images from other compatible Windows applications into AutoCAD. Just reverse the process, cutting or copying from the other application and pasting into AutoCAD.

We will undo this insertion in a moment, but first take a moment to try out the DBLIST command and see how these objects appear in the database of the new drawing.

⊕ Type "dblist".

AutoCAD will switch to the text window where you will see a series of four entity listings like this:

```
BLOCK REFERENCE    Layer: "1"
                   Space: Model space
                   Handle = D2
                   "monitor"
            at point, X=9.00 Y=5.00 Z=0.00
                 X scale factor   1.00
                 Y scale factor   1.00
       rotation angle             0
                 Z scale factor   1.00
```

You will have to press enter to see the whole list. The four pasted blocks are the only entities in the new drawing. If there were other objects, they would be listed here as well.

⊕ Press F2 to return to the drawing window.
⊕ Press U until everything has been undone.

The issue of scaling is handled differently when you paste AutoCAD objects into other applications. In those cases objects are automatically scaled to fit in the document that receives them. Most applications have their own editing feature, which allows you to adjust the size of the objects after they have been pasted.

10.5   INSERTing Blocks and External References into Other Drawings

---

GENERAL PROCEDURE

1. Prepare a drawing to be inserted into other drawings.
2. Open another drawing.
3. Enter the INSERT or XATTACH command.
4. Enter the name and path of the drawing to be inserted or referenced, or Browse to the file.
5. Answer prompts for scale and rotation.

Any drawing may be inserted as a block or external reference into another drawing. The process is much like inserting a block within a drawing, but you will need to specify the drawing location. In this task we will attach Drawing1 as an external reference in Drawing2. The process for inserting blocks into other drawings is identical to attaching an xref.

External References

Externally referencing a drawing is a powerful alternative to inserting it as a block. The principal difference between inserted drawings and externally referenced drawings is that inserted drawings are actually merged with the current drawing database, whereas externally referenced drawings are only linked. If the referenced drawing is changed, the changes will be reflected in the current drawing the next time it is loaded or when the Reload option of the XREF manager is selected. This allows designers at remote locations to work on different aspects of a single master drawing, which is updated automatically as changes are made in the various referenced drawings.

Since attaching a reference only loads enough information to "point to" the externally referenced drawing, it does not increase the size of the current drawing file as significantly as INSERT does.

⊕   You should be in Drawing2 to begin this task, with everything undone.

To switch back to Drawing1, use the open drawing list at the bottom of the Window menu, as follows.

⊕   Open the Window menu and select Drawing1, as shown in Figure 10-11.

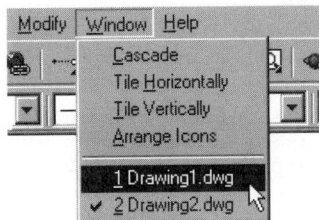

Figure 10-11

This will bring you back into your original drawing with the computer workstation objects displayed as shown previously in Figure 10-6. You could use this drawing as a block or xref without further adjustment, but using the BASE command to add an insertion base point for the drawing will be convenient. BASE works for either blocking or referencing.

⊕ Type "base".

AutoCAD prompts:

$$\text{Enter base point , } <0'-0", \ 0'-0", \ 0'-0">:$$

This indicates that the current base point is at the origin of the grid. We will move it to the lower left corner of the keyboard.

⊕ Pick the lower left corner of the keyboard.

The new base point will be registered but there will be no change in the drawing.

⊕ Open the Window menu and select Drawing2.

This will return you to Drawing2. There should be nothing on the screen.

⊕ Open the Insert menu and select External Reference....

This will open the Select Reference File dialog box, shown in Figure 10-12. This is basically the same dialog box you see when you enter any command in which you select a file.

⊕ If necessary, double click on the folder that contains Drawing1, or use the Up One Level button to locate the folder you need.

⊕ Select Drawing1 from the list of files.

Notice the preview image on the right.

⊕ Click the Open button.

This will take you to the External Reference dialog box, shown in Figure 10-13. Note that this box is nearly identical to the Insert dialog box shown previously in Figure 10-8. Drawing1 should be entered in the name box, and its Path identified below the name.

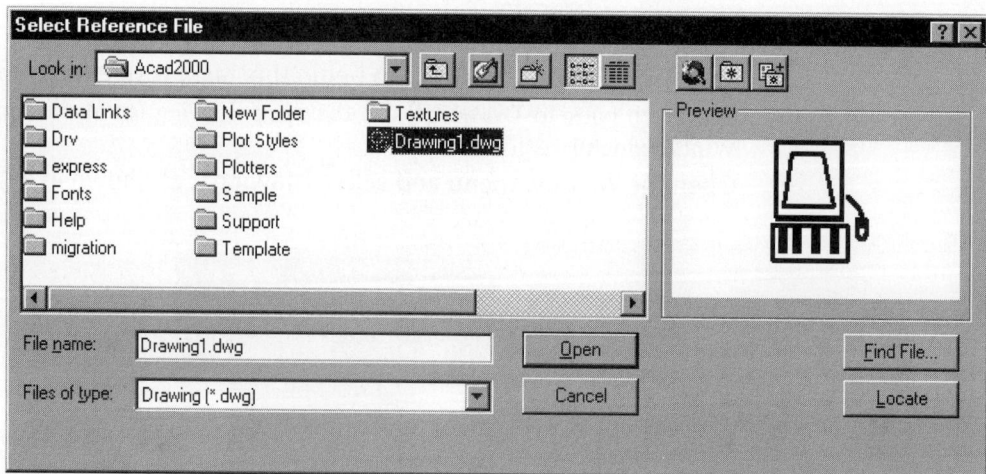

Figure 10-12

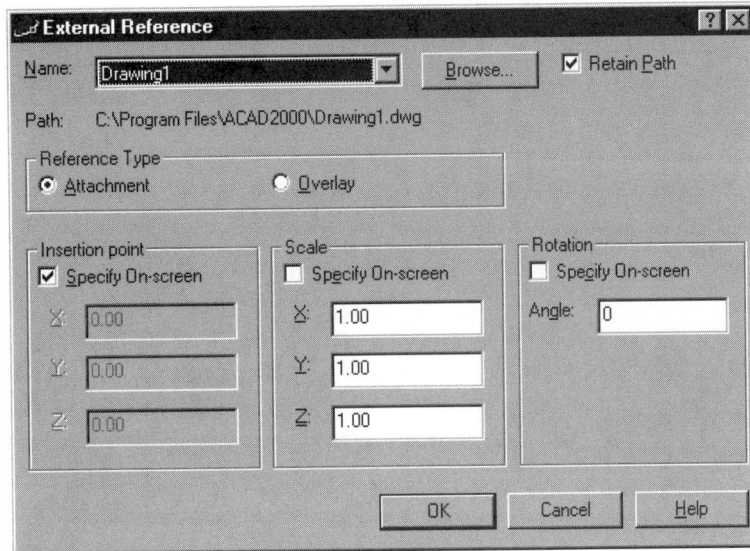

Figure 10-13

Figure 10-14

⊕ **Click on OK to exit the dialog.**

Before you return to the drawing area, you will see a message like the one in Figure 10-14. The message tells you that since Drawing1 is currently open, it cannot be "demand loaded." Demand loading is a process that can be used to increase the efficiency of large drawings with numerous xrefs. When an xref is demand loaded, only data necessary to regenerate the drawing is read in. We have no need for demand loading at this point and will accept a "full read" of the external drawing. See the *AutoCAD User's Guide* for more informaton on demand loading.

⊕ **Click OK to close the message.**

You are now back to the Drawing2 drawing window. As in the last task, you will have a very large image of the keyboard and mouse, but this time there will be a prompt for scale factors in the command area.

⊕ **Type "s" for the Scale option.**

This option will take a uniform scale factor for the complete inserted drawing.

⊕ **Type "1/8".**

You could also type .125, but it is worth noting that the INSERT and XAT-TACH commands will take fractions or scale ratios at the scale factor prompt.

⊕   Pick an insertion point near the middle of the grid.

At this scale, the workstation will appear on your screen much as it does in Drawing1. Before going on, try using the LIST command to see how the newly inserted xref is specified in the database of Drawing2.

⊕   Select the workstation.

It will only take one pick, since this is now a single entity.

⊕   Type "list".

In the text window, you will see a listing similar to this:

```
BLOCK REFERENCE  Layer: "0"
                Space: Model space
                Handle = D3
                "Drawing1"
        External reference
        at point, X=9.00 Y=5.00 Z=0.00
            X scale factor  0.13
            Y scale factor  0.13
        rotation angle      0
            Z scale factor  0.13
```

Notice that the drawing name has become the block definition name, that the block is identified as an external reference, and that the X, Y, and Z scale factors have been rounded off to .13

⊕   Press F2 to return to the drawing window.

Keep Drawing1 and Drawing2 open. Stop for a moment to consider each drawing. Drawing1 has the architectural units and limits established at the beginning of the chapter. It has four separate blocks currently assembled into a workstation. Drawing2 has our standard 1B units and limits and has one instance of Drawing1 attached as an external reference. In the tasks that follow we will continue to make changes to these drawings. Later you will see that changes in Drawing1 are reflected in Drawing2. In the next task we introduce an exciting new tool for managing drawing data, the AutoCAD 2000 Design Center.

Before leaving this section, here are two final notes.

Management of Named Objects

What happens when an externally referenced or block inserted drawing has layers, linetypes, text styles, dimension styles, blocks, or views with names that conflict with those in the current drawing? Good question. In the case of blocked drawings, name definitions in the current drawing override those in the inserted block. In the case of XREFed drawings, named objects are given special designations that eliminate the confusion. For example, if drawing A is attached to drawing B and both have a layer called FLOOR, a new layer is created in B called A|FLOOR.

Raster Images

A raster image is an image such as a picture or photograph that has been encoded as a matrix of dots or pixels. Any ordinary computer graphic image is an example.

Such images can be brought into an AutoCAD drawing much as an external reference would be. Raster images are attached and linked to AutoCAD drawings but do not actually become part of the drawing database so that they do not take up large amounts of memory. Once attached, raster images can be inserted repeatedly in the same drawing just like blocks. Raster images can be scaled as they are inserted. To insert a raster image, select Raster Image... from the Insert menu.

10.6   Using the AutoCAD DesignCenter

The AutoCAD DesignCenter is a new AutoCAD feature that enables you to manipulate drawing content similar to the way Windows Explorer handles files and folders. The interface is similar with a tree view on the left and a list of contents on the right. The difference is the types of data you will see. With the DesignCenter you can look into the contents of a drawing file and easily copy or insert content into an open drawing.

In this task we will begin by inserting blocks from Drawing1 into Drawing2. Keep in mind that in the last task we were limited to inserting or attaching a complete drawing; now we will look inside the database of Drawing1 to add blocks to Drawing2.

⊕   To begin this task you should be in Drawing2 with Drawing1 open in the background.

⊕   Click on the AutoCAD DesignCenter tool at the right end of the Standard toolbar, as shown in Figure 10-15.

By default, the DesignCenter window will open in a docked position at the left side of your screen. The window will be split into two "panes" similar to those in Figure 10-16. These are called the tree view on the left and the design palette on the right. However, if anyone has used DesignCenter on your computer you are likely to see something different, since the DesignCenter stores all changes and resizing adjustments. So, if you do not see two panes, you will need to click the "tree view" button.

⊕   If necessary, click the tree view tool, as shown in Figure 10-17.

The tree view shows the hierarchy of files in a selected location, usually your hard drive, a disk, or a CD, but possibly a remote location on a network or the internet. When a file is selected in the tree view, its contents will appear in the palette on the right.

The DesignCenter can be moved like a dialog box by using a click and drag motion with the cursor positioned on the top border. It can be resized by moving the cursor over any of the borders until you see the two way arrow cursor, and then clicking and stretching the border. We have resized our

Figure 10-15

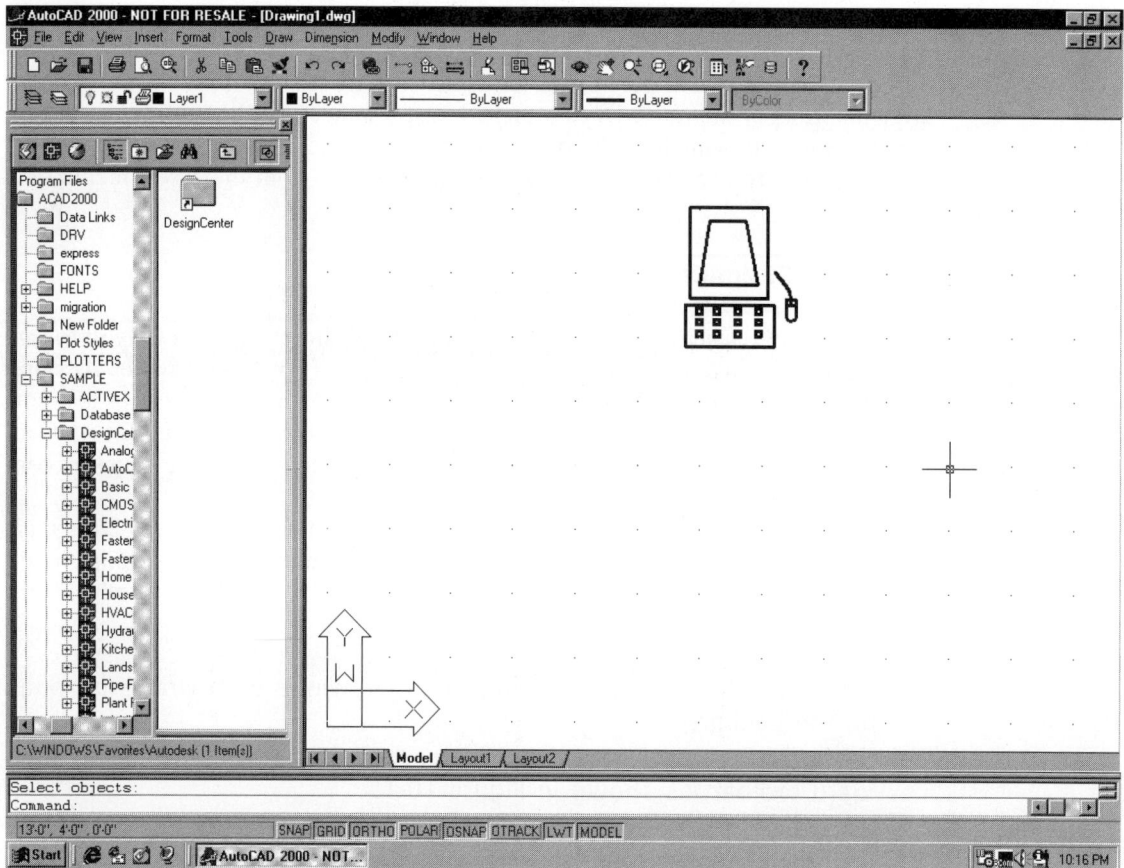

Figure 10-16

Figure 10-17

window slightly to show a wider tree view. Otherwise we will leave things in their default positions.

Along the top of the window is a series of buttons. The tree view button we have already seen. It opens and closes the tree view pane. The other buttons we will explore as we go along. On the left is the desktop button. It will probably have no effect at this point since the default for the tree view is to show the desktop hierarchy of files. We will do a quick simplification to look at open drawings only.

⊞ Select the Open Drawings tool, as shown in Figure 10-18.

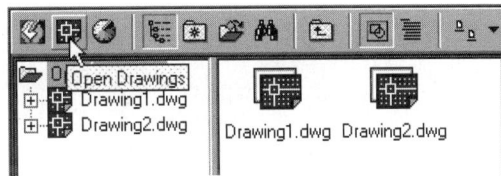

Figure 10-18

Figure 10-19

Now you will have a very simple window with the two drawings in both panes, as shown in Figure 10-18.

⊕ Click on Drawing1 in the tree view or double click on Drawing1 in the palette.

Selecting the drawing in either pane will open a list of content types as shown in the palette in Figure 10-19.

⊕ Click on the + sign next to Drawing1 in the tree view.

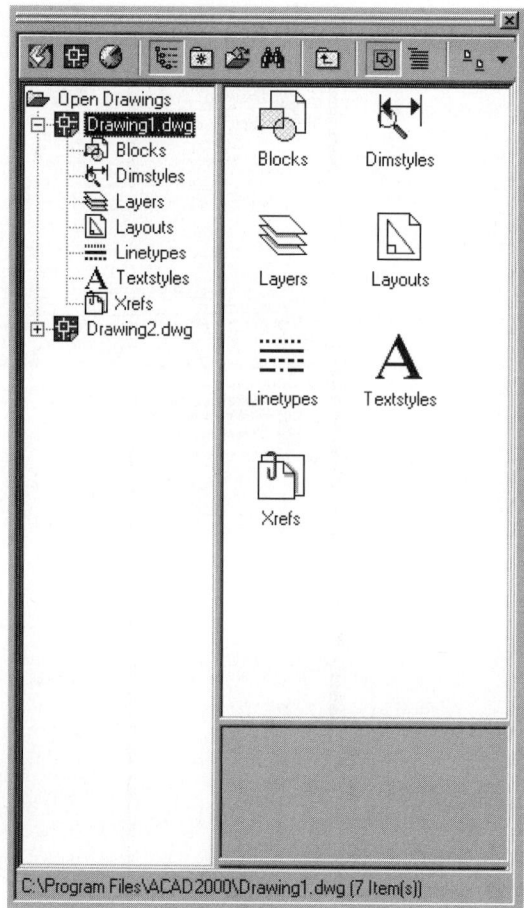

Figure 10-20

This action opens the hierarchy within the chosen file. This is similar to actions in Windows Explorer, but here we are moving down into content within files. You will see a list of content types, as shown in Figure 10-20. Notice the familiar types: Blocks, Dimension Styles, Layers, Layouts, Linetypes, Textstyles, and Xrefs. All drawings will show the same list, although not all drawings will have content defined in each category. Content in any of the categories may be copied into other drawings. This can greatly simplify layer definition, for example, when you can copy definitions from other drawings rather than re-creating them.

In the tree view, the list of types is as far as you can go. In the palette, however, there is another level.

⊕ Click on Blocks in the tree view, or double click on Blocks in the palette.

You should see a familiar set of blocks from Drawing1 in the palette, as shown in Figure 10-21. Keep in mind that Drawing2 is in the drawing area, and Drawing1 is open in the DesignCenter. There are two ways to insert a block from Drawing1 into Drawing2. Try this:

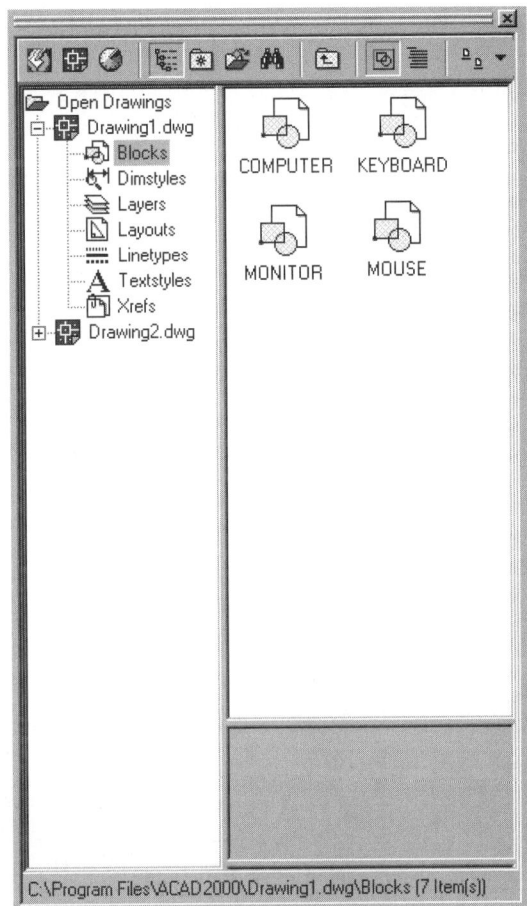

Figure 10-21

⊕ Select the computer block in the palette.

⊕ Drag the block into the Drawing2 drawing area.

As soon as you are in the drawing area you will see a very large image of the computer block. This is a now familiar scaling problem.

⊕ Return your cursor to the palette without releasing the block.

The second method will allow you to scale the block as you insert it.

⊕ Right click on the computer block.

This will open a very small short cut menu with two choices: Insert Block... and Copy.

⊕ Select Insert Block....

You will see the Insert dialog box. From here on the procedure will be just like inserting the block in its original drawing.

⊕ Check the Uniform Scale box.

⊕ Enter 1/8 or .125 in the X scale box.

⊕ Click OK.

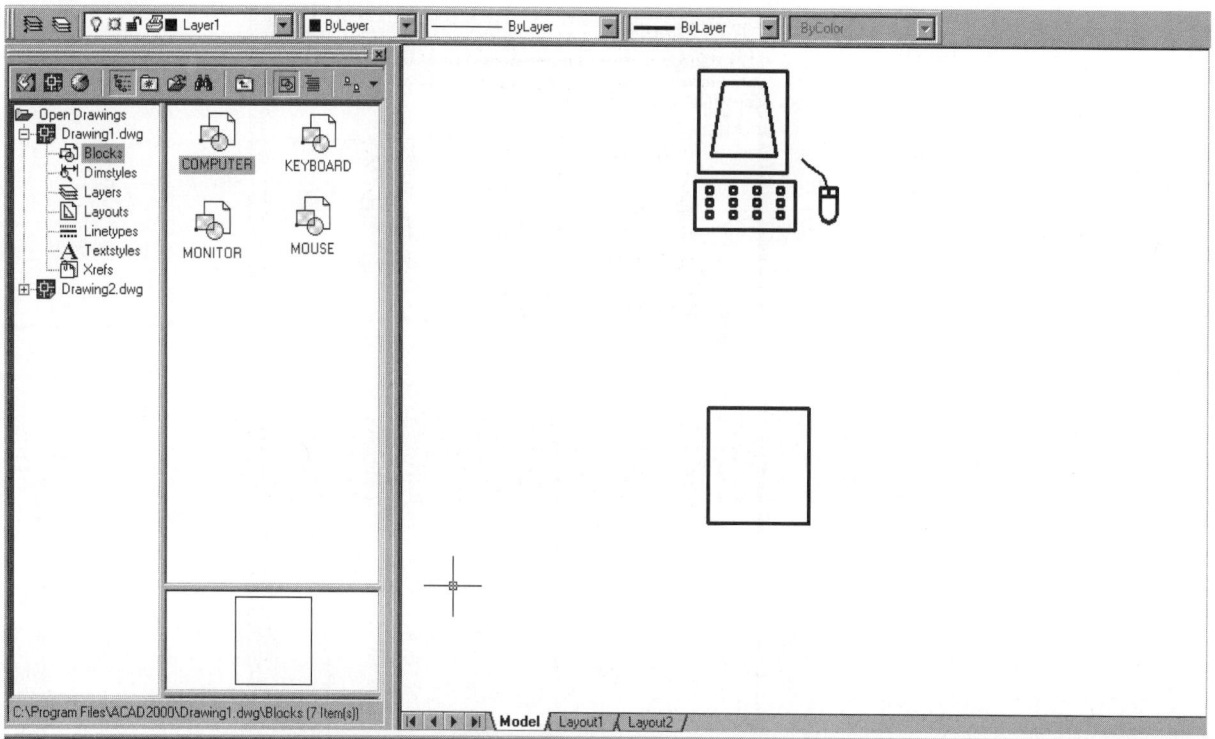

Figure 10-22

⊕ Select an insertion point below the workstation Xref, as shown in Figure 10-22.

⊕ Select Drawing2 in the tree view.

⊕ Double click the Blocks icon in the palette.

You will see that the computer block definition from Drawing1 is now in the database of Drawing2.

⊕ Double click Xrefs in the palette.

You will see that Drawing1 is present as an xref in Drawing2.

Other Features of the DesignCenter

Before leaving the DesignCenter, here are a few more features. Looking across the toolbar, the **History** tool displays the last 20 file locations opened in the Design-Center. The **Favorites** tool gives quick access to locations stored in the Windows Favorites folder. The favorites folder does not contain actual files, but short cuts to frequently accessed file locations. The Autodesk folder contains a DesignCenter folder with a set of sample drawings made up of useful blocks for all kinds of drawings from basic electronic symbols to House Design symbols. Try this:

⊕ Select the Favorites tool from the DesignCenter toolbar, as shown in Figure 10-23.

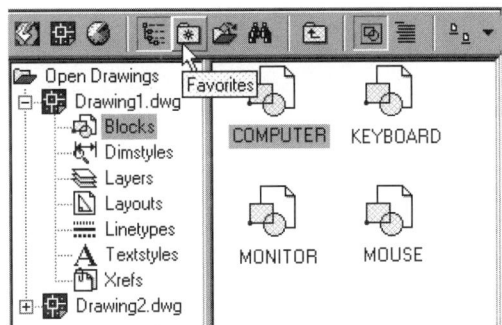

Figure 10-23

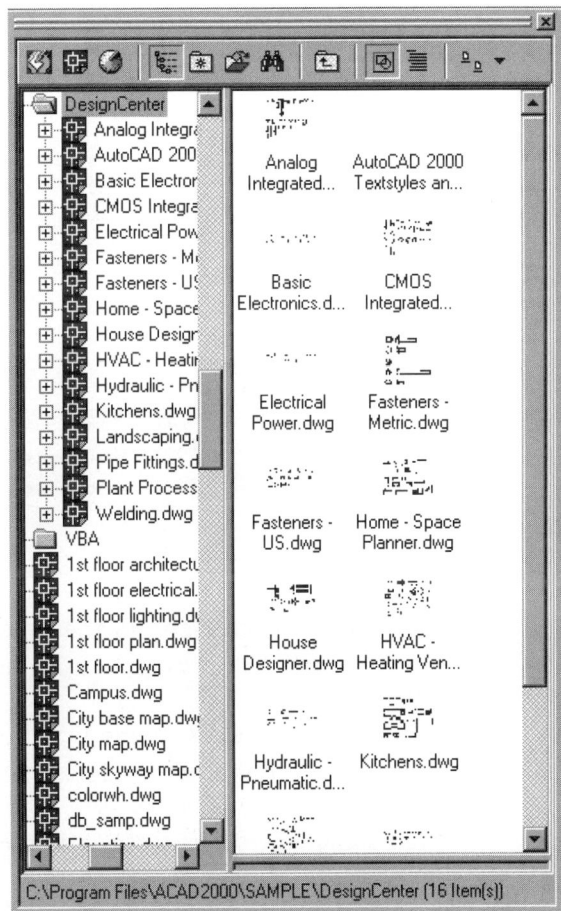

Figure 10-24

⊕ Double click the DesignCenter folder in the palette.

This brings up a list of sample files as shown in Figure 10-24.

⊕ Scroll through the list in either the tree view or the palette and open "Home-Space Planner.dwg".

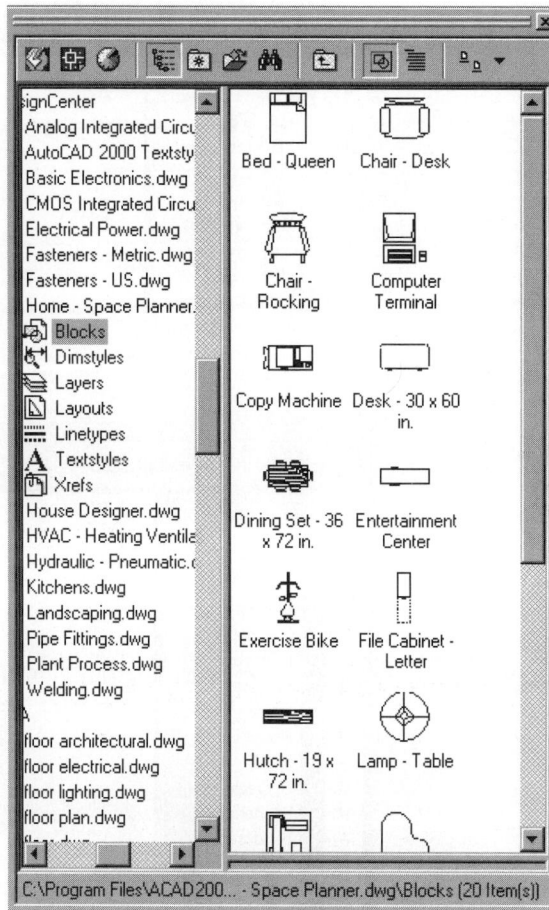

Figure 10-25

⊕ Double click the Blocks icon in the palette.

You will see a set of blocks representing household furniture, as shown in Figure 10-25.

⊕ Scroll through the blocks to the Computer Terminal.

⊕ Right click the terminal and insert it at a scale of .15, as shown in Figure 10-26.

Now you have another version of a computer workstation in Drawing2.

Continuing across the DesignCenter toolbar, the **Load** tool opens a Load Design-Center Palette dialog box. This is a standard select file dialog box that lets you browse for content on disks, networks, and the Internet. Selected locations are loaded into the DesignCenter just like the files on your hard drive you have already worked with. The **Find** button lets you search databases for text matches. You could, for example, search for layers beginning with "dim". The **Preview** tool opens a third pane at the bottom of the palette. Preview images of blocks and drawings will be shown here when objects are selected. The **Description** tool uses

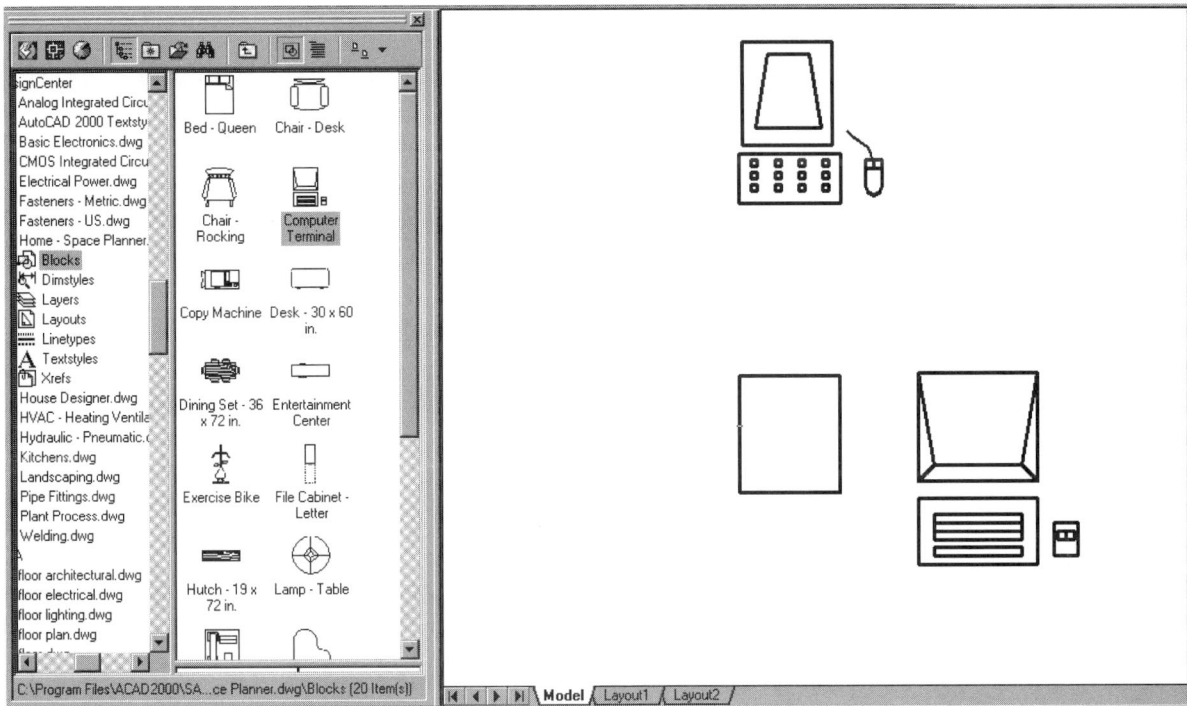

Figure 10-26

the same pane to display text descriptions that have been added to block definitions for identification purposes.

Before moving on, close the DesignCenter.

⊞   Click the close button in the upper right corner of the DesignCenter window.

10.7   Defining Attributes

GENERAL PROCEDURE

1. Select Block and then Define Attributes... from the Draw menu.
2. Specify attribute modes.
3. Type an attribute tag.
4. Type an attribute prompt.
5. If desired, type a default attribute value.
6. Include the attribute in a block definition.

We have introduced many new concepts in this chapter. We have gone from simply grouping objects together to sharing drawing content between drawings. We will explore one last level of complexity before we are done. When you add attributes to a block definition you create the ability to share drawing data between drawings and other types of nongraphic applications, typically database and spread sheet programs. Attributes hold information about blocks in a drawing in a form that can be read out to other programs and organized into reports or bills of materials. Attributes can be confusing, and you should not spend too much time worrying over their details unless you are currently involved in an application that requires their use. On the other hand, they are a powerful tool, and if you have a basic understanding of what they can do, you could be the one in your work setting to recognize when to use them.

One of the difficulties of learning about attributes is that you have to define them before you see them in action. It is therefore a little hard to comprehend what your definitions mean the first time around. Bear with us and follow instructions closely; it will be worth your effort.

In this task we will define attributes that will hold information about CAD workstations. The attributes will be defined in a flexible manner so that the workstation block can represent any number of hardware configurations. One instance of the workstation block could represent a Compaq computer with a Pentium III processor and an Acer monitor, for example, while another instance of the same block could represent an IBM computer, Pentium II processor, and an NEC monitor.

When we have defined our attributes, we will create a block called "ws" that includes the whole workstation assembly and its attributes. To accomplish this we will return to Drawing1 and add attributes to our workstation assembly there. This will also give us the opportunity later to observe the effects of editing an Xref, since Drawing1 is now an Xref in Drawing2.

⊕ **To begin this task, open the Window menu and select Drawing1.**

You should have the workstation assembly from Task 10.3 on your screen. First we will define an attribute that will allow us to specify the type of computer in any individual reference to the "ws" block.

⊕ **Open the Draw menu, highlight Block, and select Define Attributes....**

This executes the ATTDEF command and opens the Attribute Definition dialog box shown in Figure 10-27.

Look first at the check boxes at the top left in the Mode panel. We will be using all the default modes in this first attribute definition. This means that when our workstation block is inserted, the computer attribute value will be visible in the drawing (because "Invisible" is not checked), variable with each insertion of the block (because "Constant" is not checked), not verified ("Verify" is not checked), and not preset to a value ("Preset" is not checked).

Next look at the Attribute panel to the right. The cursor should be blinking in the Tag edit box. Like a field name in a database file, a tag identifies the kind of information this particular attribute is meant to hold. The tag appears in the block definition as a field name. In occurrences of the block in a drawing, the tag is replaced by a specific value. "Computer," for example, could be replaced by "IBM."

⊕ **Type "Computer" in the Tag edit box.**

⊕ **Move the cursor to the Prompt edit box.**

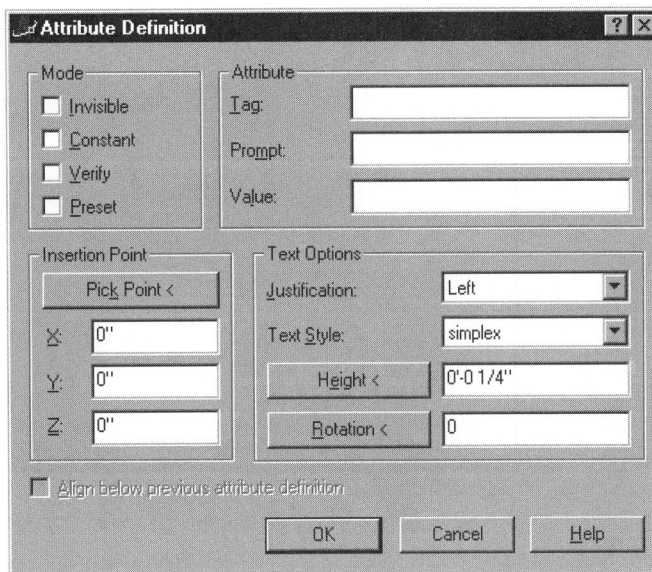

Figure 10-27

As with the tag, the key to understanding the attribute prompt is to be clear about the difference between block definitions in the drawing database and block references in a drawing. Right now we are defining an attribute. The attribute definition will become part of the definition of the "ws" block and will be used whenever ws is inserted. With the definition we are creating, there will be a prompt whenever we insert a ws block that asks us to enter information about the computer in a given configuration.

⊕ Type "Enter computer type".

We also have the opportunity to specify a default attribute value, if we wish, by typing in the Value edit box. Here we will leave this field blank, specifying no default value in our attribute definition.

The panel labeled "Text Options" allows you to specify text parameters as you would in DTEXT. Visible attributes appear as text on the screen. Therefore, the appearance of the text needs to be specified. The only change we will make is to specify a height.

⊕ Click in the edit box to the right of "Height <" and then type "4'''".

If you click on the "Height <" botton itself, the dialog box will disappear so that you can indicate a height by pointing.

Finally, AutoCAD needs to know where to place the visible attribute information in the drawing. You can type in x, y, and z coordinate values, but you are much more likely to show a point.

⊕ Click the "Pick Point <" button.

The dialog box will disappear temporarily to allow access to the screen. You will also see a "Start point:" prompt in the command area.

We will place our attributes 8 inches below the keyboard, as shown in Figure 10-28.

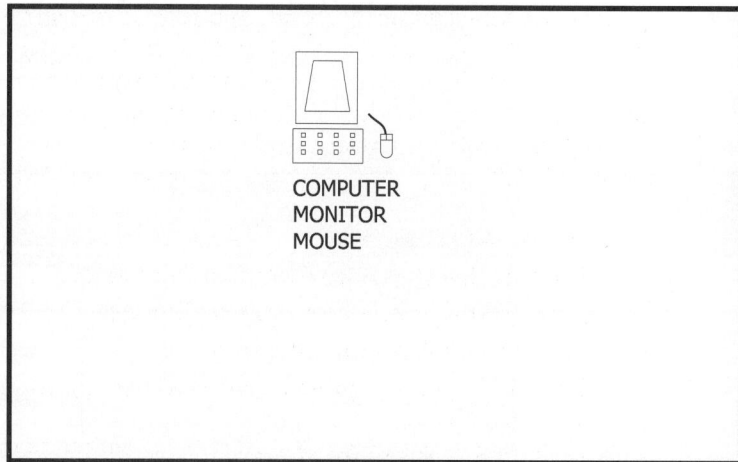

Figure 10-28

⊕ Pick a start point 8 inches below the left side of the keyboard, as shown in Figure 10-28.

The dialog box will reappear.

⊕ Click OK to complete the dialog.

The dialog box will disappear and the attribute tag "Computer" will be drawn as shown. Remember, this is an attribute definition, not an occurrence of the attribute. "Computer" is our attribute tag. After we define the workstation as a block and the block is inserted, you will answer the "Enter computer type:" prompt with the name of a computer type, and the name itself will be in the drawing rather than this tag.

Now we will proceed to define three more attributes, using some different options.

⊕ Repeat ATTDEF by pressing enter or by right clicking and selecting Repeat Define Attributes... from the short cut menu.

We will use all the default modes again, but we will provide a default monitor value in this attribute definition.

⊕ Type "Monitor" for the attribute tag.

⊕ Type "Enter monitor type" for the attribute prompt.

⊕ Type "Super VGA" for the default attribute value.

Now when AutoCAD shows the prompt for a monitor type, it will also show Super VGA as the default.

You can align a series of attributes by checking the Align below previous attribute box at the lower left of the dialog box.

⊕ Click in the check box labeled "Align below previous attribute".

⊕ Click OK to complete the dialog.

The attribute tag "Monitor" should be added to the workstation below the "Computer" tag, as shown in Figure 10-28.

Next, we will add an "invisible, preset" attribute for the mouse. "Invisible" means that the attribute text will not be visible when the block is inserted, although the information will be in the database and can be extracted. "Preset" means that the attribute has a default value and does not issue a prompt to change it. However, unlike "constant" attributes, you can change preset attributes using the ATTEDIT command, which we will explore in Task 10.8.

⊕ Repeat ATTDEF.

⊕ Click in the check box next to "Invisible".

⊕ Click in the check box next to "Preset".

⊕ Type "Mouse" for the attribute tag.

You will not need a prompt, since the preset attribute is automatically set to the default value.

⊕ Type "MS Mouse" for the default attribute value.

⊕ Click in the Align below previous attribute check box to position the attribute below "Monitor" in the drawing.

⊕ Click OK to complete the dialog.

The "Mouse" attribute tag should be added to your screen, as shown in Figure 10-28. When ws is inserted, the attribute value "MS Mouse" will be written into the database, but nothing will appear on the screen since the attribute is defined as invisible.

Finally, the most important step of all: We must define the workstation as a block that includes all our attribute definitions.

⊕ Type "b" or select the Make Block tool from the Draw toolbar.

⊕ Type "ws" for the block name.

⊕ Click the Select Objects button.

⊕ Window the workstation assembly and all three attribute tags.

⊕ Press Enter to end object selection.

⊕ Click the Pick Point< button.

⊕ Pick an insertion point at the midpoint of the bottom of the keyboard.

⊕ Click OK to end the dialog.

The newly defined block will disappear from the screen. In the next task we will insert several workstations back into Drawing1 and then use ATTEDIT to change attribute values.

10.8 Editing Attributes

> **GENERAL PROCEDURE**
>
> 1. Open the Modify menu, highlight Attribute, and select Single or Global.
> 2. Specify blocks and attributes to include in the editing process.
> 3. In one-by-one editing, specify the property to be edited and edit it.
> 4. In global editing, specify the string to change and new string.

The ATTEDIT command provides the capacity to change values and text properties of attributes in blocks that have been inserted. It does not allow you to edit attribute definitions. Block definitions and attribute definitions can be changed only by re-creating them.

There are two ways to edit attributes. Single editing allows you to change individual attribute values, text position, height, angle, style, layer, and color. Global editing allows you to change values only, but for multiple instances of the same block.

⊕ To begin this task, you should have a clear screen in Drawing1. The ws block definition with its three attributes should be present in the drawing database.

⊕ Insert three workstations, using the following procedure (note the attribute prompts):

1. Type "i" or select the Insert Block tool from the Draw toolbar.
2. Type or select "ws" for the block name.
3. Click OK to exit the dialog box.
4. Pick an insertion point.
5. Answer the attribute prompts for monitors and computers.

We specified one Pentium IV and two Pentium III computers for this exercise and retained all the monitor defaults (Super VGA). Your hardware information may be entirely different, but this exercise will be simpler if you use ours. Notice that you are not prompted for mouse specifications because that attribute is preset.

When you are done, your screen should resemble Figure 10-29.

The first thing we will do with the inserted blocks is use ATTDISP ("attribute display") to turn invisible attributes on.

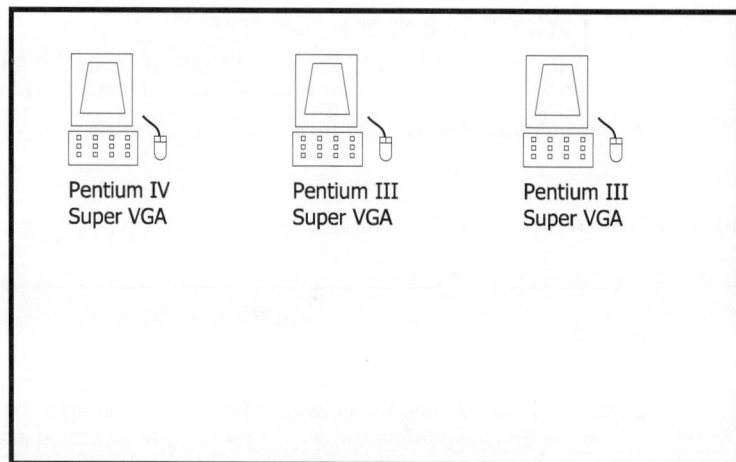

Pentium IV
Super VGA

Pentium III
Super VGA

Pentium III
Super VGA

Figure 10-29

Displaying Invisible Attributes

The ATTDISP command allows control of the visibility of all attribute values, regardless of their defined visibility mode.

⊕ Open the View menu, highlight Display, and select Attribute Display.

The submenu has three options. "Normal" means that visible attributes are visible and invisible attributes are invisible. "On" turns all attributes on. "Off" turns all attributes off.

⊕ Select "on".

Your screen will be regenerated with invisible attributes on, as shown in Figure 10-30. You can leave ATTDISP on in this exercise or turn it back to "normal".

Now we will do an edit. Imagine that these three workstations represent part of a small work site and that we just purchased a new Super VGA 20″ monitor. We could erase one of the workstations and reinsert it with new attribute information, but it will be simpler to edit just the one attribute that needs to change.

⊕ Open the Modify menu, highlight Attribute, and then select Single....

This enters the ATTEDIT command. AutoCAD will prompt you to select a block.

⊕ Select the workstation on the right.

You will see the Edit Attributes dialog box shown in Figure 10-31. Notice that all defined attributes are available, including the preset mouse attribute.

⊕ Click in the Monitor edit box and add "20″" to the text.

⊕ Click OK to end the dialog.

The attribute text will be changed as shown in Figure 10-32.

Now let's perform a global edit.

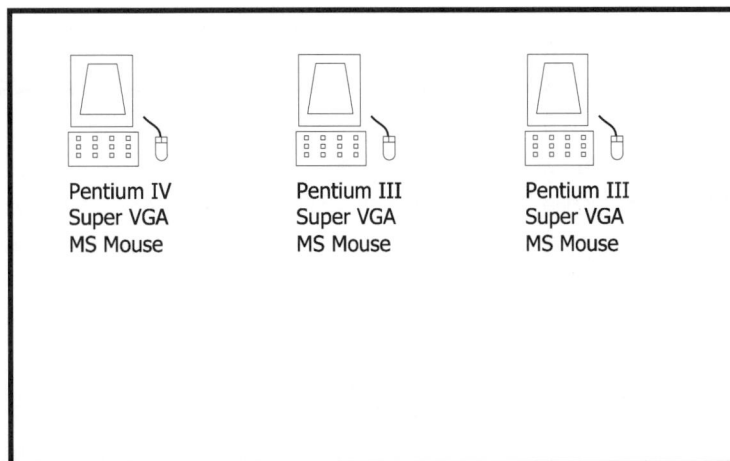

Pentium IV
Super VGA
MS Mouse

Pentium III
Super VGA
MS Mouse

Pentium III
Super VGA
MS Mouse

Figure 10-30

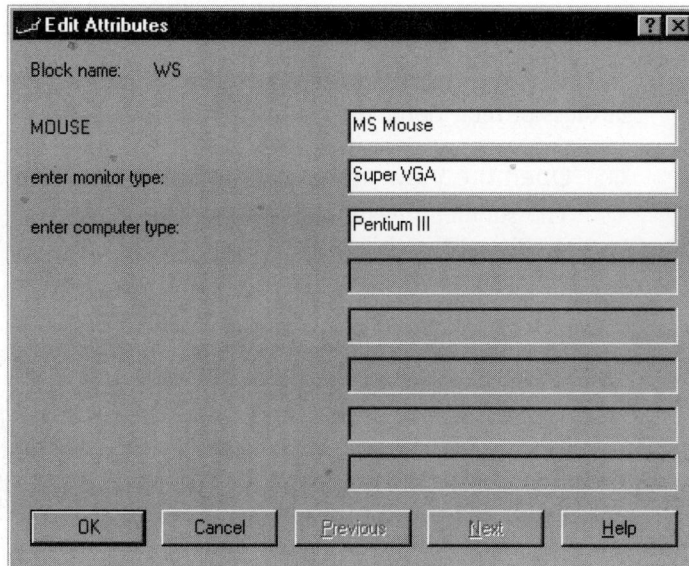

Figure 10-31

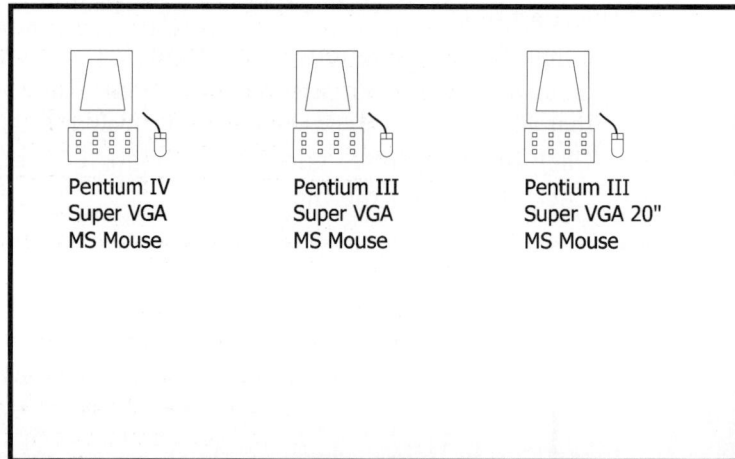

Figure 10-32

⊕ Open the Modify menu, highlight Attribute, and then select Global.
    This enters the ATTEDIT command on the command line. From here you
    have to bypass single editing to get to global editing. AutoCAD prompts

        Edit attributes one at a time? <Y>:

⊕ Enter "n" to move on to global editing.
    AutoCAD prompts

        Edit only attributes visible on the screen? <Y>

If you left ATTDISP "on", all attributes are visible.

⊕ Press Enter to edit only visible attributes.

AutoCAD issues a series of three prompts that allow you to narrow down the field of attributes to be edited.

```
Enter block name specification <*>:
```

If we had more than one type of block on the screen, we could limit editing to occurrences of whatever block we wished to name. But we have only the ws block.

⊕ Press Enter.

AutoCAD prompts

```
Enter attribute tag specification <*>:
```

This allows us to narrow the field to a single tag—all the computer types, for example.

⊕ Type "computer".

AutoCAD now prompts for an attribute value:

```
Enter attribute value specification <*>:
```

This allows us to specify only computers with the value—"Pentium III", for example. We will do this by pointing.

⊕ Press Enter.

Now AutoCAD asks us to select attributes by pointing or windowing:

```
Select Attributes:
```

⊕ Select the two Pentium III computer attributes.

Now AutoCAD knows which attributes to edit. It will allow you to change the entire text of the two attributes, or only part. It does this by requesting a string:

```
Enter string to change:
```

A string is simply a text sequence. It may be part or all of the text.

⊕ Type "Pentium III".

Now AutoCAD prompts

```
New string:
```

⊕ Type "Pentium IV".

The two selected attributes will be changed, as shown in Figure 10-33.

Extracting Attribute Information from Drawings

Although there are many good reasons to use attributes, the most impressive is the ability to create extract files (the ATTEXT command), which can be processed by other programs to generate reports, bills of materials, inventories, parts lists, and quotations. This means, for example, that with a well-managed CAD system you can do a drawing of a construction project and get a complete price breakdown and supply list directly from the drawing database, all processed by computer. To accomplish this, you need carefully defined attributes and a program such as Excel that is capable of receiving the extract information and formatting it into a useful

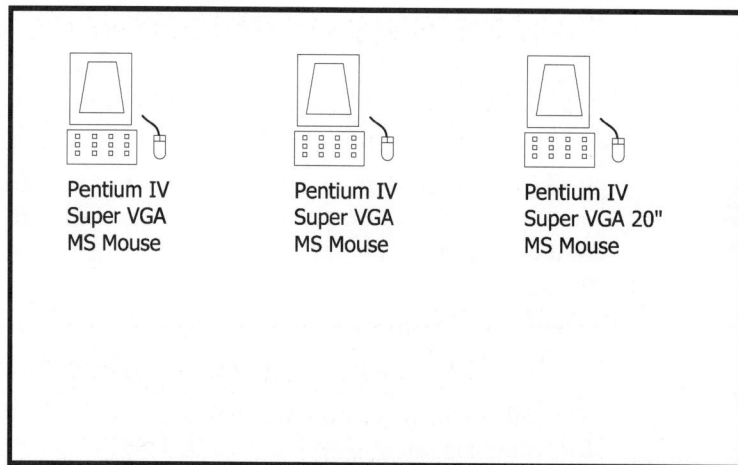

Figure 10-33

report. In addition you need to create an extraction template file in a word processor with a ASCII text format to receive the attribute information. This attribute information file receives the information from the AutoCAD drawing that is then read by the database or spread sheet application.

Since we have no way of knowing what programs are available to you and since we want to keep the focus of this book on drawing rather than programming, it is beyond our scope to create the files and formats necessary for extracting attributes. With a little imagination, however, you can see the possibilities. With a database program, for example, we could match the computer, monitor, and digitizer names in our block references to a price list contained in a database file, calculate totals and subtotals, and format an elaborate report. If you want additional information on attribute extraction, see the *AutoCAD User's Guide*.

10.9   Working with External References

In the past two tasks you have made numerous changes to Drawing1. Attributes have been added, a ws block created, and three references to the new block have been inserted into the drawing. This provides us a good opportunity to turn our attention back to Drawing2 and work with the Drawing1 external reference there to see how Xrefs work in action.

⊕   Before leaving Drawing1, click the save tool on the Standard toolbar to save your changes.

This is not just to safeguard changes. It is necessary to save changes to an Xref before the changes can be read into another drawing.

⊕   Open the Window menu and select Drawing2.

You should be back in Drawing2 with a workstation xref, a computer terminal block, and a computer block on your screen as shown previously in Figure 10-26. The first thing we will do is reload the Drawing1 Xref.

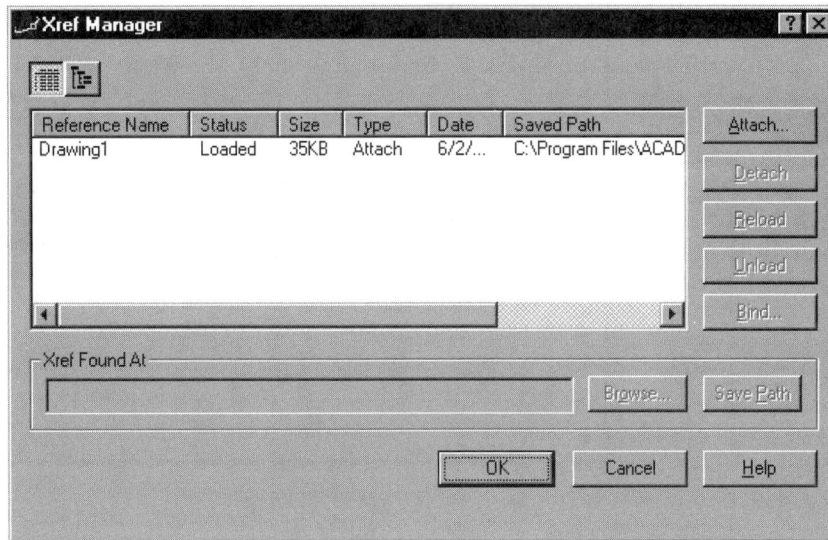

Figure 10-34

⊕ Select the workstation.

⊕ Right click anywhere in the drawing area.

This opens a short cut menu.

⊕ Select Xref Manager... from the short cut menu.

This executes the XREF command, which is also accessible by selecting Xref Manager... from the Insert menu. You will see the Xref Manager dialog box, as shown in Figure 10-34. Drawing1 is the only Reference in your drawing and the only drawing listed in the Reference Name list.

⊕ Select Drawing1 in the Reference Name list.

When a reference is selected the option buttons on the right become accessible and the Path to the reference is displayed in the Xref Found At box. Take a minute to look over these options in the Xref Manager dialog box.

Attach:	Executes the XATTACH command. Creates a link between the current drawing and another drawing. Performs the same functions as selecting External Reference from the Insert menu.
Detach:	Removes the link between the current drawing and specified external references. Detached objects are no longer present in the current drawing.
Reload:	Reloads an external reference without leaving the current drawing. Using this option, the most recent changes can be brought into the current drawing.
Unload:	Unloads the external reference from the drawing so that it is not displayed or retained in memory, but maintains the pointer data so that the xref can be reloaded quickly using the Reload option.
Bind:	Merges an external reference completely into the current drawing. The end result is the same as INSERTing a drawing, but binding does not have to occur until the final version of the drawing is complete. There is also a XBIND command that allows you to exclude certain types of information when you bind an external reference. The dimensions, for example, can be left out if they are drawn on a separate layer.

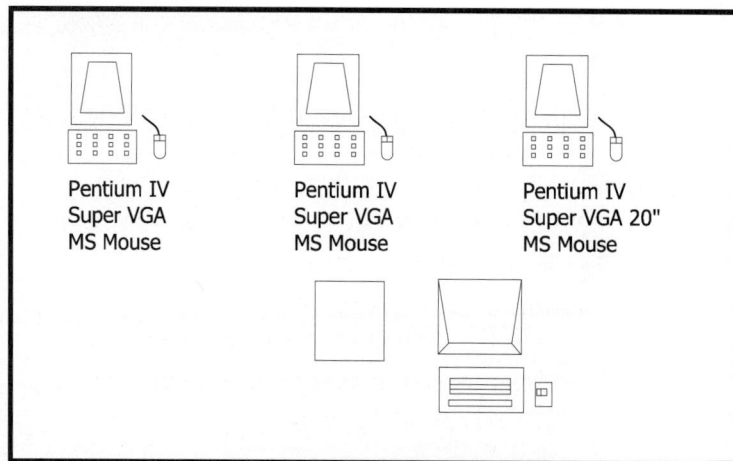

Figure 10-35

Note: The Xref Found At: edit box can be used to tell AutoCAD where to locate an existing external reference. This option can be used to update a link when file structure is changed or the externally referenced drawing is moved. Otherwise, the link cannot be maintained.

⊞   Click the Reload button.
⊞   Click OK to exit the dialog.
    You will see the Unable to Demand Load message encountered previously.
⊞   Click OK to accept a full read of the Xref.
    Drawing2 will be updated to reflect the changes in Drawing1, as shown in Figure 10-35.

Editing External References in Place

External References can be edited within the current drawing and even used to update the original referenced drawing. This should be done sparingly and for simple edits only; otherwise the current drawing will expand to take up more memory and the point of using an external reference instead of a block reference will be lost. To edit a block or external reference "in place," select In-place Xref and Block Edit from the Modify menu.

Clipping External References

External References may also be clipped so that only a portion of the referenced drawing is actually displayed in the current drawing. This would allow different users on the same network to share portions of their drawings without having to alter the original drawings to eliminate aspects that would not be useful in a master drawing. Clipping boundaries may be defined by a rectangular window, a polygon window, or by selecting an existing polyline. Clipping is performed with the XCLIP command and can be used on block references as well as external references. You can type the command, or select a reference, right click to open a short cut menu, and select Xref Clip from the Modify menu. Try this:

⊕ Still in Drawing2, select the three workstations externally referenced from Drawing1.

⊕ Right click to open the short cut menu.

⊕ From the short cut menu, select Xref Clip.

AutoCAD prompts

```
Enter clipping option
[ON/OFF/Clipdepth/Delete/generate Polyline/New boundary] <New>:
```

⊕ Press Enter or the space bar to begin defining a new clipping boundary.

AutoCAD prompts

```
Specify clipping boundary:
[Select polyline/Polygonal/Rectangular] <Rectangular>:
```

⊕ Press Enter or the space bar to define a rectangular boundary.

AutoCAD prompts for a first corner. We will place a rectangular boundary around the middle workstation and its computer attribute, clipping away the monitor attribute and the other two workstations.

⊕ Pick a first corner point as shown by P1 in Figure 10-36.

⊕ Pick an opposite corner point as shown by P2 in Figure 10-36.

Your screen should resemble Figure 10-37. Clipping an instance of an Xref does not alter the Xref definition, it only suppresses the display of the clipped objects. This particular instance of the Drawing1 xref will continue to show only the remaining objects even if the xref is reloaded, unless the clipping boundary is deleted by the XCLIP command. If another instance of Drawing1 is referenced through the XATTACH command, it will not be affected by the clipping boundaries.

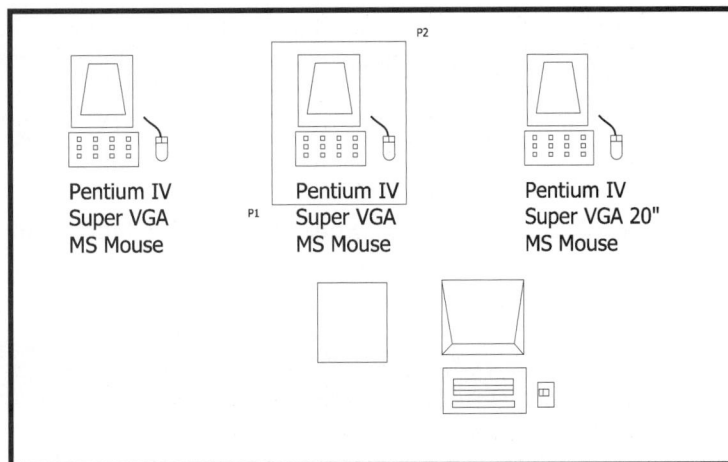

Figure 10-36

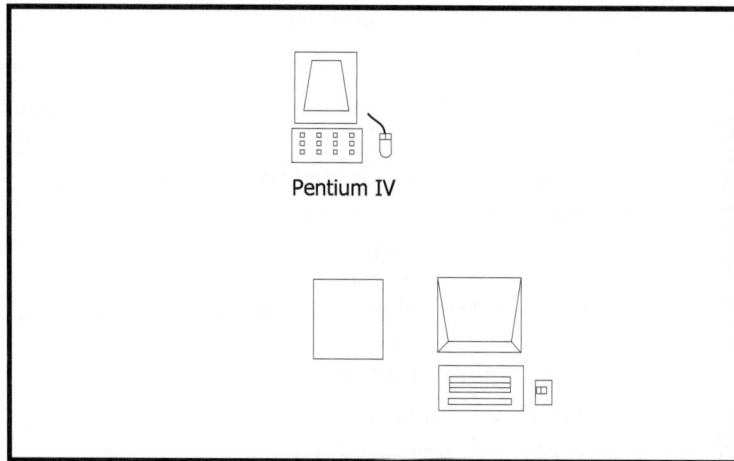

Figure 10-37

10.10 EXPLODEing Blocks

GENERAL PROCEDURE

1. Type "X", select Explode from the Modify menu, or select the Explode tool from the Modify toolbar.
2. Select objects.
3. Press Enter to carry out the command.

The EXPLODE command undoes the work of the BLOCK or GROUP command. It takes a set of objects that have been defined as a block or group and re-creates them as independent entities. EXPLODE works on dimensions and hatch patterns as well as on blocks created in the BMAKE or BLOCK commands. It does not work on externally referenced drawings until they have been attached permanently through the bind option.

⊕ To begin this task, you should have Drawing2 on your screen.

Let's try exploding the computer terminal, inserted from the Autodesk favorites House Space Planner drawing.

⊕ Type "x", select Explode from the Modify menu, or select the Explode tool from the Modify toolbar, as shown in Figure 10-38.

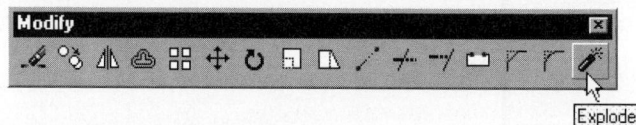

Figure 10-38

You will be prompted to select objects.

⊕ Select the computer terminal.

⊕ Press Enter to carry out the command.

⊕ Now try selecting any part of the computer terminal.

All of the component parts of the previously blocked terminal can now be selected separately.

Note: Exploding removes only one layer of block definition. If a block is made up of other blocks, these "nested" blocks remain as independent blocks after exploding. Attribute information is removed by exploding, leaving the attribute tag instead.

10.11   Review Material

Questions

1. Why is it usually a good idea to create blocks on layer 0?
2. What is the difference between a group and a block?
3. What is an insertion base point, as used in the BLOCK command? What is an insertion point, as used in the INSERT command?
4. Blocks, external references, and raster images are all inserted with a scale factor. Why?
5. Explain how you could create a complete drawing using the INSERT command only.
6. What is the difference between COPY and COPYCLIP?
7. What is an attribute tag? What is an attribute prompt? What is an attribute value?
8. What are the three settings of ATTDISP?
9. Explain the purpose of attribute extraction.
10. What other complex entities can be EXPLODEd besides blocks?
11. What happens to attribute values when a block is exploded?
12. What is the main thing you can accomplish with the AutoCAD DesignCenter that cannot be done with INSERT or XATTACH?

Drawing Problems

1. Save Drawing1 so that you can use the settings for Drawing 10-1. Open a new drawing using the IB prototype and create a hexagon circumscribed around a circle so that both have a 1.0 unit radius. These objects should be created so that when they are defined as a block, they will be inserted on layer 2 regardless of what layer is current at the time.
2. Define an attribute to go with the hexagon and circle. The tag should identify the two as a hex bolt; the prompt should ask for a hex bolt diameter. The attribute should be visible in the drawing, center justified 0.5 units below the block, with text 0.3 units high.
3. Create a block with the bolt and its attribute. Leave a clear screen when you are done.

4. Draw a rectangle on layer 1, with lower left corner at (0,4) and upper right corner at (18,8).

5. Insert 0.5 diameter hex bolts at (2,6) and (16,6). Insert a 1.0 unit hex bolt at (9,6). The sizes of each hex bolt should appear beneath the bolt.

10.12   WWW Exercise #10 (Optional)

The new material in this chapter opens the door to several new Internet access procedures. In this task we will show you how to insert hyperlinks into drawings so that anyone using your drawing can jump from an object directly to a specified Internet address. All it takes is that you insert a hyperlink and that whoever wants to use the hyperlink is connected to the internet at the time. Hyperlinks can also be used to connect to other drawing files, views, or layouts. For demonstration, we will insert a hypcrlink into Drawing1, attached to a workstation block. The hyperlink will be defined to link to our companion Web site. Then we will go through the procedure for connecting to the Web site through the hyperlink. Here we go.

⊞   To begin this task you should be in Drawing1 with three instances of the workstation block and its attributes displayed, as shown previously in Figure 10-33.

If for any reason this drawing is not readily available, any drawing will do, but the illustrations will not match.

⊞   If you have not already done so, connect to your Internet service provider.

⊞   Open the Insert menu and select Hyperlink, or select the Insert Hyperlink tool from the Standard toolbar, as shown in Figure 10-39.

Hyperlinks are connected to objects, so AutoCAD will prompt you to select objects. The prompt is plural, indicating that you can select more than one object to connect to the same hyperlink.

⊞   Select the workstation on the left.

⊞   Select the workstation on the right.

⊞   Right click to end object selection.

This brings you to the Insert Hyperlink dialog box shown in Figure 10-40.

⊞   Look over the box to see the array of options you have for linking through this feature.

⊞   Type "www.prenhall.com/dixriley" in the Link to file or URL edit box.

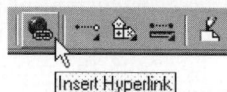

Figure 10-39

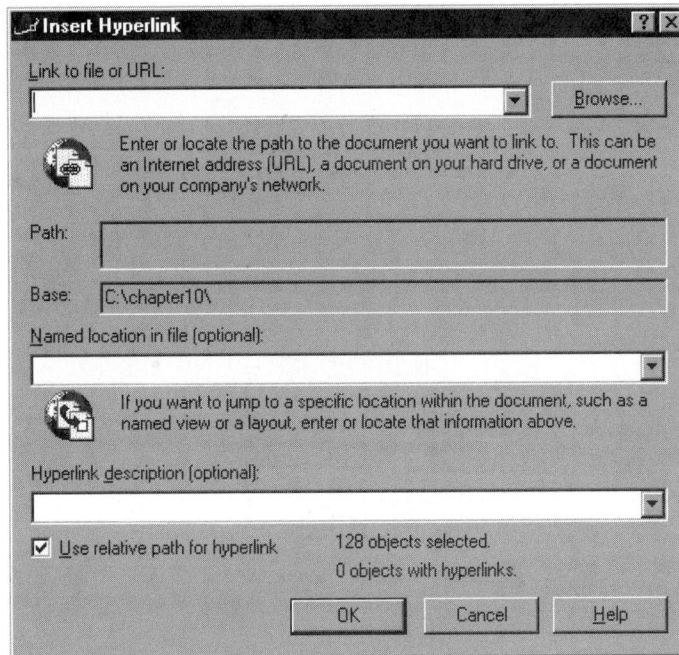

Figure 10-40

⊕ Click OK to exit the dialog.

The dialog box will disappear. The links have been inserted, but nothing will happen until you select a hyperlink.

⊕ Move your cursor over either of the selected workstations (we chose the one on the right). When you see the hyperlink cursor as shown in Figure 10-41, let the cursor rest.

You will see the hyperlink symbol and below it the hyperlink specification, as shown in Figure 10-41.

⊕ With the hyperlink symbol displayed, press the pickbutton.

The workstation will be selected but nothing else will happen.

⊕ Right click anywhere in the drawing area.

A short cut menu will appear with Repeat Hyperlink... on the top and Hyperlink on the bottom.

⊕ Highlight Hyperlink at the bottom of the short cut menu.

This will open a submenu, as shown in Figure 10-42.

⊕ Select Open "www.prenhall.com/dixriley".

We are sure you will find many uses for this great feature. See you at the Web site.

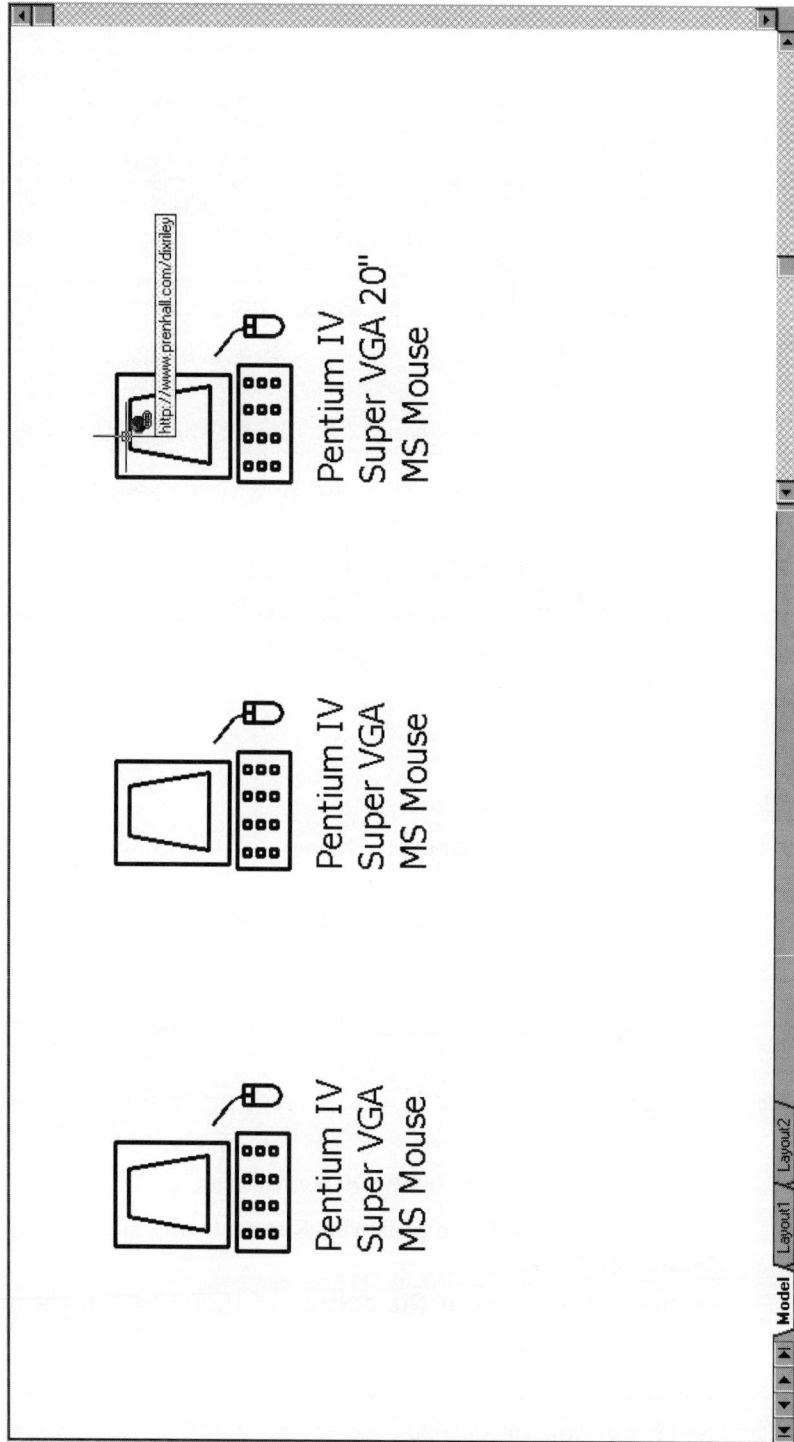

Figure 10-41

446

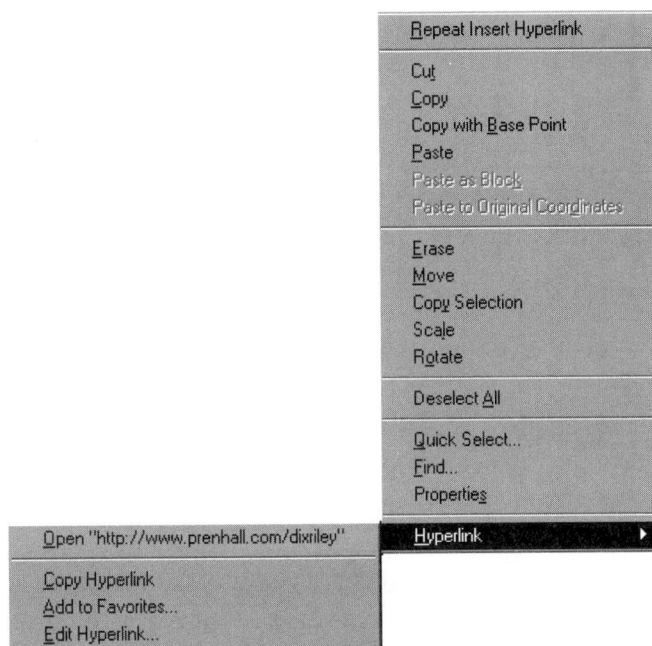

Repeat Insert Hyperlink

Cut
Copy
Copy with Base Point
Paste
Paste as Block
Paste to Original Coordinates

Erase
Move
Copy Selection
Scale
Rotate

Deselect All

Quick Select...
Find...
Properties

Open "http://www.prenhall.com/dixriley"   Hyperlink ▶

Copy Hyperlink
Add to Favorites...
Edit Hyperlink...

Figure 10-42

10.13   Drawing 10-1: Cad Room

This architectural drawing is primarily an exercise in using blocks and attributes. Use your ws block and its attributes to fill in the workstations and text after you draw the walls and countertop. New blocks should be created for the plotters and printers, as described following. The drawing setup is the same as that used in the chapter.

DRAWING SUGGESTIONS

> UNITS = Architectural, precision = 0′–0″
> GRID = 1′
> SNAP = 1″
> LIMITS = (0′,0′)(48′,36′)

- The "plotter" block is a 1 × 3 rectangle, with two visible, variable attributes (all the default attribute modes). The first attribute is for a manufacturer and the second for a model. The "printers" are 2 × 2.5 with the same type of attributes. Draw the rectangles, define their attributes 8 inches below them, create the BLOCK definitions, and then INSERT plotters and printers as shown.

  Note: Do not include the labels "plotter" or "laser printer" in the block, because text in a block will be rotated with the block. This would give you inverted text on the front countertop. Insert the blocks and add the text afterward. The attribute text can be handled differently, as described following.

- The "8 pen plotter" was inserted with a Y scale factor of 1.25.

THE MIRRTEXT SYSTEM VARIABLE

The two workstations on the front counter could be inserted with a rotation angle of 180 degrees, but then the attribute text would be inverted also and would have to be turned around using ATTEDIT. Instead, we have reset the "mirrtext" system variable so that we could mirror blocks without attribute text being inverted:

1. Type "mirrtext".
2. Type "0".

Now you can mirror objects on the back counter to create those on the front. With the "mirrtext" system variable set to "0", text included in a MIRROR procedure is not inverted as it would be with mirrtext set to "1" (the default). This applies to attribute text as well as ordinary text. However, it does not apply to ordinary text included in a block definition.

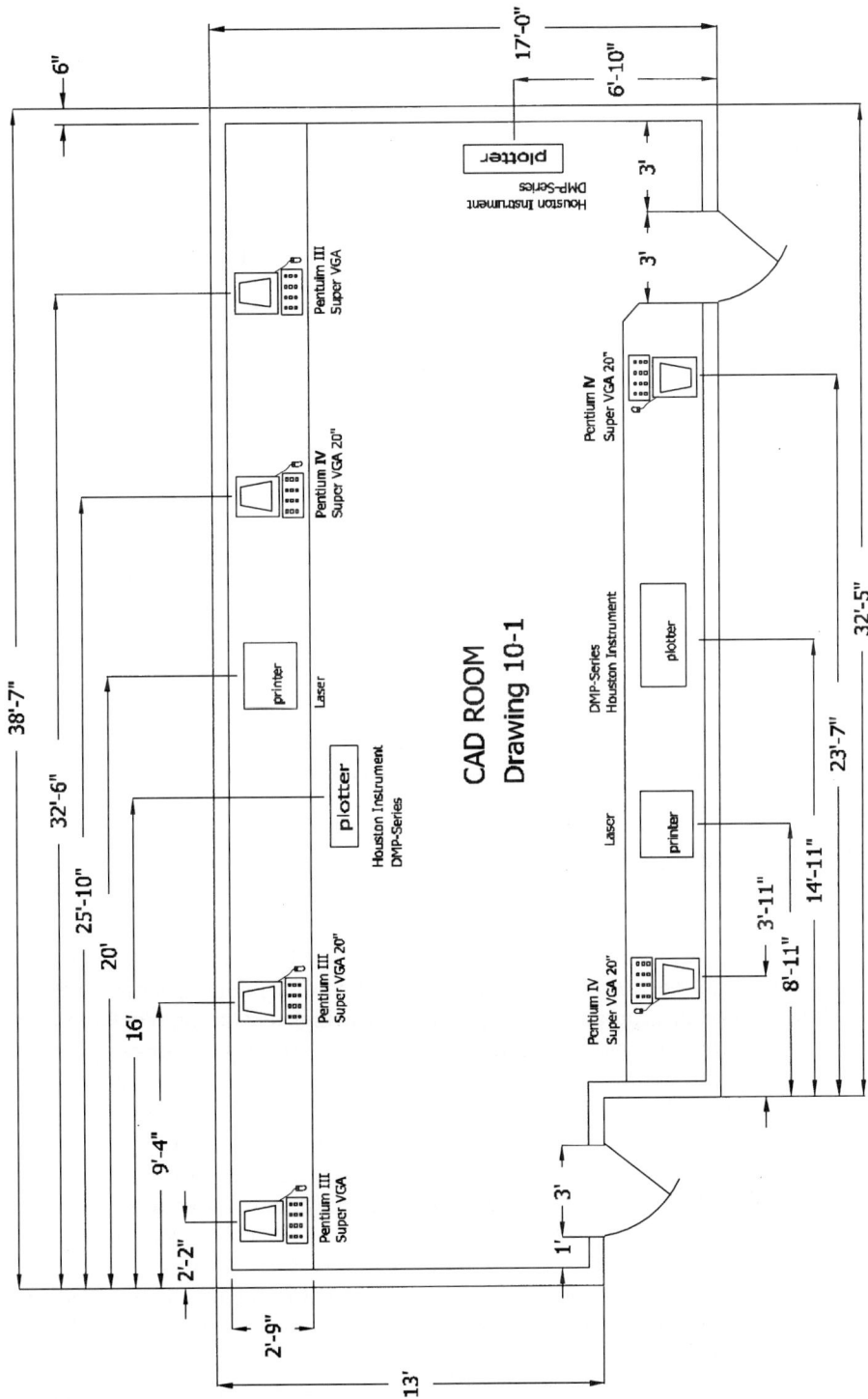

CAD ROOM
Drawing 10-1

10.14 Drawing 10-2: Base Assembly

This is a good exercise in assembly drawing procedures. You will be drawing each of the numbered part details and then assembling them into the "Base Assembly."

DRAWING SUGGESTIONS

We will no longer provide you with units, grid, snap, and limit settings. You can determine what you need by looking over the drawing and its dimensions. Remember that you can always change a setting later if it becomes necessary.

- You can create your own title block from scratch or develop one from "Title Block," Drawing 7-1, if you have saved it. Once created and SAVEd or WBLOCKed, a title block can be inserted and scaled to fit any drawing. AutoCAD also comes with drawing templates that have borders and title blocks.

USING MINSERT TO CREATE A TABLE

The parts list should also be defined as a block. Since many drawings include parts lists, you will want to be able to create a table quickly with any given number of rows. Try this:

1. Define a block that represents one row of the parts list.
2. WBLOCK it so it can be used in any drawing.
3. When you insert it, use either ARRAY or MINSERT to create the number of rows in the table (MINSERT creates an array of a block as part of the insertion process).

MANAGING PARTS BLOCKS FOR MULTIPLE USE

You will be drawing each of the numbered parts (B101-1, B101-2, etc.) and then assembling them. In an industrial application the individual part details would be sent to different manufacturers or manufacturing departments, so they must exist as separate, completely dimensioned drawings as well as blocks that can be used in creating the assembly. An efficient method is to create three separate blocks for each part detail: one for dimensions and one for each view in the assembly. The dimensioned part drawings will include both views. The blocks of the two views will have dimensions, hidden lines, and center lines erased.

Think carefully about the way you name blocks. You might want to adopt a naming system like this: "B101-1D" for the dimensioned drawing, "B101-1T" for a top view without dimensions, and "B101-1F" for a front view without dimensions. Such a system will make it easy to call out all the top view parts for the top view assembly, for example. A more detailed procedure is outlined for Drawings 10-3 and 10-4.

- Notice that the assembly requires you to do a considerable amount of trimming away of lines from the blocks you insert. This can be done easily, but you must remember to EXPLODE the inserted blocks first.

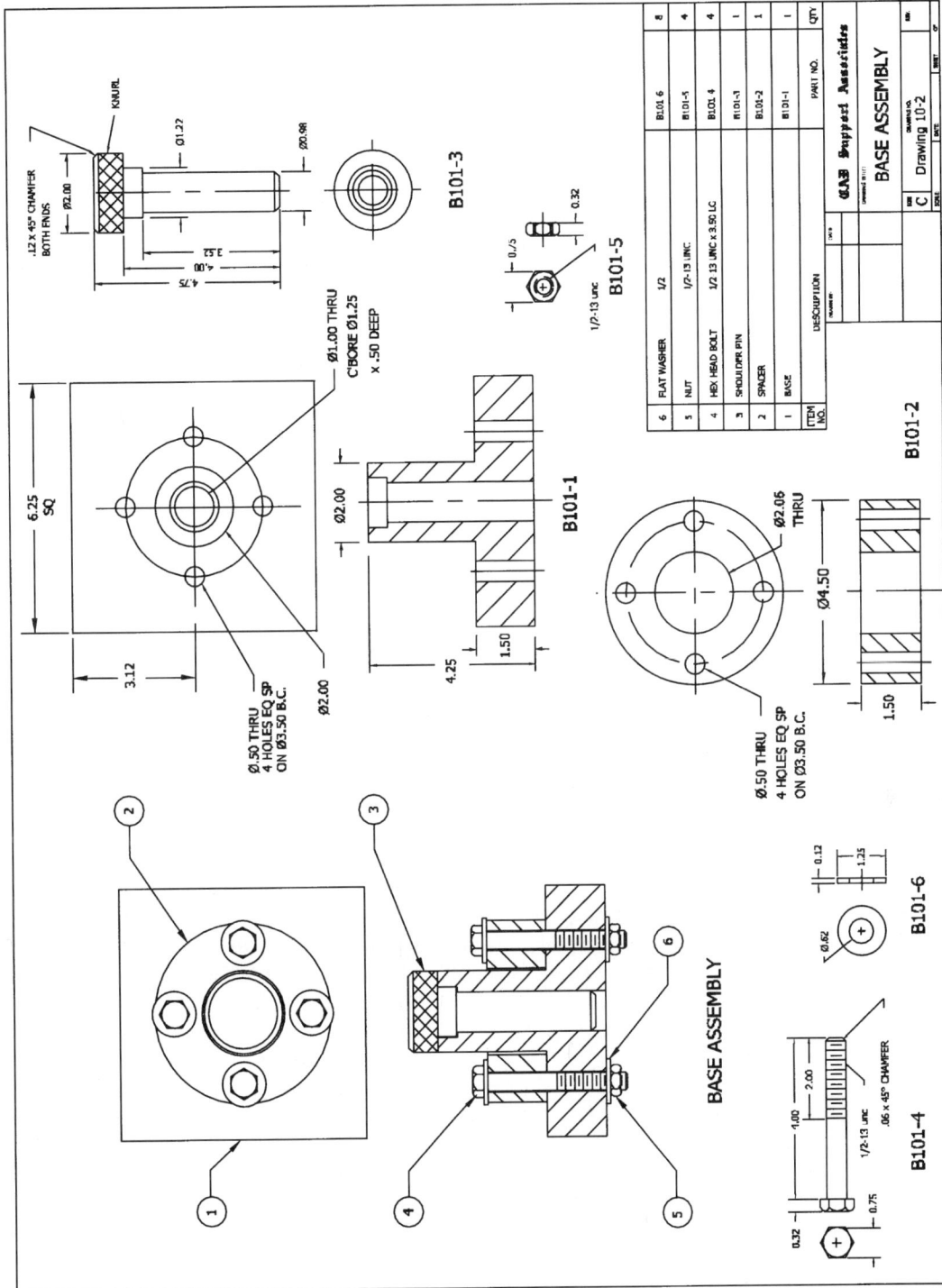

10.15   Drawings 10-3 and 10-4:
Double Bearing Assembly and Scooter Assembly

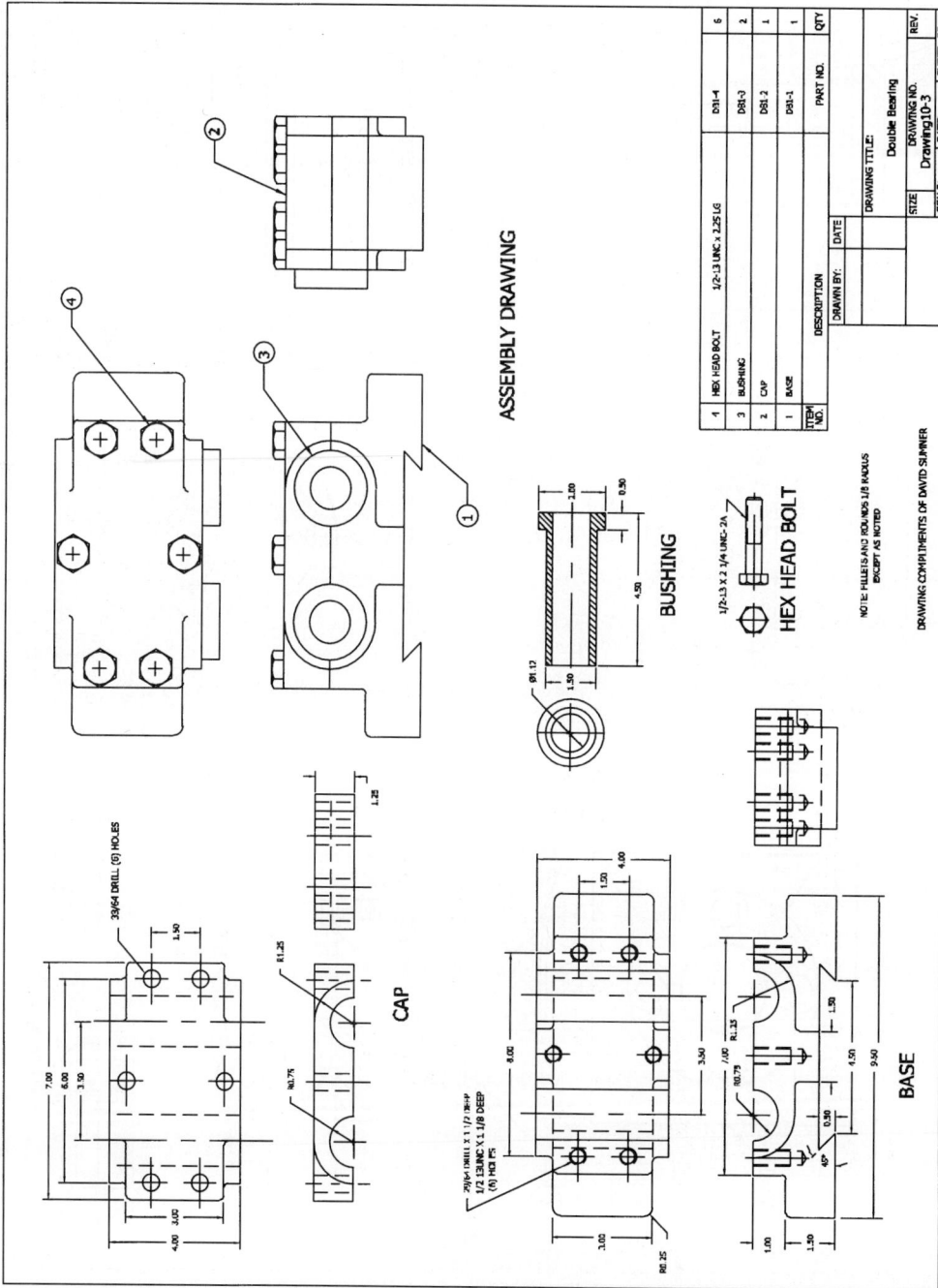

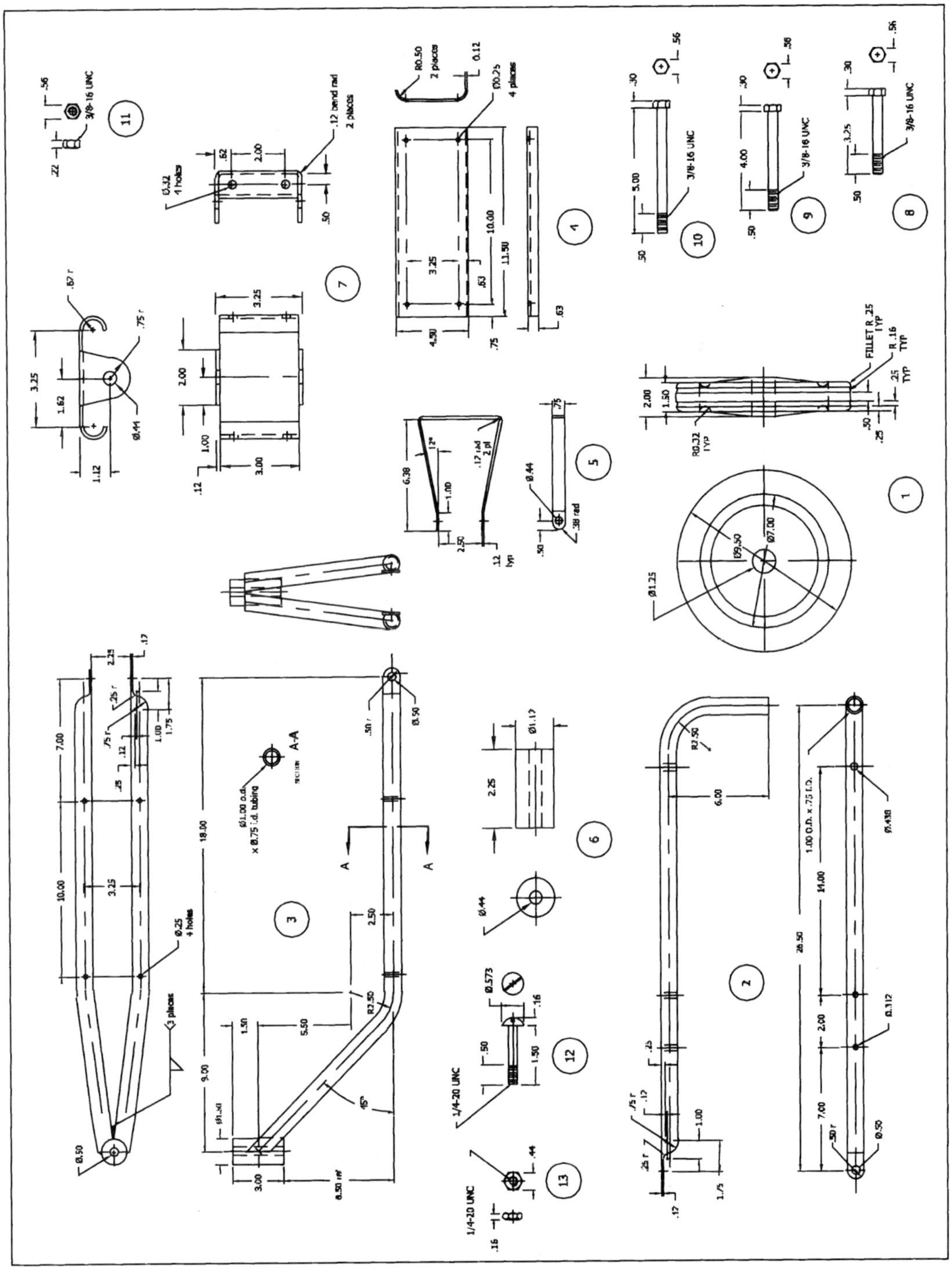
1
2
3
4
5
6
7
8
9
10
11
12
13
3/8-16 UNC
1/4-20 UNC
section A-A
Ø1.00 o.d. x Ø.75 i.d. tubing
Ø.25 4 holes
3 places
FILLET R .25 TYP
R .16 TYP
R0.50 2 places
Ø0.25 4 places
.12 bend rad 2 places
Ø.32 4 holes
1.00 O.D. x .75 I.D.
28.50
18.00
14.00
11.50
10.00
7.00
6.00
5.00
4.00
3.25
2.00
45°

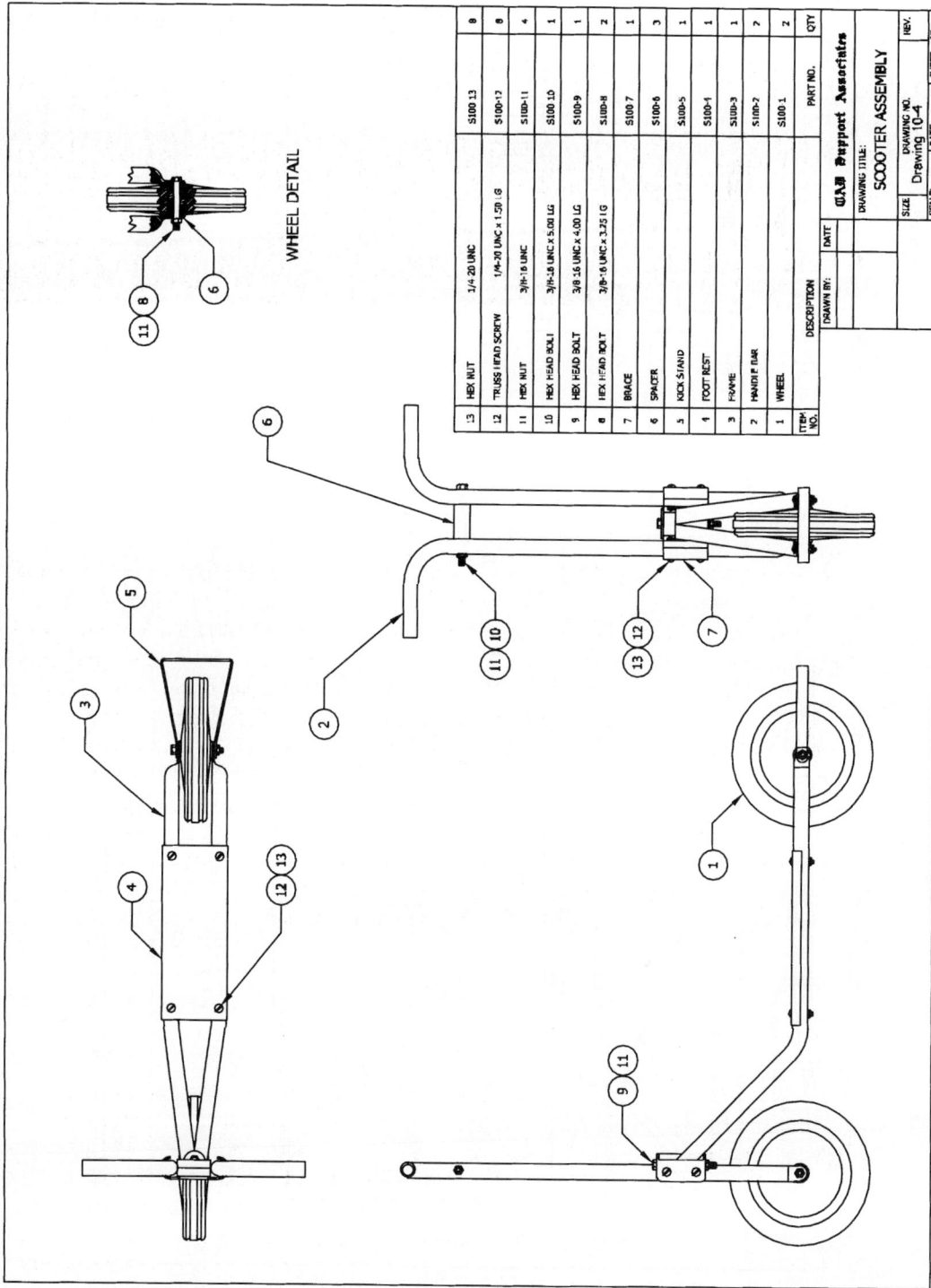

WHEEL DETAIL

ITEM NO.	DESCRIPTION		PART NO.	QTY
13	HEX NUT	1/4-20 UNC	S100-13	8
12	TRUSS HEAD SCREW	1/4-20 UNC x 1.50 LG	S100-12	8
11	HEX NUT	3/8-16 UNC	S100-11	4
10	HEX HEAD BOLT	3/8-16 UNC x 5.00 LG	S100-10	1
9	HEX HEAD BOLT	3/8-16 UNC x 4.00 LG	S100-9	1
8	HEX HEAD BOLT	3/8-16 UNC x 3.25 LG	S100-8	2
7	BRACE		S100-7	1
6	SPACER		S100-6	3
5	KICK STAND		S100-5	1
4	FOOT REST		S100-4	1
3	FRAME		S100-3	1
2	HANDLE BAR		S100-2	2
1	WHEEL		S100-1	2

WAB Support Associates

DRAWING TITLE: SCOOTER ASSEMBLY

DRAWING NO. Drawing 10-4

REV.

SIZE SHEET OF

SCALE: DATE:

DRAWN BY: DATE

PART III

ISOMETRIC DRAWING AND THREE-DIMENSIONAL MODELING

11 Isometric Drawing

COMMANDS

ELLIPSE   SNAP (isometric)   VIEW

OVERVIEW

Part III of this book will take you in a whole new direction. You will begin to use the AutoCAD drawing area in new ways to represent isometric and 3D spaces. Everything you know about two-dimensional drafting will translate and possibilities will expand as the familiar grid and snap are turned and rotated to define new coordinate systems. We will begin with simple two-dimensional isometric drawing and then move on to true three-dimensional modeling.

Learning to use AutoCAD's isometric drawing features should be a pleasure at this point. There are very few new commands to learn, and anything you know about manual isometric drawing will be easier on the computer. Once you know how to get into the isometric mode and to change from plane to plane, you will be able to rely on previously learned skills and techniques. Many of the commands you have learned will work readily and you will find that using the isometric drawing planes is an excellent warmup for 3D wireframe drawing, which is the topic of Chapter 12.

TASKS

11.1   Using Isometric SNAP

GENERAL PROCEDURE

1. Right Click on SNAP or GRID on the status bar.
2. Select Settings....
3. In the Drafting Settings dialog box, select the Isometric snap radio button.
4. Click OK.

To begin drawing isometrically you need to switch to the isometric snap style. You will find the grid and cross hairs behaving in ways that may seem odd at first, but you will quickly get used to them.

⊕   Right click on the SNAP or GRID button on the status bar.

⊕   Select Settings... from the short cut menu.

    You will see the Drafting Settings dialog box. Remember, you can also open this dialog by typing "ds" or selecting Drafting Settings... from the Tools menu.

⊕   Click the Isometric snap radio button in the Snap type & style panel.

⊕   Click OK.

    At this point your grid and cross hairs will be reoriented so that they resemble Figure 11-1. This is the isometric grid. Grid points are placed at 30-, 90-, and 150-degree angles from the horizontal. The cross hairs are initially turned to define the left isometric plane. The three isoplanes will be discussed in Task 11.2.

⊕   To get a feeling for how this snap style works, enter the LINE command and draw some boxes, as shown in Figure 11-2.

    Make sure that ortho is off and snap is on, or you will be unable to draw the lines shown.

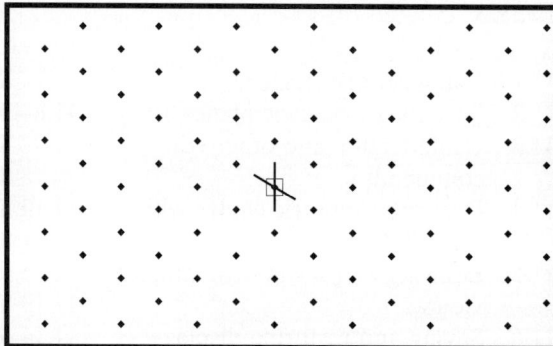

Figure 11-1

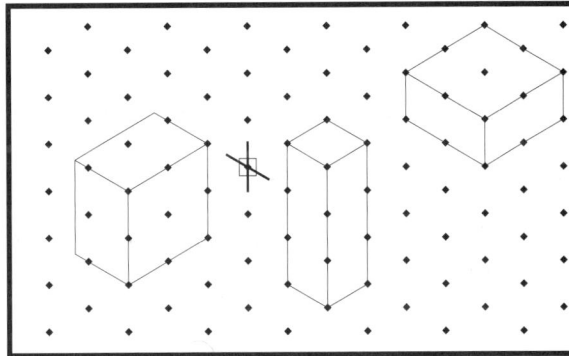

Figure 11-2

11.2   Switching Isometric Planes

GENERAL PROCEDURE

1. Press Ctrl-E or F5 once to switch to the "top" plane.
2. Press Ctrl-E or F5 again to switch to the "right" plane.
3. Press Ctrl-E or F5 again to return to the "left" plane.

If you tried to draw the boxes in Task 11.1 with ortho on, you have discovered that it is impossible. Without changing the orientation of the cross hairs, you can draw in only one of the three isometric planes. We need to be able to switch planes so that we can leave ortho on for accuracy and speed. There are several ways to do this, but the simplest, quickest, and most convenient way is to use F5 or Ctrl-E.

Before beginning, take a look at Figure 11-3. It shows the three planes of a standard isometric drawing. These planes are often referred to as top, front, and right. However, AutoCAD's terminology is top, left, and right. We will stick with Auto-CAD's labels in this book.

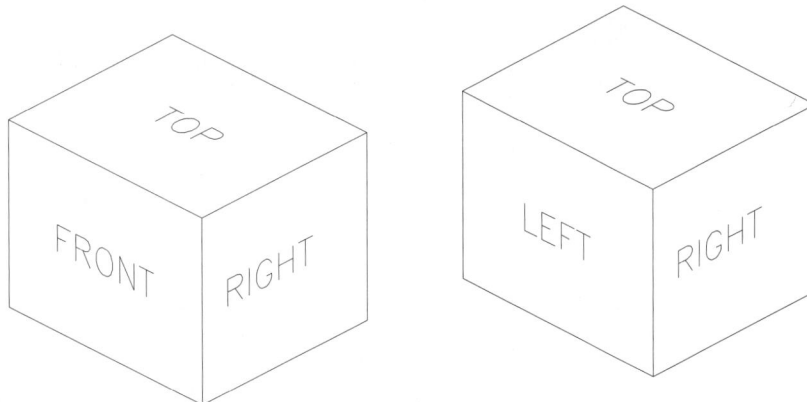

Figure 11-3

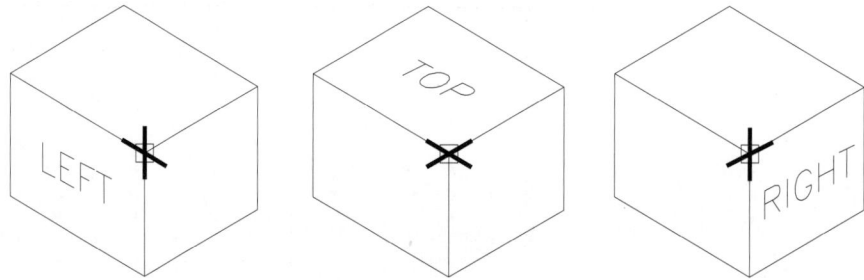

Figure 11-4

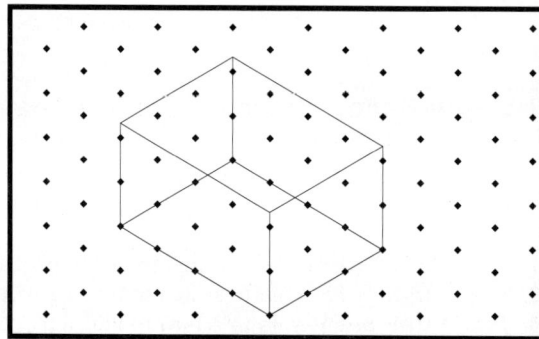

Figure 11-5

Now look at Figure 11-4 and you will see how the isometric cross hairs are oriented to draw in each of the planes.

⊕ Press F5 to switch from "left" to "top."
⊕ Press F5 again to switch from "top" to "right."
⊕ Press F5 once more to switch back to "left."
⊕ Now turn ortho on and draw a box outline like the one in Figure 11-5.
   You will need to switch planes several times to accomplish this. Notice that you can switch planes using F5 without interrupting the LINE command. If you find that you are in the wrong plane to construct a line, switch planes. Since every plane allows movement in two of the three directions, you will always be able to move in the direction you want with one switch. However, you may not be able to hit the snap point you want. If you cannot, switch planes again.

11.3 Using COPY and Other Edit Commands

Most commands work in the isometric planes just as they do in standard orthographic views. In this exercise we will construct an isometric view of a bracket using the LINE, COPY, and ERASE commands. Then we will draw angled corners using CHAMFER. In the next task we will draw a hole in the bracket with ELLIPSE, COPY, and TRIM.

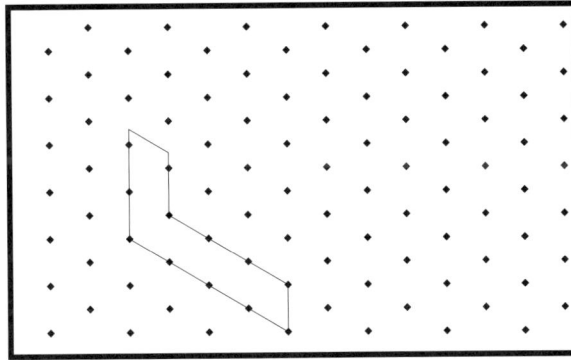

Figure 11-6

⊕ To begin this exercise, clear your screen of boxes and check to see that ortho is on.

⊕ Draw the L-shaped object shown in Figure 11-6.

Notice that this is drawn in the left isoplane and that it is 1.00 unit wide.

Next, we will copy this object 4.00 units back to the right to create the back surface of the bracket.

⊕ Select the Copy Object tool from the Modify toolbar.

⊕ Use a window or crossing box to select all the lines in the L.

⊕ Right click to end object selection.

⊕ Pick a base point at the inside corner of the L.

It is a good exercise to turn ortho on, switch planes, and move the object around in each plane. You will see that you can move in two directions in each plane and that in order to move the object back to the right, as shown in Figure 11-7, you must be in either the top or the right plane.

⊕ Pick a second point of displacement four units back to the right, as shown in Figure 11-7.

⊕ Enter the LINE command and draw the connecting lines in the right plane, as shown in Figure 11-8.

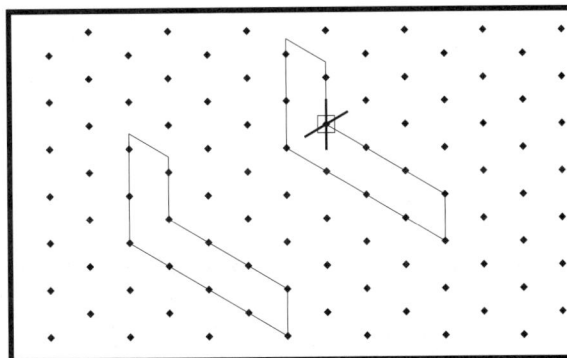

Figure 11-7

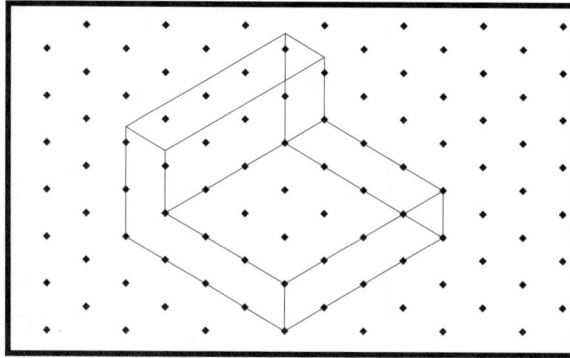

Figure 11-8

If you wish, you can draw only one of the lines and use the COPY command with the multiple option to create the others.

Creating Chamfers in an Isometric View

Keep in mind that angular lines in an isometric view do not show true lengths. Angular lines must be drawn between end points located along paths that are vertical or horizontal in one of the three drawing planes. In our exercise we will create angled lines by using the CHAMFER command to cut the corners of the bracket. This will be no different from using CHAMFER in orthographic views.

⊕ Select Chamfer from the Modify menu or the Chamfer tool from the Modify toolbar.

⊕ Type "d".

AutoCAD will prompt for a first chamfer distance.

⊕ Type "1".

⊕ Press Enter to accept 1.00 as the second chamfer distance.

⊕ Repeat the CHAMFER command.

⊕ Pick two edges of the bracket to create a chamfer, as shown in Figure 11-9.

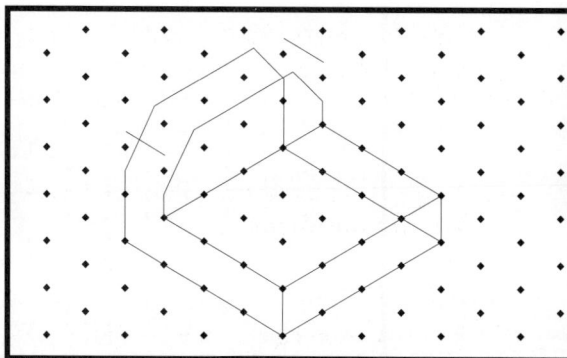

Figure 11-9

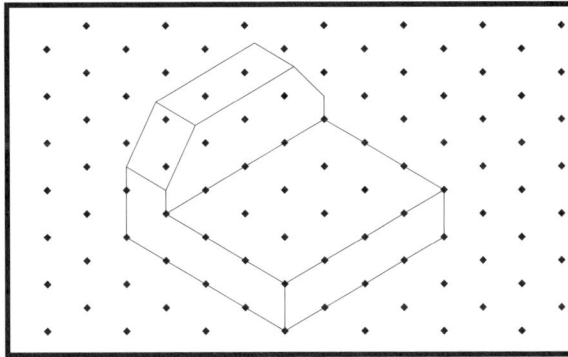

Figure 11-10

⊕ Repeat CHAMFER.

Chamfer the other three corners so that your drawing resembles Figure 11-9.

⊕ ERASE the two small lines left hanging at the previous corners.

⊕ To complete the bracket, enter the LINE command and draw lines between the new chamfer end points.

⊕ Finally, ERASE the two unseen lines on the back surface to produce Figure 11-10.

11.4   Drawing Isometric Circles with ELLIPSE

GENERAL PROCEDURE

1. Locate the center point of the isometric circle.
2. Select the Ellipse tool from the Draw toolbar.
3. Type "I".
4. Pick the center point.
5. Type or show the radius or diameter.

The ELLIPSE command can be used to draw true ellipses in orthographic views or ellipses that appear to be circles in isometric views (called "isocircles" in AutoCAD). In this task we will use the latter capability to construct a hole in the bracket.

⊕ To begin this task you should have the bracket shown in Figure 11-10 on your display.

The first thing you will need in order to draw an isocircle is a center point. Often it will be necessary to locate this point carefully using temporary lines, object snap tracking, or point filters (Chapter 12). You must be sure that you can locate the center point before entering the ELLIPSE command.

In our case it will be easy since the center point will be on a snap point.

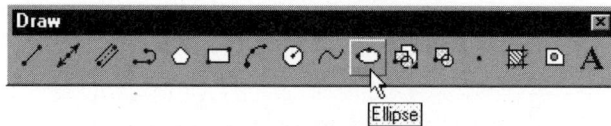

Figure 11-11

⊕ Select Ellipse from the Draw menu, or select the Ellipse tool from the Draw toolbar, as shown in Figure 11-11.

AutoCAD will prompt

Specify axis endpoint of ellipse or [Arc/Center/Isocircle]:

The option we want is "Isocircle". We will ignore the others for the time being.

⊕ Type "i".

AutoCAD prompts

Specify center of isocircle:

If you could not locate the center point, you would have to exit the command now and start over.

⊕ Use the snap and grid to pick the center of the surface, as shown in Figure 11-12.

AutoCAD gives you an isocircle to drag, as in the CIRCLE command. The isocircle you see will depend on the isoplane you are in. To understand this try switching planes to see how the image changes.

⊕ Stretch the isocircle image out and then press F5 to switch isoplanes. Observe the isocircle. Try this two or three times.

⊕ Switch to the top isoplane before moving on.

AutoCAD is prompting for a radius or diameter:

Specify radius of isocircle or [Diameter]:

A radius specification is the default here, as it is in the CIRCLE command.

⊕ Type a value or pick a point so that your isocircle resembles the one in Figure 11-12.

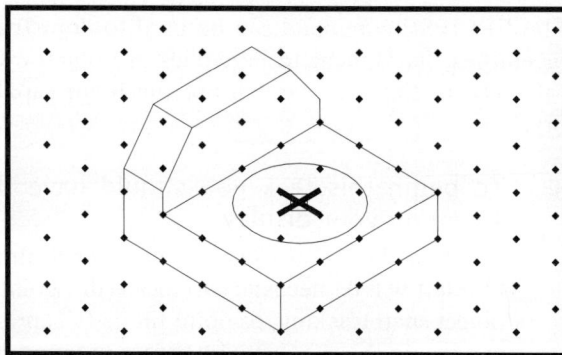

Figure 11-12

Next, we use the COPY and TRIM commands to create the bottom of the hole.

⊕ Select the Copy Object tool from the Modify toolbar.

⊕ Select the isocircle by pointing, or type "l" for "last".

⊕ Right click to end object selection.

⊕ Pick a base point.

Any point could be used as the base point. A good choice would be the top of the front corner. If you do this, then choosing the bottom of the front corner as a second point will give you the exact thickness of the bracket.

⊕ Pick a second point 1.00 unit below the base point.

Your screen should now resemble Figure 11-13. The last thing we must do is TRIM the hidden portion of the bottom of the hole.

⊕ Select the Trim tool from the Modify toolbar.

⊕ Pick the first isocircle as a cutting edge.

⊕ Press Enter to end cutting edge selection.

⊕ Select the hidden section of the lower isocircle.

⊕ Press Enter to exit TRIM.

The bracket is now complete and your screen should resemble Figure 11-14.

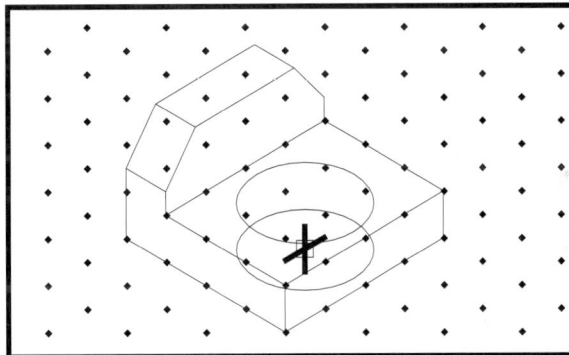

Figure 11-13

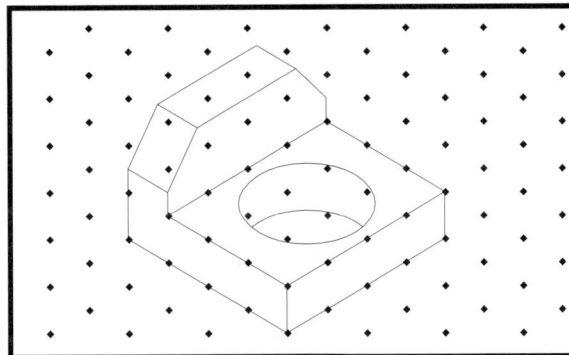

Figure 11-14

Note: Sometimes you will not get the results you expect when using TRIM in an isometric view. It may be necessary to use BREAK and ERASE as an alternative.

This completes the present discussion of isometric drawing. You will find more in the drawing suggestions at the end of this chapter.

Now we will go on to explore the nonisometric use of the ELLIPSE command and then to show you the VIEW command for saving named views in a drawing.

11.5 Drawing Ellipses in Orthographic Views

GENERAL PROCEDURE

1. Select the Ellipse tool from the Draw toolbar.
2. Pick one end point of an axis.
3. Pick the second end point.
4. Pick a third point showing the length of the other axis.

The ELLIPSE command is important for drawing isocircles but also for drawing true ellipses in orthographic views. There is also an option to create elliptical arcs.

An ellipse is determined by a center point and two mutually perpendicular axes of differing lengths. In AutoCAD, these specifications can be shown in two nearly identical ways, each requiring you to show three points (see Figure 11-15). In the default method you will show two end points of an axis and then show half the length of the other axis, from the midpoint of the first axis out (the midpoint of an axis is also the center of the ellipse). The other method allows you to pick the center point of the ellipse first, then the end point of one axis, followed by half the length of the other axis.

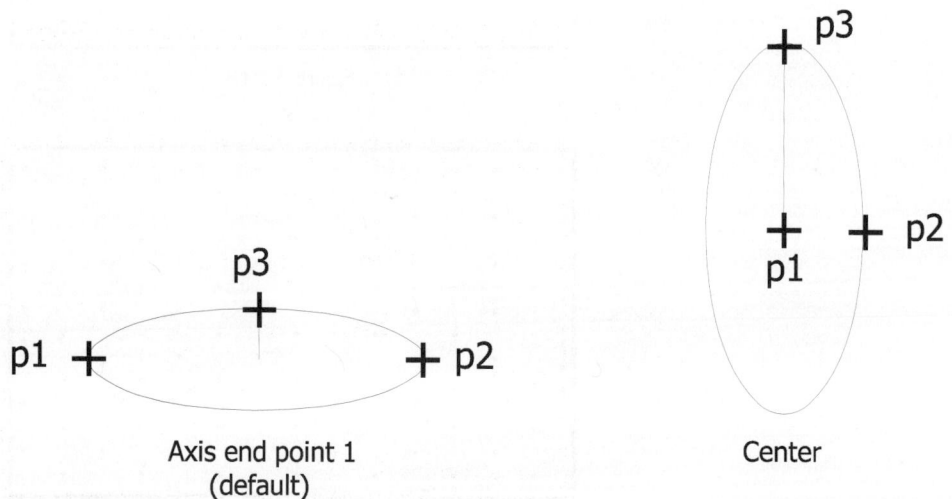

Axis end point 1
(default)

Center

Figure 11-15

⊕ In preparation for this exercise, return to the standard snap mode using the following procedure:

1. Right click on SNAP or GRID and open the Drafting Settings dialog box from the short cut menu.
2. Click the Rectangular snap radio button.
3. Click OK.

You will see that your grid is returned to the standard pattern and the cross hairs are horizontal and vertical again. Notice that this does not affect the isometric bracket you have just drawn.

We will briefly explore the ELLIPSE command and draw some standard ellipses.

⊕ Select the Ellipse tool from the Draw toolbar or Ellipse from the Draw menu.

AutoCAD prompts

```
Specify axis endpoint of ellipse or [Arc/Center]:
```

⊕ Pick an axis end point, as shown by p1 on the ellipse at the lower left in Figure 11-16.

AutoCAD prompts for the other end point:

```
Specify other endpoint of axis:
```

⊕ Pick a second end point as shown by p2.

AutoCAD gives you an ellipse to drag and a rubber band so that you can show the length of the other axis. Only the length of the rubber band is significant; the angle is already determined to be perpendicular to the first axis. Because of this the third point will only fall on the ellipse if the rubber band happens to be exactly perpendicular to the first axis.

The prompt that follows allows you to show the second axis distance as before, or a rotation around the first axis:

```
Specify distance to other axis or [Rotation]:
```

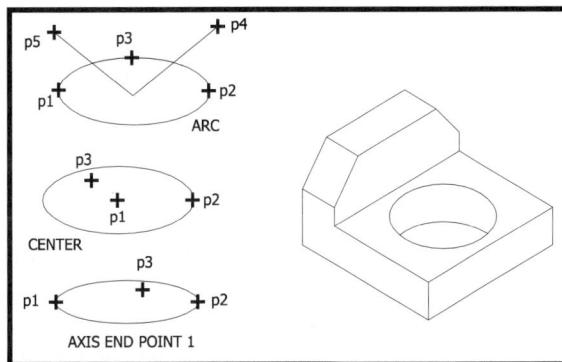

Figure 11-16

The rotation option is awkward to use, and we will not explore it here; see the AutoCAD Command Reference for more information.

⊕ Pick p3 as shown.

This point will show half the length of the other axis.

The first ellipse should now be complete. Now we will draw one showing the center point first.

⊕ Repeat the ELLIPSE command.

⊕ At the first prompt, type "c" for Center.

AutoCAD will give you a prompt for a center point:

Specify center of ellipse:

⊕ Pick a center point, as shown by p1 at the middle left of Figure 11-16.

Now you will have a rubber band stretching from the center to the end of an axis and the following prompt:

Specify endpoint of axis:

⊕ Pick an end point, as shown by p2 in Figure 11-16.

The prompt that follows allows you to show the second axis distance as before, or a rotation around the first axis:

Specify distance to other axis or [Rotation]:

⊕ Pick an axis distance, as shown by p3.

Here again the rubber band is significant for distance only. The point you pick will fall on the ellipse only if the rubber band is stretched perpendicular to the first axis. Notice that it is not so in Figure 11-16.

Drawing Elliptical Arcs

Elliptical arcs can be drawn by trimming complete ellipses or by using the arc option of the ELLIPSE command. Using the arc option, you will first construct an ellipse in one of the two methods shown previously and then show the arc of that ellipse that you want to keep. Determining arcs can be quite complicated because of the many different parameters available. You will remember this from Chapter 5, in which you learned the arc command. In this exercise we will stick to a simple procedure; you should have no difficulty pursuing the more complex options on your own.

⊕ Enter the ELLIPSE command.

⊕ Pick a first axis end point, as shown by p1 at the upper left in Figure 11-16.

⊕ Pick a second end point, p2 in the figure.

⊕ Pick p3 to show the second axis distance.

AutoCAD will draw an ellipse as you have specified, but the image is only temporary. Now you need to show the arc you want drawn. The two options are "Parameter" and "start angle". Parameter will take you into more options that allow you to specify your arc in different ways, similar to the options of the ARC command. We will stick with the default option.

⊕ Pick p4 to show the angle at which the elliptical arc will begin.
Move the cursor slowly now and you will see all the arcs that are possible starting from this angle.

⊕ Pick p5 to indicate the end angle and complete the command.

11.6 Saving and Restoring Displays with VIEW

GENERAL PROCEDURE

1. Select the Named Views tool from the Standard toolbar.
2. Select New to create a new view.
3. Type a view name.
4. Click on Define Window.
5. Select points.
6. Click OK.
7. Click OK.

The word "view" in connection with the VIEW command has a special significance in AutoCAD. It refers to any set of display boundaries that have been named and saved using the VIEW command. It also refers to a defined 3D viewpoint that has been saved with a name. Views that have been saved can be restored rapidly and by direct reference rather than by redefining the location, size, or viewpoint of the area to be displayed. VIEW can be useful in creating drawing layouts and anytime you know that you will be returning frequently to a certain area of a large drawing. It saves having to zoom out to look at the complete drawing and then zoom back in again on the area you want. It can also save the time required in creating a 3D viewpoint. In this chapter we will use 2D views only. In the next we will introduce 3D viewpoints.

Imagine that we have to do some extensive detail work on the area around the hole in the bracket and also on the top corner. We can define each of these as a view and jump back and forth at will.

⊕ To begin this exercise, you should have the bracket on your screen, as shown in Figure 11-17.

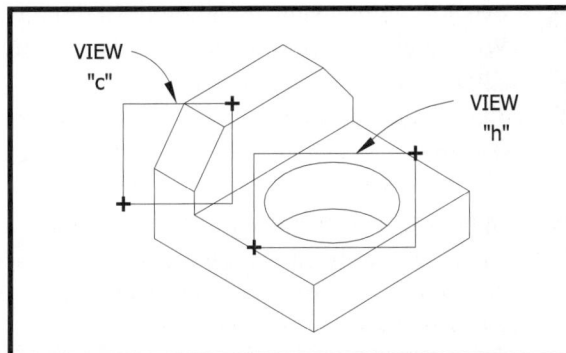

Figure 11-17

Figure 11-18

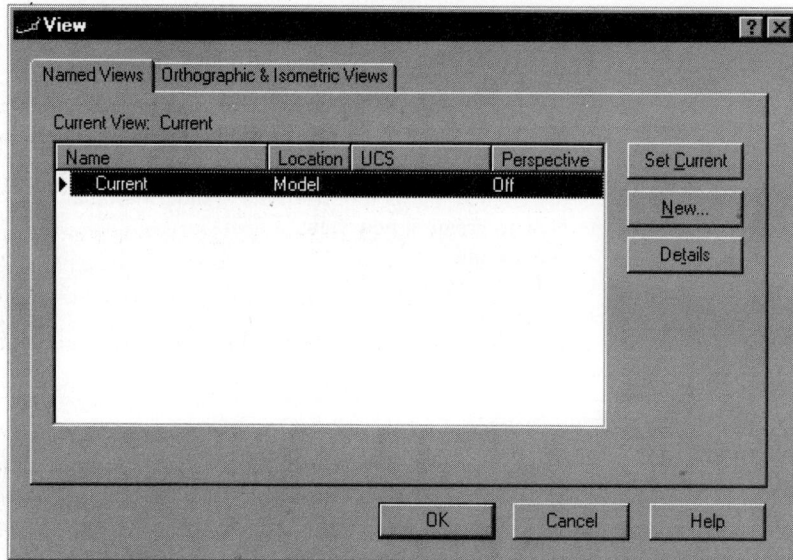

Figure 11-19

✛ Select the Named Views tool from the Standard toolbar, as shown in Figure 11-18.

This opens the View dialog box shown in Figure 11-19. There are two tabs, one for Named views and one for Orthographic and Isometric views. "Isometric" here refers to certain standard 3D viewpoints, not to the 2D isometric drawing that we are exploring in this chapter. We will introduce these 3D viewpoints in the next chapter. In this chapter we will use only the Named Views tab.

✛ If necessary, select the Named Views tab.

The first thing we need to do is define some views. Then we will see how to switch from one view to another. The first view to define is the current view. We will give it a new name and save it so that we can return quickly.

✛ Click on New....

This takes you to the New View dialog box shown in Figure 11-20. Notice that the Current Display radio button is selected. All we have to do is give the current display a name in order to save it as a named view.

✛ Type "A" in the View name edit box.

Views are designed for speed, so it makes sense to assign them short names, unless you are defining many views and need them clearly identified with longer names.

✛ Click OK.

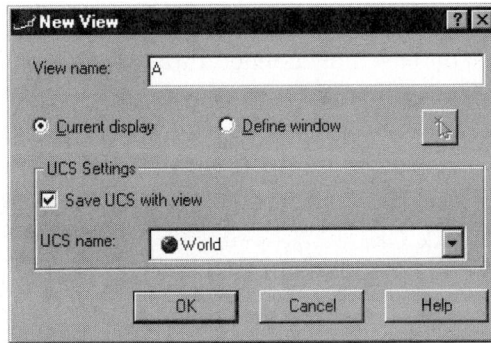

Figure 11-20

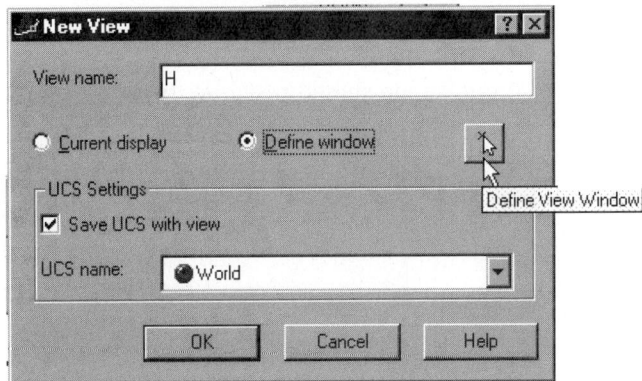

Figure 11-21

The View dialog box reappears, with "A" showing on the list of defined views. Next we will use a window to define a smaller view.

⊕ Click on "New..." to return to the New View dialog box.

⊕ Type "H" in the View name edit box.

⊕ Select the Define Window radio button.

Notice that several previously grayed out items are now accessible.

⊕ Click on the Define View Window icon, as shown in Figure 11-21.

The dialog box disappears, giving you access to the screen.

⊕ Pick first and second corners to define a window around the hole in the bracket, as shown previously in Figure 11-17.

⊕ Click OK.

You are now back in the View dialog box with A and H on the list of views. Define one more view to show the upper left corner of the bracket, as shown in Figure 11-17.

⊕ Click on New....

⊕ Type "C" for the view name.

⊕ Click the Define Window radio button.

⊕ Click the Define View Window icon.

⊕ Define a window, as shown in Figure 11-17.

⊕ Click OK.

You have now defined three views. To see the views in action we must set them as current.

⊕ Highlight "H" in the Named views list.

⊕ Click on the Set Current button.

Notice that the current view is listed above the Named view list.

⊕ Click OK.

Your screen should resemble Figure 11-22.

Now switch to the corner view.

⊕ Repeat the VIEW command.

⊕ Highlight "C".

⊕ Click on Set Current.

⊕ Click OK.

Your screen should resemble Figure 11-23.

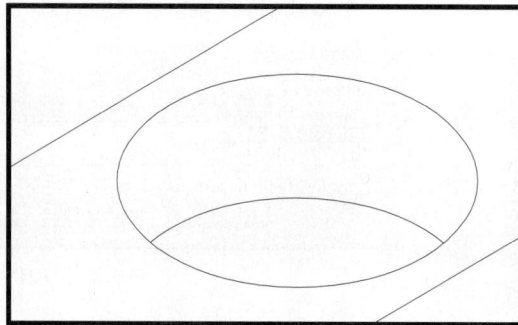

Figure 11-22

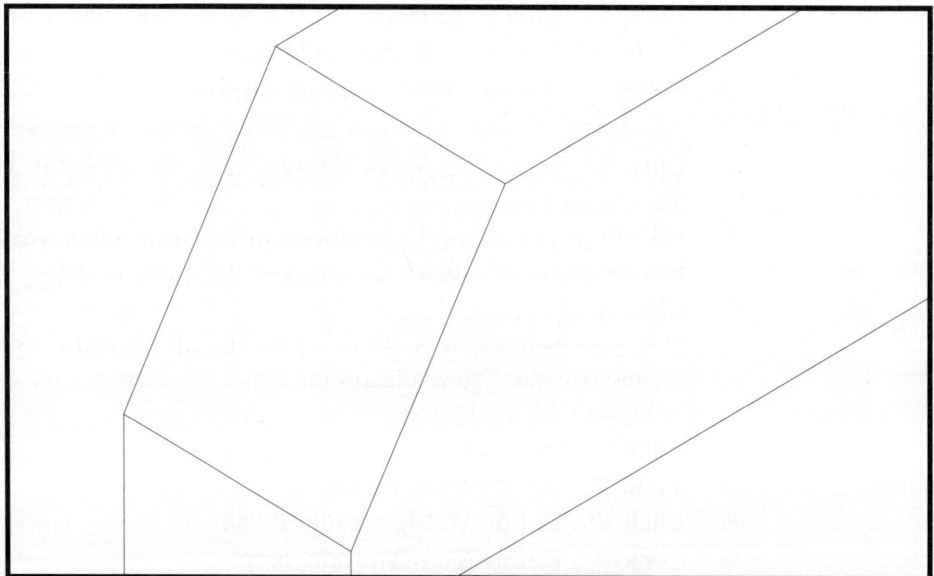

Figure 11-23

11.7   Review Material

Questions

1. What are the angles of the cross hairs and grid points in an isometric grid?
2. What function key is used to switch from one isometric plane to another?
3. What are the names for the isometric planes in AutoCAD?
4. What is an isocircle? Why are isocircles drawn in the ELLIPSE command?
5. How many different isocircles can you draw that have the same radius and the same center point?
6. How many points does it take to define an ellipse?
7. What do these points define in each of the two basic methods of drawing an orthographic ellipse?
8. What must you do before you can use the VIEW command to restore a view?
9. What are the two basic ways to define a view?
10. What tool do you use to enter the VIEW command, and where is the tool found? What is the name of the dialog box it calls?

Drawing Problems

1. Using the isometric grid, draw a 4-by-4 square in the right isoplane.
2. Copy the square back 4 units along the left isoplane.
3. Connect the corners of the two squares to form an isometric cube. Erase any lines that would be hidden in this object.
4. Use text rotation and obliquing to draw the word "Top" in the Top plane of the cube so that the text is centered on the face and aligned with its edges. The text should be 0.5 units high.
5. In a similar manner, draw the word "Left" at the center of the left side and the word "Right" at the center of the right side. All text should align with the face that it is on.

11.8   WWW Exercise #11 (Optional)

You are now ready for Chapter 11 of the companion Web site. So

⊕   Make sure that you are connected to your Internet service provider.
⊕   Type "browser", open the Web toolbar and select the Browse the Web tool, or open your system browser from the Windows 98 taskbar.
⊕   If necessary, navigate to our companion Web site at "www. prenhall.com/dixriley".

Good luck on the test.

11.9 Drawing 11-1: Mounting Bracket

This drawing is a direct extension of the exercises in the chapter. It will give you practice in basic AutoCAD isometrics and in transferring dimensions from orthographic to isometric views.

DRAWING SUGGESTIONS

- When the center point of an isocircle is not on snap, as in this drawing, you will need to create a specifiable point and snap onto it or use object snap and object snap tracking. For example, acquire the midpoints of the sides and then snap to the intersection of the two tracking lines.
- Often when you try to select a group of objects to copy, there will be many crossing lines that you do not want to include in the copy. This is an ideal time to use the "remove" option in object selection. First window the objects you want along with those nearby that are unavoidable, and then remove the unwanted objects one by one.
- Frequently you will get unexpected results when you try to TRIM an object in an isometric view. AutoCAD will divide an ellipse into a series of arcs, for example, and only trim a portion. If you do not get the results you want, use the BREAK command to control how the object is broken, and then erase what you do not want.
- There is no arc option when you use ELLIPSE to draw isocircles, so semicircles like those at the top and bottom of the slots must be constructed by first drawing isocircles and then trimming or erasing unwanted portions.
- Use COPY frequently to avoid duplicating your work. Since it may take a considerable amount of editing to create holes and fillets, do not COPY until edits have been done on the original.
- The row of small arcs that show the curve in the middle of the bracket are multiple copies of the fillet at the corner.

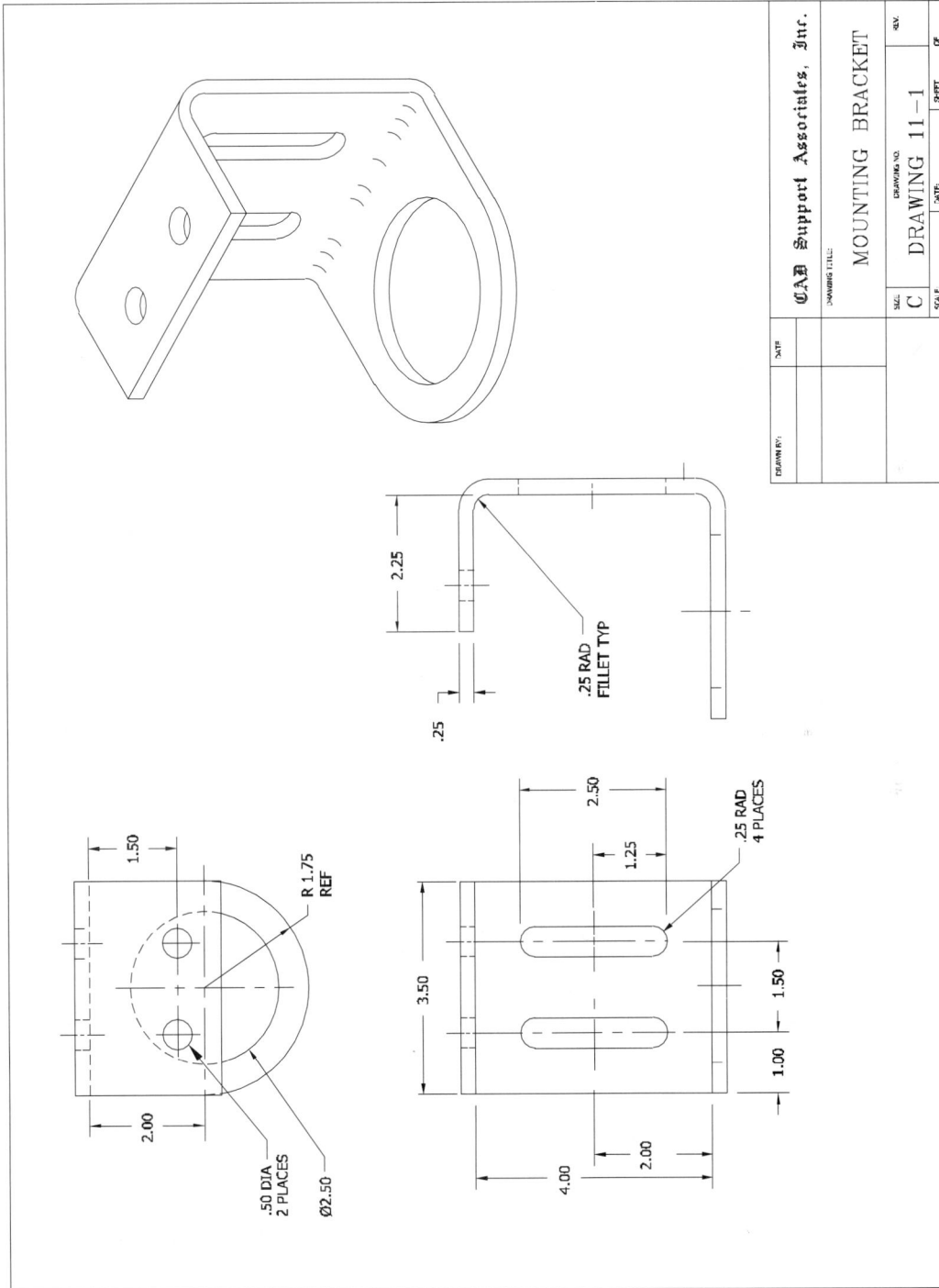

.50 DIA
2 PLACES

Ø2.50

R 1.75
REF

1.50

2.00

2.25

.25

.25 RAD
FILLET TYP

2.50

1.25

.25 RAD
4 PLACES

3.50

1.50

1.00

4.00

2.00

CAD Support Associates, Inc.

MOUNTING BRACKET

DRAWING 11-1

C

11.10 Drawing 11-2: Radio

This drawing introduces text and will be greatly simplified by the use of the rectangular ARRAY command. Placing objects on different layers so they can be turned on and off during TRIM, BREAK, and ERASE procedures will make things considerably less messy.

DRAWING SUGGESTIONS

- Use the "box method" to do this drawing. That is, begin with an isometric box according to the overall outside dimensions of the radio. Then go back and cut away the excess as you form the details of the drawing.
- The horizontal "grill" can be done with a rectangular array since it runs straight on the vertical. Look carefully at the pattern to see where it repeats. Draw one set and then array it. Later you can go back and trim away the dial and speaker areas.
- Draw isocircles over the grill and break away the lines over the speaker. When you are ready to hatch the speaker, draw another trimmed isocircle to define the hatch boundary, create the hatch, and then erase the boundary.
- The knobs are isocircles with copies to show thickness. You can use tangent-to-tangent osnaps to draw the front-to-back connecting lines.
- The text is created on two different angles that line up with the left and right isoplanes. We leave it to you to discover the correct angles.

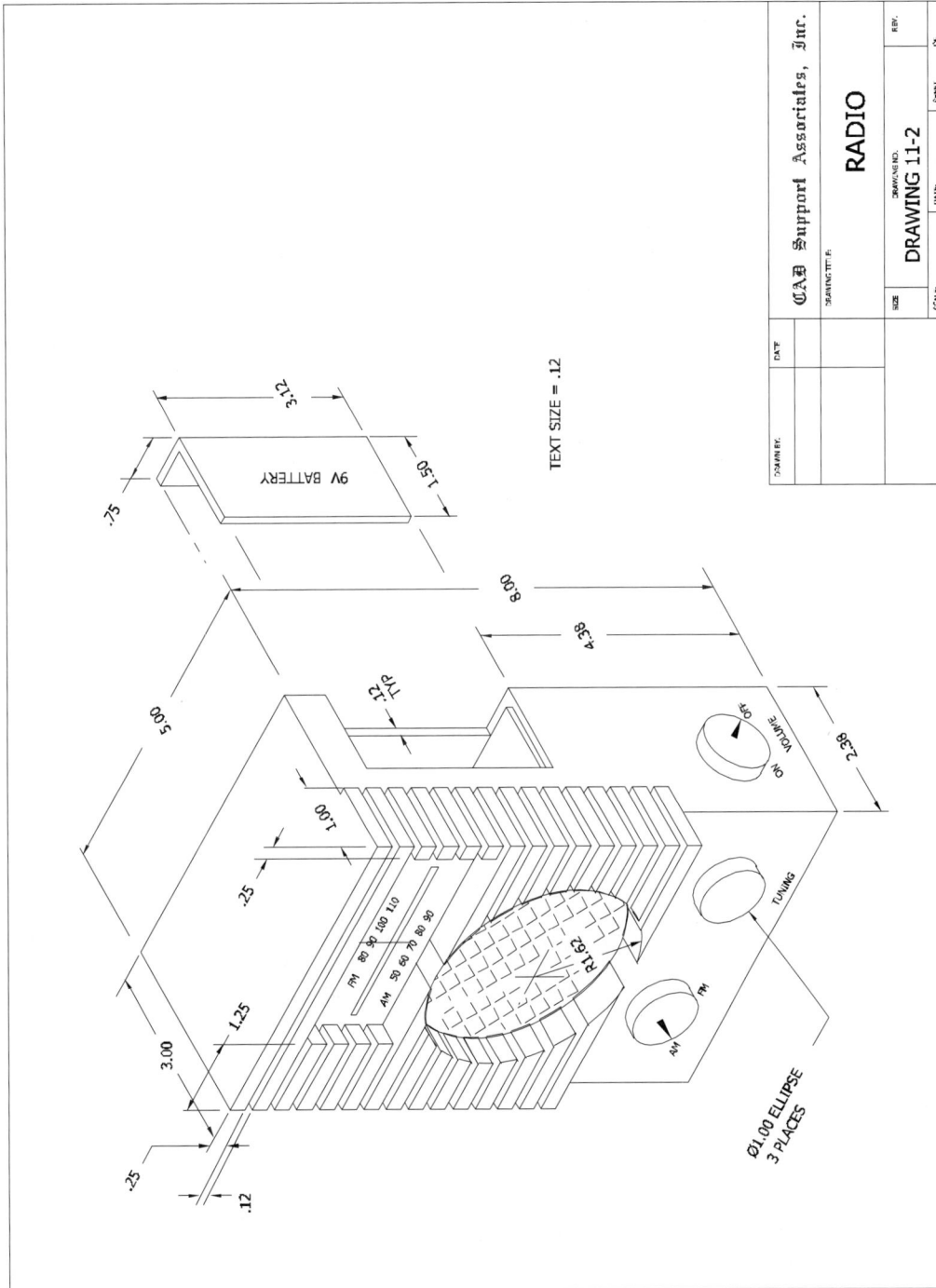

3.12

.75

9V BATTERY

1.50

TEXT SIZE = .12

8.00

4.38

.12 TYP

5.00

1.00

.25

FM 80 90 100 110

AM 50 60 70 80 90

R1.62

VOLUME

ON OFF

TUNING

FM

AM

Ø1.00 ELLIPSE
3 PLACES

2.38

1.25

3.00

.25

.12

CAD Support Associates, Inc.

DRAWING TITLE:

RADIO

REV.

DRAWING NO.

DRAWING 11-2

SHEET:

0

SIZE

DATE:

DRAWN BY:

DATE

SCALE:

11.11   Drawing 11-3: Fixture Assembly

This is a difficult drawing. It will take time and patience but will teach you a great deal about isometric drawing in AutoCAD.

DRAWING SUGGESTIONS

- This drawing can be done either by drawing everything in place as you see it, or by drawing the parts and moving them into place along the common center line that runs through the middle of all the items. If you use the former method, draw the center line first and use it to locate the center points of isocircles and as base points for other measures.
- As you go, look for pieces of objects that can be copied to form other objects. Avoid duplicating efforts by editing before copying. In particular, where one object covers part of another, be sure to copy it before you trim or erase the covered sections.
- To create the chamfered end of item 4, begin by drawing the 1.00 diameter cylinder 3.00 long with no chamfer. Then copy the isocircle at the end forward 0.125. The smaller isocircle is 0.875 (7/8), since 0.0625 (1/16) is cut away from the 1.00 circle all around. Draw this smaller isocircle and TRIM away everything that is hidden. Then draw the slanted chamfer lines using LINE, not CHAMFER. Use the same method for item 5.
- In both the screw and the nut you will need to create hexes around isocircles. Use the dimensions from a standard bolt chart.
- Use three-point arcs to approximate the curves on the screw bolt and the nut. You are after a representation that looks correct. It is impractical and unnecessary to achieve exact measures on these objects in the isometric view.

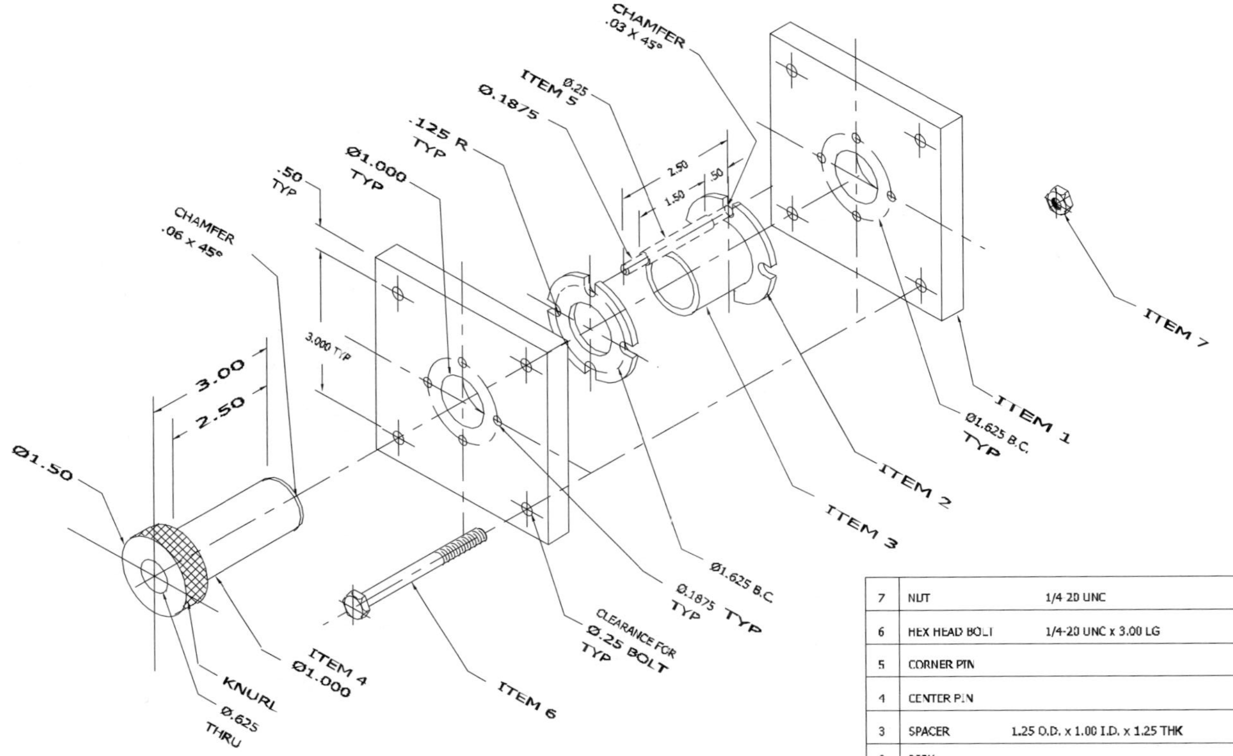

ITEM NO.	DESCRIPTION		PART NO.	QTY
7	NUT	1/4 20 UNC	F113 7	4
6	HEX HEAD BOLT	1/4-20 UNC x 3.00 LG	F113-6	4
5	CORNER PIN		F113-5	4
4	CENTER PIN		F113-4	1
3	SPACER	1.25 O.D. x 1.00 I.D. x 1.25 THK	F113-3	1
2	DISK	2.00 O.D. x 1.00 I.D. x .12 THK	F113-2	2
1	END PLATE	4.00 SQUARE x .50 THK	F113 1	2

TOLERANCE FOR HOLES AND PINS

ITEM 4 CLASS RC2 FIT
ITEM 5 CLASS LT4 FIT
ITEM 1 CLASS RC2 FIT FOR CENTER HOLE
ITEM 1 CLASS LT4 FIT FOR CORNER PIN HOLES
ITEM 2 CLASS RC2 FIT FOR CENTER HOLE
ITEM 2 CLASS RC1 FIT FOR CORNER PIN HOLES
ITEM 3 CLASS RC2 FIT FOR CENTER HOLE

CAD Support Associates, Inc.

DRAWING TITLE: FIXTURE ASSEMBLY

SIZE: D DRAWING NO.: DRAWING 11-3

11.12   Drawing 11-4: Flanged Coupling

The isometric view in this three-view drawing must be done working off the center line.

DRAWING SUGGESTIONS

- Draw the major center line first. Then draw vertical center lines at every point where an isocircle will be drawn. Make sure to draw these lines extra long so that they can be used to trim the isocircles in half. By starting at the back of the object and working forward, you can take dimensions directly from the right side view.
- Draw the isocircles at each center line and then trim them to represent semicircles.
- Use end point, intersection, and tangent to tangent osnaps to draw horizontal lines.
- Trim away all obstructed lines and parts of isocircles.
- Draw the four slanted lines in the middle as vertical lines first. Then, with ortho off, CHANGE their end points, moving them in 0.125.
- Remember, MIRROR will not work in the isometric view, although it can be used effectively in the right side view.
- Use BHATCH to create the cross hatching.
- If you have made a mistake in measuring along the major center line, STRETCH can be used to correct it. Make sure that ortho is on and that you are in an isoplane that lets you move the way you want.

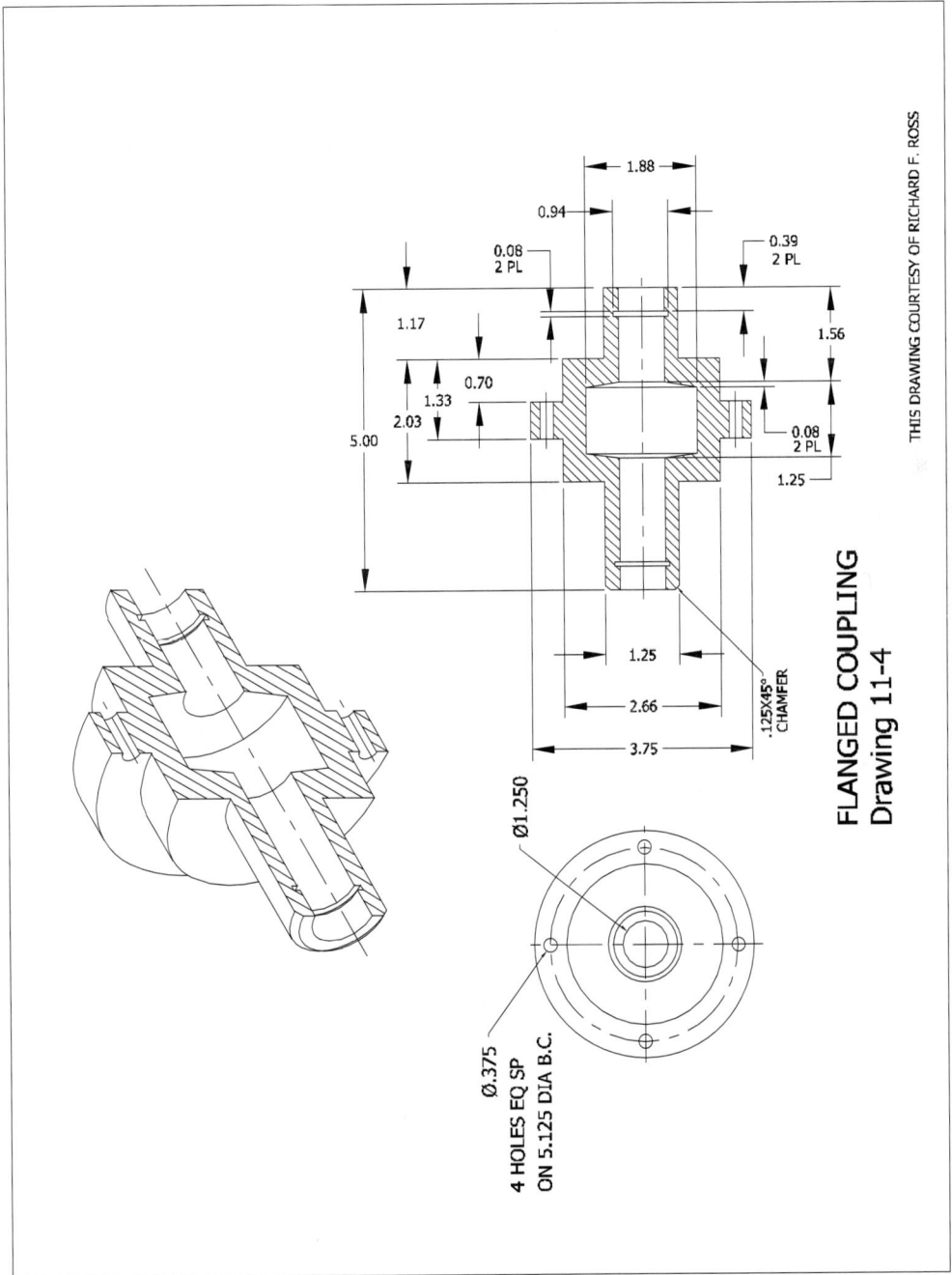

THIS DRAWING COURTESY OF RICHARD F. ROSS

FLANGED COUPLING
Drawing 11-4

11.13 Drawing 11-5: Garage Framing

This is a fairly complex drawing that will take lots of trimming and careful work. Changing the "snapang" (snap angle) variable so that you can draw slanted arrays is a method that can be used frequently in isometric drawing.

DRAWING SUGGESTIONS

- You will find yourself using COPY, ZOOM, and TRIM a great deal. OFFSET also will work well.
- You may want to create some new layers with different colors. Keeping different parts of the construction walls, rafters, and joists on different layers will allow you to have more control over them and add a lot of clarity to what you see on the screen. Turning layers on and off can considerably simplify trimming operations.
- You can cut down on repetition in this drawing by using arrays on various angles. For example, if the snapang variable is set to 150 degrees, the 22′ wall in the left isoplane can be created as a rectangular array of studs with 1 row and 17 columns set 16 inches apart. To do so, follow this procedure:
  1. Type "snapang".
  2. Enter a new value so that rectangular arrays will be built on isometric angles (30 or 150).
  3. Enter the ARRAY command and create the array. Use negative values where necessary.
  4. Trim the opening for the window.

- One alternative to this array method is to set your snap to 16″ temporarily and use multiple COPY to create the columns of studs, rafters, and joists. Another alternative is to use the grip edit offset snap method beginning with an offset snap of 16″ (i.e., press Shift when you show the first copy displacement and continue to hold down Shift as you make other copies).
- The cutaway in the roof that shows the joists and the back door is drawn using the standard nonisometric ELLIPSE command. Then the rafters are trimmed to the ellipse and the ellipse is erased. Do this procedure before you draw the joists and the back wall. Otherwise you will be trimming these as well.
- Use CHAMFER to create the chamfered corners on the joists.

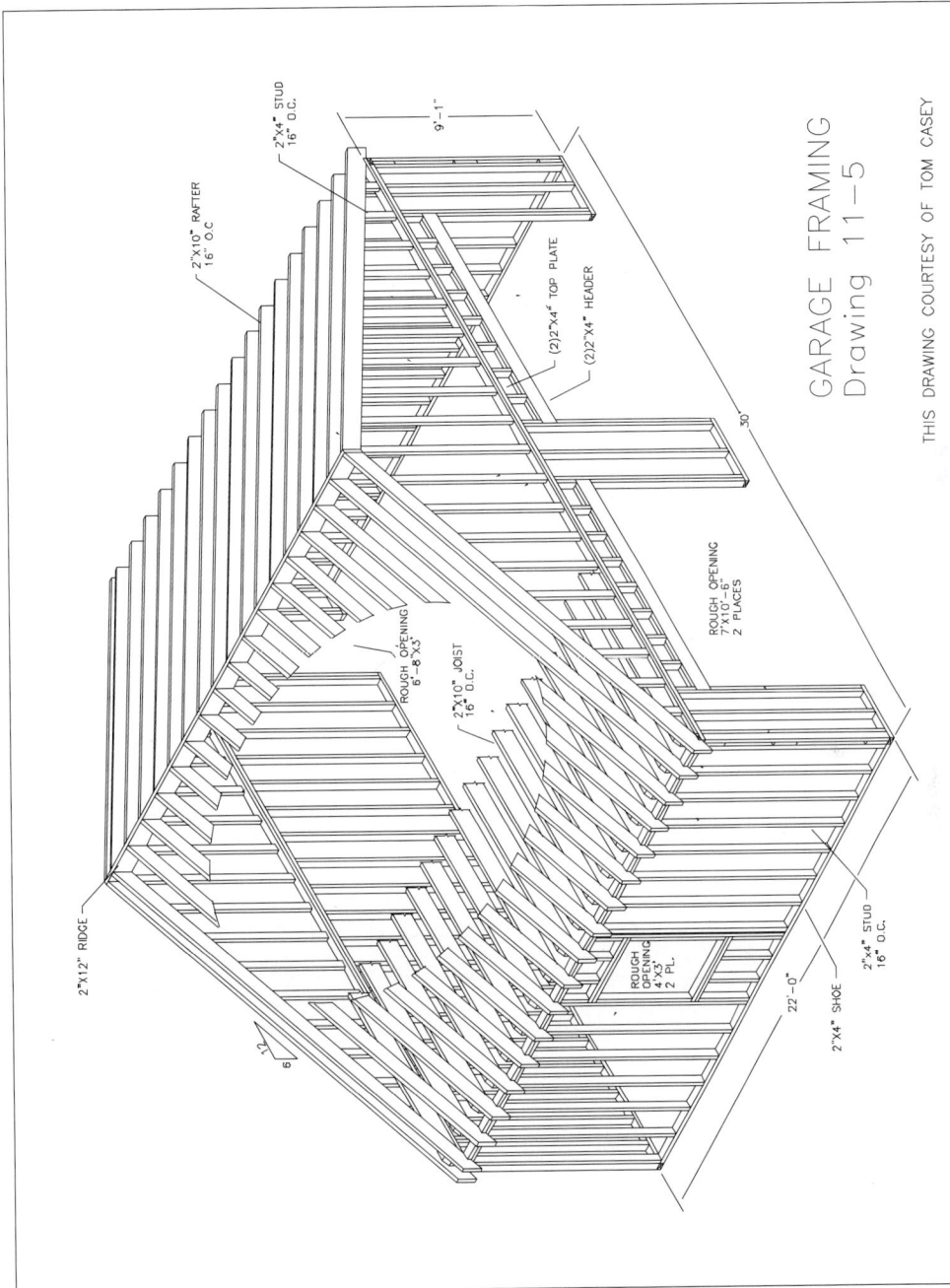

GARAGE FRAMING
Drawing 11-5

THIS DRAWING COURTESY OF TOM CASEY

2"X4" STUD
16" O.C.

2"X10" RAFTER
16" O.C

9'-1"

(2)2"X4" TOP PLATE

(2)2"X4" HEADER

30

ROUGH OPENING
7'X10'-6"
2 PLACES

ROUGH OPENING
6'-8"X3'

2"X10" JOIST
16" O.C.

2"X12" RIDGE

12
6

ROUGH
OPENING
4'X3'
2 PL.

22'-0"

2"X4" STUD
16" O.C.

2"X4" SHOE

11.14   Drawing 11-6: Cast Iron Tee

The objective of this exercise is to complete the isometric view of the tee using dimensions from the three-view drawing. Begin this isometric by working off the center line.

DRAWING SUGGESTIONS

- Be sure that ortho is on and that you are in an isoplane that is correct for the lines you want to draw. Take full advantage of object snap as you lay out this drawing.
- Draw the two major center lines as shown in isometric first. Draw them to exact length. Then draw vertical center lines at every point where an isocircle will be drawn. These center lines should be drawn longer so the isocircles will trim more easily. You will notice that OFFSET and MIRROR will not work very well in the isometric mode.
- After establishing the centers, draw the isocircles for the three flanges.
- When you have completed the flanges, draw the isocircles for the wall of the tee.
- Draw all horizontal and vertical lines and trim away all nonvisible lines and parts of isocircles. Fillet the required intersections.
- After completing the outline of the tee, use BHATCH to create the cross hatching.

5 1/2

9/16 DRILL
12 HOLES

2 1/2

7

11/16

4 3/8

7/16

7 1/2   6   3

4 1/2

7/16

3/4   3/4

9

FILLET &
ROUNDS 1/8 R

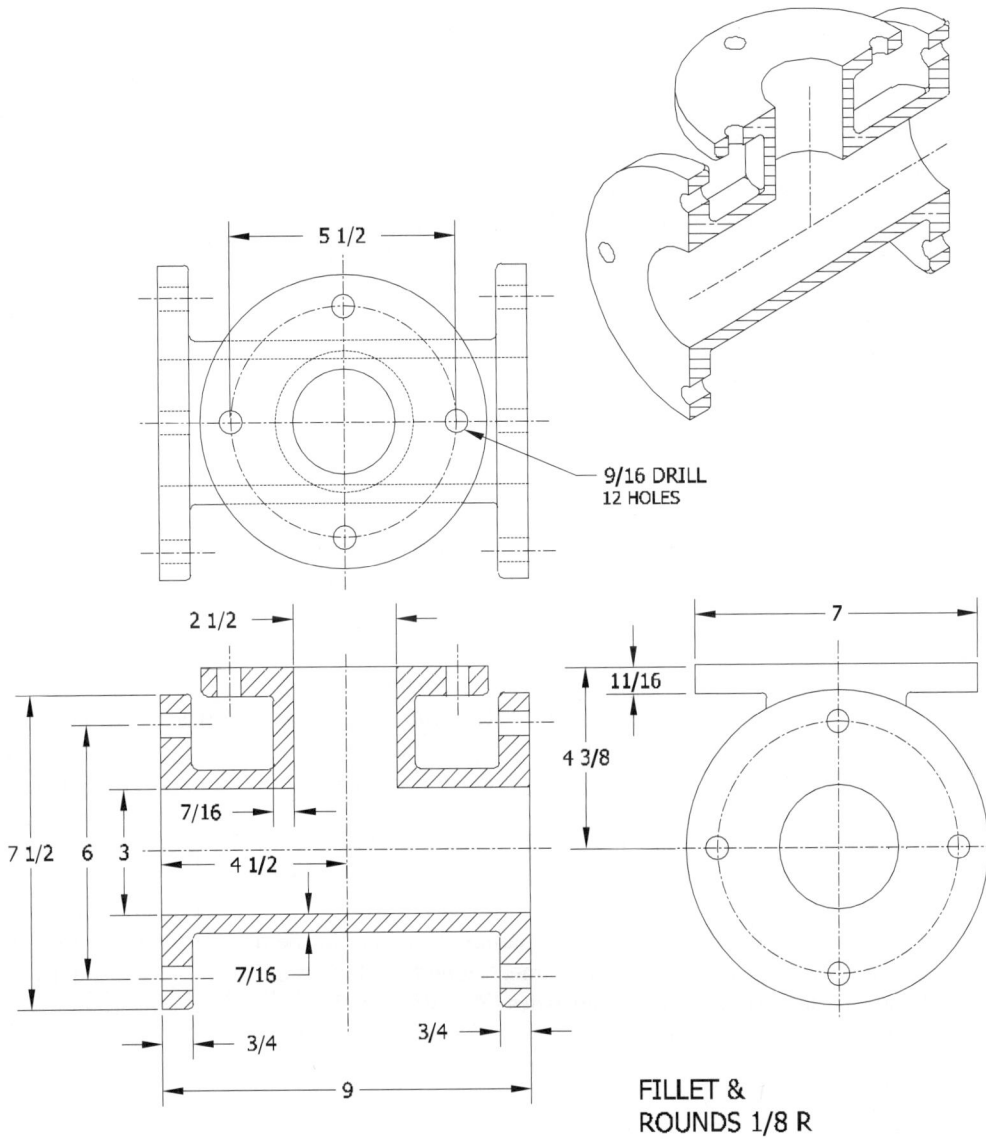

3" CAST IORN TEE
Drawing 11-6

12 Wireframe Models

COMMANDS

RULESURF   UCS   UCSICON   VPOINT

OVERVIEW

It is now time to begin thinking in three dimensions. 3D drawing in AutoCAD is logical and efficient. You can create wireframe models, surface models, or solid models and display them from multiple points of view. In this chapter we will focus on User Coordinate Systems, 3D viewpoints, and wireframe modeling. These are the primary tools you will need to understand how AutoCAD allows you to work in three dimensions on a two-dimensional screen. Tasks 12.1 through 12.5 will take you through a complete 3D wireframe modeling exercise using four different coordinate systems that we will define. As in the last chapter, there will be few new commands to learn.

If you have completed Chapter 11, you will find that working on isometric drawings has prepared you well for 3D drawing. There will be a similar process of switching from plane to plane, but there are two key differences. First, you will not be restricted to three isometric planes: You can define a User Coordinate System aligned with any specifiable plane. Second, and most important, the model you draw will have true 3D characteristics. You will be able to view it, edit it, and plot it from any point in space.

TASKS

12.1   Creating and Viewing a 3D Wireframe Box

In this task we will create a simple 3D box that we can edit in later tasks to form a more complex object. In Chapter 1 we showed how to turn the coordinate system icon (see Figure 12-1) off and on. For drawing in 3D you will definitely want it on. If your icon is not visible, follow this procedure to turn it on:

1. Open the View menu, highlight Display, and then UCS Icon, as shown in Figure 12-2.
2. Select On from the submenu.

For now, simply observe the icon as you go through the process of creating the box, and be aware that you are currently working in the same coordinate system that you have always used in AutoCAD. It is called the World Coordinate System (WCS), to distinguish it from others you will create yourself beginning in Task 12.2.

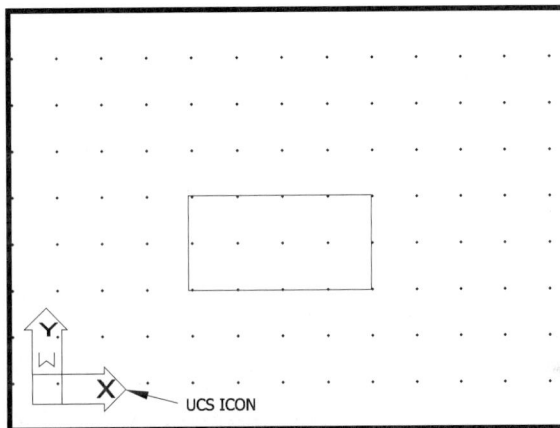

Figure 12-1

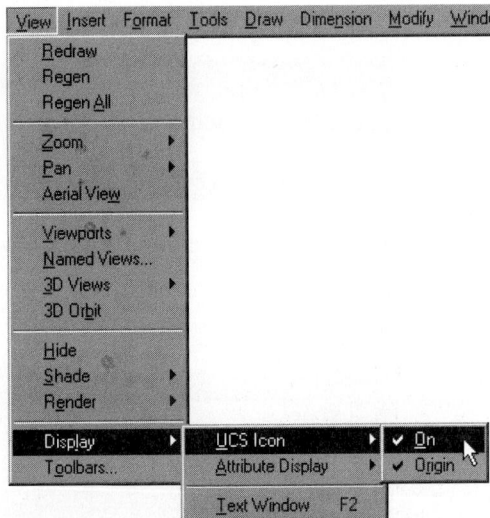

Figure 12-2

Currently, the origin of the WCS is at the lower left of your grid. This is the point (0,0,0) when you are thinking 3D, or simply (0,0) when you are in 2D. The *x* coordinates increase to the right horizontally across the screen, and *y* coordinates increase vertically up the screen as usual. The *z* axis, which we have ignored until now, currently extends out of the screen toward you and perpendicular to the *x* and *y* axes. This orientation of the three planes is called a plan view. Soon we will switch to a "front, right, top" or "southeast isometric" view.

Let's begin.

⊕ Draw a 2.00 by 4.00 rectangle near the middle of your screen, as shown in Figure 12-1. Do not use the RECTANG command to draw this figure because we will want to select individual line segments later on.

Changing Viewpoints

To move immediately into a 3D mode of drawing and thinking, our first step will be to change our viewpoint on this object. There are three commands that allow you to create 3D points of view, VPOINT, DVIEW, and 3DORBIT. 3DORBIT and DVIEW, which are discussed in Chapter 13, are best suited for creating carefully adjusted presentation images, including perspective views. The VPOINT command is simpler and best used for setting up basic views during the drawing and editing process. A good understanding of all the VPOINT options will increase your understanding of AutoCAD's 3D space. For this reason we have included at the end of this chapter an optional discussion of the different options available in the VPOINT command. There are three or four different methods, developed over time as Autodesk has tried to simplify the viewpoint definition process with each new release of AutoCAD.

The simplest and most efficient method is to use the Named Views dialog box introduced in the last chapter. For now, this is the only method you will need.

⊕ Click the Named Views tool on the standard toolbar.

This will open the View dialog box, which was used in Chapter 11 to create named views. In this chapter we will use the Orthographic & Isometric Views tab.

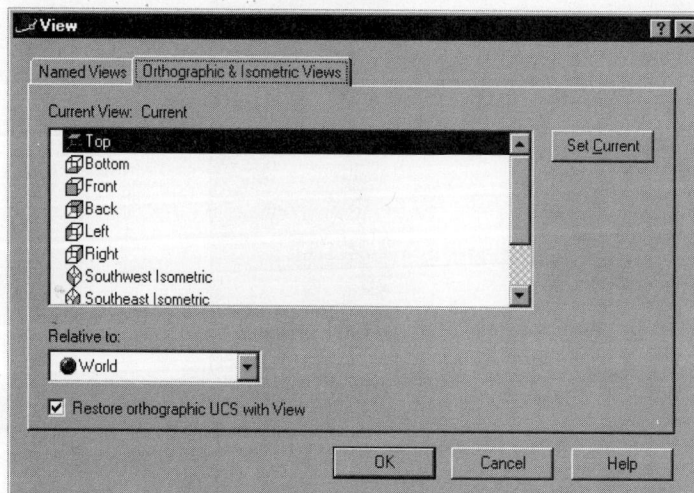

Figure 12-3

⊕   Select the Orthographic & Isometric Views tab, as shown in Figure 12-3.

This dialog box uses simple cube images to show ten standard preset views. Imagine your point of view to be perpendicular to the blue face of the cube in each case. In the six orthographic views objects will be presented from points of view along each of the six axis directions. You will see objects in the drawing from directly above (Top, positive z) or directly below (Bottom, negative z), or by looking in along the positive or negative *x* axis (Left and Right) or the positive or negative *y* axis (Front and Back).

The four isometric views present objects at 45 degree angles from the XY axis and take you up 30 degrees out of the XY plane. We will use a southeast isometric view. It is simple if you imagine a compass. The lower right quadrant is the southeast. In a southeast isometric view you will be looking in from this quadrant and down at a 30 degree angle. Try it.

⊕   Select "SE Isometric" from the list of views.

⊕   Click on Set Current.

⊕   Click OK.

The dialog will disappear and the screen will be redrawn to the view shown in Figure 12-4. Notice how the grid and the coordinate system icon have altered to show our current orientation. These visual aids are extremely helpful in viewing 3D objects on the flat screen and imagining them as if they were positioned in space.

At this point you may wish to experiment with the other views in the View dialog box. You will probably find the isometric views most interesting. Pay attention to the grid and the icon as you switch views. Variations of the icon you may encounter here and later on are shown in Figure 12-5. With some views you will have to think carefully and watch the icon to understand which way the object is being presented.

When you are done experimenting, be sure to return to the southeast isometric view shown in Figure 12-4. We will use this view frequently throughout this chapter and the next.

Whenever you change viewpoints, AutoCAD displays the drawing extents, so that the object fills the screen and is as large as possible. Often you will need to zoom out a bit to get some space to work in. This is easily done using the "Scale(X)" option of the ZOOM command.

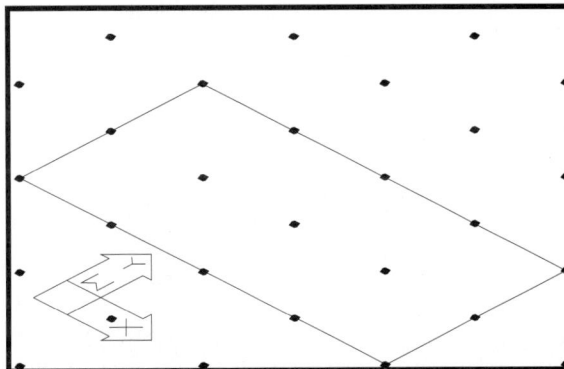

Figure 12-4

ICON	DESCRIPTION
	WCS (World Coordinate System) "W" appears on "Y" arm
	UCS (User Coordinate System) <u>NO</u> "W" appears on "Y" arm
	+ Appears in box and "W" appears on the "Y" arm if the current UCS is the same as the WCS
	Box appears at the base of ICON if viewing UCS from above its X-Y plane
	Box is missing if viewing UCS from below its X-Y plane
	Broken pencil ICON appears if viewing direction is "EDGE ON" or near "EDGE ON" X-Y plane of current UCS

Figure 12-5

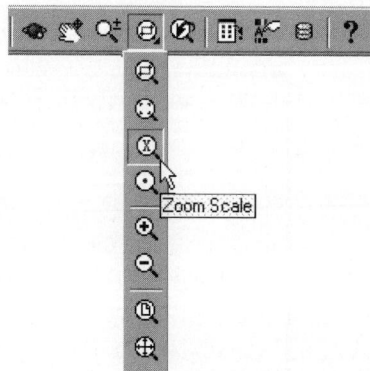

Figure 12-6

⊕ Open the View menu, highlight Zoom, and select Scale, or select the Zoom Scale tool from the Zoom flyout on the Standard toolbar, as shown in Figure 12-6.

⊕ Type ".5".

This tells AutoCAD to adjust and redraw the display so that objects appear half as large as before.

Your screen will be redrawn with the rectangle at half its previous magnification.

Entering 3D Coordinates

Next we will create a copy of the rectangle placed 1.25 above it. This brings up a basic 3D problem: AutoCAD interprets all pointer device point selections as being in the XY plane, so how does one indicate a point or a displacement in the Z direction? There are three possibilities: typed 3D coordinates, X/Y/Z point filters, and object snaps. Object snap requires an object already drawn above or below the XY plane, so it will be of no use right now. We will use typed coordinates first and then discuss how point filters could be used as an alternative. Later we will be using object snap as well.

3D coordinates can be entered from the keyboard in the same manner as 2D coordinates. Often this is an impractical way to enter individual points in a drawing. However, within COPY or MOVE it provides a simple method for specifying a displacement in the Z direction.

⊕ Select Copy from the Modify menu, or select the Copy Object tool from the Modify toolbar.

AutoCAD will prompt for object selection.

⊕ Select the complete rectangle.

⊕ Press Enter, the space bar, or the enter equivalent button on your pointing device to end object selection.

AutoCAD now prompts for the base point of a vector or a displacement value:

```
Specify base point or displacement, or [Multiple]:
```

Typically, you would respond to this prompt and the next by showing the two end points of a vector. However, we cannot show a displacement in the Z direction by pointing. This is important for understanding AutoCAD coordinate systems. Unless an object snap is used, all points picked on the screen with the pointing device will be interpreted as being in the XY plane of the current UCS. Without an entity outside the XY plane to use in an object snap, there is no way to point to a displacement in the Z direction.

⊕ Type "0,0,1.25".

AutoCAD now prompts

```
Specify second point of displacement,
or <use first point as displacement>:
```

You can type the coordinates of another point, or press Enter to tell AutoCAD to use the first entry as a displacement from (0,0,0). In this case, pressing Enter will indicate a displacement of 1.25 in the Z direction, and no change in X or Y.

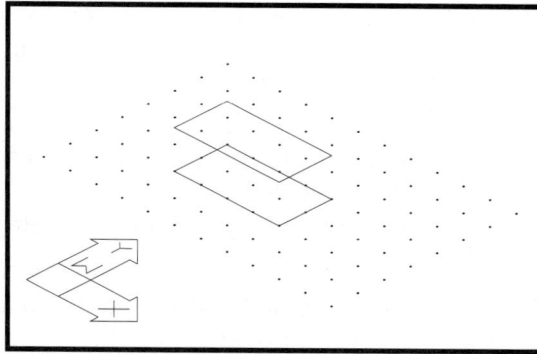

Figure 12-7

⊞ Press Enter.

AutoCAD will create a copy of the rectangle 1.25 directly above the original. Your screen should resemble Figure 12-7.

X/Y/Z Point Filters (Optional)

Point filters can be very useful in 3D, although they may seem odd until you get a feel for when to use them. In a point filter we filter out coordinates from one point and use them to create a new point. Notice that in the displacement we just entered, the only thing that changes is the Z value. Note also that we could specify the same displacement using any point in the XY plane as a base point. For example, (3,6,0) to (3,6,1.25) would show the same displacement as (0,0,0) to (0,0,1.25). In fact, we don't even need to know what X and Y are as long as we know that they don't change.

That is how an ".XY" point filter works. We borrow, or "filter," the X and Y values from a point, without pausing to find out what the values actually are, and then specify a new Z value. Other types of filters are possible, of course, such as ".Z" or ".YZ".

You can use a point filter, like an object snap, anytime AutoCAD asks for a point. After a point filter is specified, AutoCAD will always prompt with an "of". In our case you are being asked, "You want the X and Y values of what point?" In response, you pick a point, and then AutoCAD will ask you to fill in Z. Notice that point filters can be "chained" so that, for example, you can filter the X value from one point and combine it with the filtered Y value from another point.

To use an .XY filter in the COPY command instead of typing coordinates, for example, you could follow this procedure:

1. Enter the COPY command.
2. Select the rectangle.
3. For the displacement base point, pick any point in the XY plane.
4. At the prompt for a second point, type ".xy".
5. At the "of" prompt, type "@" or pick the same point again.
6. At the "(need Z):" prompt, type "1.25". The result would be Figure 12-7, as before.

> **Note:** There is a Point Filters cascading submenu on the object snap short cut menu. To access it, hold down Shift and right click anywhere in the drawing area. From the short cut menu, highlight Point Filters and select a point filter type from the submenu.

Using Object Snap

We now have two rectangles floating in space. Our next job is to connect the corners to form a wireframe box. This is done easily using Endpoint object snaps. This is a good example of how object snaps allow us to construct entities not in the XY plane of the current coordinate system.

⊕ Right click on the OSNAP button on the status bar.

⊕ Select Settings... from the cursor menu.

⊕ Click on Clear all to remove checks from all object snap boxes.

⊕ Click the check box next to Endpoint.

⊕ Click on OK.

⊕ Click the OSNAP button so that it is in the down position.

The running Endpoint object snap is now on and will affect all point selection. You will find that object snaps are very useful in 3D drawing and that Endpoint mode can be used frequently.

Now we will draw some lines.

⊕ Enter the LINE command and connect the upper and lower corners of the two rectangles, as shown in Figure 12-8.

(We have removed the grid for clarity, but you will probably want to leave yours on.)

Before going on, pause a moment to be aware of what you have drawn. The box on your screen is a true wireframe model. Unlike an isometric drawing, it is a 3D model that can be turned, viewed, and plotted from any point in space. It is not, however, a solid model or a surface model. It is only a set of lines in 3D space. Removing hidden lines or shading would have no effect on this model.

In the next task you will begin to define your own coordinate systems that will allow you to perform drawing and editing functions in any plane you choose.

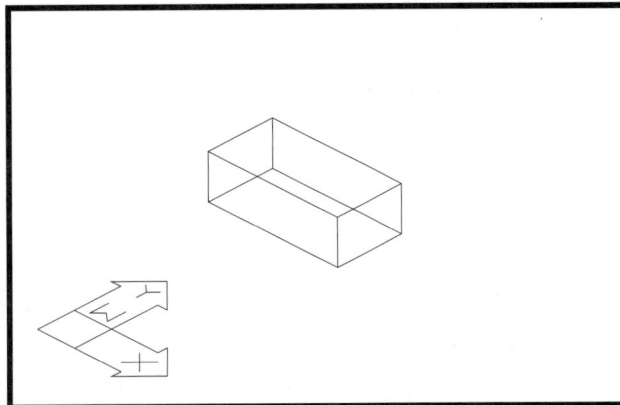

Figure 12-8

12.2 Defining and Saving User Coordinate Systems

GENERAL PROCEDURE

1. Type "UCS" or select New UCS from the Tools menu.
2. Choose an option.
3. Specify a coordinate system.
4. Name and save the new coordinate system.

In this task you will begin to develop new vocabulary and techniques for working with objects in 3D space. The primary tool will be the UCS command. You will also learn to use the UCSICON command to control the placement of the coordinate system icon.

Until now we have had only one coordinate system to work with. All coordinates and displacements have been defined relative to a single point of origin. Keep in mind that view point and coordinate system are not the same, although they use similar vocabulary. In Task 12.1 we changed our point of view, but the UCS icon changed along with it, so that the orientations of the x, y, and z axes relative to the object were retained. With the UCS command you can free the coordinate system from the viewpoint and define new coordinate systems at any point and any angle in space. When you do, you can use the coordinate system icon and the grid to help you visualize the planes you are working in, and all commands and drawing aids will function relative to the new system.

The coordinate system we are currently using is unique. It is called the World Coordinate System and is the one we always begin with. The "W" at the base of the coordinate system icon indicates that we are working in the world system. A User Coordinate System is nothing more than a new point of origin and a new orientation for the x, y, and z axes.

We will begin by defining a User Coordinate System in the plane of the top of the box, as shown in Figure 12-9.

⊕ Leave the Endpoint osnap mode on for this exercise.

⊕ Open the Tools menu and highlight New UCS.

There is also a UCS tool on the UCS toolbar shown in Figure 12-10, but you will have to open the toolbar before you can access it. If you type "ucs" or select the tool from the toolbar, you will work with prompts at the command

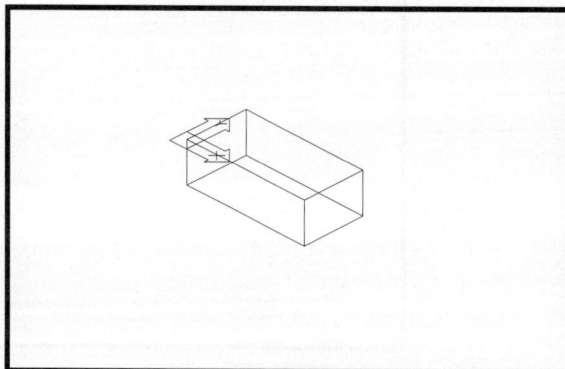

Figure 12-9

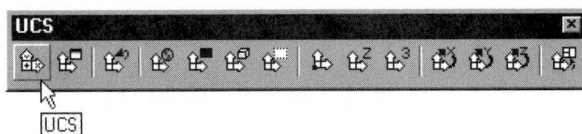

Figure 12-10

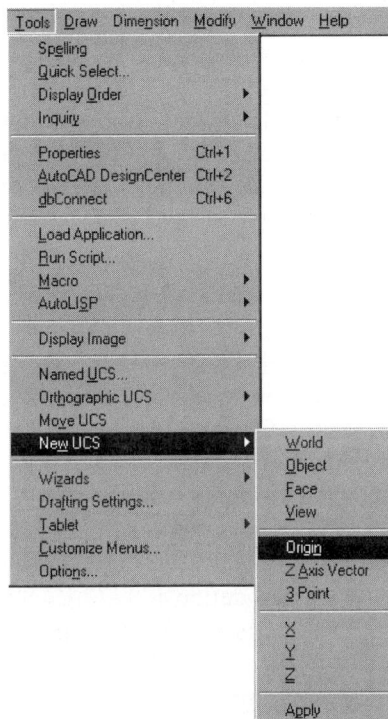

Figure 12-11

line. Here we will begin using the pull-down menu options and later use the command line as well.

On the pull-down menu, you will see options on a submenu, as illustrated in Figure 12-11. We will begin by using "Origin" to create a UCS that is parallel to the WCS.

⊕ Select Origin from the submenu.

AutoCAD will prompt for a new origin:

Specify new origin point <0,0,0>:

This option does not change the orientation of the three axes. It simply shifts their intersection to a different point in space. We will use this procedure to define a UCS in the plane of the top of the box.

⊕ Use the Endpoint object snap to select the top left far corner of the box, as shown by the location of the icon in Figure 12-9.

You will notice that the "W" is gone from the icon. However, the icon has not moved. It is still at the lower left of the screen. It is visually helpful to place it at the origin of the new UCS, as in the figure. To do this we need the UCSICON command.

⊕ Open the View menu, highlight "Display", and then "UCS Icon".

⊕ Select "Origin", so that there is a check mark next to it.

The icon will move to the origin of the new current UCS, as in Figure 12-9. With UCSICON set to origin, the icon will shift to the new origin whenever we define a new UCS. The only exception would be if the origin were not on the screen or too close to an edge for the icon to fit. In these cases the icon would be displayed in the lower left corner again.

The UCS we have just created will make it easy to draw and edit entities that are in the plane of the top of the box and to perform editing in planes that are parallel to it, such as the bottom. In the next task we will begin drawing and editing using different coordinate systems, and you will see how this works. For now, we will spend a little more time on the UCS command itself. We will define two more user coordinate systems, but first let's save this one so that we can recall it quickly when we need it later.

⊕ Open the Tools menu and highlight "Named UCS...".

The new UCS will be on the list as "Unnamed", along with World and Previous.

⊕ Select "Unnamed".

The word "Unnamed" should be selected for editing. We will name our coordinate system "top." It will be the UCS we use to draw and edit in the top plane. This UCS would also make it easy for us to create an orthographic top viewpoint later on.

⊕ Type "top" and press enter.

The top UCS is now saved and can be recalled by opening this dialog, selecting it in the name list, and clicking the Set Current button.

Next we will define a "left" UCS using the "3point" option.

⊕ Open the Tools menu, highlight New UCS, and select "3 point" from the submenu.

AutoCAD prompts

```
Specify new origin point <0,0,0>:
```

In this option you will show AutoCAD a new origin point, as before, and then a new orientation for the axes as well. Notice that the default origin is the current one. If we retained this origin, we could define a UCS with the same origin and a different axis orientation.

Instead, we will define a new origin at the lower left corner of the left side of the box, as shown in Figure 12-12.

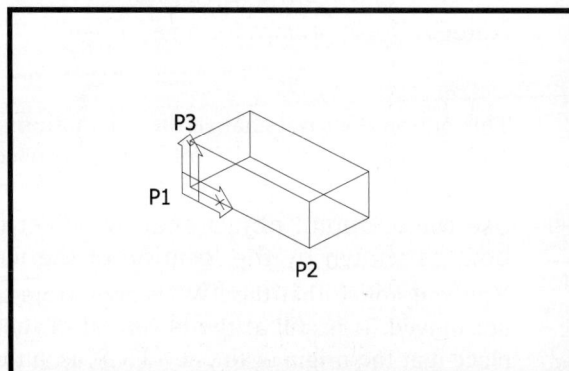

Figure 12-12

⊕ With the Endpoint osnap on, pick P1, as shown in Figure 12-12.

AutoCAD now prompts you to indicate the orientation of the *x* axis:

```
Specify point on positive portion
of the X axis <1.00,0.00,-1.25>:
```

⊕ Pick the right front corner of the box, P2, as shown.

The object snap ensures that the new *x* axis will now align with the left side of the object. AutoCAD prompts for the *y* axis orientation:

```
Specify point on positive-Y portion
of the UCS XY plane <0.00,1.00,-1.25>:
```

By definition, the *y* axis will be perpendicular to the *x* axis; therefore, Auto-CAD needs only a point that shows the plane of the *y* axis and its positive direction. Because of this, any point on the positive side of the *y* plane will specify the *y* axis correctly. We have chosen a point that is on the *y* axis itself.

⊕ Pick P3, as shown.

When this sequence is complete, you will notice that the coordinate system icon has rotated along with the grid and moved to the new origin as well. This UCS will be convenient for drawing and editing in the left plane of the box, or editing in any plane parallel to the left plane, such as the back plane.

Now save the "left" UCS, using the command line this time.

⊕ Press Enter to repeat the UCS command.

⊕ Type "s" to save.

⊕ Type "left" to name the UCS.

Finally, we will use the "Origin" and "Y" axis rotation options together to create a right-side UCS.

⊕ Open the Tools menu and highlight New UCS.

⊕ Select "Origin" from the submenu.

⊕ Pick the lower front right corner of the box for the origin, as shown in Figure 12-13.

The UCS icon will move to the selected point.

⊕ Press enter or the space bar to repeat the UCS command.

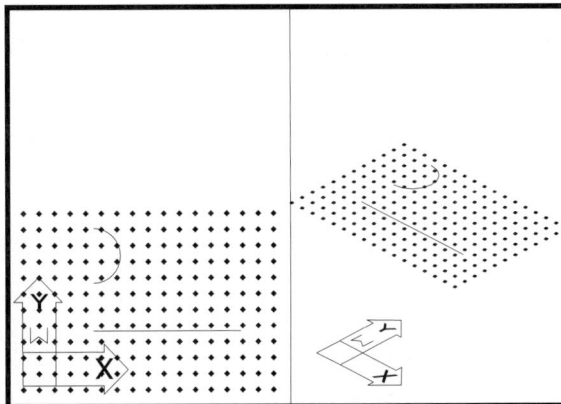

Figure 12-13

We will rotate the UCS icon around its *y* axis to align it with the right side of the box.

In using any of the rotation options ("X axis", "Y axis", and "Z axis"), the first thing you have to decide is which axis is the axis of rotation. If you look at the current position of the icon and think about how it will look when it aligns with the right side of the box, you will see that the *y* axis retains its position and orientation while the *x* axis turns through 90 degrees. In other words, since x rotates around *y*, *y* is the axis of rotation.

⊕ Type "y".

Now AutoCAD prompts for a rotation:

```
Specify rotation angle around Y axis <90>:
```

It takes some practice to differentiate positive and negative rotation in 3D. If you like, you can use AutoCAD's right-hand rule, which can be stated as follows: If you are hitchhiking (pointing your right thumb) in a positive direction along the axis of rotation, your fingers will curl in the direction of positive rotation for the other axis. In this case, align your right thumb with the positive *y* axis, and you will see that your fingers curl in the direction we want the *x* axis to rotate. Therefore, the rotation of *x* around *y* is positive.

⊕ Type "90".

You should now have the UCS icon aligned with the right side of the box, as shown in Figure 12-13. Save this UCS before going on to Task 12.3.

⊕ Press enter to repeat UCS command.
⊕ Type "s".
⊕ Type "right".

12.3 Using Draw and Edit Commands in a UCS

Now the fun begins. Using our three new coordinate systems and one more we will define later, we will give the box a more interesting "slotted wedge" shape. In this task we will cut away a slanted surface on the right side of the box. Since the planes we will be working in are parallel to the left side of the box, we will begin by making the "left" UCS current. All our work in this task will be done in this UCS.

⊕ Open the Tools menu and highlight Named UCS....
This will open the Named UCS dialog box again, with three new coordinate systems as shown in Figure 12-14. Now that we have these coordinate systems defined, this dialog box provides a simple way to switch among them.
⊕ Highlight "Left" in the dialog box.
⊕ Click on Set Current.
⊕ Click on OK.
The UCS icon should return to the left plane.

In this case we also could have used the "Previous" option since "left" was the previous UCS.

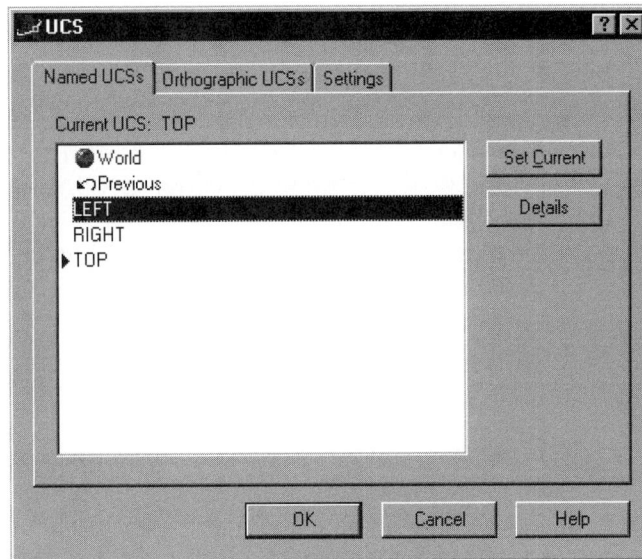

Figure 12-14

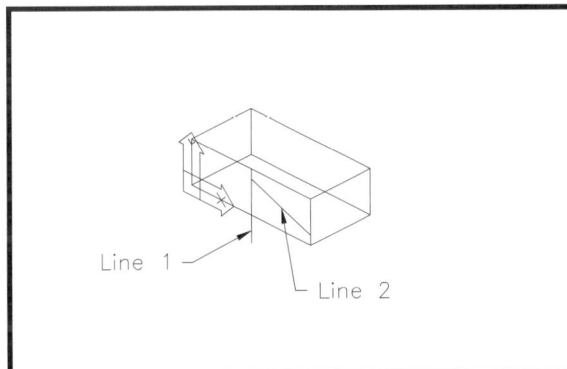

Figure 12-15

Look at Figure 12-15. We will draw a line down the middle of the left side (line 1) and use it to trim another line coming in at an angle (line 2).

⊕   Type "L" or select the Line tool from the Draw toolbar.
⊕   Hold down shift and right click to open the object snap cursor menu.
⊕   Select Midpoint.
      This will temporarily override the Endpoint object snap.
⊕   Point to the top edge of the left side of the box.
      AutoCAD will snap to the midpoint of the line.
⊕   Make sure that ortho is on (F8 or the ORTHO button).
      Notice how ortho works as usual, but relative to the current UCS.
⊕   Pick a second point anywhere below the box.

This line will be trimmed later, so the exact length does not matter.

⊕ Exit the LINE command.

Next we will draw Line 2 on an angle across the left side. This line will become one edge of a slanted surface. Your snap setting will need to be at 0.25 or smaller, and ortho will need to be off. The grid, snap, and coordinate display all work relative to the current UCS, so it is a simple matter to draw in this plane.

⊕ Turn grid snap on (F9 or the SNAP button) and check your snap setting by observing the coordinate display. Change it to .25 if necessary.

⊕ Turn ortho off.

⊕ Turn osnap off (F3 or the OSNAP button).

⊕ Enter the LINE command.

⊕ Use incremental snap to pick a point .25 down from the top edge of the box on line 1, as shown in Figure 12-15.

⊕ Pick a second point 0.25 up along the right front edge of the box, as shown.

⊕ Exit the LINE command.

Now trim line 1.

⊕ Select the Trim tool from the Modify toolbar.

AutoCAD will present the following message, though you may need to switch to the text screen to see it:

```
View is not plan to UCS. Command results may not be obvious.
```

In the language of AutoCAD 3D, a view is plan to the current UCS if the XY plane is in the plane of the monitor display and its axes are parallel to the sides of the screen. This is the usual 2D view, in which the y axis aligns with the left side of the display and the x axis aligns with the bottom of the display. In previous chapters we always worked in plan view. In this chapter we have not been in plan view since the beginning of Task 12.1.

With this message, AutoCAD is warning us that boundaries, edges, and intersections may not be obvious as we look at a 3D view of an object. For example, lines that appear to cross may be in different planes.

Having read the warning, we continue.

⊕ Select line 2 as a cutting edge.

⊕ Press Enter to end cutting edge selection.

⊕ Point to the lower end of line 1.

⊕ Press Enter or the space bar to exit TRIM.

Your screen should resemble Figure 12-16.

Now we will copy our two lines to the back of the box. Since we will be moving out of the left plane, which is also the XY plane in the current UCS, we will require the use of Endpoint object snaps to specify the displacement vector.

⊕ Select the Copy Object tool from the Modify toolbar.

⊕ Pick lines 1 and 2. (You will probably need to zoom in on the box at this point to pick Line 1.)

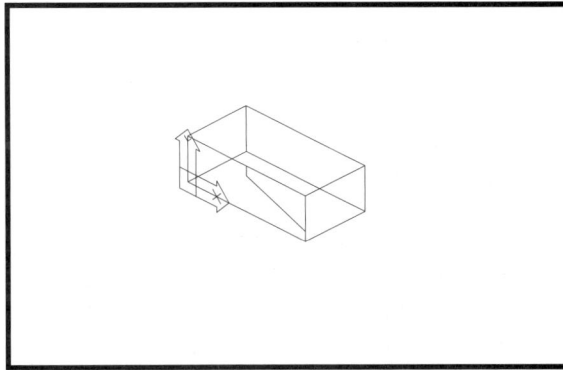

Figure 12-16

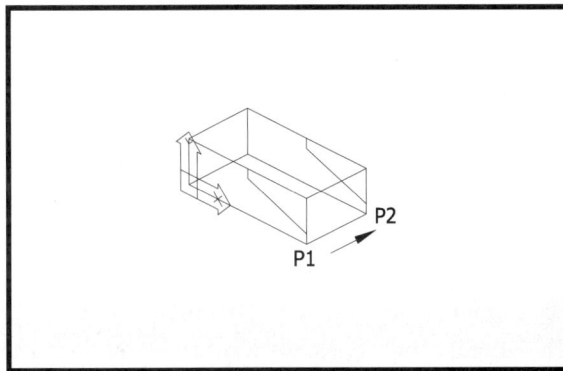

Figure 12-17

⊕ Press Enter to end object selection.
⊕ Use the Endpoint osnap to pick the lower front corner of the box, P1 as shown in Figure 12-17.
⊕ At the prompt for a second point of displacement, use the Endpoint osnap to pick the lower right back corner of the box, P2 as shown.

    Your screen should now resemble Figure 12-17.

What remains is to connect the edges we have just outlined and then trim away the top of the box. We will continue to work in the left UCS and to use Endpoint osnaps.

We will use a multiple COPY to copy one of the previously drawn edges in three new places.

⊕ Repeat COPY.
⊕ Pick the bottom right edge for copying (the edge between P1 and P2 in Figure 12-17).
⊕ Press Enter to end object selection.
⊕ Type "m" for the multiple option.

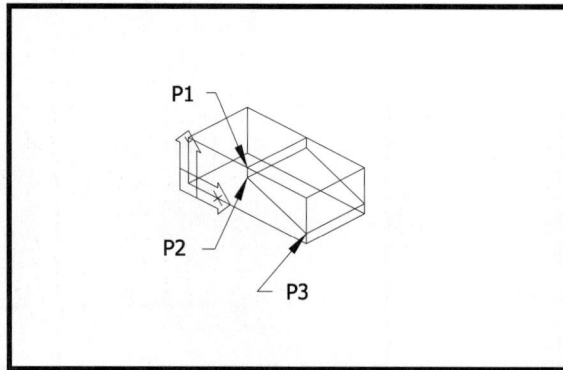

Figure 12-18

⊕ Pick the front end point of the selected edge to serve as a base point of displacement.

⊕ Pick the top end point of line 1 (P1 in Figure 12-18).

⊕ Pick the lower end point of line 1 (P2) as another second point.

⊕ Pick the right end point of line 2 (P3) as another second point.

⊕ Press Enter to exit the COPY command.

Finally, we need to do some trimming.

⊕ Select the Trim tool from the Modify toolbar.

For cutting edges, we want to select lines 1 and 2 and their copies in the back plane (lines 3 and 4 in Figure 12-19). Since this can be difficult, a quick alternative to selecting these four separate lines is to use a crossing box to select the whole area. As long as your selection includes the four lines, it will be effective.

⊕ Select the area around lines 1 and 2 with a crossing box.

Note: Trimming in 3D can be tricky. Remember where you are. Edges that do not run parallel to the current UCS may not be recognized at all.

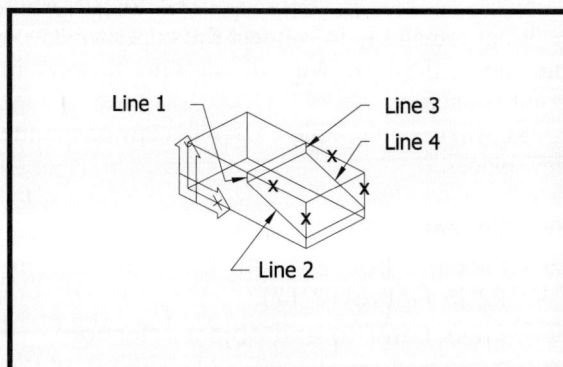

Figure 12-19

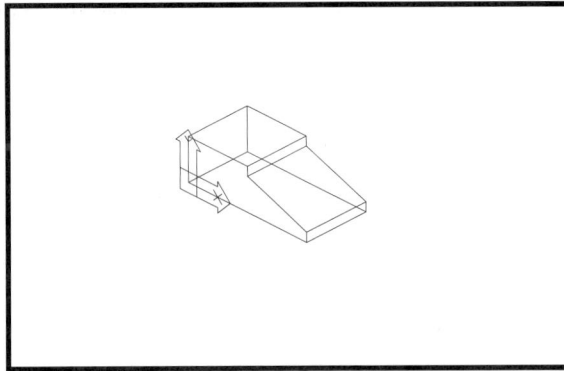

Figure 12-20

⊕ Press Enter to end cutting edge selection.

⊕ One by one, pick the top left and top back edges to the right of the cut, and the right front and right back edges above the cut, as shown by the x's in Figure 12-19.

⊕ Press Enter to exit the TRIM command.

⊕ Use the ERASE command to erase the top edge that is left hanging in space.

We use ERASE here because this line does not intersect any edges.

Your screen should now resemble Figure 12-20.

12.4 Working on an Angled Surface

In this task we will take our 3D drawing technique a step further by constructing a slot through the new slanted surface and the bottom of the object. This will require the creation of a new UCS. In completing this task, you will also use the OFFSET command and continue to develop a feel for working with multiple coordinate systems.

Begin by defining a UCS along the angled surface.

⊕ Open the Tools menu, highlight New UCS, and select "3 point".

⊕ Using the Endpoint osnap, pick P1, as shown in Figure 12-21.

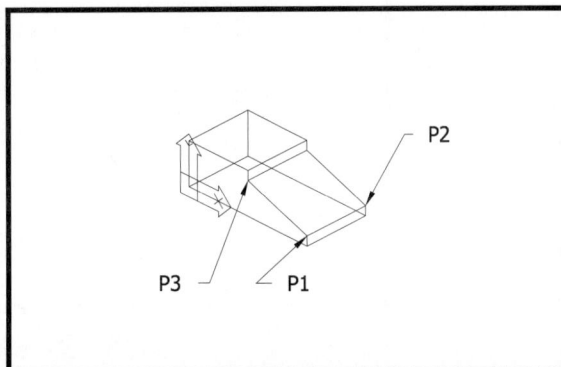

Figure 12-21

⊕ Using an Endpoint osnap, pick P2, as shown.

⊕ Using an Endpoint osnap, pick P3, as shown.

⊕ Repeat the UCS command.

⊕ Type "s".

⊕ Type "angle" for the name of the UCS.

Now we are ready to work in the plane of the angled surface.

From here on, we have moved our UCS icon back to the lower left of the screen for the sake of clarity in our illustrations. You may leave it at its origin on your screen, if you like, or move it by opening the View menu, highlighting Display and then UCS Icon, and then deselecting "Origin".

⊕ Turn osnap off (F3 or the OSNAP button).

⊕ If ortho is off, turn it on (F8 or the ORTHO button).

We will create line 1 across the angled surface, as shown in Figure 12-22, by offsetting the top right front edge of the wedge.

⊕ Select the Offset tool from the Modify toolbar.

⊕ Type or show a distance of 1.50.

⊕ Pick the top right front edge (the top edge at the tapered right end of the wedge).

⊕ Point anywhere above and to the left of the edge.

⊕ Exit OFFSET.

⊕ Draw lines 2 and 3 perpendicular to the first, as shown. They will be over 0.50 and 1.50 from the current *y* axis.

Watch the coordinate display and notice how the coordinates work in this UCS as in any other.

⊕ Turn ortho off.

⊕ Using grid snap for the top point and a Perpendicular object snap for the lower point, drop line 4 down to the bottom left front edge.

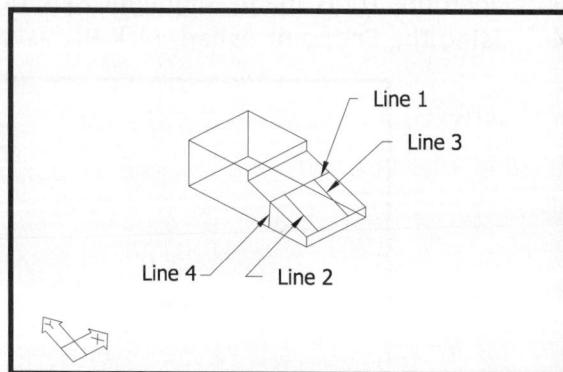

Figure 12-22

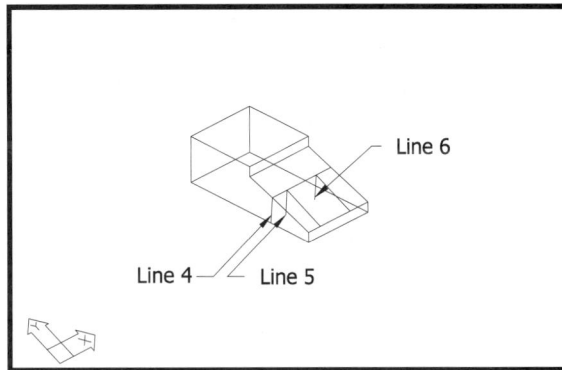

Figure 12-23

This is a single-point osnap. Use the osnap short cut menu. Notice again how object snap modes work for you, especially to locate points that are not in the XY plane of the current UCS.

⊕ Create lines 5 and 6, as shown in Figure 12-23, by making two copies of line 4, extending down from the ends of lines 2 and 3, as shown.

⊕ ERASE line 4 from the left plane.

⊕ Turn osnap on.

⊕ Using Endpoint osnaps, connect lines 5 and 6 to each other in the plane of the bottom of the object.

⊕ Using Endpoint and Perpendicular osnaps, connect lines 5 and 6 to the bottom edge of the right side.

⊕ Using Endpoint osnaps, draw two short vertical lines on the right side, connecting to lines 2 and 3.

⊕ TRIM line 1 and the two lines on the right side across the opening of the slot to create Figure 12-24.

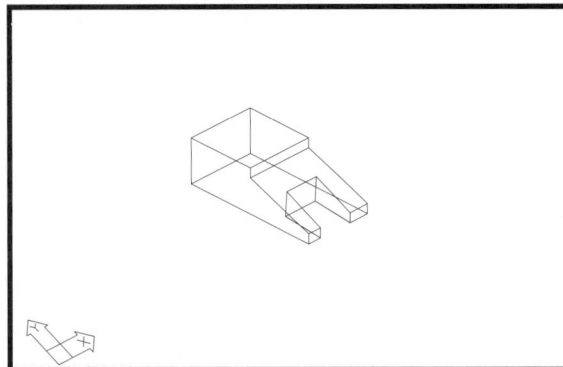

Figure 12-24

12.5 Using RULESURF to Create 3D Fillets

GENERAL PROCEDURE

1. Create fillets in two planes.
2. Open the Draw menu, highlight Surfaces, and select Ruled Surface.
3. Pick a fillet.
4. Pick the corresponding side of the fillet in the other plane.

There are two parts to completing this task. First, we will fillet the top and bottom corners of the slot drawn in Task 12.4. Then we will use the RULESURF command to create filleted surfaces between the top and bottom of the slot. RULESURF is a surface command that we will use in the next chapter, but we will use it here as the most effective way to create a 3D fillet in our wireframe model.

⊕ To begin this task you should be in the "angle" UCS, as in Task 12.4, and your screen should resemble Figure 12-24.

⊕ Select the Fillet tool from the Modify menu.

AutoCAD will prompt as usual:

        Current settings: Mode = TRIM, Radius = 0.50
        Select first object or [Polyline/Radius/Trim]:

⊕ Type "r".

⊕ Type ".25" for the radius value.

⊕ Repeat FILLET.

⊕ Pick two lines that meet at one of the upper corners of the slot.

Look at Figure 12-25 to see where we are headed.

⊕ Repeat FILLET.

⊕ Pick two lines that meet at the other upper corner of the slot.

⊕ Repeat FILLET.

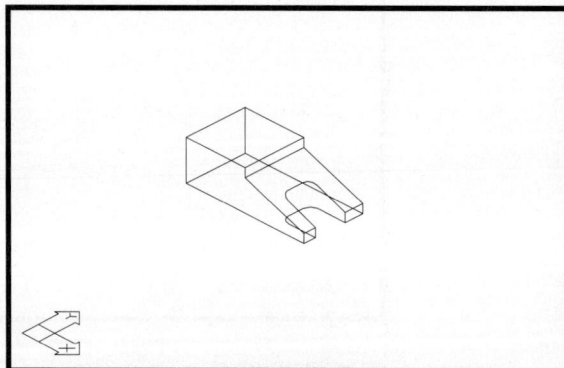

Figure 12-25

⊕ Pick two lines that meet at one of the lower corners of the slot.

⊕ Repeat FILLET once more.

⊕ Pick two lines that meet at the other lower corner of the slot.

⊕ Erase the two vertical lines left outside the fillets.

Your screen should resemble Figure 12-25.

Now we will use RULESURF to connect the upper and lower fillets with 3D surfaces. RULESURF is one of several commands that create 3D surfaces. These commands create entities called "3D polygon meshes," which are discussed in detail in Chapter 13. This quick introduction will allow you to create 3D fillets in the drawings at the end of this chapter.

The RULESURF command creates a 3D surface between two lines or curves in 3D space. Our two curves will be the upper and lower fillets at each of the two corners.

⊕ Open the Draw menu, highlight Surfaces, and select Ruled Surface.

AutoCAD will prompt

Select first defining curve:

⊕ Pick one of the top fillets, as shown by pick 1 in Figure 12-26.

AutoCAD will prompt for a second curve:

Select second defining curve:

⊕ Pick the corresponding fillet in the bottom plane, with a pickpoint on the corresponding side, as shown by pick 2 in Figure 12-26.

AutoCAD will draw a set of faces to represent the surface curving around the fillet radius, as shown in Figure 12-27.

The trick in using RULESURF is to be sure that you show a pickpoint toward one side of the curve and that you pick the next curve with a point on the corresponding side. Otherwise you will get an hourglass effect, as shown in Figure 12-28.

⊕ To complete this task, repeat the RULESURF command and draw the fillet at the other corner of the groove.

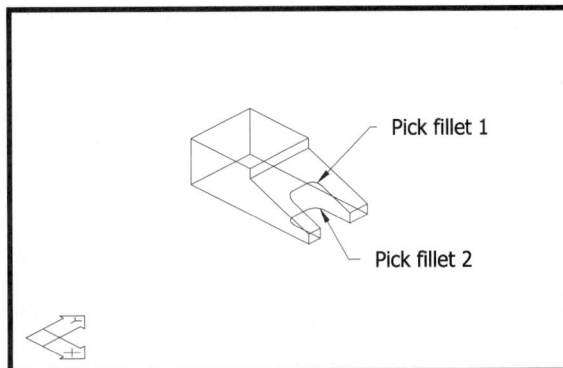

Figure 12-26

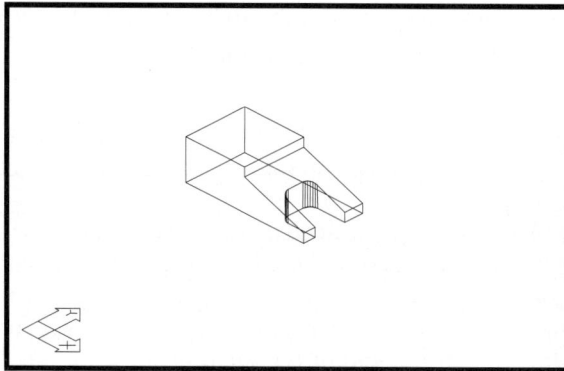

Figure 12-27

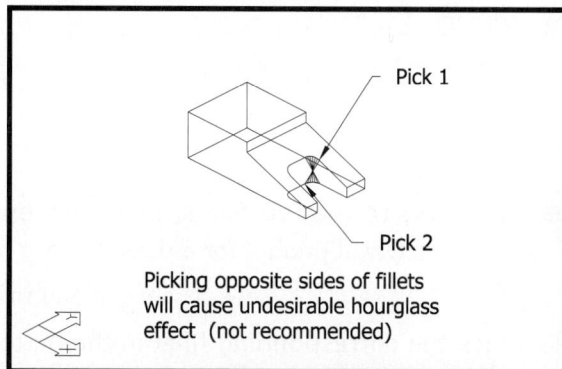

Pick 1

Pick 2

Picking opposite sides of fillets
will cause undesirable hourglass
effect (not recommended)

Figure 12-28

When you are done, your screen should resemble Figure 12-27. This completes the introduction to drawing 3D wireframe models and using User Coordinate Systems. What follows is an optional discussion of other methods for using the VPOINT command.

12.6 Exploring Other Methods of Using the VPOINT Command (Optional)

This discussion of other methods of using VPOINT is intended as a reference. The information presented here is not necessary to complete the drawings in this chapter, and no specific exercise is presented. However, if you are interested in gaining a full understanding of the VPOINT command, try creating the views described and outlined in the charts and figures in this section. In Chapters 13 and 14 you will also find exercises using the more dynamic 3DORBIT command for fine tuning and creating perspective and cutaway views.

Entering 3D Coordinates of a Viewpoint (Vector)

If you enter VPOINT by typing the command, you will see the following messages and prompts:

```
*** Switching to the WCS ***
Current view direction: VIEWDIR=1.00,-1.00,1.00
Specify a view point or [Rotate] <display compass and tripod>:
```

From the first line, you learn that all views are defined relative to the World Co-ordinate System, regardless of what UCS is current at the time the command is entered. From the second line, you see the current setting of the variable viewdir, which holds the vector definition of the current viewpoint. Assuming you are in the southeast isometric view, you will see 1.00, −1.00, 1.00. By reading this section you will understand how the vector definition relates to the view definition. The third line gives you three options: You can specify a view point by typing vector num-bers, by typing rotation specifications, or by using the compass and tripod images. The second two options are explained later in this discussion.

The default method is to type in vector specifications. If you enter the VPOINT command from the WCS plan view, the default viewpoint is given as (0,0,1). This means that you are viewing the object from a point somewhere along the positive z axis. You are at 0 in the x and y directions and at +1 in the z direction. In other words, you are directly above the XY plane looking straight down, a plan view. Think of the x coordinate as controlling right–left orienta-tion, the y coordinate as controlling back–front, and the z coordinate as con-trolling up–down.

By changing the x coordinate to 1 (right) and leaving y at 0 (neither front nor back) and z at 1 (above), you can create a viewpoint above and to the right of the object (1,0,1). Similarly, (1,−1,1) would move you to the right ($x = 1$), back you up a bit ($y = -1$) so that you are in front of the object, and raise your point of view ($z = 1$) so that you are above the object looking down. This com-mon (1,−1,1) viewpoint is the same as the southeast viewpoint used throughout this chapter.

We will explore other methods of specifying viewpoints in a moment, but first look at the viewpoint vector chart. It summarizes the effects of the x, y, and z spec-ifications and gives you combinations for some standard views. You should have a good understanding of why each view appears as it does.

We suggest that you try some of these viewpoints and experiment with others not listed. Your goal should be to get a feel for how different combinations move your point of view in relation to objects on the screen. You can use numbers oth-er than one, but precise distance relationships are difficult to follow in viewpoint definition.

X Right-Left	Y Back-Front	Z Up-Down	View Description	Vector Chart
0	0	1	Plan or Top	
0	0	−1	"Worm's eye" or Bottom	
1	0	0	Right side	
−1	0	0	Left side	
0	1	0	Back	
0	−1	0	Front	
1	1	1	Northeast Isometric	
1	−1	1	Southeast Isometric	

Rotation

A second option shown in the prompt is "Rotation". In this method, AutoCAD will prompt for two angles. The first is an angle in the XY plane. It is measured from the *x* axis, with 0 being straight out to the right, as usual.

The second angle goes up or down from the XY plane, with 0 being ground level. Thus an angle of 90 degrees from the XY plane would define the plan view.

The rotation chart will give you the rotation versions of some of the same major views shown in the Named view dialog box and the vector chart.

From X	From XY	View Description	Rotation Chart
0	0	Right side	
0	90	Plan	
90	0	Back side	
180	0	Left side	
270	0	Front	
45	30	Northeast Isometric	
−45 (or +315)	30	Southeast Isometric	
45	−30	Back, Right, Bottom	
	etc.	etc.	

DDVPOINT

Rotated views are also accessible through the DDVPOINT command, which calls the Viewpoint Presets dialog box (Viewpoint Presets... on the 3D Views submenu). This Viewpoint Presets dialog box is shown in Figure 12-29. DDVPOINT can also be initiated by typing "vp" at the command line. We will use this method to create a Northeast isometric or back, right, top view.

⊕ Open the View menu, highlight 3D Viewpoint, and click on Select....
This will call up the Viewpoint Presets dialog box, as shown in Figure 12-29.

Using this method, AutoCAD lets you choose the two angles it needs to create a new viewpoint from the two "dials" on the left and right. The angle from the *x* axis can be specified by selecting a point in the circle on the right or by typing a number in the edit box at the bottom. The angle from the XY plane can be typed or shown using the semicircle at the right of the dialog box. As you make selections by pointing in the circle or semicircle, the white "needle" will move and the angle value will be entered in the edit box.

⊕ Set the angle from the *x* axis by picking the top right box, "45" as shown in Figure 12-29.
Notice that selecting this box enters the value 45.0 in the From: X Axis edit box and moves the white pointer to 45. The angle of 45 moves us into the "back, right" viewpoint area, the northeast quadrant.

The second angle specification (the angle from the XY plane) can be shown in a similar manner by picking a point on the semicircle at the right or by typing a value in the edit box at the bottom. The angle you specify will be the *z* dimension

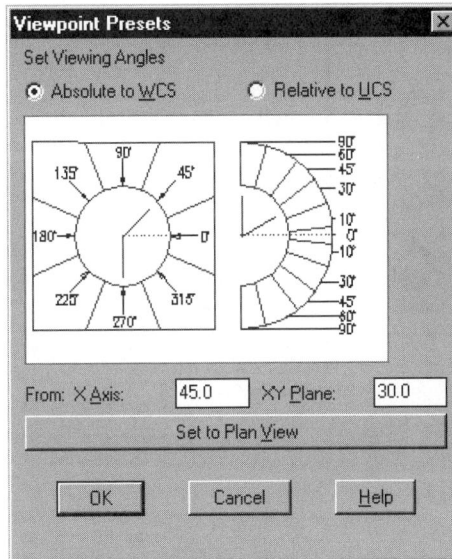

Figure 12-29

viewing position, a viewing height above or below the object. We will choose to look down at an angle of 30 degrees.

⊕ Pick the area labeled +30.

This will move the white pointer and enter the value 30 in the XY Plane edit box.

⊕ When your dialog box shows 45.0 and 30.0 as the two viewing angles, pick OK to create the new viewpoint.

Your screen should be redrawn to show a northeast isometric view.

Using the two angles in the dialog box to set rotation in the XY plane and the viewing height, you can create a large variety of points of view. We encourage you to experiment with these. Try changing the first angle to 225 to create a southwest isometric view. What two angles will give you a front view at ground level? What will a view from below the object look like? As you experiment, pay attention to the UCS icon. With some views you will have to think carefully and watch the icon to understand which way the object is being presented.

The Compass and Axes System

If you enter the VPOINT command and then press Enter in response to the prompt, you will see a display that resembles Figure 12-30.

The triple axes represent the orientation of the object. When you move your cursor, you will see these rotating. Some users may find this visualization easier to comprehend because it represents the object itself rather than your point of view in relation to the object. However, this effect is much more clearly realized in the 3DORBIT command, discussed in Chapter 13.

The other part of the display is a rather unusual representation of a globe. The horizontal and vertical axes show the X and Y dimensions, as you would expect,

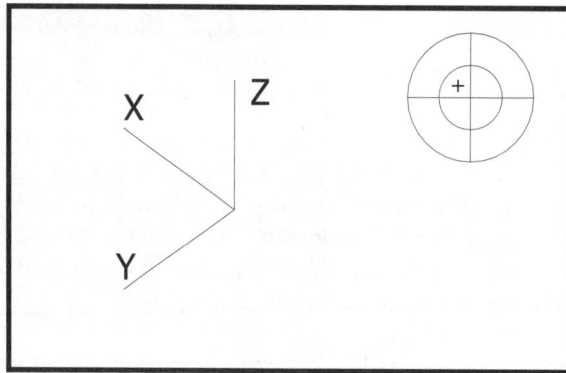

Figure 12-30

and the circles show the Z dimension. This actually shows a globe transformed into a cone and then flattened. The "north pole" of the globe has become a point at the center of the compass, while the "south pole" has been widened into a circle at the outside of the compass. In between is another circle representing the "equator," or ground 0 region.

This simply means that anywhere inside the first circle will give you a top-down view; outside the first circle will give you a bottom-up view. Anywhere on the middle circle will give you a ground-level view.

Notice that the small cross that moves as you move your cursor. This represents your point of view in the coordinate system.

Figure 12-31 gives you a summary of the compass points and how they relate to standard views. Try them out if you like.

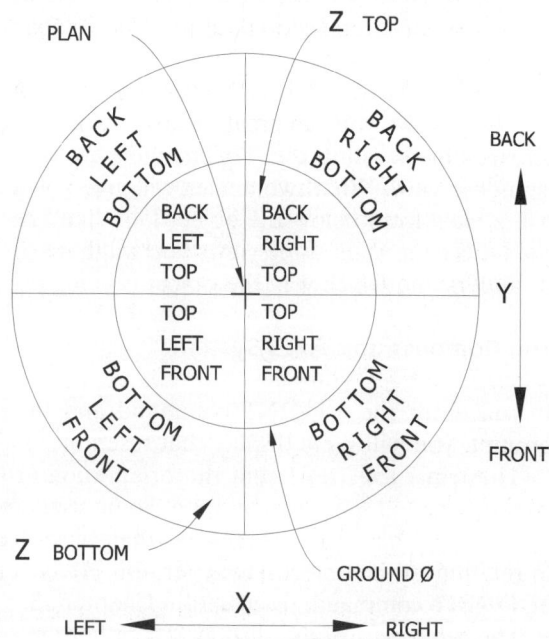

Figure 12-31

12.7   Review Material

Questions

1. It is possible to create a 3D view in which the grid is indistinguishable from an isometric snap grid. How is this grid and objects drawn on it different from the isometric grid and objects drawn on it?
2. What is a wireframe model?
3. What is the significance of the W on the UCS icon?
4. What coordinates indicate a displacement of −5 in the z direction from the point (6,6,6)?
5. Why is it usually necessary to utilize object snap to select a point on an object outside of the XY plane of the current UCS?
6. What information defines a User Coordinate System?
7. What is the right-hand rule?
8. What command did you use in this chapter that drew a surface rather than a wire entity?
9. You were apparently able to draw a line from a point in the xy plane to a point above the plane without using object snap because both points appeared to be on grid snap points. What will happen when you view this line from another viewpoint?
10. What angle from the xy plane defines a plan view?
11. What angle in the xy plane defines a front view?

Drawing Problems

1. Set up a southeast isometric 3D viewpoint in the World Coordinate System and draw a regular hexagon with a circumscribed radius of 4.0 units.
2. Create a half-sized scaled copy of the hexagon centered at the same center as the original hexagon; then move the smaller hexagon 5.0 units up in the z direction.
3. Connect corresponding corners of the two hexagons to create a tapered hexagonal prism in three dimensions.
4. Create a UCS aligned with any of the faces of the hexagonal prism.
5. Use this UCS to draw the text "Lamp Shade", at 0.3 units high, on the face that aligns with the new UCS.
6. View the object from the world plan view, the plan view of the current UCS, and a northwest isometric view.

12.8   WWW Exercise #12 (Optional)

Whenever you are ready:

⊞   Make sure that you are connected to your Internet service provider.

⊞   Type "browser", open the Web toolbar and select the Browse Web tool, or open your system browser from the Windows 98 taskbar.

⊞   If necessary, navigate to our companion Web site at "www. prenhall.com/dixriley".

12.9   Drawing 12-1: Clamp

This drawing is similar to the one you did in the chapter. Two major differences are that it is drawn from a different viewpoint and that it includes dimensions in the 3D view. This will give you additional practice in defining and using User Coordinate Systems. Your drawing should include dimensions, border, and title.

DRAWING SUGGESTIONS

- We drew the outline of the clamp in a horizontal position and then worked from a northeast isometric or back, left, top point of view.
- Begin in WCS plan view, drawing the horseshoe-shaped outline of the clamp. This will include fillets on the inside and outside of the clamp. The more you can do in plan view before copying to the top plane, the less duplicate editing you will need to do later.
- When the outline is drawn, switch to a northeast isometric view.
- COPY the clamp outline up 1.50.
- Define User Coordinate Systems as needed, and save them whenever you are ready to switch to another UCS. You will need to use them in your dimensioning.
- The angled face, the slots, and the filleted surfaces can be drawn just as in the chapter.

DIMENSIONING IN 3D

The trick to dimensioning a 3D object is that you will need to restore the appropriate UCS for each set of dimensions. Think about how you want the text to appear. If text is to be aligned with the top of the clamp (for example, the 5.75 overall length), you will need to draw that dimension in a "top" UCS; if it is to align with the front of the object (the 17 degree angle and the 1.50 height), draw it in a "front" UCS, and so forth.

- Define a UCS with the "View" option in order to add the border and title. Type "UCS", and then "v". This creates a UCS aligned with your current viewing angle.

SETTING SURFTAB1

Notice that there are 8 lines defining the RULESURF fillets in this drawing, compared to 6 in the chapter. This number of lines is controlled by the setting of the variable Surftab1, which is discussed in Chapter 13. You can change it by typing "Surftab1" and entering "8" for the new value.

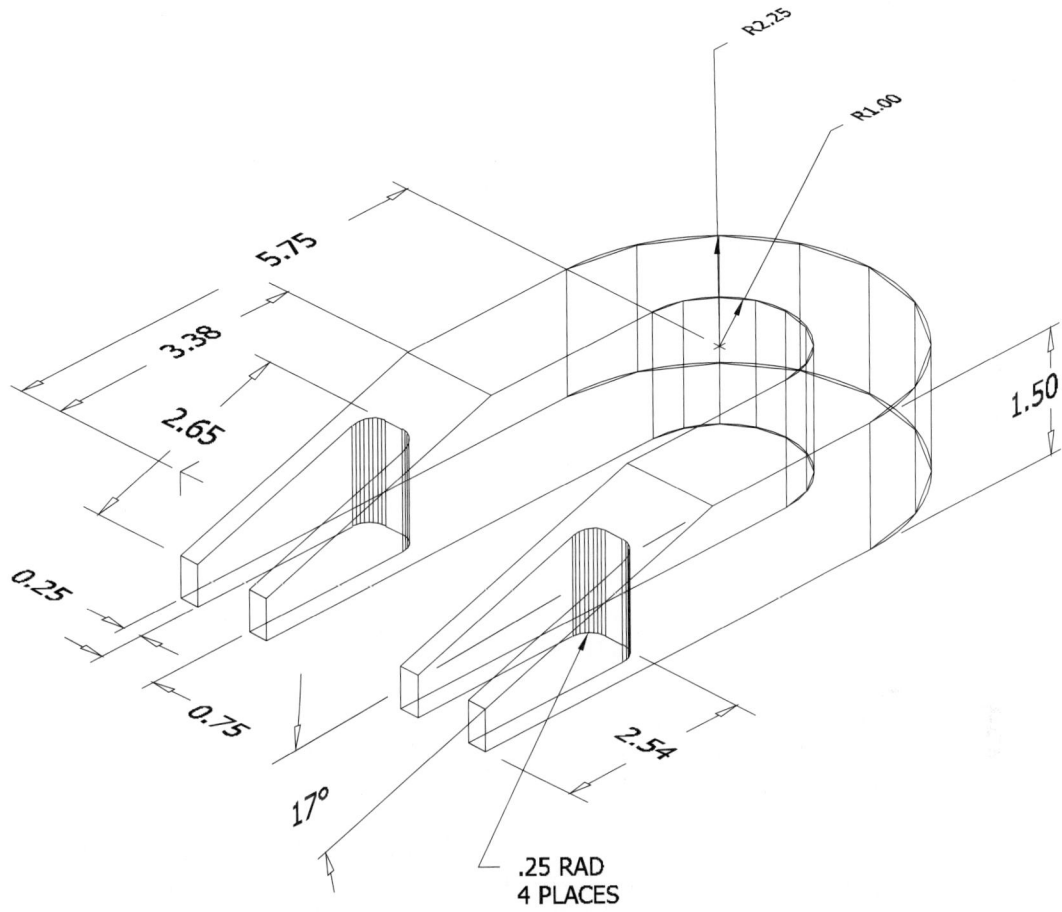

R2.25

R1.00

5.75

3.38

2.65

1.50

0.25

0.75

17°

2.54

.25 RAD
4 PLACES

CLAMP

DRAWING 12-1

12.10 Drawing 12-2: Guide Block

In this drawing you will be working from dimensioned views to create a wireframe model. This brings up some new questions: Which view should you start with? How do you translate the views into the 3D image? A good general rule is this: Draw the top or bottom in the XY plane of the WCS: otherwise, you will have trouble using the VPOINT command.

DRAWING SUGGESTIONS

- In this drawing it is tempting to draw the right side in WCS plan view first, because that is where most of the detail is. If you do this, however, you will have difficulty creating the view as shown. Instead, we suggest that you keep the bottom of the object in the WCS XY plane and work up from there, as has been the practice throughout this chapter. The reason for this is that the VPOINT command works relative to the WCS. Therefore, front–back, left–right, and top–bottom orientations will make sense only if the top and bottom are drawn plan to the WCS.
- Draw the 12.50 × 8.00 rectangle shown in the top view and then copy it up 4.38 to form the top of the guide's base.
- Change over to the same southeast isometric 3D viewpoint we used in the chapter.
- Connect the four corners to create a block outline of the base of the object.
- Now you can define a new UCS on the right side and do most of your work in that coordinate system, since that is where the detail is. Once you have defined the right-side UCS, you may want to go into its plan view to draw the right-side outline, including the arc and circle of the guide. Then come back to the 3D view to copy back to the left side.

    Tip: You can save some time switching viewpoints by using the VIEW command. When a view is saved, it includes the 3D orientation along with the zoom factor that was current at the time of the save. Also, ZOOM previous can be used to restore a previous 3D point of view. It will not, however, restore a UCS.

- Use RULESURF with Surftab1 set to 16 to fill in surfaces between the arcs and circles.

THESE VIEWS & DIMENSIONS
ARE FOR REFERENCE ONLY

GUIDE BLOCK

DRAWING 12-2

3D Wire Frame Model

12.11   Drawing 12-3: Slide Mount

This drawing continues to use the same views, coordinate systems, and techniques as the previous drawings, but it has more detail and is a bit trickier.

DRAWING SUGGESTIONS

- Draw the H-shaped outline of the top view in WCS plan.
- Copy up in the *z* direction.
- Connect the corners to create a 3D shape.
- Define a right-side view and create the slot and holes.
- Copy back to the left side, connect the corners, and trim inside the slot.
- Return to WCS (bottom plane).
- Use RULESURF between circles to create mounting holes.
- Draw filleted cutout and countersunk holes. Each countersunk hole will require three circles, two small and one larger.
- Use RULESURF to create inner surfaces of countersunk holes.

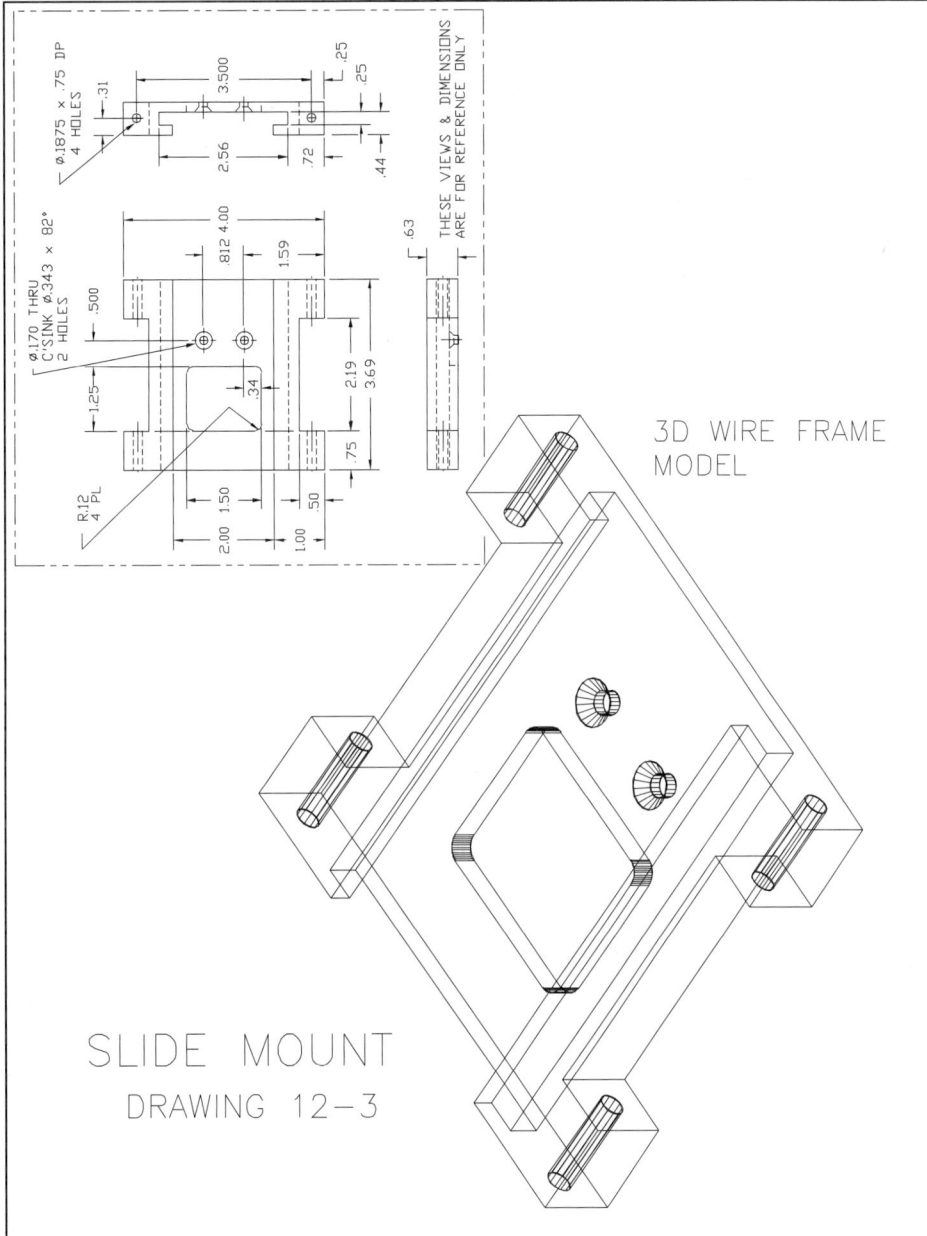

Ø.1875 × .75 DP
4 HOLES

THESE VIEWS & DIMENSIONS
ARE FOR REFERENCE ONLY

Ø.170 THRU
C'SINK Ø.343 × 82°
2 HOLES

R.12
4 PL

3D WIRE FRAME
MODEL

SLIDE MOUNT
DRAWING 12–3

12.12   Drawing 12-4: Stair Layout

This wireframe architectural detail will give you a chance to use architectural units and limits in 3D. It will require the use of a variety of edit commands.

DRAWING SUGGESTIONS

- In the WCS plan view, begin with a 2″ × 12′ rectangle that will become the bottom of a floor joist. This will keep the bottom floor in the plan view, consistent with our practice in this chapter.
- COPY the rectangle up 8″ and connect lines to form the complete joist.
- ARRAY 16″ on center to form the first floor.
- COPY all joists up 9′–6″ to form the second floor.
- Create the stairwell opening in the second floor with double headers at each end.
- Add the subfloor to the first floor.
- The outline of the stair stringers can be constructed in a number of ways. One possibility is as follows: Draw a guideline down from the front of the left double header and then another over 10′–10″ to locate the end of the run; from the right end of the run, draw one riser and one tread, beginning from the top surface of the subflooring; use a multiple copy and Endpoint osnaps to create the other steps; when you get to the top, you will find you need to TRIM the top tread slightly to bring it flush with the header.
- We leave it to you to construct the back line of the stringer. It needs to be parallel with the stringer line and down 1′ from the top tread, as shown.

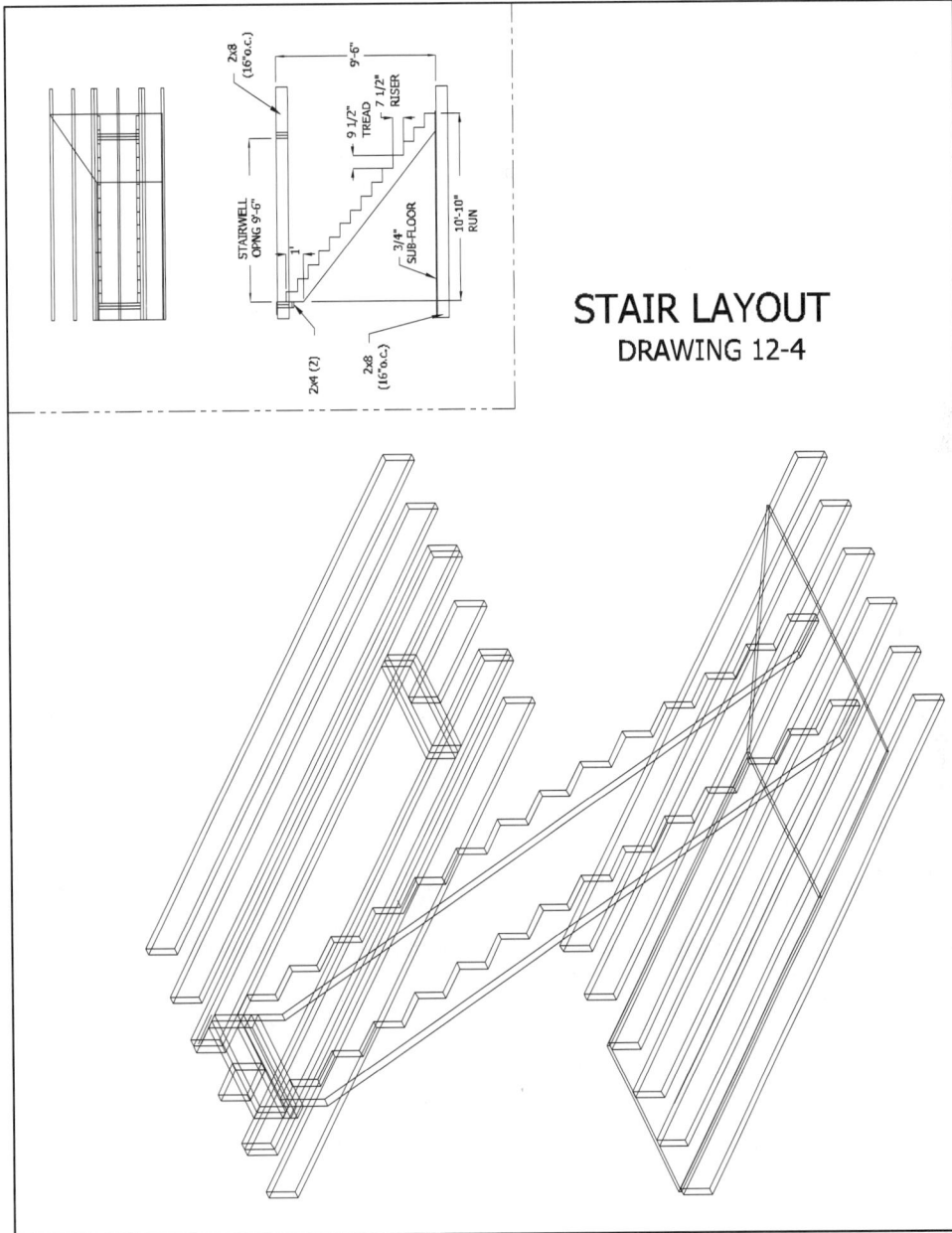

2x8
(16"o.c.)

9'-6"

9 1/2"
TREAD

7 1/2"
RISER

STAIRWELL
OPNG 9'-6"

3/4"
SUB-FLOOR

10'-10"
RUN

2x4 (2)

2x8
(16"o.c.)

STAIR LAYOUT
DRAWING 12-4

12.13 Drawing 12-5: Housing

The objective for this drawing is to create a 3D wireframe model of the housing. The RULESURF command is used extensively. If you use Section B-B as your front view, you will find it easier to create the 3D wireframe.

DRAWING SUGGESTIONS

- Draw the rectangular outline of the top view in WCS plan.
- Copy up in the z direction to the appropriate levels.
- Change the origin of the UCS in the z direction to the proper height; then create the inner rectangle.
- Fillet all corners and rulesurf as necessary to create a 3D shape.
- Use RULESURF between circles to create cylindrical pads and semicircular cutouts. Be sure to change the UCS to the appropriate position when adding detail to a particular view.
- Each counterbore hole will require three circles, two small and one larger.
- Use RULESURF to create inner surfaces of counterbore holes.

Ø1.000

1.750

2.000

SECTION   A-A

R1.125
3 pl

B

R.50

Ø1.500
2 PL

Ø .625 THRU
C'BORE FAR SIDE
Ø 1.000 x .625 DP
3 PLACES

2.750

7.500

0.500

7.000

3.500

A

A

1.000

2.250

R.75
4 PLACES

B

4.000

0.750

4.500

0.750

10.500

3.000

SECTION   B-B

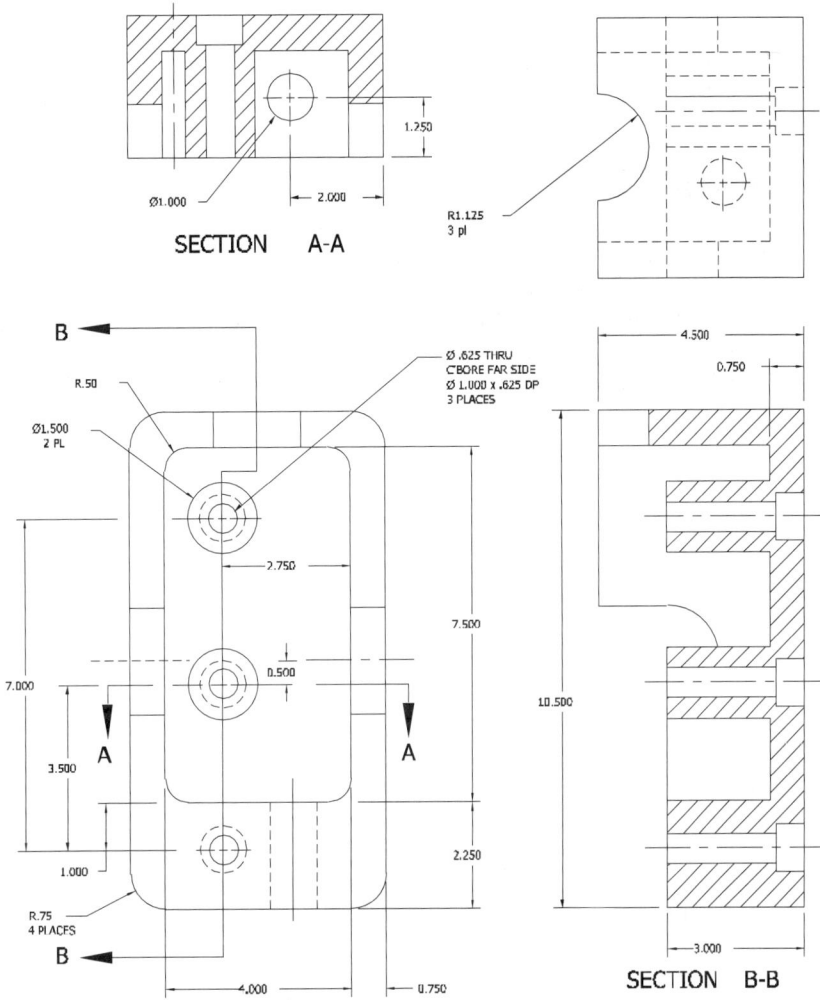

HOUSING
Drawing 12-5

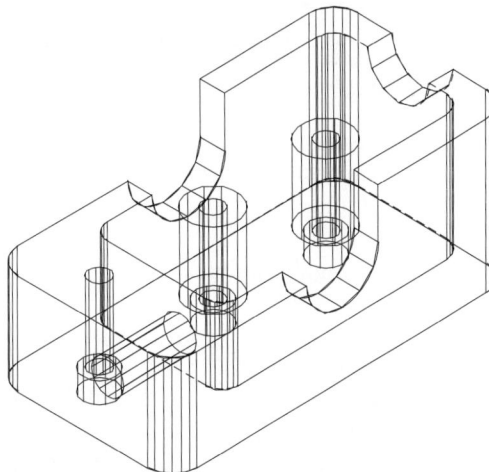

13 Surface Models

COMMANDS

3DFACE	EDGESURF	RULESURF
3DMESH	HIDE	TABSURF
3DORBIT	REVSURF	VPORTS

OVERVIEW

In this chapter you will experience a remarkable expansion of 3D drawing power as we explore AutoCAD 2000 surface modeling. You will quickly see how surface models can be used to create far more realistic images than can be done with wireframe models. Wireframe models create precise mathematical images of the edges and boundaries of objects in space. Surface models fill in the space between the lines with entities that represent the surfaces of objects. In this chapter we will introduce ways to create and present 3D surfaces. The VPORTS command will allow the creation of multiple tiled viewports so that an object may be viewed from several points of view simultaneously for more precise drawing and editing. The 3DFACE command will be introduced to draw three- and four-sided surfaces. "Polygon meshes" will be used to represent more complex three-dimensional surfaces. Most impressive of all, you will begin to use AutoCAD 2000's new 3DORBIT command, which will allow you to rotate images in 3D space in realtime as a more dynamic method of adjusting viewpoints.

TASKS

13.1 Using multiple tiled viewports
13.2 Creating surfaces with 3DFACE
13.3 Removing hidden lines with HIDE
13.4 Using 3D polygon mesh commands
13.5 Adjusting viewpoints with 3DORBIT
13.6 Hiding, Shading, and continuous orbit
13.7 Creating surface models using the "3D Objects" AutoLISP routines
13.8 Creating approximated surfaces using PEDIT
13.9 Review Material
13.10 WWW Exercise #13 (Optional)
13.11 Drawing 13-1: REVSURF Designs
13.12 Drawing 13-2: Picnic Table
13.13 Drawing 13-3: Globe
13.14 Drawing 13-4: Nozzle

13.1   Using Multiple Tiled Viewports

GENERAL PROCEDURE

1. Highlight Viewports on the View menu.
2. Select New Viewports....
3. Select number and orientation of viewports.
4. Define views in each viewport.

A major feature needed to draw effectively in 3D is the ability to view an object from several different points of view simultaneously as you work on it. The VPORTS command is easy to use and can save you from having to jump back and forth between different views of an object. Viewports can be used in 2D to place several zoom magnifications on the screen at once. More important, viewports can be used to place several 3D viewpoints on the screen at once. This is a significant drawing aid. If you do not continually view an object from different points of view, it is easy to create entities that appear correct in the current view but that are clearly incorrect from other points of view.

In this task we will divide your screen in half and define two views so that you can visualize an object in plan view and a 3D isometric view at the same time. As you work, remember that this is only a display command. The viewports we use in this chapter will be simple model space "tiled" viewports. Tiled viewports cover the complete drawing area, do not overlap, and cannot be plotted simultaneously. Plotting multiple viewports is accomplished in paper space layouts with floating viewports, as demonstrated in Chapter 6.

⊕ Highlight Viewports on the View menu.

This will open the submenu shown in Figure 13-1.

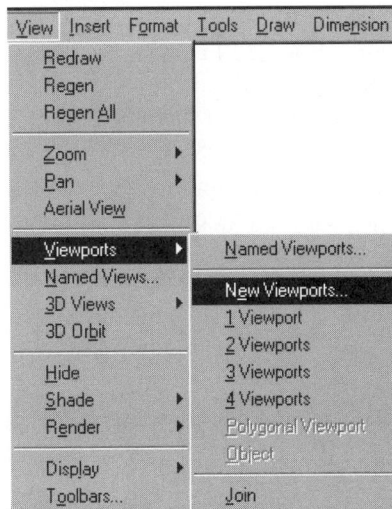

Figure 13-1

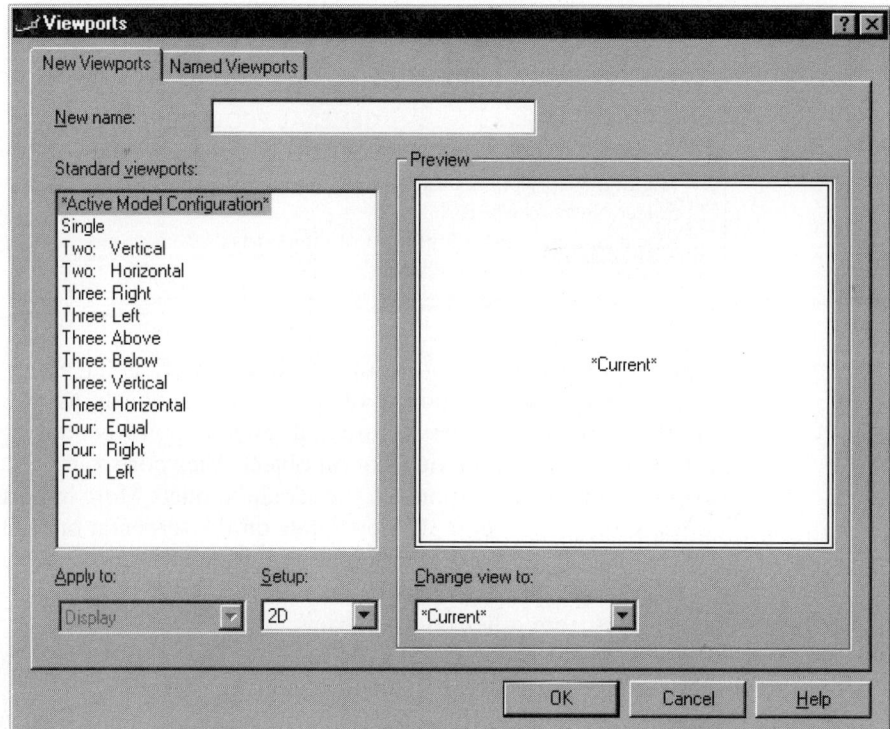

Figure 13-2

We will use the New Viewports option.

⊕ Select New Viewports....

This will open the Viewports dialog box shown in Figure 13-2. The dialog has two tabs. Since you selected New Viewports from the menu, the New Viewports tab will be showing. If you had selected Named Viewports, the other tab would be showing. The two tabs are similar, but New Viewports contains predefined options, while the Named Viewports contains viewport configurations that have been previously created and saved in your drawing.

Looking at the New Viewport tab, at the top you see an edit box so that you can give a name to a viewport configuration when you define it. This is only useful if you create a configuration that is not already on the list. The white panel on the left lists predefined configurations. Active Model Configuration is basically the current configuration in the drawing. Single is the one viewport drawing area we have been working in since the beginning. The others are defined by number and location of viewports.

⊕ Select "Two Vertical:".

The Preview on the right will change to show two vertical viewports, as illustrated in Figure 13-3. Notice that both viewports currently contain the current model space display. Look at the three list boxes at the bottom of the dialog. The Apply to list gives you the choice of applying configuration changes to the whole display or just to a selected viewport. This means you

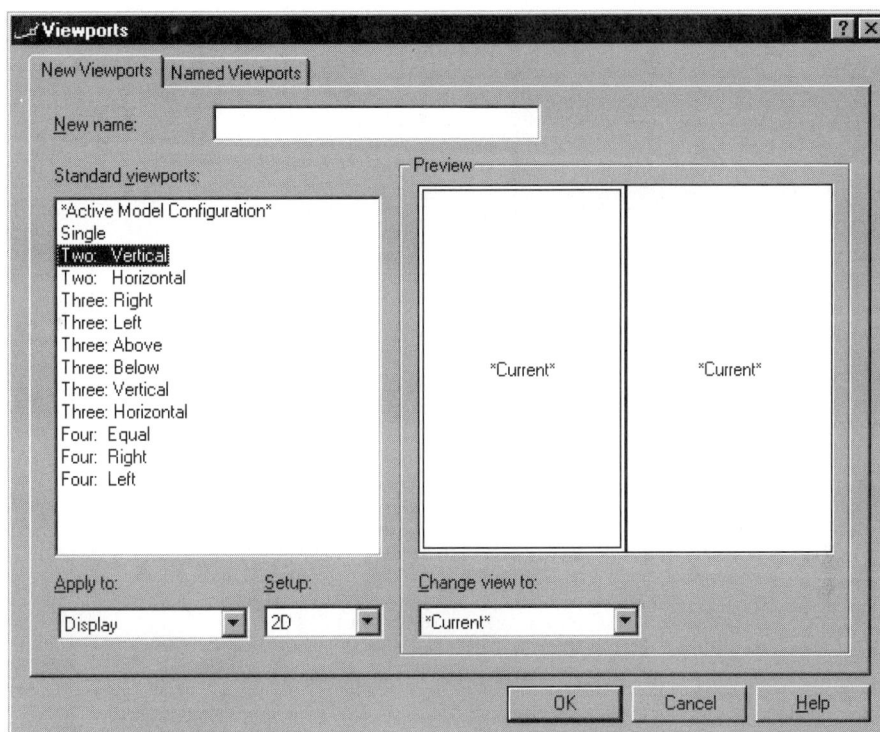

Figure 13-3

can create viewports by dividing already defined viewports. For now, display should be selected in this list.

The Setup list has two options, 2D and 3D. Standard 2D configurations will always start with the current view in each viewport. 3D configurations add standard top, front, and southeast isometric views. If you look at the third list box, labeled "Change view to:", you will see that current is the only choice. Now try this:

⊕ Open the Setup list and select 3D.

The preview will change to show a top view on the left and a southeast isometric view on the right, as shown in Figure 13-4. Notice that the top viewport is selected with a border in the preview and that "*Top*" is now showing in the Change view list.

⊕ Open the Change view to: list.

In addition to Top, you will see Bottom, Front, Back, and Left viewpoint options. These are the standard options for the left viewport in a two-viewport vertical configuration. With this list you can change the view in any selected viewport to create your own configuration. Then if you add a name in the New name edit box at the top of the dialog, the named configuration will be added to a list on the Named Viewports tab.

⊕ Select the right viewport in the preview by clicking anywhere inside it.

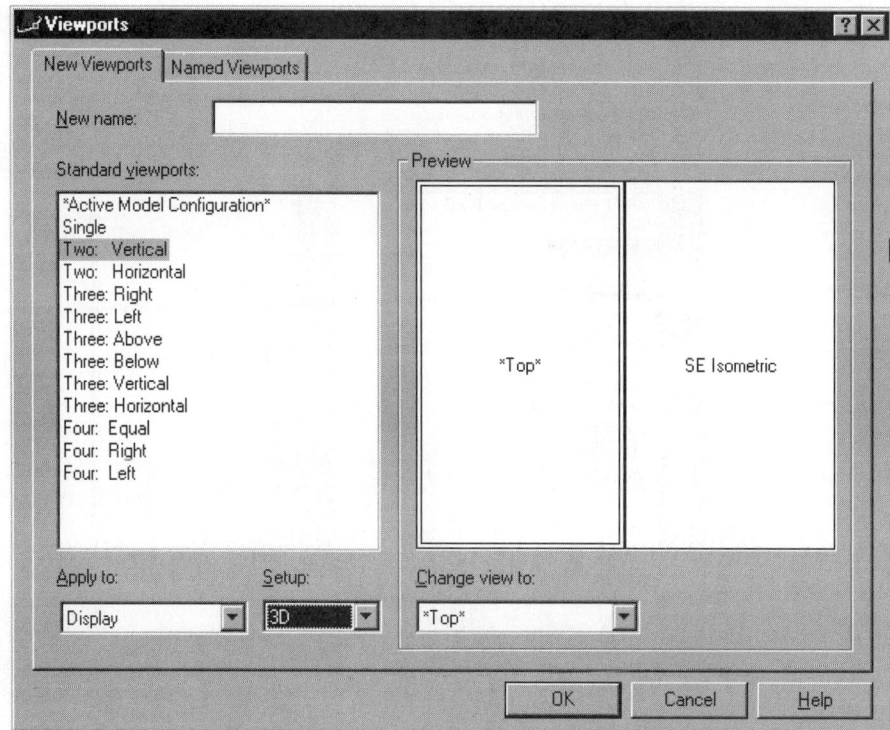

Figure 13-4

The right viewport will be selected with a border and the Change view list will show Southeast isometric. If you open the list you will see that the other options here are the four standard isometric views, SW, SE, NW, and NE.

The standard Two: Vertical 3D viewport with a top view on the left and a southeast isometric view on the right is the configuration we will be working with in this chapter, but before leaving the dialog box, look at some other options. For example:

⊕ Select "Three: Right".

Your preview will now resemble the one in Figure 13-5. This is also a very common configuration.

⊕ Select "Four: Equal", and any other configurations you wish to preview.
⊕ Select "Two: Vertical" before leaving the dialog.
⊕ Click OK to exit the dialog.

Your screen will resemble Figure 13-6, except that the grid will be off in the right viewport.

If you move your pointing device back and forth between the windows, you will see an arrow when you are on the left and the cross hairs when you are on the right. This indicates that the right window is currently active. Drawing and editing can be done only in the active window. To work in another window, you need to make it current by picking it with your pointing device. Often this can be done while a command is in progress.

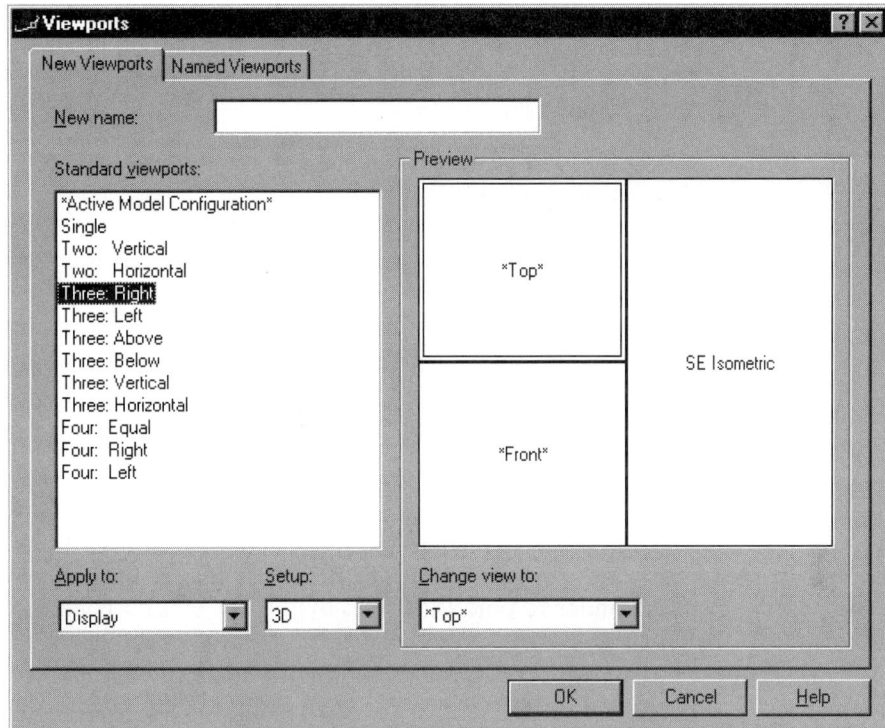

Figure 13-5

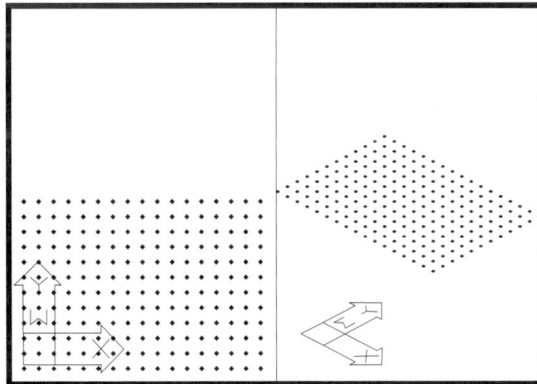

Figure 13-6

⊕ Move the cursor into the left window and press the pickbutton on your pointing device.

Now the cross hairs will appear in the left viewport, and you will see the arrow when you move into the right viewport.

⊕ Move the cursor back to the right and press the pickbutton again.

This will make the right window active again.

⊕ If the grid is off in your right viewport, turn it on (F7).

We are now ready to begin drawing in this viewport configuration. Once you have defined viewports, any drawing or editing done in the active viewport will appear in all the viewports. As you draw, watch what happens in both viewports.

13.2 Creating Surfaces with 3DFACE

GENERAL PROCEDURE

1. Open the Draw menu, highlight Surfaces, and select 3D Face, or select the 3D Face tool from the Surfaces toolbar.
2. Pick three or four points going around the face.
3. Continue defining edges or press Enter to exit the command.

3DFACE creates triangular and quadrilateral surfaces. 3D faces are built by entering points in groups of three or four to define the outlines of triangles or quadrilaterals, similar to objects formed by the 2D SOLID command. The surface of a 3D face is not shown on the screen, but it is recognized by the HIDE command and by the RENDER command and other rendering programs, such as 3D Studio.

Layering is critical in surface modeling. Surfaces quickly complicate a drawing so that object selection and object snap become difficult or impossible. Also, you may want to be able to turn layers off or freeze them to achieve the results you want from the HIDE command. You may eventually want a number of layers specifically defined for faces and surfaces, but this will not be necessary for the current exercise.

⊕ **Open the Draw menu and highlight Surfaces.**
This calls the submenu shown in Figure 13-7. There is also a Surface toolbar with a 3D Face tool, as shown in Figure 13-8.

⊕ **Select "3D Face".**
AutoCAD will prompt

Specify first point or [Invisible]:

You can define points in either of the two viewports. In fact, you can even switch viewports in the middle of the command.

⊕ **Pick a point similar to P1, as shown in Figure 13-9.**
AutoCAD prompts

Specify second point or [Invisible]:

⊕ **Pick a second point, moving around the perimeter of the face, as shown.**
Be aware that the correct order for defining 3D faces is different from the 2D SOLID command (Chapter 9). It is important to pick points in order around the face; otherwise you will get a bow tie or hourglass effect.
AutoCAD prompts

Specify third point or [Invisible]<exit>:

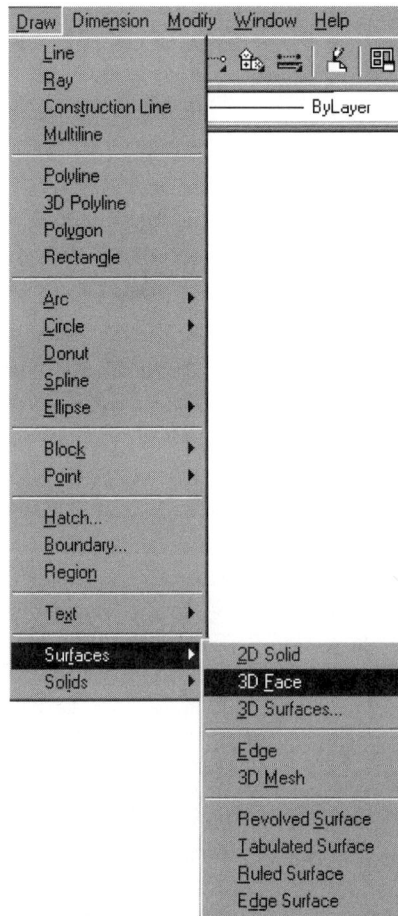

Figure 13-7

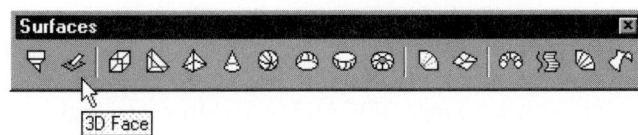

Figure 13-8

⊕ Pick a third point, as shown.

AutoCAD prompts

```
Specify fourth point or [Invisible]<create three-sided face>:
```

Note: If you pressed Enter now, AutoCAD would draw the outline of a triangular face, using the three points already given.

⊕ Pick the fourth point of the face.

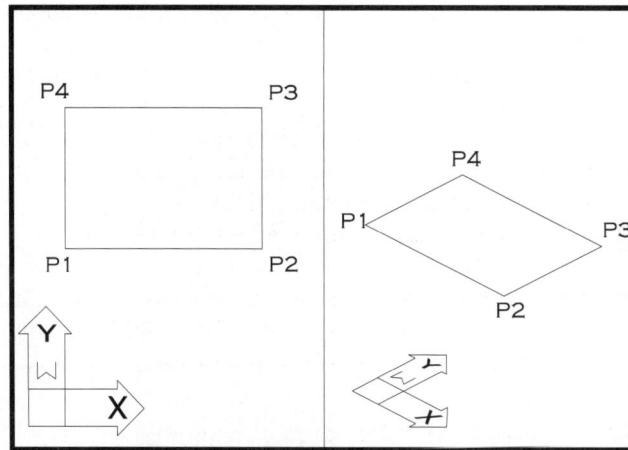

Figure 13-9

AutoCAD draws the fourth edge of the face automatically when four points have been given, so it is not necessary to complete or close the rectangle.

AutoCAD will continue to prompt for third and fourth points so that you can draw a series of surfaces to cover an area with more than four edges. Keep in mind, however, that drawing faces in series is only a convenience. The result is a collection of independent three- and four-sided faces.

⊞ **Press Enter or the space bar to exit the 3DFACE command.**

In the next task we will copy this face in order to demonstrate the HIDE command. But first, a word about invisible edges.

Invisible Edges in 3Dfaces

The edges of a 3Dface can be visible or invisible as desired. To define an invisible edge, type "i" before entering the first point of the edge. You can even define "phantom" 3D faces in which no edges are visible. There is also an EDGE command that allows you to change the visibility of edges after they have been drawn.

Take a look at Figure 13-10. This figure illustrates the need for invisible edges in 3Dfaces. Since 3DFACE only draws triangles or quadrilaterals, objects with

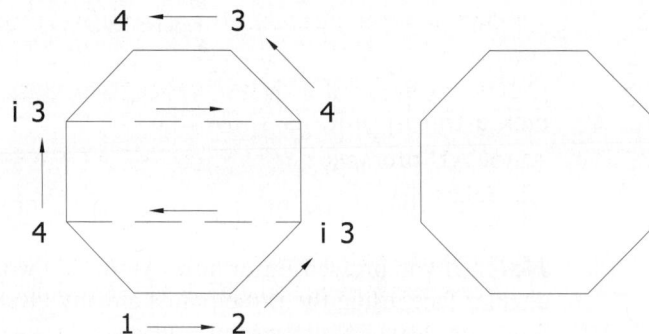

Figure 13-10

more than four edges must be drawn as combinations of three- and four-sided shapes. An octagon, for example, can be drawn as two trapezoids and a rectangle, as shown. However, you would not want the two horizontal edges across the middle showing, so the command allows you to make them invisible by typing "i" before picking the point that begins the invisible edge. This takes forethought and planning. You must remember that the end point of a visible edge also may be the starting point of the next invisible edge.

It may be easier to draw edges visible and then go back and make some invisible using the EDGE command. You can access EDGE by opening the Draw menu, highlighting surfaces, and selecting Edge. The command will ask you to select edges and then will reverse the visibility of any edge you select. It includes a Display option, which will display all edges so that they may be selected.

> **Note:** Invisible edges will be hidden if the "Splframe" system variable is set to 0, the default setting. If the variable is set to 1, invisible edges will be displayed. To change this setting, type "Splframe" and then "1".

13.3   Removing Hidden Lines with HIDE

> ### GENERAL PROCEDURE
>
> 1. Type "hi," or open the View menu and select Hide.
> 2. Wait ….

The HIDE command is easy to execute. However, execution may be slow in large drawings, and careful work may be required to create a drawing that hides the way you want it to. This is an important objective in surface modeling. When you've got everything right, HIDE will temporarily remove all lines and objects that would be obstructed in the current view, resulting in a more realistic representation of the object in space. A correctly surfaced model can also be used to create a shaded rendering. Hiding has no effect on wireframe drawings, since there are no surfaces to obstruct lines behind them.

⊕ To begin this exercise, you should have the 3Dface from the previous task on your screen.

⊕ COPY the face up 2 units in the *z* direction, using the following procedure:

1. Select the Copy Object tool from the Modify menu.
2. Select the face.
3. Right click to end object selection.
4. Type and enter "0,0,2".
5. Press Enter or the space bar at the prompt for a second point.

You now have two 3Dfaces in your drawing. Since the second is directly over the first, you cannot see both in the top view. From the southeast isometric

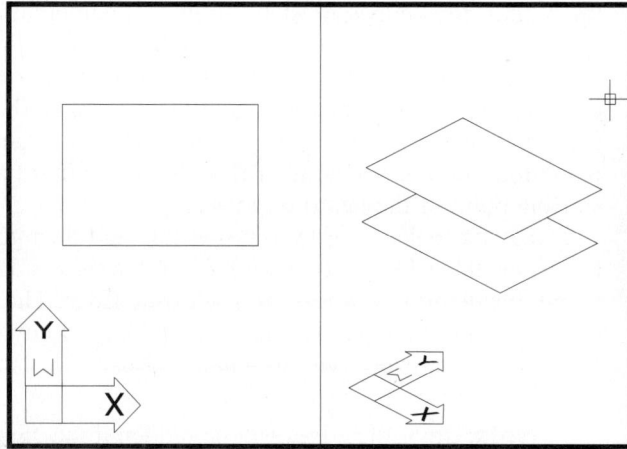

Figure 13-11

viewpoint in the right viewport, however, the second face only partially covers the first. Since these are surfaces, rather than wireframes, the top face should hide part of the lower face.

⊕ Make the right viewport active.

⊕ Type "hi" or open the View menu and select "Hide".

Your screen should be regenerated to resemble Figure 13-11. In this case the hiding and regeneration will happen very quickly. In a larger drawing you will have to wait.

Following are some important points about hidden line removal that you should read before continuing:

1. Hidden line removal can be done from the plot configuration dialog box. However, due to the time involved and the difficulty of getting a hidden view just right, it is usually better to experiment on the screen first and then plot with hidden lines removed when you know you will get the image you want.
2. The image created through hidden line removal is *not* retained in BLOCKing, WBLOCKing, GROUPing, or saving VIEWs.
3. Hidden line removal can be captured in slides (the MSLIDE and VSLIDE commands, Chapter 9). But remember, slides cannot be plotted.
4. Layer control is important in hidden line removal. Layers that are frozen are ignored by the HIDE command, but layers that are off are treated like layers that are visible. This can, for example, create peculiar blank spaces in your display if you have left surfaces or solids on a layer that is off at the time of hidden line removal.

13.4   Using 3D Polygon Mesh Commands

GENERAL PROCEDURE
1. Create geometry to be used in defining the surface.
2. If necessary, set Surftab1 and Surftab2.
3. Enter a 3D polygon mesh command.
4. Use existing geometry to define the surface.

3DFACE can be used to create simple surfaces. However, most surface models require large numbers of faces to approximate the surfaces of real objects. Consider the number of faces in Figure 13-12, the globe you will be creating when you do Drawing 13-3. Obviously, you would not want to draw such an image one face at a time.

AutoCAD includes a number of commands that make the creation of some types of surfaces very easy. These powerful commands create 3D polygon meshes. Polygon meshes are made up of 3D faces and are defined by a matrix of vertices. They can be treated as single entities and edited with the PEDIT command or exploded into individual 3D faces.

⊕   To begin this task, ERASE the two faces from the last task and draw an arc and a line below it, as shown in Figure 13-13. Exact sizes and locations are not important.

The entities may be drawn in either viewport.

Figure 13-12

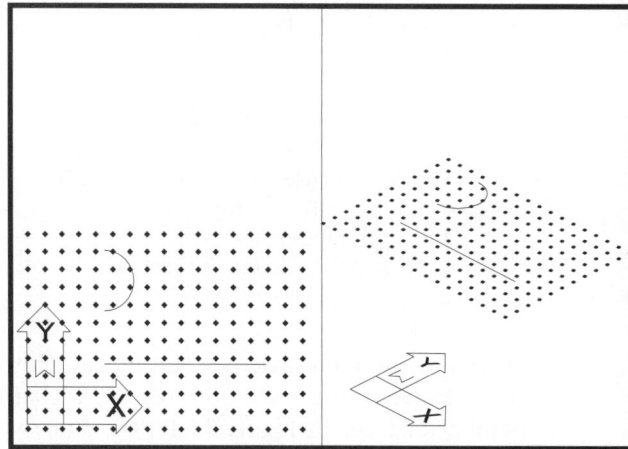

Figure 13-13

Now we will define some 3D surfaces using the arc and line you have just drawn.

TABSURF

The first surface we will draw is called a "tabulated surface." To use the TAB-SURF command, you need a line or curve to define the shape of the surface and a vector to show its size and direction. The result is a surface generated by repeating the shape of the original curve at every point along the path specified by the vector.

⊕   Open the Draw menu, highlight Surfaces, and select Tabulated Surface.

There is also a Tabulated Surface tool on the Surface toolbar, shown previously in Figure 13-8. AutoCAD will prompt

Select object for path curve:

The path curve is the line or curve that will determine the shape of the surface. In our case it will be the arc.

⊕   Pick the arc.

AutoCAD will prompt for a vector:

Select object for direction vector:

We will use the line. Notice that the vector does not need to be connected to the path curve. Its location is not significant, only its direction and length.

There is an oddity here to watch out for as you pick the vector. If you pick a point near the left end of the line, AutoCAD will interpret the vector as extending from left to right. Accordingly, the surface will be drawn to the right. By the same token, if your point is near the right end of the line, the surface will be drawn to the left. Most of the time you will avoid confusion by picking a point on the side of the vector nearest the curve itself.

⊕   Pick a point on the left side of the line.

Your screen will be redrawn to resemble Figure 13-14. Notice that this is a flat surface even though it may look 3D in the left viewport. Tabulated sur-

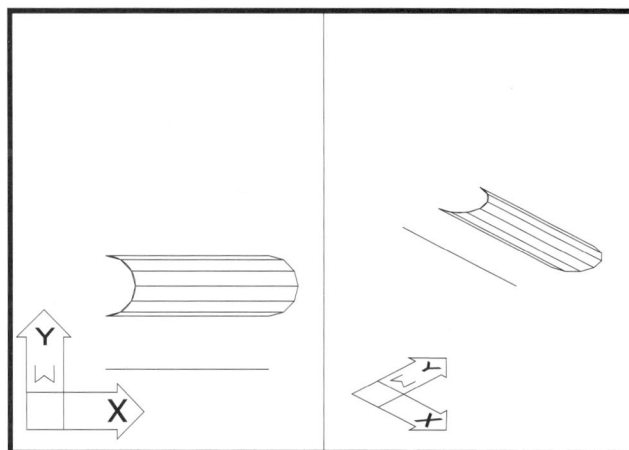

Figure 13-14

faces can be fully 3D, depending on the path and vector chosen to define them. In this case we have an arc and a vector that are both entirely in the XY plane, so the resulting surface is also in that plane.

Surftab1

You will also notice that the surface is defined by long, narrow faces that run parallel to the vector. If you zoom up on either end of the surface, you will see that the arc is only approximated by the shorter edges of these six faces. Unlike the polygons or broken curves AutoCAD often uses to display arcs and circles in order to speed regeneration time, this mesh of quadrilateral faces is the actual current definition of this surface. To achieve a more accurate approximation, we can increase the number of faces. This is done by changing the setting of a variable called "Surftab1" and drawing the object again.

Let's undo the tabulated surface so that we can draw it again with a new Surftab1 setting.

⊕ Type "u" or select the Undo tool from the Standard toolbar.
⊕ Type "surftab1".

AutoCAD prompts:

```
Enter new value for SURFTAB1 <6>:
```

The default value shows why we see six lines in the tabulated surface. When we change the setting, we will get a different number of lines and degree of accuracy.

⊕ Type "12".
⊕ Open the Draw menu, highlight Surfaces, and select Tabulated Surfaces.
⊕ Pick the arc for the path curve.
⊕ Pick the line for the direction vector.

Your screen should now resemble Figure 13-15.

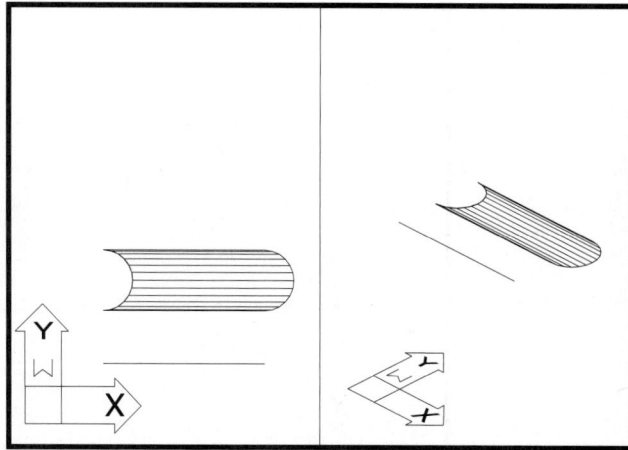

Figure 13-15

RULESURF

TABSURF is useful in defining surfaces that are the same on both ends, assuming you have one end and a vector. Often, however, you have no vector, or you need to draw a surface between two different paths. In these cases you will need the RULESURF command.

For example, what if we need to define a surface between the line and the arc? Let's try it.

⊕ Type "u" to undo the last tabulated surface.

⊕ Open the Draw menu, highlight Surfaces, and select Ruled Surface.

You are familiar with this command sequence from Chapter 12. The first prompt is

Select first defining curve:

⊕ Pick the arc, using a point near the bottom.

Remember that you must pick points on corresponding sides of the two defining curves in order to avoid an hourglass effect.

AutoCAD prompts

Select second defining curve:

⊕ Pick the line, using a point near the left end.

Your screen should resemble Figure 13-16. Again, notice that this surface is within the XY plane even though it may look 3D. Ruled surfaces may be drawn just as easily between curves that are not coplanar.

If you look closely, you will notice that this ruled surface is drawn with 12 lines, the result of our Surftab1 setting.

Some other typical examples of ruled surfaces are shown in the chart in Figure 13-22 at the end of this task.

EDGESURF

TABSURF creates surfaces that are the same at both ends and move along a straight line vector. RULESURF draws surfaces between any two boundaries.

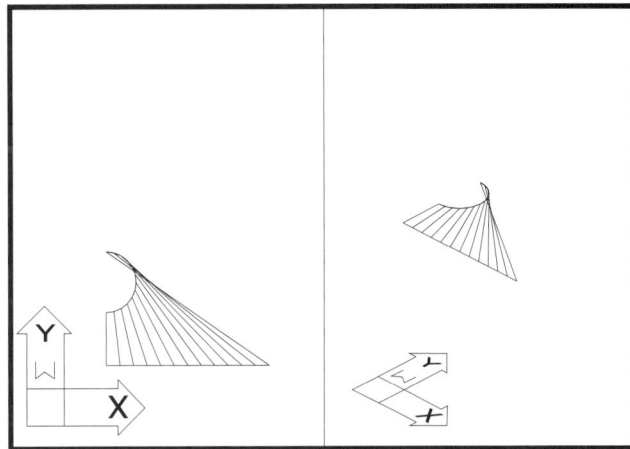

Figure 13-16

EDGESURF draws surfaces that are bounded by four curves. Edge-defined surfaces have a lot of geometric flexibility. The only restriction is that they must be bounded on all four sides. That is, they must have four edges that touch.

To create an EDGESURF, we need to undo our last ruled surface and add two more edges.

⊕ Type "u".

⊕ Add a line and an arc to your screen, as shown in Figure 13-17.
   Remember, you can draw in either viewport.

⊕ Open the Draw menu, highlight Surfaces, and select Edge Surface.
   AutoCAD will prompt for the four edges of the surface, one at a time:

            Select object 1 for surface edge:

⊕ Pick the smaller arc.
   AutoCAD prompts

            Select object 2 for surface edge:

⊕ Pick the larger arc.

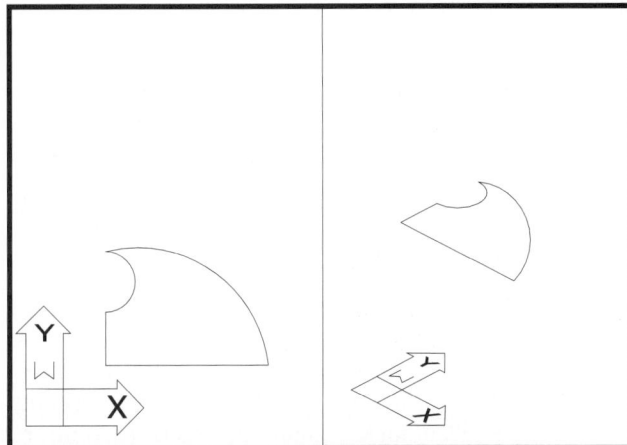

Figure 13-17

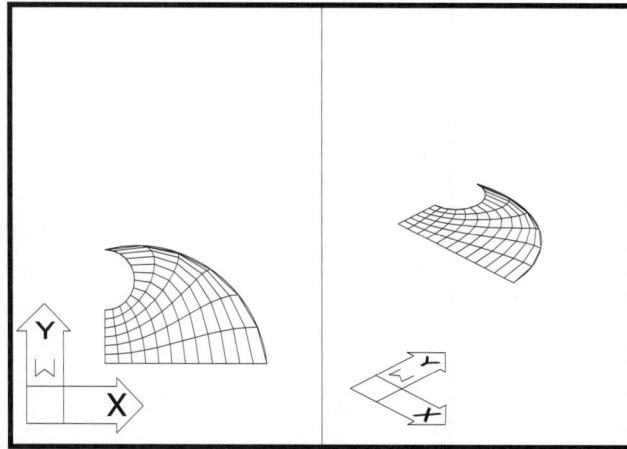

Figure 13-18

AutoCAD prompts

> Select object 3 for surface edge:

⊕ Pick the longer line.

AutoCAD prompts

> Select object 4 for surface edge:

⊕ Pick the smaller line.

Your screen should now resemble Figure 13-18.

Surftab2

There is something new to be aware of here. With TABSURF and RULESURF, surfaces were defined by edges moving in only one direction. With EDGESURF, you have a matrix of faces and edges going two ways. You will notice that there are 12 edges going one way and 6 going the other, as shown in Figure 13-18. This brings us to the variable Surftab2. If we change its setting to 12 also, we will see 12 edges in each direction.

Try it.

⊕ Type "u" to undo the EDGESURF command.
⊕ Type "Surftab2".
⊕ Type "12".
⊕ Enter the EDGESURF command and select the four edges again.

The result should resemble Figure 13-19.

REVSURF

We have one more 3D polygon mesh command to explore, and this one is probably the most impressive of all. REVSURF creates surfaces by spinning a curve through a given angle around an axis of revolution. Just as tabulated surfaces are spread along a linear path, surfaces of revolution follow a circular or arc-shaped

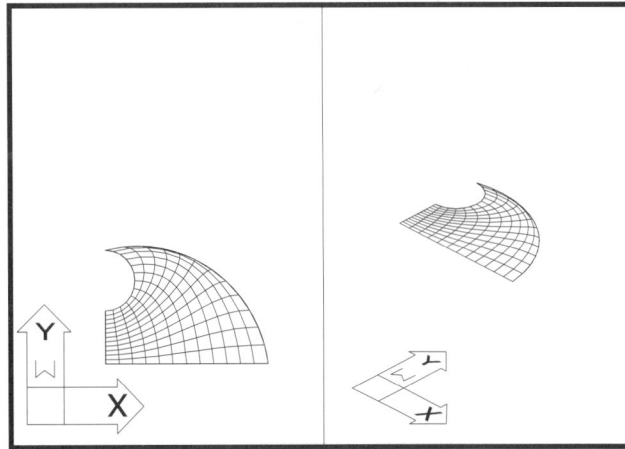

Figure 13-19

path. As a result, surfaces of revolution are always fully three dimensional, even if their defining geometry is in a single plane, as it will be here.

⊕   In preparation for this exercise, undo the EDGESURF, so that your screen resembles Figure 13-17 again.

We will create two surfaces of revolution. The first will be a complete 360-degree surface using the smaller arc and the smaller line for definition. The second will be a 270-degree surface using the larger arc and the larger line.

⊕   Open the Draw menu, highlight Surfaces, and select Revolved Surface.

AutoCAD needs an object to revolve and an axis of revolution to define the surface. The first prompt is

> Select object to revolve:

⊕   Pick the smaller arc.

AutoCAD prompts

> Select object that defines the axis of revolution:

⊕   Pick the smaller line.

AutoCAD now needs to know whether you want the surface to begin at the object itself or somewhere else around the circle of revolution:

> Specify start angle <0>:

The default is to start at the object.

⊕   Press Enter or the space bar.

AutoCAD prompts

> Specify included angle (+=ccw, -=cw) <360>:

Entering a positive or negative degree measure will cause the surface to be drawn around an arc rather than a full circle. The default will give us a complete circle.

⊕   Press Enter or the space bar.

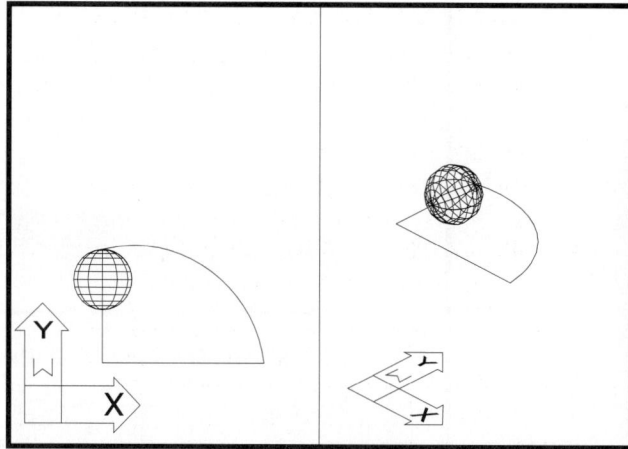

Figure 13-20

   Your screen should be drawn to resemble Figure 13-20. If you look closely, you will see that this globe has 12 lines in each direction. REVSURF, like
EDGESURF, uses both Surftab1 and Surftab2. Also notice that this command
gives us a way to create spheres. If the path curve is a true semicircle and the
axis is along the diameter of the semicircle, then the result will be a sphere.
But there is another way to create a sphere, which we will discuss in Task 13.5.

Now we will create a larger surface that does not start at 0 degrees and does not
include a full circle.

⊕   Press the space bar to repeat the REVSURF command.
⊕   Pick the larger arc as the object to revolve.
⊕   Pick the left end of the longer line for the axis of revolution.
      If you pick the right end, the positive and negative angles will be reversed in
      the two steps following.
⊕   Type "90" for the start angle.
      This will cause the surface to begin 90 degrees up from the XY plane.

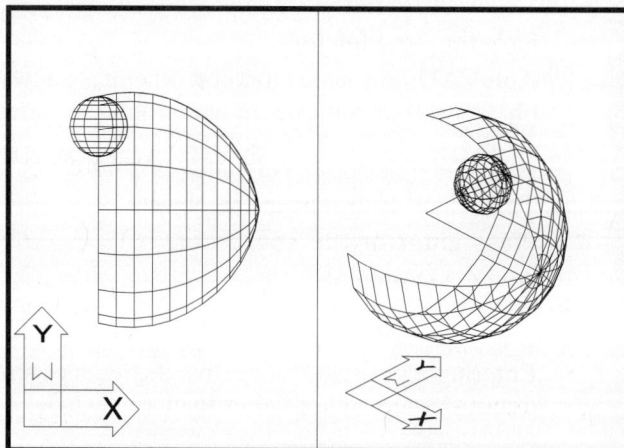

Figure 13-21

⊕ Type "−270" for the included angle.

This will cause the surface to revolve 270 degrees clockwise around the axis. The result should resemble Figure 13-21. You may have to use PAN or the scroll bars in one or both viewports to position the objects on the screen as we have shown them.

Leave this set of surfaces on your screen for the next task, where we will use them to demonstrate one of the most powerful new features in AutoCAD 2000, the 3DORBIT command. Take a look at the polygon mesh examples in Figure 13-22 before proceeding.

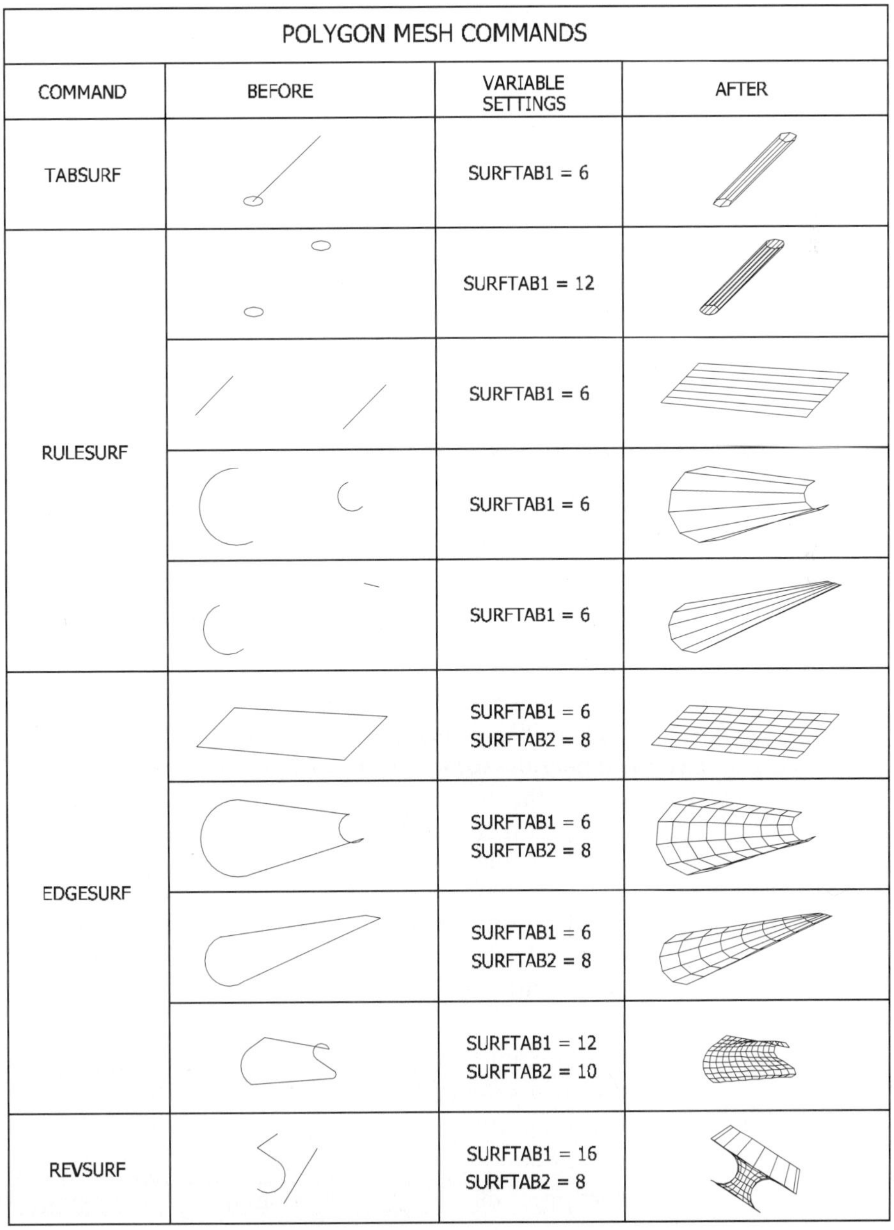

POLYGON MESH COMMANDS			
COMMAND	BEFORE	VARIABLE SETTINGS	AFTER
TABSURF		SURFTAB1 = 6	
RULESURF		SURFTAB1 = 12	
		SURFTAB1 = 6	
		SURFTAB1 = 6	
		SURFTAB1 = 6	
EDGESURF		SURFTAB1 = 6 SURFTAB2 = 8	
		SURFTAB1 = 6 SURFTAB2 = 8	
		SURFTAB1 = 6 SURFTAB2 = 8	
		SURFTAB1 = 12 SURFTAB2 = 10	
REVSURF		SURFTAB1 = 16 SURFTAB2 = 8	

Figure 13-22

13.5 Adjusting Viewpoints with 3DORBIT

GENERAL PROCEDURE

1. Center objects within the viewport.
2. Select objects for viewing.
3. Select 3D Orbit from the view menu.
4. Dynamically adjust viewpoint and shading.

The 3DORBIT command is a dramatic new method for adjusting 3D viewpoints and images. You will quickly see how much more powerful this command is than the VPOINT command and preset views we have introduced so far. This power can lead you into confusing places, however, and should be seen as a tool with its own uses that are distinct from the uses of the simpler preset views with which you are familiar. Using standard views like top, front, and isometric views is generally all you need for the creation and editing of objects, and sticking with these views will keep you well grounded and clear about your position in relation to objects on the screen. But when you move from drawing and editing into presentation, you will find 3DORBIT vastly more satisfying and freeing than the static viewpoint options.

You have on your screen an odd set of surfaces in which a large half opened globe appears to be swallowing a smaller sphere. Because this is a fully three-dimensional surface model, and no two sides of this image are the same, it is ideal for demonstrating 3DORBIT in action.

⊕   Begin by making the right viewport active.

3DORBIT makes use of a tool called an arcball, as shown in Figure 13-23. The first thing you need to do to get a feel for how the arcball works is to have your objects roughly centered within the arcball circle. You can do this precisely using Zoom Center or you can be less precise using the drawing area scroll bars. It is simple if you understand one thing: *The center of the arcball is the center of the current viewport.* Therefore, to place your objects near the center of the arcball you must place them near the center of the viewport, or, more precisely, you must place the center point of the objects at the center of the display. We will be switching back to a single viewport configuration, but it may be easier to center objects in the current setup, so we will do that first.

⊕   Using Zoom Center or the horizontal and vertical scroll bars, adjust objects in the right viewport so that they are roughly centered on the center of the viewport.

Now we will switch to a single viewport.

⊕   With the right viewport active, open the View menu, highlight Viewports, and select 1Viewport.

Your screen will resemble Figure 13-24.

Before entering 3DORBIT you must select viewing objects. 3DORBIT performance will be improved by limiting the number of objects used in view-

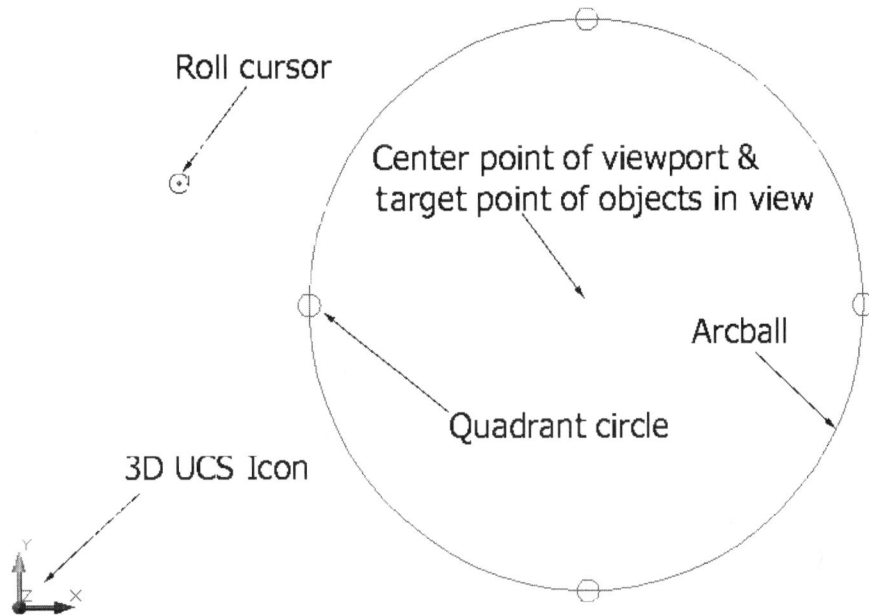

Figure 13-23

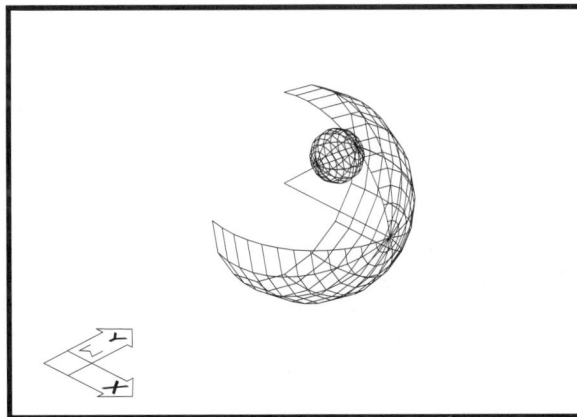

Figure 13-24

ing. Whatever adjustments are made to the viewpoint on the selected objects will be applied to the viewpoint on the entire drawing when the command is exited. In our case we have a fairly simple image to view, so we can use the whole drawing.

⊞ Open the View menu and select 3D Orbit, or select the 3D Orbit tool from the Standard toolbar, as shown in Figure 13-25.

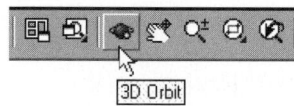

Figure 13-25

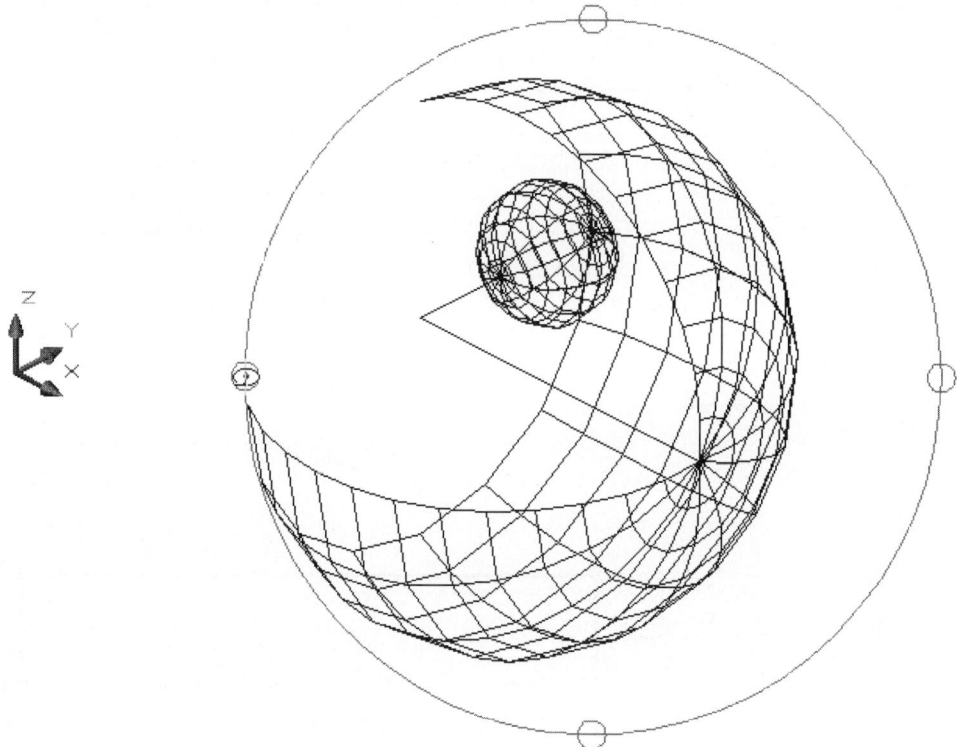

Figure 13-26

There is also a 3D Orbit toolbar with a 3D Orbit tool.

Your screen will be redrawn with the arcball surrounding your surface model, as shown in Figure 13-26. Notice also the 3D UCS icon with the x axis in red, the y axis in green, and the z axis in blue.

The Arcball and Rotation Cursors

The arcball is a somewhat complex image, but it is very easy to use once you get the hang of it. We already know that the center of the arcball is the center of the viewport, or the center of the drawing area in this case since we are working in a single viewport. AutoCAD uses a camera, target analogy to explain viewpoint adjustment. Your viewpoint on the drawing is called the **camera** position. The point at which the camera is aimed is called the **target**. In 3DORBIT, the target point is fixed at the center of the arcball. As you change viewpoints you will be moving yourself around in relation to this fixed target point.

There are four modes of adjustment, which we will take up one at a time. Each mode has its own cursor image, and the mode you are in depends on where you start in relation to the arcball. Try this:

⊕   Carefully move the cursor into the small circle at the left quadrant of the arcball, as shown in Figure 13-26.

When the cursor is placed within either the right or left quadrant circle, the horizontal rotation cursor will appear. This cursor consists of a horizontal elliptical arrow surrounding a small sphere, with a vertical axis running through the sphere. Using this cursor will create horizontal motion around the vertical axis of the arcball. This cursor and the others are shown in Figure 13-27.

⊕   With the cursor in the left quadrant circle and the horizontal cursor displayed, press the pickbutton and hold it down.

Adjustments in 3DORBIT are made by pressing the pickbutton, holding it down, and dragging across the screen.

⊕   Slowly drag the cursor from the left quadrant circle to the right quadrant circle, observing the surface model and the 3D UCS icon as you go.

As long as you keep the pickbutton depressed, the horizontal cursor will be displayed.

⊕   With the cursor in the right quadrant circle, release the pickbutton.

You have created a 180° rotation. Your screen will resemble Figure 13-28.

⊕   With the cursor in the right quadrant circle and the horizontal cursor displayed, press the pickbutton again and then move the cursor slowly back to the left quadrant circle.

If you move very slowly and watch closely you will notice that there is some ambiguity in what you are seeing. Are the objects continuing a 360° rotation, or reversing the previous 180°? Try it again without releasing the pickbutton.

⊕   Place the cursor in the left quadrant circle, press the pickbutton, drag to the right, and then move back to the left.

Observe carefully. If foreground and background suddenly shift for you, that's good. That is the ambiguity we are talking about. We will resolve this confusion in Task 13.6, but first try out the vertical rotation cursor.

⊕   Carefully move the cursor into the small circle at the top of the arcball.

The vertical rotation cursor will appear. When this cursor is visible, rotation will be around the horizontal axis, as shown in the chart in Figure 13-27.

⊕   With the vertical rotation cursor displayed, press the pickbutton and drag down toward the circle at the lower quadrant.

⊕   This time, do not release the pickbutton, but continue moving down to the bottom of the screen.

The viewpoint will continue to adjust and the vertical cursor will be displayed as long as you hold down the pickbutton. Notice that 3D Orbit uses the entire screen, not just the drawing area. You can drag all the way down through the command line, the status bar, and the Windows task bar.

⊕   Spend some time experimenting with vertical and horizontal rotation. We know you want to.

3D ORBIT CURSOR

CURSOR	DESCRIPTION
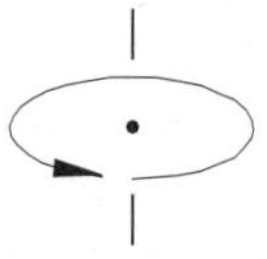 **HORIZONTAL**	Horizontal Cursor Icon displays when you move the cursor over one of the small circles on the left or right of the arcball. Clicking and dragging from either of these points rotates the view around the vertical axis that extends through the center of the arcball. The vertical axis is located on the cursor by a vertical line.
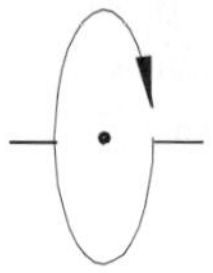 **VERTICAL**	Vertical cursor icon displays when you move the cursor over one of the small circles on the top or bottom of the arcball. Clicking and dragging from either of these points rotates the view around the horizontal axis that extends through the center of the arcball. The horizontal axis is located on the cursor by a horizontal line.
 **ROLL**	Roll cursor icon displays when you move the cursor outside the arcball. Clicking outside the arcball and dragging the cursor around the arcball moves the view around an axis that extends through the center of the arcball, perpendicular to the screen. This is called a roll.
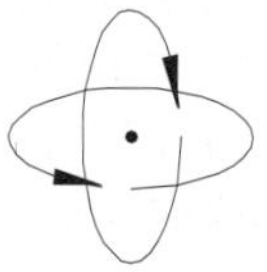 **FREE ROTATION**	Free rotation cursor icon displays when you move the cursor inside the arcball. Clicking inside the arcball and dragging the cursor around manipulates the view freely. It works as if your cursor were grabbing a sphere surrounding the objects and dragging the sphere around the target point. You can drag horizontally, vertically, and diagonally.
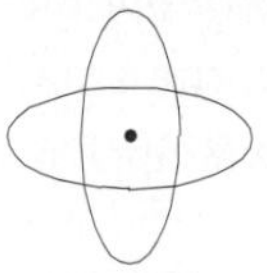 **3DCORBIT**	Continuous orbit cursor displays when you select it from the shortcut menu under (more) Click in the drawing area and drag the cursor in any direction to get the objects moving in the direction that you specify. The speed of the cursor movement determines the speed at which the objects spin.

Figure 13-27

Note that you always have to start in a quadrant to achieve horizontal or vertical rotation. What happens when you move horizontally with the vertical cursor displayed or vice versa? How much rotation can you achieve in one pick and drag sequence vertically? What about horizontally? Are they the same amount? Why is there a difference?

⌗ When you are done experimenting, try to rotate the image back to its original position, shown previously in Figure 13-26.

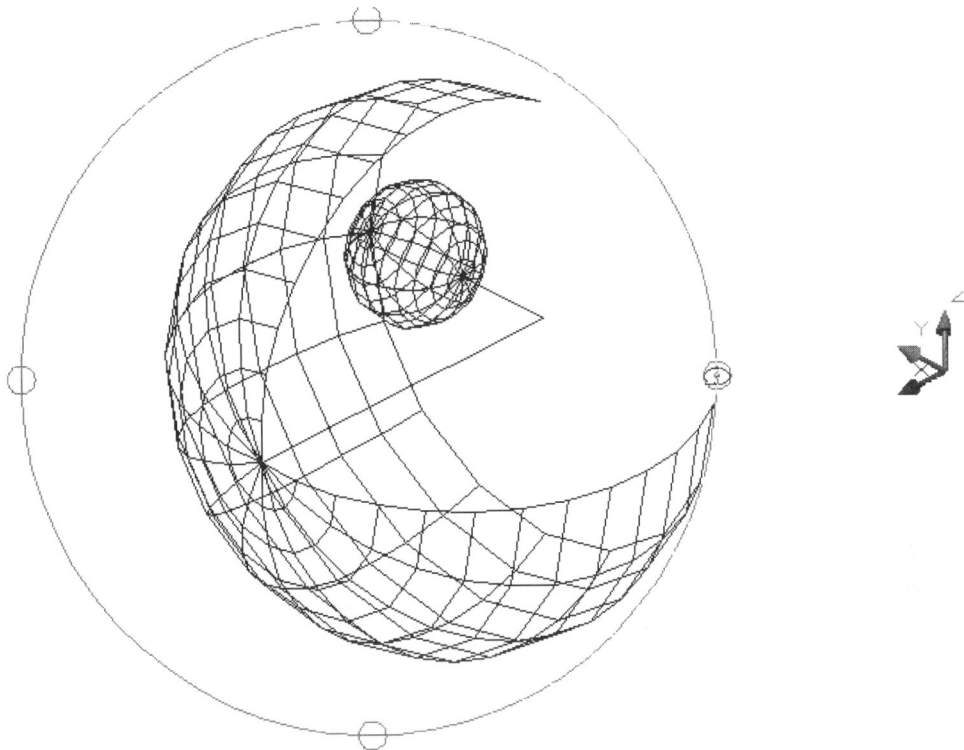

Figure 13-28

If you are unable to get back to this position, don't worry. We will show you how to do this easily in Task 13.6. Now let's try the other two modes.

⊕ Move the cursor anywhere outside the arcball.

With the cursor outside the arcball you will see the roll icon, the third icon in the chart in Figure 13-27. Rolling creates rotation around an imaginary axis pointing directly toward you out of the center of the arcball.

⊕ With the roll icon displayed, press the pickbutton and drag the cursor in a wide circle well outside the circumference of the arcball.

Notice again that you can use the entire screen, outside of the arcball.

⊕ Try rolling both counterclockwise and clockwise.

⊕ Release the pickbutton and then start again.

Note that you must be in the drawing area with the roll icon displayed to initiate a roll and that you must stay outside the arcball.

Finally, try the last cursor mode, the free rotation cursor. This is the most powerful, and therefore the trickiest form of rotation. The free cursor appears when you start inside the arcball, or when you cross into the arcball while rolling. It allows rotation horizontally, vertically, and diagonally, depending on the movement of your pointing device. Try it:

⊕ Move the cursor inside the arcball and watch for the free rotation icon.

⊕ With the free rotation icon displayed, press the pickbutton and drag the cursor within the arcball.

Make small movements vertically, horizontally, and diagonally. What happens if you move outside the arcball?

There is less room to work with the free icon, but it gives you a less restricted type of rotation. Making small adjustments seems to work best. Imagine that you are grabbing the objects and turning them a little at a time. Release the pickbutton and grab again. You may need to do this several times to reach a desired position.

⊕ Try returning the image to approximate the southeast isometric view before proceeding.

You have now explored all of the rotation modes of the 3DORBIT command. In the next task we will move on to some other options readily available in this powerful command. Leave everything as is on your screen. It is best to continue without leaving the 3DORBIT command.

13.6 Hiding, Shading, and Continuous Orbit

3DORBIT is more than an enhanced viewpoint command. It has powerful options for creating shaded views, perspective views, clipped views, and can even be used to create a continuous motion effect. We will explore some of these options now and leave the rest for Chapter 14.

⊕ To begin this task you should have objects centered within your display as shown previously in Figure 13-24. If you are not in 3DORBIT from Task 13.5, select the 3D Orbit tool from the Standard toolbar.

3DORBIT options are accessed through the short cut menu shown in Figure 13-29. We will explore these from the bottom up, looking at the lower two panels and one option from the second panel and leaving other options for Chapter 14.

⊕ Right click anywhere in the drawing area to open the short cut menu.

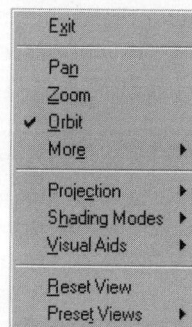

Figure 13-29

Preset and Reset Views

At the bottom of the bottom panel, there is a Preset Views option, which provides convenient access to the standard ten orthographic and isometric viewpoints we have encountered in this chapter and the last. Above this is a Reset View option. This option quickly returns you to the view that was current before you entered 3DORBIT. This is a great convenience, since you can get pretty far out of adjustment and have a difficult time finding your way back. Try it:

⊞ Select Reset View from the short cut menu.

Regardless of where you have been within the 3DORBIT command, your viewpoint will be immediately returned to the southeast isometric view shown in Figure 13-26. If you have left 3DORBIT, the view will be reset to whatever view was current before you re-entered the command. If you have attempted to return to this view manually using the cursors, you will see that there is still a slight adjustment to return your viewpoint to the precise isometric view.

Visual Aids

Moving up to the bottom of the third panel, you will see a Visual Aids selection. Highlighting this line will open a submenu with three options: Compass, Grid, and UCS icon. We will demonstrate the grid, but will not recommend either the grid or the compass because they add confusion to the image on your screen. The compass adds an adjustable gyroscope style image to the arcball. There are three rings of dashed ellipses showing the planes of the *x*, *y*, and *z* axes of the current UCS. Try this out if you like. We do not find it particularly helpful.

The grid option adds a 3D version of the grid with gridlines instead of dots, as shown in Figure 13-30. Try it.

⊞ Select Grid from the submenu.

The 3D grid will be added as shown in Figure 13-30.

⊞ Try adjusting viewpoints with any of the cursors and see how the grid moves with the objects.

⊞ When you are satisfied, right click to open the short cut menu, and select Reset View.

⊞ To turn off the grid, open the short cut menu, highlight Visual Aids, and select Grid.

The third option on the submenu turns the 3D UCS icon on and off.

Shading Modes

Shading is a very powerful feature and brings you to the essence of what surface modeling is all about. We will explore shading and rendering further in Chapter 14, but adding shading to surface objects is a simple process and there is no reason

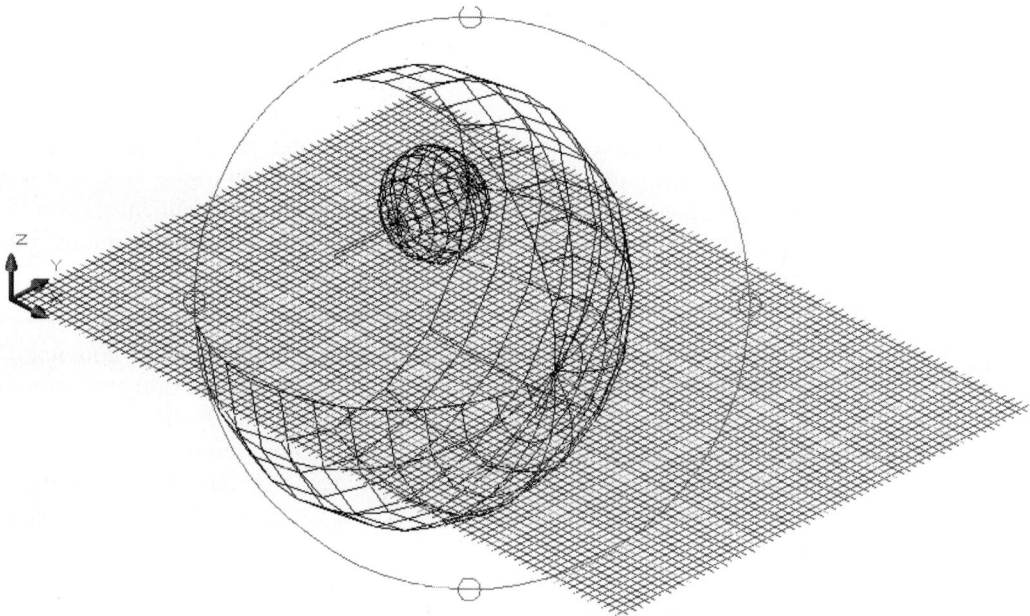

Figure 13-30

not to do it now. Shaded objects are not ambiguous in the way that wireframe images can be, so it is sometimes helpful to be able to add shading while you are adjusting viewpoints. Shading added within the 3DORBIT command is retained when you exit the command.

⊕ Right click to open the short cut menu.

⊕ Highlight Shading Modes.

This opens a submenu with six choices. Wireframe is checked. Hidden will create an image with hidden lines removed. Try it.

⊕ Select Hidden from the submenu.

Your screen will be redrawn with an image like the one in Figure 13-31. This is like the image we created early in the chapter with the HIDE command, except that now you will see that the image can be turned without losing the effect of removing hidden lines.

⊕ Rotate the image using any of the cursors.

Observe how the hidden line effect is retained as the point of view changes.

⊕ Rotate the image through 360° vertically or horizontally.

Notice that there is no longer any ambiguity about the direction of rotation.

Hidden images may be the most useful for basic view definition, but shaded views will take you to a new level of dramatic and realistic presentation. Here and in Chapter 14 when we explore rendering you will find that our black and gray illustrations cannot do justice to the images on your screen.

⊕ Open the short cut menu, highlight Shading Modes, and select Flat Shaded Edges On.

Your screen will resemble Figure 13-32. We chose this option only because it would reproduce most clearly in a gray tone illustration.

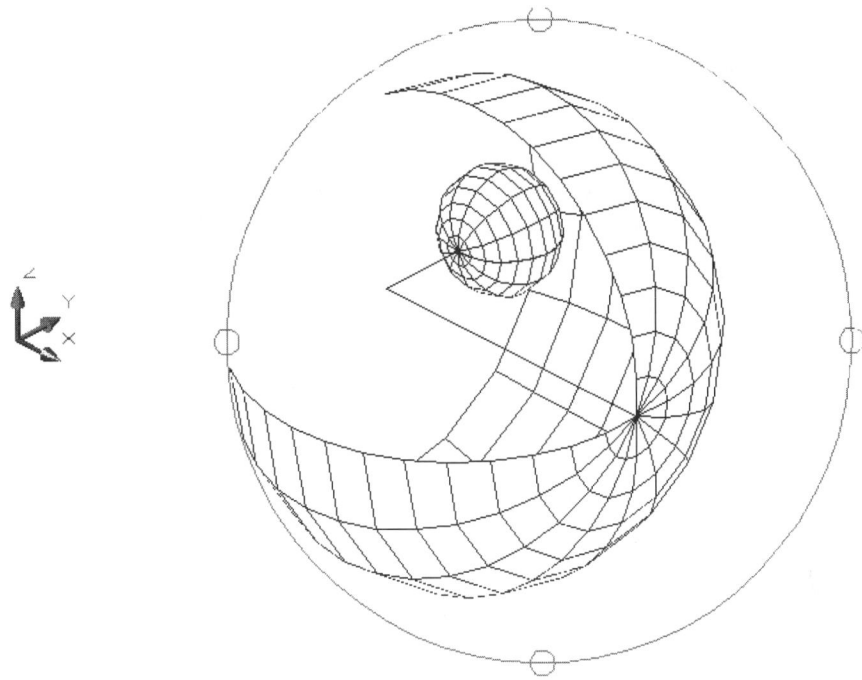

Figure 13-31

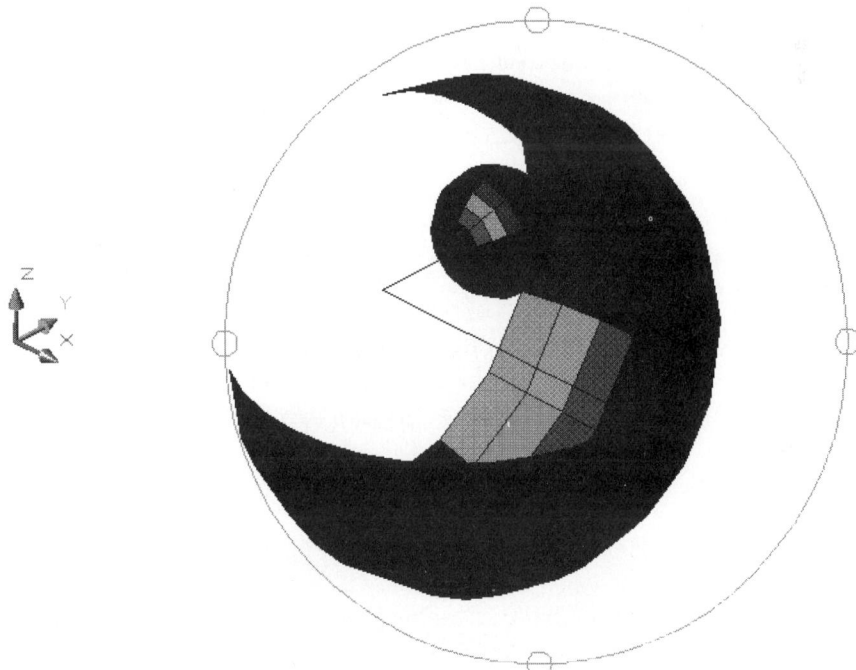

Figure 13-32

⊕ Try out the other three options as well.

As you try the other options look at the lighting effects. You will see that Flat shading adds a lighting effect in a flat, face-by-face format. The reflected light from each face is distinct from faces in adjoining regions and consistent across each face. Gourard shading produces a smooth, faceless image in which reflected light changes gradually across the object without regard to face boundaries. Both Flat and Gourard shading can be done with or without face edges displayed.

⊕ When you are done experimenting, leave objects in whatever shading and point of view you have developed.

Continuous Orbit

Continuous orbit may or may not be the most useful feature of AutoCAD 2000, but it is certainly the most dramatic and the most fun. With continuous orbit you can set objects in motion that continues when you release the pickbutton.

⊕ Right click to open the short cut menu.
⊕ Highlight More at the bottom of the second panel.

This will open a submenu with eight options. We will explore only one in this chapter. Continuous Orbit can also be initiated from the command line. The command is 3DCORBIT.

⊕ Select Continuous Orbit from the submenu.

The arcball will disappear and the continuous orbit icon will be displayed, consisting of a sphere surrounded by two ellipses as shown in Figure 13-33.

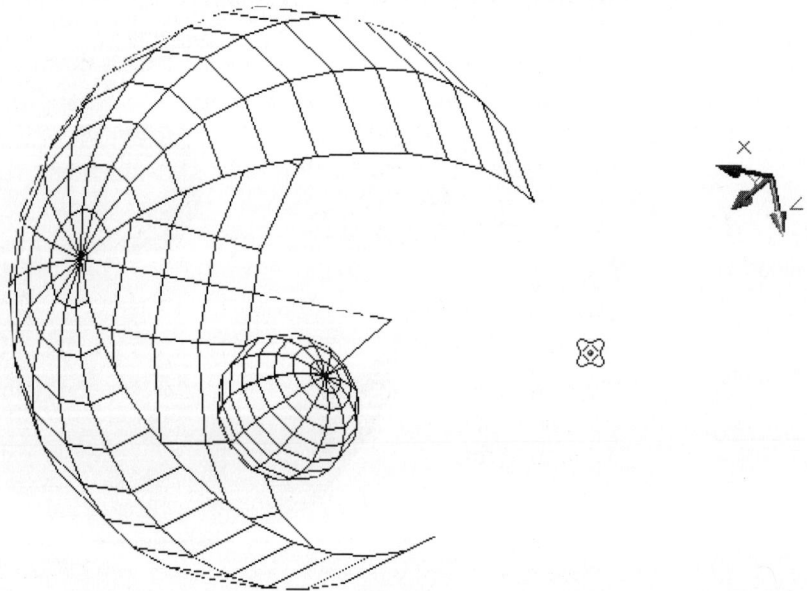

Figure 13-33

The concept is simple: Dragging the cursor will create a motion vector. The direction and speed of the vector will be applied to the model to set it in rotated motion around the target point. Motion will continue until you press the pickbutton again.

⊕ With the continuous orbit cursor displayed, press and hold the pickbutton, then drag the cursor at a moderate speed in any direction.

We cannot illustrate the effect, but if you have done this correctly, your model should now be in continuous rotation. Try it again.

⊕ Press the pickbutton at any time to stop rotation.

⊕ Press and hold the pickbutton again and drag the cursor in a different direction, at a different speed.

⊕ Press the pickbutton to stop rotation.

⊕ Press the pickbutton, drag and release again.

Now try changing directions without stopping.

⊕ While the model is spinning, press and hold the pickbutton and drag in another direction.

Have a ball. Experiment. Play. There's no way we can stop you anyway. Try to create gentle controlled motions in different directions. Try to create fast spins in different directions. Try to create diagonal, horizontal, and vertical spins.

Tip: You will find that the best way to achieve control over continuous orbit is to pick a point actually on the model and imagine that you are grabbing it and spinning it. It is much easier to communicate the desired speed and direction in this way. Note the similarity between the action of continuous orbit and the free rotation icon. The grabbing and turning is the same, but continuous orbit keeps moving when you release the pickbutton, whereas free rotation stops. Also notice that however complex your dragging motion is, continuous orbit only registers one vector, the speed and direction of your last motion before releasing the pickbutton.

One more trick before we leave. Try this:

⊕ Set your model into a moderate spin in any direction.

⊕ With your model spinning, right click to open the short cut menu.

You may have a momentary hesitation, but the model will keep spinning. Many of the short cut menu options can be accessed without disrupting continuous orbit.

⊕ Select Reset View from the short cut menu.

The model will make an immediate adjustment to the original view and continue to spin without interruption. Shading or hidden line removal will be lost, however, unless they were part of the view when 3DORBIT was entered.

⊕ Open the short cut menu again.

⊕ Highlight Shading Modes and select the shading mode of your choice.

Shading will be added and the model will keep spinning.

⊕ Open the short cut menu again and add the grid.

⊕ Open the short cut menu again and add the compass.

Pretty impressive.

⊕ When you are done playing, remove the grid and compass, and then press Enter, Esc, or the space bar to exit 3DORBIT.

You will return to the command prompt, but any changes you have made in point of view and shading will be retained. The 3D UCS icon may also be left on, but can be turned off by opening the View menu, highlighting Display, UCS Icon, and selecting Off.

Before going on you may wish to try editing or drawing with your shaded surface model in view. For example, try moving the model using the MOVE command. You will find that drawing and editing commands continue to work and do not disrupt the shading of the model. This is another extraordinary new feature of AutoCAD 2000.

Next, we will demonstrate the use of the 3D Objects dialog box, which contains commands to create nine more basic surface models. As you create these objects, you may wish to return to 3DORBIT to see how it looks with other objects in view.

13.7 Creating Surface Models Using the "3D Objects" AutoLISP Routines

---

GENERAL PROCEDURE

1. Type "3D" or open the Draw menu, highlight Surfaces, and select 3D Surfaces....
2. Choose an object and follow the prompts.

AutoCAD provides nine AutoLISP routines that create three-dimensional surface models of basic shapes. AutoLISP routines act just like commands but will only work if AutoLISP is loaded with appropriate memory allocation. If you have a problem, see the *AutoCAD Installation Guide*.

Like the 3D meshes explored in Task 13.4, the 3D surface models created this way can be treated as single entities or EXPLODEd and edited as collections of 3D faces. Each of the objects has its own set of prompts, depending on its geometry. We will demonstrate one object in this task and leave the rest for you to explore on your own.

⊕ To begin this task, clear your screen of objects left from Task 13.6.

⊕ Open the View menu, highlight 3D Views, and select SE Isometric.

Your screen should show a single viewport with a SE isometric view.

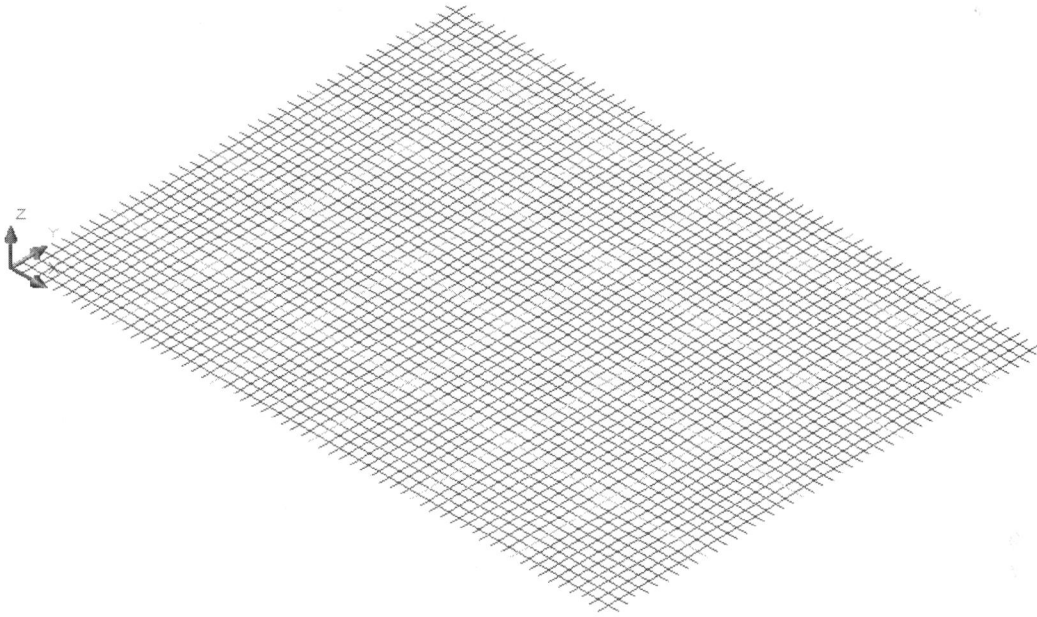

Figure 13-34

⊕ **If necessary, turn on the Grid (F7).**

3DORBIT graphics are retained after the command is exited. This includes the 3D grid and the 3D UCS icon, as shown in Figure 13-34. We recommend that you leave the 3D grid on your screen to see how it works differently from the 2D grid. You will find that the number of lines in the grid adjusts automatically to some extent as you Zoom in and out, unlike the 2D grid, which retains its density or is not displayed at all if it becomes too dense.

At some point, you will probably find the 3D grid distracting and want to return to the usual 2D image. To do this, you must return the Shademode system variable to 2D wireframe as follows:

1. Open the View menu and highlight Shade.
2. Select 2D wireframe.

The dotted grid and 2D UCS icon will now appear as usual.

⊕ **Open the Draw menu, highlight Surfaces, and select 3D Surfaces....**

This will open the 3D Objects dialog box shown in Figure 13-35. You can also select object tools from the Surface toolbar, shown previously in Figure 13-8.

Note: To create 3D surface models, you must use the 3D command, the Surfaces toolbar, or the 3D objects dialog box. Typing "sphere", "cone", "torus", etc. directly at the command line will create solid models instead of surface models. We will use these commands in Chapter 14.

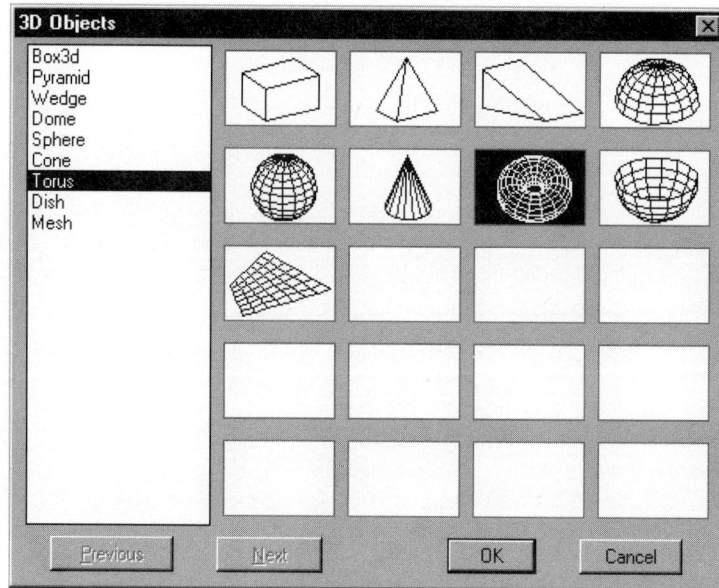

Figure 13-35

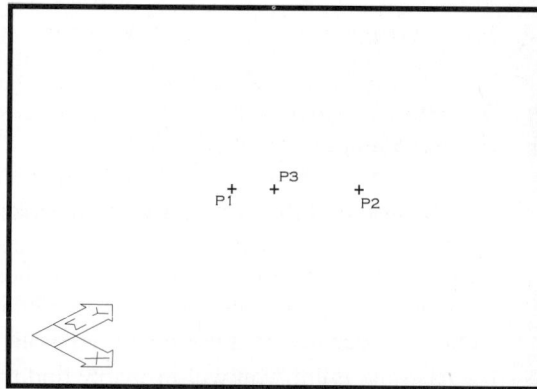

Figure 13-36

⊞ Select the torus, as shown, by clicking on the torus image or the word torus on the list.

⊞ Click OK.

This will bring you to the first Torus prompt:

        `Specify center point of torus:`

⊞ Pick a center point as shown by P1 in Figure 13-36.

AutoCAD prompts

        `Specify radius of torus or [Diameter]:`

The next point we pick will show the overall radius of the torus.

⊕ Show a radius distance of about 6.00 units, as shown by P2 in Figure 13-36.

AutoCAD prompts

```
Specify radius of tube or [Diameter]:
```

This will be the diameter or radius of the torus tube. If you specify the tube size by pointing, remember that the distance is being shown from the center point of the torus, at P1, to P3, though the tube actually will be constructed from its own center line at P2.

⊕ Show a radius of about 2.00 units, as shown by P3 in Figure 13-36.

AutoCAD prompts

```
Enter number of segments around tube circumference <16>:
```

You will be prompted for segment numbers around the tube and around the torus. These specify mesh density just like Surftab1 and Surftab2.

⊕ Press Enter to accept the default of 16 segments.

AutoCAD prompts

```
Enter number of segments around torus circumference <16>:
```

⊕ Press Enter to accept the default of 16 segments.

Your screen should resemble Figure 13-37. As in the case of the 3D polygon mesh commands, notice how much surface modeling this AutoLISP routine accomplishes through a few simple prompts.

To appreciate the nature of surface models once again, we recommend that you enter 3DORBIT, turn off the 3D grid, add Gourard shading with no edges, and practice putting the shaded torus into continuous orbit. Don't be surprised if you have a sudden craving for a donut.

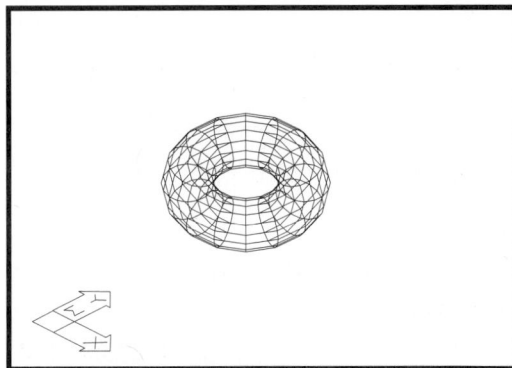

Figure 13-37

13.8 Creating Approximated Surfaces Using PEDIT

GENERAL PROCEDURE

1. Draw a 3DMESH in three dimensions.
2. Select Polyline from the Modify menu.
3. Select the mesh.
4. Enter an option.
6. Exit PEDIT.

Within the PEDIT command there are some very impressive 3D design features, which we introduce in this task. These techniques will not be needed in the drawings that follow, but your knowledge of AutoCAD and surface modeling would not be complete without them.

The techniques of curve and surface approximation are most useful when you have a curved object in mind but have not derived exact specifications for it, or when an irregular curved object passes through many different planes and would be very hard to draw face by face. You may be able to draw an outline and specify some key points, but beyond that what you conceive may be simply a smooth curve that follows the basic shape of your outline. AutoCAD provides mathematical algorithms that can translate outlines into smooth curves. This can be accomplished with 2D and 3D polylines and with 3D meshes.

3D meshes can be curved according to three different formulas, controlled by the variable "Surftype" (not to be confused with Surftab1 and Surftab2). Surftype can be set to 5 for a quadratic approximation, 6 for cubic approximation, and 8 for Bezier.

In this exercise we will create a simple rectangular 3D mesh in one plane, move two of its vertices to make it three dimensional, and then use the Smooth option of the PEDIT command to create approximated surfaces.

⊕ To begin this task, clear your screen of all objects left from the last task.

You should be in a single viewport with a southeast isometric view showing. If you have not already done so you should return to the 2D grid for this exercise.

⊕ Open the View menu and highlight Shade.

⊕ Select 2D Wireframe.

⊕ If you have been in 3DORBIT, you will probably also need to specify the SE Isometric view again.

3DMESH

The 3DMESH command allows you to create 3D polygon meshes "manually," vertex by vertex. Because of the time involved, the complete command is best used as a programmer's tool. However, there is an AutoLISP program that provides a very simple version of the 3DMESH command, which we will demonstrate here.

Those interested in the full command sequence should see the *AutoCAD Command Reference.*

⊕ Zoom in so that the grid covers most of the screen.
⊕ Open the Draw menu, highlight Surfaces, and select 3D Surfaces...
   from the submenu.

   This opens the 3D Objects dialog used in the last task.

⊕ Select "Mesh" from the list on the left, or the Mesh icon in the third row.
⊕ Click OK.

   AutoCAD prompts

   `Specify first corner point of mesh:`

   We will be prompted for four corners to define the outer boundaries of the mesh, and then for two numbers to specify the number of vertices.

⊕ Pick a corner, as shown by P1 in Figure 13-38.

   AutoCAD will prompt for another corner:

   `Specify second corner point of mesh:`

⊕ Pick a second corner, P2, 4.00 to the right of P1.
⊕ Pick a third corner, P3, 3.00 in the *y* direction from P2.
⊕ Pick a fourth corner, P4 as shown.

   When you have picked four corners, your mesh should be outlined and one side highlighted. AutoCAD is asking for the number of vertices to be defined in the "M" direction. The letters M and N are used to designate the number of vertices in the two directions in which the mesh will be defined. The M size is equivalent to the Surftab1 setting.

   `Enter mesh size in the M direction:`

⊕ Type "5".

   AutoCAD highlights a side perpendicular to the first and prompts

   `Enter mesh size in the N direction:`

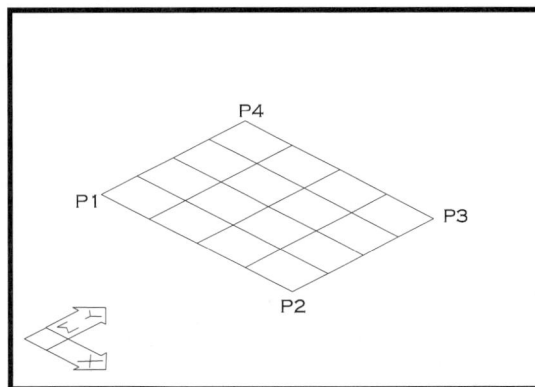

Figure 13-38

Like Surftab2, the "N" specification will determine the number of vertices in this direction.

⊕ Type "5" again.

Your screen will resemble Figure 13-38.

The mesh will be drawn with five vertices in each direction. Later we will copy it twice so that we can produce three different types of smooth surfaces, but first we need to move some vertices up and down in the z direction to give it three-dimensionality. This can be done using XY filters and the grip edit stretch mode.

⊕ Select the mesh.

The mesh will be highlighted and grips will appear at each vertex.

⊕ Pick the grip at the far right corner of the mesh (P3).

The stretch mode works the same as in previous chapters, except that now we will be moving vertices up and down out of the XY plane. If you have not previously used point filters, here is an opportunity to become familiar with this useful 3D tool.

⊕ Type ".xy" or open the short cut menu (shift + right click), select Point Filters, and then select .XY.

AutoCAD prompts

.xy of

We are going to move the vertex straight up into the z dimension, so we want the same x and y coordinates with a new z. The XY filter will take the x and y values from whatever point we specify and combine them with a new z value. We can pick the same vertex again to show x and y, or we can type "@", indicating the last point entered. The z value will need to be typed since there are no objects outside of the XY plane to snap onto.

⊕ Type "@" or pick the highlighted vertex grip again.

AutoCAD responds

(need Z):

⊕ Type "3".

This will move the corner vertex up 3.00, as shown in Figure 13-39.

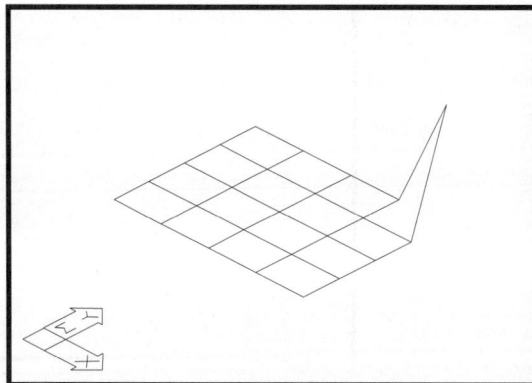

Figure 13-39

Now we will move the opposite corner down −4.00.

⊕ Pick the grip at the far left corner (P1), opposite the corner you just edited.

⊕ Type ".xy" or open the short cut menu, select Point filters, and select .XY.

⊕ Type "@" or pick the same grip again.

⊕ Type "−4".

We are now ready to create a cubic-style smoothed surface from our 3D mesh.

⊕ Open the Modify menu and select Polyline.

This executes the PEDIT command. AutoCAD will prompt for a polyline, but 3D polygon meshes may also be selected.

⊕ Pick any point on the mesh.

The mesh will not be highlighted when you pick it, but you will see the following command prompt:

```
Enter an option [Edit Vertex/Smooth
surface/Desmooth/Mclose/Nclose/Undo]:
```

The option we will be using is "Smooth surface".

⊕ Type "s".

Your screen will be redrawn to resemble Figure 13-40.

Note: If the variable "Splframe" is set to 1, your screen will show no change. Splframe shows the frame or outline used in defining an approximated curve. Because of the complexity of meshes, AutoCAD does not show a curved surface and its "frame" at the same time. With Splframe set to the default of 0, you will see the smoothed version with no frame. With a setting of 1 you see the original frame without the approximation.

Next we will make copies of the mesh and smooth the copies with the variable "surftype" set to create quadratic and Bezier surfaces.

⊕ Press the space bar to exit the PEDIT command.

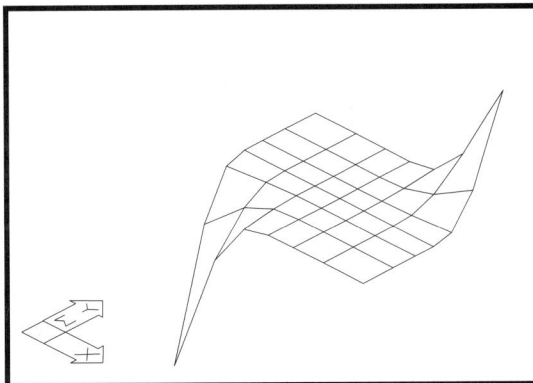

Figure 13-40

⊞ Make two copies of the mesh, to the left and right of the original.

⊞ If necessary, Zoom out to display complete copies.

⊞ Type "Surftype".

⊞ Type "5".

Surftype is 6 for cubic (the default), 5 for quadratic, and 8 for Bezier.

⊞ Open the Modify menu and select Polyline.

⊞ Select the first copy of the mesh.

⊞ Type "s".

Watch carefully. The differences between cubic and quadratic surfaces in this object will be slight. We have indicated them with arrows in Figure 13-41 for your convenience. To show a more dramatic difference, you would need to create a more dramatic 3D figure by moving more vertices up or down. If you have the time, be our guest. Also consider changing the density of surface ap-

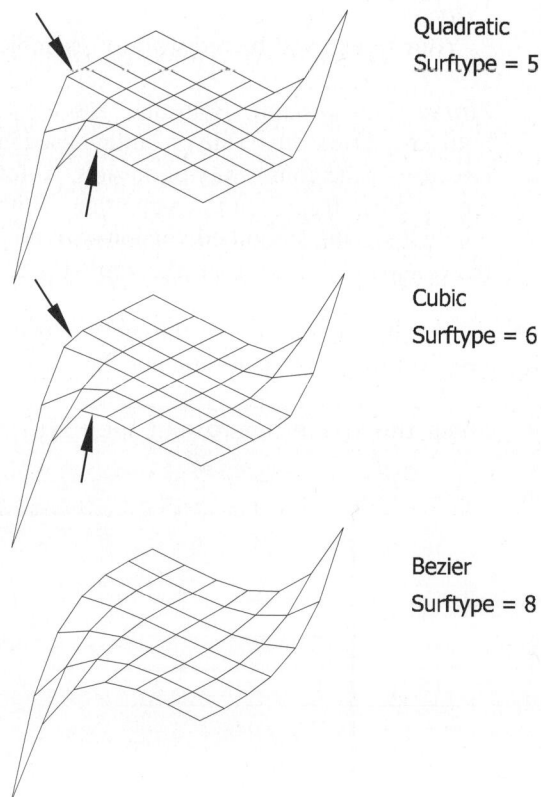

Quadratic
Surftype = 5

Cubic
Surftype = 6

Bezier
Surftype = 8

Figure 13-41

proximation through the variables "Surfu" and Surfv". For more information, see the *AutoCAD Command Reference*.

✦ Exit the PEDIT command.

✦ Type "Surftype".

✦ Type "8" for a Bezier surface.

✦ Open the Modify menu and select Polyline.

✦ Select the remaining copy of the mesh.

✦ Type "s" to smooth the mesh.

Your meshes will resemble those in Figure 13-41.

Now that you know how to create smoothed surfaces, creating two-dimensional curve approximations should be easy. We include the following discussion as a reference.

Curve Approximation

Creating approximated curves in two dimensions is analogous to smoothing surfaces in three dimensions. The process is the same, with a few changes in variable names. Instead of beginning with a 3D mesh, you begin with a polyline. Polyline frames can be curved through the "Fit" or "Spline" options of the PEDIT command. Fit replaces all straight segments of a polyline with pairs of arc segments. The resulting curve passes through all existing vertices, and new vertices are created to join the arcs. Spline curves follow the shape of their frames, but they do not necessarily pass through all vertices. Instead they pass through the first and last points and tend toward the ones between according to either the quadratic or cubic formula. (There is no Bezier option for spline curves.)

If the variable "Splineframe" is set to 1 instead of the default 0, AutoCAD will display the defining frame along with the curve. Also, the degree of accuracy of curve approximation can be varied by changing the setting of the variable "Splinesegs". This variable controls the number of segments a polyline will be considered to have in the calculations of the spline formulas.

Examples of fit, cubic, and quadratic curves are shown in Figure 13-42.

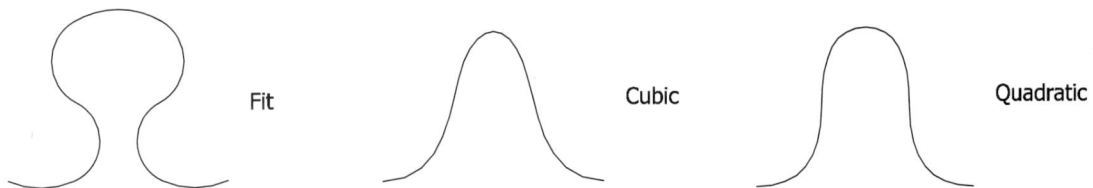

Fit   Cubic   Quadratic

Figure 13-42

13.9 Review Material

Questions

1. Why is it important to keep two or more different views of an object on the screen as you are drawing and editing it?
2. What two basic geometric shapes can be drawn as a 3DFACE?
3. How does the HIDE command treat objects on layers that are turned off?
4. What geometry is needed to define a tabulated surface? a ruled surface? an edge surface? a revolved surface?
5. What one basic surface entity makes up all AutoCAD surfaces?
6. Where is the center of the 3DORBIT arcball in relation to the screen, the drawing area, the current viewport? What else is centered at the center of the arcball?
7. What action is produced by each of the four rotation cursors in 3DORBIT?
8. Explain the camera and target metaphor used by the 3DORBIT command. How is it used to define views?
9. Describe the difference between a Flat shaded model and a Gourard shaded model.
10. What system variable do you need to change in order to return to the 2D grid after using 3DORBIT?
11. What is curve approximation? What command and what option are used to create curves from straight polylines and 3D meshes?

Drawing Problems

1. Beginning with a blank drawing using the 1B template, create a three-tiled viewport screen configuration with two viewports on the left and one viewport on the right.
2. Create a world plan view in the top left viewport, a front view in the bottom left viewport, and a southeast isometric view in the large right viewport.
3. Draw a line from (9,9,0) to (11,9,0). Draw a polyline from (9,9,0), to (7,9,0), to (7,7,0), to (6,5,0), to (4,4,0).
4. Modify the polyline so that it takes the shape of spline curve.
5. Create a 360-degree surface of revolution by revolving the spline curve around the original 2.00 unit line.
6. Make the right viewport active, enter 3DORBIT, and create a Gourard shaded image.

13.10   WWW Exercise #13 (Optional)

Whenever you are ready:

⊕   Make sure that you are connected to your Internet service provider.

⊕   Type "browser", open the Web toolbar, and select the Browse the Web tool, or open your system browser from the Windows 98 taskbar.

⊕   If necessary, navigate to our companion Web site at "www.prenhall.com/dixriley".

13.11   Drawing 13-1: REVSURF Designs

The REVSURF command is fascinating and powerful. As you get familiar with it, you may find yourself identifying objects in the world that can be conceived as surfaces of revolution. To encourage this process, we have provided this page of 12 REVSURF objects and designs.

To complete the exercise, you will need only the PLINE and REVSURF commands. In the first six designs we have shown the path curves and axes of rotation used to create the design. In the other six you will be on your own.

Exact shapes and dimensions are not important in this exercise. Imagination is. When you have completed our designs, we encourage you to invent your own.

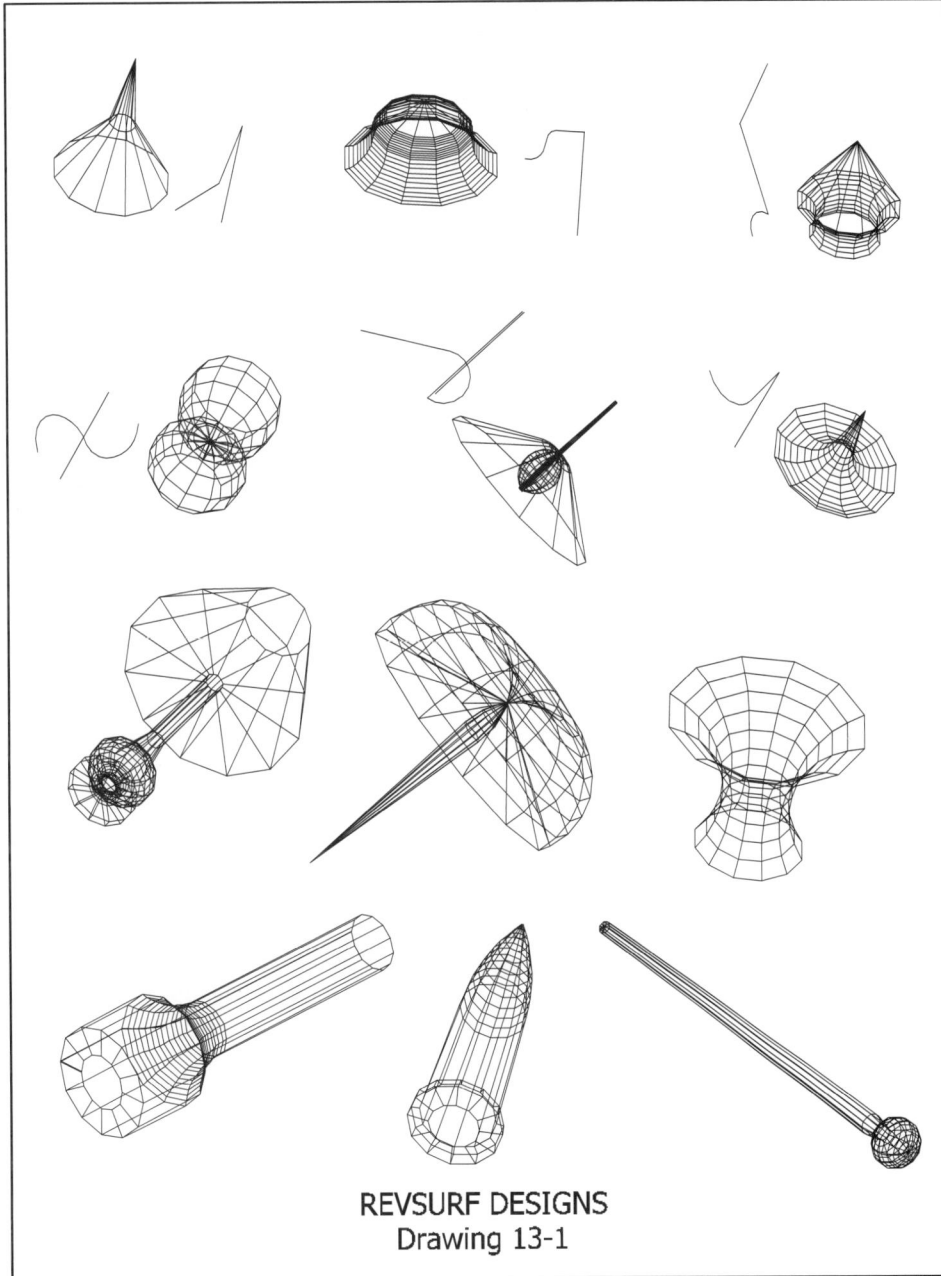

REVSURF DESIGNS
Drawing 13-1

13.12   Drawing 13-2: Picnic Table

This is a tricky drawing that must be done carefully. It requires efficient use of the UCS command along with a number of edit commands. To create an image that hides as shown in the reference, you must cover all surfaces with 3D faces.

DRAWING SUGGESTIONS

- Use a three-viewport configuration, with top (plan) and front views on the left and a 3D view on the right. Be sure to keep an eye on all viewports as you go, since it is quite likely that you will create some lines that look correct in one view but not in others.
- Use a separate layer for 3D faces and add the faces as you go. This will save you from retracing your steps. Notice that the faces on the chamfered braces are drawn with one invisible line across the middle.
- We recommend that you start with the top of the table and work down. Placing the legs directly behind the chamfered braces can be tricky. One way to do this is to draw the legs even with the side of the table first (in a UCS with its XY plane flush with a side of the table) and then MOVE them back.
- Save the angled braces for last. Once the leg braces are drawn, you can locate the angled braces by drawing a line from the midpoint of the small brace in the middle of the table top to the midpoint of the bottom of a leg brace. Then OFF-SET this line 1″ each way to create the two lower edges of one angled brace.

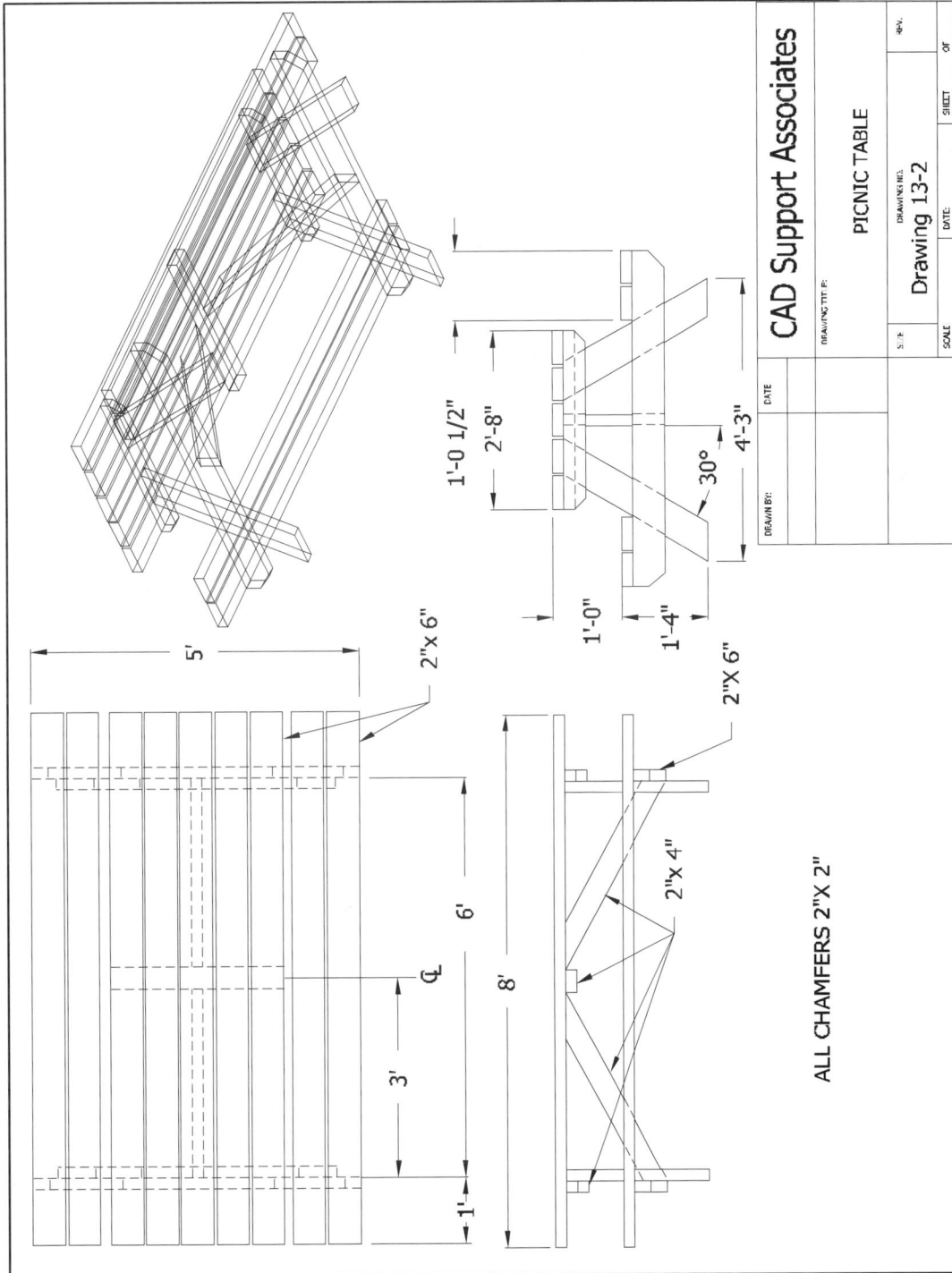

5'

2" x 6"

1'-0 1/2"

2'-8"

30°

4'-3"

1'-0"

1'-4"

2"X 6"

6'

8'

3'

1'

2"x 4"

ALL CHAMFERS 2"X 2"

CAD Support Associates

DRAWING TITLE: PICNIC TABLE

DRAWING NO.: Drawing 13-2

SIZE: SCALE: SHEET: OF

DATE: REV.:

DRAWN BY: DATE:

13.13   Drawing 13-3: Globe

This drawing uses several of the 3D mesh commands. Some of the 3D construction is a little tricky, but you may be pleasantly surprised. Follow the suggestions and you will find that this one is easier than it looks.

DRAWING SUGGESTIONS

- Use a three-viewport configuration with top and front views on the left and an isometric 3D view on the right.
- Begin with the base circles, drawing in the plan (top) view, and then MOVE the circles into place along the z axis.
- MOVE the small inner circle up 12.25 to locate the top of the shaft. Draw the center line from the center of this circle to the top center of the base. Then COPY this line on itself and ROTATE the line and circle 23.5 degrees around the midpoint of the line to position the center of the shaft.
- OFFSET the shaft center line 0.125. Later, you will TRIM a 4.00-diameter circle to this line. Then using the center line of the shaft as the axis of rotation for a REVSURF will leave a hole in the middle of the globe for the shaft.
- Draw the 4.00, 4.75, and 5.38 circles and TRIM them to the vertical, 23.5-degree, and 46-degree lines as shown.
- With your UCS parallel to the front view, COPY the 4.75 and 5.38 circles 1.25 and 2.25 in the z direction to form the two sides of the globe support. ERASE the original circles.
- TABSURF the shaft.
- RULESURF the base circles. There will be three ruled surfaces to complete the base.
- REVSURF the top of the base, using a single line from a quadrant to the center for a path curve and the vertical centerline for the axis.
- RULESURF the globe support. This will require four ruled surfaces.
- REVSURF the globe.
- Freeze all nonsurface lines before HIDEing.

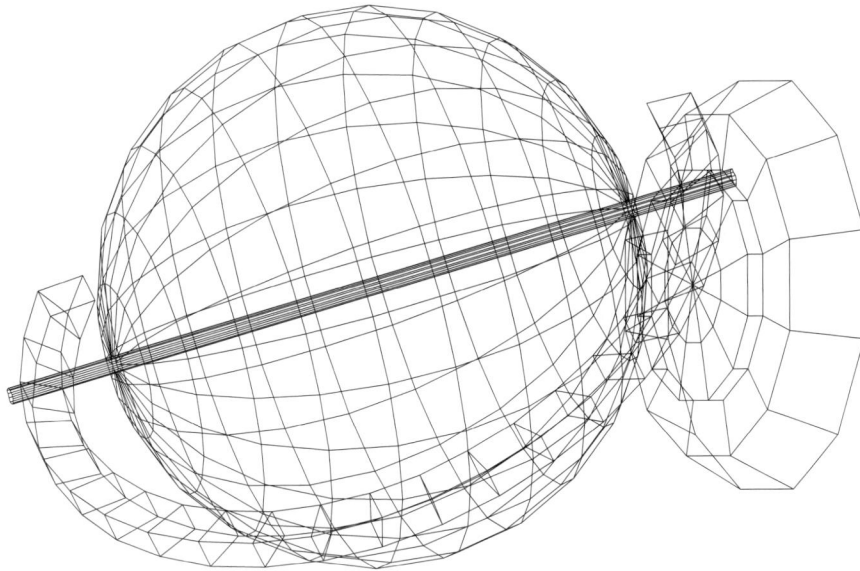

GLOBE
DRAWING 13-3

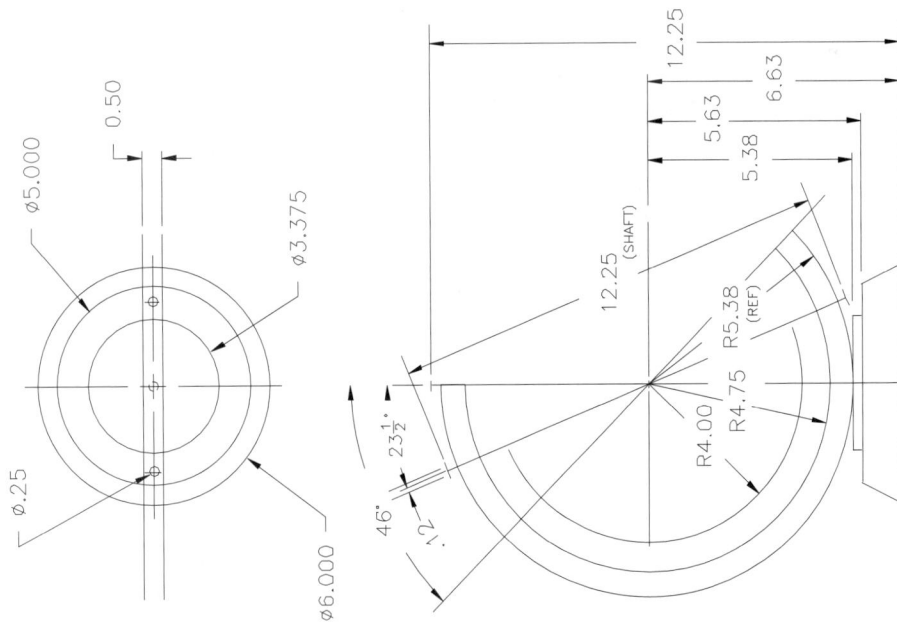

ø5.000

ø3.375

0.50

ø.25

ø6.000

12.25

5.63

6.63

5.38

12.25
(SHAFT)

R5.38
(REF)

R4.00

R4.75

46°

23½°

17°

13.14   Drawing 13-4: Nozzle

This is a tough drawing that will give you a real 3D workout. You will need to define numerous UCSs as you go. Your goal should be to create the two views A and B. Dimensioning is not part of the exercise. The dimensioned figure is not a complete wireframe, but a guide to show you the abstract relationships necessary to complete the surface model.

DRAWING SUGGESTIONS

- We began in a front, right, top view. This puts the main center line of the nozzle in the XY plane of the WCS, while the circles that show the outlines of the nozzle would be perpendicular to it. When we were done, we rotated the objects slightly to show them more clearly.
- Make ample use of COPY and OFFSET in drawing the circles and center lines of the nozzle, the hexes and circles of the knob, and the polyline curve path of the nozzle.
- The circle and center line at the right end of the 45-degree angle can be constructed using a COPY and ROTATE of the circle and center line just in front of the angle. This must be done in a UCS parallel to the WCS.
- The curve in the nozzle is a −45-degree REVSURF around the center line 1.00 to the right of the turn.
- The two darkened lines show the path curves used with REVSURF to draw the nozzle and the knob. Construct lines first and then go over them with PLINE or 3DPOLY. 3DPOLY is similar to PLINE, but it uses 3D points instead of 2D points and has no option to draw arcs. In general, 3D polylines are more flexible and can be drawn at times when the current UCS would not allow the construction of a 2D polyline.
- The center line through the knob (along the arrow) runs perpendicular to the polyline outline of the nozzle. Use a PERpendicular osnap to construct the center line and then define UCSs in relation to the center line to construct the knob.
- When this one is done you should take it into 3DORBIT, shade it, and view it from different angles.

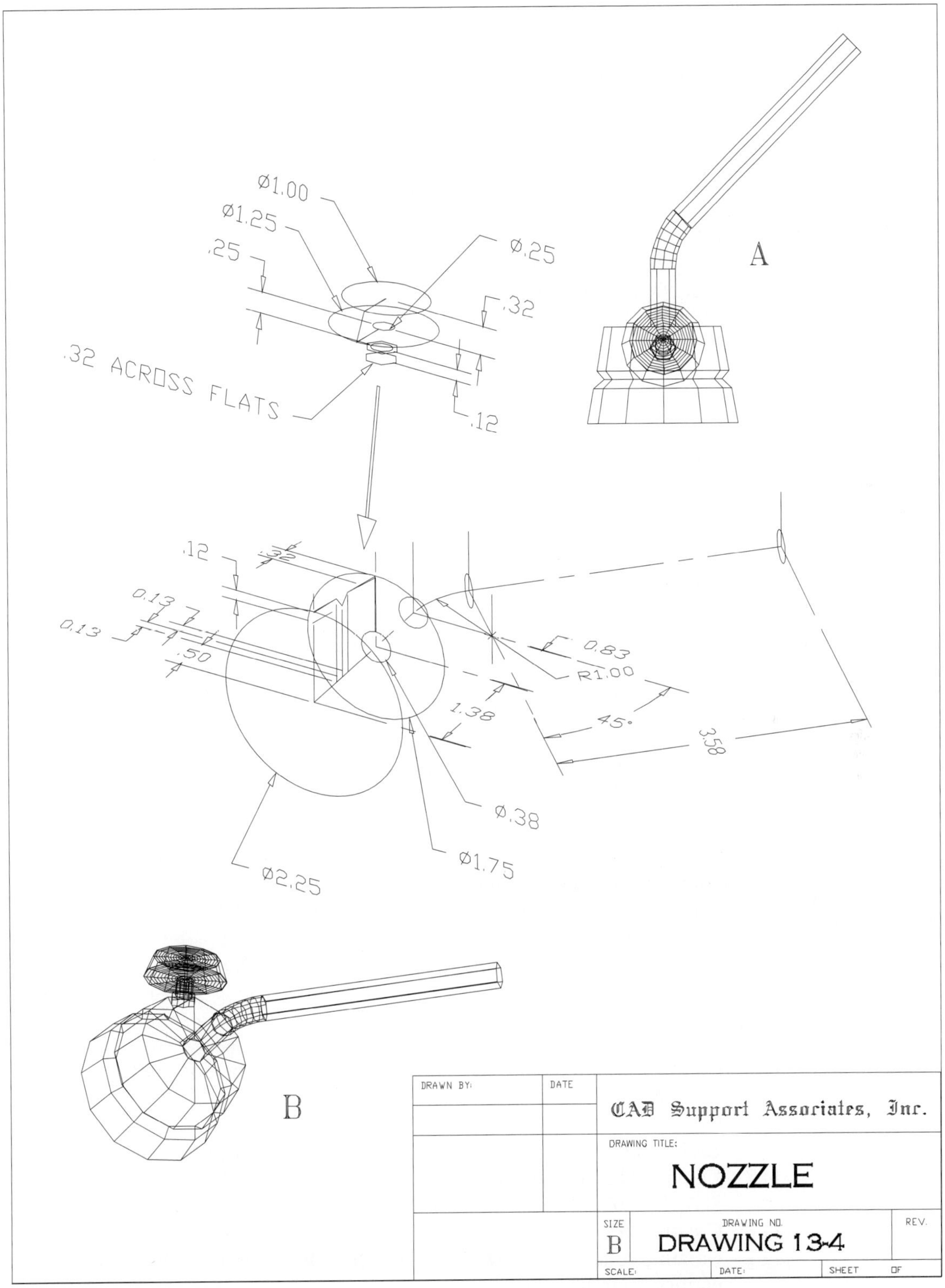

Ø1.00

Ø1.25

.25

Ø.25

.32

.32 ACROSS FLATS

.12

A

.12

0.13

0.13

.50

0.83

R1.00

45°

3.58

1.38

Ø.38

Ø1.75

Ø2.25

B

DRAWN BY:	DATE			
		CAD Support Associates, Inc.		
		DRAWING TITLE: **NOZZLE**		
		SIZE **B**	DRAWING NO. **DRAWING 13-4**	REV.
		SCALE:	DATE:	SHEET OF

14   Solid Models

COMMANDS

BOX	MATLIB	REVOLVE	UNION
CYLINDER	RENDER	SLICE	WEDGE
EXTRUDE	RMAT	SOLIDEDIT	3DORBIT
INTERSECT	SCENE	SPHERE	SUBTRACT
LIGHT	SECTION	SHADE	

OVERVIEW

Solid modeling is in many ways easier than either wireframe or surface modeling. In solid modeling you can draw a complete solid object by picking a few points, in a fraction of the time it would take to draw line by line, surface by surface. Furthermore, once the object is drawn it contains far more information than a wireframe or surface model. In this chapter you will draw a simple solid model using several solid drawing and editing commands. Then you will create sectioned, rendered, and perspective views of the model.

TASKS

14.1   Creating solid BOXes and WEDGEs

14.2   Creating the UNION of two solids

14.3   Working above the XY plane using Elevation

14.4   Creating composite solids with SUBTRACT

14.5   Creating chamfers and fillets on solid objects

14.6   Creating solid objects with EXTRUDE

14.7   Editing 3D solid faces with SOLIDEDIT

14.8   Creating 2D region entities

14.9   Creating solids by revolving 2D entities using REVOLVE

14.10   Creating solid cutaway views with SLICE

14.11   Creating sections with SECTION

14.12   SHADEing solid models

14.13   RENDERing solid models

14.14   Creating perspective and clipped views with 3DORBIT

14.15   Review Material

14.16   WWW Exercise #14 (Optional)

14.17   Drawings 14-1 through 14-5: Bushing Mount, Link Mount, 3D Assembly, Tapered Bushing, Pivot Mount

14.18   Drawings 14-6: A, B, C, and D

14.1   Creating Solid BOXes and WEDGEs

```
                    GENERAL PROCEDURE

1. Enter BOX or WEDGE.
2. Specify corner point and distances in the XY plane of the current UCS (or define a
   base plane first and then specify points).
3. Specify a height.
```

Solid modeling requires a somewhat different type of thinking from any of the drawings you have done so far. Instead of focusing on lines and arcs, edges and surfaces, you will need to imagine how 3D objects might be pieced together by combining or subtracting basic solid shapes. This building block process is called constructive solid geometry and includes joining, subtracting, and intersecting operations. A simple washer, for example, could be made by cutting a small cylinder out of the middle of a larger cylinder. In AutoCAD solid modeling you can begin with a flat outer cylinder, then draw an inner cylinder with a smaller radius centered at the same point, and then subtract the inner cylinder from the outer, as illustrated in Figure 14-1.

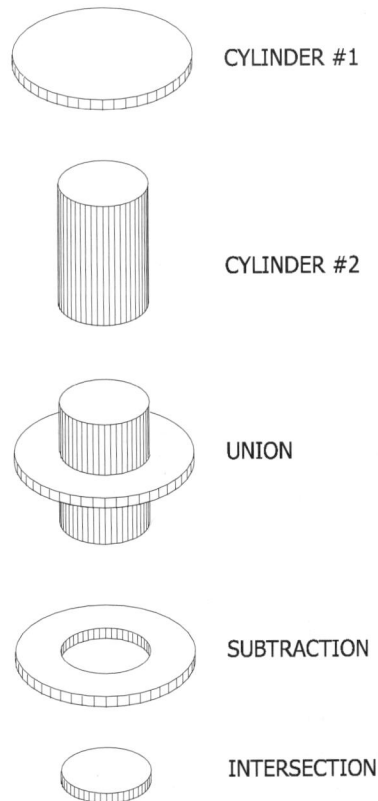

CYLINDER #1

CYLINDER #2

UNION

SUBTRACTION

INTERSECTION

Figure 14-1

This operation, which uses the SUBTRACT command, is the equivalent of cutting a hole and is one of three Boolean operations (after the mathematician George Booles) used to create composite solids. UNION joins two solids to make a new solid, and INTERSECT creates a composite solid in the space where two solids overlap (see Figure 14-1).

In this chapter you will create a composite solid from the union and subtraction of several solid primitives. Primitives are 3D solid building blocks—boxes, cones, cylinders, spheres, wedges, and torus. They all are regularly shaped and can be defined by specifying a few points and distances.

⊕ To begin this task, go into a top, right, front view (315 degrees from the *x* axis and 45 degrees from the XY plane).

Notice that this is a slightly higher viewing angle than the southeast isometric view we used in the previous two chapters. If you are unfamiliar with the use of the Viewpoint Preset dialog box, use the following procedure:

1. Type "vpoint".
2. Type "r" for "Rotate".
3. Type "315" for the angle in the XY plane from the *x* axis.
4. Type "45" for the angle from the XY plane.

⊕ Type "box" or open the Draw menu, highlight Solids, and select Box.

There is also a Solids toolbar with a Box tool, as illustrated in Figure 14-2. In the command area you will see the following prompt:

```
Specify corner of box or [CEnter] <0,0,0>:
```

"CEnter" allows you to begin defining a box by specifying its center point. Here we will use the "Corner of box" option to begin drawing a box in the baseplane of the current UCS. We will draw a box with a length of 4, width of 3, and height of 1.5.

⊕ Pick a corner point similar to point 1 in Figure 14-3.

AutoCAD will prompt

```
Specify corner or [Cube/Length]:
```

With the "Cube" option you can draw a box with equal length, width, and height by specifying one distance. The "Length" option will allow you to specify length, width, and height separately. If you have simple measurements that fall on snap points, as we do, you can show the length and width at the same time by picking the other corner of the base of the box (the default method).

⊕ Move the cross hairs over 4 in the x direction and up 3 in the *y* direction to point 2, as shown in Figure 14-3.

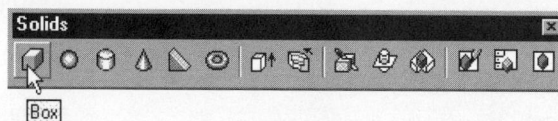

Figure 14-2

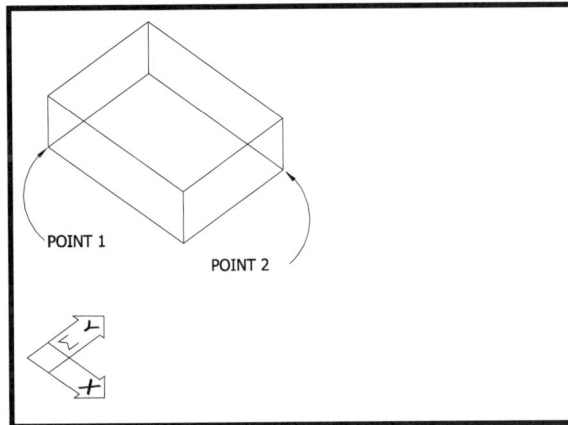

Figure 14-3

Notice that "length" is measured along the x axis, and "width" is measured along the y axis.

⊕ Pick point 2 as shown.

Now AutoCAD prompts for a height. "Height" is measured along the z axis. As usual, you cannot pick points in the z direction unless you have objects to snap to. Instead, you can type a value or show a value by picking two points in the XY plane.

⊕ Type "1.5" or pick two points 1.5 units apart.

Your screen should resemble Figure 14-3. Zoom in if you like.

Next we will create a solid wedge. The process will be exactly the same, but there will be no "Cube" option.

⊕ Type "we" or open the Draw menu, highlight Solids, and select Wedge.

AutoCAD prompts

    Specify first corner of wedge or [CEnter] <0,0,0>:

⊕ Pick the front corner point of the box, as shown in Figure 14-4.

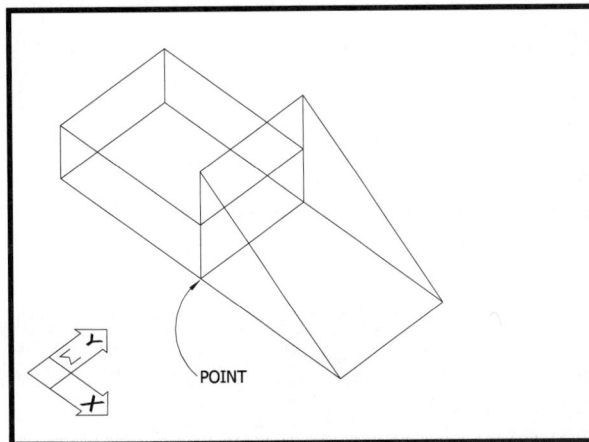

Figure 14-4

As in the BOX command, AutoCAD prompts for a cube, length, or the other corner:

Specify corner or [Cube/Length]:

This time let's use the length and width option.

⊕ Type "L".

The rubber band will disappear and AutoCAD will prompt for a length, which you can define by typing a number or showing two points.

⊕ Type "4" or show a length of 4.00 units.

AutoCAD now prompts for a width. Remember, length is measured in the x direction, and width is measured in the y direction.

⊕ Type "3" or show a width of 3 units.

AutoCAD prompts for a height.

⊕ Type "3" or show a distance of 3 units.

AutoCAD will draw the wedge you have specified. Notice that a wedge is simply half a box, cut along a diagonal plane.

Your screen should resemble Figure 14-4. Although the box and the wedge appear as wireframe objects, they are really quite different, as you will find. In Task 14.2 we will join the box and the wedge to form a new composite solid.

14.2   Creating the UNION of Two Solids

GENERAL PROCEDURE

1. Open the Modify menu, highlight Solids Editing, and select Union.
2. Select solid objects to join. (Steps 1 and 2 may be reversed if noun/verb selection is enabled.)

Unions are simple to create and usually easy to visualize. The union of two objects is an object that includes all points that are on either of the objects. Unions can be performed just as easily on more than two objects. The union of objects can be created even if the objects have no points in common (i.e., they do not touch or overlap).

Right now we have two distinct solids on the screen; with UNION we can join them.

⊕ Open the Modify menu, highlight Solids Editing, and select Union.

There is also a Union tool on the Solids Editing toolbar, as shown in Figure 14-5.

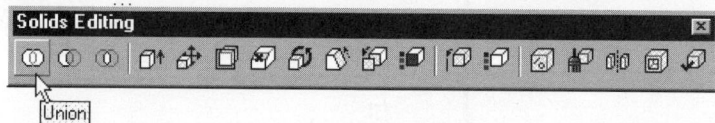

Figure 14-5

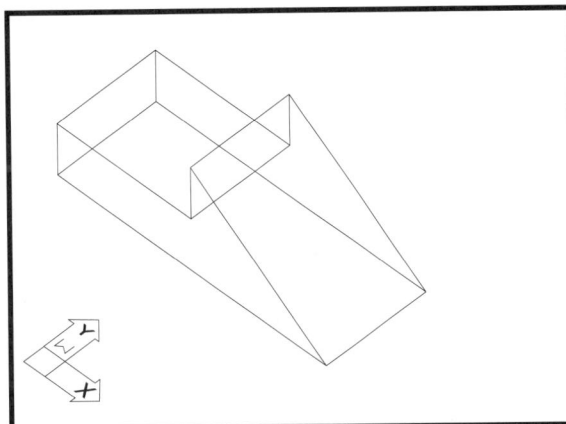

Figure 14-6

AutoCAD will prompt you to select objects.

⊕   Point or use a crossing box to select both objects.

⊕   Press Enter to end object selection.

Your screen should resemble Figure 14-6.

14.3   Working Above the XY Plane Using Elevation

GENERAL PROCEDURE

1. Type "Elev".
2. Enter elevation and thickness values.

In this task we will draw two more solid boxes while demonstrating the use of elevation to position objects above the XY plane of the current UCS. Changing elevations simply adds a single Z value to all new objects as they are drawn and can be used as an alternative to creating a new UCS. With an elevation of 1.00, for example, new objects would be drawn 1.00 above the XY plane of the current UCS. You can also use a thickness setting to create 3D objects, but these will be created as surface models, not solids.

⊕   To begin this task you should have the union of a wedge and a box on your screen, as shown in Figure 14-6.

We will begin by drawing a second box positioned on top of the first box. Later we will move it, copy it, and subtract it to form a slot in the composite object.

⊕   Type "Elev".

AutoCAD prompts

        Specify new default elevation <0.00>:

The elevation is always set at 0 unless you specify otherwise.

⊕   Type "1.5"

This will bring the elevation up 1.5 out of the XY plane, putting it even with the top of the first box you drew.

AutoCAD now prompts for a new thickness. Thickness does not apply to solid objects because they have their own thickness.

⊕   Press Enter or the space bar to retain 0.00 thickness.

This brings us back to the command prompt. If you watch closely you will see that the grid has also moved up into the new plane of elevation.

⊕   Type "Box" or open the Draw menu, highlight Solids, and select Box.

⊕   Pick the far upper left corner of the box, point 1 in Figure 14-7.

⊕   Type "L" to initiate the "length" option.

⊕   Type "4" or pick two points (points 1 and 2 in Figure 14-7) to show a length of 4 units.

⊕   Type ".5" or pick two points (points 1 and 3) to show a width of 0.5 units.

⊕   Type "2" or pick two points to show a height of 2 units.

Your screen should resemble Figure 14-7. Notice how you were able to pick points on top of the box because of the change in elevation just as if we had changed coordinate systems. Before going on, return to 0.00 elevation.

⊕   Type "elev".

⊕   Type "0".

⊕   Press Enter to retain 0.00 thickness.

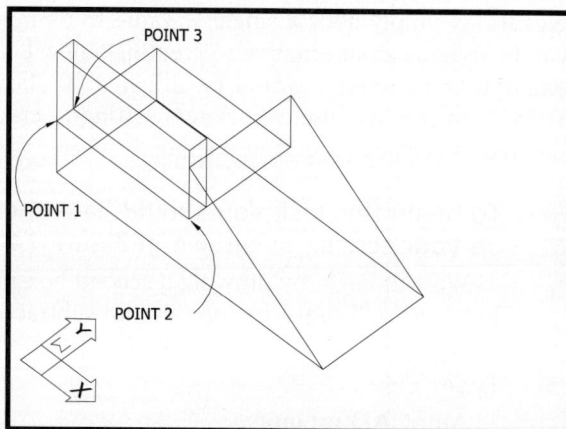

Figure 14-7

14.4 Creating Composite Solids with SUBTRACT

GENERAL PROCEDURE

1. Create solid objects to subtract and objects to be subtracted from.
2. Position objects relative to each other.
3. Type "su" or open the Modify menu, highlight Solids Editing, and select Subtract.
4. Select objects to be subtracted from.
5. Select objects to subtract.

SUBTRACT is the logical opposite of UNION. In a union operation, all the points contained in one solid are added to the points contained in other solids to form a new composite solid. In a subtraction, all points in the solids to be subtracted are removed from the source solid. A new composite solid is defined by what is left.

In this exercise, we will use the objects already on your screen to create a slotted wedge. First we need to move the thin upper box into place, then we will copy it to create a longer slot, and finally we will subtract it from the union of the box and wedge.

⊕ To begin this task, you should have the composite box and wedge solid and the thin box on your screen, as shown in Figure 14-7.

Before subtracting, we will move the box to the position shown in Figure 14-8.

⊕ Type "m" or select the Move tool from the Modify toolbar.

⊕ Select the narrow box drawn in the last task.

⊕ Right click to end object selection.

⊕ At the "Specify base point or displacement" prompt use a midpoint object snap to pick the midpoint of the top right edge of the narrow box.

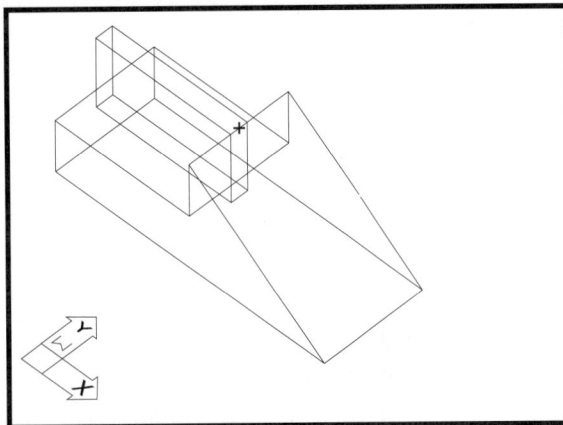

Figure 14-8

⊕ At the "Specify second point of displacement" prompt use another midpoint object snap to pick the top edge of the wedge, as shown in Figure 14-8.

This will move the narrow box over and down. If you were to perform the subtraction now, you would create a slot but it would only run through the box, not the wedge. We can create a longer slot by copying the narrow box over to the right using grips.

⊕ Select the narrow box.

⊕ Pick any of the eight grips.

⊕ If ortho is off, turn it on.

Now if you move the cursor in the x direction you will see a copy of the box moving with you. Solids cannot be stretched, so we must make a copy to lengthen the slot.

⊕ Type "c".

⊕ Move the cursor between 2.00 and 4.00 units to the right and press the pickbutton.

If you don't go far enough the slot will be too short. If you go past 4.00, the slot will be interrupted by the space between the box and the copy.

⊕ Press Enter to leave the grip edit mode.

Your screen will resemble Figure 14-9.

⊕ Type "su" or open the Modify menu, highlight Solids Editing, and select Subtract.

There is also a Subtract tool on the Solids Editing toolbar, shown previously in Figure 14-5.

AutoCAD asks you to select objects to subtract from first:

```
Select solids and regions to subtract from ...
Select objects:
```

⊕ Pick the composite of the box and the wedge.

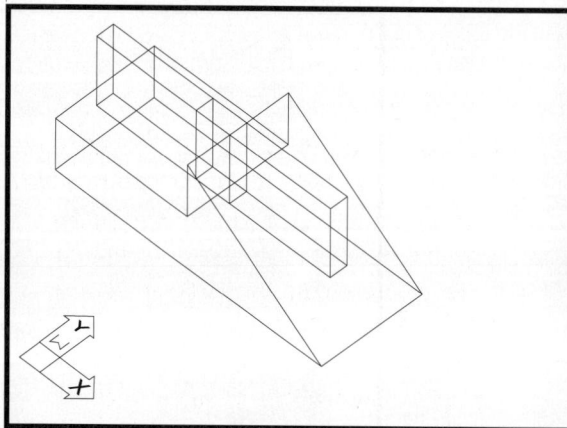

Figure 14-9

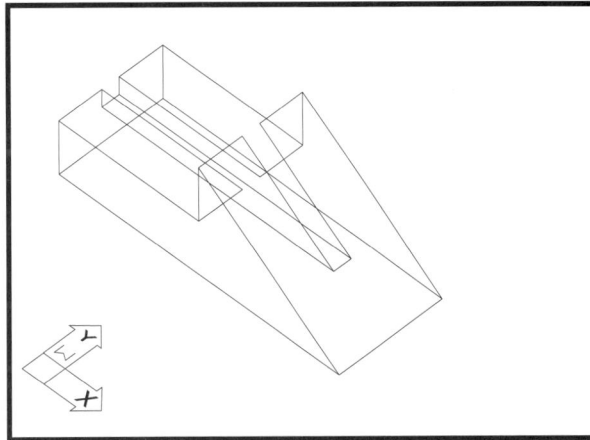

Figure 14-10

⊕   Right click to end selection of source objects.

AutoCAD prompts for objects to be subtracted:

> Select solids and regions to subtract...
> Select objects:

⊕   Pick the two narrow boxes.

⊕   Right click to end selection.

Your screen will resemble Figure 14-10.

Next we will draw a solid cylinder, move it into place, and subtract it to form a hole at the right end of the slot.

⊕   Open the Draw menu, highlight Solids, and select Cylinder.

There is also a Cylinder tool on the Solids toolbar, shown previously in Figure 14-2.

AutoCAD prompts

> Current wire frame density: ISOLINES=4
> Specify center point for base of cylinder or [Elliptical]
> <0,0,0>:

We will demonstrate the significance of the isolines setting in a moment.

⊕   Pick any convenient center point away from the composite solid.

It does not matter where the cylinder is drawn since we are going to move it to the end of the slot using a midpoint object snap.

To create a hole the same width as the slot, we need a diameter of 0.5 or a radius of 0.25.

⊕   Type ".25" for the radius value.

The cylinder must be made high enough to reach through the slot. Any height over 1.00 will do.

⊕   Type "1" for the height.

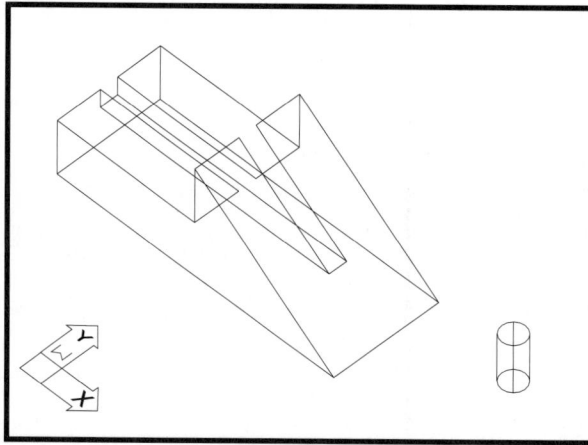

Figure 14-11

The cylinder will be drawn as shown in Figure 14-11 except that your cylinder will probably have only four vertical lines (they will actually look like two lines because they hide each other). The density of lines displayed by AutoCAD to represent curved solid surfaces is controlled by the Isolines system variable. We will change ours to show eight lines.

⊕ Type "isolines".

AutoCAD prompts

Enter new value for ISOLINES <4>:

⊕ Type "8".
⊕ Type "Regen" or open the View menu and select Regen.

Next we will move the cylinder to the end of the slot using a grip edit and a midpoint object snap.

⊕ Select the cylinder.

There will be a grip at the top and bottom centers of the cylinder. We want to move the top center to the midpoint of the end of the wedge. Zoom in if you need to.

⊕ Select the top center grip on the cylinder.
⊕ Use a midpoint object snap to move the cylinder to the end of the slot, as shown in Figure 14-12.

Now it's time to subtract.

⊕ Type "su" or open the Modify menu, highlight Solids Editing, and select Subtract.
⊕ Select the composite object.
⊕ Right click to end object selection.
⊕ Select the cylinder.
⊕ Right click to end object selection.

Your screen will resemble Figure 14-13.

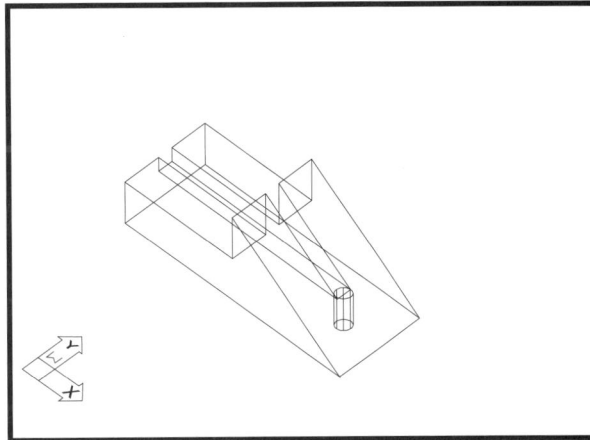

Figure 14-12

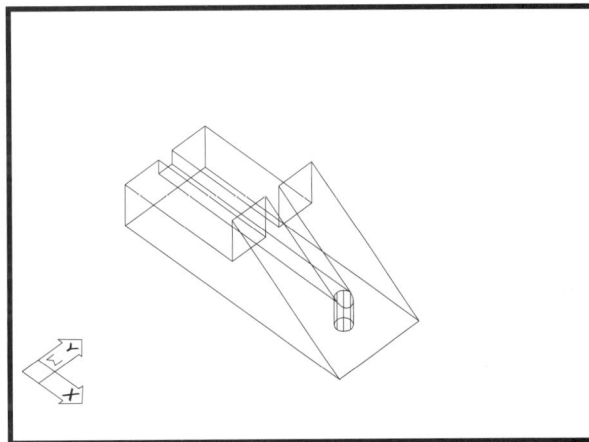

Figure 14-13

14.5 Creating Chamfers and Fillets on Solid Objects

GENERAL PROCEDURE

1. Type "cha", select Chamfer from the Modify menu, or select the Chamfer tool from the Modify toolbar.
2. Pick a base surface.
3. Press Enter or type "n" to select the next surface.
4. Enter chamfer distances.
5. Pick edges to be chamfered.
6. Press Enter to end object selection.

Constructing chamfers and fillets on solids is simple, but the language of the prompts can cause confusion due to some ambiguity in the designation of edges and surfaces to be modified. We will begin by putting a chamfer on the back left edge of the model.

⊕ To begin this task you should have the solid model shown in Figure 14-13 on your screen.

⊕ Type "cha", select Chamfer from the Modify menu, or select the Chamfer tool from the Modify toolbar.

The first chamfer prompt is the same as always:

```
(TRIM mode) Current chamfer Dist1 = 0.00, Dist2 = 0.00
Select first line or [Polyline/Distance/Angel/Trim/Method]:
```

⊕ Select point 1, as shown in Figure 14-14.

AutoCAD highlights the back left surface and prompts

```
Base surface selection...
Enter surface selection option [Next/OK (current)]
<OK>:
```

We are constructing a chamfer on the left surface of the object. However, chamfers and fillets happen along edges that are common to two surfaces. What is a "base surface" in relation to a chamfered edge? Actually, it refers to either of the two faces that meet at the edge where the chamfer will be. As long as you pick this edge, you are bound to select one of these two surfaces, and either will do. Which of the two surfaces is the "base surface" and which is the "adjacent surface" will not matter until you enter the chamfer distances, and then only if the distances are unequal. However, AutoCAD allows you to switch to the other surface that shares this edge, by typing "n" for the "Next" option.

⊕ Press Enter.

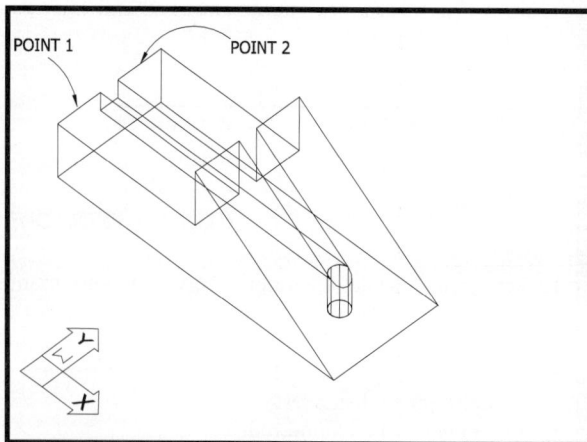

Figure 14-14

AutoCAD prompts

> Specify base surface chamfer distance <0.00>:

⊕ Type ".5" for the base surface distance.

Now AutoCAD prompts

> Specify other surface chamfer distance <0.50>:

Now you can see the significance of "base surface." The chamfer will be created with the first distance on the base surface side and the second distance on the other surface side. If the chamfer is symmetrical, it will not matter which is which.

⊕ Type ".25" for the other base surface distance.

This will construct a chamfer that cuts 0.5 down into the left side and 0.25 back along the top side.

Now AutoCAD prompts for the edge or edges to be chamfered.

> Select an edge or [Loop]:

"Loop" will construct chamfers on all edges of the chosen base surface. Selecting edges will allow you to place them only on the selected edges. You will have no difficulty selecting edges if you pick the edge you wish to chamfer again. The only difference is that you will need to pick twice, once on each side of the slot.

⊕ Pick the top back left edge of the model, to one side of the slot (point 1 in Figure 14-14 again).

⊕ Pick the same edge again, but on the other side of the slot (point 2 in Figure 14-14).

⊕ Press Enter to end edge selection (right clicking will open a short cut menu).

Your screen will resemble Figure 14-15.

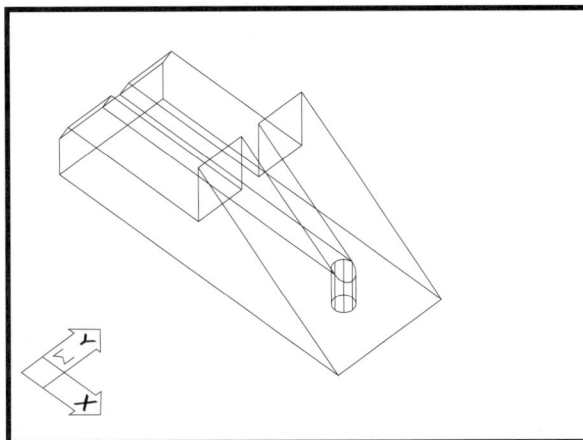

Figure 14-15

Creating Fillets

The procedure for creating solid fillets is simpler. There is one less step since there is no need to differentiate between base and other surfaces in a fillet.

⊕ Select Fillet from the Modify menu or the Fillet tool from the Modify toolbar.

> AutoCAD gives you current settings and prompts

> > `Select first object or [Polyline/Radius/Trim]:`

⊕ Pick the edge where the box and the wedge meet, point 1 in Figure 14-16.

> AutoCAD prompts

> > `Enter fillet radius <0.50>:`

⊕ Press enter or type ".5".

> The next prompt looks like this:

> > `Select an edge or [Chain/Radius]:`

"Chain" will allow you to fillet around all the edges of one side of a solid object at once. For our purposes we do not want a chain. Instead we want to select the two edges on either side of the slot.

⊕ Pick the same edge on the other side of the slot, point 2 in Figure 14-16.

> You will see this prompt again:

> > `Select an edge or [Chain/Radius]:`

The prompt repeats in order to allow you to select more edges to fillet.

⊕ Press Enter to end selection of edges.

> Your screen will resemble Figure 14-17.

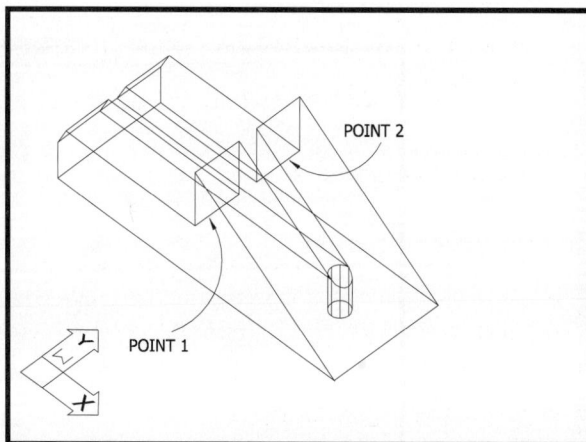

Figure 14-16

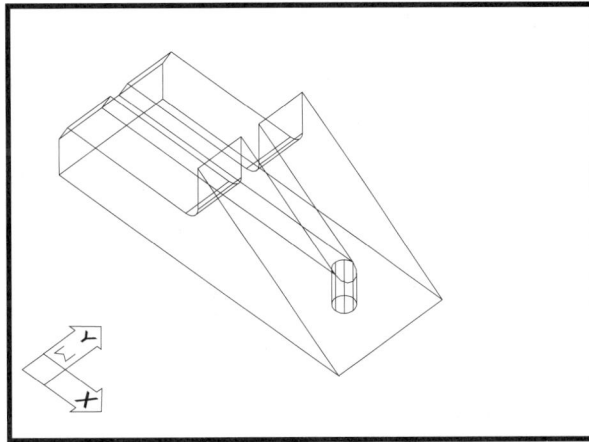

Figure 14-17

Important: *Before proceeding, save the composite wedge as a block so that you can insert it later when we use it to explore shading and rendering.*

⊕ Type "b" or select the Make Block tool from the Draw toolbar.

⊕ Type "w" for the block name.

⊕ Click the Select Objects button.

⊕ Select the composite wedge.

⊕ Right click to end object selection.

⊕ Click on the Pick Point button.

⊕ Select an insertion base point; any corner will do.

⊕ Click the Delete radio button.

⊕ Click OK.

When the block definition is complete, the wedge will disappear from the screen. We will insert this block later and use it to explore lighting and rendering techniques. But first, there are some other solid modeling commands to demonstrate.

14.6 Creating Solid Objects with EXTRUDE

GENERAL PROCEDURE

1. Create a polyline, circle, or region shape in two dimensions.
2. Open the Draw menu, highlight Solids, and select Extrude.
3. Select objects.
4. Specify an extrusion height.
5. Specify an extrusion taper angle.

AutoCAD 2000 includes two additional ways to create solid objects. First, using the EXTRUDE command, simple 2D polylines and regions can be built up or repeated along a linear path stretching up or down from the plane in which they are drawn. Second, using REVOLVE, 2D polylines and regions can be revolved around an axis along a circular or semicircular path. The REVOLVE command is very similar to REVSURF, but it creates a solid rather than a surface model.

In this task we will draw a simple polyline shape and extrude it to create a solid. In Task 14.8 we will begin working with regions.

⊕ To begin this task, your screen should be clear of all objects left from the previous task.

⊕ Draw a 2.00 by 4.00 polyline rectangle, as shown in Figure 14-18.

Be sure to use PLINE or RECTANG to create this 2D polyline. 3DPOLY, which draws 3D polylines, will not work with EXTRUDE.

⊕ Open the Draw menu, highlight Solids, and select Extrude.

There is also an Extrude tool on the Solids toolbar, shown previously in Figure 14-6.

AutoCAD will prompt you to select objects. Only regions, polylines, and circles can be extruded.

⊕ Select the rectangle.

⊕ Press Enter to end object selection.

AutoCAD prompts

Path/<Height of extrusion>:

The "Path" option is a powerful feature that allows you to create an extrusion along any pathway in the *z* direction. As in the TABSURF command, you need a line or polyline to serve as a pathway. A solid may then be created by essentially repeating the 2D object(s) at every point along the selected path.

If you use the default "Height of extrusion" option, the extrusion will be measured straight up into the *z* direction (or down if you enter a negative number).

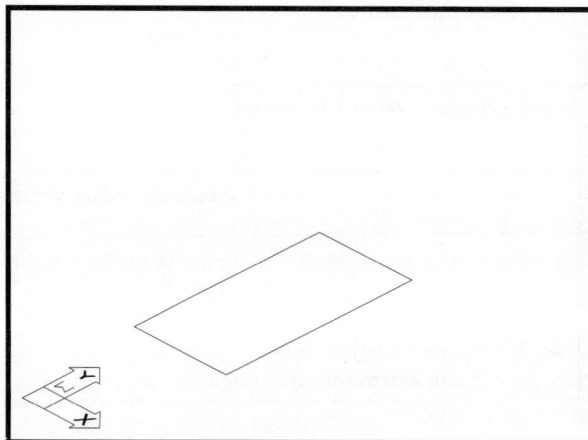

Figure 14-18

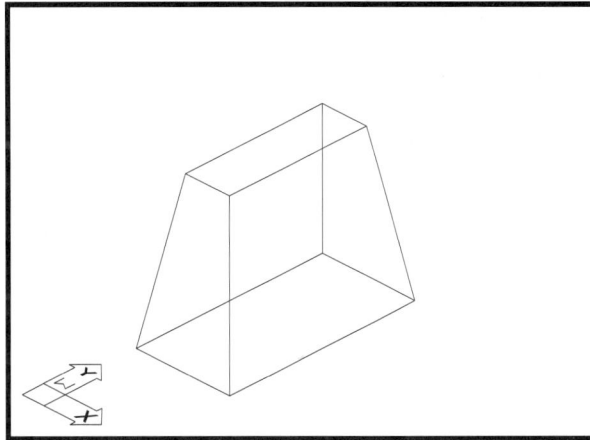

Figure 14-19

⊕ Type "3" or show a distance of 3.00 units (distance may be shown in the XY plane).

AutoCAD prompts:

```
Extrusion taper angle <0>:
```

This prompt gives you the opportunity to create a tapered extrusion by specifying an angle. This will be an angle between the *z* axis and the edge of the extruded object.

⊕ Type "10".

Your screen should resemble Figure 14-19. Be aware that if your taper angle is too large, edges may meet before the specified height is reached. In the case of an extrusion with a rectangular base, this would result in a prism, with a ridge at the top rather than a smaller rectangle.

The extruded solid you have just created will function exactly like the solid objects created earlier. It can be used in union, subtraction, and intersection with other solids to create complex solid objects. It can also be modified face by face using a set of options in the new SOLIDEDIT command, as we shall see in the next task.

14.7 Editing 3D Solid Faces with SOLIDEDIT

GENERAL PROCEDURE

1. Draw 3D solid shapes.
2. Open the Modify menu, highlight Solids Editing....
3. Select a face editing option.
4. Select faces of a solid object.
5. Follow the prompts.

AutoCAD 2000 has new features for editing the faces of previously drawn solids. This adds an extraordinary amount of flexibility and power to the whole solid modeling process. Instead of having to draw, redraw, and combine 3D primitives to create the desired model, you can move, copy, rotate, offset, extrude, taper, and even color the faces of solids in your drawing. Faces include not only the obvious exterior surfaces, but also interior surfaces, such as the cylindrical hole at the center of a nut.

The options for editing faces are extensive. We will introduce three and offer a chart, Figure 14-27, that shows what to expect from the other possibilities. We begin by extruding a face on the solid created in the last task.

⊕ To begin this task you should be in a single view with the extruded and tapered rectangle shown in Figure 14-19.

⊕ Open the Modify menu and select Solids Editing, or open the Solids Editing toolbar, as shown in Figure 14-20.

The submenu lists the same options as those available on the toolbar, and in the same order.

⊕ Select Extrude Faces, or the Extrude Faces tool from the toolbar, as shown.

Either selection enters the SOLIDEDIT command and automatically enters the Extrude Faces option. AutoCAD prompts for faces:

Select faces or [Undo/Remove]:

You can select faces by pointing within the boundary of the face, or by using a crossing window, crossing polygon, or fence. Pointing is the default; for the other methods enter c, cp, or f. In this case all windows are crossing windows so they can be shown right to left or left to right. If you point, be aware that many point selections are ambiguous. That is, the point could be in one of several different faces. This is the reason for the Undo and Remove options.

We will extrude the face on the top of the object.

⊕ Select a point similar to P1 in Figure 14-21.

If your point selection causes two or more faces to be selected, type "U" and select again, or type "R" and then select faces to remove from the selection set.

⊕ Press Enter to end face selection.

AutoCAD prompts

Specify height of extrusion or [Path]:

⊕ Type "1".

We will extrude the top face upward at a taper angle equal and opposite to the previous extrusion so that the object will funnel out at the top, as shown in Figure 14-22. AutoCAD prompts

Specify angle of taper for extrusion <0>:

What would the default taper angle look like?

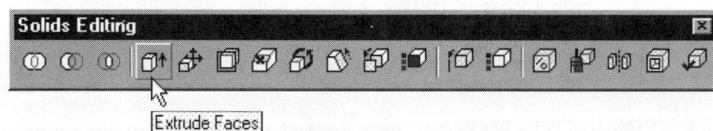

Figure 14-20

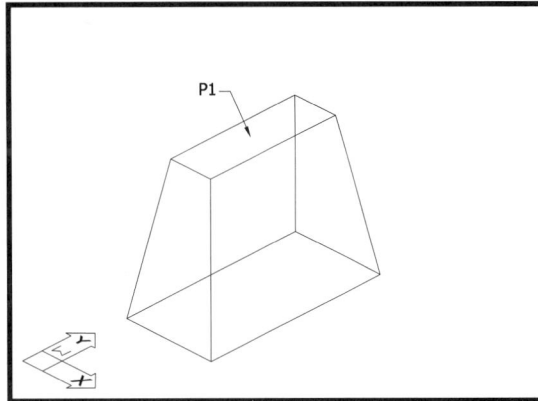

Figure 14-21

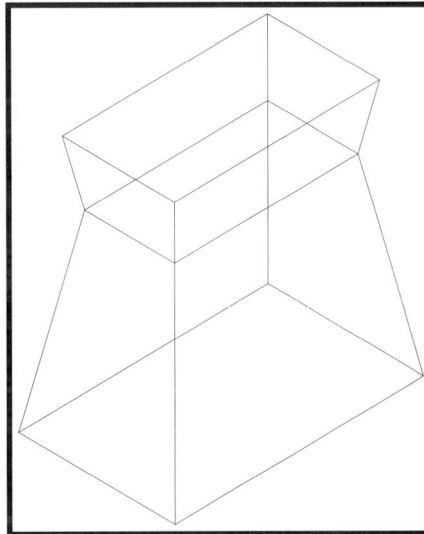

Figure 14-22

For our purpose we use –10, since we used 10 for the previous extrusion.

⊕   Type "–10".

Your screen should resemble Figure 14-22. Be aware that extrusion is directed normal to the extruded face, unless otherwise specified. Extrusion is quite flexible and can be done along paths and curves as well as normals.

Next we will move the right side faces out to widen the object. Notice that you are still in the SOLIDEDIT command.

⊕   Type "m" or select the Move Faces tool from the Solids Editing toolbar.
⊕   Type "f" to initiate a Fence selection.
⊕   Pick a point on the middle edge of the right side, similar to P1 in Figure 14-23.

Picking this edge, which is common to the two right side faces, will select both faces, as shown.

⊕   Press Enter to end object selection.

Now AutoCAD will prompt for a displacement just as in the MOVE command.

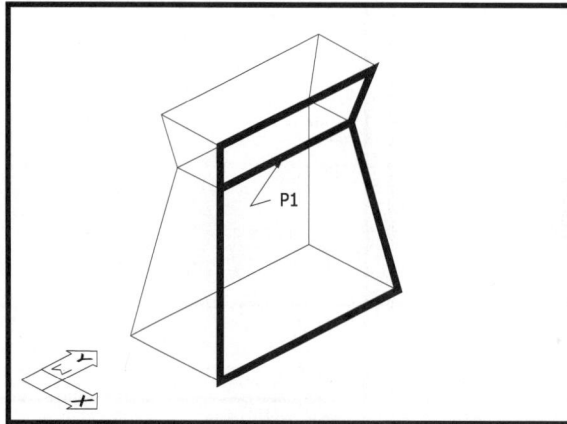

Figure 14-23

⊕ Enter two points to show a displacement of .50 unit in the *x* direction of the current UCS.

Your screen should resemble Figure 14-24.

We will perform one more edit and then leave you with the chart, Figure 14-27. In this one we will rotate the two faces on the left around the lower edge. The lower edge will stay in place and the upper and middle edges will rotate out to the left. The object will be stretched by the rotation.

⊕ Type "r" or select the Rotate Faces tool from the Solids Editing toolbar.
⊕ Pick a point on the middle edge of the left side, as shown by P1 in Figure 14-25.
⊕ Press Enter to end face selection.

AutoCAD highlights the two left faces and prompts:

```
Specify an axis point or
[Axis by object/View/Xaxis/Yaxis/Zaxis]
<2points>:
```

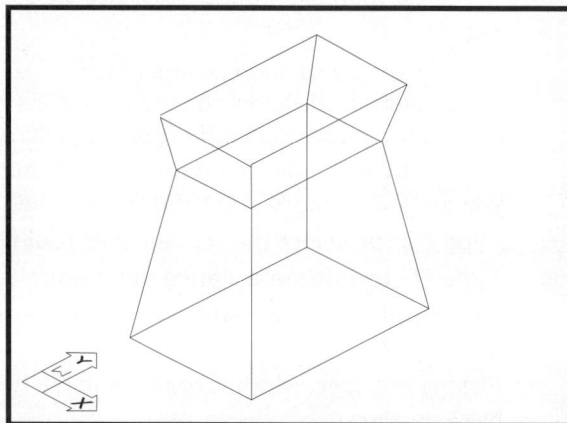

Figure 14-24

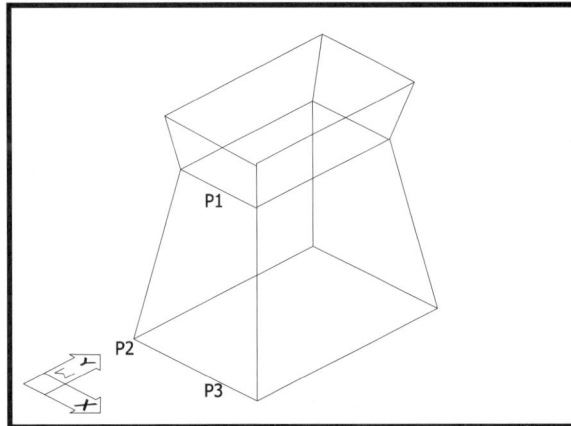

Figure 14-25

This is one of the more complex SOLIDEDIT prompts. It is asking you to define as axis of rotation by picking two point on a line, or by specifying an object or UCS axis to serve as the axis of rotation.

✛ Pick the far corner of the lower left side, P2 in Figure 14-25.

✛ Pick any other point along the lower edge of the left face, P3 in Figure 14-25.

Now AutoCAD prompts for an angle of rotation, as in the ROTATE command:

> Specify a rotation angle or [Reference]:

By rotating the faces back through 20 degrees, we can turn the lower face 10° out from the base, and stretch the top face out so that it flares even further. The rule for rotation direction is the standard AutoCAD right hand rule. Point your right thumb parallel to the axis of rotation you just defined and you will see that this outward turning of the faces is a positive angle.

✛ Type "20".

Your screen will resemble Figure 14-26.

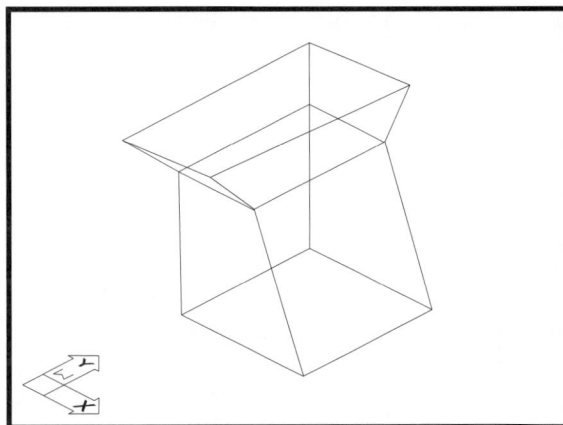

Figure 14-26

Take the time to study the SOLIDEDIT options shown in Figure 14-27. This is a very powerful command that will give you great control of solid modeling procedures.

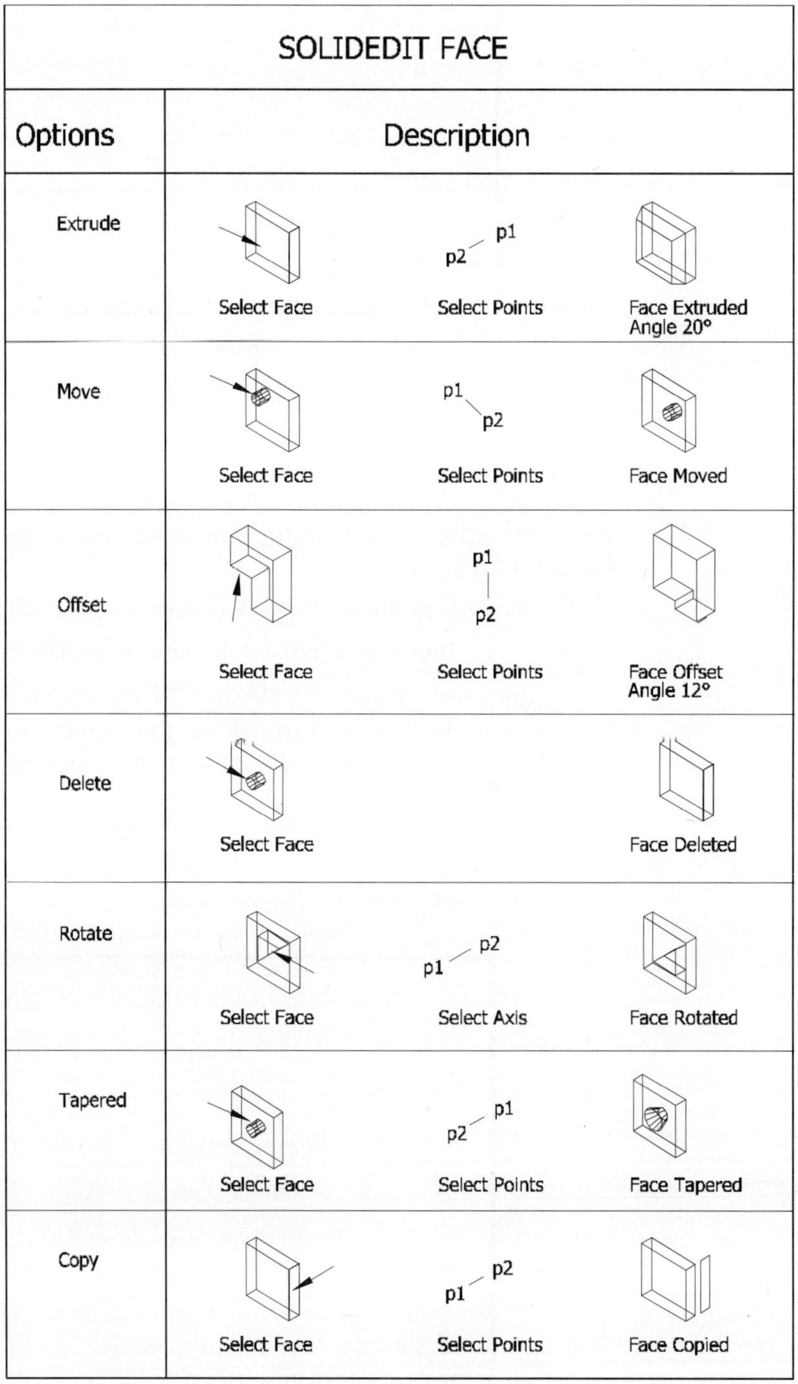

SOLIDEDIT FACE	
Options	Description
Extrude	Select Face　Select Points (p2, p1)　Face Extruded Angle 20°
Move	Select Face　Select Points (p1, p2)　Face Moved
Offset	Select Face　Select Points (p1, p2)　Face Offset Angle 12°
Delete	Select Face　Face Deleted
Rotate	Select Face　Select Axis (p1, p2)　Face Rotated
Tapered	Select Face　Select Points (p2, p1)　Face Tapered
Copy	Select Face　Select Points (p1, p2)　Face Copied

Figure 14-27

14.8   Creating 2D Region Entities

GENERAL PROCEDURE

1. Draw 2D polyline shapes.
2. Type "Region" or select the Region tool from the Draw toolbar.

Regions are the 2D equivalent of 3D solids. They can be combined through union, subtraction, and intersection using the same commands used with solids. Regions are similar to faces in that they cover 2D spaces. Like polylines, they can be extruded to form 3D solids.

In this task we will create a simple composite region from two polyline rectangles. Individual regions are created using the REGION command on previously drawn polylines, or by copying the faces of previously drawn 3D solids.

⊕   To begin this task, erase the solid from the last task and draw a rectangle again, or copy the bottom face and erase the rest to create a 2.00 × 4.00 polyline rectangle as shown previously in Figure 14-18.

If you wish to use the Copy Faces option of SOLIDEDIT as an exercise, the procedure is as follows:

1. Open the Modify menu, highlight Solids Editing, and select Copy Faces.
2. Type "c" for a crossing window selection.
3. Select the bottom face with a window that crosses a single bottom edge.
4. Type "r" and remove the adjacent face that will be highlighted.
5. Enter two points of a displacement for the copy.
6. Press enter to exit SOLIDEDIT.
7. Erase the solid.

⊕   Draw a second complete polyline rectangle, 1.00 × 2.00, centered on the midpoint of the edge of the first, as shown in Figure 14-28.

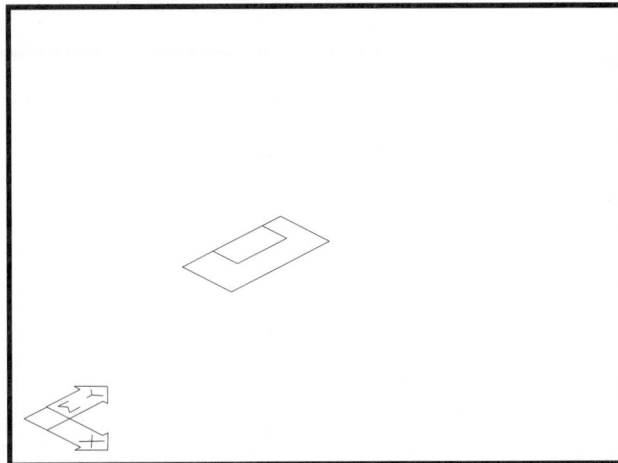

Figure 14-28

Note: You must draw all four sides of this rectangle, even though you will not see the side that lies along the left side of the larger rectangle. Regions can only be constructed from closed polyline figures.

Next we will convert the two rectangles into 2D regions. If you used the SOLIDEDIT Copy Faces procedure, the copied face is already a region, but the steps that follow will be the same.

⊕ Select Region from the Draw menu or the Region tool from the Draw toolbar.

AutoCAD prompts you to select objects.

⊕ Pick both rectangles with a window or crossing window.

⊕ Press Enter to end object selection.

You will see no change, although there will be a message in the command area that says that two regions have been created. If the face is already a region, it will say one instead.

Now if you subtract the smaller rectangle from the larger, you will see that these regions behave just like 3D solids.

⊕ Open the Modify menu, highlight Solids Editing, and select Subtract.

⊕ Select the larger rectangle as the region to subtract from.

⊕ Press Enter or right click to end object selection.

⊕ Select the smaller rectangle as the region to subtract

⊕ Press Enter or right click to end object selection.

Your screen will resemble Figure 14-29.

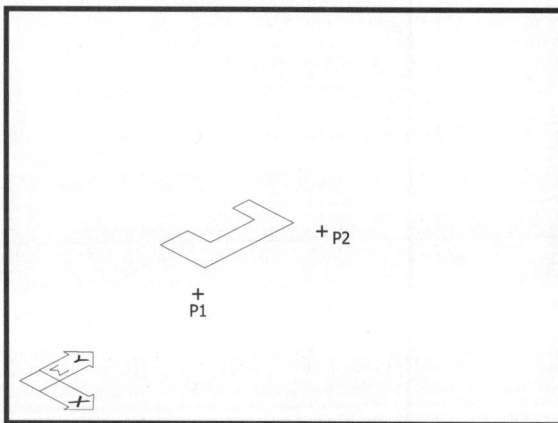

Figure 14-29

14.9 Creating Solids by Revolving 2D Entities Using REVOLVE

GENERAL PROCEDURE

1. Draw regions or 2D polyline shapes.
2. Open the Draw menu, highlight Solids, and select Revolve.
3. Select objects.
4. Specify an axis of revolution.
5. Specify an angle of revolution.

REVOLVE is a powerful solid modeling command that creates solid objects by revolving 2D polyline shapes and regions around an axis. It functions in ways very similar to the REVSURF surface modeling command.

In this task we will create a spool-shaped 3D solid by revolving the composite region from the last task around an axis in the XY plane to the right of the region.

⊕ To begin this task, you should have the composite region shown in Figure 14-29 on your screen.

⊕ Open the Draw menu, highlight Solids, and select Revolve.

There is also a Revolve tool on the Solids toolbar, shown previously in Figure 14-6.

⊕ Select the composite region.

⊕ Right click to end selection.

AutoCAD prompts

```
Specify start point for axis of revolution or
define axis by [Object/X (axis)/Y (axis)]:
```

"Object" allows you to select a line or a one-segment polyline as the axis of revolution. "X" and "Y" allow you to specify one of the axes of the current UCS. We will specify an axis by pointing.

⊕ Pick a start point 1.00 unit to the right of the region, as shown by P1 in Figure 14-29.

AutoCAD prompts for an end point of the axis.

⊕ Pick an end point like P2 in Figure 14-29.

AutoCAD prompts

```
Specify angle of revolution <360>:
```

Like REVSURF, REVOLVE gives you the option of creating only a portion of the circle of revolution. Unlike REVSURF, there is no option to begin the object somewhere other than in the plane of the region itself.

⊕ Press Enter to create the full circle.

Your screen will resemble Figure 14-30.

In the next two tasks we will continue to demonstrate methods for manipulating solids by creating a cutaway view and a section.

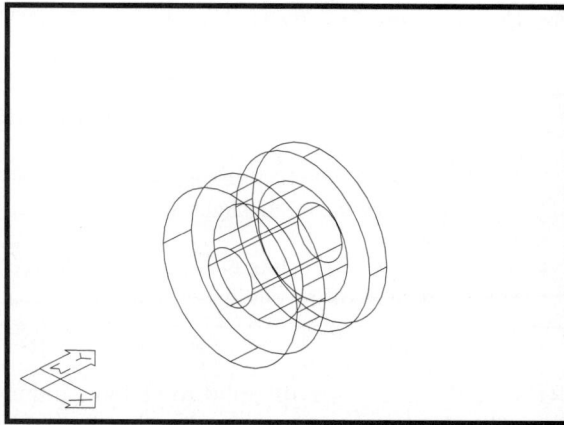

Figure 14-30

14.10 Creating Solid Cutaway Views with SLICE

GENERAL PROCEDURE

1. Open the Draw menu, highlight Solids, and select Slice, or select the Slice tool from the Solids toolbar.
2. Select objects.
3. Specify a cutting plane.
4. Specify a point on the plane.
5. Pick a side to retain.

A single solid or composite solid may be sliced along its intersection with a specifiable plane. The plane is specified in terms common to several solid commands.

In this task we will cut the object created in the last task along a plane parallel to the current z and y axes and retain the left portion so that we can view the inside of the "spool."

⊕ Open the Draw menu, highlight Solids, and select Slice.

There is also a Slice tool on the Solids toolbar, shown previously in Figure 14-6.

AutoCAD will prompt you to select objects.

⊕ Select the spool.

⊕ Right click to end object selection.

AutoCAD now prompts for plane specification:

```
Specify first point on slicing plane by
[Object/Zaxis/View/XY/YZ/ZX/3points] <3points>:
```

A similar prompt is used in the SECTION command, which we will explore next. The slicing plane requested here can be determined by an object, by a point

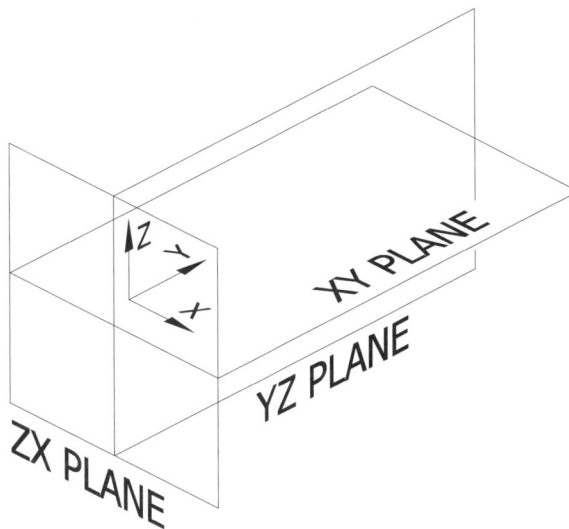

Figure 14-31

on the *z* axis, by one of the current UCS planes, or by showing three points. In this task we will use a YZ plane.

Take a look at Figure 14-31. It should help you visualize the XY, YZ, and ZX planes. The actual slicing plane will be parallel to a plane of origin in the current UCS. In other words, it does not have to have the same origin. Once you have determined which plane you want to use, the next step will be to specify a point on the plane.

⊕   Type "YZ".

AutoCAD will prompt for a point on the YZ plane. The default point is (0,0,0), which will specify the YZ plane of the current UCS. Any other point will specify a plane parallel to the current YZ plane.

⊕   Pick a point similar to P1 in Figure 14-32, so that the *y* axis of the cross hairs runs through the center of the spool.

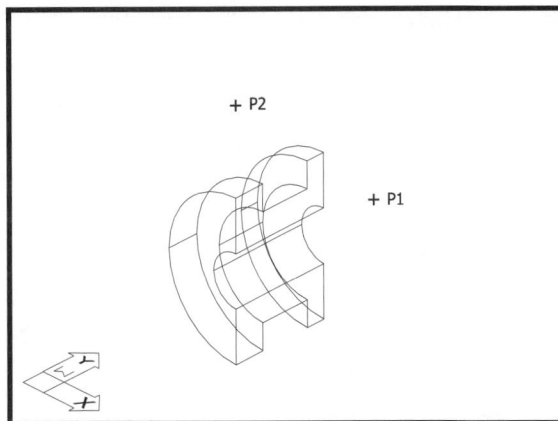

Figure 14-32

This will cause the spool to be cut along its center line.

AutoCAD prompts

```
Specify a point on the desired side of the plane or
[Keep both sides]:
```

⊕ Pick a point similar to P2 in Figure 14-32, to the left of the previous point (that is, left in the *x* direction).

This will show that you want to retain the portion of the spool that lies along the left side of the cutting plane. Your screen should resemble Figure 14-32.

Next we will create a cross section of the remaining half.

14.11 Creating Sections with SECTION

GENERAL PROCEDURE

1. Open the Draw menu, highlight Solids, and select Section.
2. Select objects.
3. Specify a sectioning plane.

Sectioning works just like slicing, but the outcome is a 2D region taken from the solid along the specified plane. In this task we will create a region section of the spool by sectioning it along the XY plane. The result will be a U-shaped block. It will look exactly like the region we used to create the revolved solid in the first place.

⊕ Open the Draw menu, highlight Solids, and select Section.

There is also a Section tool on the Solids toolbar, shown previously in Figure 14-6.

⊕ Select the cut spool.

⊕ Right click to end object selection.

AutoCAD prompts

```
Specify first point on Section plane by
[Object/Zaxis/View/XY/YZ/ZX/3points] <3points>:
```

This is the same prompt as the slicing plane prompt, except for the first word. This time we will cut along the current XY plane.

⊕ Type "xy".

AutoCAD will prompt for a point on the XY plane. Any point will do.

⊕ Press Enter for the point (0,0,0) or pick any point.

AutoCAD will create the section. To see it well, you will need to move it or move the spool.

⊕ Enter the Move command, type "L" for last and show a displacement to move the section away from the spool.

When you are done your screen should resemble Figure 14-33.

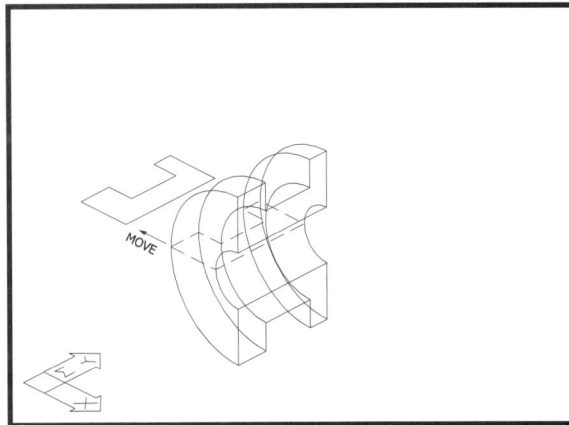

Figure 14-33

14.12 SHADEing Solid Models

GENERAL PROCEDURE

1. Adjust layers, colors, and variables to create desired effects.
2. Type "Shade" or select the Shade tool from the Render toolbar.

Shaded images are simple to create as you know from using the 3DORBIT command. There are relatively few variables to manipulate. For more dramatic and realistic images you will need to delve into the realm of rendering, introduced in the next task. Unlike shading, rendering involves a large number of variables and will require a great deal of practice before you become proficient.

In working with shaded images your only options concern the color of objects in the image, the manner in which edges are shown, the color of edges, and the relative amounts of diffuse and ambient light. In this exercise we will create a shaded image of the composite wedge from earlier in the chapter. In the next task we will use the same object for rendering.

⊕ Erase all objects from your screen.

⊕ Type "i" or select the Insert Block tool from the Draw toolbar.

⊕ Select the W block from the block list.

⊕ Click on OK.

⊕ Insert the wedge near the middle of your grid.

Since this book does not contain color illustrations, we have moved our wedge to layer 0 so that the image is shaded in gray and white. If you do the same, your screen images will more closely match our illustrations. The following procedure is provided if you wish to work with gray and white rather than color images.

1. Make layer 0 current by opening the layer list on the Standard toolbar and clicking on layer 0.
2. Explode the W block.
3. Draw a line anywhere on layer 0.
4. Use the Match Properties tool from the Standard toolbar to move the wedge to layer 0.

⊕ **Turn off the grid.**

You will not want the grid in your shaded or rendered images.

⊕ **Open the View menu and highlight Shade.**

This will open the submenu shown in Figure 14-34. There are seven options. The first three are wireframe and hidden images. The next four correspond to the four settings of the SHADEDGE variable. SHADEDGE determines whether edges of shaded objects arc outlined and the complexity of color values used.

⊕ **Select Flat Shaded.**

This will produce a shaded image similar to Figure 14-35. We suggest that you try the other three settings to see how they appear on your screen before going on to the next task. The differences will not be dramatic and may not be noticeable at all with the current light settings. At this point, you should take advantage of the 3DORBIT command to get a good look at the shaded object.

⊕ **Enter the 3DORBIT command and view the shaded image from different angles.**

⊕ **Reset the view before leaving 3DORBIT.**

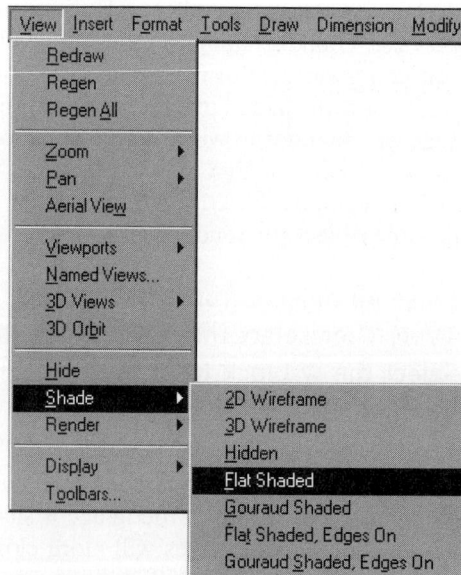

Figure 14-34

Figure 14-35

Reminder: When AutoCAD 2000 shades or renders objects it automatically changes the Shademode variable to 3D. In older versions of AutoCAD, a regen would remove shading and rendering. Not so in AutoCAD 2000. As discussed previously in Chapter 13, to remove shading or rendering in 2000, it is necessary to change Shademode back to 2D (type "Shademode" and then "2", or open the View menu, highlight Shade, and select 2D Wireframe).

14.13 RENDERing Solid Models

GENERAL PROCEDURE

1. Position lights.
2. Attach materials.
3. Adjust light intensity.
4. Render.
5. Save scene.

Rendering goes far beyond shading by creating the effect of light falling on the various surfaces of a solid or surface model. Rendering is a complex craft whose mastery requires many hours of experimentation. Most of the techniques involved concern the placement and setting of lights. There are four types of lights, and each light has its own set of variables and settings, which will dramatically affect the end result. Knowing the various lights, how to position them, and how to understand their respective settings is a good place to begin. But this knowledge alone will not take you very far. You will need to accumulate hours of experience in order to know what you want and how to achieve it.

In this task we will show you how to position lights and how to use some of the most critical settings. We will continue to use the wedge shaded in the last task and to work on layer 0.

⊕ To begin this task you should have the wedge on your screen in a southeast isometric viewpoint, as in the last task.

Ambient Light

First, we will simply render the object as is without any change in lighting. What you will see will be entirely dependent on the default ambient light setting. Ambient light is background light that fills space and is the same everywhere. It has no direction and can only be varied as to color and intensity.

⊕ Open the View menu, highlight Render, and select Render....

There is also a Render tool on the Render toolbar, shown in Figure 14-36. AutoCAD will display the Render dialog box shown in Figure 14-37. Ignore the options in the dialog box for now.

⊕ Click the Render button at the bottom.

After a few moments you will see an image similar to the one in Figure 14-38. As you can see, this image is not much of an advancement over the

Figure 14-36

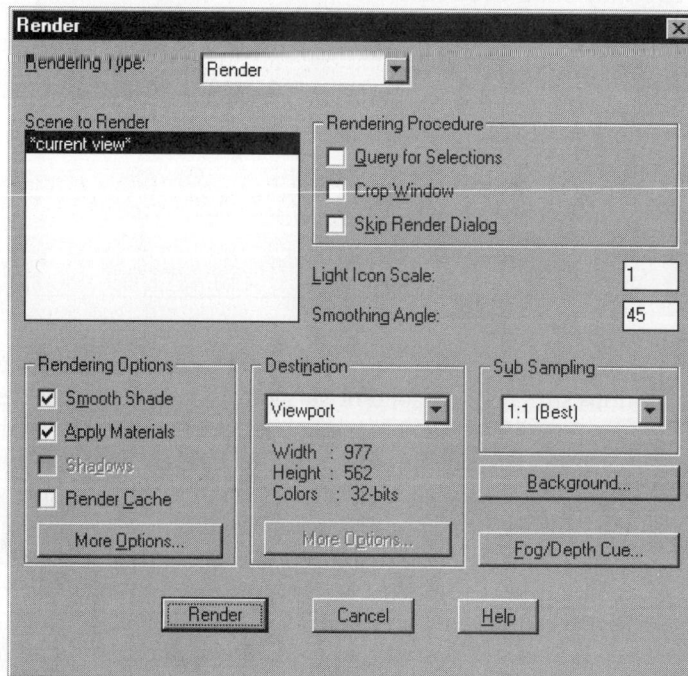

Figure 14-37

Figure 14-38

shaded images in the last task. To enhance the lighting, we need the LIGHT command.

The Lights Dialog Box

Lights are created, placed, and modified using the Lights dialog box.

⊕ Open the View menu, highlight Render, and select Lights....

There is also a Lights tool on the Render toolbar, shown previously in Figure 14-36.

The LIGHT command opens the Lights dialog box, shown in Figure 14-39. Look at the Ambient Light panel on the right. Ambient light has only color

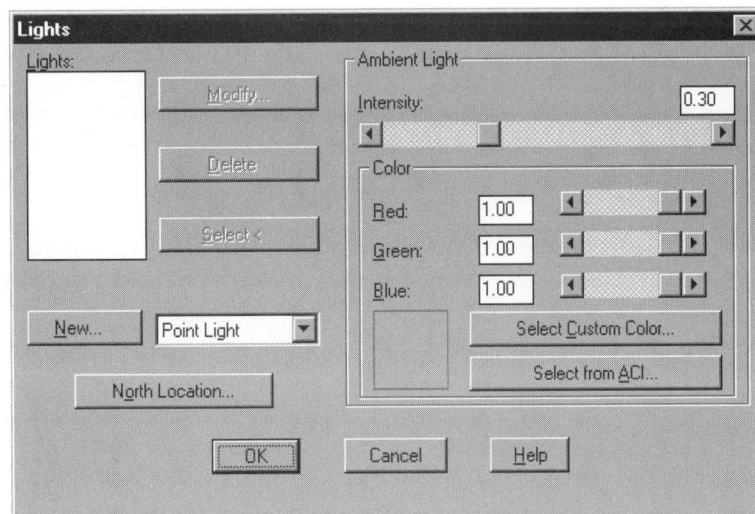

Figure 14-39

and intensity. With the scroll bar at the top you can vary the intensity from 0 to 1.00. The default setting is 0.30. Try changing the intensity using the following procedure:

1. Using the scroll bar, select greater ambient light intensity. Increase it to 1.00 to see the effect clearly.
2. Click on OK.
3. Open the View menu, highlight Render, and select Render....
4. Click the Render button in the Render dialog box.

Also in the Ambient Light box are three scroll bars for mixing the amounts of red, green, and blue light. All types of lights have these scroll bars so that you can vary the color quality of the light coming from individual light sources as well as ambient light color. Feel free to experiment with color settings at this time. The effect of the color mix is especially clear on a gray and white object like ours. For example, if you set the green and blue on 0 and leave the red at 1.00, you will see that what remains of the ambient light is shown as small red dots on the surfaces of the object. With all three set at 1.00, the default, the effect is that of white light.

Changing the Background Color

You may find that rendered images are too dark against the AutoCAD background screen color. This is particularly true if you are creating gray and white images against a black screen. You can remedy this by changing to a different background color through the Preferences dialog box. Or you can add a background to your rendering through the Background dialog box, which is part of the Rendering system. The difference is that the rendered background becomes part of the rendering, whereas the AutoCAD window background does not. The procedure for changing the AutoCAD window background is as follows:

1. Open the Tools menu and select Options from the bottom of the menu.
2. Click on the Display tab.
3. Click on Colors....
4. Select a color from the color list.
5. Click "Apply & Close".
6. Click OK.

To introduce true rendering backgrounds we will add a gradient background. Because of the colors involved, we will not be able to illustrate the results.

⊞ Open the View menu, highlight Render, and select Background....

This will call the Background dialog box illustrated in Figure 14-40. There are many possibilities available, which we will not explore here. Notice that the Solid radio button is selected and the AutoCAD background box is checked. With these two settings many options are inaccessible, and the AutoCAD window color will be used for the rendering background color.

⊞ Click on the Gradient radio button.

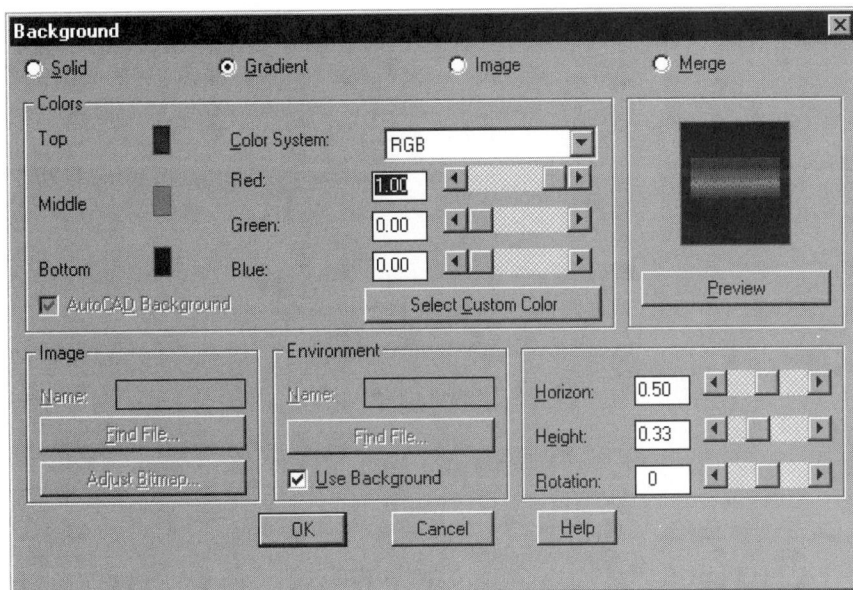

Figure 14-40

Notice that the AutoCAD background check box becomes inaccessible automatically, because it is solid and incompatible with a gradient color scheme. You will also see that the color adjustment area and the horizon, height, and rotation area are now accessible. To see what the current gradient looks like, use the Preview box.

⊕ Click on Preview.

The Preview image will appear, showing a background that grades from red to green to blue. Notice that these are the colors shown on the left next to top, middle, and bottom. One of these three will be highlighted with a dark border. The selected color can be adjusted with the three color scroll bars in the middle. These scrolls can be used like a palette to mix the amounts of red, green, and blue in the top, middle, and bottom colors. Finally, the horizon, height, and rotation scroll bars can be used to vary the proportions and orientation of color lines in the gradient.

You should experiment with these settings to get a feel for how they work.

⊕ When you are done experimenting, click on OK to retain the background you have created.

⊕ Open the View menu, highlight Render, and select Render....

⊕ In the Render dialog box, select the Render button.

In a few moments you should see your ambient light rendering with a color gradient background. Even a simple gradient background will produce a dramatic effect. Next we will add some more focused lighting.

We will be exploring three types of light placement. To define light position, it will be helpful to create a three-viewport configuration so that you can see what is happening from different viewpoints.

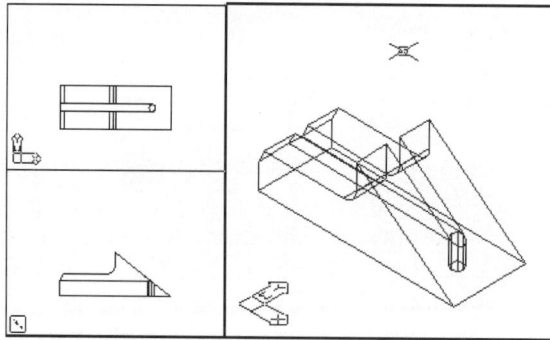

Figure 14-41

⊕ Open the View menu, highlight Viewports..., and select "New Viewports".

⊕ Select "Three: Right".

⊕ Select 3D from the Setup list.

⊕ Click OK.

Your screen will be redrawn with a three-viewport configuration, top and front views on the left, SE isometric view on the right.

⊕ Click in the top left viewport and zoom .5x.

⊕ Click in the bottom left viewport and zoom .5x.

⊕ Click in the right viewport to make it active.

Your screen should now resemble Figure 14-41, except that you will have ambient light rendered objects. Except where we are showing a specific rendering, we will continue to show wireframe images for simplicity and clarity.

Note: In AutoCAD 2000, User Coordinate Systems are defined per viewport. You can have a different UCS in each viewport if you like. The standard viewport configurations you can select from the Viewports dialog box use a convention of matching the UCS to the view in orthographic views. You will find a Front UCS in a Front view, a Top UCS in a Top view, etc. The isometric view keeps the active coordinate system, in this case, the WCS, which we have previously viewed in 2D Plan or Top view. This will mean that the Top and SE Isometric views are on the same grid and working with the same UCS, while the Front view has its own UCS. The Front UCS is derived through simple rotation of the *xyz* axis around the WCS origin and therefore has no specified relation to the objects in the drawing. In other words, the objects in the Front view will not be on the Grid at all.

Spotlight

We are going to add a spotlight on the right side of the object, aimed in along the slot. Light placement is probably the most important consideration in rendering. If you have used point filters previously, then you have already learned all you need to know in order to position lights. Keep in mind that lights will usually be positioned above the XY plane and will probably be alone in space. Point filters can be very helpful in this situation since there is nothing to snap them on to.

Before we can add a light, we must designate the light type, specify that it is new, and give it a name.

⊕ Click in the upper left window to make the Top view active.

It is extremely important that you work in either the top view or the SE isometric view. The Front view currently has a different UCS and will produce very different results. You must enter the correct viewport and therefore the desired UCS before entering the LIGHTS command.

⊕ Open the View menu, highlight Render, and select Lights....

⊕ Click the arrow next to "Point Light" at the left of the Lights dialog box.

The options will be shown as Point Light, Distant Light, and Spotlight. We begin with a spotlight because its focus and directionality make it easy to understand.

⊕ Click on Spotlight.

⊕ Click on "New...".

This will call up the New Spotlight dialog box shown in Figure 14-42. Notice first that there is a place for a name, a scroll bar for intensity, and three scroll bars for color, just as in the ambient light box. There are also panels for position, hotspot and falloff, and attenuation. We will discuss these in a moment, but first let's give the light a name and a position.

⊕ Type "Spot" in the Light Name edit box.

⊕ Type "5" in the Intensity edit box, or move the scroll bar to an intensity of about 5.00.

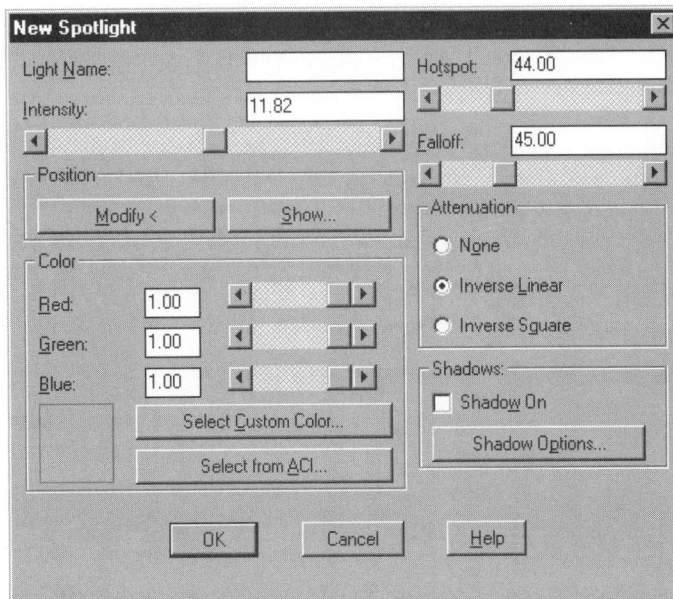

Figure 14-42

⊕ Click on "Modify <" in the Position panel.

This closes the dialog box temporarily and gives you access to your drawing. On the command line you will see the following prompt:

Enter light target <current>:

Spotlights have a target and a source position. As is the case with real spotlights, AutoCAD rendering spotlights are carefully placed and aimed at a particular point in the drawing. The light falls in a cone shape and diminishes away from the center of the cone. You can vary the size of the focal beam using the Hotspot scroll bar, and the size of the surrounding falloff area using the Falloff scroll bar.

For this exercise we will place a light above and to the right of the wedge, aimed directly into the slot. We will be using point selection and XY filters to place the target and the light source where we want them.

⊕ At the prompt for a light target, type ".xy" or hold down shift and right click to open the object snap short cut menu, highlight Point Filters, and select ".XY".

AutoCAD prompts ".xy of" and waits for you to choose a point in the XY plane.

Moving the cursor within the viewport, you will notice that AutoCAD has created a default target placement, which you can ignore.

⊕ Pick a point about 1.0 unit to the left of the cylindrical hole, as shown in Figure 14-43.

AutoCAD now prompts for a Z value:

(need Z):

To place the target point right in the slot, we will need to have a Z value of 1.00 (the bottom of the slot is 1.00 above the XY plane).

⊕ Type "1".

The target point has been specified. Now AutoCAD prompts for the spotlight location:

Enter light location <current>:

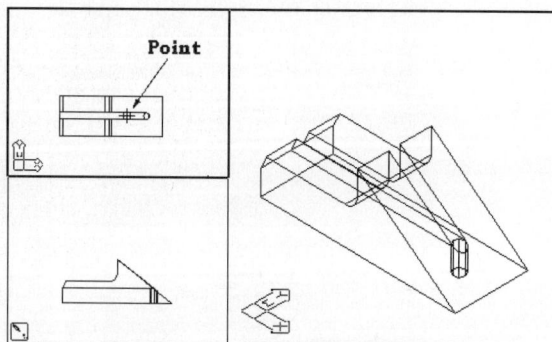

Figure 14-43

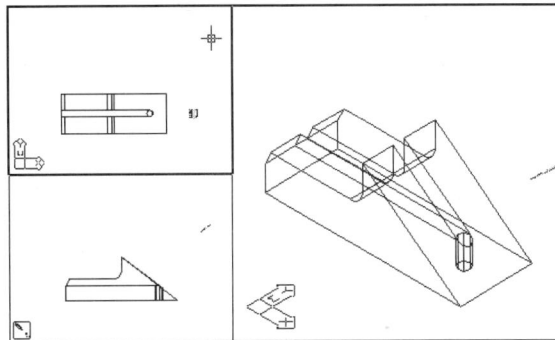

Figure 14-44

We will use an .xy filter to place the light source to the right and above the wedge.

⊕ Type ".xy" or open the short cut menu, highlight Point Filter, and select ".XY".

⊕ In response to the "of" prompt, select a point about 2.00 units to the right of the wedge, as shown in Figure 14-44.

⊕ In response to the "need Z" prompt, type "5" to position the spotlight 5.00 above the XY plane.

This will bring back the New Spotlight dialog box.

⊕ Click OK to exit the New Spotlight dialog box.

⊕ Click OK to exit the Lights dialog box.

You will now see a spotlight icon in your drawing. The three-view configuration will show clearly how it is positioned and directed. Let's render the scene again to see the spotlight in action.

⊕ Click on the right viewport to make it active.

⊕ Open the View menu, highlight Render, and select Render....

⊕ Click the Render button in the Render dialog box.

You will see a rendered image similar to the one in Figure 14-45. In this image you can clearly see how the spotlight hits the wedge just behind the hole and falls off in waves along the back of the object.

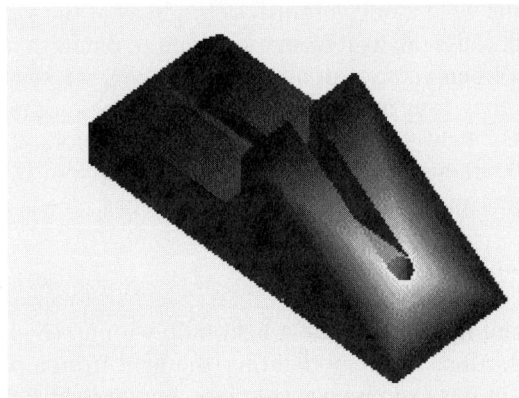

Figure 14-45

Figure 14-46

To achieve a more precise light cone, you can change from a Gouraud style rendering to a Phong rendering.

⊕ Press enter to repeat RENDER.
⊕ Select the More Options... button in the Rendering Options panel.
⊕ Select the "Phong" radio button in the Render quality panel.
⊕ Click on OK.
⊕ Click the Render button.

Your new rendered image will resemble Figure 14-46.

Next we will be adding a point light, but before going on you may want to experiment with some of the other features of spotlighting (available in the New Spotlight or Modify Spotlight subdialog of the Lights dialog box). Try varying the hotspot and falloff. Notice that the hotspot must always be smaller than the falloff. You will also see significant differences when you vary the attenuation. Attenuation is the rate at which light intensity diminishes relative to distance from the light source. In the default Inverse Linear setting, light two units away from its source will appear half as bright. If you switch to Inverse Square attenuation, light at two units will be only a fourth as bright as at the source. So switching to inverse square will cause the light from a spotlight to diminish more quickly over a shorter distance.

When you are done experimenting, we suggest that you return to our settings so that your images continue to resemble ours. These include the following: Ambient light is at 1.00 intensity and all colors are at 1.00. The spotlight is at about 5.00 intensity, all colors are at 1.00, hotspot is at 44 degrees with falloff at 45 degrees, and attenuation is inverse linear.

Point Light

Point light works like a light bulb with no shade. It radiates outward equally in all directions. Like spotlighting, the light from a point light attenuates over distance.

In this exercise we will place a point light right inside the slot of the wedge. This will clearly show the light bulb effect of a small point of light radiating outward.

- Open the View menu, highlight Render, and select Lights....

  Remember that the upper left viewport should be active before you enter the command. If the right viewport is active you can switch after entering the command because these two share the same UCS. The lower left viewport should not be active.

- Click on the arrow to the right of "Spotlight" and switch to "Point Light".
- Click on "New...".
- Type "Point" in the Light Name edit box.
- Click on "Modify <".

  For a point light you only need to specify a location, since point light has no direction other than outward from the source. The prompt is

  `Enter light location <current>:`

  We will use the same point filtering system to locate this light.

- At the prompt type ".xy" or open the cursor menu, highlight Point Filters, and select .XY.
- At the "of" prompt, pick a point in the top view at the center of the slot and about 1.00 unit behind the plane where the box and the wedge join, as shown in Figure 14-47.
- Type "1.25" for a Z value.

  Since the slot is at 1.00 from the XY plane, this will put the point light just above the bottom of the slot.

- Click on OK.
- Click on OK again to exit the Lights dialog box.
- Click on the right viewport to make it active.
- Open the View menu, highlight Render, and select Render....
- Select the Render button from the Render dialog box.

  Your rendered object will resemble Figure 14-48. In this image you can clearly see the effect of the point light within the slot along with the spotlight falling on the right side of the object.

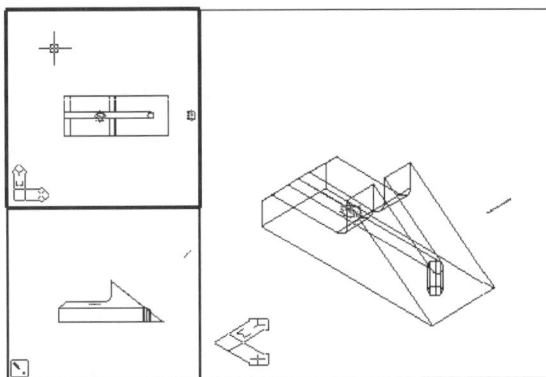

Figure 14-47

Figure 14-48

Distant Light

The last type of light is called distant light and is often used to achieve the effect of direct sunlight. In AutoCAD rendering, a distant light source emits beams of light that are parallel and travel in one direction only. Distant light does not attenuate. It is the same at any distance from the source. Distant light placement is defined by a directional vector; the command line prompt will ask for a "to" point and a "from" point. You can define this vector precisely using point filters, as we have done previously. The to point will probably be on an object or in the XY plane. The from point will be above the XY plane. Most important is the angle and direction between the two points. You can define these points using point filters, as we have done previously, or you can use the sunlight-oriented Azimuth and Altitude dials shown in the Distant Light dialog box. Since you have already used point filters, we will introduce the dial system here for variety.

⊕ Open the View menu, highlight Render, and select Lights....
⊕ Click on the arrow to the right of "Point Light" and switch to "Distant Light".
⊕ Click on "New...".

This brings up the New Distant Light dialog box shown in Figure 14-49. You will see scroll bars for intensity and color on the left. On the right you will see the Azimuth and Altitude dials and scroll bars above a light source vector modification panel. By selecting "Modify <" you could proceed to place the distant light source with to and from points using point selection and point filters. The Azimuth and Altitude system may help you to think more specifically in terms of sunlight. The Azimuth setting will determine the position of sunlight relative to the east–west horizon. In other words, it will simulate the variations of sunlight depending on your position on the planet and the time of year. The Altitude setting will simulate time-of-day variations. In the northern hemisphere in late morning, for example, the sun is coming from the south (180 degrees, opposite north on the azimuth dial) from an altitude

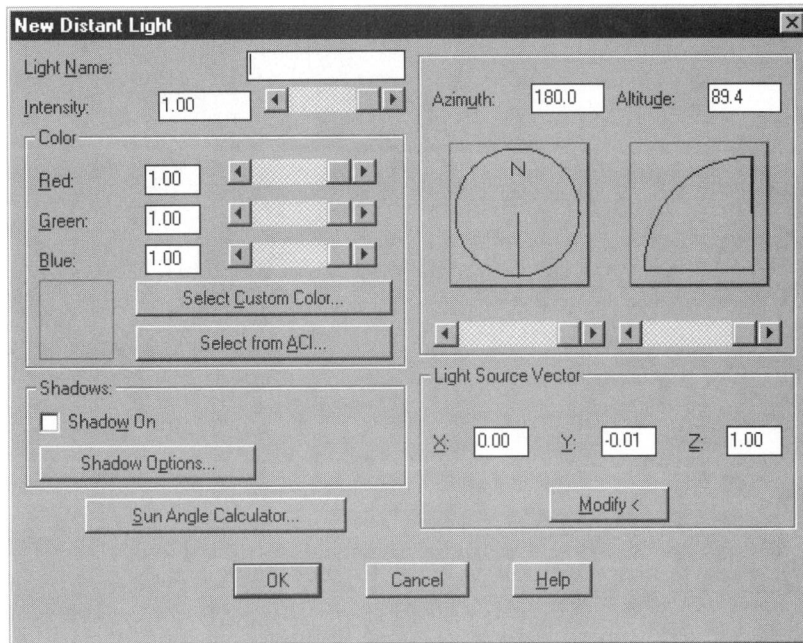

Figure 14-49

of, let's say, 65 degrees. You can use the scroll bars, points on the dials, or typing in the edit boxes to achieve these settings. You can also use the Sun Angle Calculator to find appropriate settings for different times and places.

⊕ Type "Dist" in the Light Name edit box.

⊕ Using the scroll bar, move the Azimuth setting all the way to the right so that the edit box reads 180 degrees.

⊕ Using the scroll bar, move the Altitude setting partway to the right so that the edit box shows 65 degrees.

Changes in these settings will also cause changes in the Light Source Vector box and in the dials above the scroll bars.

⊕ Click on OK.

⊕ Click on OK in the Lights dialog box.

⊕ Open the view menu, highlight Render, and select Render....

⊕ Click the Render button in the Render dialog box.

Your image will resemble the rendering in Figure 14-50. By comparing this image with the one in Figure 14-48, you can see the effect of adding distant "sunlight" to this rendering.

The Render Window

To get a full view of a rendered image, it is often desirable to send the rendering to the Render Window rather than view the rendering within a single viewport. Renderings sent to the Render window are also saved during the current drawing

Figure 14-50

session so you can quickly compare results. To use the render window, you have to make one change in the Render dialog box.

⊕ Press Enter to repeat Render.

⊕ In the dialog box, click the arrow to the right of the box that says "Viewport".

This will be in the Destination panel of the dialog box. The arrow will open a list that shows Viewport, Render Window, and File as Destination options. Rendering to a viewport you have already done; rendering to a file will send the rendering information directly to a file without displaying the image on your screen. Render files can be created in TGA, TIFF, GIF, PostScript, X11, PBM, PGM, PPM, BMP, PCX, SUN FITS, FAX G III, and IFF formats and may then be displayed in other graphics systems.

⊕ Click on Render Window.

The list will close and Render Window will be shown in the Destination box.

⊕ Click on the Render button.

In a moment the rendered wedge will be shown in the Render Window. This window has standard Windows features and can be moved, maximized, or minimized. Once it is opened there will be a label for it on the Windows taskbar. You can switch between the Drawing Window and the Render Window, as you would with other open applications.

⊕ Click on the maximize button to see a full-screen rendered image.

⊕ Click on the AutoCAD drawing name label on the Windows taskbar to return to the drawing window.

Scenes

A rendered scene is made up of a view and a set of lights. Once you have positioned lights, you may want to present the image from different points of view and use different configurations of lights. Defined scenes can be saved so that you can re-create them easily and even switch from one to another. For example, let's cre-

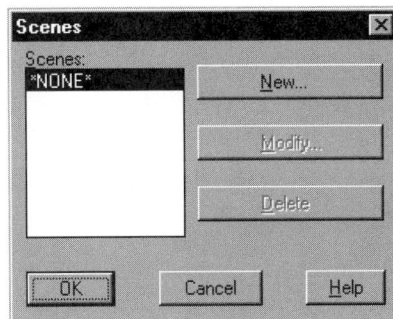

Figure 14-51

ate a scene without the spotlight to see the effect of the distant light and the point light together.

⊕ Open the View menu, highlight Render, and select Scene....

There is also a Scene tool on the Render toolbar, shown previously in Figure 14-36. This will bring up the Scenes dialog box shown in Figure 14-51.

⊕ Select "New...".

⊕ Type "NoSpot" for a scene name (spaces not allowed in names).

⊕ Highlight "Point" and "Dist" in the Lights area (hold down the shift key to highlight both names).

Make sure that "Spot" is not highlighted.

⊕ Click on OK.

⊕ In the Scenes dialog box, make sure that "NOSPOT" is highlighted and then click OK.

Now that the new scene is defined, you can create a new rendering.

⊕ Open the View menu, highlight Render, and select Render....

⊕ In the Render dialog box, make sure that "NOSPOT" is highlighted under "Scene to Render".

⊕ Click on the Render button.

Your "Nospot" scene will resemble Figure 14-52 and will be rendered to the Render window.

Figure 14-52

⊕ Click on the AutoCAD drawing name label on the Windows taskbar to return to the drawing window.

Notice that the image in the viewport is not the new rendering but the previous image with the spotlight included. The rendered image in the Render window does not affect the image in the viewport.

Attaching Materials

Materials can be created or selected from AutoCAD's materials library. Each material definition has its own characteristic color, ambient light color, reflection color, and roughness value. Materials can also be created or modified. Changing an object's material will dramatically affect the way it is rendered, so it will usually make sense to attach materials before adjusting light intensity and color. In this exercise we will simply take you through the procedure of loading materials from the AutoCAD library and attaching them to an object. When you experiment on your own, you will see color effects that we cannot show in this book.

⊕ Open the View menu, highlight Render, and select Materials....

There is also a Materials tool on the Render toolbar, as shown in Figure 14-53.

Notice that there is a Materials Library option as well as a Materials option. These two options refer to the MATLIB and RMAT commands. MATLIB opens the Materials Library dialog box and RMAT opens the Materials dialog. Materials Library is used to load Materials into a drawing, while Materials is used to attach, modify, and create materials. Since you can access the Materials library through the Materials dialog box, it may be more efficient to go this way. RMAT will call the Materials dialog box shown in Figure 14-54. Before we can attach a material, we must load at least one from the Materials Library. To use this box, select a material or materials on the right and then select Import to bring them into your drawing.

⊕ Click on Materials Library....

This will open the Materials Library dialog box shown in Figure 14-55. To load materials, they must be selected on the right and then imported.

⊕ Select "Beige Matte".

⊕ While "Beige Matte" is highlighted, select "<-Import".

The Beige Matte material definition will be loaded and you will see it on the Materials List at the left.

⊕ Click on OK.

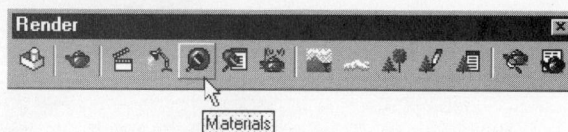

Figure 14-53

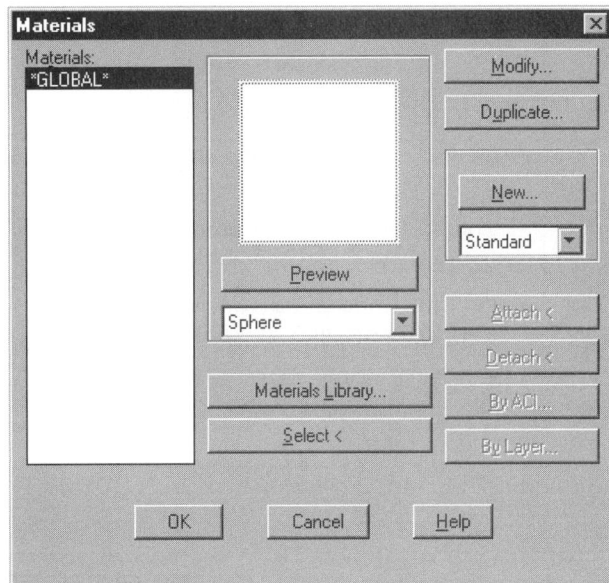

Figure 14-54

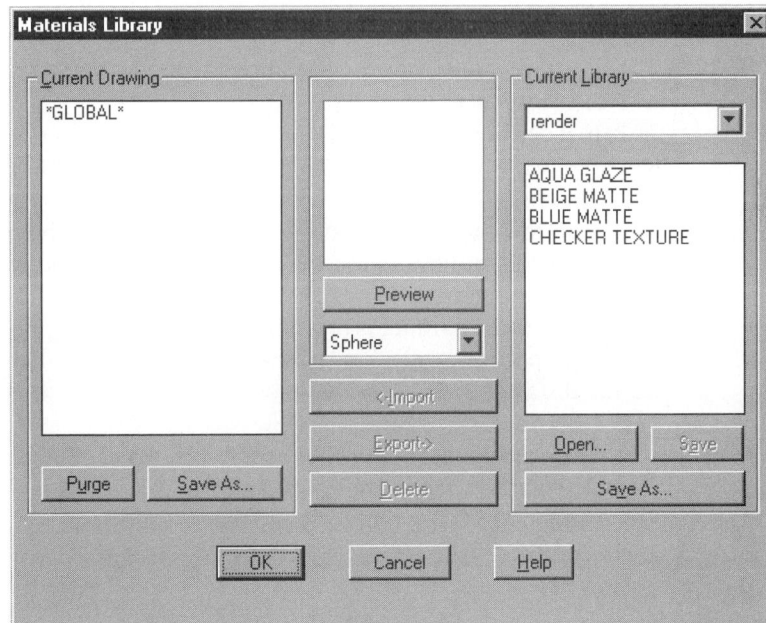

Figure 14-55

Now you must attach the material to the object you are rendering. When there is more than one object, you can attach different materials to different objects.

⊞ Click on "Attach <".

The dialog box disappears and you will see this prompt:

Select objects to attach "BEIGE MATTE" to:

⊕ Select the wedge.

⊕ Right click to end object selection.

⊕ Click on OK.

You are now ready to render.

⊕ Open the View menu, highlight Render, and select Render....

⊕ Select the Render button in the Render dialog box.

Your rendered image will be similar to the last image, but it will appear in beige tones.

14.14 Creating Perspective and Clipped Views with 3DORBIT

GENERAL PROCEDURE

1. Create objects.
2. Enter 3DORBIT.
3. Adjust viewpoint.
4. Open short cut menu.
5. Highlight Projection.
6. Select Perspective.
7. Exit 3DORBIT.

We have a few more presentation tricks to show you before we are done. In this task you will learn how to use the 3DORBIT command to create simple perspective views. In perspective projections, all parallel lines converge at one horizon point, in the usual parallel projection, parallel lines are presented as parallel on the screen. Perspective projection replicates the way the eye sees objects as they recede into the distance.

⊕ To begin this task you should have the 3D solid wedge model on your screen from the last task.

⊕ If necessary, left click in the right viewport to make it active.

⊕ Open the View menu, highlight Viewports, and select 1 Viewport.

You should have the model in a SE isometric view in a single viewport. Whatever shading or rendering you have will be fine for this task.

⊕ Using the scroll bars, center the model within the drawing area.

The next step will be to adjust the viewpoint on the object to create a "long, flat" view. This type of view will show the effect of perspective projection more dramatically than the views we have been using. This can be done by adjusting the viewpoint in the 3DORBIT command, but we will provide a method using the VPOINT command, which will allow a more precise adjustment to match our illustrations.

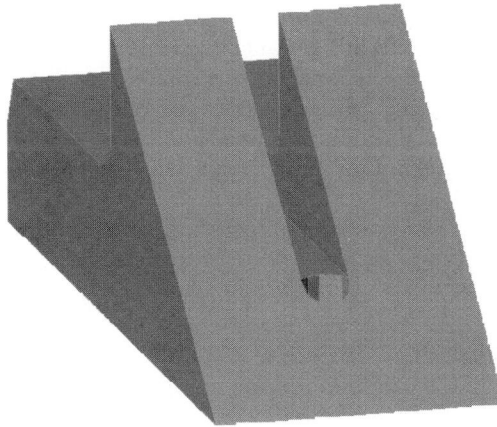

Figure 14-56

⊕ Open the View menu, highlight 3D Views, and select Viewpoint Presets....

⊕ In the Viewpoint Presets dialog box, enter 345 for the angle from the X axis and 15 for the angle from the XY plane.

Your screen should resemble Figure 14-56.

⊕ Open the View menu and select 3DORBIT.

You will see the familiar arcball, which you will not need since your viewpoint is already adjusted.

⊕ Right click to open the short cut menu.

⊕ Highlight Projection, and select Perspective.

The menu will disappear and the wedge will be presented in perspective projection, as shown in Figure 14-57. Compare this with the previous parallel projection image. If you want a little more dramatic demonstration, add the grid and then switch back and forth between perspective and parallel projections.

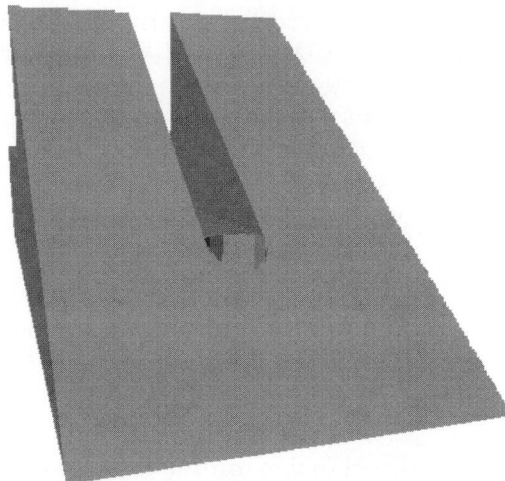

Figure 14-57

Note: Whatever projection you are in when you leave 3DORBIT will be maintained in your drawing. By leaving objects in perspective you can create perspective renderings. However, you cannot edit, pick points, zoom, or pan in your drawing while in a perspective view.

3DORBIT Zoom, Pan, and Camera Adjustments

While you are in 3DORBIT and in a perspective projection, it is a good time to explore the 3DORBIT zoom, pan, and camera adjustment options. The difference between camera adjustment and zooming, for example, will be more evident in a perspective projection.

⊕ Stay in 3DORBIT and right click to open the short cut menu.

⊕ If you have not already done so, turn on the 3DORBIT grid.

⊕ Open the short cut menu again and select Pan.

The Zoom and Pan options work just like the realtime ZOOM and PAN options you are used to. You will see the Pan hand cursor icon.

⊕ Use the cursor to pan left and right.

Notice that in perspective projection, panning actually turns the model. Try panning in parallel projection to see the difference.

⊕ Open the short cut menu and switch to parallel perspective.

You will still be in panning mode when the menu closes.

⊕ Pan left and right again.

Observe how everything shifts together in a completely parallel manner.

Now try zooming in parallel.

⊕ Open the short cut menu and select Zoom.

You will see the realtime Zoom cursor.

⊕ Click and drag the cursor up and down the screen to zoom in and out.

Notice that zoom takes you in and out of the center point of the display, so that you move directly into the grid or a point on the object. Now stay in zooming mode and switch to a perspective projection.

⊕ Open the short cut menu, highlight Projection, and select Perspective again.

You will still be in zoom mode when the menu closes.

⊕ Click and drag the cursor up and down the screen to zoom in and out.

Notice how zooming in perspective is the same as zooming in parallel because you are moving straight in and out on a single line directed at the target point at the center. Now try adjusting the camera distance.

⊕ Open the cursor menu, highlight More, and select Adjust distance.

You will see the camera adjustment cursor, which works like the realtime zoom cursor but produces a different effect.

⊕ Click and drag the cursor up and down the screen slowly to adjust camera distance in and out.

Observe how adjusting the camera distance produces a long, flat motion that brings you down along the grid, as if you were moving gradually into the scene along the lines of perspective. Now switch back to a parallel projection.

⊕ Open the short cut menu, highlight Projections, and select parallel.

⊕ Click and drag the cursor up and down the screen to adjust camera distance in and out.

In parallel projection you observe no difference between zooming and adjusting camera distance.

Before going on to the clipping plane options that will complete this task, you should also try out the Swivel Camera option. This option moves your point of view around the target point at the center of the display and adjusts your view of objects accordingly. It is probably easier to comprehend this action in the current parallel projection, but you are encouraged to experiment in perspective as well.

Adjusting Clipping Planes in 3DORBIT

The last feature of the 3DORBIT command that we will demonstrate is the clipping plane option. With this feature you can add an invisible plane in front or behind objects. With a front clipping plane, for example, any part of the object which would be in front of the plane is not displayed. In this way you can show a view of the inside of an object without actually sectioning it.

⊕ Open the short cut menu and select Reset View to return to the 345° from X, 15° from XY view with which we began this exercise (Figure 14-56 or 14-57, depending on which projection you are in).

⊕ If necessary, open the short cut menu and switch to a perspective projection, as shown previously in Figure 14-57.

⊕ Open the short cut menu again and pan to the right so that your grid and wedge are positioned similar to Figure 14-58.

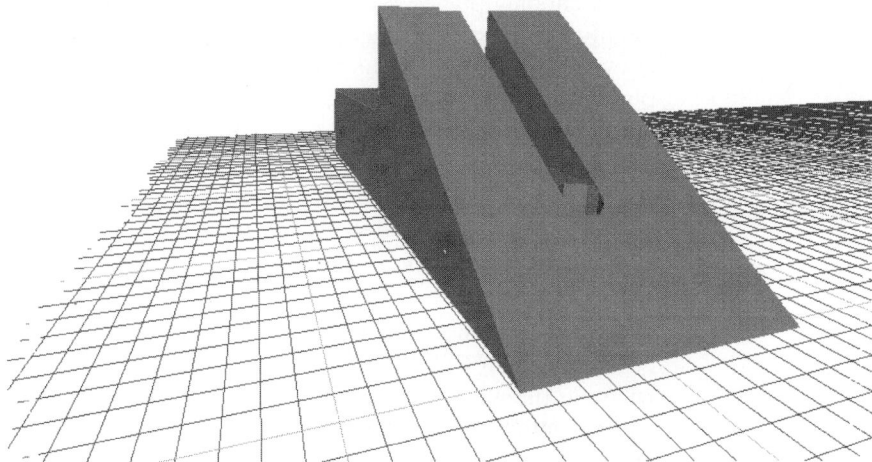

Figure 14-58

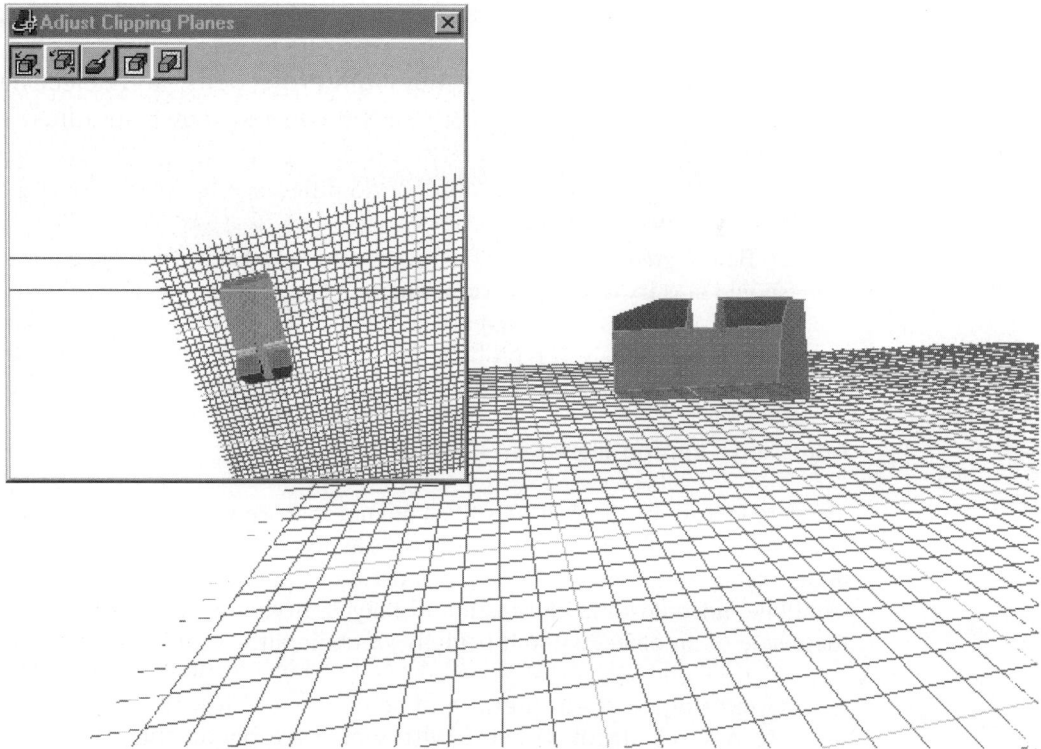

Figure 14-59

This will make it easier for you to see the clipping planes in action.

⊕ Open the short cut menu, highlight More, and select Adjust Clipping Planes.

This will open an Adjust Clipping Planes window, as shown in Figure 14-59. In this window the grid and wedge have been rotated 90°, so that you can adjust clipping planes from above. The green and white lines across the middle of the window represent the clipping plane, and the icons on the toolbar above let you control which plane you are adjusting, and also to turn clipping planes on and off. In the current default setting, the front clipping plane has been turned on and its adjustment tool is in the on position. Looking at the image in the drawing area, you will clearly see that the front part of the wedge has been clipped away. Clicking and dragging the plane in the Adjust Clipping Plane window will bring it back into view.

⊕ Click and drag the cursor up and down in the Adjust Clipping Plane window.

Observe the model as you move the plane. Notice that you don't have to be on the line of the plane to drag it. Clicking and dragging vertically anywhere in the window will cause the plane to move. When the two planes come together the back plane will move also, as if it were being pushed.

⊕ Move the front plane to create an image similar to Figure 14-60, showing the inside of the hole in the wedge.

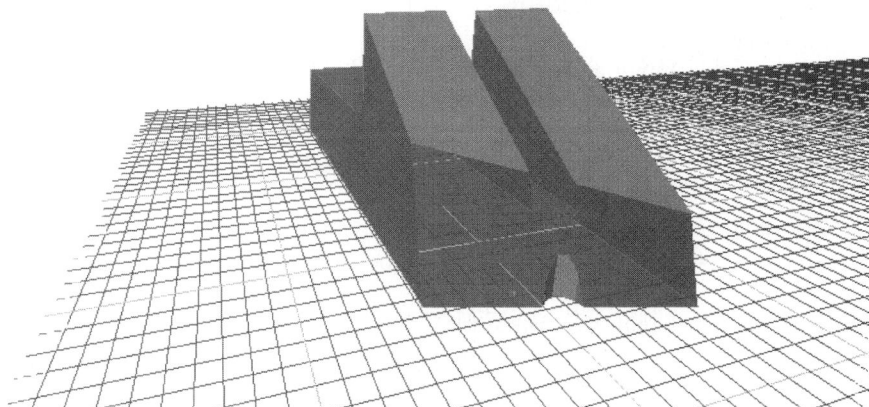

Figure 14-60

There you have it. You have now seen everything this great command can do. You have come a long way since drawing your first line in Chapter 1. You will find many drawings in this chapter and in Appendix A on which to practice your skills. Good luck!

14.15   Review Material

Questions

1. What 3D solid objects and commands would you use to create a square nut with a bolt hole in the middle?
2. What command allows you to draw outside the *xy* plane of the current UCS without the use of typed coordinates, object snap, or point filters?
3. Why is there a prompt for a base surface in CHAMFER but not in FILLET?
4. Name three ways to select faces for editing in the SOLIDEDIT command.
5. What is the difference between a REGION and a 2D SOLID? What is the difference between a REGION and a 3DFACE?
6. What options are available for the creation of different effects in shaded images?
7. What is the major additional effect available in rendered images that is not available in shaded images?
8. How would you use a point filter to place a spotlight 5.0 units above the point (3,5,0)?
9. What is ambient light?
10. What are the shapes and qualities of spotlights, point lights, and distant lights? What is attenuation, and how does it affect each type of lighting?
11. What four qualities make up a material definition?
12. What are some limitations on the capacity to manipulate perspective projection views in the drawing window?
13. Why are objects rotated 90° in the Adjust Clipping Planes window?

Drawing Problems

1. Open a new drawing with the 1B prototype, switch to a southeast isometric view, and draw a solid cylinder, centered at (9,6,0), with a radius of 3.0 units and a height of 5.0 units.
2. On layer 1, draw a solid box 2.0 × 2.0 units at the base, with a height of 5.0 units, centered at (9,6,0).
3. Subtract the box from the cylinder.
4. Create a section view of the composite object cut along the diagonal of the rectangular hole.
5. Create a rendered image with a solid blue background, a spotlight with target at (9,6,3) and source at (14,8,6), and a distant light at the default position. Ambient light should be set to full 1.00 intensity.

14.16 WWW Exercise #14 (Optional)

And now, one last time:

⊕ Make sure that you are connected to your Internet service provider.
⊕ Type "browser", open the Web toolbar and select the Browse the Web tool, or open your system browser from the Windows 98 taskbar.
⊕ If necessary, navigate to our companion Web site at "www.prenhall.com/dixriley".

See you there.

14.17   Drawings 14-1 through 14-5:
Bushing Mount, Link Mount, 3D Assembly, Tapered Bushing, Pivot Mount

We offer the following drawing suggestions for Drawing 14-1. The principles demonstrated here will carry over into Drawings 14-2 through 14-5, and you should be capable of handling them on your own at this point. In all cases you are encouraged to experiment with renderings when the model is complete.

Use an efficient sequence in the construction of composite solids. In general, this will mean saving union, subtraction, and intersection operations until most of the solid objects have been drawn and positioned. This approach allows you to continue to use the geometry of the parts for snap points as you position other parts.

DRAWING SUGGESTIONS

- Use at least two views, one plan and one 3D, as you work.
- Begin with the bottom of the mount in the XY plane. This will mean drawing a 6.00 × 4.00 × 0.50 solid box sitting on the XY plane.
- Draw a second box, 1.50 × 4.00 × 3.50, in the XY plane. This will become the upright section at the middle of the mount. Move it so that its own midpoint is at the midpoint of the base.
- Draw a third box, 1.75 × 0.75 × 0.50, in the XY plane. This will be copied and become one of the two slots in the base. Move it so that the midpoint of its long side is at the midpoint of the short side of the base. Then MOVE it 1.125 along the *x* axis.
- Add a 0.375 radius cylinder with 0.50 height at each end of the slot.
- Copy the box and cylinders 3.75 to the other side of the base to form the other slot.
- Create a new UCS 2.00 up in the *z* direction. You can use the origin option and give (0,0,2) as the new origin. This puts the XY plane of the UCS directly at the middle of the upright block, where you can easily draw the bushing.
- Move out to the right of the mount and draw the polyline outline of the bushing, as shown in the drawing. Use REVOLVE to create the solid bushing.
- Create a cylinder in the center of the mount, where it can be subtracted to create the hole in the mount upright.
- Union the first and second boxes.
- Subtract the boxes and cylinders to form the slots in the base and the bushing-sized cylinder to form the hole in the mount.

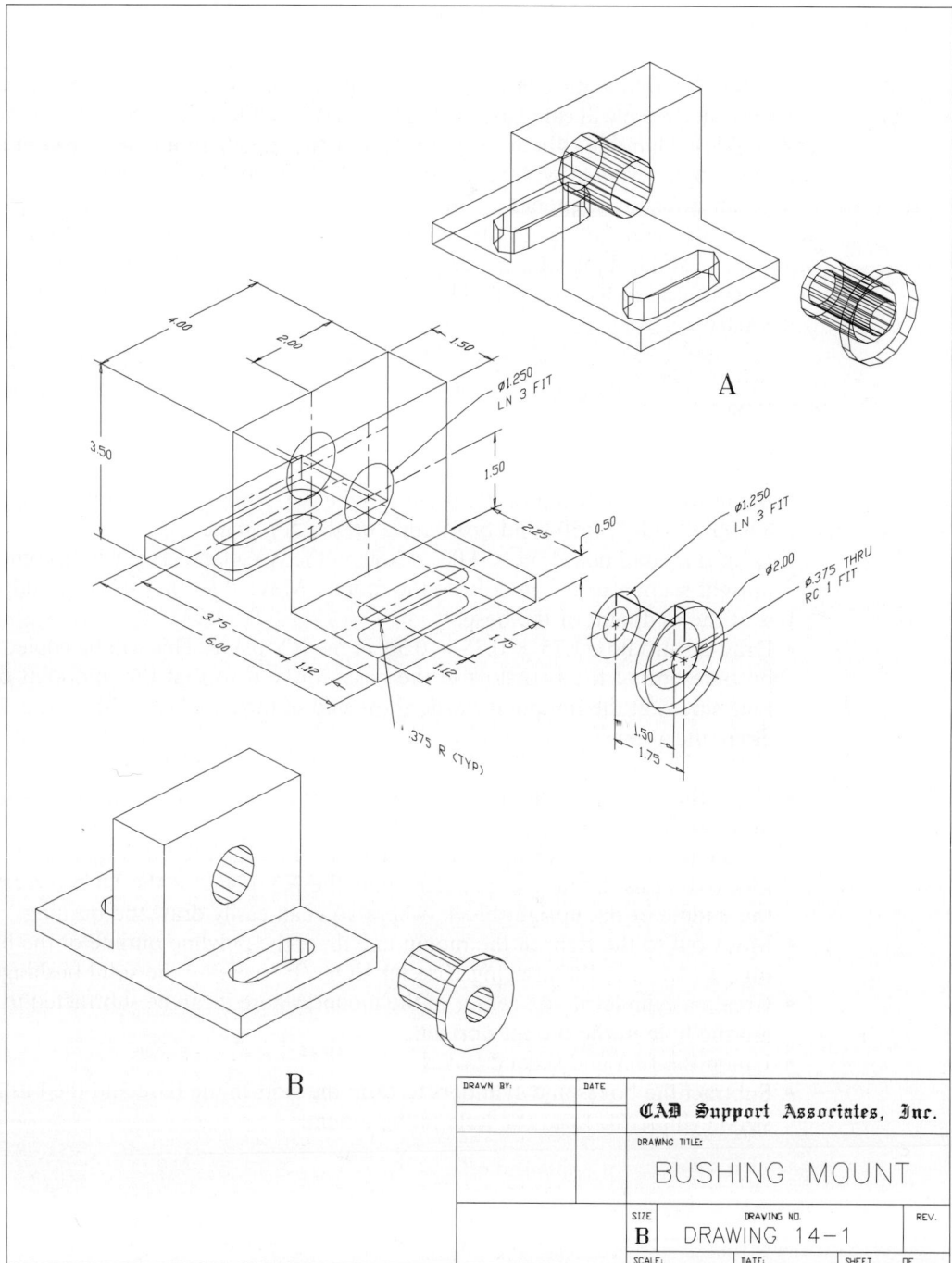

A

B

DRAWN BY:	DATE	**CAD Support Associates, Inc.**		
		DRAWING TITLE:		
		BUSHING MOUNT		
		SIZE	DRAWING NO.	REV.
		B	DRAWING 14-1	
		SCALE:	DATE:	SHEET OF

LINK MOUNT

Drawing 14-2

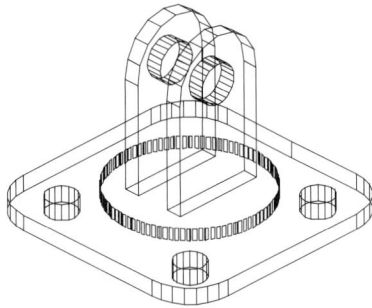

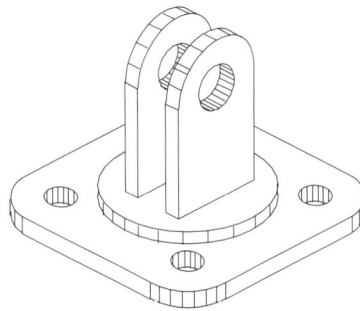

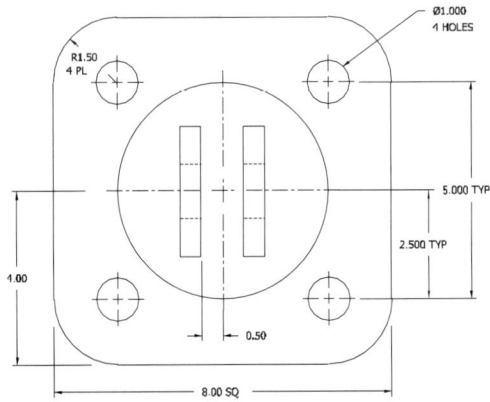

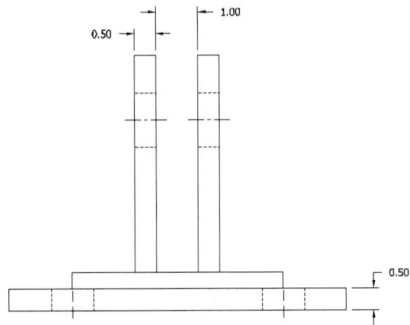

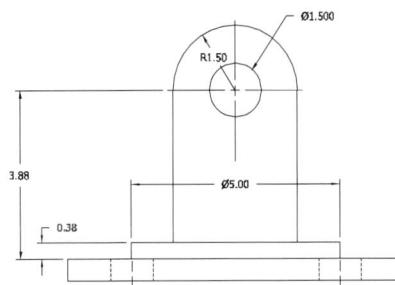

Ø2.375

.12

Ø4.75

3.00
(REF)

1.88

.12

Ø.375

1.25

.12

Ø1.500
CENTER HOLE

Ø.500
FLANGED HOLE

Ø3.5000 B.C.

HEX .56 ACROSS FLATS
(BOLT & NUT)

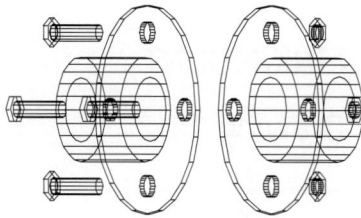

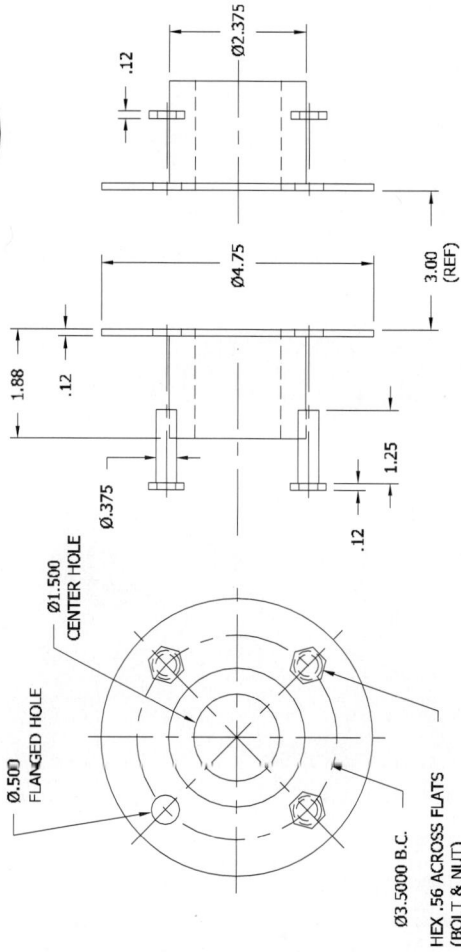

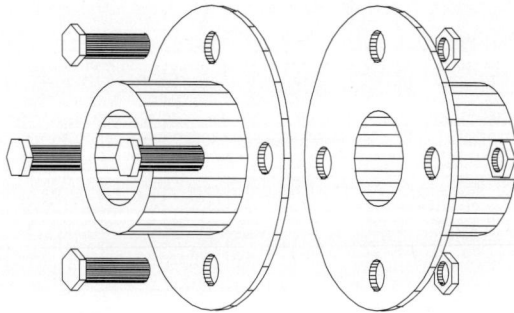

Reference 14-3

CAD Support Associates

3D ASSEMBLY

Drawing 14-3

Drawing 14-4
Tapered Bushing

Drawing 14-5
Pivot Mount

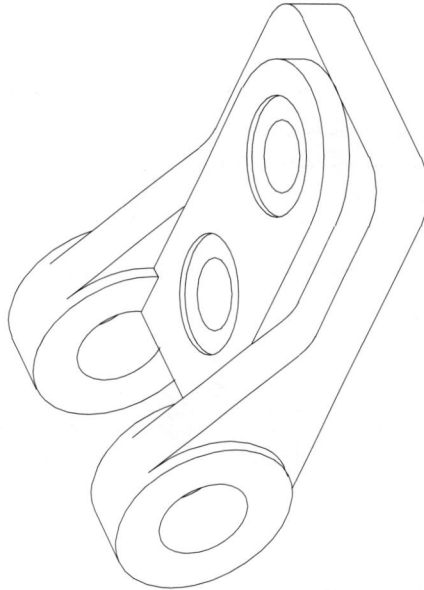

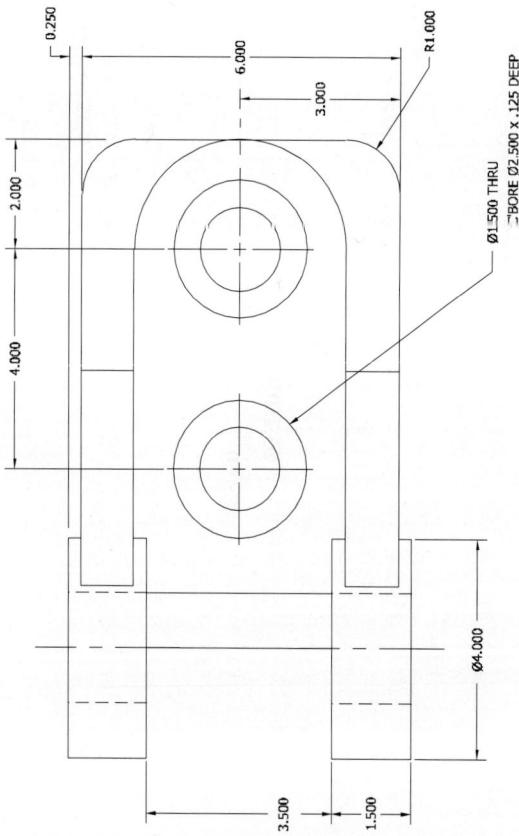

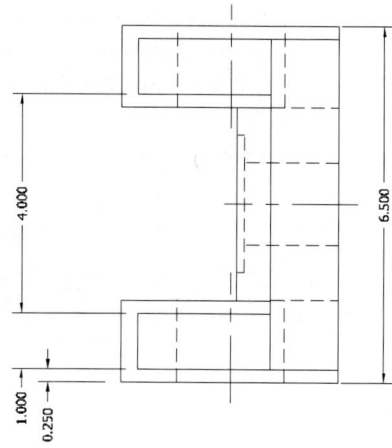

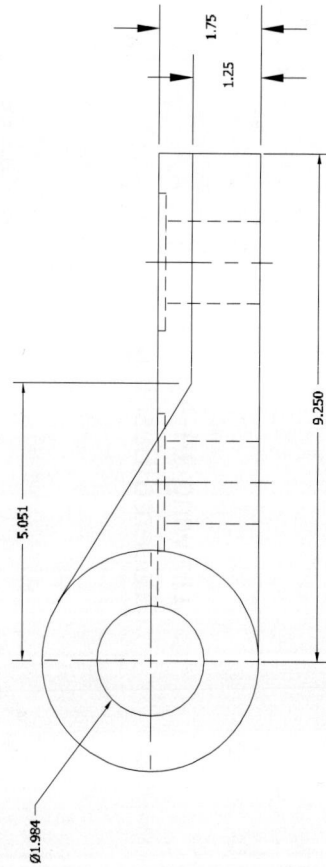

Ø1.500 THRU
⌴BORE Ø2.500 x .125 DEEP

0.250

6.000

3.000

2.000

4.000

R1.000

Ø4.000

3.500

1.500

4.000

6.500

1.000

0.250

1.75

1.25

9.250

5.051

Ø1.984

14.18   Drawings 14-6A, B, C, and D

The drawings that follow, shown six to a page and labeled 14-6 A, B, C, and D, are 3D solid models derived from drawings done earlier in the book. You can start from scratch or begin with the 2D drawing and use some of the geometry as a guide to your 3D model. Either way, the dimensions for these drawings are those shown in preceding chapters.

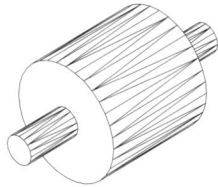

Drawing 2—2

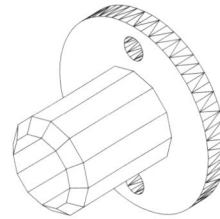

Drawing 3—4

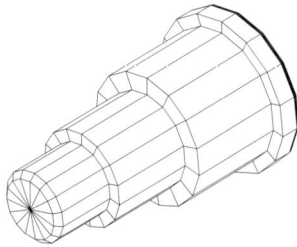

Drawing 3—2

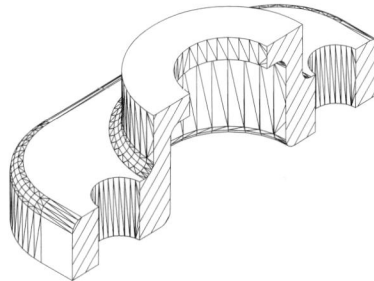

Drawing 3—6

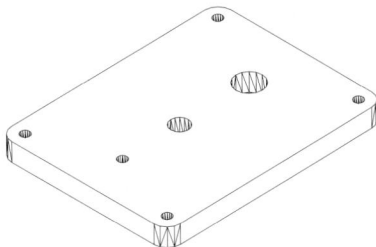

Drawing 3—3

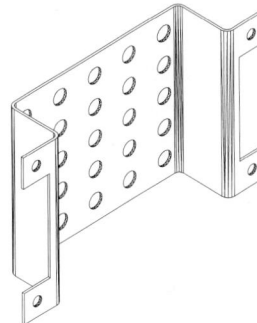

Drawing 4—4

DRAWING 14—6A

3D SOLIDS DRAWING

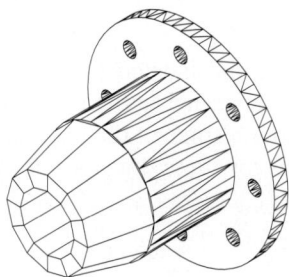

Drawing 5-1

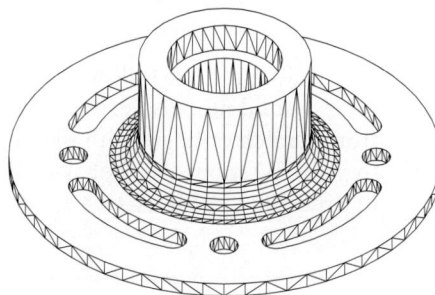

Drawing 5-6

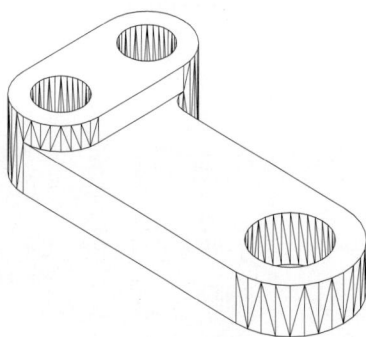

Drawing 5-2

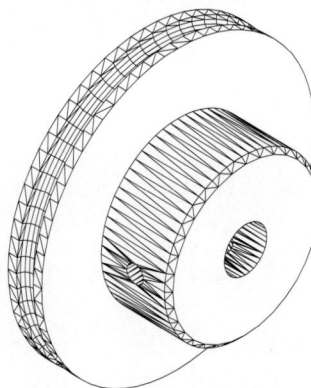

Drawing 6-4

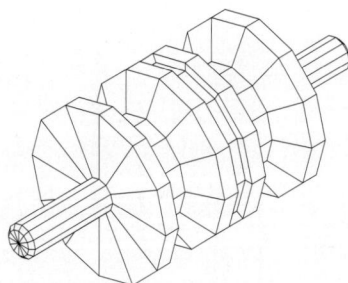

Drawing 5-4

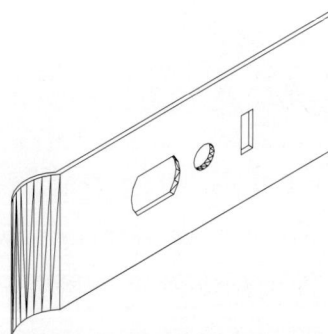

Drawing 6-5

DRAWING 14-6B

3D SOLID DRAWINGS

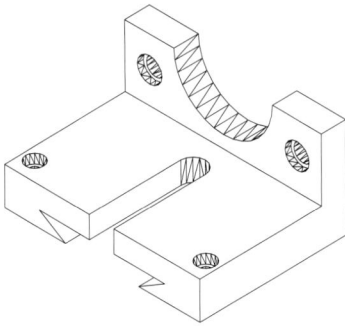

Drawing 6–7

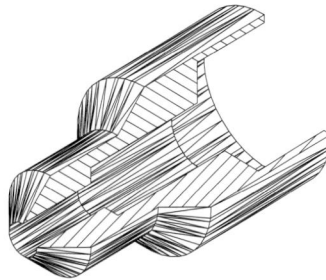

Drawing 8–3

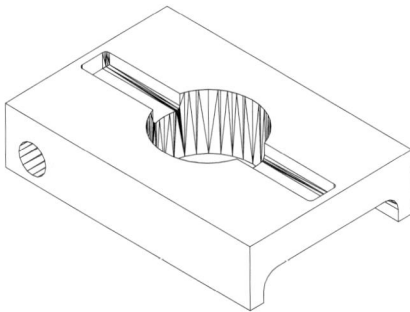

Drawing 8–1

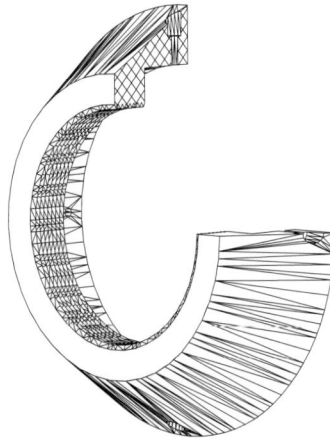

Drawing 8–4

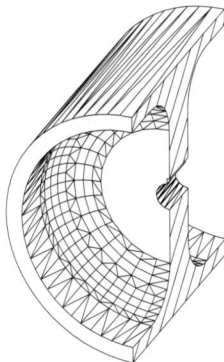

Drawing 8–2

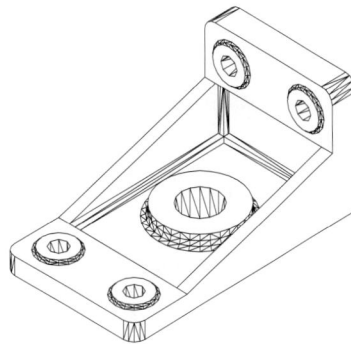

Drawing 8–7

DRAWING 14–6C

3D SOLID DRAWINGS

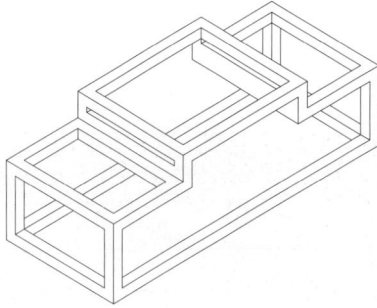

Drawing 9–6

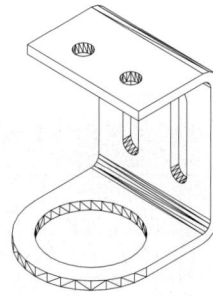

Drawing 11–1

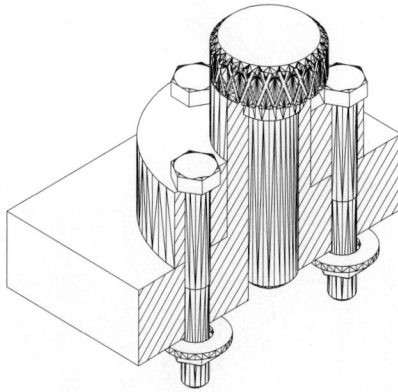

Drawing 10–2

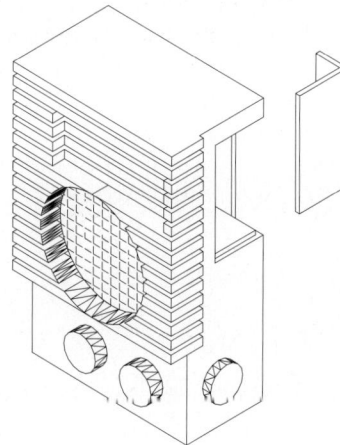

Drawing 11–2

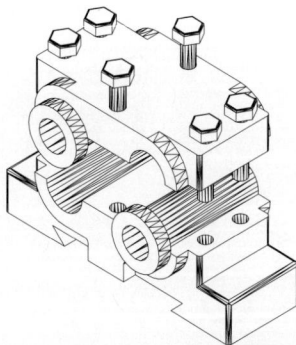

Drawing 10–3

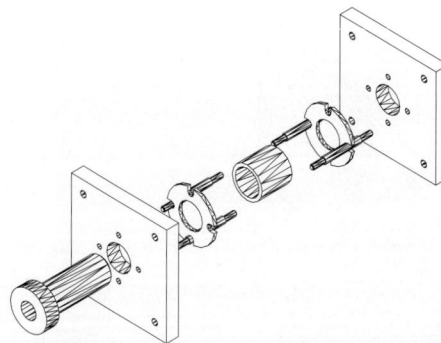

Drawing 11–3

DRAWING 14–6D

3D SOLID DRAWINGS

Drawing Projects

The drawings on the following pages are offered as additional challenges and are presented without suggestions. They may be drawn in two or three dimensions and may be presented as multiple view drawings, hidden line drawings, or rendered drawings. In short, you are on your own to explore and master everything you have learned in this book.

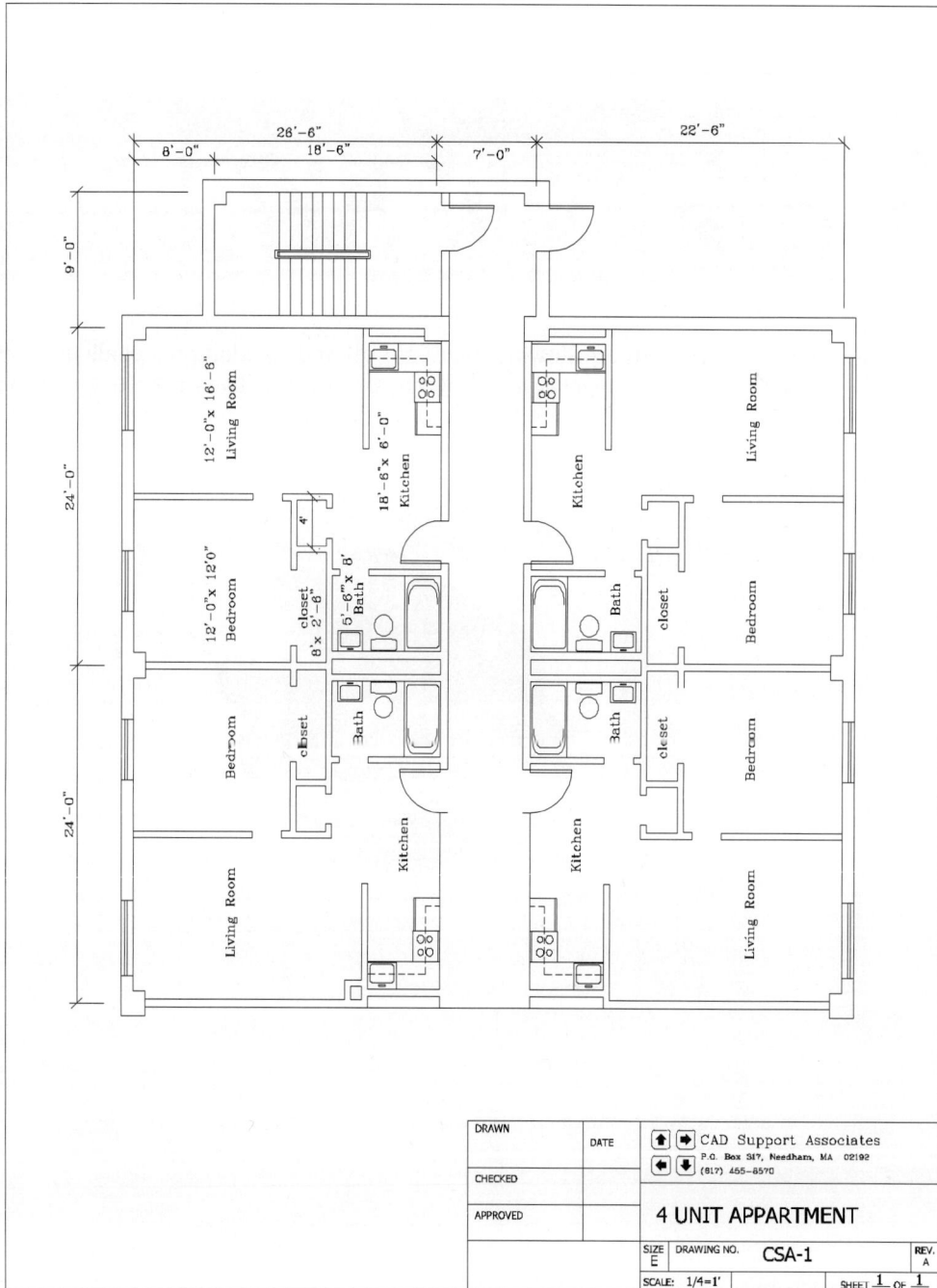

DRAWN		
	DATE	CAD Support Associates
CHECKED		P.O. Box 317, Needham, MA 02192
		(617) 455–8570
APPROVED		**4 UNIT APPARTMENT**

SIZE E	DRAWING NO. CSA-1	REV. A
SCALE: 1/4=1'		SHEET 1 OF 1

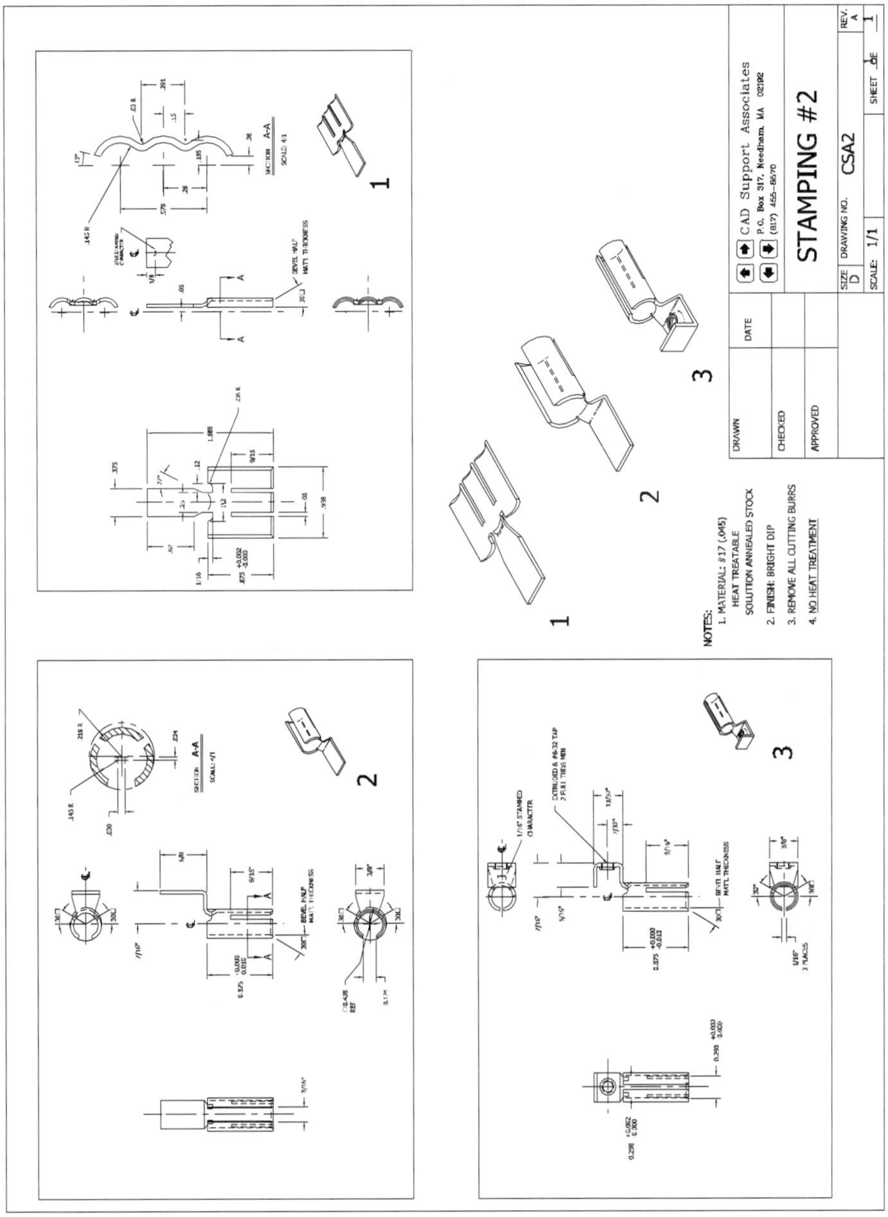

CAD Support Associates
P.O. Box 317, Needham, MA 02192
(817) 455-8670

STAMPING #2

NOTES:
1. MATERIAL: #17 (.045)
   HEAT TREATABLE
   SOLUTION ANNEALED STOCK
2. FINISH: BRIGHT DIP
3. REMOVE ALL CUTTING BURRS
4. NO HEAT TREATMENT

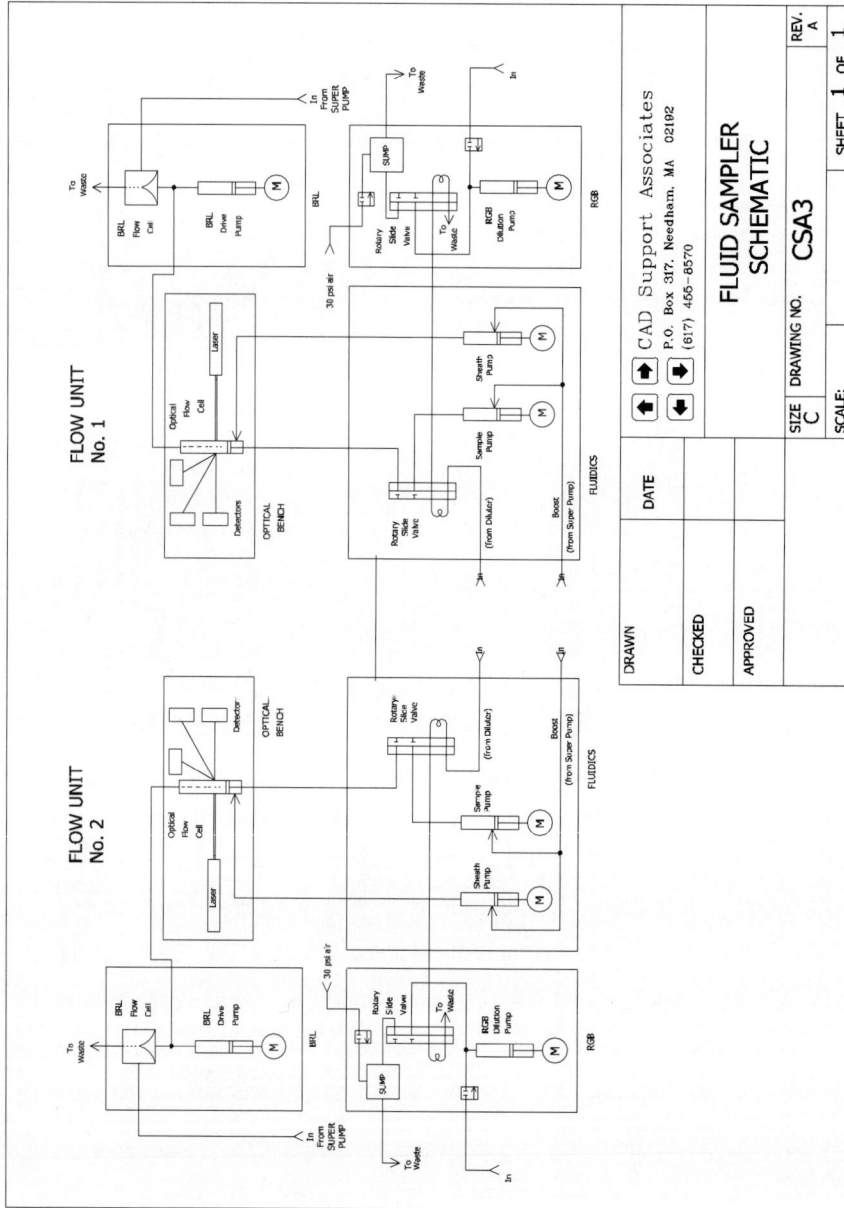

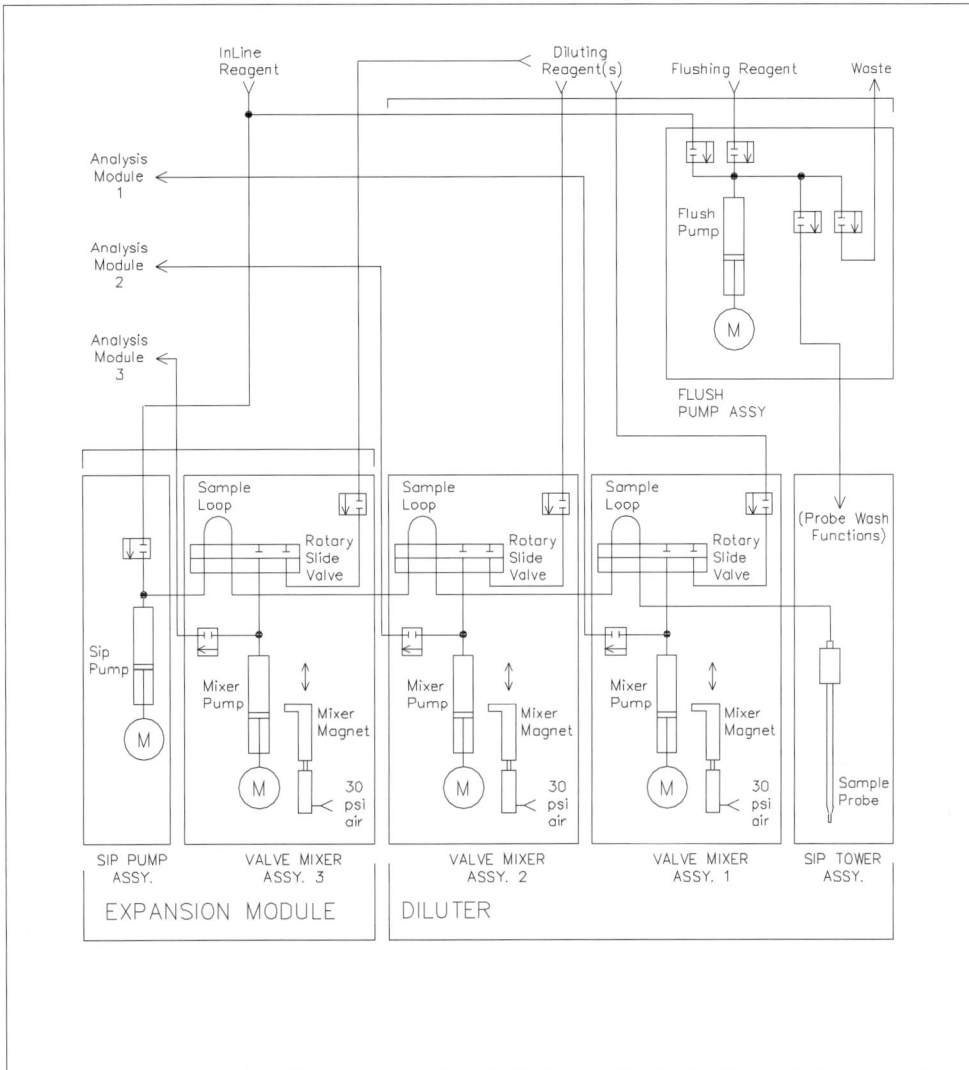

InLine Reagent

Diluting Reagent(s)

Flushing Reagent

Waste

Analysis Module 1

Analysis Module 2

Analysis Module 3

Flush Pump

M

FLUSH PUMP ASSY

(Probe Wash Functions)

Sample Loop

Rotary Slide Valve

Sample Loop

Rotary Slide Valve

Sample Loop

Rotary Slide Valve

Sip Pump

M

Mixer Pump

Mixer Magnet

M

30 psi air

Mixer Pump

Mixer Magnet

M

30 psi air

Mixer Pump

Mixer Magnet

M

30 psi air

Sample Probe

SIP PUMP ASSY.

VALVE MIXER ASSY. 3

VALVE MIXER ASSY. 2

VALVE MIXER ASSY. 1

SIP TOWER ASSY.

EXPANSION MODULE

DILUTER

DRAWN		CAD Support Associates
	DATE	P.O. Box 317, Needham, MA 02192
CHECKED		(617) 455-8570
APPROVED		DILUTER

	SIZE C	DRAWING NO. CSA4	REV. A
	SCALE:		SHEET 1 OF 1

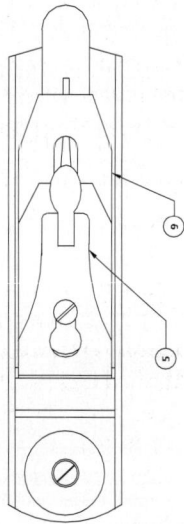

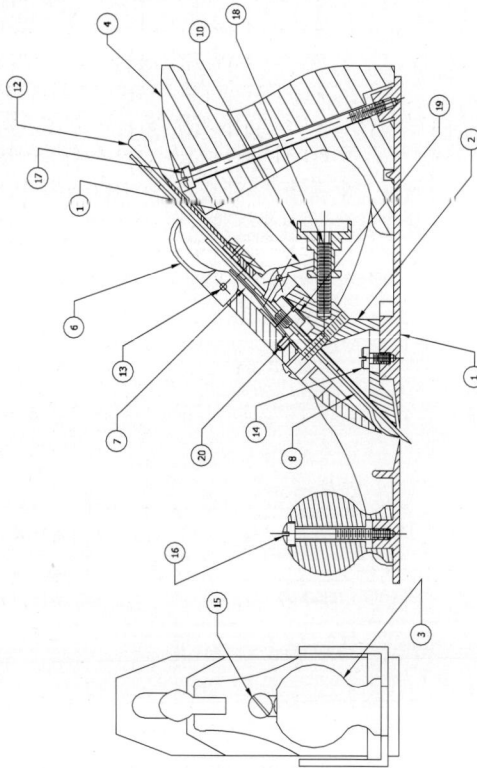

ITEM NO.	DESCRIPTION	PART NO.	QTY.
20	FLAT HD SCREW #8-32 UNC X .25 LG	D400 F7	1
19	PAN HD SCREW 5/16-18 UNC X .18 LG	D400 F6	1
18	THREADED STUD 1/4-24 UNF X 1.25 LG	D400 F5	1
17	BINDER HD SCREW #10-24 UNC X 3.75 LG	D400 F4	1
16	BINDER HD SCREW #10-24 UNC X 1.62 LG	D400 F3	1
15	TRUSS HD SCREW 1/4-20 UNC X .88 LG	D400 F2	1
14	PAN HD SCREW #10-24 UNC X .38 LG	D400 F1	2
13	PIN .12 DIA (CUT LENGTH TO SUIT)	D400 C2	3
12	ANGLE ADJUSTOR	D400 I	1
11	PIVOT	D400 H	1
10	THUMB KNOB	D400 G	1
9	BLADE	D400 E	1
8	CAP IRON	D400 D	1
7	WEDGE SPRING	D400 C1	1
6	WEDGE LEVER	D400 C	1
5	WEDGE IRON	D400 B	1
4	GRIP	D400 A	1
3	KNOB	D400F	1
2	MOUNTING PLATE	D400 K	1
1	BASE	D400 L	1

DRAWN P. RILEY DATE 5-22-87

CHECKED

APPROVED

CAD Support Associates
P. O. Box 317, Needham, MA 02192
(817) 466–8670

JACK PLANE

SIZE C   DRAWING NO. D400   REV. A

SCALE: 1/1   SHEET 1 OF 1

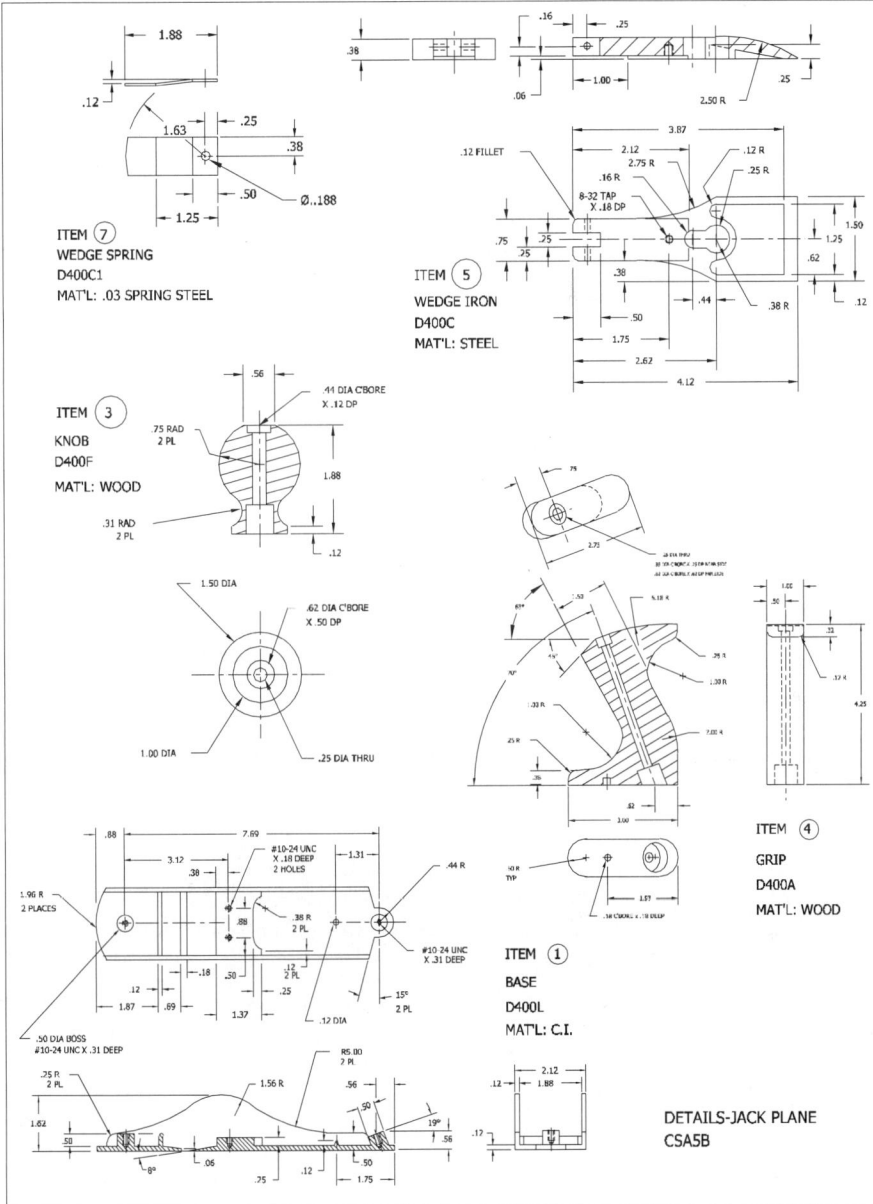

ITEM (7)
WEDGE SPRING
D400C1
MAT'L: .03 SPRING STEEL

ITEM (5)
WEDGE IRON
D400C
MAT'L: STEEL

ITEM (3)
KNOB
D400F
MAT'L: WOOD

ITEM (4)
GRIP
D400A
MAT'L: WOOD

ITEM (1)
BASE
D400L
MAT'L: C.I.

DETAILS-JACK PLANE
CSA5B

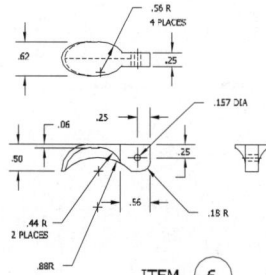

ITEM (6)

WEDGE LEVER

D400C

MAT'L: STEEL

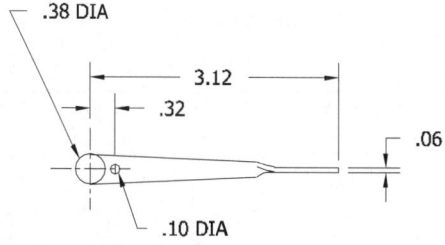

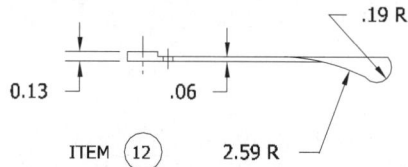

ITEM (12)   2.59 R

ANGLE ADJUSTOR

D400I

MAT'L: STEEL

ITEM (11)

PIVOT

D400H

MAT'L: STEEL

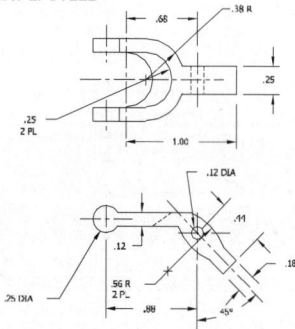

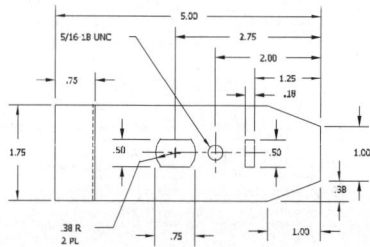

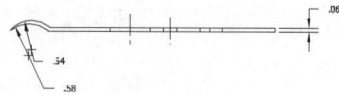

ITEM (8)

D400D

CAP IRON

MAT'L: STEEL

DETAILS-JACK PLANE
CSA5C

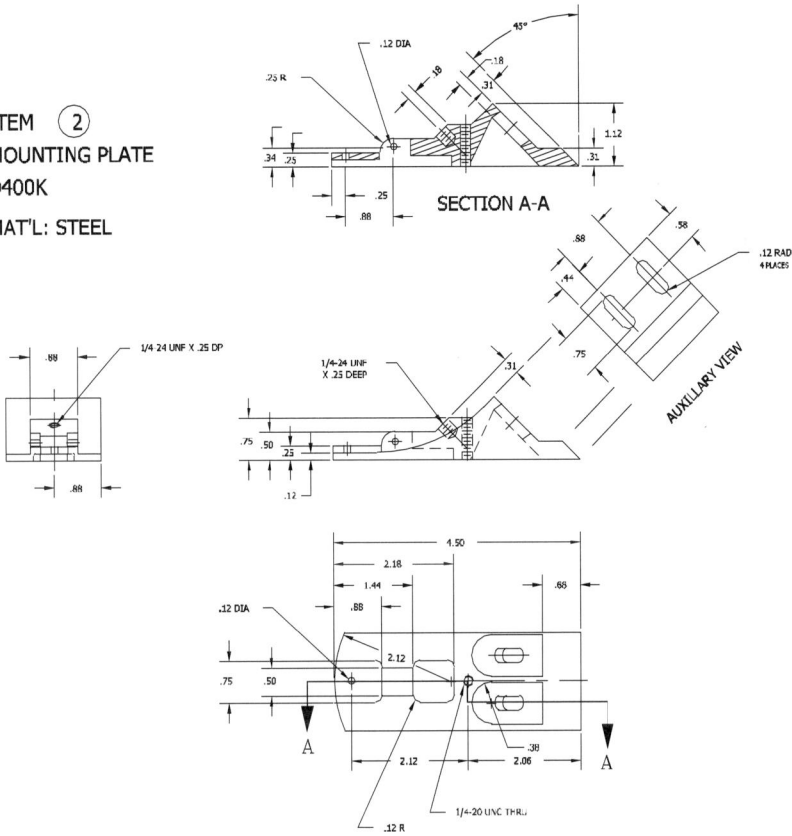

ITEM ②
MOUNTING PLATE
D400K

MAT'L: STEEL

SECTION A-A

.12 DIA

.25 R

45°

.18   .18

.31

1.12

.34   .25

.25

.88

.31

1/4-24 UNF X .25 DP

1/4-24 UNF
X .25 DEEP

.88

.75   .50

.25

.88

.75   .50

.25

.12

.31   .75

AUXILIARY VIEW

.88   .58

.44

.12 RAD
4 PLACES

4.50

2.18

1.44

.68

.12 DIA

.88

2.12

.75   .50

A

2.12

.38

2.06

A

.12 R

1/4-20 UNC THRU

ITEM ⑨
BLADE
D400E

MAT'L: STEEL

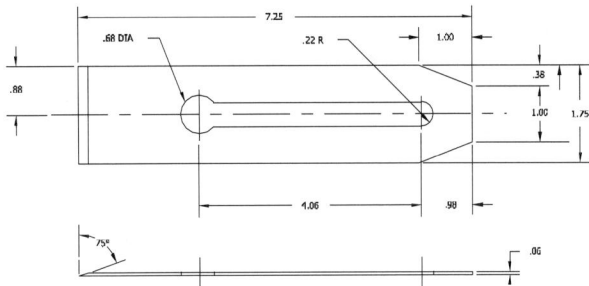

7.25

.68 DIA

.22 R

1.00

.88

.38

1.00   1.75

4.06

.98

75°

.06

DETAILS-JACK PLANE
CSA5D

ITEM (14)
D400F1
#10-24 UNC X .38 LG
PAN HD SCREW

ITEM (19)
D400F6
5/6-18 UNC X .18 LG
PAN HD SCREW

ITEM (15)
D400F2
#1/4-20 UNC X .88 LG
TRUSS HD SCREW

ITEM (16)
D400F3
#10-24 UNC X 1.62 LG
BINDER HD SCREW

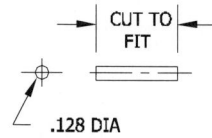

CUT TO FIT

.128 DIA

ITEM (13)
D400C2
PIN
MAT'L: STEEL

ITEM (17)
D400F4
#10-24 UNC X 3.75 LG
BINDER HD SCREW

ITEM (18)
D400F3
#1/4-24 UNF X 1.25 LG
STUD

ITEM (20)
D400F7
#8-32 UNC X .25 LG
FLAT HD SCREW

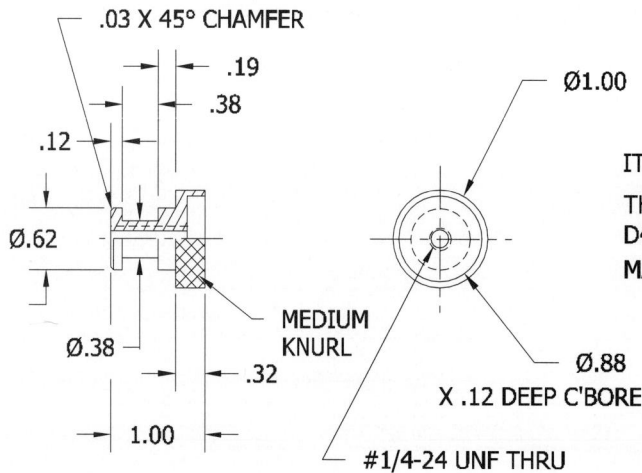

.03 X 45° CHAMFER
.19
.38
.12
Ø.62
Ø.38
.32
1.00
MEDIUM KNURL

Ø1.00

ITEM (10)
THUMB KNOB
D400G
MAT'L: BRASS

Ø.88
X .12 DEEP C'BORE

#1/4-24 UNF THRU

DETAILS-JACK PLANE
CSA5E

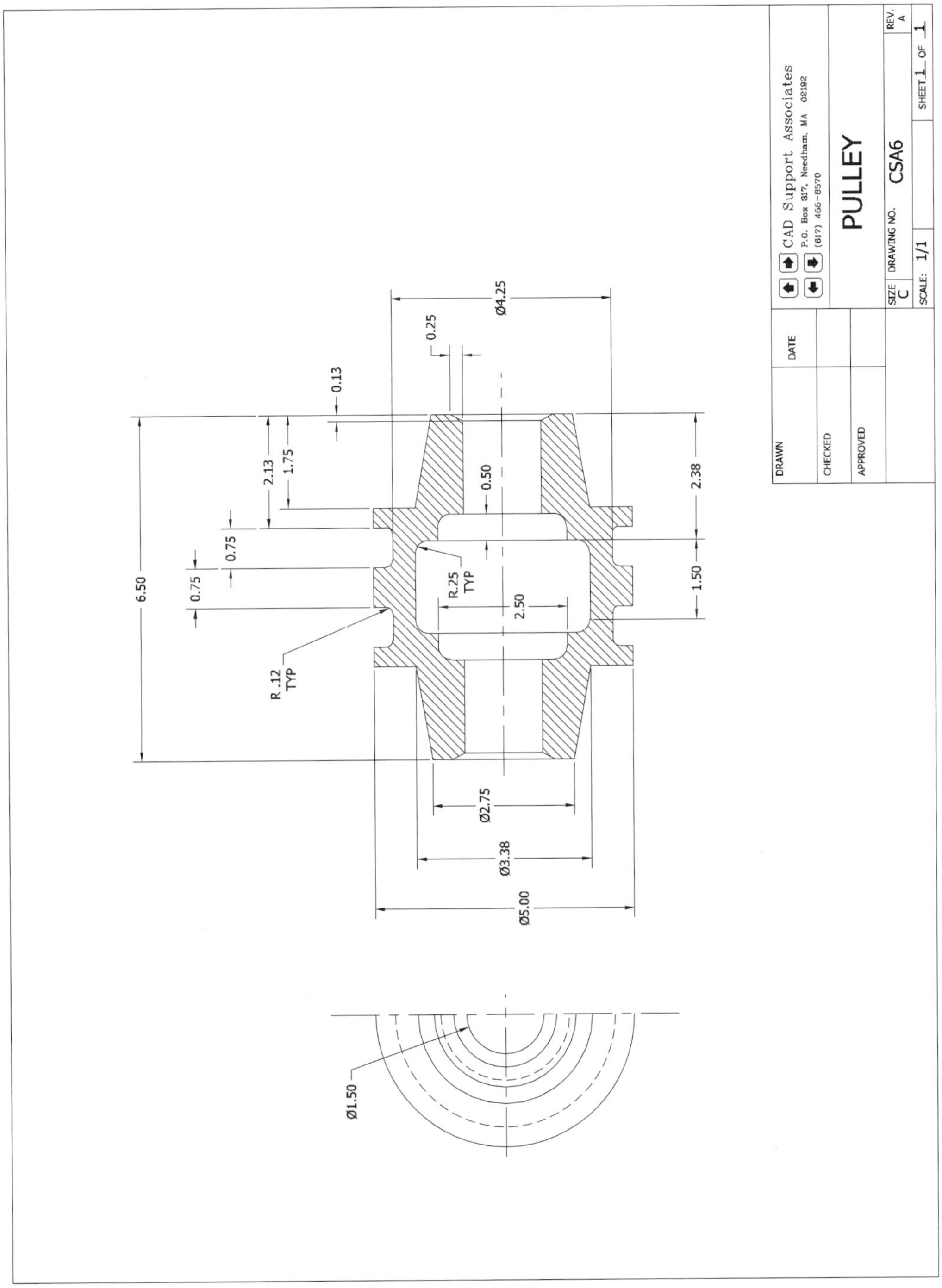

CAD Support Associates
P.O. Box 317, Needham, MA 02192
(617) 456-8570

PULLEY

DRAWING NO. CSA6

REV. A

SHEET 1 OF 1

SIZE C

SCALE: 1/1

DRAWN | DATE
CHECKED
APPROVED

Ø4.25
0.25
0.13
2.13
1.75
0.50
6.50
0.75
0.75
R.25 TYP
2.50
R.12 TYP
2.38
1.50
Ø2.75
Ø3.38
Ø5.00
Ø1.50

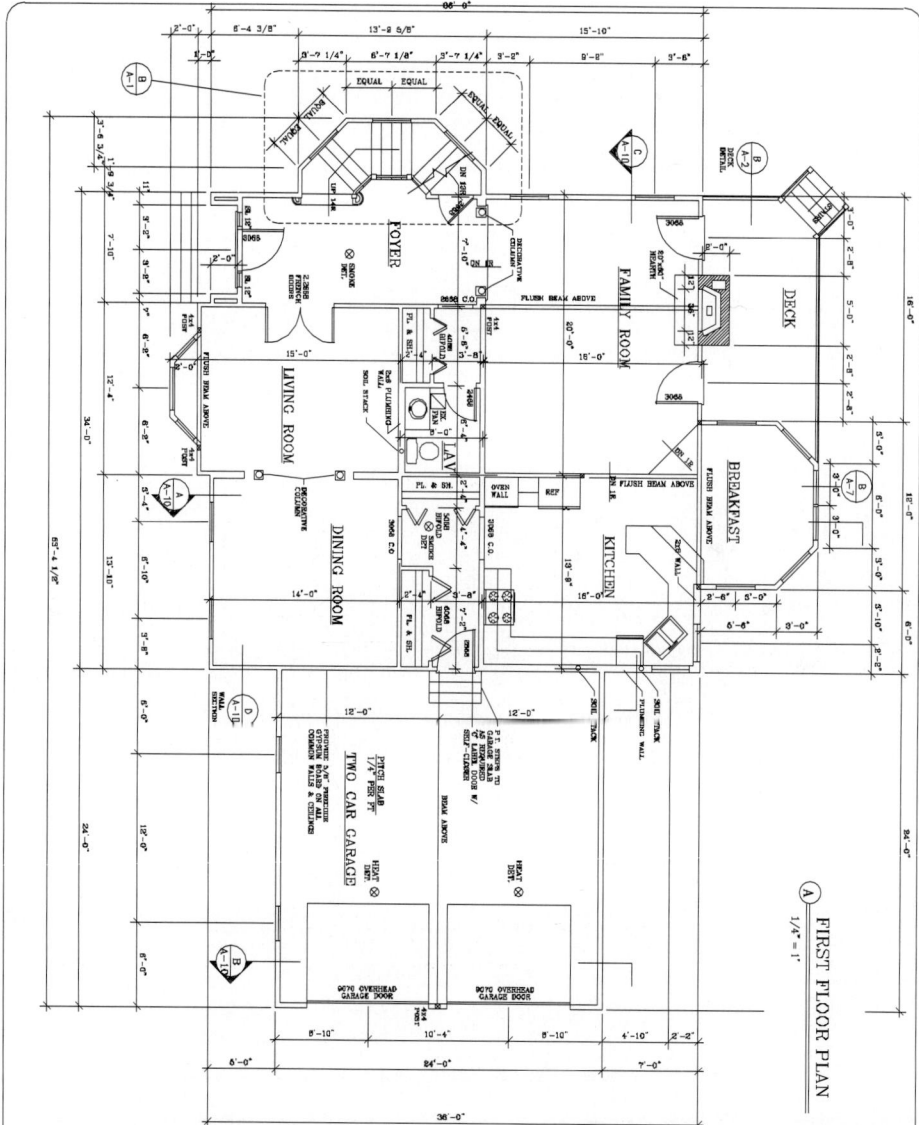

FIRST FLOOR PLAN

FIRST FLOOR PLAN

HPA DESIGN
Building Designers

1408 Providence Highway
Norwood, MA 02062
(617) 769-6001
(508) 520-3256
FAX (617) 769-7881

SHEET NO.

A-1

CSA7

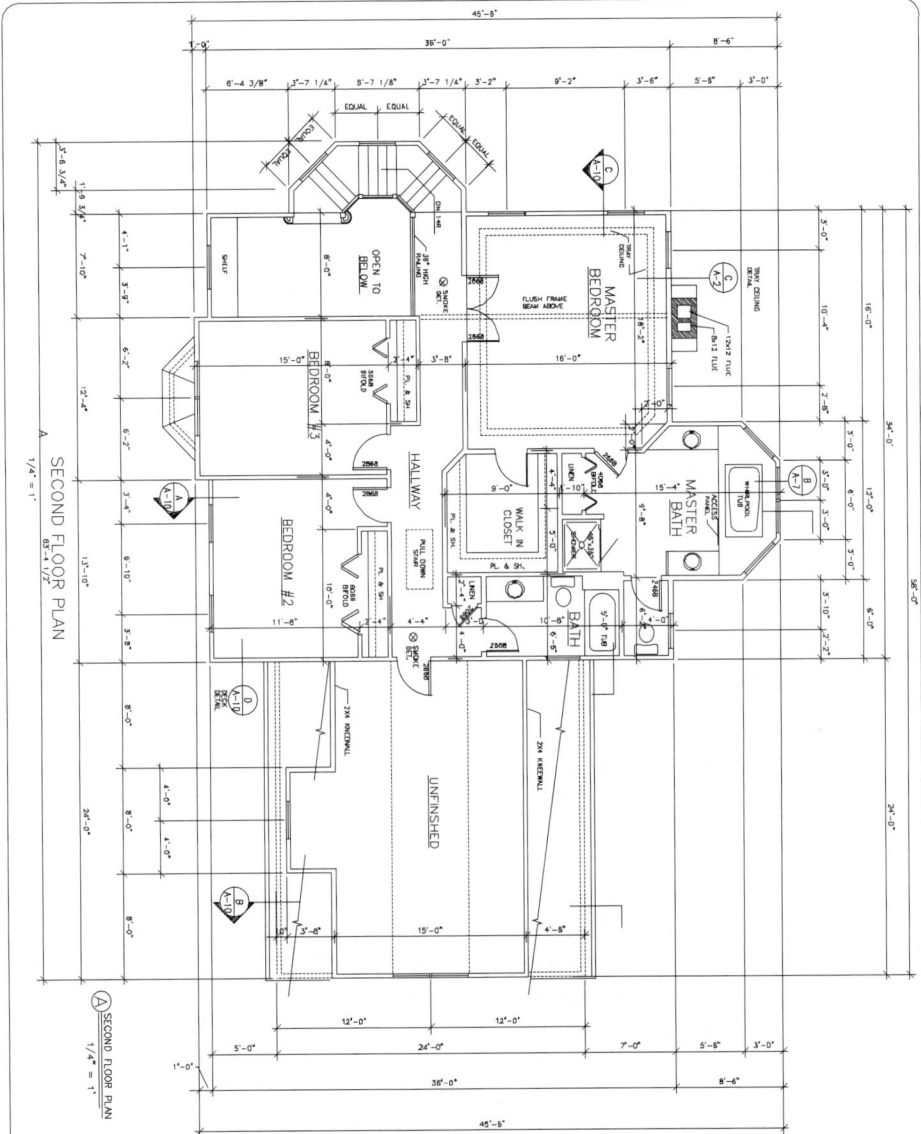

SECOND FLOOR PLAN

SHEET NO.
A-2

FRONT ELEVATION
RIGHT SIDE ELEVATION

SHEET NO.
A-4

CSAB

HPA
DESIGN
Building Designers
1408 Providence Highway
Norwood, MA 02062
(617) 769-8001
(508) 520-3256
FAX (617) 769-7881

JOB NO.   95246
DATE   DECEMBER 13, 1995
DRAWN BY   AIK
CHECKED BY   HPA
REVISION   DATE:
PATH: MCNDN/HH

SCALE   1/4" = 1'-0"

FRONT ELEVATION
A
1/4" = 1'

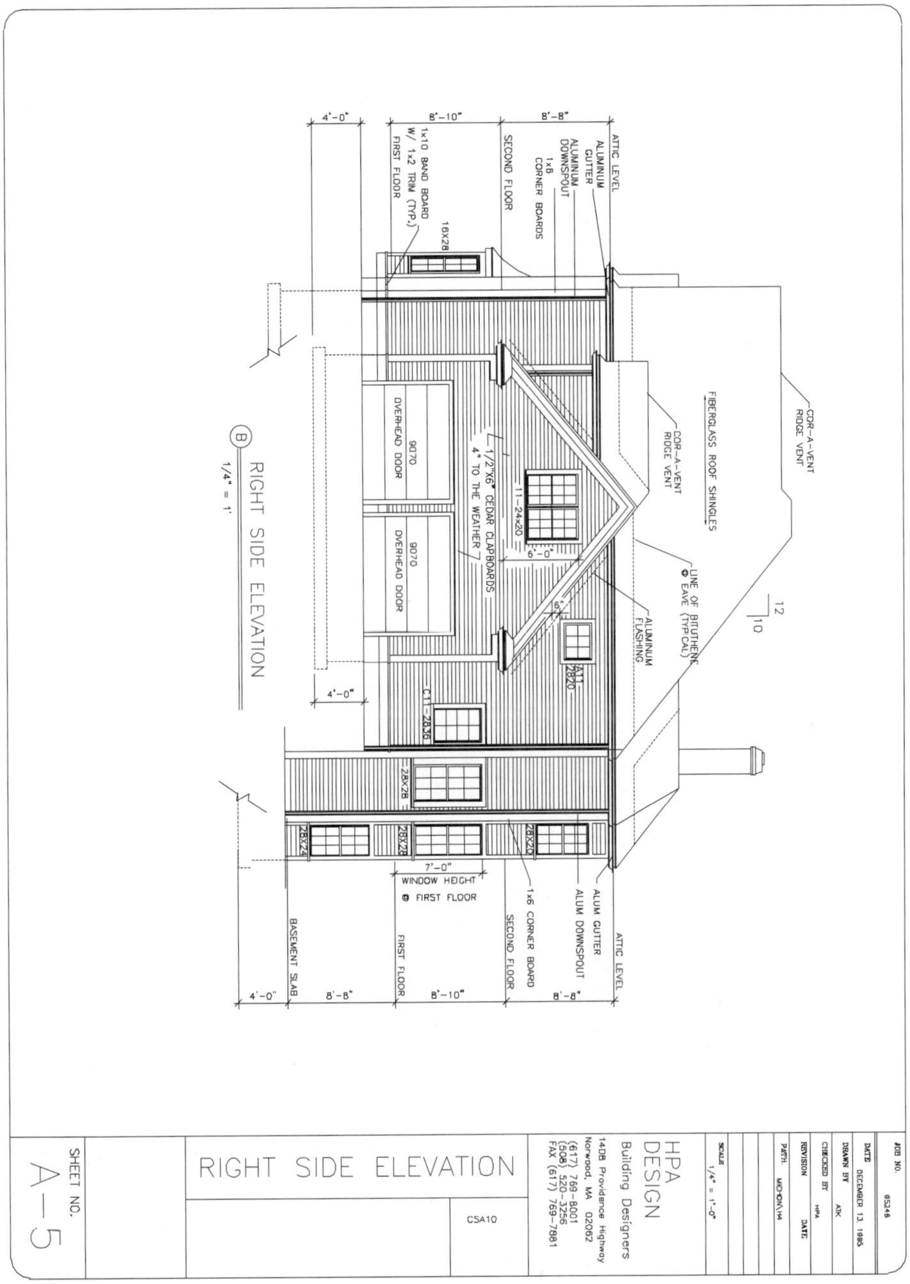

RIGHT SIDE ELEVATION

B
1/4" = 1'

Labels on drawing:
- 4'-0"
- 8'-10"
- 8'-8"
- ATTIC LEVEL
- ALUMINUM GUTTER
- ALUMINUM DOWNSPOUT
- 1x8 CORNER BOARDS
- SECOND FLOOR
- 1x10 BAND BOARD W/ 1x2 TRIM (TYP.)
- FIRST FLOOR
- 16X28
- 9070 OVERHEAD DOOR
- 9070 OVERHEAD DOOR
- 11-24x20
- 1/2"X6" CEDAR CLAPBOARDS 4" TO THE WEATHER
- 6"
- 6"
- 8"
- C11-28x36
- 4'-0"
- 2x5X28
- FIBERGLASS ROOF SHINGLES
- COR-A-VENT RIDGE VENT
- COR-A-VENT RIDGE VENT
- LINE OF BITUTHENE EAVE (TYP'CAL)
- ALUMINUM FLASHING
- 12 / 10
- 2x5X28
- 28x28
- 7'-0" WINDOW HEIGHT
- FIRST FLOOR
- 2x5X28
- 1x6 CORNER BOARD
- SECOND FLOOR
- ALUM DOWNSPOUT
- ALUM GUTTER
- ATTIC LEVEL
- BASEMENT SLAB
- FIRST FLOOR
- 4'-0"
- 8'-8"
- 8'-10"
- 8'-8"

RIGHT SIDE ELEVATION

RIGHT SIDE ELEVATION

SHEET NO.
A-5

CSA10

HPA
DESIGN
Building Designers
1402B Providence Highway
Norwood, MA 02062
(617) 769-8001
(508) 520-3245
FAX (617) 769-7881

SCALE 1/4" = 1'-0"
PATH: VACADN14
REVISION DATE:
CHECKED BY HPA
DRAWN BY ADK
DATE DECEMBER 13 1995
JOB NO. 95246

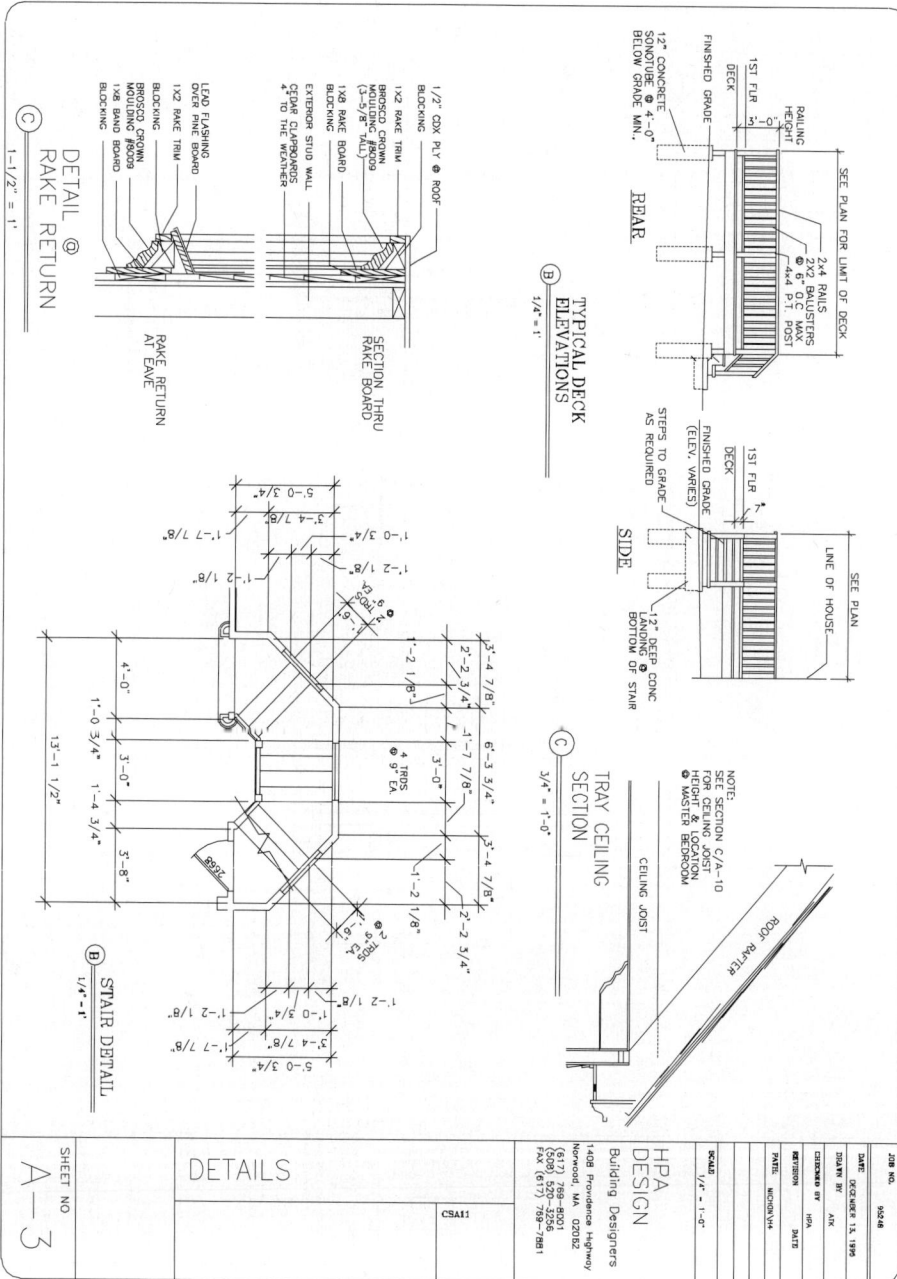

DETAIL @
RAKE RETURN

C   1-1/2" = 1'

1/2" CDX PLY @ ROOF
BLOCKING

1X2 RAKE TRIM
BROSCO CROWN
MOULDING
(3-5/8" TALL)

1X8 RAKE
BOARD
BLOCKING

EXTERIOR STUD WALL
CEDAR CLAPBOARDS
4" TO THE WEATHER

LEAD FLASHING
OVER PINE BOARD

1X2 RAKE TRIM
BLOCKING

BROSCO CROWN
MOULDING #9009
1X8 BAND BOARD
BLOCKING

RAKE RETURN
AT EAVE

SECTION THRU
RAKE BOARD

TYPICAL DECK
ELEVATIONS

B   1/4" = 1'

REAR

12" CONCRETE
SONOTUBE @ 4'-0"
BELOW GRADE MIN.

FINISHED GRADE

DECK
1ST FLR

RAILING
HEIGHT

3'-0"

SEE PLAN FOR LIMIT OF DECK

2X4 RAILS
2X2 BALUSTERS
@ 6" O.C.
4x4 P.T. POST

SIDE

DECK
1ST FLR

FINISHED GRADE

STEPS TO GRADE
(ELEV. VARIES)

FINISHED GRADE

12" DEEP CONC
LANDING @
BOTTOM OF STAIR

LINE OF HOUSE

SEE PLAN

TRAY CEILING
SECTION

C   3/4" = 1'-0"

NOTE:
SEE SECTION C/A-10
FOR CEILING JOIST
HEIGHT & LOCATION
@ MASTER BEDROOM

CEILING JOIST

ROOF RAFTER

STAIR DETAIL

B   1/4" = 1'

DETAILS

CSA11

HPA
DESIGN
Building Designers

1408 Providence Highway
Norwood, MA 02062
(617) 769-8001
(508) 520-3256
FAX (617) 769-7881

JOB NO.   95248
DATE: DECEMBER 13, 1995
DRAWN BY   AYK
CHECKED BY   HPA
REVISION   DATE
PATEL   MCKENVH+

SCALED   1/4" = 1'-0"

SHEET NO
A-3

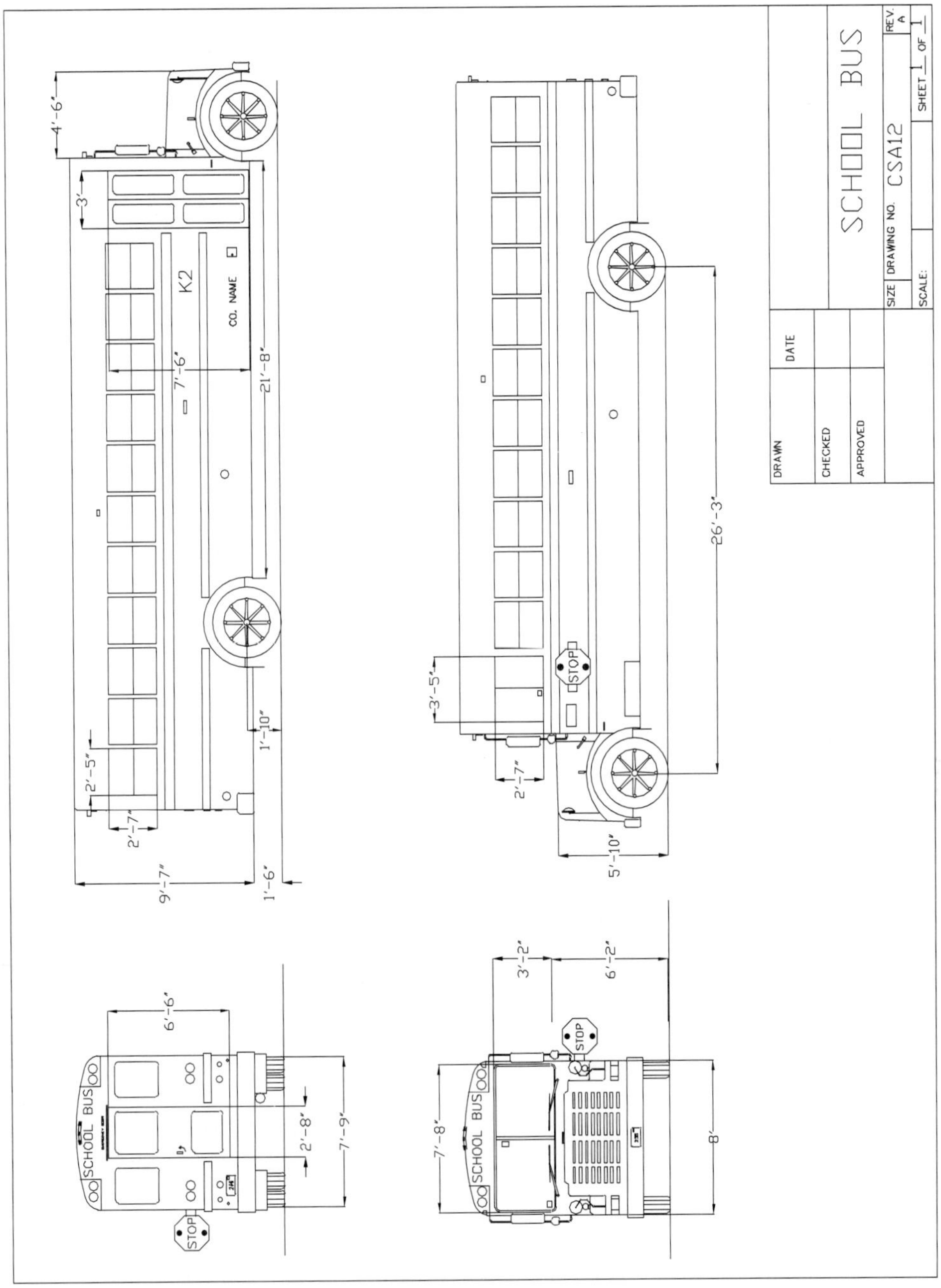
SCHOOL BUS
SIZE
DRAWING NO. CSA12
REV. A
SCALE:
SHEET 1 OF 1
DRAWN
CHECKED
APPROVED
DATE
K2
CO. NAME
STOP
SCHOOL BUS
4'-6"
3'
7'-6"
21'-8"
2'-5"
2'-7"
1'-10"
9'-7"
1'-6"
26'-3"
3'-5"
2'-7"
5'-10"
6'-6"
2'-8"
7'-9"
3'-2"
6'-2"
7'-8"
8'

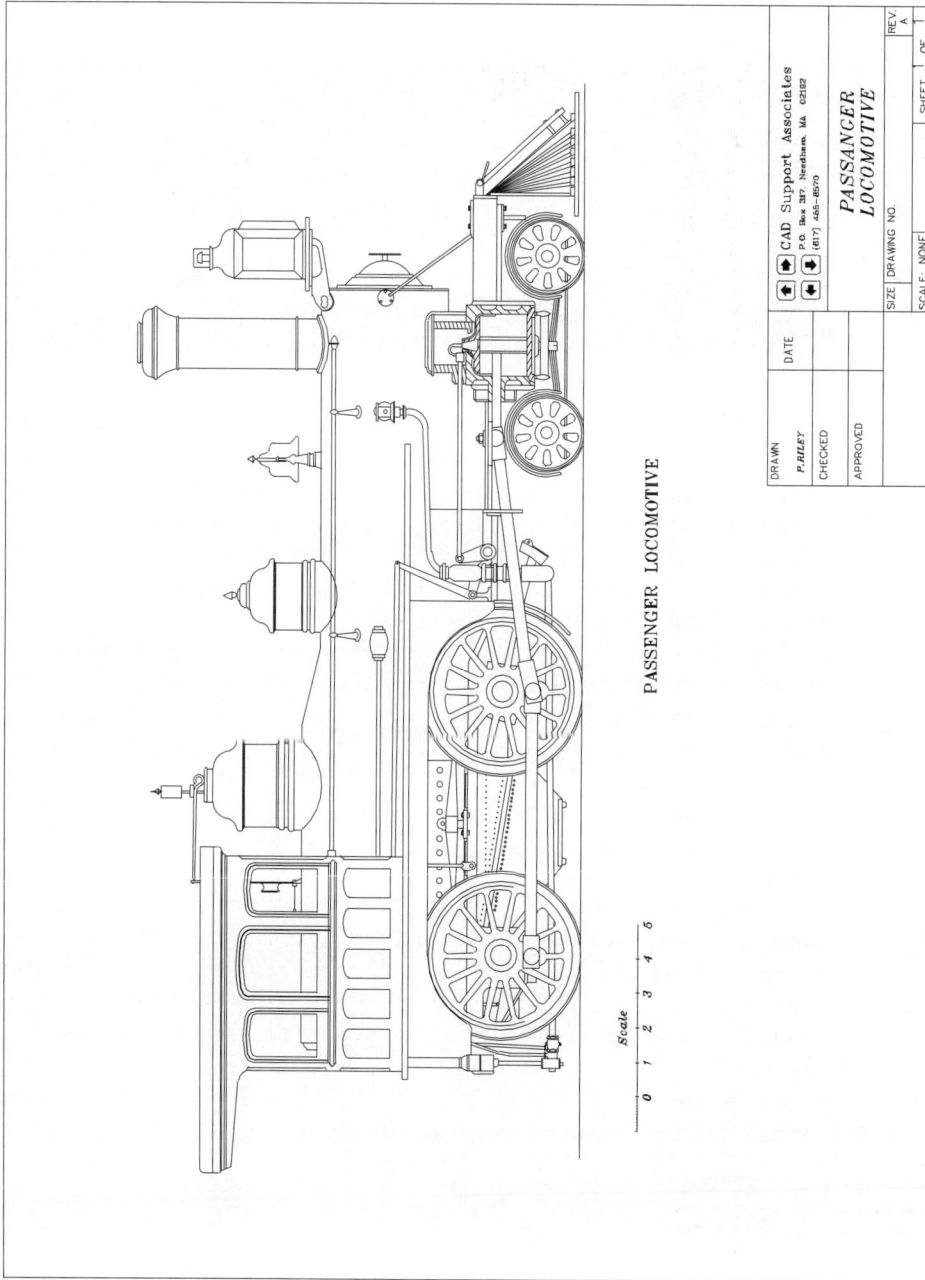

PASSENGER LOCOMOTIVE

Scale
0 1 2 3 4 5

CAD Support Associates
P.O. Box 317 Needham, MA 02192
(617) 465-8570

PASSANGER
LOCOMOTIVE

DRAWN	DATE	
P.RILEY		
CHECKED		
APPROVED		

SIZE | DRAWING NO. | REV. A
SCALE: NONE | | SHEET 1 OF 1

Appendix

B

Menus and Macros

When you begin to look below the surface of AutoCAD as it is configured straight out of the box, you will find a whole world of customization possibilities. This "open architecture," which allows you to create your own menus, commands, toolbars, menus, and automated routines, is one of the reasons for AutoCAD's success. It is characteristic of all AutoCAD releases and has made room for a vast network of third-party developers to create custom software products tailoring AutoCAD to the particular needs of various industries.

Over time, the options for customizing AutoCAD have grown and become more powerful. Many of the basics of menu structure, however, have not changed. The intention of this discussion is not to make you an AutoCAD developer, but to give you a taste of what is going on in the menu system. After reading this, you should have a sense of what an AutoCAD menu is and how it works. You should also understand that menu development is a complex subject. Before you attempt any menu development of your own, you should study the AutoCAD Customization Guide.

True to form, AutoCAD provides several different ways to accomplish most customization tasks. A customized command sequence, for example, may result from a simple keyboard macro, an AutoLISP routine, a line of DIESEL string expression language, or a C language program connected to AutoCAD through ADS (AutoCAD Development System). We will confine our discussion to the organization of a menu file and the language of macros. These are easy to learn and require little programming background. AutoLISP, DIESEL, and C, on the other hand, are topics requiring a good deal of explanation and a knowledge of programming.

What Is an AutoCAD Menu?

Most likely, every time you have begun a drawing in AutoCAD you have used either the AutoCAD standard menu or some other menu that is available on your system. This menu is what makes it possible for you to select commands off of a menu, tablet, or toolbar. Without a menu you are limited to typing commands.

Menu files have a standard format that AutoCAD can read, and standard extensions so that AutoCAD can recognize them. In AutoCAD 2000, menu file extensions include .mnc, .mnl, .mnr, .mns, .mnt, and .mnu files. For example, the AutoCAD standard menu is contained in a file called ACAD.mnc. This file is loaded when you begin a new drawing from scratch or use any template drawing that was created using ACAD.mnc. The .mnc file is an executable file compiled in machine language. But there is also an ASCII version of ACAD.mnc called ACAD.mnu. ACAD.mnc was created by compiling ACAD.mnu into machine code. The importance of ACAD.mnu is that you can look at it with a word processor and revise it if you wish. The .mnu files can be created in any word processing program or text editor with an ASCII format and are easy to read and understand once you know the syntax.

You also make frequent changes in menu items directly in the drawing area (hiding, showing, or moving toolbars, for example). These changes are retained in a new ASCII file with the same name as the .mnc and .mnu files, but with an .mns extension. Once an .mns file is created, it is continually updated and used in lieu of the .mnc file. To return to the original menu configuration, you must use the MENU command to compile a new .mnc from the original .mnu file.

There are also two files that are loaded along with the .mnc file. The .mnl file contains AutoLISP expressions that are referred to in the menu. The .mnr file contains bitmap images that are used in the menu, and the .mnt file is generated if the .mnr file is unavailable (read-only).

Once you know the language, you can create your own menu by modifying the ACAD.mnu file and giving the modified file a new name. You would make the changes to ACAD.mnu in any word processor or text editor with an ASCII format and give it a name with a .mnu extension. Then when you wanted to load it into a drawing you would follow this procedure:

1. At the "Command:" prompt, type "menu".
2. Type your menu's name with no extension.
3. Wait.

AutoCAD will create the new .mnc, .mnl, .mnr, .mnt, and .mns files and load them.

What Does a Menu Look Like?

If you go into whatever word processor or text editor you have available on your system and load the file ACAD.mnu (it usually will be located in a folder called Program Files\Acad2000\Support), you will see the first page of the menu. Menu files are quite large, and you will see only a small portion on your screen. The complete menu will be about 90 pages long. A good way to learn about menus is to print out a few pages and study them, using the list of characters in the table at the end of this appendix and the AutoCAD Customization Guide. Comparing menu lines with menu items in the drawing editor is also an essential exercise, as we will demonstrate next.

How Is a Menu Organized?

Menus consist of sections for button menus, pull-down and short cut menus, toolbars, image tile menus, tablets, the screen menu, helpstrings and tooltips, and keyboard accelerators. Each section type uses slightly different syntax, but there are certain generalizations that can be made. Take a look at this section from the AutoCAD 2000 ACAD.mnu. It creates the File pull-down menu, shown in Figure B-1:

```
***POP1
**FILE
ID_MnFile    [&File]
ID_New       [&New...\tCtrl+N]^C^C_new
ID_Open      [&Open...\tCtrl+O]^C^C_open
ID_FILE_CLOSE [&Close]
ID_PartialOp [$(if,$(eq,$(getvar,fullopen),0),,~)Pa&rtial
             Load]^C^C_partialload
             [–]
ID_Save      [&Save\tCtrl+S]^C^C_qsave
ID_Saveas    [Save &As...]^C^C_saveas
ID_Export    [&Export...]^C^C_export
             [–]
ID_PlotSetup [Pa&ge Setup...]^C^C_pagesetup
ID_PlotMgr   [Plotter &Manager...]^C^C_plottermanager
```

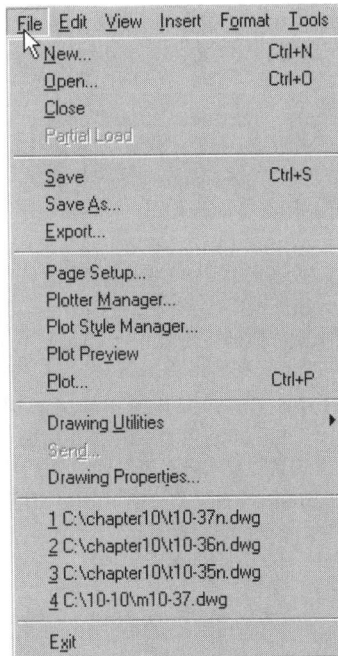

Figure B-1

```
ID_PlotStyMgr [Plot St&yle Manager...]^C^C_stylesmanager
ID_Preview    [Plot Pre&view]^C^C_preview
ID_Print      [&Plot...\tCtrl+P]^C^C_plot
              [--]
ID_MnDrawing  [-[greater]Drawing &Utilities]
ID_Audit      [&Audit]^C^C_audit
ID_Recover    [&Recover...]^C^C_recover
              [--]
ID_MnPurge    [-[greater]&Purge]
ID_PurgeAll     [&All]^C^C_purge _a
                [--]
ID_PurgeLay     [&Layers]^C^C_purge _la
ID_PurgeLin     [Li&netypes]^C^C_purge _lt
ID_PurgeTxt     [&Text Styles]^C^C_purge _st
ID_PurgeDim     [&Dimension Styles]^C^C_purge _d
ID_PurgeMln     [&Multiline Styles]^C^C_purge _m
ID_PurgeBlk     [&Blocks]^C^C_purge _b
ID_PurgePlt     [&Plot Styles]^C^C_purge _p
ID_PurgeShp     [<-<-&Shapes]^C^C_purge _sh
ID_SendMail   [Sen&d...]
ID_Props      [Drawing Propert&ies...]^C^C_dwgprops
              [--]
ID_MRU        [Drawing History]
              [--]
ID_APP_EXIT   [E&xit]
```

Using this as an example, we can make the following points about menu organization, and pull-down menus in particular:

1. Menus are organized into lines. Each line is associated with a single line on a pull-down menu, a short cut menu, a tool on a toolbar, or a box on a tablet menu. There are also single lines for helpstrings, cursor buttons, image tile menus, and user-defined accelerator key sequences.

2. The only lines that are not associated with specific menu items and functions are those added for organizational purposes. These include lines with asterisks, called section headers, and lines with double slashes (//), which are comment lines. In the POP1 menu section, for example, "***POP1" is a section header.
   - Three-star headers like this one identify major sections, including the button functions, the pull-down menus, the screen menu, toolbars, image tile menus, helpstrings, accelerators, and the four tablet areas. The pull-down menus are identified as POP1-POP11. POP0 is the object snap short cut menu. Context sensitive short cut menus are designated by POP500 and up.
   - Two-star headers identify individual toolbars and submenus of the screen menu. In this case **File identifies this section as the File pull-down menu section.

3. Menu items also have name tags. All of the ID_labels in this example are name tags. These name tags can be referenced elsewhere in the menu. One common use of the name tag is to call out Helpstrings, the short phrases on the status line that describe what a particular menu selection will do. These phrases are defined in the ***HELPSTRING section of the menu.

4. For pull-down menu sections, the words written in brackets, such as &File], control the labels that actually appear on the menu.

- The "&" character is placed before a letter that can be used as a keyboard alternative to selecting the item with the pointing device.
- "\t" is the tab character. Observe, for example, the space between "New" and "Ctrl+N" in the figure in relation to the third line of the POP1 menu section.

5. The action taken by selecting the menu item is controlled by the macro that comes after the brackets. In the fourth line of this section, "^C^C_new" is the macro. This macro is explained in the next section of this appendix.

6. The [–] lines create the line dividers in the pull-down menu.

7. The lines between ID_MnDrawing and ID_PurgeShp are the Drawing Utilities submenu. The line that calls the submenu is indicated by the characters "->"; in this case, "[->Drawing &Utilities]". The last line of the submenu is indicated by "<-<-"; in this case, "[<-<-&Shapes]".

What Is a MACRO?

The ability to define macros is available in many software packages. Macros have the function of storing frequently used sequences of keystrokes in a shorthand form. Much of AutoCAD's menu system depends on macros. To understand and create simple macros in this system, there are a few items of syntax that you need to know. In the preceding example, "^C^C_new" is the macro in the fourth line. Look at the line again:

$$\text{ID\_New [\&New...\textbackslash tCtrl+N]\textasciicircum C\textasciicircum C\_new}$$

ID_New [&New...\tCtrl+N]: These are the item name tag and the label that appears on the menu, as discussed previously.

^C^C: This appears frequently in all menus. The "^" character is read by AutoCAD as the equivalent of the CTRL key on your keyboard. So what you see here is the menu equivalent of typing CTRL-C (Cancel) twice. CTRL-C works just like the Esc key to cancel commands. This ensures that any command in process is canceled before another one is entered. Often two cancels are required to bring you all the way out of one command before you enter another.

_new: This is the NEW command. Commands on the menu are typed exactly as they would be on the keyboard except that the _ is added as a flag identifying this as the English-language command. This allows foreign-language versions of AutoCAD to use menus developed in English.

Taken as a whole, then, this line does four things. First, it identifies the item and associates it with other related items. Second, it writes the label on the pull-down menu, identifying Ctrl+N as a keystroke alternative to making the menu selection. Third, it cancels any command in progress. Fourth, it initiates the New command.

With this basic understanding, you should be able to make use of the list of macro characters included at the end of this appendix.

What Other Languages Can Be Used in Menu Development?

AutoCAD 2000 allows you to create customized routines in other languages in addition to the macro language presented here. AutoLISP is a programming language based on LISP. LISP is a "list processing" language. You will see AutoLISP statements in ACAD.mnu enclosed in parentheses. AutoCAD 2000 has a new AutoLISP programming interface called Visual LISP. AutoLISP can also be used in conjunction with DCL (Dialog Control Language) to create customized dialog boxes. Consult the Visual LISP and AutoLISP guide in online HELP for more information.

DIESEL (Direct Interpretatively Evaluated String Expression Language) is a language that evaluates strings and returns string results. DIESEL borrows many of its terms from AutoLISP, and DIESEL expressions, like AutoLISP expressions, are enclosed in parentheses. DIESEL expressions, however, are always proceeded by $. DIESEL is useful for such simple procedures as toggling the values of AutoCAD variables and writing helpstrings to the status line.

C or C++ language programs can be written and linked to AutoCAD through ARX, the AutoCAD Runtime Extension. ARX programs are read by the AutoLISP interpreter and then passed to AutoCAD as if they were AutoLISP. C is a high-level programming language. It has more power and is also significantly faster than AutoLISP. Programs written in C and run through ARX will run faster than AutoLISP programs.

In addition to these three languages, AutoCAD also includes a language for interface with database programs such as PARADOX or dBASE IV. This is called the AutoCAD SQL Extension (ASE). (SQL stands for Structured Query Language.)

How Is a Tablet Configured to Match a Menu?

AutoCAD reads the tablet sections of a menu file in a particular way that must correspond to the configuration of the physical tablet overlay that is attached to the digitizer. In ACAD.mnu there are four tablet sections, each corresponding to an area on the tablet overlay. Each line of the menu file corresponds to a box on the overlay, and boxes are read from left to right, top to bottom, area by area. This means that there must be a way to tell AutoCAD how many rows and columns are contained in each tablet area. This is done using the TABLET command and the following procedure (the tablet overlay must be securely in place on your digitizer before you begin):

1. Type "Tablet".
2. Type "cfg" (configure).
3. Enter the number of tablet areas on your overlay.
4. Type "y" to indicate that you want to realign the tablet menu areas.
5. In response to AutoCAD's prompts, point to the upper left, lower right, and lower left corners of each tablet menu area. Be sure that you do this in the same order as the tablets are named in the .mnu file.
6. After the outline of each area is specified, also specify the number of columns and rows in that area.

For additional information on tablets, see the AutoCAD Customization Guide.

What Characters Are Used in AutoCAD Menus and Macros?

The following table lists some menu and macro characters you will find in any AutoCAD menu, along with their functions.

Most Common AutoCAD Macro Characters (in order of appearance in AutoCAD 2000 ACAD.mnu)

//	Identifies a comment line for documentation. Items on these lines will not be interpreted or executed.
***	Major section header.
;	Same as pressing enter while typing.
$	Begins any screen or pull-down menu call, or a Diesel expression.
$pn=*	Pulls down the menu called for pull-down area n.
^	CTRL
^C	CTRL-C
^C^C	Double cancel: cancels any command, ensures a return to the "Command:" prompt before a new command is issued.
***POPn	Section header, where n is a number between 1 and 16, identifying one of the 16 possible pull-down menu areas. POP0 refers to the cursor menu.
[ ]	Brackets enclose text to be written directly to the screen or pull-down menu area. Eight characters are printed on the screen menu. The size of menu items on the pull-down menu varies.
[–]	Writes a blank line on a pull-down menu.
_	English-language flag.
"	Transparent command modifier.
->	Indicates the first item in a cascading menu.
<-	Indicates the last item in a cascading menu.
^P	Toggles menu echo off and on so that macro characters do not appear on the command line as they are being entered via the menu.
( )	Parentheses enclose AutoLISP and DIESEL expressions.
$S=	Calls a menu. If there is no menu name following the equal sign, the previous menu is called.
$M=	Introduces a DIESEL expression.
\	Pause for user input. Allows for keyboard entry, point selection, and object selection. Terminated by press of Enter or pickbutton.
~	Begins a pull-down menu label that is "grayed out." May be used to indicate a function not presently in use.
*^C^C	This set of characters will cause the menu item to repeat.
space	A single blank space in the middle of a line is treated as a press of the enter key.
$i=name	Calls an icon menu.
$i=*	Displays an icon menu.
+	Used at the end of a line to indicate that the menu item continues on the next line.

Data Exchange Formats

AutoCAD 2000 has the capacity to recognize and create files in a number of common file exchange formats. These allow you to translate AutoCAD drawings for use with other software and to bring drawings from other programs into AutoCAD. Following is a list of available drawing file types, listed by extenson, with descriptions of the purpose of each, followed by the commands used to import and export them.

FILE EXTENSION	PURPOSE
3DS	3d Studio. 3DS files are used by Autodesk's 3D Studio software. 3D Studio is an Autodesk rendering program with advanced lighting and material capabilities. EXPORT, 3DSOUT, 3DSIN
BMP	Bitmap. Bitmap files use a pixel by pixel digital representation of screen images. BMPOUT, PASTECLIP
DWF	Drawing Web Format. For publishing drawings on the World Wide Web. DWF files can be viewed on the Internet by others who have a Web browser and the AutoCAD plug-in WHIP! DWF files are created for viewing and publishing; they are not read by AutoCAD for editing and information exchange, as regular DWG files would be. DWFOUT, ePLOT
DXB	Drawing Exchange Binary. A binary-coded format used by AutoSHADE. DXBIN
DXF	Data Exchange Format. A text file format for exchanging drawings between different CAD programs. AutoCAD reads and writes DXF files for exchange with other systems. SAVEAS
EPS	Encapsulated Postscript. For printing and plotting on machines with postscript capability. PSOUT, PSIN
SAT	ACIS (*.sat extension) files capture regions, solids, and NURB (NonUniform Rational B-spline) surfaces in an ASCII format for exchange with other modeling software. ACISOUT, ACISIN
STL	Stereolithograph Apparatus. For translating solid object data into a format compatible with a Stereolithograph machine.

	Stereolithography is a technology that creates actual physical models from CAD solid model data. STLOUT
WMF	Windows Metafile. For saving objects in a raster or vector image format for use with other Windows programs. EXPORT, WMFOUT, WMFIN

In addition to these file types, also remember that images can be transferred among Windows applications using the clipboard (Chapter 10) and that raster images can be attached in a manner similar to external references (Chapter 10). The clipboard makes use of the CUTCLIP, COPYCLIP, and COPYLINK commands for exporting and PASTECLIP, PASTELINK, and PASTESPEC for importing. When importing through the clipboard, AutoCAD automatically recognizes and uses the most efficient format among its options of DWG, WMP, and BMP files. Raster images are attached using the IMAGEATTACH command, which supports a large number of image filetypes. See the AutoCAD Users Guide for additional information on raster images and image file types.

Creating Export Files

Although the file formats that AutoCAD can export vary widely and are used for quite different purposes, the procedure for creating them is identical. As long as you know what type of file you want to create, all you need to do is open the Export Data dialog box from the File menu (Figure C-1), give the export file a name,

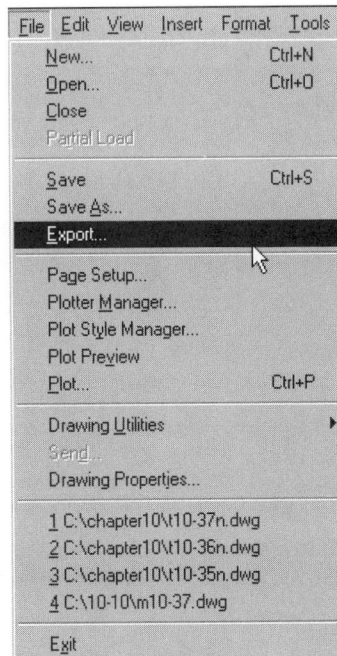

Figure C-1

and select the type of file you want to save it as. To create a 3DS (3D Studio file) for example, follow this procedure:

1. Open the File menu and select Export.
2. In the Export Data dialog box, type a name for the file.
3. Open the Save As Type list and select 3D Studio (*.3ds).
4. Click on Save.

For other drawing exchange formats, follow the same procedure, selecting the file type you want from the Save As Type file list. DWF files are created using the ePLOT feature of the PLOT dialog box.

Importing Files in Other Formats

Many of the drawing file types listed previously can be imported into AutoCAD as well. Importing most drawing file types is handled through the Insert menu. In most cases you will select a file type, select a file, and open it. An example of an import procedure for a WMF follows:

1. Open the Insert menu and select Windows Metafile....
2. In the Import WMF file dialog box, select the name of a WMF file to insert.
3. Select Open.
4. Specify an insertion point and scale factors, just as you would when inserting a block with the INSERT command.

Different types of files require different insertion specifications, as shown in their respective Import dialog boxes. File types on the Insert menu are shown in Figure C-2. DXF files are opened using the OPEN command, selecting DXF from the Files of Type list.

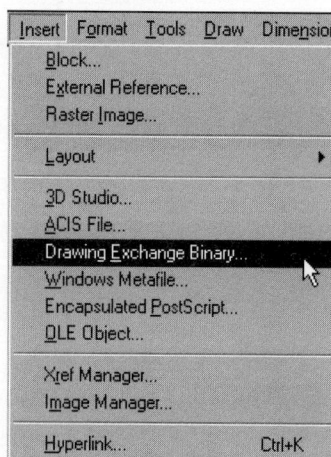

Figure C-2

INDEX